THE BIBLE
AND CIVILIZATION

LIBRARY OF JEWISH KNOWLEDGE
Geoffrey Wigoder, General Editor of the Series

The Jews of the United States
What Does Judaism Say About . . . ?
Bible and Civilization
Biblical Archaeology
Kabbalah

The New York Times
Library of Jewish Knowledge

THE BIBLE
AND CIVILIZATION

GABRIEL SIVAN
Consultant Editor: SHALOM M. PAUL

QUADRANGLE/THE NEW YORK TIMES BOOK CO.

Published in the Western Hemisphere by
QUADRANGLE/THE NEW YORK TIMES BOOK CO.
10 East 53 Street, New York, N.Y. 10022.
Distributed in Canada by Fitzhenry & Whiteside, Ltd., Toronto.

ISBN 0-8129-0348-X
Library of Congress Catalog Card Number 73-77030

Manufactured in the United States of America

CONTENTS

INTRODUCTION

by Dr. Shalom M. Paul

Turn it over and over, for everything is in it.
(*Avot* 5.22)

In the beginning there was the Book of Books. And from that beginning the record of both God's revelation to Israel and Israel's aspiration to God became immortalized within the twenty-four books of the Hebrew Bible. Throughout the vicissitudes of history, this gallery of classic masterpieces has continued to play a preeminent role in a world it originally helped to fashion. The magnetic appeal of this multi-dimensional anthology of sacred literature has never ceased to inspire mankind with its charm, simplicity, and sublimity.

The Bible is "le livre où Dieu se rend visible" (Hugo). Herein lies one of its most profound contributions. The Biblical concept of God was totally new and unique: one universal God, omnipotent, omniscient, transcendent—and yet immanent and concerned with the destiny of His creation. He was not subjected to the shackles of fate, magic, nature, or time as were the gods of other nations. The God of Israel removed chaos, and "there was light"—a light which became a "lamp to man's feet and a light on his path." And the path became the tale of history which now was given a meaning, a purpose, and a goal.

One God—one man. Diverse species of all living creatures were created, but only one human species. Man, whose life was sacred, since he alone bore the image of his creator, became the Bible's main preoccupation. Not perfect—"What is man that Thou art mindful of him, the son of man that Thou regardest him?"—but potentially perfectible—"Yet Thou has set him just a little lower than the angels"—he was a free agent, burdened with the boon of responsibility and accountable, in the long run, only to his God.

One man—one common origin of mankind, united in the utopian dream of an eventual restoration of that primeval unity—a goal clearly audible in the voice of prophecy. The prophets with their stress on the supremacy of morality, social justice, righteousness, mercy, and compassion directed their oracles to Israel as well as to the other nations, forecasting both punishment and ultimate redemption. They bequeathed as their spiritual heritage some of the most profound and noble ideas that have become an indispensable part of the religious and moral advancement of civilization.

The object of this book is to describe and illustrate the Hebrew Bible's influence on the many spheres and institutions of modern (especially Western) society. Part One deals with the Bible's impact on society, Part Two with its far-reaching effects in language and letters, and Part Three with the Biblical legacy in art and music.

In his first chapter ("From Religion to Race Relations"), Gabriel Sivan shows how the Bible's call for justice and ethical conduct penetrated both Judaism and Christianity, surveys its influence on the theory and practice of education, and also deals with its contribution to the whole range of social welfare—from the fight against poverty to the struggle for racial equality. The second chapter of Part One ("The Legal and Political Spheres") traces the Hebrew Bible's role in Western law and its emergence as a significant factor in the development of the democratic ideal, laying particular stress on issues such as resistance to tyranny and the quest for peace and international understanding.

Part Two comprises first a chapter ("The Testimony of Everyday Speech") that discusses the Bible's penetration into the vocabulary and expression of English and other modern languages, illustrating the retention or adaptation of the Biblical-Hebraic idiom in daily usage. The book's fourth, and most detailed, chapter ("Biblical Themes and Echoes in World Literature") is concerned with two interrelated subjects: the Bible's impact on the style of many great writers throughout the past two millennia, and its importance as a source for the motifs which have been chosen to express national and universal yearnings in the world's poetry, drama, and fiction.

In the third part of his book, the author devotes a chapter ("Painting and Sculpture") to Biblical representation in the fine arts, emphasizing the contribution of some of the great masters and indicating the process whereby changing social conditions and attitudes have affected the portrayal of Biblical episodes and personalities throughout the ages. The sixth and final chapter ("The Musical Tradition") deals with several key topics: settings of Biblical verses and passages in liturgical and folk music, the interpretation of Biblical themes in opera and oratorio, their influence on other forms of art music, and the adaptation of Biblical motifs in the Negro spiritual and in Jewish folk-song.

A novel aspect of this study is the emphasis laid upon the Hebrew Bible's distinctive reinterpretation by Jewish scholars, writers, artists, and musicians. In sum, the author has collected an overwhelming amount of material demonstrating the impact which the Bible has had on all dimensions of the human adventure.

Countless reading does not dim the profound insights and moral and religious fervor of the Scriptural word, for "the Bible grows more beautiful as we grow in our understanding of it" (Goethe).

FOREWORD

As its title indicates, this book explores those areas of creative human endeavor in which the Hebrew Bible's influence has been especially remarkable (and it should be noted that the Bible in this context refers to the Hebrew Bible, which has been extended to include the Apocrypha). During the last two millennia, men have "searched the Scriptures" for confirmation of their faith and for answers to vital and eternal questions. As Ralph Waldo Emerson once wrote, "the Bible is like an old Cremona; it has been played upon by the devotion of thousands of years until every word and particle is public and tunable." No other document in the possession of mankind offers so much to the reader—ethical and religious instruction, superb poetry, a social program and legal code, an interpretation of history, and all the joys, sorrows, and hopes which well up in men and which Israel's prophets and leaders expressed with matchless force and passion.

In *The Bible and Civilization* I have drawn on the wealth of information contained in the new *Encyclopaedia Judaica*, some of which passed through my hands during the five years I served on the editorial board, my particular responsibilities being World Literature, modern translations of the Bible, and Christian Hebraism. In addition, however, liberal use has been made of other authoritative sources and I have also utilized research work of my own, including articles published in the encyclopedia or elsewhere. All of this provides the interested student and layman with a detailed and systematic treatment of a unique cultural inheritance.

I wish to acknowledge the scholarly influence and warm sympathy of three of my teachers: the late Rabbi Hyman Klein, M.A. (Cantab), former Principal of the Liverpool Talmudical College; Mr. Arthur D. Crow, M.A., B. Litt., Senior Tutor of Oriel College, Oxford; and Dr. D. P. Walker, Reader in Renaissance Studies at the Warburg Institute, University of London. I also feel it appropriate to recall the inspiration

xiii

and close friendship of a great historian and man of letters, the late Professor Cecil (Bezalel) Roth, whose Hebrew name is borne by my youngest son. Special thanks are due to Dr. Shalom Paul, Senior Lecturer in Bible at the Hebrew University of Jerusalem, and to Dr. Geoffrey Wigoder, Editor in Chief of the *Encyclopaedia Judaica*, who both read my typescript and offered much valuable advice and useful criticism; a number of their suggestions have contributed to the improvement of the book. Finally, I am indebted to my wife, Viva, whose legal training was of assistance in planning the first two chapters and whose cheerful acceptance of my irregular hours of work made the process of writing far less of a burden than it might have been. To all who have brought their expertise to bear on the accompanying illustrations and the technical production of this book I am immeasurably grateful.

G. S.

NOTES FOR THE READER

The following information and the appended glossary are intended for those unfamiliar with the Hebrew language and with Jewish terminology.

The word "Bible" refers exclusively to the Hebrew Bible (from Genesis to 2 Chronicles), also styled the "Old" Testament. *Torah* ("teaching") is often used in this sense as well, although the term's basic meaning is "Pentateuch" (or the "Five Books of Moses"). Biblical citations follow the Jewish chapter and verse divisions and are mostly taken from the English translation of *The Holy Scriptures* issued by the Jewish Publication Society of America (Philadelphia, 1917). In place of "B.C." and "A.D." the abbreviations B.C.E. (=before the Common Era) and C.E. (Common Era) have been used. Hebrew terms, phrases, and quotations adhere to a simplified system of transliteration (see below), but familiar Biblical names retain their usual English spelling ("Moses," not *Moshe*, "Israel," not *Yisra'el*, etc.). Quotations from the Babylonian Talmud (e.g., *Shabbat*, 37a) are distinguishable from Mishnaic and other Rabbinic sources (e.g., *Avot*, 5.2). I have avoided the use of traditional Jewish acronyms, allowing only one exception to this rule, Rashi (for *R*abbi *S*olomon ben *I*saac), an acronym with which the non-Jewish world has also become familiar. For the purposes of this book, Apocryphal literature (Tobit, Judith, Susanna, etc.)— though outside the Jewish (and Protestant) canon—is granted a "Biblical" status.

GUIDE TO TRANSLITERATION

Hebrew Letter	Trans-literation	Approximate Value
א (aleph)	(')	takes vowel sound*
ב ,בּ (bēt, vēt)	b, v	b, v
ג (gimel)	g	g
ד (dālet)	d	d
ה (hē)	h	h
ו (vav)	v	v, u, o
ז (zayin)	z	z

Hebrew Letter	Transliteration	Approximate Value
ח (ḥet)	ḥ	as Scots, German "ch"
ט (tet)	t	t
י (yod)	i, y	vocalized "y"
כ, כֿ (kaph, khaph)	k, kh	k, or kh (as ḥ)
ל (lāmed)	l	l
מ, ם (mem)	m	m
נ, ן (nūn)	n	n
ס (sāmekh)	s	s
ע (ayin)	(')	takes vowel sound*
פ, פֿ, ף (pē, fē)	p, f(ph)	p, f
צ, ץ (ẓadē)	ẓ	ts
ק (koph, qoph)	k(q)	k
ר (rēsh)	r	r
שׁ, שׂ (shin, sin)	sh, s	sh, s
ת (tav)	t	t

* Among Ashkenazi Jews, *aleph* and *ayin* are no longer sounded and take the value of their associated vowel (thus אֶחָד ("one") = *eḥad* and זֶרַע ("seed") = *zera*). Hebrew is basically a consonantal language and the vowel points are only printed for those first learning to read (see Chapter 3). Between two vowels, the symbol ' is used to denote a glottal break (e.g., in רֵעַ, *re'a* = "neighbor"). The construction of some of the Hebrew terms in the glossary below can be gauged by referring to this transliteration guide. The reader should bear in mind that Hebrew is written from right to left.

GLOSSARY

Akedah, Heb. עקדה: the Binding (or "Sacrifice") of Isaac (Gen. 22).

Ashkenazi (plural, Ashkenazim), Heb. אשכנזי: name applied to those Jews (now the great majority of the world's Jewish population) descended from and using the ritual of the medieval German community ("Ashkenaz," see Gen 10:3); often used in contradistinction to "Sephardi."

Avot, Heb. אבות: a much-quoted tractate of the Mishnah, known in full as *Pirkei Avot,* the "Chapters ("Ethics" or "Sayings") of the Fathers."

Diaspora: a Greek term meaning "dispersion," roughly equivalent to the Hebrew *Golah* or *Galut* ("exile," i.e., Jewish communities outside the Land of Israel).

Essene(s): an ascetic Jewish religious sect of the late Second Temple period.

Etrog, Heb. אתרוג: "citron," one of the Four Species prescribed for use in the synagogue on the Tabernacles (*Sukkot*) festival; for this "fruit of goodly trees," see Lev. 23:40.

Gemara, Aramaic גמרא: commentaries on and supplements to the Mishnah, these two corpora together forming the Talmud.

Haggadah, Heb. הגדה: "narration" recited in the Jewish home on the eve of Passover and recalling the events of the Exodus. The text of the *Haggadah* used at the *Seder* service includes songs as well as Biblical and Rabbinic passages.

Halakhah (adj., halakhic), Heb. הלכה: authoritative Rabbinic law; also, the legal sections of the Talmud.

Hallel, Heb. הלל: the Psalm of "Praise" (113–118) recited and sung on festive occasions in the synagogue.

Hanukkah, Heb. חנוכה: festival commemorating the Hasmonean victory over the Syrian tyrant Antiochus Epiphanes and the restoration of the Temple.

Hasid (plural Hasidim, adj., Hasidic), Heb. חסיד: adherent(s) of Hasidism, a mass religious movement founded in Eastern Europe during the early 18th century.

Haskalah, Heb. השכלה: the "Enlightenment" movement which spread from 18th-century German Jewry to the communities of Eastern Europe.

Hazzan (plural, *hazzanim*), Heb. חזן: precentor or cantor who leads the synagogue worshipers in prayer; the art of the cantor is known as *hazzanut.*

xvii

Kabbalah (adj., kabbalistic), Heb. קבלה: the Jewish mystical tradition, exponents of which are termed kabbalists.

Kaddish, Heb. קדיש: "sanctification" which constitutes a Jewish liturgical doxology.

Kibbutz (plural, kibbutzim), Heb. קיבוץ: Israeli communal and cooperative settlements (mainly secular and socialistic, though a few are religiously inspired).

Kol Nidrei, Aramaic כל נדרי: formula recited in the synagogue on the eve of the Day of Atonement (*Yom Kippur*).

Lulav, Heb. לולב: "palm branch," one of the Four Species used on the Tabernacles festival.

Mahzor, Heb. מחזור: prayer book designed for use on the High Holidays or Pilgrim Festivals.

Megillah, Heb. מגלה: a scroll, specifically the Scroll of Esther read publicly on the festival of *Purim*.

Menorah, Heb. מנורה: the seven-branched oil lamp or "Candelabrum" used in the Tabernacle and Temple (see Ex. 25:31ff., 37:17ff.); the same term is also used to describe the eight-branched candelabrum which features in the ceremony of the *Hanukkah* festival.

Midrash (adj., Midrashic), Heb. מדרש: (mainly) homiletical interpretation of Scripture by the Rabbis.

Mishnah (adj., Mishnaic), Heb. משנה: the earliest codification of the Oral Law; together with the Gemara, it constitutes the Talmud.

Pharisee(s): the popular Jewish religious and political party of the Second Commonwealth period; exponents of the Oral Law and forerunners of the mainstream teachers of Rabbinic Judaism.

Piyyut: Hebrew derivative of a Greek word meaning "poetry," specifically denoting Jewish liturgical verse. Composers of this type of poetry were known as *paytanim.*

Purim, Heb. פורים, from a Persian word meaning "lot": festival commemorating the deliverance of the Jews from Haman's plan for their total destruction on a date determined by his casting of lots (as told in the Book of Esther).

Purim-Shpil, Yiddish for "Purim play": a masquerade, traditionally performed on the *Purim* festival, from which Yiddish drama ultimately derives.

Sadducee(s): priestly and aristocratic sect of the Second Temple era ideologically and politically opposed to the Pharisees.

Seder, Heb. סדר: ceremony observed in Jewish homes on the eve of the Passover festival in commemoration of the deliverance from Egypt (see Ex. 13:8ff.); the reading of the *Haggadah* is the central feature of the *Seder* service.

Sefer Torah, Heb. ספר תורה: handwritten Scroll of the Law (Torah scroll), comprising the Pentateuch, used for public readings in the synagogue.

Sephardi (plural, Sephardim), Heb. ספרדי: name applied to those Jews descended from and maintaining the ritual of the pre-Expulsion Spanish and Portuguese communities (see Obad. 1:20); also a popular designation for all non-Ashkenazi ("Eastern") Jews.

Shema, Heb. שמע: Judaism's confession of faith in the One God ("Hear, O Israel . . . ," Deut. 6:4).

Siddur, Heb. סדור: daily prayer book of the Ashkenazi Jews.

Talmud (adj., Talmudic), Heb. תלמוד: the principal corpus of Jewish "learning"; it comprises the Mishnah and the Gemara in two separate traditions: the Jerusalem (or Palestinian) Talmud and the more authoritative Babylonian Talmud.

Targum (plural, Targumim or "Targums"), Aramaic תרגום: the vernacular Aramaic translation of the Hebrew Bible, often in an extended paraphrase.

Torah, Heb. תורה: the "Teaching" of the Five Books of Moses; often applied in the broadest sense to all traditional Jewish learning.

Yeshivah (plural, *yeshivot*), Heb. ישיבה: Rabbinical college where students are mainly instructed in the Talmud and allied lore.

Zealot(s): a Jewish sectarian and political party of late Second Temple times advocating armed revolt against the Romans.

Zohar, Heb. זוהר: the "Book of Splendor," a mystical commentary on the Torah and the principal textbook of the Kabbalah.

Part One

THE BIBLE'S IMPACT ON SOCIETY

1

FROM RELIGION
TO RACE RELATIONS

To do justly, and to love mercy, and to walk
humbly with thy God (Micah 6:8)

Ever since Sinai, the moral imperatives of the Five Books of Moses, reinforced by the thunderous indignation of the Prophets, have provided one of the greatest inspirations for social reformers and religious idealists, motivating their perennial concern for man's physical and spiritual welfare and for the evolution of a more just and humane society. Indeed, it seems fair to say that the Hebrew Bible's influence has been especially important and profound within the whole ethical framework of Western civilization. The extraordinary potency of the Biblical catalyst in the translation of ideas into facts was stressed by the English classical scholar Benjamin Jowett, who noted that "the moral feelings of men have been deepened and strengthened, and also softened, and almost created, by the Jewish prophets. In modern times we hardly like to acknowledge the full force of their words, lest they should prove subversive to society. And so we explain them away or spiritualize them, and convert what is figurative into what is literal, and what is literal into what is figurative. And still, after all our interpretation or misinterpretation, whether due to a false theology or an imperfect knowledge of the original language, the force of the word remains, and a light of heavenly truth and love streams from them even now more than 2,500 years after they were first uttered" (*Selected Passages from the Theological Writings*, 1903).

Within the limits of this chapter an attempt will be made to describe and assess some of the more significant aspects of the Bible's impact on modern society—its influence on Judaism and the "daughter religions" to which it gave rise, on the ethical values of the West, on education, on the concept and application of social welfare, and on the relations between the races of mankind. Out of this primal fabric arose the Biblical leaven that has worked such amazing effects on those spheres of activity which form the subject of this book's succeeding chapters: legal and political thought and organization, linguistic expression, and the realms of literature, art, and music. To give any adequate account of such vast

3

fields is a formidable task in a work of this scope, bearing in mind the whole compass of our Biblical heritage. The wisdom and humanity of the Scriptures have enriched man's cultural and moral perspectives over the past three millennia and their civilizing effects have been measureless.

RELIGION AND ETHICS

The Hebrews received the basis of their religio-ethical code as "an inheritance of the congregation of Jacob" (Deut. 33:4) when Moses instructed them in the principles and practice of the commandments during their forty years in the wilderness. This code was then handed down through the eras of the Judges and Prophets, with various amplifications and refinements, until it became the possession of post-Biblical Jewry in early Rabbinic times. During the first century C.E., the ethics of ancient Israel were transmitted to Christianity by the Jewish Church of ·Jerusalem, even though the legal teachings of normative Judaism were largely discarded by Paul and later leaders of the Gentile Church. To a certain extent, the ethical legacy of the Hebrew Bible influenced Islam as well, Muhammad having borrowed many of his religious concepts from both Judaism and Christianity. The three great monotheistic religions are thus heirs to the same moral code, which has its roots in the Bible. Biblical ethics are closely associated with Biblical religion, and the ethical injunctions of the Bible have become an integral part of Western civilization. Despite the rise of skepticism, agnosticism, and even 20th century atheism (in its militant, Marxist formulation), these injunctions continue to provide the basis for much of the world's social legislation and accepted norms of conduct.

Social historians and Bible critics have often drawn attention to the high level of ethical aspiration in other cultures of the past—the Egyptian, Babylonian, and Greek in the Old World, and the Inca in the New—but in so doing they fail to take account of the Hebrew Bible's historical background and of such important details as the duties implicit in human freedom. Alone among the ethical systems of antiquity, the Biblical code placed the moral imperative at the center of religious and national values. Justice (in Hebrew, *zedek*) is the foundation of society: Abraham, whom God has selected "that he may command his children and his household after him . . . to do righteousness and justice" (Gen. 18:19), challenges the Lord's own application of the code in the case of

Sodom with the question, "Wilt Thou indeed sweep away the righteous with the wicked? . . . shall not the Judge of all the earth do justly?" (Gen. 18:23, 25). This sublime idea of justice as a combination of the rule of law and of righteous conduct in human relations is a leitmotiv of the Bible: "Justice, justice shalt thou follow" (Deut. 16:20), "Seek justice, relieve the oppressed" (Isa. 1:17), "Let justice well up as waters, and righteousness as a mighty stream" (Amos 5:24).

The ethical approach of the Hebrew Bible is rooted in the respect which it demands for the sanctity of human life. Amid the polytheism and sexual depravity of ancient society, the Bible taught that all human beings were equal in the love of God, since He "created man in His own image, in the image of God created He him; male and female created He them" (Gen. 1:27). In Prophetic and post-Biblical Judaism, this affirmation of life and respect for one's neighbor gave rise to very practical legislation that sharply contrasts with the norms of other religious systems. "At a time when the deepest night of inhumanity covered the rest of mankind, the religion of Israel breathed forth a spirit of love and brotherhood which must fill even the stranger, if he be only willing to see, with reverence and admiration. Israel has given the world true humanitarianism, just as it has given the world the true God" (C. H. Cornill, *Das Alte Testament und die Humanität,* 1895).

While justice is not the only important ethical quality in God and man, it is the basis of the universal code of morality which the Bible imparts. This notion was typically expressed by the Psalmist: "Righteousness and justice are the foundation of Thy throne; mercy and truth go before Thee" (Ps. 89:15). In Greek thought, the inequalities of human nature were emphasized, Plato's *Republic* implying that humble folk must be content to perform their allotted functions in proper subservience to their superiors and masters. The Hebrews, on the other hand, stressed that a spark of God's essence enters every human being and that every human life is sacred. Thus, all men have a fundamental right to life, honor, and the rewards of their labor; the captive idolater who has not glimpsed the true God, the malefactor, even the condemned murderer— all are entitled to the same basic consideration. After serving for his crime, the evildoer is on a par with his fellows and, even after execution, the criminal's body may not be exposed to public ignominy (Deut. 21:23). Just how advanced such an outlook was may be gauged from comparing the Mosaic legislation with the practice of Christian England even in recent centuries, when public executions were a form of popular diversion, political offenders were hanged, drawn, and quartered for exposure to the London mob, and starving men who stole a loaf of bread were sentenced to harsh punishments of various types.

For the Greeks, social justice was akin to harmony, but in Hebrew the term *ẓedek* awakened the idea of life's sanctity. Moses proclaimed that the Israelites were to be "a kingdom of priests, and a holy nation" (Ex. 19:6) and the notion of *imitatio Dei* (the imitation of God) was also taught in the Pentateuch: "Ye shall be holy; for I the Lord your God am holy" (Lev. 19:2). Ever practical, the Hebrew Bible made it clear that the way to ethical perfection lay not in philosophical abstractions, but in adhering to God's commandments. A Christian writer of the second century C.E., Aristides Mareianus, paid tribute to this Hebraic interpretation of morality's application to everyday life when he declared in his *Apology* that "Jews imitate God by philanthropy."[1] Greek ethical philosophy, addressing itself primarily to the individual, differentiated between various types of virtue (courage, generosity, etc.) and allowed for their cultivation according to the individual's particular inclination and temperament. This approach is again totally foreign to the Bible, which demands "righteousness" of everyone (Isa. 33:15–16, Jer. 9:22–23, etc.) and which makes Abraham, because of the many virtues attributed to him in the Scriptural narrative (piety, obedience, hospitality, generosity, compassion), the ideal man. Righteousness, that other sense of *ẓedek*, "exalts a nation" (Prov. 14:34) and its practice "is more acceptable to the Lord than sacrifice" (Prov. 21:3). Fundamentally, therefore, the ethics of the Bible work through three primary virtues which find their concrete application in the Scriptural text: Justice (Gen. 9:6), Loving-kindness (Lev. 19:17), and Humility (Num. 12:3, Micah 6:8). The problem is not *why* men should lead "the good life," but *how* they should do so—and it was Judaism's affirmation of the moral law that preserved the ethical structure of Western civilization.

THE COMMANDMENTS

It is no exaggeration to say that the Decalogue has had a greater impact on man's moral thinking and endeavor than all other ethical formulations known to humanity. The Ten Commandments (in Hebrew, *Aseret*

---

[1] "Philanthropy" in the original Greek sense of *philanthrōpos*, "loving mankind."

Two Tables of the Law surmount the baroque Holy Ark in Jerusalem's Italian Rite Synagogue.

ha-Dibrot, "The Ten Words"; whence, through the Greek, "Decalogue") constitute a unique summary of the duties binding on mankind, unparalleled in its simplicity, comprehensiveness, and solemnity. Ageless and sublime, these Commandments (Ex. 20:2–14; repeated almost word for word in Deut. 5:6–18) epitomize both the essential creed of Judaism and the "Natural Law" of all civilized men. Today, they constitute the moral foundation of one-third of mankind. Traditionally, the five opening Commandments (engraved on the first tablet) set forth man's duties to God, and the latter five (on the second tablet) those applicable to his fellow man. Significantly enough, the essentials of the Decalogue repeated in the Book of Leviticus (19:3ff.) as a handbook of moral instruction are prefixed by the injunction already mentioned concerning the need to imitate the righteousness and sanctity of God. Their application guarantees the stability of human society by controlling four critical "danger areas"—power, wealth, sex, and speech.

7

In Judaism, the Ten Commandments were recited during the morning service in the Temple and their representation on two tablets often forms part of the design of the contemporary synagogue. However, because of the suggestion by heretics of the Second Temple era that the Decalogue actually contained the "whole duty of man," its place in the Jewish liturgy became restricted. The Ten Commandments are accordingly recited in the synagogue only as they occur twice annually in the weekly Scriptural reading, although the text still figures in the traditional prayer book. Unlike most of the other Biblical precepts, these Commandments retained their hold on the Christian mind from the period of the Church Fathers to the Reformation (when Luther called them "so sublime that no man could attain to them by his own power"), and so on to our own time. The great French historian and Bible scholar Ernest Renan declared that "the incomparable fortune which awaited this page of Exodus, namely, to become the code of universal ethics, was not unmerited. The Ten Words are for all peoples; and they will be, during all the centuries, the commandments of God."

Biblical morality has two parallel spheres of influence and concern: social (including sexual) ethics, and the ethical conduct of each individual. The Bible primarily stresses righteous living in the context of society as a whole—man's duty toward his fellow—and lays down a comprehensive series of rules governing social behavior. Doing right by one's neighbor means the avoidance of any action prejudicial to the physical and moral welfare of the next man or of humanity at large. Since right is not automatically on the side of the strongest or the majority, one should "not follow a multitude to do evil" (Ex. 23:2), distort the truth by giving false testimony and perverting justice (Ex. 23:2), nor even allow one's natural sympathy with a poor man to wrest judgment in his favor (Ex. 23:3, Deut. 16:18–20). Servants and aliens must be assured of just and fair treatment, since the Hebrews themselves were once strangers and slaves in Egypt (Ex. 22:20, 23:9; Lev. 19:34; Deut. 10:19, 24:14–15). A constant injunction is that special care be taken of the widow, the orphan, and the needy (Ex. 22:21–23; Deut. 15:7–11; cf. Isa. 58:7). Slander and talebearing destroy social harmony (Lev. 19:16; cf. Prov. 11:13, 26:20) and harboring a grudge is also condemned (Lev. 19:17–18). Business ethics, too, are laid down in the demand for just weights and balances (Lev. 19:36, Deut. 25:13–16; cf. Prov. 20:10, 23). The ethical concern of the Scriptures also extends to animals, which must be treated humanely (Deut. 22:20, 25:4), even when they are required for food

(Ex. 23:19, etc.; Deut. 22:6–7).[2] Here, the Hebrew Bible takes up a rational position midway between the extremes of certain Eastern religions, such as Buddhism (which forbids the slaughter of any beast), and early Christianity as expounded by Paul, who commented sardonically on Deut. 25:4: "For it is written in the law of Moses, Thou shalt not muzzle the mouth of the ox that treadeth out the corn. Doth God take care for oxen?" (1 Corinthians 9:9).

Brief statements of the Bible's social morality have been traced in Amos 5:15 ("Hate the evil, and love the good . . .") and Micah 6:8 ("It hath been told thee, O man, what is good, and what the Lord doth require of thee: only to do justly, and to love mercy, and to walk humbly with thy God")—passages which inspired some famous ethical statements in Jewish and Christian literature.[3] The Hebrew Bible's stand on sexual relationships is uniquely clear-cut and severe. Incest, adultery, homosexuality, and bestiality ("the doings of the land of Egypt" and "of the land of Canaan," Lev. 18:3) are grave crimes in the eyes of Heaven incurring stern penalties; as such, they can never be viewed permissively, as they were in pagan cults, where the deities themselves behaved lewdly toward one another (not only in Near Eastern mythology, but even in the writings of ancient Greece and Rome). Through Judaism and Christianity, the Bible's outlook on sex and perversion has—with varying emphases in the social morality of the Church—influenced much of the modern world.

Various techniques are employed for the demonstration of Biblical morality: exemplary statements about "going beyond the letter of the law," citations of popular wisdom, and the use of didactic stories. "To do righteousness and justice is more acceptable to the Lord than sacrifice" (Prov. 21:3) and Job emphasizes the fact that he did not limit himself to the heeding of basic negative precepts (the "thou shalt nots"), but delighted in performing positive commandments:

---

[2] A fundamental of the Jewish dietary laws *(Kashrut)* is the repeated prohibition against "seething a kid in its mother's milk" (Ex. 23:19, 34:26; Deut. 14:21).

[3] The "Golden Rule" of the New Testament (Matthew 7:12) was anticipated both in the Apocrypha (Tobit 4.14) and by Hillel the Elder in the Talmud: "What is hateful to you, do not to another: this is the whole Law, the rest is commentary." In the tradition of the Rabbis, however, Hillel added: "Now go and study it."

I delivered the poor that cried,
The fatherless also, that had none to help him . . . .
I was eyes to the blind,
And feet was I to the lame.
I was a father to the needy;
And the cause of him that I knew not I searched out (Job 29:12–16).

A poetic passage elsewhere in the Bible couples wisdom with the concern for ethical values: "And they that are wise shall shine as the brightness of the firmament; and they that turn the many to righteousness as the stars for ever and ever" (Dan. 12:3).

In the Pentateuch and Prophetical books, the ethical commandments are to be obeyed as a duty to God, but the worldly wisdom of the Book of Proverbs points to the outcome if moral injunctions are disregarded. A servant should not be slandered in his master's hearing, "lest he curse thee, and thou be found guilty" (Prov. 30:10); and an outraged husband cannot be bought off, since "he will not spare in the day of vengeance" (Prov. 6:24–35). Perhaps the most potent method of ethical instruction in the Bible is that of the cautionary or didactic tale. Whereas, as we have seen, the patriarch Abraham is the prototype of righteous conduct ("he hearkened to My voice, and kept My charge, My commandments, My statutes, and My laws," Gen. 26:5), all the other Biblical heroes and heroines—including the Lawgiver himself—are depicted as they are, with their virtues and their human failings. Moral lessons are driven home in episodes such as Joseph's entanglement with Potiphar's wife (Gen. 39:7ff.), Moses' impatient striking of the rock (Num. 20:7–12), and David's intrigue with Uriah's wife, Bath-Sheba (2 Sam. 11:2–12:25). Significantly indeed, in view of misrepresentation in anti-Jewish polemics, the patriarch Jacob whose acquisition of Esau's birthright was accomplished by deception (Gen. 27) is punished through a similar trick at the hands of Laban (Gen. 29). This ethically uncompromising aspect of the Scriptural narrative particularly impressed the Anglo-Jewish writer Israel Zangwill: "The Bible is an anti-Semitic book. 'Israel is the villain, not the hero, of his own story.' Alone among epics, it is out for truth, not high heroics."

JEWISH AND CHRISTIAN ETHICS

One source of conflict between Judaism and Christianity lies in their diverging interpretations of the Bible's injunctions regarding the treatment of neighbors and enemies. The Biblical position presents no ambiguity: "Thou shalt not hate thy brother in thy heart; thou shalt surely rebuke thy neighbor, and not bear sin because of him. Thou shalt not take vengeance, nor bear any grudge against the children of thy people, but thou shalt love thy neighbor as thyself . . . " (Lev. 19:17–18). In other words, this "golden rule" cautions against private enmities, whether overt or concealed, and lays down that men should display love and forbearance toward one another in a godly society. Associated with this teaching is another key Biblical statement: "If thou meet thine enemy's ox or his ass going astray, thou shalt surely bring it back to him again. If thou see the ass of him that hateth thee lying under its burden, thou shalt forbear to pass by him: thou shalt surely release it with him" (Ex. 23:4–5). Here, too, the lesson is clear. Private animosities must be suppressed and a man's conduct toward an enemy and treatment of his property may not be governed by feelings of hostility. This is an ideal, but an attainable ideal. The Biblical doctrine of "live and let live" also finds expression in the injunctions not to rejoice over the downfall of an enemy (Prov. 24:17), but to answer his hostility with kindness, not in kind (Prov. 25:21–22).

Rabbinic Judaism steadily broadened the application of these commandments both within the original context of Jewish society and, by extension, within the sphere of relations with the non-Jewish world. The anger or resentment that can consume a man because of some real or imagined injury is a destructive force, *sin'at hinam* ("groundless hatred"), and to this cardinal iniquity the Talmud even attributes the fall of the Second Jewish Commonwealth: "The First Temple was destroyed because of the sins of idolatry, harlotry, and murder. The Second—despite the study of Torah and the practice of the commandments and of kindly acts—fell because of groundless hatred . . . " (*Yoma*, 9b). This assertion was based on historical experience, for during the war against Rome (68–70 C.E.) thousands perished as a result of internal political conflicts between various Jewish parties. The Rabbis also greatly developed the ethical rules governing the attitude toward Gentiles in the belief that "to rob a non-Jew is more heinous than to rob a Jew, since this involves the desecration of God's Name" (*Tosefta* to *Bava Kamma*, 10.15). They further maintained that "righteous Gentiles have a share in the world to come" (*Tosefta* to *Sanhedrin*, 13.2), a famous saying of Rabbi Joshua which became authoritative Jewish doctrine, and one sage declared: "I call heaven and earth to witness that whether it be Gentile or Israelite, man or woman, slave or handmaid, according to his or her deeds, so will the Holy Spirit rest upon the individual" (*Tanna de-Vei Eliyahu*, p. 48). The non-Jew who accepted the fundamental moral law had no need to adopt the detailed religious legislation prescribed for Israel, since the "Noachide" (or "Noachian") Laws based on God's injunctions to Noah made anyone practicing them a semi-convert who merited respect and honor in this life and a share in the hereafter.[4] As for "loving thy neighbor as thyself," Rabbinic Judaism again preached a realizable ideal—cherishing him *as* oneself, no less and no more. Jewish teaching illuminated its approach in a story about two men lost in the desert with just enough water left to keep one of them alive: in such circumstances, the one in possession of the water must use it, for otherwise, the commandment would have stated: "Thou shalt love thy neighbor *more* than thyself" (*Bava Mezia,* 62a).

The ethical approach of Jesus, as related in the New Testament, was rooted in the Hebrew Bible. However, the forbearance and comparative leniency shown in many aspects of religious life by the School of Hillel the Elder[5] now went much further in the "Nazarene" doctrine. "This is my commandment," says Jesus in the Gospel according to John, "that ye love one another, as I have loved you. Greater love hath no man than this, that a man lay down his life for his friends" (15:12–13). Another statement attributed to Jesus—"Ye have heard that it hath been said, Thou shalt love thy neighbor, and hate thine enemy . . ." (Matthew 5:43)—is, to say the least, a very curious one. The half-clause, "and hate thine enemy," has no basis whatsoever in the Bible, whether independently or in conjunction with the "love thy neighbor" rule. The Psalmist, it is true, cries, "Do not I hate them, O Lord, that hate Thee? . . . I count them mine enemies" (Ps. 139:21–22), but this is out of zeal for God and His righteous cause. The Hebrews were taught to hate idolatry, not the idolater; to destroy idols, but not the redeemable

---

[4] The "Seven Commandments of the Children of Noah" demand (1) the establishment of courts of law; (2) the outlawing of idolatry; (3) the prohibition of blasphemy and false testimony; (4) purity in sexual relationships (incest and unnatural lusts being specifically forbidden); (5) the prohibition of murder and bloodshed; (6) the interdiction of theft and robbery in every form; and (7) the prohibition of flesh cut from a living animal. In Rabbinic law, Muslims and (since the later Middle Ages) Christians have been classified as "Noachides."

[5] On Hillel and the development of Talmudic legislation, see Chapter 2.

idol-worshiper.[6] And, in the early Rabbinic period, though Shammai and his disciples (who took a more generally rigorous line than their Pharisee colleagues of Hillel's school) were staunch nationalists, they never taught hatred for one's private enemies—yet what Jesus supposedly affirmed was applicable to the private sphere. From the New Testament it is clear that Jesus himself was intolerant of money changers (Matthew 21:12; Mark 11:15; John 2:14–15) and Gentiles (Matthew 10:5–6, 15:22–26; Mark 7:24–27), and that he never said: "Love your enemies, including non-Jews." Some modern scholars therefore believe that what Jesus in fact said was probably along these lines: "The Law states, 'Love your neighbor,' but I tell you that this commandment really includes the bidding to love your enemy as well."[7]

The tearing of quotations out of their context is a dangerous practice, lending itself to mischievous abuse. Some hyperbolical statements by the Rabbis of the Talmud can be read as wholesale condemnations of women, ignorant folk, and Gentiles, while the New Testament likewise provides hostile remarks about marriage, religious ceremony, and Jews. In Rabbinic Judaism, the predominant attitude toward the non-Jewish world is—despite harsh experience—a tolerant one; and, at their best, Christian ethics have embraced men and women of other creeds. Thus, *The Book of Common Prayer* (1662) in Anglican usage calls for "mercy upon all Jews, Turks, Infidels and Heretics," and since the 19th century Christians of most denominations have shown greater understanding for the spiritual insights of other religions. Augustine's proclamation of "no salvation outside the Church" (which gave rise to the Inquisition) still motivates the endeavors of missionary societies but, so far as the broad mass of enlightened Christendom is concerned, it is a dead letter.

In the wake of the Reformation, independent thinkers like Jean Bodin (1530–1596) began to promote a new respect for the Hebrew Bible's universal moral code, a "Natural Law" untrammeled by Church dogma and New Testament polemics. Ernest Renan admitted in 1877 that "Isaiah, seven hundred and fifty years before Jesus, made bold to say that sacrifices were of little consequence, and that the one thing which

---

[6] Dean A. P. Stanley, a 19th-century English churchman, wrote that "the duty of keeping alive in the human heart the sense of burning indignation against moral evil . . . is as much a part of the Christian as of the Jewish dispensation."

[7] For a detailed study of this problematic quotation, see C. G. Montefiore, *The Synoptic Gospels* (1927; new edn. New York, 1968), vol. 2, pp. 76–80.

availed was clean hands and purity of heart." The moral inspiration of the Hebrew Prophets was also acknowledged by Renan's German colleague, Hermann Gunkel: "With trenchant power they hammered into the hearts of their people, and, through their writings, into the heart of all mankind, the truth that the essence of sin among men is oppression of the lowly, and that righteousness consists in worthy treatment of the poor and the oppressed" (*Was bleibt vom Alten Testament,* 1916).

The central role of the ethical imperative in Biblical religion has no parallel elsewhere and, transmitted through the Apocrypha and Pseudepigrapha, it penetrated Christian thought, influencing Western culture as a whole. Within post-Biblical Judaism, the ethical teachings of the Scriptures were elaborated by the Rabbis and during the past two centuries gave rise to the *Musar* ("Ethics") movement, which reinvigorated traditional Jewry. Israel's moral code is thus a source of constant stimulation, "for what great nation is there, that hath statutes and ordinances so righteous as all this law?" (Deut. 4:8).

THE BIBLE'S IMPACT ON JUDAISM

The fact that Judaism first stressed the moral basis of religion has led to its well-known definition as "ethical monotheism." The concept of an omnipotent Creator is present in the Biblical text from the very beginning of the Book of Genesis, and the unique nature of God is indeed explicit

A Jew reciting the *Shema* before he goes to bed is portrayed in this miniature from the *Jerusalem Mishneh Torah,* a manuscript written in Spain and partly illuminated in Perugia (c. 1400).

in the *Shema* (Hebrew for "hear"), which observant Jews recite each morning and evening: "Hear, O Israel: the Lord our God, the Lord is One" (Deut. 6:4). God's own qualities demand imitation—"Ye shall be holy; for I the Lord your God am holy" (Lev. 19:2)—and man should emulate His righteousness, justice, and compassion. Judaism has thus anchored itself in the Biblical word: the "Lord of all the earth" (Josh. 3:11), not some obscure tribal deity, chose Israel "to be His own treasure out of all peoples that are upon the face of the earth" (Deut. 14:2) and set this one people "for a light of the nations" (Isa. 42:6). Apart from this spiritual vocation, Israel has been promised "all the land of Canaan, for an everlasting possession" (Gen. 17:8) and there God will cause His Temple to be built, "none other than the house of God" (Gen. 28:17) where "the Lord your God shall choose to cause His name to dwell" (Deut. 12:11). As He proclaimed Himself before Moses on Mount Sinai, so do Jews continue to proclaim Him in the service of the synagogue —"The Lord, the Lord, God, merciful and gracious, long-suffering, and abundant in goodness and truth; keeping mercy unto the thousandth generation, forgiving iniquity and transgression and sin . . . " (Ex. 34:6–7).

The idea of Israel as God's "Chosen People" is thus rooted in the Scriptures: "I will take you to Me for a people, and I will be to you a God" (Ex. 6:7); "I the Lord am holy, and have set you apart from the peoples, that ye should be Mine" (Lev. 20:26); "And who is like Thy people, like Israel, a nation one in the earth, whom God went to redeem unto Himself for a people . . . " (Sam. 7:23). The notion of being "chosen" is not restricted to the Jewish people, but what distinguished the Biblical doctrine of election from the sterile nationalistic claims of other folk lies within the old question: chosen for what? Israel was chosen for a Divine vocation: to proclaim God's unity, fatherhood of man, and call to righteousness—"Ye are My witnesses, saith the Lord, and My servant whom I have chosen" (Isa. 43:10). A wry Yiddish proverb underlines the tragic experience of Jewry as a result of the world's misunderstanding of this election: "'Thou hast chosen us from among all nations'— what, Lord, did You have against us?!" History has indeed fulfilled the prophecy of Amos (3:2), and with a vengeance: "You only have I known of all the families of the earth; therefore I will visit upon you all your iniquities." The Jewish people's melancholy experiences during the centuries of dispersion following the destruction of the Second Temple and the Jewish State were constantly exploited by polemists and hatemongers in other religious camps, who derisively asked what had happened to the "Chosen" race. Ignoring all the evidence in Scripture, the British sociologist and historian Arnold Toynbee (who in general regarded the Jews as a curious historical "fossil") went so far as to denounce this "idolization of an ephemeral self" (*A Study of History*, 1939). Alluding to a famous passage in the Talmud (*Avodah Zarah*, 2b), Israel Zangwill provided a telling answer to all such misconceptions: "A chosen people is really a choosing people. Not idly does Talmudical legend assert that the Law was offered first to all other nations and only Israel accepted the yoke."[8]

A fundamental idea related to the election of Israel is that of man's partnership with God in the development of the world. This creative cooperation, expressed in obedience to God's moral law, recognizes human rights (Justice) and man's acceptance of his duties (Righteousness).[9] Through a series of three primary Covenants, the Creator revealed the outline of His Divine plan for mankind. The rainbow serves as a remembrance of the first Covenant entered into with Noah after the Flood, when the future continuity of life on earth was firmly guaranteed (Gen. 9:9–17), and it is from the primary injunctions at the beginning of Genesis that the "Noachide" laws binding on all civilized mankind take their origin. The second Covenant was made with the Hebrew patriarch Abraham, to whose descendants God bequeathed the Promised Land "from the river of Egypt unto the great river, the river Euphrates" (Gen. 15:18–21); this Covenant was reconfirmed when circumcision was ordained as a perpetual symbol of God's contract with Israel (Gen. 17:10–14) and when Abraham and his descendants were named as the Lord's agents in the service of humanity (Gen. 18:19; cf. 17:4–8, 19, 21). This second contract was ratified in the Covenant with Israel at Sinai, when God undertook to make them His own "treasure" in return for their adherence to His commandments (Ex. 19:5; the phrase recurs in Deut. 14:2, 26:18, and Ps. 135:4). Israel's universal mission was formulated in the charge that they be "a kingdom of priests" serving humanity in general, and "a holy nation" following a distinctive way

---

[8] On a popular level, W. N. Ewer's sardonic quatrian, "How odd/ Of God/ To choose/ The Jews," evoked the anonymous retort: "It's not so odd—/ The Jews chose God"!

[9] For some of the following material I am indebted to Isidore Epstein's *Judaism. A Historical Presentation* (1959).

of life (Ex. 19:6). The Sinaitic revelation—historically unique as an experience shared by an entire people—thus lent final authenticity to the claims of the patriarchs and of Moses, converting tradition into everlasting certainty and faith. This fundamental idea of God's contract with Israel also finds expression in the Prophets, where its universal significance (and conditional nature) is invariably stressed: "I the Lord have called thee in righteousness, and have taken hold of thy hand, and kept thee, and set thee for a covenant of the people, for a light of the nations . . . " (Isa. 42:6).

BIBLICAL TRADITION

Judaism as a faith[10] rests on two dynamic pillars—Torah ("teaching," i.e. the Pentateuch and, by extension, the entire written and Oral Law) and Prophecy. The religio-moral code and the knowledge of God and His purpose which the Torah imparted were reinterpreted and redirected by Israel's Prophets in a way that established their universal relevance and appeal: penetrating to the core of the Biblical ethic, the Prophets made religion something more than the observance of mere ritual—a matter of justice and righteousness in the life of the individual and the community. With the overthrow of the Israelite and Judean kingdoms, Judaism faced—and met—the great challenge of exile under the inspiration of its spiritual resources. The traumatic effect of the Babylonian Captivity was to purify and confirm Israel's faith and traditions to the extent that the Return to Zion under Ezra and Nehemiah marked a new and decisive era in Jewish religious history. On the occasion of the solemn New Year in 444 B.C.E., Ezra instituted the public reading of the Torah and, in order to make its meaning clear to everyone, expounded the written text in accordance with the demands of new times and circumstances. "And they read in the book, in the Law of God, distinctly; and they gave the sense, and caused them to understand the reading" (Neh. 8:8). The Jewish sages shrewdly took "they read in the book" to denote the original Hebrew text and "distinctly" to imply a vernacular (Aramaic) translation that was more easily grasped by the returned exiles. Ezra's great achievement was to ensure continuous revelation

[10] The term "Judaism" is Hellenistic, not Biblical. Torah and "Faith [or "Tradition"] of Israel" more adequately convey the essence of the Jewish "way of life."

through the development of an Oral Law. The Torah—enthroned in the heart and mind of the Jewish people—became the ultimate source of every precept and usage that found a place in everyday life, affecting religion, morality, society, economics, politics, and the home.

During the Hellenistic period, the Pharisees (champions of the strict application of the Oral Law and of democracy in religious affairs) opposed the assimilationist, compromising party of the Sadducees, whose strength lay in the priestly and landowning classes, although a number of the more learned priests joined the Pharisaic opposition. The essential difference between the two parties lay in their outlook and doctrines. For the Sadducees, God was a Supreme Being committed entirely to Israel and the notion of an afterlife was anathema; for the Pharisees, God was a universal Being, the God of all mankind, and the soul's survival was implicit in the individual's responsibility toward his Maker in an imperfect world. The conflict between the aristocratic Sadducees and the popular Pharisees had serious repercussions in both religious and political life under the later Hasmonean rulers, and the civil wars that ensued finally brought the Herodian dynasty to the throne and the Romans to Judea.

Both these parties were heirs to the tradition of the Maccabees, whose revolt against the Syrian tyrant Antiochus Epiphanes in the second century B.C.E. temporarily restored Jewish national independence and reasserted Judaism's pure expression. The Sadducees emphasized the national at the expense of the spiritual, the Pharisees held fast to the universal aspects of the Prophetic faith. Under the Hasmonean (Maccabean) kings, a synthesis of Judaism and Hellenism was attempted and this had far-reaching consequences in Hellenistic Jewry's scattered colonies, from the populous and influential community of Alexandria in Egypt to Greece, Asia Minor, and the coast of North Africa. As practiced by many of these Hellenized communities, Judaism appealed to under-privileged Gentiles who could read the Bible in its new Greek version (the Septuagint, or "Book of the Seventy," which popular legend ascribed to a group of 70 or 72 Jewish translators in Alexandria acting on the suggestion of one of the Ptolemaic rulers). The Bible's social message, especially those passages relating to the emancipation of slaves, proved highly attractive to the fringe elements in Greek society. A "mission to the Gentiles" was thus in full swing long before Jesus and Paul began reshaping the religious structure of the ancient world. Most of the neophytes were only semi-converts (in Hebrew, *gerei ha-sha'ar,* or "proselytes of the gate") who undertook to observe the seven "No-achide Laws." In his *De Vita Mosis* ("Life of Moses"), the Alexandrian Jewish philosopher Philo Judaeus (c. 20 B.C.E.–50 C.E.) significantly observed that "our laws . . . attract and win the attention of all, of barbarians, of Greeks . . . of the whole inhabited world from end to end."

The Pharisees of Judea sought proselytes of a more committed sort (in Hebrew, *gerei ha-zedek,* "proselytes of righteousness"), whose prototype was Ruth, the Moabite ancestress of King David. A parallel to Philo's account may be found in *Contra Apionem* ("Against Apion"), an apology for Judaism written by the historian Josephus Flavius (c.38–after 100 C.E.): "There is not any city of the Greeks, nor any of the barbarians, nor any nation whatsoever, whither our custom of resting on the seventh day has not come, and by which our fasts and lighting of lamps, and many of our prohibitions as to our food, are not observed; they also endeavor to imitate our mutual accord, and the charitable distribution of our goods . . . and as God Himself permeates the universe, so the Law has found its way among all mankind." The contemporary effect of this "mission to the Gentiles" may be seen in the conversion to Judaism of the royal house of Adiabene in the East and of certain Roman patricians in the West, phenomena which drew a somewhat grudging tribute in the Gospels: "Ye compass sea and land to make one proselyte" (Matthew 23:15). Judaism in the Second Commonwealth era thus accepted and even promoted two levels of religious propaganda among interested Gentiles, confirming the Bible's significance and appeal at a time of increasing social and moral unrest and in a world where paganism was on the decline. Yet Hellenistic Jewry's role was increasingly irrelevant to the course of Judaism and Jewish history: Philo's conception of the *Logos* ("Word" or "son of God" in the sense of an instrument of Divine creation) was thoroughly un-Jewish and, like other aspects of Hellenistic Jewish thought, influenced early Christianity. The substitution of Greek for Hebrew was perhaps the ultimate cause of Greek-speaking Jewry's disappearance from the main stream of the faith, and the accession of proselytes—though never actually halted—became something quite exceptional in Judaism, subject as it was to the pressures of a hostile environment.[11]

---

[11]Notable Jewish proselytes have included Count Valentine Potocki in Poland, the English aristocrat and politician Lord George Gordon, and the U.S. diplomat Warder Cresson, as well as various Arab and Berber tribes and the ruling elements

JEWISH BIBLE COMMENTARY

From the period of Ezra onward, the main preoccupation of Jewish scholarship was with the systematic development of the law *(Halakhah)*[12] to be deduced from the Bibilical text or with the non-legal interpretation of Scripture *(Aggadah)*, which comprises homiletic exposition of the Bible, anecdotes and legendary material, folklore, maxims, and kindred subjects. Until about the sixth century C.E., these two parallel streams constituted the old Rabbinic literature; the Oral Law thus supplemented the written Torah and indicated its proper interpretation according to two basic methods of exegesis known as *peshat* (the plain meaning of the text) and *derash* (the exposition of its underlying significance where this was not immediately clear). The term *derash* comes from a Hebrew verb meaning "to seek, investigate," and Ezra—"a ready scribe in the Law of Moses"—assumed the role of a commentator, reading the Law "distinctly" (Neh. 8:8) and setting out "to seek *(li-drosh)* the law of the Lord, and to do it, and to teach in Israel statutes and ordinances" (Ezra 7:10). From this same root the Rabbis later coined the noun *Midrash*—signifying the legal or homiletic interpretation of Scripture. There are, in fact, earlier traces of such exposition in certain Biblical books, as when Ps. 106:33 explains why Moses came to strike the rock (Num. 20:10ff.) or when 2 Chron. 7:8–10 elucidates an obscure dating in 1 Kings 8:65–66. Many other clarifications of earlier Biblical passages can be found in the Book of Chronicles. Ezra began this process of interpretation and Hillel and his successors later formulated its guiding principles. The Hellenistic scholars of Alexandria, who called the Torah God's "Law" (or the "Law of Moses" or "Law of Israel") and coined the term "Holy Bible," wed Greek thought and Jewish religious concepts in their allegorical exegesis, a field in which Philo particularly excelled. In their missionary zeal, these Alexandrians

---

of the Khazar people. In many cases, however, these converts to Judaism had no Jewish sponsors or "missionaries" to guide them and had to travel a lonely—and often perilous—road to their new faith. Under the Mussolini regime, many inhabitants of San Nicandro, an Italian village, embraced Judaism and they eventually found their way to Israel. The 20th century has seen the growth of a more flexible attitude toward the conversion issue within most streams of Judaism.

[12] See below and, for a more detailed discussion, the first part of Chapter 2.

even went so far as to suggest that Homer, Socrates, and Plato had somehow had access to a lost Greek translation of the Pentateuch; and one Greek-speaking Jew, Ezekiel the Poet, used the Septuagint and contemporary homiletics as the basis for his drama about the Exodus.[13]

After the second century C.E., the focus of Jewish scholarship shifted to Mesopotamia ("Babylon"), where great new Talmudic academies modeled on that founded by Johanan ben Zakkai at Yavneh (after the fall of Jerusalem) came into being. Normative Judaism had to face a crisis in the eighth century, when the heretical Karaites (*Benei Mikra*, "students of the Scripture") rejected the whole body of Oral Law, paying close attention to the Biblical text alone. The challenge posed by Karaite literalism and by Muslim polemics led to a consolidation of Judaism and to a regrouping of the traditionalists (or "Rabbanites," as they were called) under the leadership of Sa'adiah Gaon (892–942). Abandoning the old homiletic approach, Sa'adiah made Bible study an independent discipline, using the latest secular knowledge and philological and other forms of investigation in his objective analysis of the Scriptural text. The methods which Sa'adiah pioneered were fostered by the medieval Sephardi ("Spanish") and Ashkenazi ("German") communities, each of which developed its own distinctive cultural and liturgical tradition. In Spain, Abraham Ibn Ezra (1089–1164) used linguistic criteria to elucidate the Bible's meaning (some of his conclusions actually foreshadowing later Biblical criticism); in France, the new rationalist school of Jewish exegesis found its leading exponent in Rashi (Solomon ben Isaac of Troyes, 1040–1105), who wrote commentaries on almost the entire Hebrew Bible, as well as on the Talmud. Rashi, the greatest of all Jewish Bible commentators, relied on the unadorned, literal meaning of a word or passage and used philological and grammatical data to elucidate obscurities (occasionally supplying an Old French equivalent in Hebrew transliteration) in the course of his logical and concise exposition; he also made reference to the Midrash in order to elucidate points under discussion. David Kimḥi (c. 1160–1235) combined the speculative and linguistic methods of Spain with Rashi's plain interpretation, his own lucid commentary later aiding Christian scholars who made ample use of it in a Latin translation.[14] A similar

---

[13] See Chapter 4.

[14] For Nicholas de Lyre's use of Rashi's Biblical commentary, see Chapter 4 (France).

technique was adopted by Naḥmanides (Moses ben Naḥman, 1194–c. 1270), the preeminent Spanish Talmudist and a courageous champion of his faith, who also injected a mystical element into his exegesis deriving from the Kabbalah. In the Zohar, a mystical commentary on the Torah, this kabbalistic literature reached a climax soon after Naḥmanides' death.[15] From the 14th century until the Age of Enlightenment, Jewish Bible interpretation went into a decline, except for the influential and original (if prolix) commentary of Don Isaac Abrabanel (1473–1508), a statesman and scholar who found refuge in Italy after the Spanish Expulsion of 1492.

THE "WAY OF LIFE"

Israel's free and grateful acceptance of the Torah and the "yoke of the kingdom of Heaven" derives from a distinctive conception of life and ultimate responsibility. The "Law" is in fact "a river of God full of living water" (Ps. 65:10) and "a tree of life to them that lay hold upon it" (Prov. 3:18). The Psalmist's call to "serve the Lord with gladness" (Ps. 100:2) was to inspire the Rabbinic idea of "the joy of the Commandment" (*Shabbat,* 30b), which imbues both the ritual and the ethical prescriptions of Judaism. In his *Geschichte des Volkes Israel* ("History of the People of Israel," 1925), the German Christian scholar Rudolph Kittel freely confessed that "anyone who has had the opportunity of knowing the inner life of present-day Jewish families that observe the Law of the fathers with sincere piety and in all strictness will have been astonished at the wealth of joyfulness, gratitude, and sunshine, undreamt of by the outsider, which the Law animates in the Jewish home."

The Talmud (literally, "Learning") is the great repository of Rabbinic law and lore, the work of the Rabbis who taught the average Jew to understand his faith and love his God. Aware of the dangers of literalism —acting only on the letter, and not also on the spirit, of the Law—the Rabbis proclaimed the need for continual Oral interpretation of the Torah in the form of what they called *Halakhah* ("the way of life").[16] "Without the zeal of the Rabbis," wrote the Anglo-Jewish scholar Adolf Büchler, "the Bible would never have become the guide of every Jew.

---

[15] An outline of the Kabbalah is given below; other points of interest are contained in Chapters 3 and 4.

[16] The Talmud and Jewish Law are discussed more fully in Chapter 2.

They translated it into the vernacular for the people, and expounded it to the masses. They taught them not to despair under the tortures of the present, but to look forward to the future. At the same time they developed the spirit of the Bible and never lost sight of the lofty teachings of the Prophets. It is the immortal merit of the unknown Rabbis of the centuries immediately before and after the common era that they found and applied the proper 'fences' for the preservation of Judaism, and that they succeeded in rescuing real morality and pure monotheism for the ages that were to follow."

As a "way of life," Judaism is not simply a revealed religion but, as the German philosopher Moses Mendelssohn phrased it, "revealed legislation." The Decalogue epitomizes the Law, but the 613 Commandments *("Taryag Mizvot")* which the Rabbis deduced from the Scriptures regulate every aspect of life, both physical and spiritual, from prayer and study to food and marital relations. Some of these laws (e.g., those relating to the Temple) are not currently applicable, while others govern only the lives of Jews resident in the Land of Israel, the natural home of the people and the focus of its legal code and national and Messianic yearnings. From the Bible Judaism thus derives moral precepts concerned with man's duty to God and to his fellow, ritual laws intended to train human character, and other injunctions for which no explanation is available. The Rabbis made *gemilut hasadim* ("acts of kindness") a practical application of the old *imitatio Dei* ideal, noting that the Creator, at the beginning of the Torah, clothes Adam (Gen. 3:21) while, at the end, He buries Moses (Deut. 34:6).

Centuries of prejudice and ignorance have increased popular misconceptions as to the Biblical origin and moral value of Israel's ceremonial precepts. That "cleanliness is next to godliness" finds practical demonstration in the rules of hygiene and ritual ablution which Jews have observed since time immemorial. Although hygienic considerations may be present in the Jewish dietary laws, an element of spirituality governs the choice and preparation of meat, fish, fowl, and other foods, requiring the avoidance of blood (Gen. 9:4), the complete separation of meat and milk in both diet and kitchen (Ex. 23:19), and the elimination of "unclean" species (Lev. 11:2–30, 41–45) and carrion (Lev. 11:39–40). Perpetual awareness of Israel's election as "a kingdom of priests and a holy nation" is ensured by the circumcision of boys (Gen. 17:10–14) and the symbols of consecration to God: the fringed garment worn under the shirt *(zizit)* and, as the "prayer shawl" *(tallit),* in

Man touching the *mezuzah* as he leaves a house. Detail from illustration in the *Rothschild Miscellany,* North Italy, Ferrara (?) (c. 1470).

the synagogue (Num. 15:37–40); the phylacteries (*tefillin*) worn during weekday morning prayers on the head and arm (Deut. 6:6–8); and the doorpost sign *(mezuzah)* which one passes when entering and walking through the Jewish home (Deut. 6:9).

The laws governing Sabbath observance, based on God's hallowing of the seventh day of Creation (Gen. 2:3; Ex. 20:8–11; Lev. 23:3; Deut. 5:12–15), ensure that the loyal Jew "shall keep the Sabbath, to observe the Sabbath" in every .generation (Deut. 31:16). This "perpetual covenant" between God and His people has, perhaps more than anything else, guaranteed the survival of the Jews throughout all the tragic vicissitudes of their history; in the telling phrase of a modern Hebrew essayist and philosopher, Aḥad Ha-Am (Asher Ginsberg, 1856–1927), "More than Israel kept the Sabbath, the Sabbath has kept Israel." Far from inflicting an intolerable burden on the Jew, its pious observance makes him "call the Sabbath a delight" (Isa. 58:13). Men and women of today are often oblivious of the fact that the institution of the Sabbath revolutionized ancient society, freeing man from perpetual drudgery, although its wide appeal alarmed the Greeks and Romans, who condemned Sabbath observance as a subversive superstition. The seventh Day of Rest, the proper enjoyment of which Jews see as a foretaste of the Messianic age and the world to come, eventually became the Christian "Lord's Day" (Sunday) and the Muslim Friday of communal devotion. The idea that the Jewish Sabbath is a day of gloom derives from its peculiarly rigid adoption as the Nonconformist "Lord's Day." The British theologian William Booth Selbie has stressed the folly of such confusion: "To the Jews it is a day of happiness. The synagogue liturgy of the Sabbath is full of the joyous note. It is marked by gay dress, sumptuous meals, and a general sense of exhilaration. The Puritans knew little or nothing of synagogue worship or of Jewish homes. They had no experience of 'the joy of the commandment'—a phrase often on Jewish lips and in Jewish hearts. They interpreted the Scripture injunctions in their own dour spirit."[17]

Historical and symbolic motifs dominate the solemn and festive occasions in the Jewish year. The "Days of Awe" (or "High Holidays") comprise the New Year *(Rosh ha-Shanah)*, when the ram's horn *(shofar)* is sounded (Lev. 23:24–5; Num. 29:1), and the Day of Atonement *(Yom Kippur)*, a sunset to sunset fast (Lev. 23:27–32; Num. 29:7–8). Colorful ceremonies reminiscent of Biblical times distinguish the Three Pilgrim Festivals—Passover *(Pesaḥ)*, when the *Seder* service in the home and the eating of unleavened bread *(maẓẓot)* commemorate the Exodus from Egypt (Ex. 12:14–20, 13:3–10; Lev. 23:5–8; Num. 28:16–18); Pentecost *(Shavu'ot)*, celebrating the ingathering of the harvest and the traditional date of the Sinaitic Revelation (Ex. 19:1ff., 34:22; Lev. 23:21); and Tabernacles *(Sukkot)*, when the "four species" (palm branch, myrtle and willow stems, and citron) are ceremonially waved and shaken in the synagogue and "booths" are erected next to the home in memory of Israel's journey through the wilderness (Lev. 23:34, 39–43). Joy and thankfulness mingle in the festival of Purim (Esther 9:20–28), commemorating the Jewish people's narrow escape from Haman's murderous trap.

[17] From "The Influence of the Old Testament on Puritanism," in *The Legacy of Israel* (1927), p. 423.

TORAH AND PRAYER

As we have seen, public readings from the Torah were first instituted by Ezra and the Hebrew Bible occupies a central position in Jewish study and devotion. With the exception of the Five Scrolls (Song of Songs, Ruth, Lamentations, Ecclesiastes, and Esther), which are recited on prescribed occasions during the year, only the Pentateuch is read in its entirety in the synagogue service. Extracts from the Prophets and Writings form "additional readings" *(haftarot)* to the weekly Torah portion *(sidrah,* or *parashah)*. Until recently, the Jewish preacher almost invariably based his sermon on the prescribed Torah reading for the Sabbath and at one time the Pentateuch was read from end to end within one year in Babylon and over a period of three years (the "triennial cycle") in the Land of Israel. Although the Babylonian system is currently the norm, a modified version of the triennial cycle has been adopted by Reform (and some Conservative) congregations. After mastering the Hebrew alphabet, the Jewish child begins his religious studies with the Five Books of Moses and is later introduced to the Bible commentaries of Rashi and other scholars; only when he is thoroughly familiar with the Pentateuch and Prophets does he normally proceed to the Mishnah, Gemara, and other higher studies.[18] Oriental Jewry's Biblical expertise derives from the fact that the great Spanish luminary Maimonides differed from the Rabbis of medieval France and Germany in laying at least as much stress on the value of Torah study as on knowledge of the Talmud.

The focal point of synagogue worship is the Holy Ark or Ark of the Law *(aron ha-kodesh* or *tevah)* housing one or more copies of the Pentateuch *(Sefer Torah)*. Each Torah scroll is made up of numerous lengths of parchment inscribed by hand with the text of the Five Books. A special script (varying slightly from one rite to another) is used and the work entailed, which can require a year's patient and devoted effort, is entrusted to a professional *sofer* (scribe) who executes it with loving care, checking each letter and flourish against a perfect copy as he proceeds from *"Be-reshit"* ("In the beginning"), the first word of Genesis,

---

[18] Torah study is an essential part of Judaism, which takes its authority for this from the Five Books of Moses (Ex. 13:8–9; Deut. 4:10, 6:7) and from the Book of Proverbs (1:7; cf. Ps. 111:10): "The fear of the Lord is the beginning of knowledge."

to *"Yisra'el"* ("Israel"), the last word of Deuteronomy. If, after constant use, any letter of the text becomes illegible or ambiguous, the Torah scroll is rendered invalid *(pasul)* and must be handed to a qualified *sofer* so that the necessary correction(s) can be made without delay. Only a perfect scroll may be employed for public reading in the synagogue. The *Sefer Torah* is wound on wooden rollers and, in Ashkenazi communities, it is swathed in an ornamented velvet mantle *(me'il);* over this are placed two silver appurtenances, a plaque or breastplate *(tas)* and a pointer *(yad,* literally "hand") used by the reader to indicate the place. Fruit-shaped silver or gilded ornaments surmount the tops of the rollers when the *Sefer Torah* is not in use and these are known as *rimmonim* ("pomegranates"); sometimes they are replaced by a large silver or gilded crown *(keter* or *atarah),* signifying the Torah's majesty. The scroll itself is bound tight with a cloth or velvet binder *(mappah)* to prevent damage to the parchment. Oriental and most Sephardi communities replace the mantle and ornaments with an ornate wooden or metal case *(tik)* which opens on hinges for the Torah reading. It is considered a great honor for a congregant to be called upon to raise or bind up the scroll after the prescribed Scriptural portion has been

A Yemenite *sofer* (scribe) at work on a Torah scroll in Israel.

Rejoicing of the Law (*Simḥat Torah*) in a Tel Aviv suburb.

concluded. On weekdays, three worshipers are called to the reading of the Law, on festivals five, and on Sabbaths seven; on Sabbaths and festivals, an additional person is honored with the final portion *(maftir)*, which entails his recitation of the Prophetic reading, generally from a "pointed" (vocalized) text, the Torah itself being unpointed. Jewish congregations endeavor to acquire as many Torah scrolls as possible, all of which are joyously carried around the synagogue on the *Simḥat Torah* (Rejoicing of the Law) festival. Great reverence is shown for every *Sefer Torah* and any damage to it caused by fire, desecration, or vandalism is regarded as a public calamity. The Ark in which the scrolls are kept is situated on the synagogue's eastern wall to face Jerusalem; it is usually fronted by a velvet ornamented curtain *(parokhet)* and before it hangs the *ner tamid* ("eternal light"), a lamp fed by oil or powered by electricity which must be constantly alight in memory of the fire that burned perpetually on the altar of the Tabernacle (Lev. 6:6). This lamp also symbolizes the radiance of faith and formerly served various purposes,

28

Torah scroll collection in the Holy Ark of the Central Synagogue, Manhattan.

such as the ceremonial rekindling of lights after the conclusion of the Sabbath.

The basis of prayer is the belief in a personal God with Whom each individual can communicate, expressing his quest for the Divine and his wish to unburden himself before his Maker. Judaism's three statutory services are homiletically traced to the Pentateuch: the morning service *(Shaharit)* from the fact that "Abraham rose early in the morning" (Gen. 22:3); the afternoon service *(Minhah)* because "Isaac went out to meditate in the field at the eventide" (Gen. 24:63); and the evening service *(Arvit* or *Ma'ariv)* from the fact that Jacob "lighted upon[19] the place [Beth-el], and tarried there all night" (Gen. 28:11). There are said to be no less than 85 complete prayers in the Bible, the shortest of which is Moses' plea to God on his sister Miriam's behalf: "Heal her now, O God, I beseech Thee" (Num. 12:13). The *Hallel* ("Praise") recited on the Three Pilgrim Festivals and certain other occasions comprises Psalms 113–118, and each day of the week has its allotted Psalm "which the Levites used to recite in the Temple." Apart from these daily Psalms and the six of the *Hallel,* the only Scriptural passages in regular liturgical use during the Talmudic period were those making up the *Shema* creed (Deut. 6:4–9, 11:13–21; Num. 15:37–41), but many more have been added to the Jewish prayer book since that time. Thus, the Song of Moses (Ex. 14:30–15:18) is now recited in the morning and Ps. 126 is generally sung before grace after meals. Congregational singing of prescribed Biblical passages precedes and follows the reading of the Torah, which is displayed to the assembled worshipers who then proclaim: "And this is the Law which Moses set before the children of Israel" (Deut. 4:44). Appropriate Scriptural texts are also contained in the special prayer invoking God's blessing on the monarch or president and on the government.

One of the few privileges still reserved for Jews of priestly descent (the *Kohanim*) is blessing other worshipers in the synagogue.[20] In Jerusalem this ceremony forms part of the daily service, in the rest of Israel it takes place on Sabbaths and festivals, and in the lands of the

---

[19]"Lighted upon" was interpreted to mean "prayed," the Hebrew verb *paga* containing the sense of both.

[20] A *Kohen* is still instrumental in the ceremonial Redemption of the Firstborn Son *(pidyon ha-ben),* based on Ex. 34:20; and, if present in the synagogue, he is called first to the reading of the Torah.

Priestly Benediction before a large assembly at the Western Wall, Jerusalem.

Diaspora it is reserved for the major festivals only. A treasured relic of the ancient Temple ritual, the Benediction of the Priests is pronounced while the *Kohanim,* standing before the holy ark, envelop themselves in the fringed *tallit* and the congregation piously avert their gaze. The source of the Benediction is Numbers 6:24–26:

> The Lord bless thee, and keep thee;
> The Lord make His face to shine upon thee, and be gracious unto
> thee;
> The Lord lift up His countenance upon thee, and give thee peace.

Particular significance is attached to the *Shema Yisra'el* ("Hear, O Israel") creed recited morning and evening, before retiring at night, when the Torah scrolls are taken out of the holy ark, and at the end of the Atonement *(Yom Kippur)* fast. The first phrase taught to children and the last uttered on the deathbed, Israel's *Shema* has been a password in every age and the martyr's agonized confession of faith—a "sanctification of the Divine Name"—ever since the era of the Maccabees. It defied the torturers of Syria and Rome, of the medieval Church and the

31

Spanish Inquisition, of the Russian pogroms and the Nazi death camps. In her famous "Zionist" novel, *Daniel Deronda* (1876), George Eliot displayed an enlightened Christian's insight when she made her hero say: "The *Shema,* wherein we briefly confess the divine Unity . . . made our religion the fundamental religion for the whole world; for the divine Unity embraced as its consequence the ultimate unity of mankind."

As we have already observed, the homiletic interpretation of Scripture serves as a parallel and complement to the legal (halakhic) prescriptions of the Gemara. The roots of this homiletic literature may be found in the Talmudic *Aggadah* (or *Haggadah,* "narrative")—all the legendary, allegorical, historical, metaphysical, and edifying material which intersperses the strictly legal discussions of the Rabbis. Out of this literary tradition arose the Midrash (from a Biblical term meaning "commentary," see 2 Chron. 13:22, 24:27), best translated as "history," a body of lore ranging over many eras and countries which bears traces of much external influence. The Midrash illuminated the underlying sense of the Bible and often served to produce a Scriptural basis for established laws and customs. Although Midrashic elements are prominent in the Talmud, an independent literature also grew up in the form of specific compilations (*Midrash Rabbah, Tanḥuma, Pirkei de-Rabbi Eliezer, Tanna de-Vei Eliyahu, Midrash Ha-Gadol,* etc.) arranged in accordance with the Biblical order of the verses treated. Here, the heroes and villains of the Bible were given a new, symbolic role—Abraham as the embodiment of courage, Esau of enmity toward Israel, David of unqualified righteousness, Solomon of limitless wisdom—and the realism of their portrayal, despite frequent anachronism, brought them vividly to life in popular imagination.

In early Rabbinic times, the Jewish preacher *(darshan)* used a translation of the weekly Torah reading into the Aramaic vernacular *(Targum)* and often resorted to the Midrash in order to elucidate or embellish his text. The sermon (*derashah:* another word allied to *derash,* the homiletic method of interpreting the Bible), eventually abandoned the *Targum,* which survived only as a written (or later as a printed) accompaniment to the Hebrew source. The sermon was, however, a vehicle of vast importance for the popular exposition of Scripture, enabling the preacher to furnish all sections of the population with a basic knowledge of the Torah, to strengthen the Jewish faith, and to refute heresy. Both Christianity and Islam were to base their own sermonic traditions on this Jewish model. At times, the preacher would employ various techniques to capture the attention of his audience, which often flocked to hear the entertaining addresses of a favorite *darshan*. Some preachers used a Biblical text to scold transgressors or denounce social evils, and in more recent centuries they often exploited their text in order to attack dangerous tendencies that they saw on the immediate horizon. During the 19th century, sermons in German Reform temples were first preached in the vernacular, reflecting the influence of the Evangelical pulpit. Although Orthodox communities resisted this innovation, sermons in English, French, German, and other languages have since replaced the old-time Yiddish *derashot* in most traditionalist Ashkenazi communities. Another 20th-century change has been the virtual disappearance of the professional *darshan,* whose place has been taken by the incumbent Rabbi or "minister." On the other hand, hallowed techniques have been preserved: the prescribed weekly portion is often the sermon's point of departure, although current affairs and other topics may largely engage the preacher's attention.

A mystical outgrowth of the Midrash was the literature of the Kabbalah (literally, "tradition"), partly foreshadowed in some passages of Ezekiel and Daniel. From the Apocalyptic writings (Enoch, 2 Esdras, the Sibylline Oracles, etc.), this mystical current emerged in time as a separate body of lore, producing the early mystical *Sefer Yezirah* ("Book of Formation"), the 12th-century *Sefer Ha-Bahir* ("Book of Brightness"), and the Kabbalah's greatest single monument, the Zohar (*Sefer Ha-Zohar,* "Book of Splendor"). The alleged antiquity of the Zohar has been hotly disputed, but most of it seems to have been written toward the end of the 13th century, the final redaction being credited to a Spanish Rabbi and mystic, Moses de Leon (c.1240–1305), who wrote a number of other kabbalistic books. The Zohar is ostensibly a mystical commentary on much of the Pentateuch and three of the Five Scrolls, the authorship being ascribed to the second-century teacher, Simeon bar Yohai. The Torah was interpreted in accordance with four exegetical methods— *peshat* (the plain sense), *remez* (allegory), *derash* (homiletical exposition), and *sod* (secret wisdom)[21]—the last of which especially preoccupied the kabbalists. Homilies, parables, hidden meanings, and lengthy discourses all intermingle in the Zohar, which achieved special importance

---

[21] The initials of these four terms spell *Pardes* ("orchard"), a word that assumes a special mystical significance in the Zohar. For further (linguistic and literary) information about the Kabbalah, see Chapters 3 and 4.

after the Spanish Expulsion of 1492, when it was used to bolster the faith of Sephardi exiles. The Ḥasidic movement, too, later venerated this mystical work, portions of which have entered the Jewish liturgy. In the Oriental and Ḥasidic worlds, the Zohar has been accorded a place of supreme importance, ranking next to the Bible and Talmud. Although its author(s) probably never trod the soil of the Holy Land, it is the Palestine of early Rabbinic times that forms the legendary background to the Zohar. Medieval Spain was also the birthplace of a glorious new tradition of Hebrew secular and religious poetry, the creators of which (notably Judah Halevi) often exploited Biblical themes and echoes without resorting to an artificial "Biblical" style.[22] A good deal of this verse has also found its way into the service of the synagogue.

MODERN TRENDS IN JUDAISM

Talmudic and kabbalistic pursuits overshadowed study of the Bible in the Jewish world during the 16th–18th centuries, although the pioneer Hebrew grammarian Elijah Levita (1468–1549), the eminent commentator Obadiah Sforno (1475–1550), and other men of learning managed to preserve the light of Bible scholarship in Italy. However, even when the Talmud exclusively preoccupied the Jewish student in the countless *yeshivot* (Rabbinical academies) of Central and Eastern Europe, all authority in the spheres of Jewish law and literature had its basis in the Hebrew Bible. Biblical studies as such might be neglected, but the Jew still familiarized himself with the Bible through a host of quotations in the Talmud. Moreover, the weekly Torah portion (read in full on the Sabbath and in part on Mondays and Thursdays) and its associated commentaries kept a knowledge of the Pentateuch and of sections of the Prophets and Writings (the *haftarot* or "additional readings") alive in the consciousness of the Jew. In his poem, *Ha-Matmid* ("The Talmud Student," 1894–95), the Hebrew writer H.N. Bialik[23] thus recalled his own early training when he rhapsodized: "Nor rock nor flint can e'er in hardness vie/ With a Jewish boy whose Torah is his fare."

The modern revival of Bible study and exegesis among the Jews was inaugurated by Moses Mendelssohn (1729–1786), who published a Pentateuch in German translation (though, for the reader's convenience,

----

22 On the Bible in medieval Spanish poetry, see Chapter 4.
23 On Bialik and the Hebrew renaissance, see Chapter 4.

in Hebrew transliteration) together with a Hebrew commentary, this *Bi'ur* (or *Be'ur*) appearing in 1780–83. Mendelssohn also wrote other translations and commentaries at this period, but some of the modern conceptions which he introduced—and which his disciples subsequently developed—provoked serious opposition in more rigidly Orthodox circles. Since Mendelssohn and his emulators wrote in German, their impact on the Jewish masses of Eastern Europe was negligible, and it was only after the rise of the *Haskalah* ("Enlightenment") movement in the 19th century that the new spirit of criticism and enquiry began to have any effect further afield. While Moses Mendelssohn was himself an observant Jew, loyal to Orthodox tradition, many of his followers promoted the religious Reform movement which spread from Germany to other parts of Europe and especially to the United States. Reform Judaism was initially motivated by a genuine concern for the faith's survival in a changing world and, to counteract the allurements of secular culture, Protestant worship, and skepticism, various innovations were attempted: improved and more decorous services, vernacular prayers and sermons, and certain liturgical and ritual modifications. The spirit of the age also led to a new stress on religious and social ethics to match the idealism of Reform's leadership. Deploring the "aridity" of Talmudic studies, which were rooted in the legal aspects of the Pentateuch, the Reform movement reemphasized the message of the Prophets and proclaimed Judaism to be "ethical monotheism"—a definition which it has consistently maintained in its theological stand. Soon, however, other changes were made in the fabric of traditional Judaism: much of the Oral Law was abandoned as an anachronism which placed an unnecessary and inconvenient burden on the modern, "enlightened" Jew; references to the resurrection of the dead and the Messianic hope of a return to Zion were jettisoned; and separate seating for men and women was abolished in Reform temples. Some radicals, no longer content even with the authority of the written Torah, went so far as to repudiate the Saturday Sabbath and its observances, the dietary laws, and the hallowed rite of circumcision. In Europe, these excesses met opposition not only from traditionalists but also from wide sections of the Reform movement itself. Radical Reform lost influence and a more moderate and "conservative" spirit eventually prevailed, manifesting itself in German Liberalism, Hungarian Neology, and English Reform Judaism, the leaders of which sought to avoid the dangers of a final break with tradition. In the United States, radical Reform also encountered similar opposition, but its appeal (formulated in the famous "Pittsburgh Platform" of 1885) proved decisive and the dissenters were forced to reorganize as a minority group that was to be the forerunner of Conservative Judaism.

The challenge of Reform, first felt in the West, brought about a significant revival of Jewish studies and teaching in the traditionalist or "Orthodox" camp. Although seminaries for the training of Reform Rabbis were established in Berlin (1870) and Cincinnati (1875), the overwhelming majority of these Rabbinical colleges were of Orthodox or Conservative affiliation,[24] and systematic instruction in the Bible formed an important part of the curriculum. Journals and publications for the promotion of the conflicting ideologies came into being and educational reforms were undertaken in an effort to stem the rising tide of ignorance and religious indifference. In Meir Leibuoh (Löb) Malbim (1809–1879), whose commentary on the Bible appeared during the years 1845–76, Orthodoxy found a vehement champion and Jewish Biblical scholarship an exegete of stature. Reform Judaism readily embraced 19th-century Biblical Criticism and used its findings to batter away at doctrines and assumptions long cherished by traditional Jewry. The Orthodox, for their part, made a stand on the doctrine of Divine Revelation—*Torah min ha-Shamayim* ("Torah from Heaven") or *Torah mi-Sinai* (the "Torah of Sinai")—which reaffirms that continuous process of authoritative Scriptural interpretation which the Rabbis of old made fundamental to Jewish belief. They quoted in support of their position

[24] The first seminaries were in fact Orthodox foundations: the Collegio Rabbinico Italiano (1829) and the Ecole Rabbinique in France (1830). These were followed by Jews' College in London (1855), the Berlin Rabbinical Seminary (1873), the Vienna Rabbinical Seminary (1893), and the Rabbi Isaac Elchanan Theological Seminary in New York (1897; now part of Yeshiva University). The Conservative approach was propagated in the Breslau Rabbinical Seminary (1854), the National Rabbinical Seminary of Budapest (1877), and the Jewish Theological Seminary of America (1886). The main teaching centers of Reform Judaism were the Berlin "Hochschule" (1872), Hebrew Union College in Cincinnati (1875), and the Jewish Institute of Religion in New York (1922; merged with Hebrew Union College in 1950). Reform and Liberal Jews in England are served by Leo Baeck College in London (1956). The Berlin, Breslau, and Vienna seminaries were liquidated by the Nazis; others of secondary importance have not been mentioned above.

the eighth and ninth of the classic Thirteen Principles of the Faith which Maimonides had formulated in the 12th century:

> I believe with perfect faith that the whole Torah, now in our possession, is the same that was given to Moses our teacher, peace be unto him.

> I believe with perfect faith that this Torah will not be changed, and that there will never be any other Law from the Creator, blessed be His name.[25]

These theological conflicts over the centrality of the Torah and Oral Law in Jewish belief and observance have given rise to the three main streams in contemporary Judaism. Orthodoxy, which has modernist wings attuned to the culture of the West alongside the most rigid and "fundamentalist" sectors of piety, adopts the stand of Rabbinic tradition; Reform, which has latterly retreated from the ultra-radicalism of the past, claims the right to question and modify established concepts and observances in the light of modern outlook and research; while Conservatism, originally America's answer to militant Reform, takes a theological position midway between Orthodoxy and Reform and a halakhic (legal or ritual) stand fairly close to that of the traditionalist right. A minor American trend, Reconstructionism, often outbids Reform in its theology and, while approving many of the halakhic precepts, sees their justification not in Divine sanction, but in their psychological hold on Jewry, furthering the sense of Jewish peoplehood. During the 19th century, Reform sometimes described itself as a Mosaism," implying that the movement signified a return to the "pure" faith of the Bible, and styled its house of worship a "temple." Some elements in Western Orthodoxy, also sensitive to the call for intellectual progress, imitated this tendency by calling themselves "Israelites" and their synagogues "Hebrew congregations"—a phenomenon that still persists in the English-speaking world.

One result of the religious controversies that marked the 19th century was the growth of "Judische Wissenschaft" (the "Science of Judaism," i.e., Jewish scholarship pursued on modern scientific lines), the exponents

---

[25] These Thirteen Principles entered the Jewish liturgy in the form of the popular *Yigdal* hymn (c. 1300).

of which paid special attention to the Bible and to Jewish liturgy. The Reform movement mainly concentrated on revisions of the prayer book, while translations of the Bible were often the work of specialists in the traditionalist camp. The Jewish Publication Society of America's widely distributed edition of *The Holy Scriptures* (1917)[26] was, however, the fruit of much devoted effort by a panel of Orthodox, Conservative, and Reform scholars. Two particularly influential annotated Pentateuchs were issued by Samson Raphael Hirsch (1808–1888), the leader of German Orthodox Jewry, and Joseph Herman Hertz (1872–1946), a master of popular Jewish scholarship, who was Chief Rabbi of the British Empire. The "Science of Judaism" set out to restore, among other things, Jewish scholarly proficiency in the Biblical field. The works of Samuel David Luzzatto (1800–1865) proclaim him to have been both an erudite exponent of Orthodoxy and a religious precursor of Zionism. He prepared an Italian version of the Pentateuch with Hebrew commentary (1871–76) and various other annotations to the Bible. While accepting the textual sanctity of the Pentateuch, Luzzatto did not hesitate to amend other portions of the Scriptures, the Divine inspiration of which he nevertheless maintained. Modern Jewish Bible scholarship has evolved its own distinctive approach to the Scriptural text, repudiating the 19th-century theories associated with the Graf-Wellhausen school,[27] together with certain other features of non-Jewish criticism. Umberto (Moses David) Cassuto (1883–1951), who served as professor of Bible at the Hebrew University of Jerusalem (from 1939) and as first editor-in-chief of the Hebrew *Biblical Encyclopedia,* thus used textual and linguistic analysis to affirm the existence of an ancient oral tradition and the Hebrew Bible's unitary character. Similarly, Yeḥezkel Kaufmann (1889–1963), who also became head of the Bible department at the Hebrew University, asserted that Israel's monotheistic tradition began with Moses and combated many critical theories about the Bible in his monumental eight-volume *Toledot Ha-Emunah Ha-Yisre'elit* (1937–57; *The Religion of Israel,* 1960). Kaufmann also published a number of important essays, commentaries, and studies relating to Biblical books and texts and shedding new light on the Scriptures.

The age-old yearning for a Return to Zion which fortified Jewish hopes of restoration and renewal lay behind many attempts to resettle the Land

[26] The J.P.S.A.'s revised Pentateuch appeared in 1962.
[27] See below.

of Israel—from the Jewish pilgrims of the Middle Ages and the Safed kabbalists of the 16th century to the Hasidic and other pioneering immigrants of more recent times. Religious impulses have been strong in this desire for a freer Jewish life in the ancient homeland and for a fruitful rebirth of Jewish culture on the ancestral soil. Theodor Herzl's political Zionism, which from the 1890s inspired the most eventful trend in recent Jewish history, set in motion a whole train of activity—the wider promotion of Hebrew as a living language, intensive study of Jewish literature, and worldwide Zionist activity ranging from the Orthodox Mizraḥi movement to the radical Socialist left. Both in the State of Israel and in the major communities of the Diaspora *(Golah* or *Galut)*, the Hebrew Bible is studied with an interest and fervor unknown in the Jewish sphere for centuries past. Whether their teachers are religious or secular, Israeli schoolchildren are made to realize that the Bible is their birthright, their greatest literary treasure, and their main title to their land. It is the first chapter of their history, the foundation of their daily language, and the basis of their geography. Bible study finds an ally in the national pastime of archaeology, indicative of the new generation's search for roots. Children are given Biblical names long forgotten, and new villages and settlements revive the names of ancient Biblical localities. International and local Bible contests for adults and youngsters are regular events; Bible study groups meet at the homes of the nation's leaders; and the traditional text read at the conclusion of each evening's television program is often chosen from the prescribed weekly portion of the Torah or from some other Biblical book. For the first time in two millennia, the language of the Scriptures is also that of Israel's masses and, to some degree also, of many committed Jews overseas. These momentous developments, together with the shift of several important institutes of Jewish learning to the Land of the Bible, lend fresh significance to the cherished hope and belief that "out of Zion shall go forth Torah, and the word of the Lord from Jerusalem" (Isa. 2:3).

THE BIBLE IN CHRISTIANITY

Originally one of several sects within normative Judaism, "Nazarenism" —the faith taught by Jesus—remained loyal to the spirit and to most of the letter of the Law. It was only after Paul brought about a doctrinal break with the parent faith that the teachings of Jesus were transformed

A Pre-Raphaelite impression of *The Finding of Christ in the Temple* (1862) by the English artist William Holman Hunt.

into the basis of an entirely separate religion, Christianity, which nevertheless preserved many of the concepts of Judaism, such as the basic idea that it alone was the true faith and that the Bible, God's blueprint for humanity, was its own special inheritance. Paul announced that the crucifixion had abrogated the authority of the Torah in its literal and oral form and that God's Grace and the "law of love" now constituted the foundation of the Christian's life. With the completion of the "New" Testament, Christians came to view the Pentateuch merely as the "old" Israel's preparatory discipline and the Prophetical books as a source from which the Messianic nature of Jesus' life on earth might be confirmed. Church Fathers, such as Justin Martyr (c. 100–c. 165), held that the "new covenant" of the Gospels was the ordained fulfillment and replacement of God's ancient pledge to the Jewish people who, having rejected Jesus, might continue to read the Scriptures but would fail to "catch the spirit that is in them." To a large extent, this remained the characteristic approach of all Christian churches toward Judaism and its adherents.

Jesus himself was raised in the Pharisaic tradition, to which many of his sayings are directly traceable.[28] Despite the propagandist and polemical intent of the Gospel writers, there is much evidence in the New Testament of that vital stream of religious and ethical thought which links the teachings of Jesus with those of the early Rabbis. Thus Matthew, whose Gospel was aimed at Christians of Jewish origin, reports that Jesus admonished his disciples and wider following to obey the precepts of the Torah: "The scribes and Pharisees sit in Moses' seat: All therefore whatsoever they bid you observe, that observe and do" (23:2–3). This injunction is elsewhere elaborated with reference to both the ceremonial and the moral code of Israel: "Think not that I am come to destroy the law, or the prophets: I am not come to destroy, but to fulfil .... Whosoever therefore shall break one of these least commandments, and shall teach men so, he shall be called the least in the kingdom of heaven .... For I say unto you, That except your righteousness shall exceed the righteousness of the scribes and Pharisees, ye shall in no case enter into the kingdom of heaven" (Matthew 5:17–20).

What Jesus himself preached—and what many of his later followers tried hard to obscure—was both the authority of the Mosaic precepts and the need to give greater emphasis to the ethical cry of the Prophets. As the 19th century German Bible critic Julius Wellhausen observed, "Jesus was not a Christian, he was a Jew. He did not proclaim a new faith, but taught men to do the will of God. According to Jesus, as to the Jews generally, this will of God is to be found in the Law and the

[28] Recent scholarship inclines to the view that Jesus was a Pharisee with leanings toward the monastic Essene sect, which practiced an ascetic communal life with frequent ritual immersion. The mystical outlook of the Essenes, who had pronounced Messianic and eschatological beliefs and who generally abstained from marriage and politics, evidently links them with many of the early Judeo-Christians. Jesus himself, however, did not stress abstinence and did not aim to form any monastic brotherhood, while the "Nazarenes" (unlike the Essenes) took no part in the war against Rome (see Joseph Klausner, *Jesus of Nazareth*, 1925). The Judean Desert sect, whose Dead Sea Scrolls were discovered at Khirbet Qumran in 1947, had much in common with the Essenes; its adherents produced an apocalyptic literature in which these "Sons of Light" warred with the forces of darkness under the leadership of a mysterious, Messianic "Teacher of Righteousness" *(moreh ẓedek)*. John the Baptist may once have belonged to the Qumran sect, which conceivably influenced the circles in which Paul the Apostle and John the Evangelist were active. This Jewish sectarian background sheds much new and important light on the origins of Christianity.

other canonical Scriptures" (*Einleitung in die drei ersten Evangelien,* 1905). The ethical teachings of Jesus were rooted in the Bible and prompted him to denounce those hypocritical elements among the "scribes and Pharisees" of his time who made a public demonstration of their piety, while neglecting the imperatives of the moral code (Matthew 23:4–5). Some of his ethical injunctions (e.g., on pacifism and God's regard for the sinner) were hyperbolical, but in general they served as an emphatic repetition of what the Prophets had said centuries previously.[29] This fact was underlined by another Christian Bible scholar, Renan, who wrote that "the first founder of Christianity was Isaiah. By introducing into the Jewish world the concept of ethical religion, of justice, and of the relative unimportance of sacrifices, he antedated Jesus by more than seven centuries" (*Le Judaisme comme race et comme religion,* 1883).

A study of the Gospels also reveals that Jesus deviated from the main lines of Pharisaic teaching in regard to the observance of the Oral Law, which he made subordinate to inward piety. His dispute with the Rabbis of his day centered in particular interpretations of the *Halakhah*—the Jewish "way of life" formulated by authoritative scholars—and involved his personal belief that conscience might best determine how the "Law" should be applied. Jesus insisted that his own lenient approach was an improvement on that of the Rabbis and antagonized other teachers by claiming ancient authority for some of his controversial statements on ritual and legal matters (Matthew 12:1–14, 15:11, 20; Mark 2:23–3:6; Luke 6:1–11). The prolonged critique of Pharisaic Judaism in the Synoptic Gospels—Mark (c. 54 C.E.), Luke (c. 75 C.E.), and Matthew (c. 90 C.E.)—betrays an underlying awareness of those beliefs and attitudes which Jesus and the Rabbis held in common and which therefore imperiled the successful propagation of the "Nazarene" doctrine. For the Pharisees, too, held that "the Sabbath was made for man, and not man for the Sabbath" (Mark 2:27);[30] where they differed from Jesus was in their approach to "the Law." Thus, Jesus campaigned against the Pharisees (and not against the worldly Sadducees or the monastic Essenes) precisely because the Pharisees "were so nearly right,"

---

[29] In Wellhausen's phrase, "Micah 6:6–8 and Psalm 73:23–28 give us the complete Gospel."

[30] The Talmudic version of this saying is: "The Sabbath is committed to you, not you to the Sabbath" (*Yoma,* 85b).

while the Rabbis condemned his attempt to rewrite aspects of the *Halakhah* and to win over the half-educated Jewish masses to his way of thinking.[31] What was at stake was not their personal prestige so much as the final authority of the Oral Torah, the established and tested "way of life." Yet despite the later editing and comment that are apparent in the Gospels, it is noteworthy that Jesus' own muted Messianic claims excited only minor controversy among the Pharisees,[32] who are not mentioned in connection with the political trial (staged by Caiaphas and other Sadducees) that led to the crucifixion; and that certain Pharisees even showed extraordinary tolerance and protectiveness in their dealings with Jesus and his early followers.[33]

[31] James Parkes, *Judaism and Christianity* (1948), p. 59. The second chapter of Parkes's book constitutes an informative analysis of the relationship between Jesus and his teachings and the Judaism of his time.

[32] Jesus was not the first Jew, nor the last, to believe he was the Messiah. Zerubbabel w s addressed as the Lord's "chosen one" by the prophet Haggai (2:21–23) and in similar terms by Zechariah (4:6–10). A more explicit Messianic role was accorded to Hezekiah by the prophet Isaiah (11:1–10), as the Rabbis later confirmed (*Sanhedrin*, 99a). The Zealot leader Judah the Galilean, who died a few years after the birth of Jesus, and his son Menahem, who captured the fortress of Masada during the early stages of the war against Rome (66–73 C.E.), seem to have been regarded as the Messiah by their respective followers; Menahem apparently adopted a deliberate Messianic pose. A figure of even greater significance in this context was Simeon Bar Kokhba, commander of the last great anti-Roman revolt (132–135 C.E.), whom the prestigious Rabbi Akiva hailed as "the king Messiah" (Jerusalem Talmud, *Ta'anit*, 4.8). In later times, Jews periodically rallied to a pseudo-Messiah who claimed Davidic descent and announced his advent as a deliverer: among these charismatic figures were David Alroy in 12th-century Persia (the hero of one of Disraeli's novels), the 16th-century adventurer David Reuveni, and the 17th-century Turkish impostor Shabbetai Zevi, whose pretensions (even when he embraced Islam) still had serious repercussions long after his death. For a fuller discussion, see Joseph Klausner's *The Messianic Idea in Israel* (1955) and Abba Hillel Silver's *History of Messianic Speculation in Israel* (1927; second edn. 1959). Jesus was thus one of several claimants to the "Messiah" title during the last decades of the Second Jewish Commonwealth; where he differed was in his renunciation of temporal rule ("My kingdom is not of this world," John 18:36).

[33] Pharisees warn Jesus against a plot by Herod in Luke 13:31; Gamaliel defends Peter in Acts 5:34–39; and Pharisees even exonerate Paul in Acts 23:9. On the other hand, Jesus took care to influence his followers against them (Matthew 23:3ff.).

JEWISH AND GENTILE CHRISTIANITY

After Jesus was put to death by the approved Roman method—crucifixion—his immediate disciples remained loyal to Judaism and, for the remainder of their history, upheld Jewish observances such as the Sabbath, circumcision, and dietary regulations. They worshiped in their own synagogues wherever possible, adapting the traditional liturgy to their own sectarian needs (e.g., in references to the coming of the Messiah), and until the destruction of the Temple they were an accepted part of the Jewish scene. These "Nazarenes" or "Ebionites" (from the Hebrew *evyon,* "poor") sometimes differed among themselves over questions such as the admission of proselytes as wholehearted observers of *Halakhah* or merely of the "Noachide Laws" (Acts 15:13–21), but they bitterly opposed Paul's negative attitude to the Torah and his policy on the conversion of Gentiles. The rigorists among them were even critical of the apostle Simon Peter (Galatians 2:11–14), whom James and the "Nazarene" community (or church) of Jerusalem thought unduly lax in his contacts with non-Jews.[34] The Judeo-Christians eventually had to face and suffer the consequences of their ambiguous religious position: rejection by the orthodox Jews during and after the tensions of the war against Rome, and hostility on the part of the more powerful Gentile church, culminating in the expulsion of these Jewish "heretics" from the Christian community less than a century after the end of the Second Commonwealth. Remnants of the Judeo-Christians were still to be found in Syria and Transjordan during the third century C.E. Their accounts of Christianity's early beginnings and of the activities of Paul, whom they detested, have a staunchly pro-Jewish and anti-Roman coloring; they condemn the abandonment of the Torah and equate Jesus, the prophet whom they saw announced in Deut. 18:15, with the lawgiver Moses. As the Gospel of John already indicates, by the end of the first century C.E. the teachings of Jesus had been converted into the basis of an entirely separate faith, which severed its last links with Judaism, sealing the division with a "New" Testament in replacement of the "Old." Furthermore, the cross—symbolizing man's redemption through the suffering and death of Jesus—now became for Christianity what the Torah was, and has remained, for Judaism.

---

[34] Jesus himself occasionally displayed less universalism than most Pharisees (see Matthew 10:6, 15:24ff.; Mark 7:25ff.).

The "parting of the ways" between the two religions was almost entirely the work of Paul, the Apostle to the Gentiles, who at first tried to stifle his own spiritual uncertainties by persecuting the "Nazarenes." Proud of the fact that he was "a Pharisee, the son of a Pharisee" (Acts 23:6), Paul combined the Greek culture of his native Tarsus with some degree of Rabbinic scholarship, which he is said to have imbibed in Jerusalem "at the feet of Gamaliel" (Acts 22:3).[35] Yet, as C. G. Montefiore, a Liberal Jewish New Testament scholar, has pointed out, "no one misunderstood Judaism more profoundly than Paul." Unlike those who had lived in Jesus' company and proclaimed his message both during and after his lifetime, Paul declared that the crucifixion had abrogated the Law of Moses (Romans 4:15; 2 Corinthians 3:6–11; Galatians 3:10–14), redeeming man from its "curse." Cautioning against any "Judaistic" reverence for the "Old" Testament, he maintained that only those in receipt of "grace" could gain a true insight into the spiritual message of the Hebrew Bible and that the death of Jesus had also spelled the end of Judaism as a Divinely ordained religion. These assertions naturally outraged Judeo-Christians who loyally observed the commandments and strenuously objected to Paul's accommodation with the paganizing tendencies of Gentile neophytes.[36] In his Epistle to the Hebrews (probably aimed at the Judeo-Christians of Asia Minor),[37] Paul also acclaimed Jesus as "the mediator of the new covenant" (12:24) first prophesied by Jeremiah (Jer. 31:31–34; cf. Hebrews 8:8–13). However much Judeo-Christians believed in the messiahship of Jesus and however lax some Hellenistic Jewish communities may have been in their observance, they were at one in protesting against the essence of Paul's theology: "By him [i.e., Jesus, the risen savior] all that believe are justified from all things, from which ye could not be justified by the law of Moses" (Acts 13:39). Through such "justification by faith," Paul opened the way to salvation to everyone, regardless of "good works" (adherence to the precepts) or formal acceptance of Judaism. By making his interpretation of Jesus' teachings "Judaism for the multitude" Paul

---

[35] This Gamaliel may have been Rabban Gamaliel the Elder, a grandson of Hillel.

[36] Through concepts which he adopted, such as the Greco-Roman doctrine of the God-Man. Judeo-Christian polemics against Paul's ideas have been detected in the "synagogue of Satan" imagery of the Apocalypse (Revelation 2:9, 3:9).

[37] Some claim that this was not actually written by Paul.

thus proclaimed "circumcision of the heart" a substitute for "circumcision of the flesh" (Romans 2:25–29).

The second-century Church Father Justin Martyr emulated Paul's fondness for allegory by discovering innumerable Biblical prophecies which Jesus could be shown to have fulfilled and by seeing prefigurations of the cross in many passages in the Scriptures. Repelled by such "Midrashic" excesses, his contemporary, Marcion, insisted that a literal understanding of the "Old" Testament betrayed its un-Christian character. To his mind, Jesus had really come to destroy the Law, and it was through fear that this view might prevail that orthodox Christian opinion played down the antinomian undercurrents in the Pauline doctrine, and branded Marcion as a heretic. While Paul himself abandoned the "Law," he did not reject his former coreligionists, the Jews. It was, nevertheless, his hostility toward Judaism which influenced the theology of the Church and its unyielding attitude toward both the faith and the people of Israel. As the centuries passed, Christians were taught to regard the Jews not as the "holy nation" from whom Jesus sprang, but as graceless, blaspheming rebels who had long ago closed their eyes to the light of the Gospel, deicides and "Christ-killers" (though centuries separated them from the events described in the New Testament) whose very survival testified either to the Wandering Jew's well-deserved homelessness or to the Christian charity of those who tolerated them in their midst.[38] So far as the Jews were concerned, few remembered to apply the words of the Apostle: "Some indeed preach Christ even of envy and strife; and some also of good will" (Philippians 1:15).

Justin Martyr did not have far to look in his search for Biblical parallels with, or sources for, Christian doctrine: many were usefully at hand in the text of the Gospels ("that it might be fulfilled which was spoken by the prophets," etc.), particularly in the writings of Matthew. Hosea's "out of Egypt I called My son" (11:1), referring to the Exodus, was applied to the flight of Joseph and Mary with their infant son into Egypt (Matthew 2:13–15); Jeremiah's "Rachel weeping for her children" (31:15) to Herod's massacre of the children in Bethlehem (Matthew 2:16–18); Isaiah's vision of Israel as God's servant (42:1–4) was seen as a prediction of Jesus (Matthew 12:17–21); and Zechariah's prophecy of a savior-king "riding upon an ass" (9:9) was carefully fulfilled in

---

[38] A prime source of medieval anti-Semitism may be seen in the condemnation of "the Jews" in the Gospel according to John.

the entry of Jesus into Jerusalem (Matthew 21:1–9). Similarly, the circumstances attending the crucifixion (Matthew 27:34–35; John 19:24) closely resemble the phrasing of Ps. 22:19, and this same Psalm forms a poignant background to the whole crucifixion episode, since Jesus apparently quotes its opening ("My God, my God, why hast Thou forsaken me . . . ?") in his death throes on the cross.[39] The picture of the "suffering servant" in Isaiah (53:1–12) was interpreted as referring to the vicarious suffering and atoning death of Jesus, while there seems little doubt that the Sermon on the Mount (Matthew, chapters 5–7) forms a New Testament parallel to the Sinaitic revelation. In the traditional theology of the Church, Isaiah's prophecy of a symbolic Immanuel ("with us is God") to be born in the reign of Ahaz was naturally reinterpreted to signify the nativity of Jesus: "Therefore the Lord Himself shall give you a sign: behold, the young woman shall conceive, and bear a son, and shall call his name Immanuel . . . " (Isa. 7:14). As all Bible scholars are now agreed, however, the Hebrew word *almah* means any "young woman" (not "virgin," as the *King James Version* renders the word, which in Hebrew is *betulah*), and so Isaiah provides no authority for the virgin birth, nor can this passage be applied anachronistically to the Roman era.

CHRISTIAN HEBRAISM

Although Jerome (c. 340–420), one of the four great "doctors of the Church," was orthodox enough in his theology, he advocated a sober, literal understanding of the Bible and learned Hebrew in order to grasp fully the original meaning of its text. Jerome's new Latin translation of the Bible, known as the Vulgate, was destined to replace all older versions of the Scriptures in the West. Together with his lexicons of the names of Biblical persons and places, the Vulgate provided an important impetus for the study of Biblical Hebrew during the Middle Ages. Jerome's knowledge of Hebrew and Aramaic was mainly gained from Jewish scholars with whom he had friendly relations in Palestine, and his Vulgate also leaned on the Greek Scriptural translations of Aquila, Symmachus, and Theodotion—Jewish works originally undertaken to supersede the

---

[39] In Hebrew, the crucial words are: *Eli, Eli, lamah azavtani?* The Gospels according to Matthew (27:46; *Eli, Eli, lama sabachthani?*) and Mark (15:34; *Eloi, Eloi, lama sabachthani?*) give this in the vernacular Aramaic form.

Septuagint, which arbitrary exploitation by the Church had made unacceptable to Greek-speaking Jews in the early centuries of the common era.[40] Jerome became convinced that only the Hebrew Bible and the New Testament deserved incorporation in the canonical Scriptures and that the Apocryphal books ought to be excluded. Rome disregarded Jerome's opinion and the Apocrypha remained in the Catholic Bible, although the Protestant churches later followed Jerome. The Septuagint also remained in honor for centuries, despite the fact that the Church Father Origen, as well as Jerome, noted its frequent divergence from the original Hebrew text.

Throughout the Middle Ages, the principal motivations of Christian Hebraism were anti-Jewish polemics and an overwhelming desire for the conversion of the Jews. Rabbinical sources were not neglected by Christian propagandists, although an arsenal of useful Biblical quotations was ever at hand and a host of Jewish renegades offered their services to interested churchmen, frequently inventing or corrupting texts in order to "prove" the superior truth of the Christian faith. Because of the weighted evidence against them, Jews normally came off worst when they were compelled to defend their beliefs at public disputations—a favorite entertainment of medieval Europe. The revival of Hebrew learning as an aid to Christian Bible study may be traced to the activities of Nicholas de Lyre (c. 1270–1349), whose commentary on the whole Bible (*Postillae Perpetuae,* written in 1322–30) was the first of its kind to see print (Rome, 1471–72). In his search for the exact sense of the Scriptural text, Nicholas boldly consulted the commentaries of Rashi and other Jewish scholars, and in this he was later to be emulated by other Christians such as Wycliffe and Luther.

During the latter half of the 15th century, Hebrew studies received a sudden and curious impetus from Christian scholarship's growing preoccupation with the mysteries of the Kabbalah. Interwoven with various forms of Biblical exegesis in the kabbalistic classics was a good deal of numerology, popularly known as *gematria* (cf. the Greek *geometria*), a technique involving the interpretation of a word or phrase in accordance with each letter's numerical value in the Hebrew alphabet.[41] Hence

---

[40] Theodotion and Symmachus (a Samaritan convert to Judaism) lived in the second century; Aquila, a pagan who converted first to Christianity and then to Judaism, in the third.

[41] These values rise in accordance with the order of the Hebrew alphabet. Thus

the Rabbinic interpretation that the verb *garti* ("I have sojourned") in Gen. 32:5 ("Thus shall ye say unto my lord Esau . . . I have sojourned with Laban, and stayed until now") lends itself to the numerological interpretation: "I have kept the 613 Commandments" (the four Hebrew consonants of *garti* together amounting to the sum of 613). This technique was greatly exploited by the kabbalists in their effort to discover ever more hidden meanings in the Biblical text and, since Christological ideas could also be "discovered" by such means (particularly the doctrine of the Trinity), the dawn of the Renaissance saw the birth of a strange new "science"—Christian Kabbalah. Wherever Jewish experts could be found (Spain, Italy, Provence), Gentile enthusiasts arranged their own initiation into these Hebraic mysteries or "arcana."

The founding father of Christian Kabbalah was Giovanni Pico della Mirandola (1463–1494), an outstanding Renaissance humanist who acquired his knowledge of Oriental languages from Jews or Jewish apostates. One of the famous "900 Theses" which Pico offered to substantiate at a public debate in Rome (1486) which never took place was that "no science can make us more certain of Christ's divinity than magic and Kabbalah." There are Jewish mystical elements in a number of Pico's writings, notably his *Heptaplus* ("The Seven Days," 1489), an account of the Creation. In many instances, this obsession with the Kabbalah proved to be a major factor in the development of Hebrew studies during the 16th century, when the Renaissance spirit of enquiry left no avenue of potentially useful knowledge unexplored. Even more significant, perhaps, was the gradual emergence of a more objective approach to Rabbinic literature, which arose from the intuitive belief that everything Jewish scholarship had to offer might not have vanished with the advent of Jesus. In any case, self-respecting humanists felt the need to acquire at least a smattering of Hebrew in addition to the Greek and Latin on which they prided themselves, and "Colleges of the Three Languages" were established at Alcalá in Spain and in Paris, Oxford, and other European cities.

The prestige enjoyed by Pico della Mirandola ensured that Christian Hebraism found a ready home in Italy, where Cardinal Egidio (Aegidius)

---

aleph (א) = 1, *beth* (ב) = 2, etc., as far as *tet* (ט) = 9, after which *yod* (י) = 10, *kaph* (כ) = 20, etc., until *tsade* (צ), the eighteenth letter (= 90); *koph* or *qoph* (ק), *resh* (ר), *shin* (ש), and *tav* (ת) are respectively equal to 100, 200, 300, and 400. Higher values can be obtained by the use of "final" letter forms and various diacritical marks.

An extract from Agostino Giustiniani's polyglot *Psalterium octaplum* (Genoa, 1516). The marginal Latin commentary to Ps. 19:5 includes an interesting reference to Columbus and his voyages of discovery.

da Viterbo (1465–1532) dabbled in Kabbalah and befriended the Hebrew grammarian Elijah Levita. Santes Pagnini (1470–1536) gained eminence as one of the foremost Christian Hebraists of the age and published the first translation of the Hebrew Bible since Jerome's time that was based directly on the original text (*Utriusque instrumenti nova translatio,* 1528). Agostino (Pantaleone) Giustiniani (c. 1470–1536), a friend of Erasmus, Pico, and Sir Thomas More, began work on what he hoped would be the first modern polygot Bible,[42] but only succeeded in issuing a Psalter in five languages with commentary (1516). He taught at the new "Collège trilingue" in Paris (1517–22) and published various works on Hebrew grammar and literature, together with some kabbalistic writings which later appeared in *De arcanis catholicae veritatis* ("The Secrets of Catholic Truth," 1518), a mystical compendium widely exploited by Christian kabbalists throughout the 16th century. The compiler of this work, Pietro Columna Galatinus (1460–1540), was a heretical Italian friar and an ardent admirer of Reuchlin, the great German Hebraist. Galatinus' exact contemporary, Francesco Giorgio (or Zorzi; 1460–1540),

---

[42] The first Polyglot to see print was the "Complutensian Bible" conceived and produced by Cardinal Jiménez de Cisneros (1436–1517) at Alcalá de Henares in Spain (1502–17).

also wrote a voluminous work (*De Harmonia Mundi,* 1525) full of Biblical, Rabbinic, and kabbalistic material. By then, however, Hebrew scholarship had begun to make its mark elsewhere.

Both before and after the Lutheran Reformation, Christian Hebraism scored some of its major triumphs in Germany. Johann Reuchlin (1455–1522) first turned to Hebrew and Kabbalah at the suggestion of Pico della Mirandola. His two studies of the kabbalistic mysteries, *De Verbo mirifico* ("On the Wonder-working Word," 1494) and *De arte Cabalistica* ("On the Kabbalistic Art," 1517), are monuments of scholarship; they also reveal the author's religious objectivity. Reuchlin is perhaps best known for his involvement in the "Battle of the Books" as a champion of free enquiry. Braving Catholic reaction and the "obscurantists," he refused to condemn the Talmud and other Rabbinic classics and his stand brought many humanist admirers to his side. By 1517, Hebrew books had been saved from the inquisitional flames and soon Biblical and Rabbinic studies in the Hebrew language were no longer subject to rigid control. Reuchlin's pupils included Sebastian Münster (1489–1552) and Johann Forster (or Föster; 1495–1556). Next to Reuchlin, Münster was the outstanding Christian Hebraist of the century, publishing some 40 works on a variety of subjects—Hebrew and Aramaic grammar, extracts from Jewish literature, and original Hebrew translations of the Apocryphal Book of Tobit (1542) and the Gospel according to Matthew (*"Torat Ha-Mashi'aḥ,"* 1537). His *Hebraica Biblia* (1534–35) was the first Protestant version of the Hebrew Bible taken directly from Hebrew into Latin. Forster, a diligent Hebraist, issued a pioneering Hebrew-Latin dictionary in 1557. Something of a wandering scholar, Conrad Pellicanus (Pellikan or Kürschner; 1478–1556) also abandoned holy orders to become a Protestant and teach Hebrew at Zurich. Widely read in the Christian Kabbalah, Pellicanus translated many Rabbinic works and assisted the great Swiss Reformer Ulrich Zwingli in his preparation of a German Bible. He was also the first Christian to publish a Hebrew grammar (1504). Paulus Fagius (Paul Büchelin, 1504–1549) was a pupil of Elijah Levita, two of whose works on grammar he himself translated. He ran his own Hebrew press for a time, publishing parts of the Targum, Kimḥi's commentaries on the first ten Psalms (1544), and a Hebrew-Latin version of the Book of Tobit. He eventually became professor of Hebrew at Cambridge, where he died.

In France, Kabbalah and normative Christian Hebraism also developed side by side. François Vatable (c. 1490–1547), Jean Mercier (died

1570), and Jean Cinqarbres (died 1587) were three distinguished teachers and scholars, Mercier translating most of the Targum on the Prophets. Guillaume Postel (1510–1581), who mastered an amazing variety of languages, was one of the outstanding exponents of the Christian Kabbalah and attracted many disciples.[43] His mystical visions, which led him to resurrect Judeo-Christianity and to proclaim himself a reincarnation of the prophet Elijah, resulted in his spending the last 20 years of his life in protective custody. Rabbinic and kabbalistic "proofs" abound in works such as his multilingual treatise on the *Menorah* (Temple Candelabrum), first published in 1548. Postel also wrote an annotated version of part of the Zohar (manuscript now in the British Museum) and countless speculative treatises, most of which never reached the censor. Through some of his agents, Postel also had an unauthorized hand in the "Catholic" Antwerp Polyglot Bible of 1568–72. His principal lieutenant, the French poet Guy Le Fèvre de la Boderie (1541–1598),[44] injected much kabbalistic material into his patriotic verse; La Boderie produced French metrical versions of various Psalms "turned" from the Hebrew and was also one of the editors of the Antwerp Polyglot, to which he contributed an Aramaic lexicon. The Polyglot itself, a masterpiece of Renaissance book production, was printed by Christophe Plantin (c. 1520–1589), a French rival of Daniel Bomberg (died 1549), the eminent Venetian printer-publisher of the Rabbinic Bible and Talmud. Although their enterprise had the patronage of Philip II of Spain, Plantin and many of his editors were secret heretics and some copies of the Polyglot Bible were specially designed for Protestant readers.

The origins of Christian Hebraism in England date back to Andrew of St. Victor (12th century) and Herbert of Bosham (died after 1190), who had an important successor in Nicholas Triveth (or Trevet; c. 1258–1328), the first recorded student of Maimonides in Britain and the author of commentaries on parts of the Pentateuch and on Psalms. Like François I in France, King Henry VIII of England promoted humanism and appointed Robert Wakefield (died 1537) first professor of Hebrew at Oxford in 1530. Wakefield's pioneering Latin work "On the Value of Arabic, Aramaic, and Hebrew" (1524) was the earliest English publica-

---

[43] On Postel, see also Chapters 3 and 5.
[44] La Boderie's works are discussed in greater detail elsewhere—in Chapters 3, 4, and 5.

Three Hebrew pane-
gyrics introducing Vol-
ume 1 of the Antwerp
Polyglot (*Biblia Sacra,*
Antwerp, 1568–72),
printed by Christophe
Plantin. These poems
by Gilbert Génébrard
(right) and Jean Benoît
(left) praise the Bible's
patron, Philip II of
Spain, its chief editor,
Arias Montano, and
one of the leading con-
tributors, Guy Le Fèvre
de la Boderie.

HÆC sua Hebraica sic Latinè adumbrauit Gilbertus Gene-
brardus Theologus Parisienfis, & Lutetiæ diuinarum Hebrai-
carúmque literarum professor Regius.

ANTIQVIS *bini quod vix potuere diebus*
Reges, nunc Regum maxime solus agis.
Persa Cyrus Domino sacratam condidit edem,
Dona Dei populo, iuráque multa dedit.
Vulgauit Pharius diuina volumina princeps
Septenim decies percitus arte virûm.
Sancta patri Caroli soboles tu vincis vtriûque,
Cum Persa à Mauris diruta templa pias.
Cum Rege Ægypti toti das Biblia mundo,
Pluribus & linguis, pluribus atque typis.
Sic sanctam aedificas duplici ratione Sionem,
Vinat vt exterius, vinat & interius.
Ergo quod Numen Regem tunc rexit vtriûque,
Nunc te in perpetuâ dirigat vsq́, & amet.

IN EDITIONIS SYRIACÆ
ἐγκώμιον psallebat F. Iochannes Benedictus
Gallus, necnon instituti Francifcani alumnus.

tion to contain Hebrew printing. Thomas Wakefield (died 1575), the
author's younger brother, was appointed first Regius Professor of
Hebrew at Cambridge (1540). Unlike the Catholic Wakefields, William
Tyndale (c. 1490–1536) was a Protestant Hebraist and martyr. Tyndale
translated the entire Bible into English, but only one part of it (Pentateuch, 1530; Jonah, 1531) appeared in his lifetime; the rest of his manuscript apparently inspired later efforts by Miles Coverdale (1535) and
others. It is largely as a result of Tyndale's remarkable feeling for the
two idioms that so much Hebraic color entered the English language.
Once England turned Protestant, the study of Hebrew became a general
scholarly pursuit, especially in Puritan circles. Bryan Walton (1600–1661)
modeled his London Polyglot Bible (*Biblia Sacra Polyglotta,* 1654–57) on
a work of the same type published in Paris (1645), but his proved to be
the outstanding multilingual Bible and it retains much value and interest
even today. The texts included the Hebrew "Old" Testament, the Greek
Septuagint, the Latin Vulgate, and rare versions such as the Samaritan
Pentateuch and a Persian translation of the same. Among the contribu-

tors to the London Polyglot were Edmund Castell (1606–1685), a leading Orientalist and lexicographer, and John Lightfoot (1602–1675), a specialist in Biblical and Rabbinic literature. Lightfoot also published a work on Herod's Temple (1650) and various studies, including an objective assessment of the New Testament's Rabbinic sources and background (*Horae Hebraicae et Talmudicae,* 1658–74).

The great Protestant Reformers—Luther, Calvin, and Zwingli—fostered Christian Hebraism and, rejecting the infallibility of the Pope, made their stand on the infallibility of the Bible. Whereas Roman Catholicism based its authority on Church tradition as well as on Scripture, Protestantism in its various streams made the Bible alone its authoritative statement of revealed truth—"God's word written," as the Thirty-Nine Articles of the Anglican Church laid down. Even before England finally cut its ties with Rome, Henry VIII—whom a grateful Pope had once exalted as the "defender of the faith"—sent emissaries abroad to consult Venetian Rabbis (and Christian Hebraists like Francesco Giorgio) in the hope of obtaining a favorable verdict on the basis of Biblical law when he sought to rid himself of his Spanish wife, Katherine of Aragon. Calvinists and Puritans turned to the "Old" Testament and reverted to Biblical precedents for the regulation of their daily life.[45] So far as Hebrew studies in the Christian milieu were concerned, the humanist and Protestant example was soon followed by Catholics, a few of whom—like Giulio Bartolocci (1613–1687)—made notable contributions to Hebrew scholarship. After the 17th century, however, ecclesiastical influence in this sphere rapidly declined, and investigation of the Bible became an independent pursuit. The battle which Reuchlin so courageously fought on the eve of the Reformation had become a victory for men of every creed, or none at all.

THE PURITAN SPIRIT

The English Puritans and French Calvinists drew much of their religious inspiration directly from the pages of the Hebrew Bible. Its language and the ideas it expressed fortified their social and political doctrines, confirming the widespread ultra-Protestant belief that the war they fought against Rome was a sacred task and that "Jehovah Lord of Hosts" would help them smite the Amalekites hip and thigh. The Church of

[45] See especially Chapter 2.

Rome was Babylon, the statues of Mary and Jesus in Catholic shrines were idolatrous images, and ecclesiastical vestments were "relics of the Amorites." In his *Short History of the English People* (1874), John Richard Green describes the astonishing moral change that affected Elizabethan England, especially after the glorious defeat of the Spanish Armada: "Elizabeth might silence or tune the pulpits, but it was impossible for her to silence or tune the great preachers of justice, and mercy, and truth, who spoke from the Book which the Lord again opened to the people. The effect of the Bible in this way was simply amazing. The whole temper of the nation was changed. A new conception of life and of man superseded the old. A new moral and religious impulse spread through every class." For the Puritans, whose influence increased year by year, the English were God's chosen people, and their mainly Calvinistic theology—expressed in terms of Biblical legalism—emphasized the idea of a solemn Covenant to which God and His people were parties. Their creed, with its doctrines of Grace, Faith, and Predestination, was a grim one, but it suited the mood and needs of the time and created strong men—men like Oliver Cromwell, whose Ironsides went into battle with Bible and sword in the service of the Lord and of Gideon. The English Civil War was for the Puritans a struggle against tyranny, and Parliament's victory confirmed that love of liberty which the Roundheads acquired from their reading of the Scriptures.[46]

This "chosen people" idea was also dominant in the religious and political struggles of the Huguenots, Dutch patriots, and American Pilgrim Fathers, all of whom based their libertarian ideals on the Hebrew Bible. For many of these soldierly "servants of the Lord" the Bible was, however, something very different from what it had become for the modern descendants of the Israelite nation. The righteousness and mercy to which men were called by the Prophets found less response than their demand for justice; the Puritan Sabbath (still strictly maintained in some parts of the world) made Sunday an occasion for gloom rather than joy; and a literal belief in the power of witchcraft encouraged fanaticism and cruel persecution, one notorious instance being the witch-hunt at Salem, New England, in 1691–2, when hundreds of innocent people were arrested and tried and twenty of them put to death. Puritanism's excesses also led to the degenerate manifestations of the late Commonwealth period, when England was assailed by Ranters, Levellers, and

[46] This is discussed at greater length in Chapter 2.

Fifth Monarchy Men. Yet despite such bibliolatry, Puritanism left many positive imprints on the conscience and outlook of the English and American peoples. In the words of the U.S. economist Henry George, the spirit of the Bible "strengthened the Scottish Covenanter in the hour of trial, and the Puritan amid the snows of a strange land. It charged with the Ironsides at Naseby; it stood behind the low redoubt on Bunker Hill."

The fact that the Protestant churches made the vernacular Bible known to tens of millions, "familiar in their mouths as household words," proved to be of immense significance in the language and psychology of many Western nations.[47] This is particularly the case with the Psalter, which has left a deep and powerful imprint on Protestant thought and hymnology. The 16th-century continental translations of Luther, Marot, and others inspired English hymn writers who adapted Biblical poetry to the needs of Protestant devotion. Miles Coverdale's *Goostly Psalms and Spiritual Songs* (1539), Thomas Sternhold's English psalmody, the New England *Bay Psalm Book* (1640), and the metrical Psalms of the Church of Scotland were some of the milestones in this momentous process. Although more moderate Anglicans (such as Archbishop Laud) in the royalist camp also set great store by the Psalms, it was the Roundhead cavalry that galloped into battle singing "David's songs." Oliver Cromwell's letters and addresses contained whole passages from the Psalter and the speech he delivered at the opening of his second Parliament mainly consisted of an exposition of Psalms 46 and 85. This was entirely natural and inevitable in the man, and not the "cant" of Puritanism in its decadence. Nor should one overlook the fact that John Milton, who served the Lord Protector as Latin Secretary, translated many of the Psalms into English. The Scottish *Gude and Godlie Ballatis* of the 16th century were steeped in the language of the Bible and the Scots Covenanters martyred after the Restoration died with the Psalms on their lips, while the austere French Huguenots, too, found courage in the inspiring verses of this Biblical book. Indeed, the spiritual strength of English Puritans and Quakers, Scots Presbyterians, New England pioneers, and French and Dutch Calvinists derived in large measure from their reading and interpretation of the Hebrew Bible. So, for that matter, did much of their narrow-mindedness and proverbial intolerance. In a more tranquil era, Psalm 90 inspired Isaac Watts' verse paraphrase, *"O God,*

---

[47] See Chapter 3.

Our Help in Ages Past" (1719), and its musical setting ensured this hymn's lasting popularity among English-speaking Protestants.

THE LEGACY OF THE "OLD" TESTAMENT

In the wake of the Reformation, independent thinkers turned their attention to the legislative and social organization of ancient Israel and also came to appreciate the Biblical concepts of justice and morality as expounded by the Rabbis even after the time of Jesus. The "Old" Testament thus became the model for the concepts and ideals of a world feeling its way toward democratic government (in the best sense of that much misused term), and this was to lead to a new respect for the Jews of the modern era—an attitude reflected in the paintings of Rembrandt, the Biblical dramas of Racine, and in Christian support for Jewish emancipation. By the 19th century, dogmatism had declined to such an extent that the Bible could be viewed merely as great literature or as a source book for humanitarian endeavor. Thomas Carlyle (1795–1881), the "sage of Chelsea," called the Book of Job "one of the grandest things ever written with pen" and stressed Protestant Christianity's indebtedness to the Bible: "What built St. Paul's Cathedral? . . . that divine Hebrew Book—the word partly of the man Moses, an outlaw tending his Midianitish herds, four thousand years ago, in the wilderness of Sinai!" (*On Heroes, Hero-Worship, and the Heroic in History,* 1840).

A new, critical approach to the Scriptures was inaugurated by Jean Astruc (1684–1766), pursued with vindictive prejudice by Voltaire and the French Encyclopedists, and finally erected into a system by Graf, Wellhausen, and others of the German 19th-century "Higher Critical" school, who challenged the assumptions of both Judaism and Christianity. The Pentateuch and other Biblical books were ascribed not to Moses and other inspired writers, as tradition maintained, but to a host of anonymous authors and editors of a much later period, who supposedly reworked the Biblical prophecies and "higher" morality to accord with the history and outlook of their own times. Divine revelation was thus repudiated and "documentary" evidence painstakingly amassed in an effort to prove that man's insight into religious truth was only the outcome of a protracted evolution toward a loftier ethic and civilization. Research modified many of the confident assertions and often contradictory hypotheses of "Higher Criticism," making way for modern Christian scholarship's more sober critical view of the Biblical texts.

Many vital elements in the ritual and outlook of Christianity are of Biblical origin. The Ten Commandments often form part of church architecture; Protestant houses of worship are sometimes known as "temples"; and British Nonconformists have their "bethel," American Mormons their "tabernacle." Christians also hold statutory services partly on the Jewish pattern (matins and vespers or evensong) and the ancient Priestly Benediction is recited by officiating clergy over the assembled worshipers, to whom a lesson is often read from the "Old" Testament. Baptism and confirmation recall the Jewish ceremonies of *tevilah* (ritual immersion) and *bar mitzvah* (religious initiation at the age of 13), while the Eucharist—reenacting the Last Supper which, as the Synoptic Gospels make clear, was a Passover *Seder*—contains such traditional Jewish elements as the breaking of bread and the sacramental drinking of wine. While Protestants in general honor the Second Commandment by their ban on images, and the Fourth by the cessation of business on Sundays, Unitarians go further by rejecting the doctrine of the Trinity and Seventh Day Adventists by observing their Sabbath— like the Jews—on Saturday.[48] The Biblical concept of *zedakah* ("righteousness," extended to mean philanthropy in Judaism) finds practical Christian application in offertory boxes, charitable work, and church campaigns on behalf of the poor, the underprivileged, and the lonely. Sexual permissiveness in respect of adultery, promiscuity, and even homosexual marriage–though occasionally tolerated or excused by "advanced" Catholic and Protestant clergymen—is not condoned in most Christian circles, where Scriptural morality remains the basis of life and social values. On the other hand, clergymen protesting against all forms of social and political injustice habitually invoke the radicalism of the Hebrew Prophets.

Since the 19th century, Christian scholars of many denominations have increasingly emphasized those aspects of the Biblical heritage which Jews and Christians preserve and proclaim in common. The British scientist Thomas Huxley (1825–1895) expressed liberal Christianity's new and more appreciative view of its Biblical-Hebraic roots when he

---

[48] Although the Church Fathers transferred the "Lord's Day" from Saturday to Sunday, Puritanism revived many aspects of Jewish Sabbath observance, often in an extreme form. The rigid Sunday Sabbatarianism of the "Pennsylvania Dutch" and of the "Wee Frees" (members of the Free Church of Scotland) has become proverbial.

wrote that, "of all the strange ironies of history, perhaps the strangest is that the word 'Pharisee' is current as a term of reproach among the theological descendants of the sect of Nazarenes who, without the martyr spirit of those primitive Puritans, would never have come into existence." Close attention is now paid to the milieu in which Christianity first developed and much more objective study is devoted to the Hebrew Bible. More selectivity is exercised in respect to what is taught in Sunday schools and popular traditions rooted in medieval anti-Semitism are slowly being eradicated. Such progressive moves have not gone un-challenged, particularly where they ran counter to established conceptions in the Catholic world or to missionary endeavors supported by Protes-tants. Much valuable work has been done by organizations such as the National Conference of Christians and Jews in the U.S.A. and the Society of Christians and Jews in Great Britain. In response to the feelings of guilt engendered by the Nazi extermination of European Jewry, a significant new attitude toward the "Old" Testament and Jewish his-torical continuity has also begun to emerge. Despite the once fashionable "God-is-dead" movement and an alarming degree of indifference toward the issue at stake in Israel's Six-Day War (1967), the Protestant churches of the West (especially in America and Britain) have produced spokesmen and thinkers of great enlightenment and objectivity. In some instances, Jews and Protestants have collaborated in Biblical projects (e.g., the *Revised Standard Version* of the "Old" Testament, 1952); and in many cases Protestant scholarship has come to accept the Jewish rendering of certain terms and phrases in the Hebrew Bible.

There is also much evidence of new thinking in the Catholic Church. The Fathers and Sisters of Zion, two orders founded in the mid-19th century, were prominent in the fight against Nazi persecution of the Jews and have latterly opposed the missionary spirit in dealings with the Jewish people. These orders favor Christian-Jewish understanding and Bible study in Hebrew and have adopted a particularly friendly attitude toward the State of Israel. Although a few of his predecessors expressly condemned anti-Semitism (thus, in 1938, Pius XI told visiting Belgian pilgrims, "spiritually, we are Semites"), John XXIII (Angelo Giuseppe Roncalli, 1881–1963) went much further by evincing a warm regard for Judaism and the Jews and by initiating a significant reevaluation of the Catholic approach toward the "Chosen People." When an American Jewish delegation met him at the Vatican in 1960, the Pope greeted them with a Hebrew quotation from the Bible: "I am Joseph your brother"

(Gen. 45:4). Through the patient efforts of John XXIII and Cardinal Augustin Bea, a declaration entitled *Nostra aetate* ("In Our Time") was eventually promulgated by the Second Vatican Council in 1965, stressing Christianity's debt to "Abraham's stock," which had given the world its precious revelation of God's message: "Since the spiritual patrimony common to Christians and Jews is thus so great, this sacred synod wishes to foster and recommend that mutual understanding and respect which is fruit, above all, of Biblical and theological studies as well as of fraternal dialogues." Despite certain modifications (introduced to placate the conservative members of the Council), this declaration has helped to inject a new spirit into Catholic reading of the Hebrew Scriptures.[49]

Christianity's unenviable history of intolerance and persecution—affecting not only Jews, but Muslims, Arians, Albigenses, Anabaptists, anti-Trinitarians, Quakers, and Mormons as well—derives from its firm belief that the world must be converted to one faith and that there is "no salvation outside the Church." Yet Christianity has also presented a nobler vision of humanity and, in recent times, a profounder awareness that, as John Donne once phrased it, "no man is an island," since "any man's death diminishes me, because I am involved in mankind." The Biblical injunction to love one's neighbor, reiterated by the Rabbis and by Jesus, might be ignored or narrowly interpreted by medieval clerics and more recent churchmen, but Christians endowed with true compassion did not shut their eyes to its full implication. Recalling a conversation he once had with a Rabbi about the Sermon on the Mount, the Russian novelist Tolstoy ruefully acknowledged the force of the Rabbi's enquiry as to whether Christians "resist not evil," recording: "I had nothing to say in reply, especially as at that particular time Christians, far from turning the other cheek, were smiting the Jews on both of theirs." The same test awaited Christianity during the Nazi era, when far greater moral courage was displayed by humble priests and pastors and by laymen than by many eminent ecclesiastics. While millions throughout the world remained silent or even gave aid to Hitler's butchers, many anonymous heroes and heroines sheltered and rescued

---

[49] The search for a new relationship with Judaism and the Jewish people is limited to the Western (Catholic and Protestant) churches. Russian Orthodoxy has largely remained oblivious to these trends, while some of the Oriental (Uniate) churches actively opposed the Vatican "declaration on the Jews."

those outlawed and condemned to death or (in a few instances) bore witness to their faith by sharing the doomed victims' last journey to the crematoria.

Today, the Hebrew Bible appears in edition after edition for Christians of every denomination. English versions of the 20th century include the Catholic Bible of Monsignor Ronald Knox (1944–49), S.H. Hooke's *Bible in Basic English* (1941–49), and the *New English Bible* edition of the "Old" Testament (1970). The *Confraternity Version* (1946–52) serves American Catholics and the *Revised Standard Version* (1946–52) American Protestants. By the late 1960s, the British and Foreign Bible Society had published complete Bibles in well over 200 languages and individual Biblical books in about 1,000 tongues—making the Hebrew Scriptures accessible to almost every man and woman on earth. Century after century, Christian pilgrims have journeyed to the Holy Land and visited places familiar and sacred to them from their reading of the Bible. Since 1967, most of the holy places have been under the State of Israel's control and the experience of a prolonged encounter with Jewish national and religious revival in this ancient land has been a novel one for many of these pilgrims. Christian visitors also gain much from their meetings with Israeli lecturers on Bible and archaeology and from tours of kibbutzim,[50] where the Biblical precepts are given practical application with a communal framework.

BIBLICAL INFLUENCES IN ISLAM

Unlike Judaism and Christianity, Islam has never accorded a central place in its religious literature to the Hebrew Bible. Muslim tradition has borrowed many themes and figures from the Scriptures, but their treatment is largely dependent on Rabbinic lore—a legacy of Muhammad's own secondhand knowledge of the Bible, acquired in the course of his extensive contacts with the native Jewish community in the land of his birth. According to some traditions, Jews first arrived in Arabia during the era of King Solomon and their early existence and activity in the Arab world find testimony in a New Testament reference

---

[50] Those kibbutzim affiliated to the religious pioneer movements (Ha-Po'el ha-Mizraḥi and Po'alei Agudat Yisra'el) endeavor to bring out the contemporary relevance of the Torah and *Halakhah*.

(Acts 2:11). Under their influence, wholesale conversions to Judaism took place in various localities, giving rise to the powerful Jewish settlements in Khaibar, Yathrib-Medina, and other towns and oases of the Arabian peninsula. Thus, long before Muhammad, the books of the Bible were no mystery for Arabian poets, although the illiteracy prevalent among the pagan tribes of the region restricted the spread of Biblical knowledge beyond the confines of native Judaism and Christianity.

Muhammad was a witness to the theological conflict between Jews and Christians in Mecca, and his early awareness of the Bible's significance in the two monotheistic religions led him to call followers of these faiths *ahl al-Kitāb* ("the people of the Book"). Though convinced that Judaism, as he knew it, could never be a universal religion and that Christianity, as taught in Arabia, was far too close to idolatry, Muhammad was impressed by the fact that both Jews and Christians possessed books in which the word of God was revealed to men, and from these sources he was to accept some of the principal miracles— the plagues of Egypt, the Sinaitic revelation, and even the wondrous birth of Jesus. Depressed by the superstition and ignorance which dominated life in Arabia, Muhammad devoted many years to meditation, from which he at last emerged at the age of forty (c. 610) in the conviction that God had called him to serve as a teacher and prophet for his fellow Arabs. Secretly at first, and then in the open, he struggled to destroy old heathen beliefs and customs and to build a new religious community that would unite all men in a monotheistic faith anchored in that of the patriarch Abraham. Like Judaism, this faith would have its Divine authority in a *tawrat* (Torah) containing, in this case, proofs of the special mission to which Muhammad had been called: the *umm al-Kitāb* ("mother of the Book"), a notion found both in the Bible (Ex. 32:32, etc.) and in the Midrash. Ultimately, this holy text was to take earthly shape as the Koran (Arabic *Qur'ān,* "recital").

Abraham's central role in Islam (a term signifying the individual's submission to the will of God and to His decrees) was not the outcome of some mere whim on Muhammad's part. Historically remote from Moses, the patriarch was a Hebrew and not a Jew; nor could he be too closely associated with Jesus and Christian tradition. Moreover, the fact that Abraham was the father of Ishmael immediately removed the disgrace of ancestral paganism from the Arabs, Ishmael's traditional descendants. Even more important was the reverence paid to Abraham in Rabbinic literature: the patriarch's momentous break with idolatry and his courageous entry into a new life in the service of God marked a turning point in the religious history of mankind (the story of Abraham's destruction of the idols, related in the 21st Sura of the Koran, is borrowed from the Midrash), and these events could be seen to foreshadow Muhammad's own destruction of the images in the Ka'ba at Mecca after his triumphal return to that city in 629. Abraham, the "merciful Friend," became known as the "Beloved of God" *(el Khalil)*, and his burial place in Hebron was destined to become a center of Muslim, as well as Jewish, pilgrimage and devotion. Muhammad thus postulated an original, pure religion from which Judaism had later deviated and which Christianity, too, had theologically perverted.

At first, Muhammad sought Jewish support, claiming that the Islam which he preached was simply an interpretation of Judaism for the Arab nation. As the prophet whose coming was foretold by Moses in the Pentateuch (Deut. 18:15–19), Muhammad had been given the task of confirming the Torah and this he attempted to do by approving many injunctions and practices of the Mosaic Law (circumcision, Sabbath observance, the moral code, and certain elements of the dietary regulations). His conflict with Judaism resulted from the obvious imperfection

Mosque housing the tombs of the Patriarchs in Hebron (19th century engraving).

of his Biblical doctrine and from his limited knowledge of the written texts of Scripture—failings which led Jewish and other opponents to mock his teachings and pretensions because of the errors and misconceptions which they contained (and which were later a source of embarrassment to Muslim commentators of the Koran). Such inaccuracies often arose from the political and social objectives which Muhammad had in view, whereas the central monotheistic creed proclaimed by Islam differed little from that of Judaism. Nevertheless, there is only one quotation in the Koran (Sura 21:105)—" . . . 'The earth shall my righteous servants inherit' " (cf. Ps. 37:29)—which mentions its Biblical source, all the rest remaining somewhat free translations that nowhere refer to their Hebrew original.

Although Jewish exegesis was a vital factor in Muhammad's exposition of the Biblical stories and traditions, his narrative is a strange mixture of popular Jewish oral lore, original adaptation, and entirely new insights and conclusions. Adam is God's first representative on earth (khalifa) and Moses (Musa) the first recipient of a full-fledged book of Divine Law, although Abraham (Ibrāhīm) and Ishmael (Ismā'īl) were presented with "holy scrolls" in earlier generations. The true significance of Joseph's dream (Gen. 37:5–7) is not clear from its Islamic context, only from Rabbinic interpretation, and because Muslims misunderstood the Hebrew term Yosef Ha-Ẓaddik ("the righteous Joseph), associating ẓaddik with the Arabic saddiq ("truthful"), he became "Joseph the Truthful Interpreter of Dreams" (Yusuf el Saddiq)! Many Biblical figures have had their names modified under Greek or Syrian linguistic influence: Ismā'īl (Ishmael, cf. Isrā'īl for Israel), Ilyās (Elijah), Sulaymān (Solomon). Others are never directly named (the sons of Noah, Joshua, Balaam) or are given entirely different appelations in the Koran (Āzar for Terah). Muhammad's fondness for like-sounding couples produced Hābīl and Qābīl (Abel and Cain), Hārūn and Qārūn (Aaron and Korah), and Yājūj and Mājūj (Gog and Magog), yet, strangely enough, Miriam (Moses' sister) is confused with Mary (the mother of Jesus), while the four matriarchs of Israel (Sarah, Rebekah, Rachel, and Leah), Ishmael's mother (Hagar), and the three greatest Hebrew prophets (Isaiah, Jeremiah, and Ezekiel) are never mentioned at all! In post-Koranic Muslim literature, many attempts were made to correct defects, clarify obscurities, and bridge obvious gaps in Muhammad's presentation of the Biblical narrative. As part of this process of completion and exegesis, begun immediately after the death of the Prophet, those legends of

Muslims at prayer
facing the *miḥrab* in the
Mosque of Jazzar Pasha
in Acre.

Jewish origin *(Isrā'iliyyāt)* were collected and edited by scholars such
as Abu Ja'far Muhammad al-Tabarī (c. 838–992), Wahb ibn Munabbih
(seventh–eighth century), and al-Tha'labī (died 1035). A good deal of
apocryphal and romantic material (e.g., about Balkis or Bilqīs, the
Queen of Sheba) was later added to these Biblical anthologies.

In its doctrines and ceremonial and social legislation, Islam has
preserved much of the Biblical-Hebraic heritage which Muhammad
accepted or which Jewish converts to the faith insisted on importing.
Like Judaism's *Shema*,[51] Islam's creed—proclaimed five times each day
to the faithful—is an affirmation of God's uniquness: *Allah akbar!*
("Great is Allah!")—*la ilaha ill' Allah!* ("There is no God but Allah!"), [52]
to which the Muslim adds: *anna Muḥammad Nabina rasul Allah!* ("and
Muhammad our Prophet is Allah's messenger!"). To combat idolatry
Islam not only advanced the concept of one God (as *Raḥman,* "the
Merciful"), but also that of the Day of Judgment when the righteous
will receive their reward in Paradise and the wicked their deserts in
Hell. The way to salvation is through Faith, Repentance, Good Works,
and Meditation on Allah and His word (a notion close to that of the

[51] See above.
[52] Biblical sources for this phrasing may be found in Isa. 44:6, 45:5, etc.

Hebrew Prophets and Rabbinic Judaism). Also akin to the Jewish outlook is the Muslim belief that offenses against the ceremonial law weigh as heavily as those against the moral code, a view rooted in the Pentateuch. Islam's ritual injunctions, at first closely modeled on Judaism's Oral Law, were later arbitrarily changed in various respects in order to differentiate between the "true" faith and that of the obstinate Jews. Thus, the *kibla* (direction of prayer) was moved from Jerusalem to Mecca, the day of the weekly devotion from Saturday (the Jewish Sabbath) to Friday, and the fast of the tenth of Muharram (corresponding to *Yom Kippur*, the tenth of Tishri) to the entire month of Ramadan. The words of earlier prophets are true, but Muhammad is the "Seal of the Prophets," and the Arabic language (in which the Prophet wrote the Koran) is the vehicle of the Muslim faith. As in Judaism and Christianity, moral laws must also govern the functioning of society and stress is laid on business ethics and general honesty, friendly relations with family and neighbors, sexual purity of women, and on the practice of alms-giving (*sadaqa*, a term akin to the Hebrew *zedakah*, "righteousness").

As Islam spread by propaganda and force of arms from Arabia to Western Asia and North Africa, it made inroads into many old-established Jewish communities—a repetition of Christianity's earlier onslaught on the Jewish settlements of the Roman era. These Jewish converts did much to influence Islam's return to greater conformity with the obser-vances of Judaism: the eating of unclean foods such as the flesh of swine, blood, and carcasses was prohibited; a form of ritual slaughter involving the beast's consecration with a blessing, was adopted; circumcision (the "Covenant of Abraham") was generally prescribed; set times and manners of prayer were established; and sexual purity and ceremonial washing were made mandatory. A parallel to the Talmud was also constituted in the Islamic *Hadith*, namely what the Prophet said and did to lay the foundations of Koranic law. The *Hadith* even adopted the Rabbinic idea of *Halakhah le-Moshe mi-Sinai* ("the way of life as pre-scribed in the Law of Moses") in the notion that "whatever conforms with the Koran is from Muhammad, whether he actually mentioned it or not." Other Biblical influences on Islam which approximate to Jewish norms include the obligation to marry (celibacy being considered a disgrace); ritual bathing as a prelude to conversion; and Islam's re-ligious organization on the basis of a kind of rabbinate rather than priesthood, a system which contrasts with the "Old" Testament sacer-dotal hierarchy of Christianity. In much of its structure and ceremony

Islam is thus close to Judaism, although its inner life has felt more of the impact of Eastern Christian Orthodoxy.

At the same time, however, Jewish converts to the Muslim faith contributed to its growing theological hostility to Judaism, the Jews being accused of having tampered with their own Holy Writ in order to falsify the sources on which the Prophet based his claims and refute the predictions of his coming (a charge often leveled against Christianity as well). After Muhammad's time, the Hebrew Bible was mainly known to Muslims through secondhand quotations in polemical works directed against the Jews. Set passages were apparently furnished by Jewish apostates or possibly also by Christian converts who promoted the anti-Jewish tenor of Muslim polemics. During the Jewish "Golden Age" in Muslim-dominated medieval Spain, some progress was made toward a more reasoned and mutually respectful dialogue between Judaism and Islam. Arab militancy vis-à-vis the State of Israel has, however, precluded the development of a healthier and more cordial relationship between the two monotheistic faiths.

THE BIBLE'S ROLE IN EDUCATION

Although several of the world's ancient cultures stressed the importance of education—a hallmark of man's civilized and civilizing endeavor—it was the Hebrew Bible that hammered home the idea that the transmission of ethical values and religious concepts and practices was inseparably bound up with the quest for knowledge and the training of the young. This concern for education became a central feature of Judaism and, through the agency of Christianity, it eventually molded the outlook and development of Western society as a whole. Though based on Biblical injunction, the Hebraic concept of education did not evolve in isolation from the mainstream of similar thought in the ancient world: the Egyptians, Babylonians, Persians, Greeks, and Romans all contributed to ideas that have their source in the Scriptures and in Talmudic literature. The undoubted importance of Greek educational theory has, however, unfairly obscured the part played by Biblical thought in determining many fundamentals not only of the Jewish "way of life," but also of modern educational development. Goethe once wrote: "The greater the intellectual progress of the ages, the more fully will it be possible to employ the Bible not only as the foundation, but as the instrument, of education."

In Biblical times, education was essentially *religious* education, since "the fear of the Lord is the beginning of knowledge" (Prov. 1:7). Instruction in "the good and the right way" (1 Sam. 12:23) had a twofold aim: to make each individual a faithful servant and mirror of the Creator, and to weld Israel into an exemplary people. Hence the constant Biblical exhortations not to forsake God's Law, but to transmit it from father to son and from generation to generation. According to the optimistic view of humanity and of man's potential which pervades the Hebrew Bible, everyone is capable of improvement through the acquisition and practical application of learning:

Happy is the man that findeth wisdom,
And the man that obtaineth understanding.
For the merchandise of it is better than the merchandise of silver,
And the gain thereof than fine gold . . .
Her ways are ways of pleasantness,
And all her paths are peace.
She is a tree of life to them that lay hold upon her,
And happy is every one that holdeth her fast (Prov. 3:13–18).

The ethical motivation proclaims the equal importance of knowledge and of observance, since God's statutes and ordinances are handed down "that ye may learn them, and observe to do them" (Deut. 5:1), and there is also a hint that education brings a reward of its own: "And all thy children shall be taught of the Lord; and great shall be the peace of thy children" (Isa. 54:13). The fact that the educational process can only be effective if it involves the child from its earliest years is emphasized in the Book of Proverbs: "Train up a child in the way he should go, and even when he is old, he will not depart from it" (22:6). And the idea that education is a continuous process "from the cradle to the grave," to be applied at every time and in every place, is constantly reiterated: "And these words, which I command thee this day, shall be upon thy heart; and thou shalt teach them diligently unto thy children, and shalt talk of them when thou sittest in thy house, and when thou walkest by the way, and when thou liest down, and when thou risest up . . . " (Deut. 6:6–7; cf. Deut. 11:18–19). In a generalized sense—"meditating in the Law day and night"—this concept is frequently to be met with elsewhere in the Bible (Josh. 1:8; Ps. 1:2, 119:97, etc.). Other fundamentals of the Biblical concept of education were the belief that parents and the community in general share responsibility for its implementation; that the influence of the home and of sound companionship are powerful inducements to learning; and that Scriptural history is an important plank in the educational program (Ps. 44:2, 78:1–4). Individual differences in temperament and ability were also recognized, since "even a child is known by his doings, whether his work be pure, and whether it be right" (Prov. 20:11).

An element of prime importance in the Biblical blueprint for education is the influence of the parent and home: "Hear, my son, the instruction of thy father, and forsake not the teaching of thy mother" (Prov. 1:8). The Biblical-Hebraic inculcation of respect for parents and teachers finds reflection in a poetic chapter of the Book of Deuteronomy which enjoins:

Remember the days of old,
Consider the years of many generations;
Ask thy father, and he will declare unto thee,
Thine elders, and they will tell thee . . . (32:7).

The first and most lasting classroom is the home, in which the father teaches his son how to prepare for the journey into life and manhood, and the mother instructs her daughter in the skills of domestic virtue and industry. From the time of Abraham onward (Gen. 18:19), parents are expected to set an educational example and to supervise the child's training—a training of the mind and instinct as well as the cultivation of a thirst for knowledge. The religious ceremonies and festivals are designed to appeal to the child's imagination as reenactments of solemn historic events in Israel's national history, worship combined with dramatic recollection. A remarkable instance of this educational method is the Passover ritual, designed to provoke interest and questioning on the child's part, as the Biblical text itself clearly indicates: "And it shall come to pass, when your children shall say unto you: What mean ye by this service? that ye shall say: It is the sacrifice of the Lord's passover, for that He passed over the houses of the children of Israel in Egypt, when He smote the Egyptians, and delivered our houses" (Ex. 12:26–27).[53] Other Biblical passages which throw light on the educa-

---

[53] The *Seder* service, a combination of Biblical narrative, Rabbinic lore, and folk song, annually commemorates the Exodus from Egypt in a festive Passover

tional relationship of parent and child include Proverbs 31:1–9 and Job 1:5.

Since the art of writing was almost always the exclusive concern of initiated priests in antiquity, illiteracy was widespread not only among serfs and common folk, but even among the warrior caste and aristocracy. Nor was the ability to read and write common in the Near East and Europe until recent times—Muhammad even prided himself on his ignorance in this respect,[54] while popular education in the West was a long-delayed outcome of the Reformation. Only among the Hebrews was literacy a national virtue and ignorance a disgrace; from king to commoner, a knowledge of reading and writing was made available to all (Deut. 6:9, 17:18–19, 24:1; 2 Kings 5:7). The Semitic alphabet, invented by the Hebrews' kinfolk in Phoenicia some time in the second millennium B.C.E. and exported to Greece in about the ninth century B.C.E., never had the momentous impact on the Hellenistic world that it had on the Jews. To teach a child to read and write was a parent's and teacher's primary duty, the youngster's first hesitant steps perhaps being graphically described in the sarcastic diatribe of the Prophet's contemporaries:

Whom shall one teach knowledge?
And whom shall one make to understand the message?
Them that are weaned from the milk,
Them that are drawn from the breasts?
For it is precept by precept, precept by precept,
Line by line, line by line;[55]
Here a little, there a little.
For with stammering lips and with a strange tongue
Shall it be spoken to this people . . . (Isa. 28:9–11).

The entire Book of Proverbs very nearly constitutes a Biblical textbook for schools: many passages contain words and aural aids to the memory (25:4ff., 30:11–14, 15–33, 31:10–31). One of these "proverbial" sayings,

---

ritual prescribed for the Jewish home. The youngest participant asks "Four Questions" relating to aspects of the ceremony.

54 Koran, Suras 4:162, 7:156, 40:78.

55 Although their view is contested, some scholars have seen an allusion in "precept" (Hebrew *ẓav*) to the letter *ẓadē* and in "line" *(kav)* one to the letter *kof (qof)*.

unfashionable at the present day, is "He that spareth his rod hateth his son; but he that loveth him chasteneth him betimes" (13:24; whence "Spare the rod and spoil the child"). Vocational and professional training is often alluded to in the Bible. The intensive education which scribes, as civil servants, underwent involved a knowledge of reading and writing, administrative procedure, and of the drawing up of legal deeds and contracts (Deut. 24:1–3; Isa. 50:1; Jer. 32:10–14, etc.). Other essentials were a training in diplomacy, for which the lingua franca of Aramaic had to be learned (2 Kings 18:26; Dan. 1:4),[56] and in engineering (2 Kings 20:9–11; 2 Chron. 26:15, 32:30)! Nor was the education of women neglected. They were certainly taught the domestic sciences (Prov. 31:10–31), midwifery (Ex. 1:15–21), cooking (1 Sam. 8:13), and singing (2 Sam. 19:36; Eccles. 2:8).

Although there is a Scriptural allusion to public instruction by King Solomon (Eccles. 12:9), an educational system organized with the support of the community only began to take shape in the late Biblical (Hellenistic) period. In the first century B.C.E., Simeon ben Shetah, the Pharisee president of the Sanhedrin and brother of Queen Salome Alexandra, established schools in Jerusalem and other Judean towns and decreed that attendance at these be made compulsory for teenagers. The system was rapidly extended by the appointment of salaried teachers and by the institution of primary schooling for children—hitherto the sole concern of parents. Thus, free universal education first came into existence in the early Rabbinic period. In his *Outline of History* (1920), the English novelist H. G. Wells observed that "the Jewish religion, because it was a literature-sustained religion, led to the first efforts to provide elementary education for all children in the community." In fact, an intensified interest in and concern for the training of the young became evident after the Return from Babylon. There are numerous references to educational needs in the Apocrypha, which condemns failure to devote every effort to the instruction of one's children as "the grossest form of neglect" (*Letter of Aristeas*, 248) and recommends that youngsters be taught to read and write, "that they may have understanding all their life, reading unceasingly the Law of God" (*Testaments of the Twelve Patriarchs, Levi*, 13.2).

[56] Aramaic is the "Chaldean" of the Bible.

AMONG JEWS

The most significant outcome of the fall of the Second Jewish Commonwealth was the reestablishment of the Rabbinical academy at Yavne
(Jamnia), which adjusted itself to the new political reality by laying
stress on scholarship as the key to Judaism's survival.[57] This outlook is
reflected in the Talmud: "Rabbi Hamnuna said: 'Jerusalem was destroyed only because they neglected [the education of] school children'
. . . . Resh Lakish said in the name of Rabbi Judah the Prince: 'The
world endures only for the sake of the breath of school children' . . ."
(Shabbat, 119b). The focus of religious life was transferred from the lost
glory of the Temple to the synagogue (bet ha-keneset, "the house of assembly"). This democratic institution, already in existence while the
Temple still stood, enabled "laymen" to gain knowledge and participate
in scholarly discussions concerned with the traditional interpretation
of the Written and Oral Law. Portions of Scripture were read and, in time,
religious worship was introduced, transforming the "house of assembly"
into a house of prayer. Next to the home, the synagogue became the main
center of Jewish educational activity, whether for children or adults,
and it has retained its importance throughout the dispersion of the Jewish
people. To this day, Jewish religious instruction at the primary level is
bound up with synagogue life and organization in most parts of the
world.

The priority which Jews give to education has become proverbial.
In both Christendom and the lands of Islam, free schooling was maintained by each Jewish community and the most gifted students were
enabled to attend colleges of higher learning (yeshivot). The Rabbis of
Second Temple times established the tradition whereby the pursuit of
scholarship was combined with some profession or vocation, so that
the Torah might not become "a spade to dig with" (Avot, 4:7).[58] In
medieval Europe, Jewish "laymen" were more familiar with the Bible

---

[57] The Talmud records that the Romans granted the farsighted request of
Johanan ben Zakkai: "Give me Yavne and its sages" (Gittin, 56b).

[58] From their designation in the Talmud (Isaac Nappaḥa ["the smith"],
Johanan ha-Sandelar ["the sandal-maker"], etc., the occupations of many
Rabbis are clear. Hillel the Elder was a woodchopper and his rival, Shammai,
was a builder. A professional Rabbinate only came into being as a result of
modern social conditions.

than most Christian clerics and science, medicine, and philosophy were mainly transmitted to the West by scholarly Jews who translated Arabic books into Latin, thus disseminating much of Greek culture in its Muslim adaptation. The provisions made for primary schooling in the most obscure Jewish community far surpassed anything to be found in the towns of such "enlightened" countries as England, Germany, or America during the 18th century. Each week fathers tested their children's knowledge of the *sidrah* (portion of the Law) and Jacob Ashkenazi's *Ze'enah u-Re'enah* (literally, "Go forth and see," cf. Song of Songs 3:11; published 1620), a popular Yiddish work, comprising stories and Midrashic lore on the Pentateuch provided women and girls with an attractively written handbook to the Pentateuch or *Humash* ("Five Books" of Moses). The rest of the Bible was, however, increasingly neglected. By the age of seven or eight, boys were made to study Talmud, bypassing even the Mishnah and rarely completing the weekly *sidrah*. In 1637 a Frankfurt Rabbi sadly observed that some of his colleagues had never received a thorough grounding in the Hebrew Bible, and voices were heard calling for some far-reaching educational reforms, as yet to no avail. Italian and Sephardi Rabbis deplored this emphasis of Talmudic study at the Bible's expense among their Ashkenazi brethren.

The changed social and cultural atmosphere of the 19th century finally brought about a long-delayed overhaul of the Jewish educational syllabus. Samson Raphael Hirsch, the German Orthodox leader, established a coeducational school in Frankfurt (1855) where the Bible, Hebrew, and general subjects were taught, and regular Bible classes were instituted in the religion schools of Western Jewry. Yet it was not until after World War I that similar reforms were undertaken in Eastern Europe (with the exception of Communist Russia); Bible studies and spoken Hebrew entered the curriculum in the educational networks established by the Tarbut (general Zionist) and Yavneh (religious Zionist) organizations of Poland, Rumania, and the Baltic states. Since the 1920s, Zionism has been a powerful factor in the expansion of the Jewish day school system both in the New World and elsewhere. Elimination contests aimed at selecting the national representatives who attend each year's International Youth Bible Contest in Jerusalem have also done much to promote a wider and deeper knowledge of Scripture. The Bible's central role in Israeli education has already been stressed.[59] At

[59]   See above.

Bar Ilan University, a religious foundation in the Tel Aviv suburb of Ramat Gan (neighboring Tel Aviv), all students are required to attend lectures and courses in both Bible and Talmud, whatever their major field of study, and Bible study groups are fostered by kibbutzim, private societies, a Bible Readers' Union, and the Israel Defense Forces. Such widespread interest in and absorption of the Biblical word provides Jewry with an assurance that "this book of the law shall not depart out of thy mouth, but thou shalt meditate therein day and night . . . for then thou shalt make thy ways prosperous" (Josh. 1:8).

AMONG CHRISTIANS

Literacy and learning were also prized by the early Christians, who modeled their own house of worship, the church (Greek *ekklésia*, "assembly"; cf. the Hebrew term *kenesiyah*), on the Jewish synagogue. The rift between Judaism and the Gentile Church induced Christian educators to seek their ideas and inspiration in Classical sources, as well as in the Bible. The educational concepts of Greece and Rome provided an inevitable stimulus to the thinking of Gentile Christians, for whom Rabbinic norms were something foreign at best and, at worst, notions deriving from the Devil. Church leaders nevertheless disagreed about what ideas should or should not be borrowed from pagan literature: in the eyes of the Latin hierarchy of the West, Greco-Roman writings were suspect because of their emphasis of the physical to the detriment of the spiritual. Thus, architecture, medicine, and much of science and philosophy were subjects banned from the schoolroom by the Western Church precisely because they glorified life on earth and the power of man's intellect.[60] On the other hand, there were subjects that could be of service to the Church and these were in time granted a place in the educational syllabus—languages, history, and the seven liberal arts comprising the trivium (grammar, rhetoric, and logic) and the quadrivium (arithmetic, geometry, music, and astronomy). In Christian schools of the Middle Ages, the trivium formed the basis of elementary education and the quadrivium that of study for a master's degree at the university. From this it is clear that, despite its anxiety to save man's soul from the

[60] According to his own admission, Jerome, the great "Doctor of the Church," abandoned his secular studies after a harrowing vision of the torments that awaited him for so indulging his unspiritual appetite!

perdition of earthly pursuits in order to preserve it for the salvation of life after death, the medieval Church insulated pupils from the dangerous contamination of the Scriptures. Only those entering holy orders were allowed to study theology and delve into Holy Writ. Unsupervised, independent exploration of the Bible was tantamount to heresy and only clerics in good standing were permitted to expound Scripture from a Latin text incomprehensible to the Christian masses.

This emphasis of faith, at the expense of knowledge, was dominant in Christianity until the Reformation. Though in theory favorably disposed to Hebrew studies, the Church Father Augustine (354–430) helped to canonize the Latin Vulgate of Jerome and disparaged secular learning in terms that became the stock-in-trade of medieval ecclesiastics. Augustine (in *De doctrina Christiana*) declared that, "just as poor as the store of gold and silver and garments which the people of Israel brought with them out of Egypt was in comparison with the riches which they afterward attained at Jerusalem, and which reached their height in the reign of King Solomon, so poor is all the useful knowledge which is gathered from the books of the heathen when compared with the knowledge of Holy Scripture . . . " Since, for over a millennium after Augustine's death, the vast majority of Christians could not read, not even this opinion as to the importance of Bible study (which was, furthermore, written in Latin) could reach the eyes and ears of the ordinary Christian layman. It was thus practical awareness of Christian education's limitations that moved the French theologian Peter Abelard (1079–1142) to urge his ex-wife Heloïse and her nuns to learn Hebrew in order to understand their Bible, and a similar awareness that inspired the Abelard School's bold remark (in *Commentary to Paul's Epistle to the Ephesians,* ch. 6; c. 1141): "A Jew, however poor, if he had ten sons would put them all to letters, not for gain as the Christians do, but for the understanding of God's law, and not only his sons, but his daughters."

Renaissance scholarship's rediscovery of classical literature led, among other things, to the disinterment of works on the theory of education by writers of antiquity (Plutarch, Cicero, etc.), the study of which eventually brought about a decisive revolution in Western attitudes to the training of the mind. The old curriculum was discarded and new subjects (such as Greek, the sciences, and medicine) were taught at the lively new universities of Italy to which students flocked from all parts of Europe. Hard on the heels of the Renaissance came the Reformation, with its new, unfettered exploration of the Scriptures in their original tongues. Hebrew

studies, as an essential aid to Bible scholarship, became popular throughout of the lands of the West[61] and had an immense influence on basic
religious thought and on popular education. The vernacular text of the
Bible was often the greatest school primer, determining the future course
of linguistic development and the national aspiration and outlook of
entire peoples. This was particularly the case in the English-speaking
world. In his *Educational Essays* (1870), Thomas Huxley drew attention
to "the great historical fact that for three centuries this Book has been
woven into the life of all that is best and noblest in English history;
that it has become the national epic of Britain, and is familiar to noble
and simple, from John o' Groat's to Land's End; that it is written in the
noblest and purest English, and abounds in exquisite beauties of a merely
literary form . . . . By the study of what other book could children be so
much humanized, and made to feel that each figure in that vast historical
procession fills, like themselves, but a momentary space in the interval
between the Eternities; and earns the blessings or the curses of all time,
according to its effort to do good and hate evil?"

Expert opinion has in recent years increasingly acknowledged the
debt which the modern theory and practice of education owe—directly
and indirectly—to the Hebrew Bible. The importance of the home
background, of parental concern and example, and of the individual's
readiness to continue learning throughout his or her life are all educational factors on which the Scriptures first laid emphasis. And study's
effects on morality and character through the positive influence of the
family and community received their earliest description in the Book
of Proverbs. The educational program of the Bible, developed and
amplified in the Talmud, led to the recommendation that primary education begin at the age of five or six (*Avot*, 5.23; *Bava Batra*, 21a) and the
National Education Association of the United States has cited Talmudic
authority (*Bava Batra*, 21a) for the maximum size of a class to be 25
pupils. The educational principles of the Bible have thus played a significant part in the evolution of ideas concerned with "teaching children
diligently" throughout the civilized world.

[61] See Chapter 4.

SOCIAL WELFARE

The Hebrew Bible's ethical and compassionate approach to society's "have-nots" was revealed in practical injunctions governing the proper treatment of the poor and the underprivileged. The Code of Hammurabi and other legal formulations of antiquity certainly regulated the State's handling of citizens and slaves, but only the laws of Israel made both society and the individual accountable to God for the welfare of those in their charge. The English philosopher Sir Francis Bacon (1561–1626) declared that "there never was found, in any age of the world, either religion or law that did so highly exalt the public good as the Bible." The Hebrew term *zedakah* ("righteousness" or "justice"), which constantly recurs in the Scriptures, is the source of our concept of charity (Latin, *caritas,* "dearness"), to which the Church added the sense of "Christian love." From the idea of God as the Creator of all things—and hence as the source of all wealth—arose the Biblical notion of nature's bounty as a Divine trust, from which all men are entitled to receive their rightful share. Provision must be made for the poor (Lev. 25:25ff.) and the tithe apportioned to the widow, orphan, and stranger (Deut. 14:28–29), while landowners are obligated to set aside for the less fortunate the harvest of the corners of the fields (Lev. 19:9), the gleanings (Lev. 23:22), the forgotten sheaf (Deut. 24:19), and the crops that grow of themselves in the Sabbatical year (Ex. 23:10–11). In his *Controverted Questions* (1892), Thomas Huxley paid a remarkable tribute to the advanced social thinking that motivated this type of legislation in the Pentateuch: "The Bible has been the Magna Charta of the poor and of the oppressed; down to modern times no State has had a constitution in which the interests of the people are so largely taken into account, in which the duties so much more than the privileges of rulers are insisted upon, as that drawn up for Israel in Deuteronomy and Leviticus; nowhere is the fundamental truth that the welfare of the State, in the long run, depends on the uprightness of the citizen so strongly laid down."

The Israelite belief that God cared sufficiently about men to intervene in history and liberate an obscure people from perpetual slavery directed concern toward the whole issue of human welfare. The Pentateuch's social legislation forms part of God's contract with Israel: observance of the commandments can bring about a moral change resulting in the conquest of poverty (Deut. 15:4–5), "for the needy shall not always be forgotten, nor the expectation of the poor perish for ever" (Ps. 9:19).

The realization that things are not as they should be is the basis of the Bible's social protest; and it was the characteristically Hebraic affirmation of the good things of life that led the Prophets to proclaim that the grave inequalities which they saw in the distribution of wealth called for rectification. Material possessions, far from being "the root of evil," are so good that everyone should enjoy them. Thus the Mosaic idea of their constituting a Divine trust was strongly echoed in the Prophetic books—"The earth is the Lord's, and the fulness thereof" (Ps. 24:1), "Mine is the silver, and Mine the gold, saith the Lord of hosts" (Haggai 2:8), "Both riches and honor come of Thee" (1 Chron. 29:12). Renan called attention to the fact that "Israel's sages burned with anger over the abuses of the world. The prophets were fanatics in the cause of social justice, and loudly proclaimed that if the world was not just, or capable of becoming so, it had better be destroyed—a view which, if utterly wrong, led to deeds of heroism and brought about a grand reawakening of the forces of humanity" (*Histoire du peuple d'Israël*, 1887–93).

The Bible's concern for human welfare was also motivated by the need to imitate God and His holiness—"that ye may remember and do all My commandments, and be holy unto your God" (Num. 15:40). Man's nature can reduce him to the level of the beasts over which his Creator first gave him dominion, but the ethical impulse—man's willingness to be a partner in Creation—can raise him to the highest level of achievement and nobility, since "Thou hast made him but little lower than the angels." In Hebrew, this phrase ("but little lower than the angels") is *me'at me-Elohim,* literally "but less than God," a bold development of the "image of God" idea in the Biblical account of Creation (Gen. 1:27). Again and again the Pentateuch stresses the call for man to imitate God's solicitude for the less fortunate, since "He doth execute justice for the fatherless and widow, and loveth the stranger, in giving him food and raiment" (Deut. 10:18). Dealing righteously with the underprivileged is a fundamental of the Torah, a view reiterated in the Prophets: it is the key to Israel's redemption (Isa. 1:27) and to the establishment of Zion (Isa. 54:14); together with the practice of just laws, compassion for the needy "is more acceptable to the Lord than sacrifice" (Prov. 21:3). How such compassion should be translated into action is vividly described in Ezekiel 18:5–9: "If a man be just, and do that which is lawful and right . . . and hath not wronged any . . . hath given his bread to the hungry, and hath covered the naked with a garment . . . hath withdrawn his hand from iniquity, hath executed true justice between man and man

. . . he is just, he shall surely live, saith the Lord God." And the Book
of Proverbs emphasizes the concept of *imitatio Dei* in a telling phrase:
"He that is gracious unto the poor lendeth unto the Lord" (19:17).
Equally vivid is the portrayal of the fate in store for the heartless—the
"iniquity of Sodom" (Ezek. 16:49–50), God's punishment of the wicked
(Ps. 37:12–15), and the shortlived "joy of the godless" (Job 20:4–29).

RIGHTEOUSNESS IN ACTION

The Biblical concept of *ẓedakah* envisages an obligatory act, a duty to
give help and support in witness to God's own love and concern for
mankind: "Thou shalt not harden thy heart, nor shut thy hand from thy
needy brother" (Deut. 15:7). It is in no way an act of grace or special
favor, a view which finds emphasis in Proverbs 3:27–28: "Withhold not
good from him to whom it is due, when it is in the power of thy hand to
do it. Say not unto thy neighbor: 'Go, and come again, and tomorrow
I will give;' when thou hast it by thee." This duty to "uphold" one's
less fortunate neighbor (Lev. 25:35)[62] is reiterated by the Psalmist ("I
know that the Lord will maintain the cause of the poor, and the right of
the needy," Ps. 140:13), and the example and concern shown by God
find poetic expression in another book of the Prophets:

> The Lord maketh poor, and maketh rich;
> He bringeth low, He also lifteth up.
> He raiseth up the poor out of the dust,
> He lifteth up the needy from the dung-hill,
> To make them sit with princes,
> And inherit the throne of glory;
> For the pillars of the earth are the Lord's,
> And He hath set the world upon them (1 Sam. 2:7–8).

Prophetic Judaism championed the cause of the distressed, seeing in
their plight not some fault of their own but the effects of a vicious social
order. Two Biblical episodes dramatize the revolutionary nature of
prophetic intervention in the affairs of the state and of society in their

---

[62] Judaism interprets "that thy brother may live with thee" in the following
verse (Lev. 25:36) to mean, quite literally, that one's fellow man should not
be allowed to endure, let alone die from, starvation.

time. When David seduced Bath-Sheba and contrived the death of her husband, Uriah, Nathan the prophet used his parable of the poor man's lamb to condemn the king out of his own mouth (2 Sam. 11:2–12:15). The extraordinary aspect of this incident is Nathan's courageous disregard of David's royal prerogatives: God's demand for absolute justice applies to both king and commoner and his concern extends to the alien (Uriah being a Hittite), as well as to the Israelite. No less astounding is the prophet Elijah's condemnation of Ahab after Jezebel disposes of Naboth so that her husband can gain possession of the vineyard he covets (1 Kings 21:1–29). Like Nathan, Elijah had no official status or authority; yet Ahab wilted under the prophet's violent condemnation and acknowledged his sin. The U.S. archaeologist and Bible scholar William F. Albright asserted that the Prophets set a pattern and created an atmosphere that "put Hyde Park and the best days of muckraking newspapers to shame." Their only concern was for social justice and, "protected by religious sanctions, the prophets of Judah were a reforming political force which has never been surpassed and perhaps never equalled in subsequent world history" (*Approaches to World Peace,* 1943).

Nathan and Elijah were two of the "pre-writing" Prophets whose names are not commemorated in any book of the Bible. The "writing" Prophets—Amos, Hosea, Micah, Isaiah, Jeremiah, and the rest—did not erupt into history to condemn particular cases of injustice, but voiced a general protest against the evils which they saw about them. Isaiah fulminated against empty sacrifices, urging his contemporaries to "cease to do evil; learn to do well; seek justice, relieve the oppressed, judge the fatherless, plead for the widow" (1:16–17); "what mean ye," he asked, "that ye crush My people, and grind the face of the poor?" (3:15). Jeremiah complained that "every one is greedy for gain; and from the prophet even unto the priest every one dealeth falsely. They have healed also the hurt of My people lightly, saying: 'Peace, peace,' when there is no peace" (6:13–14). From Jeremiah came once again the demand for "justice and righteousness," so that men should "do no wrong, do no violence, to the stranger, the fatherless, nor the widow, neither shed innocent blood" (22:3). Malachi proclaimed that God would be "a swift witness against the sorcerers, and against the adulterers, and against false swearers; and against those who oppress the hireling in his wages, the widow, and the fatherless, and that turn aside the stranger from his right, and fear not Me" (3:5). Echoing Isaiah's denunciation of hollow ritual, the prophet Micah crystallized Israel's lofty social ethic in the famous prescription: "It hath been told thee, O man, what is good, and what the Lord doth require of thee: Only to do justly, and to love mercy, and to walk humbly with thy God" (6:8). The sense of outrage and anxiety that welled up in the cry of the Prophets was to inspire much of Judaism's legal code and many attitudes and institutions developed within Christianity and Islam. "All modern social legislation is an outcome of the prophetic spirit, and the spirit of these Hebrew teachers will continue to urge the nations to ever fresh reforms" (H. Gunkel, *Was bleibt vom Alten Testament,* 1916).

The concept of *ẓedakah* is thus the very basis of social teaching in the Bible. The Israelite celebrating his festivals must invite not only his family and friends, but also the Levite (a servant of the community), the stranger (who, being landless, is presumably disadvantaged), and the widow and orphan (Deut. 16:11, 14). The "woman of valor" stretches out her hand to the poor and needy (Prov. 31:20); Nehemiah and Ezra, instructing the people in the Torah, tell them to rejoice on the New Year and "send portions unto him for whom nothing is prepared" (Neh. 8:10); while Mordecai makes "sending portions one to another, and gifts to the poor" an obligatory part of the Purim festival (Esther 9:22). "The great concern of Moses was . . . . to lay the foundation of a social state in which deep poverty and degrading want should be unknown" (Henry George, *Moses,* 1878). Commenting on the verse, "Withhold not good from him to whom it is due . . . " (Prov. 3:27), C. H. Cornill noted that the words "him to whom it is due" are conveyed in the Hebrew term *ba'al* (literally, "owner" or "proprietor"): "Here the needy appears as the *ba'al* of the good deed, as having a God-given, legal claim to it, as being by natural right its proprietor. Truly an unfathomable depth of philanthropy," he concluded, "is expressed in this single and apparently innocent word" (*Das Alte Testament und die Humanität,* 1895). Poverty and starvation were an accepted feature of ancient life, in which the "haves" rarely showed concern for the fate of the "have-nots," but the worst aspects of impoverishment seem to have been obviated in Hebrew society. Despite the stern language of the Prophets, Scriptural legislation evidently prevented the growth of mendicancy among the Israelites, since there is in fact no Biblical Hebrew word for "beggar."[63]

---

[63] The one occurrence of "beggar" in the *Authorized Version* results from a mistranslation of *evyon* ("needy") in 1 Sam. 2:8.

ZEDAKAH IN JUDAISM

Apart from the tithes prescribed for the landless Levites (Num. 18:21ff.) and for the needy (Deut. 14:28–29), no comprehensive system of philanthropy developed in the Biblical period, although many of the Scriptural passages cited above make it clear that almsgiving was regarded as a natural obligation, and care for the underprivileged a matter of general concern. Josephus (in *Contra Apionem*) reveals how the post-Biblical notion of *zedakah* had developed under the inspiration of the Pharisees: "He who refuses a suppliant the aid which he has the power to give is accountable to justice." Among the 613 Commandments which the Rabbis deduced from the Torah were several relating to social welfare: giving alms to the poor; providing interest-free loans to the needy (Ex. 22:24); restoring the pledge needed by a poor man on the same day (Ex. 22:25–26; Deut. 24:12–13); prompt payment of a laborer's wages (Deut. 24:14–15); and allowing a hired man to eat from the produce he is harvesting (Deut. 23:25–26) By the first century C.E., population increase coupled with social stresses under the Romans made begging commonplace, as numerous references in the Mishnah and in the New Testament (blind Bartimaeus in Mark 10:46; Lazarus in Luke 16:20; the lame beggar at the Temple gate in Acts 3:2) clearly reveal. These mendicants—not infrequently impostors (the more cheerful of whom can be seen as prototypes of the classic Jewish *shnorrer* of later centuries) —forfeited their right to benefit from organized relief if they persisted in public begging. For, by the early Talmudic era, an official *kuppah* ("charity fund") was in operation, the first public relief system in history, which kept the worst manifestations of poverty within bounds and limited begging by Jews for many centuries.

Equally important, however, was the way in which charity was given or administered. A poor man's sensitivity must be respected, since the Psalmist declared: "Happy is he that *considereth* the poor" (Ps. 41:2), for which reason it is best to give charity in secret (*Shabbat*, 104a; *Bava Batra*, 9b) so as to avoid embarrassing the recipient (*Hagigah*, 5a). Referring to Prov. 11:4 (cf. Prov. 10:2, Tobit 12.8), Johanan ben Nappaha extended this to mean that "charity delivers from death" only when the giver and the receiver are unaware of each other's identity (*Sanhedrin*, 10b); the Mishnah recommended that the poor be "members of one's household" (*Avot*, 1.5); while the Talmud records the opinion that charity grants might even be determined on the Sabbath (*Shabbat*,

150a) and the Rabbinic decision that, "to promote peace, we support the poor of the Gentiles, visit their sick, and bury their dead, along with the poor, the sick, and the dead of Israel" (*Gittin,* 61a). These statements have remained characteristic of Judaism's approach to charitable questions. In later centuries, the Zohar was to give a homiletical interpretation to Gen. 12:5—"He who helps the poor is their creator. It is said of Abraham and his servants, 'the souls that they had made' " (Zohar, Ex. 198a). Maimonides, in his *Mishneh Torah,* laid down the modern welfare approach: "There are eight rungs in charity. The highest is when you help a man to help himself" (*Yad: Matnot Aniyim,* 10.7). The Biblical teachings which Jews imbibed through the Mishnah, Talmud, and codes from earliest childhood have made the practice of charity a vital rule rather than a dead letter. Every festive or family occasion, every celebration or sad event, provided a reason for almsgiving, making *ẓedakah* second nature to the Jew—from the communal welfare schemes of the Middle Ages, when his life was disrupted by persecution, to the philanthropic trusts and foundations of the 20th century.

CHRISTIAN CHARITY

Charitableness and charity occupy an important place in early Christian teaching. In its social doctrine "Nazarenism" was, perhaps, closer to the concepts of Essene piety (with its withdrawal from general life) than to those of the Pharisees, whose idealism was tempered with a more realistic assessment of man's innate capabilities. As the Synoptic Gospels and certain other New Testament writings reveal, early Christianity's outlook on poverty and the practice of charity was nevertheless close to that of the Prophets and Rabbis. Through the Greek *agapē* ("love"), *ẓedakah* was rendered *caritas* in Latin, whence the term "charity" that occurs so frequently in the New Testament. Charity in this sense signifies "love to God and good will to men," leading to patience and forbearance with others, a readiness to pursue the welfare of all, even at some cost or discomfort to the individual. For the Christian, charitableness is the equivalent of *gemilut ḥasadim* among Jews, and it is a virtue that accompanies those who practice it beyond the grave (cf. "the stock remains for him in the world to come," Mishnah, *Pe'ah,* 1). A detailed "hymn to charity" is contained in 1 Corinthians 13: "Though I speak with the tongues of men and of angels, and have not charity, I am become as sounding brass, or a tinkling cymbal. And though I have the gift of prophecy, and understand all mysteries, and all knowledge; and though I have all faith, so that I could remove mountains, and have not charity, I am nothing . . . Charity suffereth long, and is kind . . . Rejoiceth not in iniquity, but rejoiceth in the truth . . . And now abideth faith, hope, charity, these three; but the greatest of these is charity."[64] A reflection of one Talmudic statement already mentioned (*Bava Batra,* 9a) may even be seen in the New Testament opinion that "the end of the commandment is charity out of a pure heart, and of a good conscience, and of faith unfeigned" (1 Timothy 1:5).

An examination of the Gospels and other New Testament sources also reveals how closely the early Christians adhered to the "charitable" injunctions of the Pharisees and Rabbis. Clear evidence of this is available in Matthew 6:1–4: "Take heed that ye do not your alms before men, to be seen of them: otherwise ye have no reward of your Father which is in heaven . . . But when thou doest alms, let not thy left hand know what thy right hand doeth: That thine alms may be in secret: and thy Father which seeth in secret himself shall reward thee openly." Instances of charitable donations to the poor may be found in Acts 24:17, Romans 15:26, and Galatians 2:10. Jesus' hyperbolical injunction to "sell all that thou hast, and distribute unto the poor" (Luke 18:22; cf. Matthew 19:21, Mark 10:21)[65] is certainly a departure from normative Jewish tradition, which maintains that "charity begins at home" (*Bava Meẓia,* 71a) and that no more than one fifth of one's means should be disbursed on charity at any one time (*Ketuvot,* 50a). The conditions linking Deut. 15:4 and 11(that obedience to the commandments will banish poverty from the land) are also disregarded in the statement by Jesus to the effect that "ye have the poor always with you; but me ye have not always" (Matthew 26:11; cf. Mark 14:7, John 12:8). On the other hand, Luke's version of the opening declaration of the Sermon on the Mount (6:20)— "Blessed be ye poor: for yours is the kingdom of God"—has its equiva-

---

[64] This delineation of "charity" has an early Rabbinic parallel in the Mishnah's summary of those "commandments that have no fixed measure," which concludes that "the study of the Torah leads to [or "is equivalent to"] them all" (*Pe'ah,* 1).

[65] For the Judeo-Christian elaboration of this episode (in the *Gospel of the Hebrews*), see Hugh J. Schonfield, *The Authentic New Testament* (1962), p. 73.

lent in the Midrash: "Who are God's people? The poor" (Exodus Rabbah, 31.5, on Ex. 22:24).[66]

Despite widespread Christian admiration for the charitable practices of the Jews (evident from Roman times and the era of the Church Fathers to the Middle Ages and down to the present day), stress was laid doctrinally on the notion of poverty's spiritual virtue (rooted, perhaps, in passages such as 2 Corinthians 8:9).[67] This is very much at variance with the outlook of the Bible (Prov. 15:15), the Apocrypha (Wisdom of Ben Sira 34.21), and the Talmud (*Bava Meẓia,* 59a; *Avodah Zarah,* 5a). The Midrash states that "poverty outweighs all other troubles" (Exodus Rabbah, 31.14) and an old Yiddish proverb has it that "poverty is no disgrace, but neither is it an honor," since Judaism has never seen anything particularly virtuous in self-imposed impoverishment. The "holy poverty" which motivated the lives of monks, friars, and hermits in medieval Christendom (and of the monastic *kalandar* beggars of *Arabian Nights* fame in the lands of Islam) had no basis in the social thinking of the Hebrew Prophets, who never appealed to reward and punishment in an afterlife but hungered for justice in this world, giving form "to the cry of the people, to the plaint of the poor, to the obstinate demand of those who 'hunger and thirst after righteousness' . . . " (Renan, *Histoire du peuple d'Israël*). And it may well have been his awareness of the social ethic which Christianity, like Judaism, owed to the Bible that made the great Franco-Jewish commentator Rashi tell a monk whom he had cured of an ailment: "Divided as we may be by religion, we are united by charity."

The poor relief legislation which he enacted in 315 C.E. made the Emperor Constantine Europe's first ruler to promote social welfare; but his measures were actually repealed by Justinian after a mere two centuries. From the early 1560s, English Protestantism made charity a duty of the State, yet this owed more to the letter, than to the spirit, of the Scriptures, and its effect was only to make pauperism increase. Charity, in the Biblical sense—aimed at preserving the recipient's self-respect and at encouraging "self-help"—was not put into operation. If anything, organized Christianity's acquiescence in the established

---

[66] Matthew 5:3 gives "Blessed are the poor in spirit: for theirs is the kingdom of heaven."

[67] Cf. James 2:5. It is noteworthy that one of the Judeo-Christian sects took the name "Ebionite" (literally, "poor people").

economic order actually bred further poverty, deriving its unscientific approach to the problem from the sayings of Jesus and Plato. The modern theory and practice of social welfare in the Christian West owes more to Spinoza's belief that "care of the poor is incumbent on society as a whole" (*Ethics*, 1677) and to the economics of Thomas Malthus and David Ricardo. Despite the inadequacies of the early 19th-century English Poor Laws, the institution of the workhouse which these inspired was a move away from outdated attitudes. Social and political reform, compulsory education at the elementary level, and the working man's dawning awareness of his moral and economic rights provided a long-delayed response to the revolutionary legislation and protest which the Hebrew Bible had first enshrined centuries and millennia before; and many other states were to follow England's example.

HUMANITARIANISM

Assistance to the poor and underprivileged is not limited to financial support in the Pentateuch and Prophets: many other fields of humanitarian endeavor are also delineated, ranging from the care of strangers and prisoners to the proper treatment of the aged. The Hebrews made their social legislation applicable to the alien as well as to their own people and asserted the human dignity of the slave and hired laborer. Writing in 1846, the French political economist Pierre Joseph Proudhon observed that "the whole Bible is a hymn to Justice—that is, in the Hebrew style, to charity, to kindness to the weak on the part of the strong, to voluntary renunciation of the privilege of power."

The practice of hospitality is inculcated in the Bible. The patriarch Abraham hastens to welcome strangers and travelers (Gen. 18), but the men of Sodom display notable contempt for the hospitality code (Gen. 19). Even the sly Laban opens his door to the wayfarer (Gen. 24:29–32), and this tradition is maintained by Jethro (Ex. 2:20), Manoah (Judges 13:15), and the kindly Shunammite woman who gave shelter to Elisha (2 Kings 4:8–11), while Job declares that no stranger whom he encountered had to "lodge in the street" (31:32). A significant extension of the right of hospitality is contained in the Biblical law establishing cities of refuge for the manslaughter (Num. 35:9–34). Except in the case of Jael (Judges 4:17–24, 5:24–27), breaches of the hospitality code are severely condemned (Judges 8:5–9, 19:14–30; 1 Sam. 25:2–38). Welcoming the traveler and sojourner is also bound up with Israel's

Abraham offers hospitality to the three angels in this mosaic from Santa Maria Maggiore, Rome.

historical experience in foreign bondage, "for ye know the heart of a stranger, seeing ye were strangers in the land of Egypt" (Ex. 23:9). In Rabbinic times, children were taught the virtue of hospitality and host and guest were expected to adhere to prescribed standards of conduct laid down in the Talmud (*Berakhot*, 58a; *Pesaḥim*, 86b; *Kiddushin*, 32b, etc.). The Passover *Seder* service incorporates R. Huna's classic invitation to the wayfarer, "Let all who are hungry enter and eat," and travelers were cared for in the synagogue through the public recitation of the blessing over wine *(Kiddush)*. In the late patriarchal era, the Bible refers to "lodging-places" (inns) where wayfarers could find provision for their needs (Gen. 42:27, 43:21), and although Joseph and Mary discovered that "there was no room for them in the inn" at Bethlehem (Luke 2:7), the New Testament records Jesus' parable of the "good Samaritan" who brought "the man who fell among thieves" to such a lodging-place and cared for him there (Luke 10:34). The tradition of Abraham also finds an echo in the early Christian injunction: "Be not forgetful to entertain strangers: for thereby some have entertained angels unawares" (Hebrews 13:2). It has, furthermore, become part of Muslim social teaching, exemplified in the proverbial hospitality which Beduin of the desert readily extend to the stranger. Welcoming guests is now a virtue among Jews, Christians, and Muslims alike.

During the Middle Ages, sick and needy persons were often lodged in "hospitals" (hostels), but infirmaries for the treatment of the ailing were set up long before "hospital" acquired its modern sense. In the Bible, God's appearance before Abraham by the terebinths of Mamre (Gen. 18:1) is traditionally interpreted as an exemplary visit to the sick (the patriarch having just obeyed the injunction to circumcise his household and himself)[68] and references to healing wounds and ailments are scattered throughout the Scriptures. The patriarch Jacob is embalmed by Egyptian "physicians" at Joseph's command (Gen. 50:2) and King Asa, suffering from a disease of the feet, "sought not to the Lord, but to the physicians" (2 Chron. 16:12). God promises the Israelites that He "will take away from thee all sickness; and He will put none of the evil diseases of Egypt, which thou knowest, upon thee" (Deut. 7:15; cf. Ex. 23:25), while the prevalence of leprosy and other maladies in the ancient world is frequently apparent in the Bible. For these, Israel's hygienic regulations must have proved an invaluable remedy. The spiritual afflictions which only the Prophets and righteous men can cure are alluded to metaphorically in the Book of Jeremiah:

---

[68] According to the Rabbis, visiting the sick is a basic social duty (*Pe'ah*, 1, *Nedarim*, 41a; cf. Ben Sira 7.35), neglect of which is equivalent to murder (*Nedarim*, 40a).

Is there no balm in Gilead?
Is there no physician there?
Why then is not the health
Of the daughter of my people recovered? (8:22).

Although the "dwelling without the camp" (the lepers' quarantine,
Lev. 1346, Num. 5:2, etc.) does not constitute proof of the existence
of infirmaries for the sick in Biblical times, it does show some basic
awareness of the need to isolate infection. Operating theaters ("marble
rooms") operated for the Jewish sick in the Talmudic period, and the
Rabbis made the support of both Jewish and Gentile patients a communal
responsibility (Jerusalem Talmud, *Gittin,* 5.9). According to the New
Testament, the miracles performed by Jesus included the cure of various
diseases, his dispute with the Pharisees centering on one occasion in a
question of "light" and "weighty" precepts—the healing of sick people
(as opposed to those gravely ill) on the Sabbath day (Matthew 12:10;
Mark 3:2; Luke 6:7, 14:3). He also instructed his disciples themselves
to "heal the sick, cleanse the lepers, raise the dead, cast out devils"
(Matthew 10:8).[69] By early Rabbinic times, institutions for the treatment
of the sick were apparently known as "terebinths of Abraham," and
Jerome mentions that these had been established in the Holy Land long
before his own day, praising a woman who opened the first such hospital
in Rome as having thereby "transplanted the terebinth of Abraham to
Ausonian shores." In the medieval period, Maimonides was foremost
among those Jewish physicians who revolutionized the medical practice
of the West through the application of Arab science, and whom Pope
Boniface IX is said to have praised for being "good-natured and obliging,
swift to help the poor and needy . . . and highly experienced in their
art." It is a far cry from the hospices of antiquity to the hospital complexes
of today, but the humanitarian concern which motivated Biblical injunctions about care for the sick has played its part in the modern
development of health clinics, public health authorities, and national
health schemes ("socialized medicine") of the Welfare State type.

---

[69] The old "lazar-house" or lazaretto (meaning "a hospital for contagious
diseases" or "quarantine") seems to derive from a confusion of Lazarus (John
11:2ff.) and the Venetian church of Santa Maria di Nazaret, which maintained
a hospital of its own. The New Testament saying, "Physician, heal thyself"
(Luke 4:23), is an old Jewish proverb, quoted as "Physician, heal your own
limp!" in the Midrash (Genesis Rabbah, 23.4).

THE DIGNITY OF LABOR

While the Bible, in common with other documents of antiquity, regarded labor as man's destiny, part of the natural scheme of things (Gen. 2:5, 15), God Himself was visualized as the "fashioner" of everything (Jer. 10:16) and the heavens as His "handiwork" (Ps. 8:4, 102:26). For this reason, the Hebrews were taught to see merit, not disgrace, in the need to work. However normal such an attitude may seem to people of today, it was by no means "normal" to regard labor as a human virtue in antiquity. Idleness was the badge of aristocracy in the ancient world, when the nation's own serfs and the slaves it took in war were reduced to perpetual drudgery and left to eke out a miserable existence. In Greece and Rome, the laborer was nothing more than an "animated tool," bereft of rights. This has no parallel in the Bible. God's own cessation of labor after His six days of Creation (Gen. 2:2-3; Ex. 20:11) provides both grounds for *imitatio Dei* and the basis for the laws of Sabbath rest (Ex. 20:8ff., etc.).[70] As previously shown, the institution of the Sabbath was a social revolution, running counter to the whole "natural" order of the ancient world. "Our modern spirit, with all its barren theories of civic and political rights, and its strivings toward freedom and equality, has not thought out and called into existence a single institution that, in its beneficial effects upon the laboring classes, can in the slightest degree be compared to the Weekly Day of Rest promulgated in the Sinaitic wilderness" (Proudhon, *De la célébration du dimanche*, 1850).

Israel's Sabbath gave everyone—Jew and Gentile alike—one day of freedom and leisure each week, one precious day exempt from toil and overwhelming fatigue. Among the laborers of ancient Israel—as among modern Jews, Christians observing their Sunday, Muslims their Friday, and even the Soviet proletariat—the minimal one free day in the working week is now taken for granted. The eminent German philosopher Hermann Cohen claimed that, "had Judaism brought into the world only the Sabbath, it would thereby have proved itself to be a producer of joy and a promoter of peace for mankind. The Sabbath was the first step on the road which led to the abrogation of slavery" (*Die Religion der Vernunft*, 1919). But labor is not slavery: many of the Bible's heroes began their careers as humble working folk—Moses and David were

[70] Cf. Gen. 3:17, 19; Haggai 2:4; Job 5:7.

shepherds, Gideon a farmhand, Saul and Elisha were plowers, Amos a herdsman. The Book of Proverbs praises honest work and condemns idleness (20:4; 28:19, etc.), bids the sluggard "go to the ant" and "consider her ways" (6:6–8), and extols the diligent man (22:29) and the hardworking "woman of valor" (31:10ff.). The preacher Koheleth refers to the "sweet sleep" of the laborer (Eccles. 5:11) and elsewhere there is the assurance that "when thou eatest the labor of thy hands, happy shalt thou be, and it shall be well with thee" (Ps. 128:2). Indeed, Judaism's notion that there is an element of holiness in labor may partly arise from the fact that in Hebrew "work" and "worship" are conveyed in the same word, *avodah*.

The essential dignity of labor, and of the laborer, is guaranteed by the laws of the Pentateuch. An employee must be paid on time: "the wages of a hired servant shall not abide with thee all night until the morning" (Lev. 19:13); "in the same day thou shalt give him his hire, neither shall the sun go down upon it; for he is poor, and setteth his heart upon it; lest he cry against thee unto the Lord, and it be sin in thee" (Deut. 24:15). This applies to the Gentile laborer as well as to the Israelite (Deut. 24:14), and their right to eat of the produce they are harvesting is protected (Deut. 23:25–26), while the Mosaic labor laws ensure a master's realization that he does not "possess" his employees, "for unto Me the children of Israel are servants; they are My servants whom I brought forth out of the land of Egypt: I am the Lord your God" (Lev. 25:55). Violation of these laws is denounced by Malachi (3:5) and by Jeremiah, who condemns "him that buildeth his house by unrighteousness, and . . . that useth his neighbor's service without wages, and giveth him not his hire" (22:13). Further protection was given to farmers and laborers through the laws governing debt and the Jubilee year, but there is evidence in the Prophets that the Israelite kings followed local Canaanite practice in conscripting their subjects for forced labor or corvée, particularly under Solomon (1 Kings 5:27ff.) and Asa (1 Kings 15:22). The injunction to treat hired laborers in a kindly fashion is repeated in the Apocrypha (e.g., Tobit 4.14), but hints of the future conflicts between Sadducean patricians and Pharisee populists are discernible in the Wisdom of Ben Sira, where the worker and craftsman are made subordinate to the learned scribe (38.32–34).

The Pharisees and Rabbis were staunch believers in the ennobling effects of hard work and in the dignity of labor, often setting an example by choosing humble vocations (see above). The first half of the Fourth

Commandment ("Six days shalt thou labor") was given the status of a separate injunction, and the virtue of work as a means of ensuring economic independence was constantly stressed—"Hire yourself out to a work which is beneath you rather than become dependent on others" (Jerusalem Talmud, *Sanhedrin*, ii, f. 30b; cf. *Pesaḥim*, 113a; *Bava Batra*, 110a); "No labor, however humble, is dishonoring" (*Nedarim*, 49b). The dangers of idleness prompted the Rabbinic saying that "he who does not teach his son a trade virtually teaches him to be a robber" (*Kiddushin*, 29a), while the dignity of labor inspired the ruling that "artisans are not required to stand up in the midst of their labor when a scholar passes" (*Kiddushin*, 33a). A minority view was that the study of Torah necessitated one's being freed from worldly employment "in order to serve one's Maker"—enshrined in the saying of Simeon ben Eleazar: "Hast thou ever seen a wild animal or bird practicing a craft? Yet they find their sustenance without trouble, though they were created only to serve me . . . " (Jerusalem Talmud, *Kiddushin*, 4.14; cf. *Berakhot*, 35b).[71] The Rabbinic ideal was, however, formulated by Rabban Gamaliel (in *Avot*, 2.2): "An excellent thing is the study of the Torah combined with some worldly occupation, for the labor demanded by them both causes sin to be forgotten. All study of the Torah without work must in the end be futile and engender sin."

In the practical sphere, the Rabbis sided with the employee where his rights conflicted with those of his employer (*Bava Meẓia*, 77a) and ruled that "a laborer may withdraw from his job even in the middle of the day" (i.e., at any time) in defense of his rights (*Bava Kamma*, 116b). On the other hand, certain rulings were clearly designed to prevent the laborer's exploitation of his employer (*Berakhot*, 46a). In recent times, Rabbinical authorities have upheld the worker's right to strike and to organize in trade unions, also citing Biblical texts in support of social welfare legislation governing unemployment, sickness, and old age. Biblical and Rabbinic thinking on the virtue of labor and its effects on human life also find reflection in the New Testament, which states Jesus' view that "the laborer is worthy of his hire" (Luke 10:7) and the Christian

[71] It is interesting to compare this saying with one by Jesus: "Behold the fowls of the air: for they sow not, neither do they reap . . . yet your heavenly Father feedeth them. Are ye not much better than they?" (Matthew 6:26). This follows a typically ascetic statement about "taking no thought for one's life" (but has had less effect than those quoted subsequently above).

idea that, since all men are "God's husbandry" (i.e., His partners in Creation), "every man shall receive his own reward according to his own labor" (1 Corinthians 3:8–9). Although serfdom was widespread in the Dark Ages and not entirely abandoned in Europe until recent centuries (not until 1881 in Russia), the more advanced thinkers of the West championed the cause of the toiling masses, Jesuits protecting the enslaved Indians of Spanish America and liberal Protestants advocating new, enlightened economic policies in Europe. Voltaire (in *Candide*) unconsciously echoed the Scriptural source which he derided when he wrote that "work banishes those three great evils: boredom, vice, and poverty" (*"Le travail éloigne de nous trois grands maux: l'ennui, le vice et le besoin"*). The spirit of the Bible also rings through that lofty expression of Social Democracy: "From each according to his ability, to each according to his needs."

ELIMINATION OF SLAVERY

Although the laborer who hired himself out to an employer had little protection in ancient society, the slave had no rights to speak of in practice. If he fell into debt or committed certain crimes, a free commoner could be sold into slavery under Babylonian law. Whatever his origin, a slave was branded with his owner's name, had no freedom of movement and no right of sanctuary; anyone helping him to escape was sentenced to death. The Hebrew commonwealth, on the other hand, was an association of free individuals, "in which none should be condemned to ceaseless toil; in which for even the bond-slave there should be hope; in which for even the beast of burden there should be rest. It is not the protection of property, but the protection of humanity, that is the aim of the Mosaic Code . . . Everywhere, in everything, the dominant idea is that of our homely phrase, 'Live and let live' . . . " (Henry George, *Moses,* 1878). In ancient Greece, even artisans, laborers, and tradesmen—lacking the protection of a *genos* (clan)—could be oppressed with impunity and they had no redress before the law. The feudal aristocracy of Sparta ruled over an enslaved peasantry and, before Solon reformed the legislation of Athens in the sixth century B.C.E., peasants in that "birthplace of democracy" were also largely reduced to slavery. Even a century later, in the age of Pericles, Athenian "democracy" was built on the back of a slave population; nor did Socrates, Plato, or Aristotle influence the Greeks against this abuse of their fellow men. Thus, as Nietzsche pointed out, "it was with the Jews that the revolt of the slaves begins in the sphere of morals" (*Zur Genealogie der Moral,* 1887).

The very word "slave" in Hebrew *(eved)* derives from the root meaning "to work," establishing the fact that he is a worker and not a chattel. According to the Law of Moses, he only differs from the hired laborer in three respects: his work is unpaid; he belongs to the household of his master; and the latter may choose a wife for him, exercising proprietary rights in respect to the couple. Hebrew slaves, committed to servitude by court order or of their own free will, had to be liberated after six years had elapsed (Ex. 21:2; Deut. 15:12) and provided with sustenance from the master's property (Deut. 15:13–14). In the event that a Hebrew slave preferred to stay with his owner, his ear was pierced in token of his perpetual servitude and as a sign of his rejection of freedom (Ex. 21:5–6; Deut. 15:16–17). Alien slaves (bondmen) could be acquired from Gentiles (Lev. 25:44–45) and kept in servitude throughout their lifetime, even inherited from father to son (Lev. 25:46). Impoverished debtors could give themselves in bondage to their creditors, but had to be treated like hired servants (Lev. 25:39) and were freed in the Jubilee year (Lev. 25:40–42). Thieves unable to make restitution (Ex. 22:2), prisoners of war (Deut. 20:10–11), and women (Ex. 21:7) could also be sold into slavery, but captives were probably not placed in private servitude and women had to be granted their matrimonial rights or else freed (Ex. 21:11). The status of the parents devolved upon the children of slaves (Ex. 23:12; Lev. 22:11). In every case, ill-treatment or severe injury obliged the master to free his slave (Ex. 21:26–27), and if he or she escaped, the runaway could not be returned to the master (Deut. 23:16–17)—in marked contrast to the Code of Hammurabi, which rigorously prohibited such emancipation.

As members of the master's household, slaves enjoyed special rights and were subject to specific duties. They were obliged to observe the Sabbath and festivals (Ex. 20:10, 23:12; Deut. 5:14–15, 12:18, 16:11–14) and males had to be circumcised (Gen. 17:12–13). Though the property of their master, they could inherit his estate if he died childless (Gen. 15:3) and own property (cf. 1 Sam. 9:8, 2 Sam. 9:10, etc.), redeeming themselves when they acquired the means to do so (Lev. 25:29). A slave's death, even at the hand of his master, incurred the penalty imposed in the case of a freeman (Ex. 21:20) and all slaves had to be treated with respect and consideration (Lev. 25:43ff.; Deut. 23:17), a view reflected by Ben Sira (33.28ff.). Kidnapping a man or woman for the purposes of slavery was a capital offense (Ex. 21:16; Deut. 24:7). In practice, the laws relating to the release of slaves in the Sabbatical year seem to have been neglected in later times and the prophet Jeremiah castigated those who, after obeying Zedekiah's injunction to free their slaves in accordance with the law, took them back into servitude (Jer. 34:8–20). The effect of this Mosaic legislation was to protect slaves, discourage the practice of slavery, and make it a risky and expensive institution. One outcome of the enslavement of a thief—perhaps in one sense an advance even on contemporary legislation—was the fact that, instead of wasting months or years in prison, he helped to compensate his victim through the product of his labor. The unique humanity of the Torah's approach to a prevalent, but noxious, institution has impressed social historians down the ages. The German theologian Carl H. Cornill confessed that he could not "recall an instance in Hebrew literature where the master of slaves is designated as *baal* ['owner'] . . . . He is always referred to as *adon* ('possessor'), and thus the Hebrew language, as an involuntary vehicle of the Hebrew spirit, asserts that slavery is a relationship not founded in natural law . . . but merely an empirical condition, something that came into being and may properly go out of existence" (*Das Alte Testament und die Humanität*, 1895).

In the post-Biblical period, hostility toward the enslavement of Gentiles and Jews alike steadily developed and the Pharisees and Rabbis enacted increasingly stringent decrees governing the slave's treatment and the master's responsibilities. Among the Hellenists of Alexandria, who lived in daily contact with slavery's worst manifestations, Philo Judaeus believed that such "servants rank lower in fortune, but in nature can claim equality with their masters, and in the law of God the standard of justice follows nature, not fortune." He also advocated behaving toward slaves "as you pray that God may behave toward you." The regulations of the Talmud made the owning of slaves a considerable hardship: "The Merciful One demands that your servant be your equal. You should not eat white bread, and he black bread . . . you should not sleep on a feather-bed, and he on straw. Hence it was said, 'Whoever acquires a Hebrew slave, acquires a master' . . . " (*Kiddushin*, 20a). Jews were also reminded that they "were permitted to have slaves for labor, not for humiliation" (*Niddah*, 47a) and warned not to compel a slave or hired man to work in any trade other than his own (*Mekhilta* to Ex. 21:2). The first abolitionist in history was a Rabbi, Eleazar ben Parta, whom the Romans imprisoned for the "seditious" crime of freeing his slaves unconditionally. Another Rabbinic enactment granted automatic emancipation to any slave, Jew or Gentile, who fled to the Holy Land (*Gittin,* 45a) on the basis of a verse from the Pentateuch, "Thou shalt not deliver unto his master a bondman that is escaped from his master unto thee" (Deut. 23:16). This ruling was later codified by Joseph Caro in a section of the *Shulḥan Arukh* (1564), but after the fall of the Second Jewish Commonwealth slavery among Jews was rigorously controlled.

Two other matters associated with the practice of slavery were the treatment of women captives and the rights of prisoners of war. A woman's status in ancient Israel was in general superior to that granted her even in English law until recent times. Wife-beating is not even mentioned in the Bible, but it was prevalent in Europe long after the Middle Ages; and the sale of wives (vividly depicted in Thomas Hardy's novel, *The Mayor of Casterbridge,* 1886) still survived in early 20th-century England. In the advanced view of the Hebrews, women were not mindless chattels or "objects" for the sexual gratification of their menfolk. The Commandment to "honor thy father and thy mother" extended to the enjoining of respect for women in general, and Biblical and Rabbinic legislation aimed to enhance their status and protect their interests. Together with her brothers, Moses and Aaron, Miriam is mentioned in the Prophets as one of Israel's emancipators (Micah 6:4) and the role of the matriarchs and later heroines of Biblical history inspired the Talmudic admonition: "Be careful not to cause a woman to weep, for God counts her tears. Israel was redeemed from Egypt on account of the virtue of its women." The spoils of war included the enemy's womenfolk in antiquity (cf. the words attributed to Sisera's mother in the Song of Deborah, Judges 5:30) and the Middle Ages; even in later centuries history records ghastly instances of mass rape and of the torture and bestial slaughter inflicted on a conqueror's "legitimate prey"—from the Crusades to the Third Reich. The Law of Moses, by contrast, demands respect for the female captive: if desired, she may be taken to wife, but only after being given a month to "bewail her father and mother." Furthermore, if the husband loses interest in her, he may not mistreat her or sell her into slavery but must let her go free, since he (like the rapist in Deut. 22:29) has "humbled her" (Deut. 21:10–14). The Rabbis developed the Biblical legislation affecting women slaves to guarantee their exemption from many of the general provisions of servitude. Thus a woman might not sell herself, nor might others sell a woman thief who could not make restitution; and the piercing of the contented slave's ears also did not apply to women. Moreover, since the Talmud laid down that a female Hebrew slave could only be a minor (below the age of 12) who had to be released at puberty or on the death of her master, the whole practice of female slavery fell into early disuse and even Gentile women were rarely acquired as slaves after early Rabbinic times.

In the ancient world, prisoners of war were subjected to barbarous indignities, the mutilations and atrocities committed by the Assyrians outraging even the unenlightened nations who surrounded them. Captives were often beheaded or flayed alive and the Carthaginians and Romans regularly crucified their prisoners. Among many peoples of antiquity, captives were sacrificed to the victorious nation's idols and the French novelist Gustave Flaubert portrayed many such cruelties in his famous tale of ancient Carthage, *Salammbô* (1863). These abominable practices were outlawed by the legislator of Israel, who prohibited tattooing (Lev. 19:28) and demanded consideration even for animals and birds. The sanctity of human life necessitated respect even for the corpse of a criminal, whose remains might not be left hanging on a tree overnight (Deut. 21:22–23), since this constituted "a reproach unto God." From this verse, the Rabbis derived their prohibition against the mutilation of a corpse and the same commandment has even been used more recently in campaigns against the performance of autopsies, though with rather less justification. An exemplary instance of the Bible's advanced approach to the treatment of captives may be seen in the account of the war between Aram (Syria) and Israel (2 Kings 6:8–23), when a detachment of the enemy was trapped in the Israelite capital of Samaria. In face of their helplessness, the king of Israel asked Elisha whether he should annihilate the Arameans, but the prophet prescribed a form of treatment that few modern nations have ever adopted. He advised that, instead of killing his prisoners, the Israelite monarch "set bread and water before them, that they may eat and drink, and go to their master." A kind of moral lies in the wording of this episode, since (after such provision had been made for the captives) they departed to their master "and the bands of Aram came no more into the land of Israel."

There are also a few Scriptural references to the ransoming of captives, although specific injunctions were only worked out by the Rabbis, who often had to evolve laws and sanctions to secure the release of persons kidnapped by robbers or held to ransom by their Roman oppressors. The redemption of Jewish captives was considered a prime duty and was often made necessary in later times, when merchants and travelers fell into the hands of Muslim pirates or Christian extortioners, such as some rulers of the medieval West. A public fund for the ransoming of such prisoners became one of the central institutions of Jewish life in the Middle Ages and the spirit which motivated this humanitarian enterprise in now an established feature of civilized society. Kidnapping persons in order to secure ransom money remains a favorite technique of the gangster, however, and in 1972 the Soviet government made extortion an instrument of State policy by setting a price on the head of each Jewish academician who wished to leave for Israel.

Like Hellenistic Jewry, the early Christians gained many converts from the ranks of imperial Rome's slave population and the Church honored the memory of those slaves who became martyrs for the faith. In time, the Jews of Gaul and other lands of the West were forbidden to own or deal in Christian slaves, although Christians themselves were permitted to acquire them. That slavery was a normal part of life under the Church is clear from the *Ecclesiastical History* of the Venerable Bede (673–735), who records Pope Gregory I's famous remark on seeing English slaves exposed for sale in Rome, simplified as *"Non Angli sed Angeli"* ("Not Angles, but angels"). On the other hand, the early Church Father Tertullian praised the Biblical freeing of slaves in the Sabbatical year as a humanitarian precept and England's King Alfred the Great, basing many of his *Dooms* on the "Old" Testament, obliged the purchaser of a Christian slave to free him gratis and prohibited any man from selling his daughter into foreign captivity, while the slave whose eye or tooth was knocked out had to go free. These were only a few of the provisions which Alfred drew from Biblical legislation and which bear witness to his remarkable appreciation for the Mosaic code.

Although the institution of slavery as such disappeared in most European lands by the end of the Middle Ages, the profitable slave trade which English pirates first brought to Spanish America persisted well into the 19th century. While liberal opinion hardened against this vicious exploitation of human misery during the Age of Enlightenment, particularly in England and France, political reform was long delayed through the pressure of vested interests. Even so, the poet William Cowper (1731–1800) probably had in mind cases of runaway slaves finding sanctuary in his homeland when he wrote in "The Timepiece," that "Slaves cannot breathe in England; if their lungs/ Receive our air, that moment they are free;/ They touch our country, and their shackles fall."[72] The slave trade was finally abolished in all parts of the British Empire in 1833, and in 1848 the French followed suit by ending slavery throughout their overseas dominions.[73] In the U.S.A., however, it was the Southern states' unwillingness to abolish plantation slavery that provided one of the main reasons for their secession from the Union, which led to the American Civil War. Opinions were nevertheless divided in the North and South: New England's Daniel Webster scorned abolitionists like John Brown and mobs in Boston and Illinois attacked the more prominent opponents of slavery; on the other hand, many leading Confederates had emancipated their own slaves years before. Judah Philip Benjamin (1811–1884), the "brains of the Confederacy" and the secessionists' attorney general and secretary of state, had expressed strong feelings on the subject while appearing in a law case in 1845: "What is a slave? He is a human being. He has feelings and passions and intellect. His heart, like the white man's, swells with love . . . aches with sorrow, pines under restraint and . . . ever cherishes the desire for liberty." As a Jew, Benjamin had his ancestral principles to guide his thinking, but there were a few other Jews (including Rabbis)—as well as dozens of Christian preachers—in the North who claimed Scriptural authority for slavery's perpetuation. Such were the paradoxes of the age. England's William Wilberforce (1759–1833), a pious supporter of the British and Foreign Bible Society, also encountered indifference in church circles toward his campaign for the abolition of slavery, which entered the English statute book in 1803. Despite the indignation aroused by the horrors described in Harriet Beecher Stowe's novel, *Uncle Tom's Cabin* (1851), it was a non-denominational Christian, President Abraham Lincoln, who issued the Emancipation Proclamation of 1863 and who declared that, "in giving freedom to the slave, we assure freedom to the free."

Slavery, though disfavored in most of the Muslim world, has not been wholly abolished and is still practiced in some states such as Saudi Arabia. The mutilation of prisoners, though not countenanced by enlightened Muslims, remains a barbarous feature of Arab warfare in

---

[72] The Rabbinic precedent for this British policy is mentioned above.

[73] Addressing an International Anti-Slavery Congress in 1840, the French statesman Adolphe Crémieux noted that the Jewish Essene sect "first declared slavery to be a crime"

the Middle East and, during the 1970s, the hijacking or murder of "enemy" civilians became a familiar and odious development of the old kidnapping and extortion techniques of medieval piracy. It must also be noted that crimes of this type were also commonplace under the Nazi regime—whose postwar influence in certain Arab states is well known—and that brutal treatment of prisoners of war still disfigures other parts of the globe.[74] The pressure of world opinion may eventually lead to the universal outlawing of these practices, which the Biblical concepts of human freedom and dignity urge all civilized people to abhor and condemn.

RACIAL HARMONY AND HUMAN BROTHERHOOD

Implicit in the Biblical doctrine of one God is the belief that the human race which He created is also one. At the beginning of Genesis, God creates man "in His own image"—not white, black, or yellow men, not Semites or Aryans, but *Man*. And when the Bible demands that "thou shalt love thy neighbor as thyself" (Lev. 19:18), the Hebrew word for "neighbor" *(re'a)* means not the Israelite or Jew only, but "neighbor" in the broadest sense, the same term being applied to members of other national or ethnic groups (e.g., the Egyptians in Ex. 3:22, 11:2). Moreover, "the stranger *(ger)* that sojourneth with you" (Lev. 19:34) is not, as prejudiced critics once asserted, only the alien who identified with the Israelites by embracing monotheism (the "Noachide Laws"), but the foreigner of any creed, since the Israelites themselves were once "strangers in the land of Egypt" (Ex. 23:9; Lev. 19:34; Deut. 10:19). The rights which the Torah bestowed on aliens were unprecedented in antiquity precisely because the Israelites were taught to regard all men as the descendants of Adam, and hence as brothers. "As for the congregation, there shall be one statute both for you, and for the stranger that sojourneth with you" (Num. 15:15) is an exemplary statement of this humanitarian and universalist outlook. "Implicit in Hebraism lay a belief in human brotherhood which cannot be reconciled with racial or sectarian enmities. Indeed it may be said that the world as a

---

[74] History also records Napoleon's massacre of 1,400 Turkish captives at Jaffa in 1799, Stalin's killing of 10,000 Polish officers at Katyn in 1939, and the murder of Allied prisoners by the Germans and Japanese during World War II.

whole has not yet risen to the height of this great Hebraic argument"
(W. B. Selbie).

The injunction to love and not vex the stranger (Ex. 22:21; Lev. 19:33,
etc.) occurs thirty-six times in the Scriptures, more often in fact than any
other of the commandments. The patriarch Abraham tried to avert
God's wrath from a people as depraved as the Sodomites (Gen. 18:23ff.);
Jonah was made to realize that the welfare of the inhabitants of Nineveh
was also God's concern (4:11); and Balaam and Job were endowed with
the gift of prophetic insight in common with those whom God chose
from among Israel. Furthermore, although the Hebrews had good reason
to remember their sufferings under foreign rulers, they were ordered not
to abhor an Edomite or an Egyptian, because the Edomites were of
common stock and the Egyptians once gave shelter to Joseph and his
brethren (Deut. 23:8). "The Lord is good to all; and His tender mercies
are over all His works" (Ps. 145:9), while in time to come "many nations" will turn to God's teachings (Micah 4:2) and "join themselves
to the Lord" (Zech. 2:15). "Ten men . . . out of all the languages of the
nations" will tell the Jews: "We will go with you, for we have heard that
God is with you" (Zech. 8:23). The universalism of the Hebrew Prophets
finds eloquent expression in a famous appeal to human brotherhood:

Have we not all one father?
Hath not one God created us?
Why do we deal treacherously every man against his brother,
Profaning the covenant of our fathers? (Malachi 2:10).

Jeremiah's rhetorical question as to whether the Ethiopian can "change
his skin" (13:23) makes it plain that the "Cushites" were known to be
black men. The Bible's indifference to race or color is first revealed in the
punishment inflicted on Miriam for condemning the marriage of Moses
and a Cushite woman (Num. 12:1ff.), an episode that gave rise to various
legends, and this anti-racist outlook lends significance to the ethical
query of the Prophet:

Are ye not as the children of the Ethiopians unto Me,
O children of Israel? saith the Lord.
Have not I brought up Israel out of the land of Egypt,
And the Philistines from Caphtor,
And Aram from Kir? (Amos 9:7).

The Rabbis, too, insisted on the fundamental unity of mankind. "Adam was created single, to teach us that to destroy one person is to destroy a whole world, and to preserve one person is to preserve a whole world; that no man should say to another, 'my father was superior to yours!' . . . that though no two men are exactly alike, God stamped us all with the same mold, the seal of Adam; that everyone must say, The world was created for my sake!" (Mishnah, *Sanhedrin,* 4.5). Stressing the fact that "a righteous God is not a tribal God," the Anglo-Jewish writer Israel Zangwill pointed out that "the very first line of Genesis is universal . . . . The genealogy of all races and colors from Adam strikes the same broad note, while Abraham, the founder of Judaism, actually asks God, in what I have always considered the epoch-making sentence in the whole Bible, 'Shall not the Judge of all the earth do right?' . . . " (*War for the World,* 1915). Even in the "ritualistic" cult of the Temple this concern for humanity at large was uppermost, according to a Rabbinic tradition: "On the festival of Tabernacles, Israel would offer seventy bullocks, corresponding to the seventy nations of the world, and prayed that they might live in tranquility" (*Pesikta de-Rav Kahana,* 175b; cf. *Midrash Tehillim,* 243a, *Tanḥuma* to *Pineḥas,* 78b, etc.) The Rabbis also pointed out that the Revelation at Sinai was specifically located in the wilderness—no-man's-land—and was heard by all the inhabitants of the earth; so that all should understand the Torah's message, "each word uttered by God split itself into the seventy languages of the world" (*Shabbat,* 88b; Exodus Rabbah, 5.9). While Jewish Reformers of the 19th century were at pains to emphasize the universalist aspects of their faith, the staunchly Orthodox Samson Raphael Hirsch also stressed Judaism's breadth of vision when he declared, in his *Neunzehn Briefe über Judenthum* ("The Nineteen Letters of Ben Uziel," 1836), that "Israel's most cherished ideal is the universal brotherhood of mankind."

The Hebraic belief in the common ancestry and essential unity of all men was taken over by Christianity and constitutes one of the pillars of Christian belief that all are equal before God. Although Jesus himself directed his message to "the lost sheep of the house of Israel" (Matthew 10:6, 15:24), his disciples declared that "all men" sought him (Mark 1:37) and Paul proclaimed that "there is neither Jew nor Greek, there is neither bond nor free, there is neither male nor female: for ye are all one" (Galatians 3:28). The Church Fathers Origen and Tertullian also stressed the broad conception of the brotherhood of man, which Jews,

Christians, and Stoics shared in common. Periodically, however, racial prejudices were fanned by religious and economic factors: the anxiety to "win souls," the "holy war" ideology of the Crusades, fear of Jewish competition in trade and commerce. The feudal system of the Middle Ages was sometimes justified on the ground that the "Germanic blood" of the predominantly Teutonic rulers and aristocracy of the West made them the "natural" overlords of "lesser breeds," and the spurious doctrine of a superior "blue blood" thus came into being. This idea of a higher racial caste conflicted with Christian universalism and, after the final expulsion of professing Jews and Muslims from Spain in 1492, led to a policy of undisguised racial discrimination. "Old Christians" refused to marry "New Christians" (whose ancestors were of Jewish and Moorish origin) and official statutes protected the *limpieza de sangre* (racial purity) of the "original" Christian families, despite the baptism and frequent religious zeal of their converted *(converso)* brethren. Ironic echoes of such popular prejudice and discrimination may be detected in Cervantes' *Don Quixote*. Throughout the 16th–18th centuries, racial considerations dominated Spanish policy in the social and economic spheres, and it was only after much theological wrangling that the basic human rights of the Indians were recognized in Spain's American empire.

A more systematic attempt to define and justify the "racial superiority" of the European was made by anthropologists, whose "findings" received wide publicity from the 18th century onward. The Biblical concept of man's fundamental unity was jettisoned so as to attribute different origins to various ethnic groups on the basis of their physical characteristics. The mental and moral nature of the white European, associated with anthropological data, was interpreted to prove the "innate superiority" of the white man and the "natural inferiority" of all colored races. At this stage, the Jews were still grouped among the whites, but the racist nonsense of 20th–century theorists was foreshadowed in the "enlightened" Voltaire's claim that the Negroes constituted an intermediate stage between white humanity and the anthropoid apes! During the 19th century, Germany became the focus of pseudo-scientific "research" on racial origins, although otherwise responsible figures in England and France were also affected by this new and absurd preoccupation. Even Disraeli followed the trend, creating a Jewish counterpart to Germany's "Aryan" superman in the shape of Sidonia, the hero of his novel *Coningsby* (1844), who declares his belief in the idea that "race is everything."

For all his use of fashionable jargon, Disraeli concentrated on the beneficial effects which his own conception of ethnic differences might hold in store for humanity as a whole. The Pan-Germanic movement, on the other hand, seized on the new discovery of an Indo-European group of languages to proclaim the superiority of Indo-European or "Aryan" man, deliberately confusing the entirely separate categories of anthropology and linguistics. The "Aryan" race was, in its moral fiber and mental originality, the pick of mankind and the purest and highest form of Aryanism could be seen in the German people. In his *Essai sur l'inégalité des races humaines* (1853–55), Count Joseph Arthur de Gobineau popularized these theories and his belief that the Jews and Latins—unlike the "Germans"—had become racially decadent provided useful ammunition for his more extreme successors. Parallel, if opposing, theories in other countries suggested that the mingling of races produced ethnic superiority—a view propounded, for example, in the United States by advocates of the "melting-pot" philosophy as a means of undermining Anglo-Saxon dominance in public life. Such obsessions seem all the more strange in men and women who, as Christians, were heirs to the Biblical tradition and who were clearly impervious to its universalist moral outlook. Few were aware that the Hebrew genius had once inspired the question: "What is an honorable race? The race of men! . . . that fears the Lord. What is a race without honor? The race of men! . . . that transgresses the commandments" (Ben Sira 10.19).

Although responsible scientific opinion gradually abandoned such prejudiced theories toward the end of the 19th century, the apostles of "Aryanism" increasingly exploited their outdated ideas in a widespread and violent popular campaign against the "Semitic" (though European) Jews, who, while admittedly to some degree "superior" to the black and yellow men, were nevertheless more tangible "racial adversaries." The most fanatical systematization of the supposed eternal struggle of "Aryan" goodness and purity against "Semitic" evil and impurity appeared in *Die Grundlagen des neunzehnten Jahrhunderts* ("Foundations of the Nineteenth Century," 1899), which was the work of the Anglo-German racist Houston Stewart Chamberlain, one of Hitler's early admirers. It was from sources such as this that the whole racial claptrap of National Socialism—with its *Herrenvolk* perversion of the "chosen people" concept—steadily developed. Chamberlain's extraordinary claim that Jesus (a Galilean) was obviously of "Gallic" origin may have provided one section of the German Evangelical Church with an excuse for its wholehearted collaboration with the Nazis. "Race" and "blood" became the criteria for membership when Hitler laid down his manifesto of German nationhood in the National Socialist Party program of 1920: "None but members of the Nation may be citizens of the State. None but those of German blood . . . No Jew, therefore, may be a member of the Nation . . . Anyone who is not a citizen of the State may live in Germany only as a guest and must be regarded as being subject to the Alien laws."[75] The fact that such provisions ran counter to the whole spirit and teaching of the Scriptures did not bother most of the Evangelical hierarchy (although a more courageous minority did in fact secede to form the Lutheran "Confessional" Church). Nor did it prevent State Secretary Cardinal Pacelli (later Pope Pius XII) from signing a Concordat with the Nazi government in July 1933 on the Vatican's behalf. Five years later, a solemn declaration of loyalty to the Reich, hailing its "social policy," was initialed by Austria's Catholic bishops, headed by Cardinal Innitzer of Vienna, who called on "all faithful Christians to recognize their duty to their people," and Innitzer's covering letter concluded with the Nazi greeting, "Heil Hitler!" The moral reputation of the Christian churches in German-occupied Europe was fortunately redeemed by men of integrity, such as Michael Cardinal von Faulhaber of Munich (1869–1952) and those Catholic and Protestant clergymen who refused to collaborate with the Nazis, often sacrificing their lives in the maintenance of Christian principle. Cardinal Faulhaber, a vigorous opponent of racism and intolerance, was the main force behind Pope Pius XI's encyclical *Mit brennender Sorge* ("With Burning Anxiety," 1937).

Racial friction has often worked in partnership with economic exploitation, whether in Europe, North America, or the colonial empires of the great powers. The American Civil War made the white man's respect for the rights of the black a major social and political issue and, even then, the racial theories of European agitators were imported to serve the interests of slavery. Extreme fundamentalists justified the (generally benevolent) servitude of Southern blacks by referring to the crime and punishment of Ham, traditionally regarded as the ancestor of the Negroes: "Cursed be Canaan; a servant of servants shall he be unto his brethren . . . God enlarge Japheth, And he shall dwell in the tents

---

[75] From the infamous Nuremberg Laws of 1935 it was only a short step to the Nazi genocide program (involving the annihilation of Jews, Slavs, gypsies, and other "undesirables"), the final outcome of perverted science.

of Shem; and let Canaan be their servant" (Gen. 9:25–27). Here, Canaan stands for his father Ham, whose lack of filial piety provoked Noah's curse: this could be interpreted to mean that Ham's descendants would be servile, although the Rabbis tended to give the whole episode an ethical and allegorical interpretation. However, opponents of racial integration in the United States chose to adopt a narrow, literalist view of this Biblical text (hardly an injunction to oppress) and their stand has also been that of the Dutch Reformed Church in South Africa, which sees Divine sanction for the doctrine of *apartheid* in many other Scriptural passages as well. Thus, believing themselves to be God's "chosen people"—called to bring order and the Gospel into darkest Africa—the Boers felt that they were refighting Israel's ancient battles against the idolatrous Canaanites, those children of Ham, whom the Lord commanded the Israelites to dispossess (Ex. 23:23ff., etc.) and ostracize (Gen. 24:3). The pro-Nazi sympathies of many Afrikaner nationalists during the Hitler era exacerbated the fundamentalist assumptions of many white Protestants in South Africa—assumptions still shared by ostensibly pious Baptists in the Southern states of the U.S.A.

Outside these areas, few genuine Christians subscribe to any form of racial doctrine, whatever its alleged or real basis, believing that God "hath made of one blood all nations of men for to dwell on all the face of the earth" (Acts 17:26).[76] Civilized men and women of every religion will prefer to share the vision of Martin Luther King, a martyr for the cause of equality and mutual respect, who foresaw a day when "black and white, Jew and Christian, Protestant and Catholic" would finally live together in peace, harmony, and friendship.

CONCLUSION

The relevance and the practical application of the Bible's ethical and social message find constant demonstration in many spheres of human life. The Decalogue and its associated commandments, the outspoken

---

[76] A storm of protest rocked the Church of England after the late Archbishop of Canterbury, Dr. Fisher, toured South Africa and publicized his impressions of *apartheid*. "All men," he declared, "are equal in the love of God, but not in the sight of God."

protest of the Hebrew Prophets, and the humane teachings of the Pharisees and Rabbis fashioned those concepts of morality, social justice, and welfare that provide a daily guide to Jews, Christians, and Muslims alike. More than any other code or philosophy, past or present, the Bible has urged men and women imbued with a social conscience to tackle the age-old problems of poverty, suffering, and inequality. William Wilberforce fought slavery; Florence Nightingale reformed nursing and Elizabeth Fry prison conditions; Lord Shaftesbury protected the juvenile laborer; Lewis Gompertz pioneered animal welfare; William Booth's Salvation Army redeemed men from the gutter; Jean Henri Dunant made the Red Cross a delivering angel for the victims of war. James Ramsay MacDonald, later Britain's first Labor prime minister, thus observed that, "whilst the organization of Israel could not withstand the world pressure of its time, its spiritual and moral characteristics have always remained as enticing ideals in the minds of men, and thereby provide not only a proof that they are to find another opportunity of expression in society, but an earnest that the world pressure will change so as to aid rather than stultify that opportunity" (*The Socialist Movement,* 1911).

Millions of underprivileged persons in country after country have been rescued from squalor and misery thanks to the humanitarian instincts and philanthropic work of great idealists for whom the reforming spirit of the Hebrew Bible was a lasting inspiration. The injunction to love and care for one's fellow man was one of those "enticing ideals" that motivated private charity and social initiative in the past. Whether the State's assumption of what was once the individual's responsibility is to be viewed as a sign of progress may be open to dispute. The Bible's use of the term "congregation" to emphasize collective responsibility does not imply that the individual is exempt from the fulfillment of his own duty: man and society must work hand in hand. Thus, State promotion of welfare schemes for all citizens can be regarded as a long-delayed response to the Hebraic call for "righteousness and justice, loving-kindness and truth" on the part of society as a whole, in order to ensure the widest and fairest distribution of man's common, God-given patrimony.

THE LEGAL AND POLITICAL SPHERES

The king by justice establisheth
the land (Proverbs 29:4)

Since the time when the patriarch Abraham confronted God outside Sodom and insisted that the merciful Judge of all the earth could not destroy the innocent together with the guilty, man's sense of justice has invariably assumed the tones of Biblical and Prophetic rebuke. For the Jews of old, Torah meant both religious "teaching" and the overriding principle of "law and order." Only on the basis of legality could men realize the ideal of a just society and enjoy those liberties which maintain human dignity in the midst of injustice and depravity. Lord Acton affirmed that "the example of the Hebrew nation laid down the parallel lines on which all freedom has been won—the doctrine of national tradition and the doctrine of the higher law; the principle that a constitution grows from a root, by process of development, and not of essential change; and the principle that all political authorities must be tested and reformed according to a code which was not made by man" (*Freedom in Antiquity*, 1877). This point was again stressed by the U.S. preacher and publicist Lyman Abbott in his *Life and Literature of the Ancient Hebrews* (1901): "It would be impossible to mention any people of even a much later age . . . whose law and constitution embodied an ideal so noble as that embodied in the Hebrew civil laws, or any people whose history shows the existence of political institutions so essentially just, free, and humane." Abbott elsewhere stressed how great a debt the world owes to the Hebraic notions of righteousness and justice, which did not remain mere abstract concepts but found immediate practical application to the problems of ethical existence. "We Gentiles owe our life to Israel," he declared. "It is Israel who, in bringing us the divine law, has laid the foundation of liberty. It is Israel who had the first free institutions the world ever saw . . . . When sometimes our own unchristian prejudices flame out against the Jewish people, let us remember that all that we have and all that we are we owe, under God, to what Judaism has given us."

LAW

The Law of Moses and the legislation of the Hebrew Bible as a whole were preceded by several ancient legal collections, those formulated by the Sumerians, Babylonians, Assyrians, and Hittites. Of these, the so-called "Code of Hammurabi" (dating from the 18th century B.C.E.) is the most famous. How far any of these pre-Mosaic legal systems influenced other cultures is subject to scholarly debate, but it is indisputable that the Law of Moses left a unique imprint on the subsequent legal concepts of the civilized world.

JUSTICE IN THE BIBLE

The uniqueness of Biblical law lay in its basic Weltanschauung: *imitatio Dei*, the need for personal holiness ("the imitation of God"), consideration for the poor and underprivileged, respect for human life, freedom, and dignity, and concern for *justice*. "It is not the protection of property, but the protection of humanity, that is the aim of the Mosaic code. Its sanctions are not directed to securing the strong in heaping up wealth so much as to preventing the weak from being crowded to the wall" (Henry George, *Moses*, 1878). The word *zedek* expresses the Biblical concept of absolute justice, whether in dealings between man and man or in the administration of the law. Above the Central Criminal Court at London's Old Bailey stands an allegorical figure of Justice holding evenly weighted balances in her hand. In the minds of those who erected this statue were two verses from the Pentateuch: "Ye shall do no unrighteousness in judgment, in meteyard, in weight, or in measure. Just balances, just weights, a just ephah, and a just hin, shall ye have: I am the Lord your God . . . " (Lev. 19:35–36). This notion of *zedek* acquires tremendous force in the subsequent injunction concerning the legal procedure of Israel: "Judges and officers shalt thou make thee in all thy gates . . . and they shall judge the people with righteous judgment . . . Justice, justice shalt thou follow, that thou mayest live . . ." (Deut. 16:18–20). J. H. Hertz observed that "these passionate words may be taken as the keynote of the humane legislation of the Torah, and of the demand for social righteousness by Israel's Prophets, Psalmists, and Sages. 'Let justice roll down as waters, and righteousness as a mighty stream,' is the cry of Amos . . . 'Righteousness and justice are the foundations of Thy throne,' says the Psalmist: the whole idea of the Divine rests on them . . . Nor is justice limited to the relation between individuals. It extends to the relation between group and group, and it asserts the claims of the poor upon the rich, of the helpless upon them who possess the means to help. And even as there is *social* justice, prescribing the duties of class to class, so there is *international* justice, which demands respect for the personality of each and every national group, and proclaims that no people can of right be robbed of its national life or territory, its language or spiritual heritage . . ."[1]

Injunctions such as "in righteousness shalt thou judge thy neighbor" (Lev. 19:15) and "justice, justice shalt thou follow" (Deut. 16:20) powerfully influenced the Hebrews, and their impact was later felt in the wider human community. Isaiah, Jeremiah, Ezekiel, Amos, Micah, and Zephaniah imbued Israel with a love and desire for justice, the administration of which Jews always recognized as a paramount factor in human existence. The judicial system established under the prophet Samuel's direction seems to have been a highly organized one. Samuel's recorded journeys to Bethel, Gilgal, and Mizpah (1 Sam. 7:16) have been interpreted by some scholars as annual visits to the Hebrew courts of law, and the Biblical statement that "he went from year to year in circuit" was once thought to have inspired the old English "circuit" system of local assizes.[2] Samuel himself officiated as a judge at Ramah (1 Sam. 7:17). Later, King David administered law and justice among the Israelites (2 Sam. 8:15) and 6,000 of the 38,000 Levites chosen to serve in the running of the Temple were specifically appointed as judges and law officers (1 Chron. 23:4). King Solomon, who asked God for "an understanding heart to judge Thy people, that I may discern between good and evil" (1 Kings 3:9), also functioned as a judge and decided cases such as that of the two women who quarreled over the possession of the living child (1 Kings 3:16–28). His notion that the true mother is the one who would rather give up her son than see him divided and slain has parallels in the literature of other nations.[3]

---

[1] *Pentateuch*, pp. 820–821.

[2] On the antiquity of English Common Law's "trial on circuit," see G. R. Y. Radcliffe and Geoffrey Cross, *The English Legal System*, third edition (London, 1954), p. 90ff.

[3] The recurrence of this motif has been studied by Friedrich Thieberger (in *King Solomon*, 1947), who—on the basis of a caricature found at Pompeii—suggests that it was widely known in the ancient world.

The Judgment of Solomon by Rubens, the 17th-century Flemish master.

The idea of a "contract of the people" or "Covenant" (Hebrew, *berit*)[4] between God and Israel is one of the foundations of Biblical legislation; the discovery of treaty patterns in the ancient Near East merely confirms God's kingship as one of the most genuine and ancient of Hebrew doctrines. The exclusive loyalty demanded by the "covenantal" idea was unique and the Hebrew prophets frequently expressed it in terms of the fidelity which a man and his wife are expected to maintain with one another (see especially Ezek. 16:8, Hosea 2:21–22). Moreover, when the Hebrews periodically violated their contract with God, the prophets often voiced their reproaches in terms of a plaintiff's suit in a court of law (Jer. 2:4ff.; Amos 3:13; Micah 6:1ff.). That there could be no allowance for any dual loyalty is plain from the expression,

---

[4] For a fuller discussion of the "Covenant" idea, see the second half of this chapter.

111

"I the Lord thy God am a jealous God" (Ex. 20:5, Deut. 5:9; cf. Ex. 34:14), where the word "jealous" (Hebrew *kanna*) derives from a root elsewhere used to denote the "jealousy" of a husband who suspects his wife of adultery (Num. 5:14). The Pentateuch and Prophetical books thus make Israel's relationship with God a legal contract enforceable by the rigors of the law.[5]

Two distinctive features of Mesopotamian law, as it developed in the course of the third and second millennia B.C.E., were the metadivine nature of its supposed origin and its concern with economic, rather than religio-moral, issues. The law was something beyond the deities themselves, who did not hand enactments to human beings through any direct process of revelation, but merely granted men the ability to perceive them. The standard representation shows the god Shamash, with a rod and ring in his outstretched hands, symbolically transferring his authority to the Babylonian king. In the epilogue to his "Code," Hammurabi therefore declares that he himself compiled the laws contained in it "in order that the mighty might not harm the under-privileged, that justice might be dealt to the orphan and widow."[6] This clearly stated human authorship of the "Code of Hammurabi" —a secular legislation based on unquestioning obedience to an earthly king's will—is entirely at variance with the Divine nature of the Torah's "covenantal" principle. The special relationship between God and His people is enshrined in a covenant (Ex. 19:3–6), the detailed terms of which are thereafter set forth in the Ten Commandments and the religiously motivated legislation of Israel. The election of the Hebrews is not some political act by a human agency, but a revelation of the Creator's will, for "only in Israel is there an inextricable relationship between covenant and law."[7] The distinctions between the Torah and other ancient legal systems are therefore clear-cut: the Law is given to the entire nation of Israel and not merely to some chosen and favored

[5]   In compiling this section I have gleaned some of my material from two sources which deserve special acknowledgment: Rabbi K. Kahana Kagan's *Three Great Systems of Jurisprudence* (London, 1955) and Prof. Julius J. Marke's (unpublished) essay, "The Influence of Jewish Law on Other Legal Systems" (1966).

[6]   G. R. Driver and J. C. Miles, *The Babylonian Laws* (Oxford, 1960), vol. 1, p. 37.

[7]   Shalom M. Paul, *Studies in the Book of the Covenant in the Light of Cuneiform and Biblical Law* (Leiden, 1970), p. 30.

ruler; God being the sole Legislator, Israel is responsible to Him and not to any human power; and offenses against the Law count as sins, as well as crimes. The Torah, in short, is not simply just another corpus of law, but a unique appeal to man's innate conscience.

The legislation of Israel also differed from that of other ancient cultures in another important respect. When Assyria, Babylon, and the empires that succeeded them were overthrown, their entire civilization—including their judicial system—collapsed and disappeared. With the Jews, on the other hand, loss of political sovereignty did not lead to cultural oblivion. The Torah accompanied Israel's exiles into their dispersion after the destruction of both the First and the Second Commonwealth, and its study and everyday application survived the nation's separation from its homeland. Even when the Jews were condemned to what seemed perpetual homelessness, their laws (though lacking the sanction of secular enforcement) still remained dominant and mandatory in the life of the people.

ETHICS AND EQUITY

Morality is practically inseparable from the Biblical concept of law, since the principles of both have exactly the same source. The object of Torah was to educate toward holiness. Biblical law and its traditional Jewish interpretation were distinguished by a high moral tone and humanitarian spirit, the Torah prescribing regulations and precepts leading to the pursuit of justice and equating injustice with offense against God. The Bible inculcated a lofty system of moral behavior far in advance of anything known elsewhere in antiquity. Jewish judges thus refused to enforce the primitive, but prevalent, law of family liability for violations of the legal code, insisting on the sole responsibility of each individual offender. Biblical law comprised those injunctions mandatory on Jews and those (later interpreted as seven in number) which other men were obliged to observe. In a letter of 1770 to the Swiss pastor J. K. Lavater, Moses Mendelssohn asserted that "the written and oral laws, which jointly form our revealed religion, are binding on our nation only. 'Moses commanded *us* a law' [Deut. 33:4]. All the other nations of the earth, we believe, have been bidden by God to be guided by the laws of Nature and the religion of the patriarchs. Those who regulate their lives according to the laws of this natural and rational religion are called 'the virtuous of other creeds,' and are 'children of eternal salvation' . . ."[8] Through the teachings of Jesus and the Church Fathers, law and morality were also woven together in the fabric of Christian thought; they not only impressed themselves on the Canon Law of medieval Christendom, but even on the development of Civil Law far beyond the bounds of the Church. Thus, in a secular context, the British Socialist Harold Laski could maintain that "the roots of valid law . . . are, and can only be, within the individual conscience" (*The State in Theory and Practice*, 1935), while Chaim Weizmann, first President of the State of Israel, declared that "a law is something which must have a moral basis, so that there is an inner compelling force for every citizen to obey" (*Trial and Error*, 1949).

The natural imperfection of man-made laws has invariably obliged those administering them to devise "remedies" for the protection of the individual, since cases of unforeseen hardship or injustice are otherwise bound to arise. The Romans had their *jus praetorium* (Praetorian Law) to complement and correct civil legislation and, by the early 14th century, England had the rudiments of Equity—a system originating in the English Chancery and consisting of rules intended to supplement or override Common Law in defense of a man's rights. Equity, or "equitable principles," operated not according to legal precedents, but according to conscience, morality, and common sense; the English Chancellor thus applied remedial justice to those cases previously heard and decided on in the narrow and rigid framework of the Exchequer or King's Bench Court or in the Courts of Common Pleas. Hebrew law had none of this built-in rigidity: it was neither like "the law of the Medes and Persians, which altereth not" (Dan. 6:9, 13; cf. Esther 1:19) nor as inflexible as the civil laws of the Romans and the English. There was no machinery of intervention such as that of the Praetor or Chancellor, simply because of Hebrew law's very nature and distinctiveness. Whereas other legal systems found it difficult to identify the concept of law with the idea of natural justice, the lawyers of Israel never had to make any such distinction between the two notions, since for them law and justice were in perfect harmony.

---

[8] On the "Noachide Laws," see also Chapter 1 and more detailed discussion below.

EQUALITY BEFORE THE LAW

In one final respect the Mosaic Code again differed from, and revealed its superiority to, other legal systems of antiquity: in its zealous concern for the equality of all men[9] before the law. Hammurabi enacted legislation for three separate social strata—freemen, dependents, and slaves. For offenses against property (burglary, theft, looting) the penalty was death, but where capital punishment could be commuted by payment the thief had to make "restitution" of thirty times the value of anything purloined from the royal estate or temple, and of ten times the value if the wronged party were a private gentleman.[10] Class distinctions and social status determined an individual's fate and privileges in ancient Mesopotamia. The same was broadly true of the laws of Rome, both in regard to the rights of aliens and to those of citizens.

Among the Hebrews, administration of the law was sternly impartial and evenhanded. Moses, who acted as a magistrate for his people (Ex. 18:13) and who—on the advice of Jethro (Ex. 18:17–23) and on his own initiative (Deut. 1:9–18)—delegated his judicial powers to "rulers of thousands, rulers of hundreds, rulers of fifties, and rulers of tens" (Ex. 18:21), reserved only the most difficult cases for himself. Israel's judges had to be "able men, such as fear God, men of truth, hating unjust gain" (Ex. 18:21), "wise men, and full of knowledge" (Deut. 1:15). Furthermore, Moses specifically instructed the judges whom he appointed to "hear the causes between your brethren, and judge righteously between a man and his brother, and the stranger that is with him. Ye shall not respect persons in judgment; ye shall hear the small and the great alike; ye shall not be afraid of the face of any man; for the judgment is God's . . ." (Deut. 1:16–17). Judges and witnesses were further warned against the fabrication of evidence, currying favor with the majority opinion by perverting justice, and against "bending over backward" through sympathy with the weaker party irrespective of the merits of his case ("neither shalt thou favor a poor man in his cause," Ex. 23:2–3). Biblical law also accorded unprecedented equality to the alien: "One law shall be to him that is home-born, and unto the stranger that sojourneth among you" (Ex. 12:49);

---

[9] This was almost an absolute rule; in Biblical times, slaves and women did not enjoy the rights of freemen as witnesses in courts of law.

[10] Paul, *op. cit.*, p. 86.

"And a stranger shalt thou not oppress; for ye know the heart of a stranger, seeing ye were strangers in the land of Egypt" (Ex. 23:9). Such injunctions constantly recur in the Pentateuch (Ex. 22:20; Lev. 24:22; Num. 9:14, 15:15), proving that "the Jewish codes were more favorable to strangers than those of any other people" (Johann Döllinger, *Heidentum und Judentum,* 1857). This aspect of Hebrew justice was strikingly brought out by Josephus: "The Lacedaemonians [Spartans] made a practice of expelling foreigners and would not allow their own citizens to travel abroad, in both cases for fear that their laws might be corrupted . . . We, on the contrary, while having no desire to emulate the customs of others, yet gladly welcome any who wish to share our own" (*Contra Apionem,* 2.36).

Inequality before the law was not peculiar to the societies of antiquity: it remained a distressing feature of the "civilized" world until much more recent times and there are still some countries in which a fair hearing is denied to religious, ethnic, or political "undesirables." In 18th-century England, Oliver Goldsmith saw how "laws grind the poor, and rich men rule the law" (*The Traveller,* 1764), while Alexander Pope (in his satire, *The Dunciad,* 1728–42) denounced the legal corruption of his own day: "Poetic Justice, with her lifted scale,/Where, in nice balance, truth with gold she weighs, /And solid pudding against empty praise." Not for at least another century could English legal administration be shown to more nearly resemble that of the Bible in its concern for impartiality.

The legislation of Israel has impressed itself on man's sense of justice, law-abidingness, and morality, often inspiring the very pattern of his thoughts on legal matters. "Where is the God of justice?" (Mal. 2:17) is a familiar rhetorical question, and Philo's affirmation that "those who live in accordance with law are free" has scarcely been modified by modern teachers of ethics. There are few happier coinages than Disraeli's phrase, "justice is truth in action." More practical aspects of Hebrew law have often inspired social and political reformers like J. Ramsay MacDonald, who believed that "we have in the Mosaic code and its amplifications the most careful safeguards against slavery and a deadening poverty" (*The Socialist Movement,* 1911). Yet Biblical law, through its reinterpretation and application to everyday life, also remained an integral part of post-Biblical Jewry's heritage. The U.S. jurist Arthur L. Goodhart (the first American to be appointed Master of an Oxford college) accordingly declared that "the passion to shape the forms of justice has been one of the dominant forces in the life of the Jewish people from the time of the mighty tablets to the days in which we now live" (*Five Jewish Lawyers of the Common Law,* 1949). The adaptation of Biblical law to the Jewish people's later needs and circumstances was the work of the Rabbis.

JEWISH LAW—FROM SINAI TO THE STATE OF ISRAEL

In Hebrew sources there is no accepted term describing legal norms pertaining exclusively to relations between man and man (in the sense of "English Law"), simply because Jews regard both the laws governing such relations and the precepts relating to man and God as having a single, common source—the Bible. Torah, a word which Christianity translates as "the Law," actually means "teaching" and was originally applied to the Five Books of Moses only; in time, Torah came to signify the whole body of Biblical legislation and instruction, together with its traditional exposition. *Halakhah* ("the way of life," from the root *h-l-kh,* "to go") is the generic post-Biblical term used to describe the whole legal system of Judaism embracing all the detailed laws and observances. A third term, *Mishpat Ivri* (literally, "Hebrew law"), is a modern coinage signifying the laws governing relations between man and man. According to the traditional Jewish concept, Torah—the Written Law—is a revelation of God's will which expresses itself in a collection of legal, religious, and ethical statutes. This Law comprises positive and negative injunctions (*miẓvot*) numbering 613 in all, according to Rabbinic tradition. Judaism's fundamental belief that Divine command is the source of the Torah's authority gave rise to the "basic norm" of Jewish legislation that everything set forth in the Written Law is binding on the Jewish legal system. This norm is the foundation of authority and the starting point for the entire halakhic system, with all the changes and evolutions that have occurred over the centuries.

Some examples of legal direction in the Bible are Abraham's acquisition of land (for Sarah's burial place, Gen. 23:3–20); the Ten Commandments and supplementary ordinances (Ex. 20–23; Deut. 5); the laws relating to offenses for which atonement must be made (Lev. 5); sexual and ritual laws and the "holiness code" (Lev. 18–21); the rules governing female inheritance (Num. 27, 36); and the laws of the festivals, the judiciary, and the monarchy (Deut. 16–17). Commandments or injunctions which have their source in the Prophets or Hagiographa are also considered to be authoritative on the assumption that they were "received interpretation" or "*Halakhah* given to Moses at Sinai." Among these regulations are those pertaining to the laws of acquisition (Ruth 4; Jer. 32); the limitations of monarchical government (1 Sam. 8, 1 Kings 21); and laws restricting criminal responsibility to the transgressor (2 Kings 14:6).

As with all other legal codes, the passage of time necessitated expert opinion to elucidate the inner meaning of the Torah after the death of Moses. Successive generations of teachers and scholars received exclusive authority to interpret the Written Law, as the Bible itself makes clear: "If there arise a matter too hard for thee in judgment . . . thou shalt come unto the priests the Levites, and unto the judge that shall be in those days; and thou shalt inquire; and they shall declare unto thee the sentence of judgment . . . and thou shalt observe to do according to all that they shall teach thee . . ." (Deut. 17:8–10). Out of this process of interpretation came the development of an Oral Law, which the Rabbis intimately linked with the written Torah and also traced to the Sinaitic revelation. Even in the generation in which they were given, the statutes of the Written Law were difficult to obey in their literal form for lack of clarity and definition. Thus, the prohibition of "any manner of work" on the Sabbath (Ex. 20:10; Deut. 5:14) did not specify the nature of such work. Nor, to take yet another example, was there any indication as to how "ye shall afflict your souls" on the tenth day of the seventh month (Lev. 16:29–31, 23:27, 32; Num. 29:7). The Oral Law therefore laid down that, from the time of revelation, the Written Law was entrusted to the judgment of human intelligence in the person of legal scholars: "The Torah itself gave the sages a mind to interpret and declare" (*Sifre* to Numbers, 134); and the vitality and development of the Jewish legal code were determined by the nature of the Oral Law. Moses Hess, a pioneer of "ethical" Socialism, stressed that "it is to this oral development of the Law that Judaism owes its existence during the two thousand years of exile" (*Rom und Jerusalem*, 1862).

Between the lifetime of Ezra in the mid-fifth century B.C.E. and the era of the Hasmoneans some three centuries later, there arose a group of religious leaders known as the *Soferim* (Scribes). The *Soferim* laid the foundations of the Oral Law, "read in the book, the Law of God, distinctly; and they gave the sense" to the people (Neh. 8:8), and trained a new generation of scholars. Through the devoted activity of the *Soferim*, Jewish law was taken out of the hands of the priests and Levites and its development and interpretation became the province of "lay" experts—the Men of the Great Assembly ("Men of the Great Synagogue"). During the period of the free Hasmonean state, new material was added to the mass of legal interpretation accumulated under the *Soferim*. The development of commerce now called for the establishment of a code of civil law and it became clear that the plain text of the Bible offered only limited aid to such legislation. A huge quantity of textual material was nevertheless detached from Scripture and studied separately, thus conferring an independent existence on the Oral Law. Among the Pharisees who succeeded the *Soferim* was Hillel the Elder, whose seven hermeneutical (interpretative) rules were amplified by Rabbi Ishmael[11] and later teachers. Hillel dedicated himself to the science of law and to its history, explanation, and interpretation. Courts of law had been set up after the Return from Babylon and judicial power was eventually entrusted to a high court of justice with 71 members, known as the Great Sanhedrin. Judges were recruited for the Sanhedrin and its subordinate and district courts by means of a system of apprenticeship and promotion in schools of religious law. The judgments arrived at in these courts and the arguments put forward there were committed to memory by students and only put in writing at a much later date. Between the third and the sixth centuries C.E., the reports of all recorded cases (together with various commentaries) were assembled in two authoritative collections—the Mishnah (c. 200 C.E.) compiled by Rabbi Judah ha-Nasi and the Gemara, the Mishnah's elaboration. The 63 tractates of the Mishnah clarified Judaism's entire legal system and certain portions (such as the civil and criminal code) left their mark far beyond the bounds of purely Jewish law. The Mishnah and Gemara together form the Talmud, of which there are two separate editions: the Palestinian (*Yerushalmi*, c. 400 C.E.) and the more authoritative and influential Babylonian (*Bavli*, c. 500 C.E.).

TALMUDIC LAW AND TRADITION

Avot (the "Ethics" or "Sayings of the Fathers"), the best known Mishnaic tractate, relates the beginning of the process of legal transmission: "Moses received the Torah on Sinai, and handed it down to Joshua;

[11] Ishmael (ben Elisha) was something of a literalist, maintaining that "the Torah speaks the language of men" (or "uses human idiom," *Keritot*, 11a).

Joshua to the Elders; the Elders to the Prophets; and the Prophets handed it down to the Men of the Great Assembly" (1.1). Jewish tradition asserts that the Written Law's interpretation was transmitted in its entirety down to the last detail. Hence the contention of Maimonides that ritual and legal rules in the Talmud and other Rabbinic works reflect the authoritative legislation "handed down from person to person from the mouth of Moses our Teacher at Sinai." This traditional interpretation of Torah and *Halakhah* includes that regarded as undoubtedly handed down at Sinai and that inherent in the written word and made manifest by means of accepted hermeneutical rules.

The Talmud (literally, "Learning") is the classic repository of Rabbinic law and lore, "the written story in Hebrew and Aramaic dress of Biblical interpretation, of the making of bylaws, and of the adding to the store of practical guidance and wise counsel, which the intellectual and religious leaders of the Jewish people taught during a period of almost one thousand years, from the time of Ezra to the end of the fifth century of the Common Era. As such, it might be compared to the History of the British Parliament . . . a summary account of what has been done, spoken, and debated in the British legislative assembly since its earliest days to the present time."[12] *Halakhah*, which makes up the bulk of the Talmud, built "a fence round the Torah" (*Avot*, 1.1) and its vital role in the preservation of Judaism found reflection in the Talmudic maxim that, "since the Temple was destroyed, the Holy One has only the four cubits of *Halakhah* in this world" (*Berakhot*, 8a). In *Yesod Mora* ("The Foundation of Awe"), a work written in London in 1158, the great Spanish Bible commentator Abraham Ibn Ezra stressed the fact that, "were it not for the men of the Great Assembly and the men who produced the Mishnah and the Talmud, the Torah of our God would long since have been lost and forgotten. It was they who confirmed the commandments and elucidated them thoroughly." Nearer our own time, the historian Heinrich Graetz paid tribute to the Talmud's centrality in Jewish religious and moral life: "It held out a banner to the communities scattered in all corners of the earth, and protected them from schism and sectarian divisions; it acquainted subsequent generations with the history of their nation; finally it produced a deep intellectual life which preserved the enslaved . . . and

[12] Epstein, *Judaism*, p. 132.

lit for them the torch of science" (*Volkstümliche Geschichte der Juden,*
1893 edn., vol. 2).

Legal decisions were arrived at through the debates of rival Talmudic
schools, such as those of Hillel and Shammai, but Jewish law constantly
had to adapt itself to new exigencies and social pressures. One way out
of the impasse was Hillel's masterly resort to the "legal fiction"; another
was the issue of fresh and authoritative codifications of *Halakhah.*
The first great comprehensive post-Talmudic code was Maimonides'
Mishneh Torah ("Repetition of the Law") in the 12th century, a work
known also as the *Yad ha-Ḥazakah* ("Strong Hand," cf. Ex. 13:9).
Here, Maimonides restated the Oral Law doctrine when he affirmed
in his introduction that "all the precepts were given to Moses at Sinai
with their interpretations." This has remained Orthodox Judaism's
position down to the present day. The 14 books of the *Mishneh Torah,*
written in a very lucid form, include two mainly devoted to civil law and
dealing with the laws of torts and crime, property, contract, and procedure. However, Maimonides was severely criticized for following
a pattern independent of the order of the Talmud and for his failure to
provide citations of source or proof. Unlike Maimonides, Jacob ben
Asher omitted from his *Tur* (properly, *Arba'ah Turim,* "Four Rows")
legal matter that had no practical application after the destruction of

A rabbinical law court *(bet din)* in session. A miniature from a 15th-century
Italian manuscript of Jacob ben Asher's *Arba'ah Turim.*

the Temple and the fall of the Jewish State. This 14th-century code set the Ashkenazi ("German") tradition against the Spanish one of its predecessor. The *Bet Yosef* ("House of Joseph") which Joseph Caro, a refugee Spanish codifier and kabbalist of Safed in Palestine, based on the *Tur* grew into the most popular and widely used of these three great codes—the *Shulḥan Arukh* ("Prepared Table"). It is this work of the 16th century (later adapted for the use of Ashkenazi Jews as well) which now forms the basis of most everyday legal procedure in the Rabbinate. Maimonides systematized the Oral Law, Caro unified it.[13]

A necessary adjunct to these codes is the Responsa literature—records of decisions taken by the Rabbis in cases submitted to them and formulated as *she'elot u-teshuvot* (literally, "questions and answers"). These "replies" by Jewish legal scholars, for which there are parallels in Roman Law (the *Responsa Prudentium*) and English Common Law (the Opinion of Counsel), date back to the ninth century C.E. and were an indispensable means of dealing with the problems that arose from changing social and economic circumstances in many parts of the Diaspora. Such Jewish case-law, which left its imprint on the great codes, supplements the *Mishneh Torah* and *Shulḥan Arukh* by finding precedents in earlier Talmudic legislation through a subtle process of reinterpretation to meet the needs of a particular era. More than 100,000 different Responsa are known, many of which have become accepted law because of the eminence and authority of the "decisor." Classic Responsa were written by the *rishonim* ("earlier authorities") of the 12th–15th centuries; the Responsa of the *aḥaronim* ("later authorities") have dealt with modern issues such as birth control and the use of electricity on the Sabbath,[14] the bulk of 20th-century *teshuvot* emanating from the U.S.A. and Israel. So far, however, no Rabbi has attempted to follow Maimonides and Caro by recodifying the *Halakhah* in the light of available Responsa.

---

[13] Louis Ginzberg, *On Jewish Law and Lore* (1962), pp. 183–4.
[14] The concept of *hassagat gevul* ("encroachment") has thus been extended by the Rabbis from the original Biblical law against trespass on land (Deut. 19:14) to the economic and commercial fields—unfair competition in trade and the protection of a publisher by means of copyright.

MODERN RABBINIC ENACTMENTS

The thirst for justice which inspired the Talmudic saying, "Let the law pierce through the mountain!" (*Yevamot*, 92a),[15] accompanied the Jews into the Diaspora, where autonomous courts regularly functioned and a vast legal literature was built up. Until 1948, religious and civil litigation was handled in Rabbinical courts *(battei din)* if the parties concerned sought a halakhic decision; but the establishment of the State of Israel heralded a break with this tradition. Two court systems operate simultaneously in Israel—the religious and the secular—and each has its own supreme tribunal. The ordinary courts administer the laws passed in Israel's parliament, the Knesset; unlike the secular legislation of the Knesset, Jewish law is administered by Rabbinical courts, which have jurisdiction in matters of personal status (marriage, divorce, etc., and in some cases adoption, maintenance, and inheritance) according to the Knesset Law of 1953. However, specifically religious elements (based wholly or partly on *Halakhah*, and hence on Biblical injunction) have entered the general Israeli statute book. In 1948, the Provisional Council of State made it lawful to supply only *kasher* (ritually fit) food to soldiers of the Israel Defense Forces, and the provisions of the Law and Administration Ordinance of the same year laid down that the Sabbath and Jewish festivals be prescribed days of rest in the State, although non-Jews were accorded the right to observe their own day of rest and holidays. A law of 1962 prohibits the raising or slaughter of pigs, except in specified areas of Israel with a mainly Christian population.

Even though the Biblical system is not applicable in the State,[16] Israeli legislation has followed the principles of Jewish law in a number of cases. These include an employer's obligation to pay his workers on time (cf. Lev. 19:13), a man's duty to maintain needy relatives as well as his own wife and children (an extension of the *ẕedakah* ideal), and the granting of equal inheritance rights to the children of the deceased, whether they were born in or out of wedlock. Jewish law has also been integrated into that of the State through case law, particularly

---

[15] Cf. the maxim attributed to the Emperor Ferdinand I (1503–1564): *Fiat justitia, et pereat mundus* ("Let justice be done, though the world perish").
[16] The legal system of Israel has drawn largely from Ottoman and English Common Law, a legacy of the British Mandate.

through decisions of the Israel Supreme Court. Recalling Article 46 of the Palestine Order of Council (which stated that Jewish law be applied where no solution was obtainable from the existing legislation), some sections of Israeli legal opinion criticize the present-day dependence on English Common Law and the principles of Equity, favoring reference to the *Halakhah* in case of any lacuna in the law of the State. Israeli law's lack of firm roots is keenly felt and the unhomogeneous system now in operation is widely deplored. Orthodox Jews, mainly represented in the National Religious Party, advocate the restoration of traditional Jewish law, allowing for contemporary needs and conditions. In the sphere of religious legislation, some Rabbis of Israel and the West have long favored the reestablishment of the ancient Sanhedrin in order to rationalize and update the application of *Halakhah* in modern society. Biblical law proved its worth in antiquity and Jewish law might well bridge a severe gap in the legal system of modern Israel. Such a thought may well have inspired Abraham Isaac ha-Kohen Kook, first Chief Rabbi of the Holy Land during the British Mandate, when he expressed his belief that, "even as there are laws of poetry, so there is poetry in law."

THE INFLUENCE OF BIBLICAL LAW ON OTHER LEGAL SYSTEMS

To what extent Jewish law has impressed itself on the legal concepts of the Western world is still largely a matter for conjecture, and scholarly circles remain sharply divided over this question. Superficial resemblance between particular characteristics of one independent legal system and those of another does not provide sufficient reason for the assumption that this is the result of imitation or derivation. The old belief that modern law owes its origin to one ancient code has no basis in fact. Jurists of the not so distant past enthusiastically traced the practice of sending English judges "on circuit" (i.e., to hear cases in different towns) to the prophet Samuel's method of dispensing justice (1 Sam. 7:16);[17] the twenty-fifth section of Magna Carta (dealing with weights and measures) was said to betray the influence of the twenty-fifth chapter of Deuteronomy; the practice of giving sanctuary to political refugees supposedly originated in the Biblical provision that a runaway

[17] See above.

slave was not to be delivered up to his master (Deut. 23:16–17); and the English jury's "twelve good men and true" were still more oddly linked with the Biblical fondness for the figure twelve!

It was once fashionable to attribute the development of the arts and humanities to Greece, of ethical monotheism to Israel, and of law to Rome. Yet although Roman Law is traditionally regarded as the source of law in the West, it has long been established that the legal concepts of Rome were never universally accepted in Europe. The influence of Roman Law in England, for example, was only of minor significance and even in those countries where it was in fact adopted important modifications affected the development of that system. Many special codes were developed independently in the civil law of European lands (especially in the field of commercial law), precisely because Roman Law had nothing to say about corporate organization for private purposes, negotiable instruments, or the modern concept of agency. Roman legal principles could not cope with the needs of the newly emerging European nations, whether in regard to the law of torts (i.e., civil wrongs), family law, or constitutional and international law. Hence the modern suggestion that the laws of these states not only betray a move away from the spirit and substance of Roman Law, but actually reveal a greater kinship with those of the Jews in a number of instances. In his *Pensées sur la religion* (1670), the French philosopher Blaise Pascal was not guilty of extravagance, therefore, when he wrote: "I think it strange that the first law of the world happens to be the most perfect, so that the greatest legislators have borrowed their laws from it." And if Western law's debt to Rome has been greatly exaggerated, the contribution of Jewish law to other legal systems down the ages (and to the whole development of jurisprudence) has probably been underestimated.

IN ANTIQUITY

The Torah made a strong impression on the Classical world. Hecataeus of Abdera, a fourth-century B.C.E. Greek historian, had a high regard for the Mosaic constitution and its hold on the Jews: "Neither the slander of their neighbors . . . nor the frequent outrages of Persian kings and satraps can shake their determination; for these laws they, though naked and defenseless, face torture and death in its most horrible form, rather than abandon the religion of their forefathers." The Greco-Jewish clash in Alexandria soon gave rise to much less favorable comment, however, and the growing anti-Jewish prejudice was intensified by the Torah's stand against idolatry, which incensed many traditionally minded Greeks and Romans. The patricians of Rome were particularly outraged by the "indolence" induced by Sabbath observance, which not only freemen but even Judaizing slaves claimed the right to maintain. Seneca the Younger (c. 5 B.C.E.–65 C.E.), a Stoic philosopher and confidant of the Emperor Nero, referred to the fact that "this abominable nation has succeeded in spreading its customs throughout all lands; the conquered have given their laws to the conquerors" (*De Superstitione*, fragment 36; quoted by Augustine in *De Civitate Dei*, 6.11).[18]

Seneca's gibes were echoed by the satirist Juvenal (Decimus Junius Juvenalis, c. 50–c. 130.C.E.) and the historian Tacitus (c. 55–c. 120 C.E.). Despite his diatribes against the Jews for weakening traditional Roman "morality" and teaching their new adherents to scorn the gods of Rome, Tacitus lets slip some grudging admiration for the laws of Israel. "Jews," he relates, "worship with the mind alone. They believe in one God, supreme and . . . immortal, and deem it impious to fashion effigies of God out of perishable matter and after the likeness of men" (*History*, 5.5). A more unstinted tribute was paid by Dio Cassius (c. 150–235 C.E.), a Roman historian who wrote in Greek. His statement that "all those who observe the Jewish law may be called Jews, from whatever ethnic group they derive" demonstrates the Jewish people's transformation into a worldwide religious community through the steady absorption of Gentile proselytes. Confirmation of the Torah's widening appeal may be found in the propagandist writings of Philo and Josephus. According to Philo, "nations of the East and West, of Europe and Asia, of the whole inhabited world from end to end" were being attracted to Judaism, while Josephus (in *Contra Apionem*) drew attention to the fact that, "as God Himself permeates the universe, so the Law has found its way among all mankind." The sudden arresting of this process is attributable both to the successful competition of a less demanding Christianity and to the rival faith's ultimate triumph under Constantine

---

[18] Both Philo and Josephus provide evidence of their own relating to such trends; see below.

the Great (c. 280–337), when imperial enactments brought an end to Jewish missionary activities.[19]

CANON LAW

Although some Roman legal notions may have been absorbed by the early Church, the principal ingredient of law among the "Nazarenes" was, quite naturally, Biblical or Rabbinic. Paul may have negated "the [Mosaic] law" and the norms of Rabbinic Judaism, but he also condemned those who, "having a matter against another, go to law before the unjust [i.e., the pagan Romans], and not before the saints . . . brother goeth to law with brother, and that before the unbelievers" (1 Corinthians 6:1–6). The first churches were modeled on the contemporary Jewish synagogue (a school and place of assembly as well as a house of prayer); the early Christian clergy functioned not as a hereditary priesthood, but as teachers and judges on the Rabbinic pattern–qualified by learning and authority. "Benefit of clergy" found doctrinal justification for its political independence and temporal prerogatives in Scriptural texts such as Ps. 105:14–15: "He suffered no man to do them wrong, yea, for their sake He reproved kings: 'Touch not Mine anointed ones, and do My prophets no harm' . . ." (cf. 1 Chron. 16:21–22). The claims of the medieval papacy lay in Biblical passages of this kind. The weapon of excommunication which Popes brandished against Emperors also drew its authority from the Bible: herem ("proscription") was a penalty invoked against a variety of willful offenders, contempt of duly constituted government resulting in sequestration of property and "separation from the community" after the First Exile (Ezra 10:8). In practice, however, total excommunication was avoided and lesser forms of social pressure were invoked, except in the case of notorious heretics and political and religious slanderers in foreign pay. Public censure, subjection to anathema, and (finally) excommunication were stages in the legal enforcement of the Biblical ban; reflections may be seen in the New Testament narrative, where self-confessed followers of Jesus were, at a later stage, reportedly "put out of the synagogue" (John 9:22, 12:42; cf. 16:2) and upright Christians were exhorted to refrain from social contact with fornicators, drunkards, extortioners, and the like (1 Corinthians 5:11). Herem was the sanction

[19] See Chapter 1.

which, appropriated and refashioned by the Bishop of Rome, was to rock Europe and some of its crowned heads.

The Priests and Levites, whose duties precluded them from working the land, were entitled to receive tithes from the rest of Israel (Lev. 27: 30ff.; Num. 18:21, 24; Deut. 14:22ff.). In post-Biblical times, as well, Jews made voluntary offerings for the upkeep of the Temple and the maintenance of the priests, and these donations were sent to Jerusalem even from the most distant parts of the Jewish Diaspora. The early Church continued this Jewish practice of the freewill offering and charitable donation, but eventually found the system inadequate and introduced a compulsory tax, or tithe, levied on all Christians. Until the English jurist John Selden proved that such payments had not been enacted by the primitive Church, it was long believed that this compulsory tithe had ancient sanction and directly continued the old Jewish practice. Legal recognition of the Church tax was, in fact, first extended by Charlemagne (742–814), whose successors and emulators modified the system so drastically over the centuries that its original Biblical prototype was completely obscured.

In practice, as we have seen, the Church never followed Paul in his rejection of "the law" (which "worketh wrath: for where no law is, there is no transgression," Romans 4:15); indeed, many provisions of its own Canon Law derive from the Torah and from Jewish legal procedure. The Sabbath became the Lord's Day (and in its Puritan form was sternly enforced by law as a day of rest); regulations against deliberate birth control were inspired by the sin of Onan (Gen. 38: 9–10); forbidden degrees of marriage were based on the Pentateuch (Lev. 20:14, 17, 19–21). Canon Law also found Scriptural authority for its rules on a daughter's inheritance,[20] on the prohibition of usury (Ex. 22:24; Lev. 25:36–37; Deut. 23:20–21), on monetary compensation for injury (Ex. 21:18ff.), and on the furnishing of verbal evidence (Num. 35:30; Deut. 17:6; cf. 2 Corinthians 13:1).[21] The "two-witness

---

[20] Sir Frederick Pollock, the British jurist, wrote that the case of Zelophehad's daughters (Num. 26:33, 27:1–11; Josh. 17:3–4) resulted in the earliest recorded instance of a legal ruling that still retains authority.

[21] The prohibition of usury threatened the very foundations of medieval economic life and gave rise to the hypocritical practice of making the "infidel" Jews royal bankers, who might serve the exchequer without offending Christian scruples.

rule," unknown in English Common Law, now applies to the attestation of wills. Many more examples of Biblical influence can be cited from the provisions of Canon Law. When courts of law and Equity dealt with mortgages, they were guided by previous Church procedure in allowing "a redemption for the land" (Lev. 25:23–4) on the basis of Biblical law; and even trial by ordeal (abandoned after the Fourth Lateran Council of 1215) invoked the Scriptural precedent of the priest's administration of the "water of bitterness" to the suspect wife (Num. 5:11–31). The pre-Reformation law of divorce ("What therefore God hath joined together, let no man put asunder") depended on a New Testament interpretation ("Midrash") of Gen. 2:24 to the effect that "a man . . . shall cleave unto his wife, and they shall be one flesh" (Matthew 19:3–9; cf. Mark 10:2–12).

At times, Canon Law had to combat the logical extension of such Biblical norms into "Judaistic" practices. The persistence of Jewish Christianity and its adherence to much of the Torah and early *Halakhah* may in part explain certain phenomena, such as the Latin Church Father Tertullian's heterodox permit for the killing of a fetus in order to save the mother's life (cf. the Mishnaic ruling in *Oholot*, 7.6). Pope Eugenius IV's bull of 1441 shows that some Christians still practiced circumcision, while others retained customs such as the avoidance of blood. Throughout the past two millennia, heretical Christian sects have periodically reverted to an assortment of proscribed Jewish rituals, always on the basis of Scriptural authority. One case in which the laws of medieval Europe harked back to Hebrew Common Law (or perhaps even to earlier heathen custom) was in the revival of the right of sanctuary, misuse of which was prevalent in Biblical times (see Ex. 21:14; 1 Kings 1:50–51, 2:28ff.). This concept does have some basis in Biblical law, but it was preeminently a Roman idea that a criminal might find asylum in the precincts of a temple. Violations of the law of sanctuary outraged churchmen and ordinary folk alike, as when supporters of England's King Henry II assassinated Thomas à Becket, the Archbishop of Canterbury, in his own cathedral (1170). This odd "right" was finally done away with in the late 18th century. During the English Reformation, however, Henry VIII made another incursion into Scriptural law with his establishment of seven cities of refuge or privilege on the Levitical model (1540).

The development of Canon Law and the demands and privileges which it claimed made it increasingly difficult to lay down firm lines of demarcation between the spiritual and temporal domains, between "the things which are Caesar's and the things that are God's." A legal history of practically every European land might be compiled merely on the basis of the struggle of civil courts to wrest authority from the tribunals of a powerful Church. At an early stage in this struggle, the clerics had a monopoly of learning, but later they had to fortify their position by seeking justification in the Scriptural word. If a particular offense (defamation, perjury, usury) was also demonstrably a sin, then it fell within the jurisdiction of the Church; if not, then the other side asserted its secular prerogatives. Defamation ceased to be the concern of the English Church in the 17th century, but probate and divorce matters remained under its exclusive jurisdiction until as late as 1857. The significant fact was that, as the State assumed control of legal issues that had previously been the concern of the Church, some of the principles of Canon Law also passed into the realm of civil legislation and procedure (the "two-witness rule," land mortgage, etc.). This was to have interesting consequences from the 17th century onward, particularly in England and the New World.

LEGAL CONCEPTS IN MEDIEVAL ENGLAND

The Jews scattered throughout Western Europe during the early Middle Ages found themselves deprived by law of any free contact with their Christian neighbors either socially, economically, or politically. Forced in upon themselves, they drew on the knowledge and experience which the *Halakhah* provided in order to develop legal institutions, devices, and practices of an independent sort and capable of allowing for a viable organization of their everyday business needs and livelihood. The innovations which the Jews introduced found a notable reflection in legal documents and record-keeping practices which were sometimes copied by astute Christians with whom they did business. Strictly speaking, these Jewish legal instruments and developments were, of course, Rabbinic, but their roots were nevertheless often clearly in Biblical law. The hired servant who must be freed in the Jubilee Year may not be treated as a mere slave, "for," says the Lord, "unto Me the children of Israel are servants" (Lev. 25:55). Rashi's commentary gives a legal turn to this injunction: "My document [deed of purchase] is of earlier date" (cf. Rashi on Lev. 25:42). In the Sermon on the Mount, this idea acquires a popular religious form as "No man can serve two masters" (Matthew 6:24); and, in modern law books, it reappears in the context of the absolute loyalty demanded of an agent. Similarly, the Talmudic maxim that "one's agent is like one's self" (*sheluḥo shel adam kemoto*; *Mekhilta* to Ex. 12:3) may well have inspired the central doctrine of representation in English and European law, *Qui facit per alium, facit per se* ("He who acts through another, acts for himself"). This Latin expression, one of many such cryptic sayings in the *Liber Sextum Decretalium* of Canon Law, cannot be located in the legislation of Rome.

Some modern legal authorities have therefore asserted that a comparatively large number of formulae passed from Jewish into general use.[22] Among these are the mortgage system of the later Middle Ages and the introduction of negotiable instruments, now generally attributed to Jewish commercial enterprise. Mishnaic references make it clear that, from the Babylonian period onward, Jews were familiar with such instruments; moreover, the bills of exchange used by Jewish merchants in medieval England trading with their brethren in Spain had no equivalent among their non-Jewish contemporaries. Negotiable paper forms were later adopted by Christian merchants and bankers, especially the Lombards, who made use of the "gage" device as security for the repayment of loans. The presence of Jewish commercial devices in the English legal system of the Middle Ages is fully attested, and once such securities were validated in courts of law they were apparently incorporated in Canon Law procedure, their true origin soon disappearing from view. Ecclesiastical pressure against Christian moneylending prompted England's Angevin kings to grant the lucrative monopoly of banking to their Jewish wards (or "chattels"), from whom immense taxes might be levied when the royal exchequer needed funds for war or other affairs of state. The Jewish "gage" brought a new, foreign influence to bear on English feudal law, revolutionizing many aspects of commercial practice. Had Edward I not expelled his exploited Jewish "chattels" in 1290, the mortgage system which they introduced might well have simplified English Common Law. One legal formula that derives from Jewish usage was the *Jus Gazaga* ("*Gazaga* Law"), a system of tenant right or right of possession that became current throughout Western

---

[22] For a fuller assessment of these matters, see Nathan Isaacs' essay, "The Influence of Judaism on Western Law," in *The Legacy of Israel* (1927), especially pp. 396–403.

Europe. Based on the Talmudic principle of *ḥazakah* ("established claim" or "law of possession"), the *Jus Gazaga* became a kind of lease-hold right for Jews in the overcrowded ghettos of Italy and the Popes, aware of its value, made it binding on Christian landlords renting their property to Jewish tenants.

To medieval Englishmen, a *Starr* (in Latin, *Starrum*) was any Jewish business deed or bond, especially one written in Hebrew. This term, a modification of the Mishnaic word *shetar* ("document"), entered English legal history and parlance; of the 500 or more *Starrs* that have survived (almost as many of which were written in Latin as in Hebrew), a large proportion relate to property transactions as well as to the recording of debts.[23] At one time, it was thought that the notorious Star Chamber (abolished by Parliament in 1641) acquired its name from the *Starrs* deposited there, but the earlier Latin designation, *Camera Stellata* ("Starred Chamber"), points to a less mysterious origin. No less intriguing is the term *archa* ("ark" or "treasure chest"), signifying the place in which Anglo-Jewish merchants were, at their own request, allowed to deposit private records and documents for safekeeping between 1194 and 1290. Since the kings of England had a personal interest in the preservation of such deeds, those relating to loans were executed in duplicate and one copy placed in *archae* under royal supervision in a number of towns. *Arkei* (from the Greek *archē*, "rule, government") is a Mishnaic term for a record office (*Kiddushin*, 4.5), and its plural form, *arka'ot* ("Archaoth"), occurs in a well-known Rabbinic ruling to the effect that "all *shetarot* issuing from non-Jewish *arka'ot* . . . are valid" (*Gittin*, 1.5). The Gemara to the same Talmudic tractate (*Gittin*, 44a) also refers to the "*arka'ot* of the Gentiles." However novel the *archa* may have been in English legal procedure, its Jewish equivalent had a time-honored place in the *Halakhah* and through it the Jews thus gave England its first "archive" or collection of public records. When the moneylending activities of the Lombards commended themselves to the English crown, the Jews were ruthlessly expelled from the realm and, after 1290, Jewish security devices (pledges, mortgages, and public record-keeping) were taken over by the more inflexible

---

[23] See M. D. Davis, *Shetaroth: Hebrew Deeds of English Jews before 1290* (1888); Herbert Loewe, *Starrs and Jewish Charters* (1930–32); and V. D. Lipman, *The Jews of Medieval Norwich* (1967), especially pp. 82–3.

Lombard immigrants. The development of English commercial law thus owes a great deal to Jewish initiative.

HEBRAIC ELEMENTS IN ANGLO-AMERICAN LAW

The unprecedented revival of Biblical and Jewish legal norms in the Puritan age came at a time when the medieval Jewish contribution to English law was long forgotten and when the few Jews actually living in the realm found it best to disguise themselves as foreign Christian refugees.[24] Puritanism, of course, marked a return to the Bible —especially to the "Old" Testament—and quite a number of its adherents carried their doctrine of the "new Israel" embattled in the cause of the Lord of Hosts to its logical extreme.[25] A few adopted "Judaistic" practices and, fleeing to Amsterdam, finally embraced Judaism; most advocated a more moderate "Hebraic" policy, involving partial acceptance of the Jewish dietary laws, the alteration of the Lord's Day to the Biblical (seventh day) Sabbath, and other literalistic measures. The widespread belief that the final Redemption could only begin when the Jewish dispersion was complete (cf. Deut. 28:64; Dan. 12:7), wedded to the view that the original children of Israel were now only absent from Britain, even forged an alliance between certain Puritan mystics and the Dutch Rabbi Menasseh Ben Israel, who together campaigned for the readmission of the Jews. Although the Council of State rejected their petition, Oliver Cromwell (the Lord Protector of the Commonwealth) gave his informal sanction in 1656. Meanwhile, some Puritan theologians had come to accept, in part, the Jewish axiom that the Torah and *Halakhah* embodied a perennially significant message to human society in general. The institutions of Rabbinic Judaism, encoded in the Mishnah and the Maimonidean ordinances, derived their authority from Holy Writ and were therefore the legitimate concern of true Christians as well as Jews.

[24] These Spanish and Portuguese "New Christians" bore the brunt of the anti-Semitic storm aroused by the trial and execution of Dr. Roderigo Lopez, Queen Elizabeth's physician, on a trumped-up treason charge (1594). Reflections of that partisan trial may be seen in Shakespeare's play, *The Merchant of Venice* (1596).

[25] On the Puritans and Puritanism, see also Chapter I and the section on Politics (below).

For the first time in the history of Christendom, men sensed the continuity of the Old and the New Dispensations and felt that Jews and Christians alike had a share in Divine Revelation and the Scriptures. The adoption of Biblical usages and the Puritan identification with ancient Israel did not signify any exclusion of the modern Jews from God's grace. The language of the Psalmist and the Prophets was on men's lips, thousands studied Hebrew, theologians commended the Mosaic legislation, and moral offenses were sometimes treated as crimes to be punished by the magistrate. The religious vehemence and moral rectitude of English Puritanism and its political establishment were firmly anchored in the belief that Israel's God was also a Lawgiver. Men's lives must be regulated by the precepts given on Sinai and failure to obey them incurred an appointed penalty. So, in the spirit of the Law, everyday life was subject to positive and negative injunctions. Proceeding beyond the Scriptures, some Puritans honored post-Christian, Rabbinic enactments and concepts. In *The Christian Synagogue*, a book published during the 1620s, the Scotsman John Weemse embellished his interpretation of the Bible with quotations from the Talmud, which he clearly regarded as possessing no less authority than the works of the Church Fathers. If the Puritan Sabbath and similar "killjoy" manifestations marked the decline of early Puritan moral idealism, England had nevertheless absorbed some of the more beneficial elements of Biblical and Hebraic teaching. The just society was founded on a Covenant between God, the government, and the people; and the rule of law was universally regarded as essential for the maintenance of the body politic and national welfare.

The technical nature of English Common Law and the reflections of medieval feudalism and tyranny which men saw in it made the early American colonists look elsewhere for the basis of their legislation. Between 1620 and about 1700, most of the "first settlers" administered justice according to their own independent system, unless custom or specific statutes adopted English law; Georgia, New Jersey, Virginia, and perhaps New York were the only exceptions to the rule established by the Puritans of New England. Hebraic legal norms were closely followed by many of the colonists; Cotton Mather was later to declare that, as with the Israelites in the wilderness, these new settlers' "laws were still enacted, and their wars were still directed by the voice of God, as far as they understood it, speaking from the Oracle of the Scriptures." Their notion of government was a theocratic one, their ideal was a commonwealth ruled by the Mosaic Code. An *Order of the General Court of Massachusetts* (1636) and the *General Lawes of Plymouth Colony* (1658) laid down that divines and magistrates (laymen trained in Hebrew) should decide cases as far as possible in accordance with the Law of God or of Moses. Insofar as it was observed at all, English Common Law was checked for its agreement with "the word of God." Cases were often decided by reference to Scripture and, as the early records show, arguments of counsel and even deliberations of the General Court (or Legislature) took more heed of Mosaic injunction or Prophetic wisdom than of the Lord High Chancellor's decisions.

Whether "the word of God" was really ever more influential than the law of England in early American courts is still in dispute, some historians suggesting that the invoking of Biblical authority actually represented an attempt to confirm the application of the law in particular situations. There is, however, no doubt as to the influence of Scripture in matters of inheritance, the maintenance of churches and schools, and in criminal cases. In Pennsylvania, an eldest son at one time inherited a double portion of the estate (cf. Deut. 21:17); in New Haven, prisoners were cautioned with the text, "He that covereth his transgressions shall not prosper; but whoso confesseth and forsaketh them shall obtain mercy" (Prov. 28:13); and officials were read appropriate passages (such as Ex. 18:13–26) before being formally installed. In Massachusetts, Connecticut, New Haven, and West New Jersey, judges were instructed to inflict the penalties ordained in the "Law of God." Nathaniel Ward's *Body of Liberties* (1641) laid down that magistrates be guided by "the word of God" rather than Common Law when no guidance could be obtained from the existing code; similar directives appeared in the *Fundamental Agreement of the Colony of New Haven* (1639), in the *Fundamental Orders* and resolutions of 1638 and 1639, and in the legislation of Plymouth and Rhode Island. John Cotton's *Abstract of the lawes of New England* (1641) was a reworking of his unsuccessful proposal for the Massachusetts Bay Colony (*"Moses His Judicials,"* 1636) and was provided with marginal references to Scriptural authority. The code adopted (*The Body of Liberties*), America's first law book, contained a chapter entitled "Capital Laws" and this, too, included marginal notes referring to the Pentateuch; of its 48 laws, all but two were taken directly from the Hebrew Bible. When former Puritan generals sought refuge in the New World after the Restoration of 1660, John Davenport successfully invoked Scripture in their defense, quoting

Isa. 16:3–4 ("Hide the outcasts; betray not the fugitive. Let Mine outcasts dwell with thee"). It was on his motion that "the word of God," as revealed in the Bible, was proclaimed the only rule to be observed in executing the duties of government in New Haven (1639). In Massachusetts, as in New Haven, English Common Law was replaced by Biblical rulings; for the Puritans of New England, the Pentateuch was *the* authoritative statute book and this explains the preponderance of Scriptural ordinances in *The Body of Liberties*.

By the beginning of the 18th century, however, this "Law of God" had given way to the Common Law of England, whence Washington Irving's quip that the New Englanders had seen fit to be governed by the laws of God until they were able to devise better laws for themselves. Puritan experiments with Biblical legislation were generally shortlived and often disastrous. Their legacy was seen in the oppressive Blue Laws governing behavior on Sunday, in the persecution and expulsion of "heretics," in the Salem trials and judicial murder of "witches," and in the legal procedure of Puritan Elders so graphically described in Nathaniel Hawthorne's novel, *The Scarlet Letter* (1850). A more enlightened American society could not stomach such excesses and the progress of time made English Common Law infinitely more attractive to men of a new era. Municipal and county administration and trial by jury were only two "innovations" which answered modern demands for sound government in line with English norms. This process of reversion did not, however, mean that the Bible had ceased to be a potent factor in the legal conscience of America. Along with Hebrew, Biblical and even Rabbinic studies were pursued by generations of scholars in New England and lawyers as well as preachers received a grounding in "the Divine Law" at Yale, Harvard, and other colleges. When the British soldiers responsible for the massacre at Boston were tried there in 1770, Justice Oliver cautioned the jury against deciding the case on the Biblical principle that "whoso sheddeth man's blood, by man shall his blood be shed" (Gen. 9:6). The Israelites of old, he observed, had cities of refuge to which a manslayer might flee from the avenger of blood (Num. 35:6–15) and Moses had designated this sanctuary for those who killed without enmity or premeditation. The supremacy of law, a basic tenet of Anglo-American legislation, can also be traced to older Jewish procedure. Enunciated in clauses of the U.S. Constitution's Fifth and Fourteenth Amendments ["No person shall be deprived of life, liberty, or property without due process of law"], this tenet is generally derived from the 39th clause of Magna Carta ["No freeman shall be taken or imprisoned ... except by the lawful judgment of his peers or by the law of the land"]. Such protection of human rights against arbitrary power is remarkably similar to the principles expressed in the *Mishneh Torah* of Maimonides (*Hilkhot Melakhim*), which was compiled 35 years before Magna Carta (in 1180), and some scholars believe that English Jews—smarting under the extortionate policies of King John—may have suggested such a clear restriction of the royal powers in the charter of liberties which the king was made to sign.

A final, and most significant, Biblical contribution to the concepts and practices of English and American law may be seen in the idea of a contract between the government and the people assuring the preservation of individual freedom. This notion, enshrined in the American Bill of Rights, goes back to the Puritan doctrine of Covenant, and this in turn was based squarely on the covenants between God and the Hebrew Patriarchs and the Sinaitic covenant between God, Moses, and the people of Israel. This social contract, a vital element in political thinking from the 16th century onward,[26] owes much to the devoted advocacy and example of those inspired Englishmen who made "government by consent" one of the fundamental laws of the modern democratic State.

NATURAL LAW CONCEPTS AND INTERNATIONAL LAW

As far as the non-Jewish world is concerned, the Bible's outstanding contribution to law has been in the field of jurisprudence (i.e., legal philosophy). A universal code was developed from the seven "Noachide Laws" which Rabbinic scholars deduced from the Torah.[27] The first written evidence of this code is available in the pseudepigraphical Book of Jubilees (7.20ff.), although the actual details vary from those contained in later Rabbinic literature. The classic reference occurs in the Talmud: "Seven precepts were imposed on the descendants of Noah [i.e., all mankind]: civil justice, the prohibition of blasphemy, idolatry, incest, murder, and theft, and the prohibition of eating flesh cut from a living animal" (*Sanhedrin*, 56a). This formulation amounts

---

[26] See below.

[27] The main source of these laws in the Bible is Gen. 9.

to what medieval jurists called the *jus naturale et gentium* ("Natural Law"). The Rabbis taught that "the righteous among the Gentiles" who adhered to these commandments would have a share in the world-to-come and Maimonides later declared that "whoever wishes to adopt Judaism ... is constrained to accept, not the Torah and precepts, but the Noachide laws." Modern Jewish philosophers, such as Moses Mendelssohn (in his correspondence with Lavater, 1770) and Hermann Cohen (*Die Religion der Vernunft,* 1919), have proclaimed that these universal injunctions form the common ground of Israel and all humanity in the sphere of ethics and reason.

Early Christianity shared Judaism's belief that the "Noachide" laws implied no necessary acceptance of the Mosaic Code as a whole by the Gentile world. Paul therefore recommended "that we trouble not them, which from among the Gentiles are turned to God: but that ... they abstain from pollutions of idols, and from fornication, and from things strangled, and from blood" (Acts 15:19–20). He also maintained that, while the Jews were subject to the Torah, non-Jews were required to observe a separate discipline, "for when the Gentiles, which have not the law, do by nature the things contained in the law, these, having not the law, are a law unto themselves ..." (Romans 2:14ff.). The Rabbinic concept of a "Natural Law" was subsequently adopted by the Church Fathers, who made the "Noachide" commandments the standard norm of Christian morality. Tertullian spoke of the pre-Mosaic "law of nature" honored by the Hebrew Patriarchs; Eusebius quoted Midrashic views about the precepts which Abraham observed; and Jerome, who detected traces of this "Natural Law" in Isa. 24:5 ("The earth also is defiled under the inhabitants thereof; because they have transgressed the laws, violated the statute, broken the everlasting covenant"), asserted that Adam and Eve, Cain, and the Pharaoh of the Exodus all showed an awareness of having sinned against a universal code. In general, the early Christians developed a formula for the acceptance or rejection of specific aspects of the Torah by declaring that whatever features of the "Old Covenant" amounted to the "law of nature" were still binding on members of the Church. Thus, despite wholesale repudiation of the Torah and *Halakhah*, Christianity preserved some basic injunctions (the Ten Commandments, the forbidden degrees of consanguinity and affinity in Leviticus, etc.), and these were eventually absorbed by Canon Law.

Once Christianity became the state religion of the Roman Empire, those Biblical regulations adopted by the Church made their way into Roman Law and were later absorbed by the legal codes of Western Europe.[28] The Eastern Emperor Justinian's *Corpus juris civilis* ("Body of Civil Law," sixth century C.E.), which transmitted Roman Law as a universal code, included references to the Mosaic legislation in the glosses to its *Codex* and *Digest*. Both the ecclesiastical and the civil law codes of the Middle Ages followed this lead, and the study of secular law—revived in Italian universities of the 12th century—was mainly based on Justinian's Byzantine regulations. Thus transformed, Roman Law gave rise to the concept of universal justice, a development that was to have lasting significance. Scriptural precedent was quoted by the Irish collection of Canon Law, by the *Leges Barbarorum* ("Foreigner's Laws") of Charlemagne's time (c. 800), and by the late ninth-century Anglo-Saxon Code of Alfred the Great. Though mainly intended as a learned gloss or as an exhortation to adopt "the good life," Alfred's use of Biblical passages (the Ten Commandments and the "Book of the Covenant" in Exodus) was both extensive and illuminating; apart from the Pentateuch, the Books of Kings, Psalms, Proverbs, and Job are all cited, as well as Apocryphal and New Testament sources.

While scholars continue to argue about the extent to which the "Noachide" concept influenced "Natural Law" ideas of the Middle Ages and the 16th–18th centuries, there is no denying the fact that the notion of a discoverable "law of nature" in the universe was the major force in the shaping of modern European law. Jurists from the later Middle Ages to the Age of Enlightenment shared this assumption. François Hotman, one of the leading French Huguenots,[29] declared that the ideal code would be based on Roman and philosophical authorities, court practice, and those portions of the Mosaic legislation that accorded with the concepts of his day. The Dutch statesman and jurist Hugo Grotius, commonly regarded as "the father of International Law," believed that the "law of nature" was a human quality independent of God and that modern states might deduce principles of conduct from the idea of "consent" and from the concept of "Natural Law." Grotius' theory of natural rights, expounded in his famous work on war and peace, *De jure belli et pacis* (1625), was mainly based on Stoic

---

[28] The practice whereby a witness takes the oath on the Bible indicates the Bible's penetration into legal procedure, as well as concepts of law.

[29] Similar political views are discussed later in this chapter.

philosophy and Roman legal principles, but often cited Mosaic law as a fundamental authority. For Grotius, "Natural Law" was inviolable and not subject to the changes constantly affecting civil legislation. Rejecting Grotius' ideas on the freedom of the seas (*De mari libero*, 1609), the English lawyer John Selden opposed the Dutchman's reliance on Roman Law and sought other evidence in Jewish literature. Reputedly the most learned man of his time, Selden dealt with the "Noachide" code and its universal application in his *De jure naturali et Gentium juxta disciplinam Ebraeorum* ("The Law of Nature and of Nations according to the Hebrews," 1640), where he managed to find Biblical justification for the English position. Echoes of Grotius are detectable in Montesquieu's *L'Esprit des lois* (1748) and in a curious work of the same period by Christian von Wolf, entitled *Institutiones Juris Naturae et Gentium in quibus ex ipsa hominis natura continuo nexu omnes obligationes et jura omnia deducuntur* ("Institutes of the Law of Nature and of Nations in which, by an unbroken argument, all obligations and all laws are deduced from man's own nature").

On the European continent, a sublimated Roman Law won acceptance as "Natural Law," but Biblical-Hebraic concepts provided all systems with a common element and were drawn on more and more heavily as the "law of nature" and Divine regulation were increasingly felt to be identical. Since some of the Mosaic code was universally relevant, any human laws that negated "Natural Law" were invalid, and even the doctrine of Divine revelation found a place in the English scheme. From "Natural Law" English jurists evolved principles that led to the development of Equity, the French and other European nations drew their 19th-century legislative codes, and the American revolutionaries took their constitutional ideas. Burke spoke of "that law which governs all law, the law of our Creator, the law of humanity, justice, equity—the law of nature, and of nations." The American Declaration of Independence appealed to "the laws of Nature and of Nature's God." And some Frenchman, delving far beyond the Reformation, the Renaissance, Classical antiquity, and even the Gospels, found in the Torah of Moses "the prime source of 1789 . . . the new decalogue of the Rights of Man that proceeds from the tablets brought down from Sinai, and . . . a distant, involuntary echo of Horeb" (Anatole Leroy-Beaulieu, *Israël chez les nations*, 1893).

An analysis of the Hebrew Bible does, in fact, substantiate the claim that laws governing the conduct of states and relations between nations can be deduced from Scripture. Such "international justice" may be seen in passages transcending the immediate scope of the "Noachide" laws. The Pentateuch declares that foreigners are entitled to just treatment (Lev. 19:33–34) and that the rights of neutrals must be respected (Num. 20:14ff.; Deut. 2:4ff.). A variety of Biblical sources lay down a civilized code of war, where war proves inevitable (Deut. 25:17–19); maintain the inviolability of ambassadors (2 Sam. 10); and demand the honoring of treaties (Gen. 21:23, 26:28–29; Josh. 9:15; 2 Sam. 21).[30] Even the idea of a "League of Nations" can be deduced from the Prophets (Isa. 2:3–4; Micah 4:2–3; cf. Zeph. 3:9, Zech. 9:10). Texts such as these, when combined with the Roman doctrine of a *jus gentium* ("law of nations"), transformed the original concept of a universal and unchanging "Natural Law" into the foundation of international law and justice. Furthermore, Grotius and Selden were both equipped to dig deep into post-Biblical Jewish lore as well, the former citing the Talmud, Targum, Rashi, and Maimonides, the latter displaying all the wealth of his remarkable Rabbinic learning—in the cause of "the law of nature and of nations."

Some mention must finally be made of the Biblical and Jewish legislation on crime. The *lex talionis*, popularly known as the law of "an eye for an eye and a tooth for a tooth" (Ex. 21:24–25; Lev. 24:20), has already been mentioned (see above). The Sixth Commandment, which the world still mistakenly translates as "Thou shalt not kill," is actually a prohibition of willful killing or murder (in Hebrew, *lo tirẓaḥ*, from the root *r-ẓ-ḥ*, meaning "to murder, culpably slay"). Hebrew law carefully differentiated between deliberate, premeditated killing of another human being in a state of peace and unintentional homicide; the manslaughterer was protected by law and could seek asylum in one of the appointed cities of refuge, while no vengeance might be taken on the killer's innocent family. The Bible also provided no legal justification for the torture of suspects or condemned men and, even after execution, the human body had to be treated with respect (Deut. 21:22–23).

Compared with the general humaneness of Hebrew legislation, the practices not only of ancient and medieval times but even of our own

---

[30] On treaties, Josephus (in his *Antiquities*) quotes the unparalleled example of the Jews who defied Alexander the Great because of their oath of allegiance to Darius. A number of these principles were later formulated by Maimonides in his *Hilkhot Melakhim* ("Laws of Kings"), a section of the *Mishneh Torah* code.

day often display much inequity, if not downright cruelty. As late as the 19th century, English courts made transportation to Australia ("Botany Bay") a common sentence for petty theft and French law could prescribe equally savage punishment (cf. the fate of Victor Hugo's hero Jean Valjean in *Les Misérables*, 1862). In recent centuries, other European states allowed offenders to be mutilated, "rebels" to have their tongues clipped or torn out, and prostitutes to be branded with a "mark of shame."[31] Public executions, which ceased to entertain Western mobs in the last century, are still staged periodically in Arab states (Syria, Iraq) and have served "educational" purposes in Communist China. The blood feud or vendetta is a time-honored feature of life in some Latin countries, and "lynch-law" was long dominant in the American South and West. As an instrument of the State, judicial murder has disposed of heretics (both religious and political), insubordinate officials, and rebels of every kind under the Inquisition, in Tudor and Elizabethan England, and under a dozen assorted tyrannies ranging from Imperial Russia to Falangist Spain, Nazi Germany, and the Soviet empire. Genocide, too, was "legalized" by Hitler and has been sanctioned by the ruling circles in one or two newly emergent African countries. Gestapo-type methods are still employed by the secret police of many totalitarian regimes, which subject their victims to physical and psychological torture in an effort to extract "confessions," expose them to public humiliation, and terrorize their families and associates.

Even in those enlightened states where the "rule of law" is enforced, concepts of justice and the existing penal system generally fall short of the Biblical ideal. To "let the punishment fit the crime" requires far more serious thought and attention than it has hitherto received. Jewish law demanded not merely restitution of stolen property and compensation for loss of life or injury, but sanctions that would ensure the

---

[31] In October 1972, it was reported that the Libyan government had decreed a new punishment for highway robbery: amputation of the offender's right hand and left foot. Common thieves above the age of 18 would be subject to a "lighter" sentence—their hand alone being cut off. Castration and beheading were two especially brutal penalties facing Allied prisoners of war in Japan (1941–45) and Israelis captured by Arab irregulars (from 1948 onward). The forms of torture and mutilation employed by the Nazis against inoffensive civilians defy enumeration.

reeducation of offenders and legal action calculated to make certain that justice would "not merely be done, but be seen to be done." Much lip-service has been paid to fundamentals such as human rights and international law, but misuse or misrepresentation of the "natural" code which the Bible inspired does not rob it of validity. Two provisions of "the law of nature and of nations" which Israel so obviously called forth are the principle of equality before the law and the law's operation in defense of any individual or group menaced by a tyrannical government. The Biblical contribution to our notion of justice and legal consciousness has been widely acknowledged and jurists see in the Scriptures one of the main foundations of Western civilization and the "rule of law." Woodrow Wilson firmly believed that "it would be a mistake . . . to ascribe to Roman legal conceptions an undivided sway over the development of law and institutions during the Middle Ages. The Teuton came under the influence, not only of Rome, but also of Christianity, and through the Church there entered into Europe a potent of Judaic thought. The laws of Moses as well as the laws of Rome contributed suggestions and impulse to the men and institutions which were to prepare the modern world; and if we could have but eyes to see . . . we should readily discover how very much besides religion we owe to the Jew" (*The State*, 1890).

POLITICS

The "art" of politics is as old as society itself, long predating the philosophical writings of Plato. Political theory was certainly an invention of the Greeks, but there are far earlier traces of practical politics in the Hebrew Bible, beginning perhaps with the ideological duel between Moses on the one side and Pharaoh and his advisers on the other. For the Hebrews, political aspirations were largely bound up with the thirst for freedom and independence—freedom to conduct their own distinctive "way of life," and the preservation of that national independence which they first won from their Egyptian oppressors. The Biblical account of that fight for liberty has been the inspiration of men of many creeds throughout the centuries, sharpening and motivating their demand for social justice, freedom of thought and expression, and for equal opportunity. "Since the Exodus, Freedom has always spoken with a Hebrew accent," Heine observed. Despite differences of opinion as to the best form of human government, Israel's leaders were united in their demand for the safeguarding of human rights and in their unyielding opposition to tyranny, whether by their own or by foreign rulers. The English poet Coleridge paid tribute to the role of Israel's emancipators and idealists in shaping man's political thinking when he wrote: "I persist in avowing my conviction that the inspired poets, historians, and sententiaries of the Jews are the clearest teachers of political economy . . . their writings are the statesman's best manual, not only as containing the first principles and ultimate grounds of State-policy, whether in prosperous times or in those of danger and distress, but as supplying likewise the details of their application, and as being a full and spacious repository of precedents and facts in proof" (*A Lay Sermon*, 1816).

THE BIBLICAL CONCEPT OF GOVERNMENT

Just as the Divine examples of justice and righteousness lent sublimity to the Biblical notion of law and unique grandeur to the Hebraic vision of society, so did the ever-present idea of man's copartnership with God mold Israel's conception of government and the development of its political institutions. The Hebrews had not been "chosen from among all peoples," redeemed from slavery in Egypt against all the laws of the "natural" order, and led to their Promised Land merely to copy and perpetuate all the social and moral evils afflicting the ancient world. The perennial freshness of the freedom which they had won was preserved by constant injunctions to remember the Covenant to which they were party—injunctions which faced them at every turn and in every crisis, recalling the fact that it was God's intervention and not their own strength or virtue that rescued them from enslavement in order to lay the foundations of a just, free, and equal society. In this new society there was to be no room for new oppressors, no place for tyranny: allegiance was owed only to God and government was established only in His laws. Yet so great was the insistence on freedom that even God's laws had first to be freely accepted by the people of Israel. Here, for the first time in man's history, lie the foundations of what we now call democracy—government by consent—and what may well be the earliest form of social contract, a notion of supreme importance in later European thought. As President Woodrow Wilson once remarked, "not a little of the history of liberty lies in the circumstance that the moving sentences of this Book were made familiar to the ears and the understandings of those people who have led mankind in exhibiting the forms of government and the impulses of reform which have made for freedom and self-government among mankind."

THEOCRATIC RULE

The evolution of Israel's just society necessitated the development of a new system of government, begun under Moses and continued under the Judges. Josephus (in *Contra- Apionem*) used a Greek term to describe this type of constitution—"theocracy: placing all sovereignty and authority in the hands of God." To the modern ear the word "theocracy" has distinctly pejorative overtones, suggesting the rule of some oppressive priestly caste, "government of a state by immediate Divine guidance or by officials regarded as divinely guided," to quote a standard definition. Yet, unlike certain other systems known in antiquity, "the 'Theocracy' of Moses was not a government by priests, as opposed to kings; it was a government by God Himself, as opposed to the government by priests or kings" (Dean Arthur Stanley, *A History of the Jewish Church*, 1862). The U.S. jurist and statesman Oscar Straus, a close associate of President Theodore Roosevelt, also stressed this point in his study of American culture's indebtedness to the Hebraic concept: "The very fact that . . . with the single exception of Eli, no priest was ever elected to the magistracy during the entire period of the Commonwealth, decidedly negatives any such interpretation" (*The Origin of the Republican Form of Government in the United States of America*, 1887).

In its initial stage, Israel's theocracy was of short duration, lasting from the period of the Exodus until the election of Saul as the first Hebrew king barely 200 years later. The direct rule of God was freely confirmed by the people assembled at Sinai; and, as a renewal of the ancient covenants with the Patriarchs, it involved both the acceptance of God as supreme Legislator and the peculiar role of Moses, Joshua, and their successors (the Judges) as charismatic guides and rulers regarded as having been chosen by the Lord. Thus Moses presents God's conditions to the elders of the people: at that stage, the answer is "All that the Lord hath spoken we will do" (Ex. 19:8). After the giving of the Ten Commandments and the detailed precepts, Moses "took the book of the covenant, and read in the hearing of the people;

and they said: 'All that the Lord hath spoken we will do, and obey'"
(Ex. 24:7).[32] The Torah becomes a source of perpetual law and guidance,
commanding Israel's loyalty not only because of its Divine origin,
but also because of its wisdom, understanding, and righteousness
(Deut. 4:6–8). And Moses and Joshua inaugurate the process of theocratic government, being appointed by God and confirmed in office
by the free will of the people (Ex. 3:10, 4:29–31; Joshua 1:2, 16–18).

The Hebrew Judges were not lawgivers, but instruments of the Divine
will, empowered to rule for a longer or shorter period of time by God's
decree (cf. the call of Gideon in Judges 6:11ff.). As such, their function
may be compared to that of the early dictators of Rome, who quit
their daily labors to restore national morale and ward off military
peril, only to return to the plow once the danger had passed. While the
form of rule which the Israelites experienced under Joshua's successors
was in many respects democratic, it also proved to be chaotic and an-
archical; it lacked stability and continuity (Judges 18:1, 19:1) and
"every man did that which was right in his own eyes" (Judges 21:25).
Time and again, the death of a leader was followed by a return to the
evil ways of the past and only the rise of a new Judge restored order
and discipline among the people. When Samuel grew old, it was the
people's craving for greater national security that prompted the demand
for "a king to judge us like all the nations" (1 Sam. 8:5). This demand
amounted to a rejection of the theocratic system of government, rather
than of Samuel himself, as God points out when he orders Samuel to
grant the people's request, "for they have not rejected thee, but they
have rejected Me, that I should not be king over them" (1 Sam. 8:7).
Samuel's forebodings about the despotic type of monarchy that will
emerge are prophetically expressed in a detailed warning: "This will
be the manner of the king that shall reign over you: he will take your
sons, and appoint them unto him, for his chariots, and to be his horsemen

---

[32] In Judaism, this "instant and instinctive response to carry out the will of
God" is a key phrase, expressing submission to the Creator and dedication to
His Covenant: na'aseh ve-nishma (literally, "we will do and we will hear").
A Rabbinic legend, of which there are several versions, tells how God offered
the Torah to each of the seventy nations of the world in turn; but because of
some commandment to which they took exception, all of them refused to accept
it apart from Israel, whose response was: "na'aseh ve-nishma" (see Mekhilta to
Ex. 20:2 and cf. Avodah Zarah, 2b, Pesikta de-Rav Kahana, 17a, etc.).

... and to plow his ground, and to reap his harvest ... And he will take your daughters ... your fields, and your vineyards, and ... your men-servants, and your maid-servants, and your goodliest young men, and your asses, and put them to his work ... And ye shall cry out in that day because of your king whom ye shall have chosen you; and the Lord will not answer you in that day" (1 Sam. 8:11–18). Only when it is clear that the warning has fallen on deaf ears does God finally instruct Samuel to establish the basis of Israel's new monarchical system, with important consequences for the Hebrew Commonwealth.

THE DEVELOPMENT AND DECLINE OF THE MONARCHY

The anointing of Saul marked the beginning of a constitutional monarchy, since the election of the king was once more subject to contract (1 Sam. 10:17–25). A monarch's prerogatives and responsibilities had been laid down in the Pentateuch, where the Israelites were warned that, if they did choose a king "like all the nations that are round about," he must be one of themselves, not greedy for wealth or power, and God-fearing, so that "his heart be not lifted up above his brethren, and ... he turn not aside from the commandment, to the right hand, or to the left" (Deut. 17:14–20). Samuel later reminded the people that, while God had acceded to their demand for a king, the old contract between them remained in force: if Israel voided it, "ye shall be swept away, both ye and your king" (1 Sam. 12:24–25). This important lesson was not forgotten by the Israelites. Their king ruled "by the grace of God," and not instead of Him, and he was to be Israel's royal servant, not a despotic master. Authority had hitherto resided in the Judges and the "elders" or "men of Israel" (Joshua 9:6–7, Judges 20:11ff.) and, like Saul, David had later to be confirmed in office by popular acclamation (2 Sam. 3:21, 5:3). When his image as a "judge" began to fade and the people sensed that he had become aloof and indifferent toward their old democratic institutions, David was confronted with a widespread revolt against his centralized monarchy. Absalom won popular support by reviving the authority of the tribal bodies, but how long this policy would have continued had David been defeated it is hard to say. This prince was himself an ambitious autocrat and it is doubtful if he would have been content to share his powers with the "men of Israel" who flocked to his standard (2 Sam. 15:13, 16:15, 17:24). During the Biblical period there was no such limited monarchy in Israel; the covenant with the Lord was what kept the king's powers in check.

Yet the people were no herd to be regimented and oppressed as the king saw fit. The Queen of Sheba reminded Solomon that, because God "loved Israel for ever, therefore made He thee king, to do justice and righteousness" (1 Kings 10:9). And, when Rehoboam contemptuously rejected the elders' plea for the royal yoke to be lightened ("My father chastised you with whips, but I will chastise you with scorpions," 1 Kings 12:14), the Israelites took up the ancient slogan of revolt: "What portion have we in David? neither have we inheritance in the son of Jesse; to your tents, O Israel" (1 Kings 12:16; cf. 2 Sam. 20:1 and 2 Chron. 10:16). They were prepared to be a "rebellious" people, if circumstances warranted it, even at the risk of dividing the kingdom, for their allegiance was to God and not to a tyrant—even a tyrant of Davidic descent.

The uniqueness of Israel's constitutional monarchy can only be gauged by comparing the Hebrew idea of kingship with other forms of this institution in the ancient world. Whether the king ruled in the empires of Egypt, Babylon, or Assyria, or in the city-states of the Canaanites, he was regarded either as a god or son of a god or as the god's agent on earth—and his will as an embodiment of the national deity's will. The Egyptians held their monarchy to be an essential part of the natural order, while the Sumerians believed that theirs was a legacy from heaven.[33] Though in time influenced by the regal trappings and authoritarianism of the monarchical systems surrounding them, the Israelites' notion of kingship was very different; for the Hebrews, monarchy was not essential to the world scheme, but a later historical development, in many ways inferior to the theocratic government of the tribes and clans under Saul's predecessors. Indeed, Saul himself—for all his faults—was far less despotic and "regal" than those who came after him, more of a judge than a king of Israel. (1 Sam. 10:6, 10–13; 11:6–7, 13; 14:24, 37ff.; 19:23–24).

However, while there is evidence of earlier attempts to make the rule of a leader hereditary (e.g., Gideon in Judges 8:22), such attempts were stoutly resisted, and it was the hereditary principle implicit in

---

[33] The Sapa Inca ("Sole Emperor") of Peru was also thought to be divine ("Son of the Sun"), while the Japanese Mikado was, of course, revered as the "Son of Heaven."

kingship that constituted a repudiation of the contract with God as sole ruler over the people. The sacrifices which, as Samuel foresaw, Israel would have to make in order to establish the monarchy constituted a surrender of individual liberty, bringing the Hebrew kingdom into line with the prevailing system of "all the other nations." Despite Israel's adoption of the external paraphernalia of royalty in the coronation ceremonies of Solomon and his successors (1 Kings 1:33–48, 2 Kings 11:10–14), the Hebrew monarch was invested with the "testimony" (Hebrew *edut*, also translated as "law," "covenant," or "statute"), a document outlining the terms of his covenant (cf. Deut. 17:18ff., 1 Sam. 10:25). Moreover, the act of consecration with oil had a special, perhaps mystical character: the king immediately became "the Lord's Anointed One" (literally, "Messiah"; in Hebrew, *Meshiaḥ* YHVH),[34] and the ceremony bestowed "the spirit of the Lord" on Saul (1 Sam. 10:9ff.) and David (1 Sam. 16:13).

The parallels and contrasts between Israelite and pagan concepts of kingship make it clear that the institution of monarchy was a concession to the demands of national policy, rather than an acceptance of some ordained system of government. The dynastic principle came into force under King David, when Solomon was anointed in his father's lifetime so as to ensure his succession to the throne (1 Kings 1:28–48), but the heir apparent could be set aside if he failed to live up to the supreme demands of kingship (1 Kings 11:31ff., 16:3ff., 21:21ff.; 2 Kings 9:1–10). Monarchy, in contrast to the prevailing ancient view, was an earthly institution, neither permanent nor God-given, yet the king was "the Lord's anointed" and whoever harmed him was liable to be punished (1 Sam. 24:7; 2 Sam. 1:14, 19:22). Even the murderers of Saul's son, Ish-Bosheth, whose succession to the throne had been barred, were condemned to death by King David (2 Sam. 4:9–12). We have seen earlier how, in regard to the promulgation of law, the Mesopotamian king enacted statutes "in order that the mighty might not harm the underprivileged"—statutes which he himself devised and which the god Shamash never directly inspired. The kings of Israel had no such authority. "Law in Israel has a divine authorship; it is not a 'humanly authored safeguard of cosmic truth' . . . God alone is the ultimate source and sanction of law . . .[He] 'is not merely the custodian of justice or the dispenser of "truths" to man, He is the

---

[34] For further discussion of these terms, see Chapter 3.

fountainhead of the law; the law is a statement of His will . . . The only legislator the Bible knows of is God' . . . "[35] Moreover, it is not some human ruler who issues decrees to the people, but the supreme Arbiter of Israel's destiny, for God "is not merely the guarantor of the covenant, as the deities are in the epilogues to Mesopotamian legal collections and treaties; He is the author of the covenant who directly addresses His people."[36]

Ancient rulers usually functioned as high priests of the cult, as well as absolute kings. A reflection of this tradition may be seen in the Psalmist's phrase, "Thou art a priest for ever after the manner of Melchizedek" (Ps. 110:4), which links the Davidic dynasty with that rather mysterious king of Salem (an early name for Jerusalem) who greeted Abraham after the patriarch's victory over Amraphel and his allies (Gen. 14:18). While the kings of Israel sometimes performed priestly duties—offering sacrifices (2 Sam. 6:14–18; 1 Kings 9:25) and blessing the people in the manner of Aaron and his sons (2 Sam. 6:18; 1 Kings 8:55ff.)—they were, nevertheless, in no way substitutes for the legitimate Hebrew priests.

Kingship in Israel therefore amounted to monarchical rule by Divine covenant—a twofold contract between God on the one side and the king and the people on the other, and between the king and the people (2 Kings 11:17). A pact between David and the elders thus preceded his second (public) anointing (2 Sam. 5:3), while the Israelite monarch was obliged to keep God's commandment (Deut. 17:19; 1 Kings 3:14). The king was, however, responsible to God and not to the people, while God alone could bring an evil dynasty to an end (1 Sam. 13:13–14; 1 Kings 14:7ff.). The eternal covenant of kingship (based on the prophet Nathan's vision in 2 Sam. 7:8–9) is that the monarchy will remain for ever with the house of David (Ps. 132:11–12; cf. 1 Chron. 28:5–7). Until the destruction of the First Temple, this promise remained in force and it was against an idealized background of the Davidic line of kings that the Prophets foretold the advent in days to come of "a shoot out of the stock of Jesse" who would restore the kingdom, "assemble the dispersed of Israel . . . from the four corners of the earth"

---

[35] Shalom Paul, *Studies in the Book of the Covenant* . . ., pp. 36–37. The internal citations are from M. Greenberg's essay, "Some Postulates of Biblical Criminal Law," in the *Yehezkel Kaufmann Jubilee Volume* (Jerusalem, 1960), pp. 11–12.
[36] Paul, *ibid.*

(Isa. 11:1–16), save Judah (Jer. 23:5–6), act as a shepherd toward the people (Ezek. 37:24), and "raise up the tabernacle of David" (Amos 9:11). This ideal sovereign, envisioned in terms of old symbols and concepts, would also reign over the whole earth (Zech. 9:10) and restore universal harmony, since he would be the redeemer of all mankind. He would be named *Avi-ad* ("Everlasting Father") and *Sar-Shalom* ("Ruler of Peace"), signifying "that the government may be increased, and of peace there be no end, upon the throne of David, and upon his kingdom, to establish it, and to uphold it through justice and through righteousness from henceforth even for ever" (Isa. 9:5–6).

POLITICAL ACTION FROM THE PROPHETS
TO THE SECOND COMMONWEALTH

Despite this idealization of kingship, the older, democratic tradition retained vitality and there was a constant undercurrent of popular objection to the harsh realities of monarchical rule. "Harem intrigues" during the reign of King David first sowed the seeds of moral decay, and these began to sprout when Solomon, flouting the Biblical injunction against multiplying wives and horses (Deut. 17:16–17), forced his subjects to finance his luxurious administration. Corvée (compulsory labor), the division of land, and the stark contrast between life at court and among the peasantry were the outcome of Solomon's absolutist rule. Rehoboam, as we have seen, tried to "go one better" by placing himself above the law and the popular revolt which this move sparked off had a distant sequel in the English Parliament's repudiation of Charles I some 2,500 years later.[37]

Democracy was kept alive by an alliance of the people and the Prophets, the latter insisting that the kings of Israel and Judah reigned not by "Divine right" but by "the grace of God." Israel's Magna Carta lay in the restraints imposed by Deut. 17:18–20 (which was to be one of the pillars of constitutional monarchy), and the concept of ideal kingship found expression in a poetic text (Psalm 72) written for, or possibly by, King Solomon himself. From the time of David onward, those who commanded the armies of Israel retained some of the functions of the old Judges. In the Northern kingdom, from Baasa (1 Kings 15) to Pekah (2 Kings 15:25), army officers engineered insurrections against

[37] See below ("Resistance to Tyranny").

kings and changes of dynasty—a phenomenon which has its counter-
tutions, which long antedated the monarchy. Here tribal and regal
their authority from the people and their power from its ancient institutions, which long antedated the monarchy. Here tribal and regal
prerogatives often collided. In the Southern kingdom of Judah, there
was a closer identification of tribal and monarchical interests and structures and the dynasty was a far more stable political factor; it was
thus only in times of acute danger or unrest that the army invoked its
popular authority. In general, the Hebrew Prophets remained close
to the power element in tribal and military affairs. The fact that popular
dissatisfaction with a particular regime often arose from a king's attempted repudiation of the contract governing his reign led the Prophets
to become the spokesmen of democracy. *Vox populi, vox Dei* ("The
voice of the people is the voice of God") was never in Israel a call for
mob-rule, as the eighth-century English theologian Alcuin felt that
slogan to be: for Nathan, Elijah, and Isaiah it was more akin to the
"still small voice" of social and religious conscience.

Centuries before Aristotle declared that "man is by nature a political
animal," Israel's Prophets were creating political history by making
and unmaking kings and by acting as unofficial counsellors of state.
Nor was their status always entirely unofficial: Nathan and another
prophet, Gad (2 Sam. 24:11ff.; 1 Chron. 29:29), seem to have had
some sort of court appointment, Gad being specifically entitled "the
king's seer" (2 Chron. 29:25). Samuel was the great "kingmaker,"
selecting first Saul and then David for the throne of Israel; Nathan
made David's affair with Bath-Sheba an issue of political gravity (2 Sam.
12:10–12) and later engineered Solomon's proclamation as heir apparent
(1 Kings 1:11ff.); while Ahijah proclaimed the division of the kingdom
(1 Kings 11:31–32). Sometimes their "meddling" in affairs of state
proved dangerous for the prophets: the seer Hanani, who condemned
Asa's political shortsightedness, was imprisoned for his temerity (2
Chron. 16:7). Here the "righteous" King Asa's high-handed treatment of
Hanani oddly contrasts with Ahab's deferential attitude toward Elijah,
whose censure of that "wicked" ruler (1 Kings 21: 21ff.) was far more
violent and uncompromising. Other instances of the Prophets' involvement in governmental and political matters may be seen in the activities
of Hanani's son Jehu (1 Kings 16:1–7; 2 Chron. 19:2–3), Elisha (2 Kings
6:22, 9:3ff.), and Eliezer the son of Dodavahu (2 Chron. 20:35–37).

After the Return from Babylon, Hellenism corrupted the priests and perverted religious and legal administration, a baneful development already apparent in the era of the prophet Malachi (2:7–9). Yet Nehemiah's political sagacity in warding off the perils of the incipient Samaritan heterodoxy provided a lesson for future Jewish leaders (Neh. 13:28). Democracy's reassertion in the revolt of the Maccabees marked the last stage in Jewish governmental experiment before the long night of dispersion. Here was an ideal combination of constitutional monarchy and responsible theocracy, embodied in the dynasty of Mattathias' descendants who ruled the people as kings, generals, and high priests at one and the same time. The U.S. jurist Louis D. Brandeis affirmed that, "as part of the eternal world-wide struggle for democracy, the struggle of the Maccabees is of eternal world-wide interest" and the historian Joseph Klausner pointed to the ultimate historical significance of the Hasmonean rebellion, stressing that, "but for the heroism of the Maccabees, the heathen must, finally, have swallowed up the Jews" (*Jesus of Nazareth*, 1926).

The decree confirming the titles and hereditary rights of the Hasmonean rulers was passed by the Great Assembly in 140 B.C.E. This Assembly, the forerunner of the Sanhedrin (Israel's supreme religious, judicial, and political body in Roman times), can also be regarded as the Biblical model for England's Parliament—especially as that popular legislature developed in the 16th and 17th centuries. The Great Assembly was at the helm of Jewish administration during the period of the Second Temple and, through the opportunity which it gave for the people's self-expression, made politics the rightful concern of every Jew. "This experiment . . . constitutes the most remarkable theory of government that came out of the ancient world and at the same time an ideal that rebukes and challenges the distressing imperfection of our boasted modern democracy" (William A. Irwin, *The Old Testament: Keystone of Human Culture*, 1952).

LATER POLITICAL THOUGHT AMONG THE JEWS

Although there was always basic agreement among Jews as to the checks and safeguards which sound and just government required, attitudes toward specific issues and forms of administration often differed very sharply. The Third Book of Maccabees reflects a widespread popular movement against the whole institution of monarchy, noting with pride that the Jews "stand alone among nations in their stiff-necked resistance to kings." Philo regarded democracy as "the best of constitutions"—a belief which he elaborated in his statement that, "of cities, there are two kinds: the better one enjoys a democratic government, which honors equality and has law and justice for its rulers—such a constitution is a hymn to God; the worse . . . is mob-rule." Living in Alexandria, where he was subject to a Hellenistic administration, Philo spoke from practical experience of conflicting political ideologies in the outside world. Under the later Hasmoneans and the Roman procurators, religious differences accentuated the political conflicts between the aristocratic and conservative Sadducees on the one hand and the Pharisee democrats and their sectarian offspring on the other. Lord Acton believed that the example of the Essenes "testifies to how great a height religious men were able to raise their conception of society without the succor of the New Testament" (*Freedom in Antiquity*, 1877); but the political and national extremism of the Zealots, so far removed from the moderate approach of the Pharisees from whom they sprang, led directly to Jerusalem's ultimate destruction by Titus. It was, strangely enough, a member of this political group, Simon the Zealot, who joined the apocalyptic "Nazarenes" and became one of Jesus' Twelve Apostles (Luke 6:15; Acts 1:13). The Zealots' conviction that the old order was about to be overturned may well have motivated Simon's astonishing change of loyalty. The sense of realism which guided the Pharisees made them pragmatists in political affairs and this proved the salvation of Judaism, enabling it to survive exile, persecution, and universal mockery of its cherished ideals. The U.S. theologian Felix A. Levy thus observed that "the world owes the Bible with its Psalms, the Sabbath, the hospital, and the gospel of love to these modest and self-sacrificing servants of the Lord" (*Crossroads in Judaism*, 1954).

Even among the Rabbis, however, there was no unified stand on political issues. Their belief in a Messiah who would be of royal Davidic stock clashed with the harsh reality of Roman imperial rule. The deputy high priest Ḥanina, one of the more conservative Rabbis, had the melancholy example of the Zealots and Sicarii (another militant group) before him when he enjoined: "Pray for the welfare of the ruling power, since but for fear of it men would have swallowed each other alive" (*Avot*, 3.2). In fact, this view subsequently led to the composition of a special prayer for the government, which Jews traditionally recite after the reading of the Torah in the synagogue. On the other hand, the many parables in the Talmud and Midrash contrasting the mortal "king of flesh and blood" with the "Supreme King of Kings, the Holy One blessed be He" were clearly aimed at the Romans, and one of the Rabbis actually declared that the removal of the "yoke of the monarchy" would herald the arrival of the Messianic age (*Sanhedrin*, 91b). The majority probably favored a limited monarchy on the ideal, Biblical pattern, as the Midrash nostalgically recalled: "Judah's royal throne had six steps leading to the seat, which were to remind the king, as he ascended, of the six commandments for rulers: not to multiply horses, wives, and gold [Deut. 17:16–17], and not to wrest judgment, respect persons, or accept bribes [Deut. 16:19]. Above the throne was a sign reading: Know before Whom you sit!" (Esther Rabbah, 1.12; *Pesikta de-Rav Kahana,* 6b). The Rabbis of old looked beyond polemics to the ultimate aims of the opposing parties and shrewdly trusted in the judgment of history, as an anonymous Mishnaic scholar reflected: "Every controversy that is in the name of Heaven shall in the end lead to a permanent result; but every controversy that is not in the name of Heaven shall not . . . Which was in the name of Heaven?—that of Hillel and Shammai. And which was not?—that of Korah and all his company" (*Avot,* 5.20).[38]

Monarchical sentiment is thus quite firmly embedded in later Jewish thought. On the whole, it may be attributed both to the concept of God as King of the Universe and to the age-old Messianic yearning for the restoration of the throne of David. It finds vivid reflection in the liturgy, in grace after meals, and even in a Talmudic expression (*Rosh ha-Shanah*, 25a) that became a cherished folksong: "David, king of Israel, is alive and vigorous!" Maimonides, that many-sided genius of medieval Spain, was a confirmed royalist, devoting an entire section of his *Mishneh Torah* code to the laws relating to kingship; and, until more recent times, few Jewish religious leaders took a more unorthodox political stand. One notable exception was Don Isaac Abrabanel, whose republican sympathies were deepened, if not originally forged, by the Spanish Expulsion of 1492—the most momentous legislative act signed by any of the monarchs who decreed the banishment of the Jews. In his commentary on the Torah (1495), Abrabanel —hitherto a loyal servant of the Spanish crown—asserted that "a

---

[38] Hillel and Shammai headed rival schools of Rabbinic thought; for Korah, see Num. 16.

monarch is unnecessary, harmful, and very dangerous" and that "kings were first set up not by popular vote, but by force" (annotations to Deut. 17:15). This was, however, as yet an untypical opinion.

When the era of Enlightenment and Emancipation dawned for the Jews of Western Europe, political outlook again varied from country to country according to the prevailing system or its rejection. Not long after he had taken refuge in Paris, Heine maintained that "should the political revolution break out among us . . . freedom will be able to speak everywhere, and its language will be Biblical." In his essay on Jessica (*Shakespeares Mädchen und Frauen*, 1839), Heine also sardonically recalled that Josephus' history mentioned the existence in Jerusalem of "republicans who opposed the royally-inclined Herodians, fought them fiercely, called no man 'master,' and hated Roman absolutism most bitterly. Their religion was freedom and equality. What madness!" And in his *Geständnisse* ("Confessions," 1853), the poet asserted—with his usual dash of irony—that, "were not all pride of ancestry a silly inconsistency in a champion of the Revolution and its democratic principles, the writer of these pages would be proud that his ancestors belonged to the noble house of Israel, that he is a descendant of those martyrs who gave the world a God and a morality, and who have fought and suffered on all the battle-fields of thought."

Like Heine, Benjamin Disraeli scorned the bourgeoisie and the capitalist system, but his view of history was undisguisedly romantic and the political reform which he master-minded was on the right. Disraeli's novels were the vehicle for his ideology, which haughtily dismissed "the fatal drollery called a representative government" (*Tancred*, 1847) and defined his philosophy of progressive Conservatism: "Tory men and Whig measures" (*Coningsby*, 1844). Disdaining democracy, he nevertheless sought the advancement of the masses, objecting to the worst features of the English class structure—"I was told that the Privileged and the People formed Two Nations" (*Sybil*, 1845). In *Coningsby*, Disraeli also stressed the social pressures that had motivated his own people's political attitudes over the centuries: "The Jews . . . are a race essentially monarchical, deeply religious, and . . . yet you find the once loyal Hebrew invariably arrayed in the same ranks as the leveller and latitudinarian, prepared to support the policy which may even endanger his life and property, rather than tamely continue under a system which seeks to degrade him." His conclusion, which—as we have seen—has much basis in past history and experience, was (as he put it) that "the Jews . . . are essentially Tories."

Although he could not know it, Disraeli had a rather surprising ally in the German Socialist and trade union pioneer Ferdinand Lassalle, who in 1864 wrote that "nothing could have a greater future or a more beneficent role than the monarchy, if it could only make up its mind to become a social monarchy." Though estranged from Judaism, Lassalle was undoubtedly influenced by the English constitutional system, which had its roots in the Puritan interpretation of Biblical kingship. Outside Britain, however, most modern Jewish political thinkers have opted for the republican form of government which libertarianism established in the United States, France, and other Western countries. This was not necessarily an acceptance of the inevitable, but rather a pragmatic resignation to the demands of the new age and to the realities of human nature and society. Thus in 1949, when Dr. Chaim Weizmann, the first president of the new State of Israel, opened its first constituent assembly, the Knesset (a name borrowed from that Great Assembly (*Keneset Gedolah*) which governed the Second Jewish Commonwealth), he declared that "the authority of the king of Israel was limited by law and tradition . . . and in this sense the ancient Hebrew polity was the mother of constitutional government in the modern age."

RESISTANCE TO TYRANNY

The Biblical concept of God's paramount sovereignty was the principal justification for Israel's continued resistance to earthly tyranny. National memory (of Egyptian bondage) and firsthand experience (of recurrent oppression) made such resistance a religious and political virtue. While far more powerful nations succumbed to foreign tyrants, Israel alone fought doggedly to preserve culture and identity in face of what must often have seemed to be overwhelming odds. In the downfall of successive despots the Hebrews saw the hand of God, whose Law stressed human dignity and the value of freedom. The ultimate punishment of the wicked and the short-lived reign of tyrants were visible truths which the Prophets hammered home in their social message:

How hath the oppressor ceased!
The exactress of gold ceased!

> The Lord hath broken the staff of the wicked,
> The sceptre of the rulers,
> That smote the people in wrath
> With an incessant stroke,
> That ruled the nations in anger,
> With a persecution that none restrained . . . (Isa. 14:4–6).

At times, the voice of resistance did not hesitate to reproach God Himself for His apparent inaction and to call for His intervention in the affairs of men in order to restore justice and order to the world (Hab. 1:1, 6–13). It was therefore inevitable that the standard of revolt was first set up by Jewish hands when Mattathias slew the arrogant officer of Antiochus and cried: "Whosoever is zealous for the law, and maintaineth the covenant, let him come forth after me" (1 Macc. 2.15–28). The fruits of a righteous rebellion were in fact enjoyed under the heroic priest's sons, when the Jews "tilled their land in peace . . . and they sat each man under his vine and his fig tree, and there was none to make them afraid . . ." (1 Macc. 14.4–15).

THE JEWISH EXAMPLE

The moral and political lessons of the Hasmonean era were always fresh in the mind of Jews in the Rabbinic period. The Rabbis emphasized the vast difference between the King of Kings, who spoke "face to face" with Moses and who "does not deal despotically with His creatures" (*Avodah Zarah*, 3a), and earthly kings who behaved otherwise. The hope which the Rabbis held out for a time when tyranny would be banished from the world was expressed in a prayer attributed to the third-century Babylonian teacher Rav (Abba Arikha), which Jews still recite in the New Year liturgy: "Then shall the just also see and be glad, and the upright shall exult, and the pious triumphantly rejoice, while iniquity shall close her mouth, and all wickedness shall be wholly consumed like smoke, when Thou makest the dominion of arrogance to pass away from the earth. And Thou, O Lord, shalt reign alone over all Thy works . . ." During the Middle Ages, Maimonides stressed the lesson of history once again when he wrote in his message of comfort and encouragement to the oppressed Jews of Yemen (*Iggeret Teman*, c. 1172) that, "ever since the time of Revelation, every despot or slave that attained to power has made it his first aim and ultimate purpose to destroy our Law and to vitiate our religion by the sword, by violence, and by brute force . . . Tyranny oppresses us and kings are hard on us, but they cannot destroy us."

The example set by Daniel, the three Hebrews whom Nebuchadnezzar cast into the fiery furnace, and by Hannah and her heroic seven sons was followed by later Jewish apostles of freedom when the armed might of Rome swept over Asia Minor and the Near East. The law which "the Senate and the People of Rome" proclaimed to the ancient world certainly extended privileges to citizens of many ethnic origins, but it was a thoroughly destructive instrument of imperialism. The Romans annihilated every culture which they encountered—Greek, Carthaginian, Celtic, or Germanic—and the boasted unity of their imperium meant the enslavement of a hundred other nations. Not a single architectural monumant of Greek or Semitic civilization escaped the intolerant fire of Roman tyranny. When the Emperor Caligula threatened all who refused to acknowledge his divinity with swift death, the Jews stood firm. "It is," Renan averred, "to the eternal glory of the Jews that, in the midst of this ignoble idolatry, they uttered the cry of outraged

Shadrach, Meshach, and Abed-nego cast into the fiery furnace by the Babylonian tyrant. Hovering above them is the archangel Gabriel. A miniature from a 13th century Armenian manuscript.

conscience . . . Alone affirming their religion to be the absolute religion, they would not bend to the odious caprice of the tyrant" (*Les Apôtres*, 1866). Such was the road which they also trod under Vespasian and Hadrian.

Military repression and bureaucratic rapacity finally drove the Jews to open revolt. Their war of survival did not command universal support in Judea, which makes the duration of Jewish resistance all the more remarkable. For the Zealots and their sympathizers, the struggle took on an apocalyptic character as a predicted war against the powers of darkness (Edom or Gog Magog), and their amazing stand against Roman legions hastily flung into the battle from many parts of the Empire had an undisguisedly religious motivation. Josephus, a Pharisee patriot turned quisling, had no love for the ultra-nationalists, but the final section of his *Jewish War* admiringly records the (possibly apocryphal) speech of Eleazar ben Ya'ir calling on besieged Masada's last defenders to seal their resistance with the defiance of suicide: "Long ago we resolved to serve neither the Romans nor anyone else but God, who alone is the true and righteous Lord of men: now the time has come to prove our determination by our deeds . . . we were the first of all to revolt, and we shall be the last to break off the struggle . . ." This desperate response to a brutal and pitiless tyranny—*kiddush ha-Shem* ("sanctification of God's name")—has scarcely a parallel in ancient history; such acts of heroism were emulated by the early Christian martyrs under Nero and they have since inspired countless other "freedom-fighters" in other lands.

Much as Biblical and Rabbinic teaching honored such exemplary resistance and martyrdom, Jewish thought also counselled prudent acceptance of a foreign ruler's laws, so far as conscience allowed. This policy, based on one of the "Noachide Laws" (enjoining respect for established legality), produced the Rabbinic doctrine of *dina de-malkhuta dina* ("the law of the country is binding"). Where such law clashed with his religion, the Jew had to stand by his faith, whatever the cost; yet, in an era of violent, rather than peaceful change, there were some who preferred short-term oppression to the uncertainties of anarchy and political revolution. Kings and governments came to power or passed out of existence at God's pleasure and man should accept this as a natural phenomenon.

EARLY CHRISTIAN PACIFISM

Out of this more passive approach to political reality was born the quietist doctrine of early Christianity. Whereas Judaism wished to establish God's rule on earth, whatever its imperfections, Jesus declared: "My kingdom is not of this world: if my kingdom were of this world, then would my servants fight . . ." (John 18:36; cf. James 4:4). As we have seen previously, some aspects of the "Nazarene" teaching were close to Pharisaic and Rabbinic thought.[39] This is true of Jesus' injunction to "render unto Caesar the things which are Caesar's; and unto God the things that are God's" (Matthew 22:21; cf. Mark 12:17, Luke 20:25), implying that without the indispensable functioning of government the essentials of normal life are ruled out.[40] It is, moreover, also true of Jesus' extension of the Sixth Commandment in the Gospels: "Ye have heard that it was said by them of old time, Thou shalt not kill; and whosoever shall kill shall be in danger of the judgment; But I say unto you, That whosoever is angry with his brother without a cause shall be in danger of the judgment; and whosoever shall say to his brother, Raca, shall be in danger of the council . . ." (Matthew 5:21–22).[41]

Now just as Jesus stressed his differences with other Jewish teachers on matters relating to "light" and "weighty" precepts, so was he at pains to demonstrate his negation of earthly power, whether Roman or Jewish. Hyperbole in speech and nonconformity in practice were the means to this end. At times, he restricted himself to words, as in the parable of the "good Samaritan" and the "man fallen among thieves" (Luke 10:30–35), since he actually shared the common prejudice against the heretical Samaritan sect (Matthew 10:5–6). Much the same was true of his attitude toward the Romans and their Jewish collaborators. Thus, while he aroused popular controversy by eating in the

---

[39] See the section on Christianity and the Bible in Chapter 1.
[40] Cf. the Rabbinic views mentioned earlier, notably the maxim of Ḥanina. Paul was later to advise that one "render to all their dues: tribute to whom tribute is due . . . fear to whom fear; honor to whom honor" (Romans 13:7).
[41] Here, in Matthew's Gospel, *raka* ("Raca") is the colloquial Aramaic for "scoundrel," and the "council" means the Sanhedrin. Cf. the Talmudic admonitions, "Throw yourself into a blazing furnace rather than shame a neighbor in public" (*Berakhot,* 43b) and "Shaming another in public is like shedding blood" (*Bava Meẓia,* 58b).

company of "publicans" and sinners (Matthew 9:10–11; cf. 11:19), declared that "publicans" and harlots would enter the kingdom of God before the priests and Pharisees (Matthew 21:31–32), and told a parable unfavorably contrasting a Pharisee with yet another "publican" (Luke 18:9–14), Jesus nevertheless maintained that an incorrigible sinner should be treated "as an heathen man and a publican" (Matthew 18:17). There is much significance attached to this term, "publican," the real meaning of which is "tax-collector," not least perhaps because the Gospel–writer Matthew was himself such an official (Matthew 10:3). Above all, the issue of Roman tax-farming and tax-collection in Judea exposed the essentials of the "Nazarene" doctrine of non-resistance to evil. Jesus opposed armed revolt against the foreign tyrant, believing that the kingdom of God could not be hastened by violence. This was an idealistic political line at a time when, in Rome and its overseas empire, Tiberius was making cruelty and oppression *the* system of government. It is true that certain Rabbis also favored the "line of least resistance" under the Romans, stressing the purifying effect of persecution—"Belong ever to the persecuted rather than to the per-secutors" (Abbahu in *Bava Kamma,* 93a); "He who has never been persecuted is not a Jew" (Rav in *Hagigah,* 5a);—while others warned that "God adjured Israel not to rebel against the governments" (Yose ben Hanina in *Ketuvot,* 111a). But there was no unanimity, and Rabbi Akiva, as we have seen, later supported the ill-fated revolt of Bar Kokhba. Jesus, on the other hand, not only said "blessed are they which are persecuted for righteousness' sake" (Matthew 5:10), but also demanded that his followers "resist not evil" (Matthew 5:39).[42]

This "Nazarene" doctrine was not calculated to gain wide support among a population daily subject to the insults and felonies of Roman officials, Jewish informers, and pagan mercenaries. For Jesus preached something less than passive resistance to the foreign tyrant—"turning the other cheek" to his hated tax-collectors (Matthew 5:39) and patient acceptance of any other indignities to which the oppressed Jewish peasant was exposed, as a careful reading of the Sermon on the Mount

---

[42] Cf. also his admonition that "all they that take the sword shall perish with the sword" (Matthew 26:52). Within the Jewish community Jesus was less pacific, however, as when he drove the money-changers out of the Temple (John 2:14–16).

will reveal (Matthew 5:38–48; cf. Luke 6:27–35). Hermann Gunkel was one modern Christian scholar who drew attention to the striking contrast between the Weltanschauung of Judaism and of early Christianity: "When the gigantic Roman Empire was endeavoring to wean its provinces from all independent political action . . . the only message of the New Testament is subjection to the State . . . There is a different message in the Old Testament . . . a magnificent combination of piety and patriotism." The Jews, he noted, "felt most deeply the fate of their nation and took part with all their might in public affairs in the name of their God" (*Was bleibt vom Alten Testament*, 1916).

Paul's elaboration of the teachings of Jesus emphasized that "the powers that be are ordained of God" and that "whosoever therefore resisteth the power, resisteth the ordinance of God," for which reason "they that resist shall receive to themselves damnation" (Romans 13:1–2). The Christian doctrine of non-resistance to evil, which has to some extent inspired the philosophy of pacifism, takes its authority from sources in both the Hebrew Bible and the New Testament. From the former this doctrine finds justification in a misguided interpretation of the Sixth Commandment (not to "kill"), in the idea that God warns men that "vengeance is Mine, and recompense" (Deut. 32:35), and in the view of Jesus as the "Prince of Peace" foretold in Scripture (Isa. 9:5). From the latter it quotes the injunctions to love one's enemies and pray for the persecutor (Matthew 5:44), the notion that the kingdom to which Jesus laid claim "is not of this world" and that his servants do not fight (John 18:36), and the Pauline exhortation to "overcome evil with good" (Romans 12:21). In practice, however, this idealistic doctrine did not always stand up to the pressures of historical circumstance. The thousands of Christian martyrs who perished in Roman arenas as witnesses for their faith certainly entered a glorious fellowship of death with the Jews who "sanctified God's name"; but once Constantine made Christianity the official religion of the Empire self-sacrifice of this kind was more rarely demanded. The political interests of the Church actually made resistance to tyranny a far less praiseworthy course of action.

In medieval Europe, Christian heretics and non-Christian "infidels" shared the same fate under tyrannical overlords who conveniently forgot the injunction and the example of Jesus of Nazareth. "By the torture prolonged from age to age . . . By the badge of shame, by the felon's place,/ By the branding tool, by the bloody whip,/ And the summons to Christian fellowship"[43] new despots (both secular and spiritual) mocked the teachings of "good will to all men." Popes fought Emperors, kings and princes levied their mercenaries and conscripts against each other, and the feudal system ensured that the wretched peasant drained the bitter draft of servitude and oppression so generously meted out by his suzerain. The *droit du seigneur* ("right of the overlord") enslaved the body and soul of each subject and the *jus primae noctis* ("law of the first night") dishonored a bride before her wedding night, trampling on human dignity and moral responsibility. There is great significance, therefore, in the fact that the first major rebellion against the social iniquities of the Middle Ages had both economic and religious roots.[44] The Peasants' Revolt which almost overturned England's established order in 1381 was led by Wat Tyler, a charismatic populist, and John Ball, a Lollard preacher inspired by the reformist ideas of John Wycliffe. The text for Ball's sermon at the outbreak of the revolt was at once Biblical and democratic: "When Adam delved and Eve span,/ Who was then the gentleman?" Tyler was assassinated and Ball drawn and quartered, but within a year there were other popular uprisings in Florence, Ghent, and Paris. However, armed rebellion made little headway for another century and a half.

REFORMATION PROTEST AND THE QUESTION OF OBEDIENCE

It is a popular fallacy that the leaders of the Reformation, standing foursquare on a rediscovered "Hebrew truth," gave the signal for Protestantism's revolt against State, as well as Church, authority. Martin Luther was a practitioner of *Reapolitik*, first pinning his hopes on the German Emperor, then turning to the princes and city-oligarchs. The common people played only a minor part in his political calculations.

[43] Citation from Robert Browning's poem, "Holy Cross Day" (1855).

[44] History knows of several earlier revolts against tyranny: those of the Carthaginian mercenaries in the third century B.C.E., the Roman slaves led by Spartacus two centuries later, and the Swiss against their Hapsburg overlords nearly 100 years before the English Peasants' Revolt. William Tell, the legendary Swiss hero, has become a symbol of independence and valor among small nations. But the two ancient rebellions were lacking in ideology and that of the Swiss, though ultimately successful, had more basis in nationalism than morality; any Biblical inspiration in the saga of William Tell owes more to Schiller's classic drama than to the facts of history.

Indeed, when the German Peasants' Revolt broke out in the early 1520s, Luther advised his feudal supporters to butcher the insurgents, for fear that such rebellion would shatter the secular power. Paul, whom Luther admiringly followed, had laid down that resistance to that power amounted to the denial of God. Thus, when the radical movement of Anabaptism also swept Germany, Lutherans and Catholics joined forces against the theocratic anarchy which John of Leyden and his Anabaptist followers briefly established at Münster. Lutheranism tended to deify the authority of any ruler who embraced the Evangelical faith and, after the Thirty Years' War of 1618–1648, made its peace with the Imperial doctrine of *cuius regio, eius religio* ("a man's religion accords with the ruler's"). Yet the Anabaptists were far closer to the original doctrine of Jesus, maintaining that Christians had no right to brandish the sword, even in self-defense.

Calvin was no more of a revolutionary than Luther, although the implications of his *Institute of the Christian Religion* (1536) were more ambiguous. The theocracy which he labored to build in Geneva supervised the life of the community, subordinating the magistrate's authority to the word of God as the Reformer interpreted it; but it was the business of government to suppress heresy by force, if need be, as in the condemnation and burning of Servetus (an anti-Trinitarian) in 1553. Calvin firmly opposed resistance to kings and civil administration, if lawfully elected, provided these did not confront subjects with a clear-cut choice between apostasy and rebellion. However tyrannically princes and civil authorities might act, they were responsible to God alone and the injustice which they committed was, perhaps, an ordained chastisement of the people. Yet Calvin did admit that God had sometimes intervened to free His people from oppression, either through the agency of foreign powers or through the call of Moses and other "avenging prophets" —a significant admission in an age when the prophet's role was still very much of a reality. In the 1559 edition of his *Institute* (iv, 20), the Genevan Reformer specifically alluded to the prophet Daniel's refusal to obey the godless edict of Darius (Dan. 6:5ff.), because that king had "virtually abnegated his power" by exalting his horn against the Lord*("et en ce faisant s'estoit demis et degrade de toute authorite")*. Calvin certainly made it clear that this disobedience was only passive (Daniel being thrown into the lions' den) and presumably meant that only this particular edict called for limited resistance; but the implication was not lost on his followers. The ambiguity of Calvin's statement may have been occasioned by John Knox's *Appellation* of 1558 (a prelude to the outbreak of Protestant rebellion in Scotland)[45] and by the impending political crisis in France: in face of these developments the Reformer was conceivably wavering on the question of justifiable resistance to a persecuting ruler. In any case, Calvinists everywhere thereafter believed that a resort to arms was authorized by their religious leadership.

The fragmentation of Germany and Italy into comparatively small, warring states or principalities and the intolerant autocracy of Spain left only England and France to theorize and experiment in government during the 16th and 17th centuries. Under François I, political thinkers began to favor a strong central regime anchored in the king's absolute authority As Calvinism gained strength in France, however, religious conflict delayed the implementation of this process. The enlightened French chancellor, Michel de l'Hôpital, advocated a constitutional monarchy on the Biblical pattern and both Huguenots and Catholics sought Scriptural justification for their rival views of kingship. The St. Bartholomew Massacre of 1572 turned the Calvinists against absolutism and their pamphleteers proclaimed that a tyrannical king who, like Charles IX, treacherously massacred his subjects might justly be deposed or even assassinated. Jean Bodin's *Six livres de la république* (1576), inspired by Platonic and Biblical notions of government, only maintained the right of disobedience in the event that a king rejected God's laws; armed revolt was strictly forbidden. On the other hand, a Divine right of rebellion was formulated in *Vindiciae contra tyrannos* (1578)—a work attributed to the Huguenot leader Philippe de Mornay (Duplessis-Mornay)—and this theory was to influence English political thinkers of the following century. As the French Wars of Religion tore the realm apart, Calvinist propaganda and the zealotry of the ultra-Catholic League made monotonous use of Biblical injunctions and admonitions about kingship. The moderate center party of the *Politiques*, one of whose spokesmen was the great essayist Montaigne, expressed doubts as to whether either Rome or Geneva could claim a monopoly of truth and became skeptical of any attempt to model the State on ideas drawn from the plain text of the Bible.

Two important factors motivated the emerging alliance of *Politiques* and Huguenots: the reckless program of the League, which preferred

---

[45] See below.

the domination of Spain to the rule of a French Protestant king and the paramount authority of the Pope to an independent French Catholic Church;[46] and the Huguenots' realization that their champion, Henry of Navarre, would sooner or later succeed to the throne. By about 1590, the old positions had been reversed: the Leaguers were now prepared to throw the French monarchy overboard, while the Huguenots (and their allies) pragmatically abandoned the slogans of the *Vindiciae* and eagerly embraced the prospect of royal absolutism. William Barclay, an expatriate Scotsman, worked out the doctrine of the Divine right of kings in his *De Regno et Regali Potestate* ("On Kingship and the Royal Authority," 1600), asserting secular authority's origin in the will of God as outlined in hackneyed passages of the Bible and New Testament. No legitimate monarch could be regarded as a tyrant, unless he could be proved insane, and no popular assembly could lawfully depose a king who—even if excommunicated by the Pope— must still be obeyed by his subjects. Barclay's theory, which became dominant in France under Henri IV, was both religious and utilitarian: since the sovereign's right was Divine, it must be grounded in law and the duty to God. The political interpretation of this theory under Louis XIV in fact negated the *Divine* right of the monarch and was responsible for the decline of responsible government under the Bourbons.

Whereas French national sentiment worked in favor of a Catholic absolutism, English political theory was entirely bound up with the Protestant cause. Under Henry VIII, that erstwhile "defender of the [Catholic] faith," no one as yet questioned the subject's duty to obey the king, William Tyndale even affirming that "he that judgeth the king judgeth God; and he that resisteth the king resisteth God and damneth God's law and ordinance" (*The Obedience of a Christian Man*, 1528).[47] The English Protestants saw in the monarchy a bulwark against their national and religious enemies (Catholic in both cases) and, until the last years of the Elizabethan era, the Puritans, too, laid no claim to Divine sanction for any revolt against the established order. The only rebellion against a system of government devised by God was that implicit in the claims of the Papacy, according to the arguments of

---

[46] "Gallicanism"—French Catholic opposition to Papal suzerainty—was a powerful current in 17th-century France.
[47] Cf. Romans 13:1ff.

Tyndale and others who defended royal supremacy in the "Very and True Commonweal" of Tudor England. Despite vigorous Catholic opposition, popular opinion rallied to the belief that Henry VIII's assumption of power as titular head of the English Church merely renewed the ancient prerogatives of the crown, which the Popes had unlawfully usurped. This union of Church and State, which still remains a feature of the English constitutional system, was firmly established under Queen Elizabeth. However, by the time James I succeeded to the throne in 1603, the practical results of royal supremacy had alienated Puritans as well as Catholics, and the seeds of rebellion—leading to the Catholic Gunpowder Plot (1605) and to the downfall of Charles I (1649)—had been well and truly sown.

THE PURITAN REVOLT AND ITS AFTERMATH

The earliest rebellion against the existing social and political order was, as we have seen, that of the German peasants, whose example was followed a decade later by the Anabaptists. When Protestantism, in its turn, began settling accounts with earthly rulers, the first insurrection was at Magdeburg, where the Lutherans—repudiating the quietism of their late shepherd—turned to armed revolt. Their *Bekenntnis* ("Confession") of 1550 denounced any ruler seeking to destroy true religion as an agent of Satan and called on the German princes to defend their common Evangelical faith against the mounting attacks of the Emperor. However, once Charles V's attempt to root out Protestantism had failed, the Lutherans quickly discarded their revolutionary doctrine of a Divine right of rebellion, which was then taken over and applied with greater force by the French and Scottish Calvinists.

It has often been asserted that the early Protestant defenders of civil liberty derived their political principles mainly from the Hebrew Bible, while the champions of despotism took theirs from the New Testament. Although this claim is not entirely justified by the facts of history, it does fairly reflect trends of thought among the doctrinal Puritans. In Scotland, John Knox and his followers frequently used the analogy of the Hebrew Prophets to justify the defense of liberty and the right of rebellion against human authority. Thus, in a letter written in 1554, Knox declared: "The Prophet of God sometimes may teach treason against kings, and yet neither he, nor such as obey the word spoken in the Lord's name by him, offends God." In *The First*

Blast of the Trumpet against the Monstrous Regiment of Women (1558) Knox invoked Scriptural authority and the "laws of nature" in a furious attack on the right of female succession to the throne. For men to recognize the rule of a woman was unnatural; and the reign of a queen amounted to rebellion against God. Thus, England's Mary Tudor, that "cursed Jezebel," was no lawful sovereign but the means whereby her country was to be handed over to the arch-enemy, Catholic Spain; while Scotland's Mary Stuart, the "Roman harlot" (as he was later to defame her), was plotting to surrender her realm to Catholic France. In his *Appellation* (1558), an appeal against his condemnation by "the false Bishops and Clergie of Scotland," Knox went further still, asserting that the Book of Deuteronomy made it an absolute religious duty for the true Christian to take arms against an idolatrous ruler. Indiscreet royal love affairs added fuel to the flames of Calvinist wrath and, by 1567, Mary Queen of Scots could no longer oppose the movement of national self-determination which united the Scottish nobility and commoners against her. Mary's execution for treasonable activities, fearfully decreed by Queen Elizabeth in 1587, was a grave and momentous historical precedent.

England in the late 16th century was a haven of comparative peace, and the Elizabethan idealization of monarchy was dramatically portrayed in the hero of Shakespeare's *Henry V* ("we are no tyrant, but a Christian king"). The political crisis that faced the Scots in the 1550s did not confront their coreligionists south of the border for another 70 years. For the first time, however, the conflict was within Protestantism, though between two opposing philosophies of life and government. Economic as well as political factors played their part in the clash between Charles I and Parliament, just as Archbishop Laud's "reformed" Anglicanism and Puritanism's "Old Testament" conscience battled against each other in the issue of the Divine right of kings and the right to representative government. Apart from Laud, Charles I had a compliant servant in Thomas Wentworth, the Earl of Strafford, who for eleven "years of tyranny" after Parliament's Petition of Rights (1628) seemed bent on applying Richelieu's autocratic methods to the governing of England. Charles' genuine belief in his own Divine authority smacked of Louis XIV's despotism as the *Roi soleil* ("Sun King"); and Puritan suspicions were heightened by the fact that the queen, Henrietta Maria, was a Bourbon. The Scots revolt against episcopalian control in the Church; the signing of the National Covenant of Scottish allegiance to the reformed (Calvinist) faith with its declaration of war on the king; and the stormy sessions of Parliament culminating in the royal attempt to arrest the "five members" were decisive milestones in Puritan resistance to the king's authority. "In just the same manner as the oppression of Israel by the Court of Samaria had been against God's expressed will, so (imagined the Puritans of the 17th century) they were fulfilling the desire of God when they fought against arbitrary government. Elijah's reproof of tyranny on the part of Ahab applied no less (they considered) to the unconstitutional attempts of Charles I. They read an indictment of the Star Chamber in the thunderings of Amos, and found that Ship Money was condemned implicitly in the episode of Naboth's vineyard. The Bible, moreover, was in diametrical opposition to the idea of the Divine descent of kings, which was at the basis of primitive absolutism."[48] John Milton expressed his fellow Puritans' uncompromising devotion to the Bible when he declared that "there are no songs comparable to the songs of Zion; no orations equal to those of the prophets; and no politics like those which the Scriptures teach."

In the Civil War which broke out in 1642, Cromwell's New Model Army with its Psalm-singing Ironsides brought the moral fervor of the extreme Puritans into the battle, although the more moderate Presbyterians were at first disposed to reach some agreement with King Charles. This increasingly became a holy war of the righteous servants of the Lord God of Hosts executing judgment on the heathen enemies of the Divine Avenger. After his defeat at Naseby in 1645, the king sought refuge among the Scots, who promptly handed their Stuart kinsman and doctrinal foe over to Parliament. Yet though he had forfeited popular sympathy by his autocratic conduct, Charles achieved something like the status of a martyr when he was condemned and executed in 1649. For the first time in modern history, the "Anointed of the Lord" had been put to death and this act horrified the religious and social conscience of the age. In theory, the Divine right of rebellion was all very well, but its practical outcome was not to the liking of most Englishmen. Great though Cromwell's services were to the English nation and to the international Protestant cause (the Duke of Savoy's persecution of the Italian Waldenses ended at one threatening sign from the Lord Protector), royalist sentiment steadily revived during the 1650s. By the time the dead monarch's son was welcomed back from

[48] Cecil Roth, *The Jewish Contribution to Civilization* (1956), p. 9.

France and enthroned as Charles II, England was heartily sick of the Republican experiment with its combined tyranny of Puritan extremism and military rule. But the Commonwealth had effected one sweeping change, which the English thereafter jealously maintained: the fundamental right to free political expression and constitutional government. These hard-won liberties no one was prepared to surrender. It is symbolic of Parliament's triumph over royal despotism that, until the German bombing of World War II, British MPs proudly showed visitors the dents which Charles I's men-at-arms had made long before on the locked door of the House of Commons when the king sought to arrest his opponents—and the place outside where, from the Restoration onward, the royal messenger was obliged to halt when he humbly invited the Commons to hear the speech from the throne in the House of Lords.

Reverberations of English Puritanism's successful campaign against despotism were felt throughout the civilized world during the next 150 years. P ilosophers of the 18th century pondered the implications of regicide and the virtues of republican government, while more practical minds across the Atlantic applied the lessons of the Cromwellian era to the problems raised by King George's administration in the North American colonies. "Calvinism was not merely a discipline but a self-discipline . . . it believed in committees, in the rule of law, in constitutional organs . . . From the stifling parade-grounds of presbytery and synod, Sea Beggar and Huguenot, Puritan and Covenanter marched out to battlefields where at least some of the great issues of human freedom lay at stake."[49] The Hebraic conception of a tripartite agreement between God, His people, and the ruler—which lay behind the triumph of constitutional government in mid-17th-century England —was taken over by the fathers of the American Revolution, for whom the language and teachings of the Hebrew Bible were as inspiring and relevant as they had been for the Pilgrim Fathers in the New England colonies. Benjamin Franklin and his fellow revolutionaries were imbued with Hebraic concepts stemming from the Covenant doctrines of the early American settlers. "It was Hebraic mortar (to quote a famous phrase) that cemented the foundations of the Republic; and not without reason did the first seal it adopted depict the overthrow of Pharaoh in the Red Sea, with the motto: 'Rebellion to Tyrants is Obedience

---

[49] A. G. Dickens, *Reformation and Society* (1966), p. 180.

to God.'...."[50] In 1789, the American example was followed by the French revolutionaries, who issued their Declaration of the Rights of Man and of the Citizen and who, in 1793, executed their own king, Louis XVI; but a deistic philosophical background, unlinked to the Bible, here led to the Reign of Terror which far surpassed the worst excesses of Bourbon rule. The conceptions of 1642 and 1776 inspired the rise of parliamentary government in many countries throughout the 19th century and, even today, still need to be applied in those states enslaved by totalitarianism.

The 20th century has seen the emergence of tyrannies far worse than any royal despotisms of the past. Millions of people have been repressed, brainwashed, or "liquidated" by regimes which made a god of the dictator and his State apparatus—Fascist Italy with its *Duce*, Nazi Germany with its *Führer*, and the gigantic Communist empires of Russia and China with their Stalinist and Maoist idols. Instances of determined resistance to these grim new imperialisms are instructive history, sometimes melancholy (Czechoslovakia and Tibet), sometimes glorious (Abyssinia and Finland). In the presidency of Charles de Gaulle, the French war chief turned politician, a mystical identification of State and self and glimmerings of the old belief in a Divine right to rule may even be detected. The underground and partisan movements of World War II, the Finnish people's stand against the USSR in 1939–40, and the Warsaw Ghetto uprising of 1943 were all of them inspiring and dramatic examples of resistance to tyranny. The Hebrew belief that despotism and its associated evils constituted a challenge to man's instinct for justice and freedom was allied to the conviction that no oppressor was immortal and that all tyranny would ultimately perish. The poet Shelley's lines recalling the sculpted admonition of a forgotten tyrant —"My name is Ozymandias, king of kings:/ Look on my works, ye mighty, and despair!"—may thus be placed in the ironic tradition of the Prophets, who boldly mocked the despot's pride that would surely be succeeded by his fall:

> Is this the man that made the earth to tremble,
> That did shake kingdoms;
> That made the world as a wilderness,

[50] Roth, *op. cit.*, pp.9–10. This first design (by Thomas Jefferson) was not definitive; its motto is a quotation from Oliver Cromwell.

And destroyed the cities thereof;
That opened not the house of his prisoners? . . .
But thou art cast forth . . .
Because thou hast destroyed thy land,
Thou hast slain thy people;
The seed of evil-doers shall not
Be named for ever . . . (Isa. 14:16–20).

DEMOCRACY AND OTHER POLITICAL PHILOSOPHIES

The ancient Greeks evolved their concept of *dēmokratia* (popular or majority government) through the conclusions of their philosophers; the Hebrews were imbued with the idea that the common people were party to a social and political contract deriving from God's covenants with the Patriarchs and with Moses and the congregation of Israel. The unity of God, of the world, and of mankind found a parallel in one single moral code to which all men were subject, and from this the Prophets and Rabbis deduced their notion of an inherent right to freedom and social justice. The Bible itself was a social, as well as a religious, document for all time, "proclaiming liberty" to Israel and mankind as a whole. Democracy in its modern sense thus owes its origin both to the Greeks and to the Hebrews; for this amalgamation of popular sovereignty and the rule of law stems from the Biblical conception of a "kingdom of priests" as well as from Plato's *Republic* and Aristotle's *Politics*.

A quotation from the Book of Zechariah (7:9) provides the caption for an English cartoon by Vicky (Victor Weisz) following the capture of Adolf Eichmann, the Nazi war criminal, in 1960.

"THUS SPEAKETH THE LORD OF HOSTS, SAYING, EXECUTE TRUE JUDGMENT AND SHEW MERCY . . ."

Early Christianity's rather negative attitude toward earthly government found expression in Augustine's *De Civitate Dei* which maintained that man's worldly rule was more a "state of the devil" than the "City of God." Although this view persisted throughout the Middle Ages, Thomas Aquinas led the way toward modern concepts of democracy when he emphasized, in the 13th century, that the people had a sovereign right to restrict or abolish royal power, if it were abused. Dante, Machiavelli, and Bodin promoted the new political thinking of the later Middle Ages and the Renaissance, while the Calvinists of the 16th century and the Natural Law philosophers of the 17th century took a more radical—sometimes revolutionary—line, based on the notion of an original covenant or social contract by which individuals joined together and formed a state by mutual agreement. This idea of Covenant has, of course, a Biblical basis, reflected in the English reformer John Wycliffe's preface to his translation of the Scriptures (1384): "The Bible is for the government of the people, by the people, and for the people." In his *Tractatus Theologico-Politicus* (1670), a rationalist critique of revealed religion coupled with a plea for religious and intellectual freedom, Benedict (Baruch) Spinoza asserted that democracy was "of all forms of government the most natural, and the most consonant with individual liberty. In it no one transfers his natural right so absolutely that he has no further voice in affairs; he only hands it over to the majority of a society, whereof he is a unit. Thus all men remain, as they were in the state of nature, equals." Foreshadowing the views of later champions of the democratic ideal, Spinoza also maintained that "the ultimate aim of government is . . . to free every man from fear, that he may live in all possible security," since the true aim of proper government is liberty.

THE AMERICAN EXPERIMENT

Over 2,000 years after the Covenant of Deuteronomy (27:14–26), when the Israelites signified their consent ("Amen") to the theocratic system of Moses, the Pilgrim Fathers rediscovered and transmitted the Bible's social contract in their Mayflower Compact (1620): "We . . . doe by these presents solemnly and mutually in ye presence of God, and of one another, covenant and combine our selves togeather into a civill body politick" in order to frame "just and equall lawes." Since these refugee Puritans saw their new religious society as a "continuation and extension of the Jewish church," they held their responsibility to be not to kings or bishops but to God Himself. These "new Israelites" had been led into their Promised Land from Egyptian bondage in England and they firmly believed that the Prophets spoke as much to them as they had to the Hebrews of old. Their first Thanksgiving celebration (1621) was more a Jewish fast and day of prayer than the traditional festivity of modern times; in the nature of his authority their elder or minister was more like a Rabbi than an Anglican priest; and their Sabbath observance and church practice found a model in what they knew of Jewish ceremonial from the Bible. In civil and ecclesiastical government the will of the majority was law, and even trial by jury was rejected as having no Scriptural basis and precedent. The Mosaic Law was adopted in the Connecticut Code of 1650 and half of the statutes in the Code of the New Haven Colony (1655) refer to the "Old" Testament.

As yet, however, New England was a theocratic and republican society, not a democracy in the modern sense of the term. Even after more liberal views began to prevail, the Bible was law for Scottish Presbyterian settlers and, in times of stress, days of prayer and fasting were proclaimed on the basis of Scriptural texts (e.g., 1 Sam. 23:3–4). The dominant Hebraic impulse may also be seen in the Hebraism of Cotton Mather, who wrote that the conduct of magistrates should be *"Beàhavah Veyirah, cum mansuetudine ac Timore"* ("motivated by love and fear of God"). In time, practical considerations led New Englanders to modify their type of government, abandoning theocratic rigidity for a more workable and egalitarian system. The 18th-century colonies were, in fact, closer to the Biblical model and example than the old Puritan commonwealth had been. For this, much credit is due to Roger Williams of Providence, whose vision of a free republic was grounded in liberty of conscience ("forced worship stincks in God's nostrils"). Unlike most of his Puritan contemporaries, Williams showed practical tolerance toward the Jews and his denial of the Massachusetts Bay Colony's "right" to appropriate Indian lands first led this Salem pastor to seek refuge elsewhere and to found the more democratic society of Rhode Island.

In Europe, meanwhile, the theorists of democracy had become political pacemakers in monarchical (though constitutional) England and in a more autocratically monarchical France. In his *Two Treatises on Government* (1689), John Locke recapitulated some of the ideas which the Pilgrim Fathers and Roger Williams had already translated into practice with their doctrine of a social covenant entered into by mutual consent. But Locke argued against the Divine right of kings and blind obedience to the Church and Biblical authority, maintaining that political sovereignty rested on the subject's will and consent. Aware that "new opinions are always suspected, and usually opposed . . . because they are not already common" (*An Essay on Human Understanding*, 1690), he nevertheless advocated complete freedom of thought and speech in his *Letter concerning Toleration* (1689): "Neither Pagan nor Mahometan nor Jew ought to be excluded from the civil rights of the Commonwealth because of his religion." The growing belief in an original "State of Nature" in which all men had enjoyed equal reciprocal rights was eloquently expressed by Jean-Jacques Rousseau, the spiritual father of 18th-century political idealism. Rousseau's conception of popular sovereignty was much more democratic than that of his English predecessors and involved the idea of a "general will" in which each individual had a rightful share. After proclaiming his republican and democratic sympathies in the *Discours sur l'origine de l'inégalité parmi les hommes* (1753), Rousseau mounted his campaign against despotism and privilege with a series of famous works, notably *Le Contrat social* (1762), which revived and broadened the old Puritan doctrine of Covenant, beginning with the celebrated pronouncement: *"L'homme est né libre, et partout il est dans les fers"* ("Man is born free, and everywhere he is in chains").

Abhorrence of monarchy was a focal point of political agitation in Massachusetts throughout the 17th and 18th centuries, largely under the impact of European social doctrine and the hard experience of native radicals. Preaching on the repeal of the Stamp Act in 1766, Jonathan Mayhew of Boston gave a contemporary significance to the prophet Samuel's reservations about kingship: "God gave Israel a king (or an absolute monarch) in his anger, because they had not sense enough and virtue enough to live like a free commonwealth, to have Himself for their king . . ." Biblical sources again played an important part in determining political attitudes during the fateful years 1775–6, as the draft Seal of the United States (which Franklin and Jefferson devised) amply reveals.[51] The spirit of the Hebrew Scriptures also found a resounding echo in the American Declaration of Independence, which affirmed the duty of the government to uphold the Right, as ordained

[51] See above.

by Divine Law. The preamble to Thomas Jefferson's original draft, though slightly modified in the definitive Declaration, thus proclaimed that "We hold these truths to be sacred and undeniable; that all men are created equal and independent, that from that equal creation they derive rights inherent and inalienable, among which are the preservation of life, and liberty, and the pursuit of happiness." The U.S. Constitution, quoting the Declaration of Independence, stresses that "governments are not laws unto themselves, that they can not create right, that they are accountable to a Higher Power," and that men "are endowed by their Creator" with "unalienable rights." So it was that the U.S. Bill of Rights (1789) had its roots in the old Puritan idea of a "solemn agreement of the people," which was in turn based on the ancient Biblical notion of Covenant.

ENGLAND AND FRANCE

How deeply even conservative politicians in England were affected by the events in America may be gauged from Edmund Burke's speech on conciliation with the rebellious colonists (March 22, 1775): "I do not know the method of drawing up an indictment against a whole people," he declared; "a nation is not governed, which is perpetually to be conquered." When, however, the successful revolt of the Thirteen Colonies was followed by the bloody excesses of the French Revolution, Burke (and most Englishmen) took a distinctly hostile line. The outbreak of the "swinish multitude" against the rule of law and order was not a popular expression of the call for democracy and representative government, but a descent into evil; and "kings will be tyrants from policy when subjects are rebels from principle" (*Reflections on the Revolution in France,* 1790). Burke nevertheless voiced the new ideas of the age when he declared in a speech of 1794 that "there is but one law for all, namely, that law which governs all law, the law of our Creator, the law of humanity, justice, equity—the law of nature, and of nations." There was a sound basis for this careful distinction between the two great 18th-century revolts: that of the Americans was a protest motivated by Biblical and humanitarian considerations; that of the French by doctrines which substituted the worship of Reason for belief in a benevolent Creator, and which proclaimed the "religion of humanity." Democracy was, however, now taking a more radical direction outside France as well: while Tom Paine found a more congenial home in revolutionary France, where he wrote *The Rights of Man* and joined the National Convention, the Scots poet Robert Burns vigorously attacked all hereditary privilege, seeing real nobility in "the pith o' sense, an' pride o' worth," and predicting that "It's coming yet, for a' that,/ That man to man the world o'er/ Shall brothers be for a' that."

The French revolutionary slogan, "Liberty, Equality, Fraternity," no less than the English and American ideals, has inspired democratic action throughout the 19th and 20th centuries. But it has had varied fruits—promoting both the Social Democracy of the liberal West and the "People's Democracies" of the Marxist East. The "Anglo-Saxon" democratic experiments, for all their imperfections, have still afforded the most enduring and practical opportunity for liberty of speech and thought, despite George Bernard Shaw's snide comment that "democracy substitutes election by the incompetent many for appointment by the corrupt few." The American Civil War was, after all, substantially a conflict between human dignity and slavery, as Abraham Lincoln made clear in his Gettysburg Address (Nov. 19, 1863): "Four score and seven years ago our fathers brought forth, upon this continent, a new nation, conceived in Liberty, and dedicated to the proposition that all men are created equal . . ." His conclusion repeated, almost word for word, Wycliffe's stirring declaration of five centuries before, elaborated in the prayer "that this nation, under God, shall have a new birth of freedom; and that government of the people, by the people, for the people, shall not perish from the earth." Though undenominational in his Christian faith, Lincoln was well aware that the American libertarian tradition drew largely from the Bible-reading habits of the first settlers—or, as President Andrew Jackson reputedly confessed, that "that book . . . is the rock on which our republic rests." Nearer our own time, Franklin D. Roosevelt also alluded to the Scriptural foundations of American democracy in a broadcast message of 1935: "We cannot read the history of our rise and development as a nation, without reckoning with the place the Bible has occupied in shaping the advances of the Republic . . . where we have been truest and most consistent in obeying its precepts, we have attained the greatest measure of contentment and prosperity . . ."

In Britain, too, powerful Biblical impulses have operated in the political sphere, guiding liberal and democratic aspirations over the past three centuries. Disraeli's great antagonist and fellow premier,

William Ewart Gladstone, who described one European tyranny as "the negation of God erected into a system of government," was conscious of the old social contract idea that linked the 17th-century English Commonwealth with his reformist Liberalism. In a speech delivered in his burgeoning native city, Liverpool (June 28, 1886), he declared that, "all the world over, I will back the masses against the classes." And the British Labour Party theorist Harold Laski stated that "the basis of democratic development is . . . the demand that the system of power be erected upon the *similarities* and not the *differences* between men," believing that "every State is known by the rights it maintains" (*A Grammar of Politics*, 1925). Nonconformism was strong in Gladstonian Liberalism, just as the Christian Socialism of Charles Kingsley and Archbishop William Temple had more to do with the Labour Party's outlook than anything Marx or Engels ever wrote. These were the undercurrents that moved Lord Beveridge, Britain's social insurance pioneer, to write: "The object of government . . . is not the glory of rulers or of races, but the happiness of the common man." In the world of today, those who enjoy the blessings of democracy and of the "Four Freedoms" which President Roosevelt wrote into history[52] do so only because their political systems honor that ancient "covenant with the people" and "proclaim liberty throughout the land unto all the inhabitants thereof" (Lev. 25:10).

SOCIALISM

The belief that the welfare of each individual is the rightful concern of the State and that natural wealth and the means of production are the common heritage of all men long predates the "doctrinaire" Socialism of the 19th century. In a rudimentary form, such "practical" Socialism was operative among the Essenes and early Christians and, as administrative policy, it flourished among the Incas of Peru well before Columbus first set foot in the New World. Although, as Shakespeare observed, "the devil can cite Scripture for his purpose," a welldefined social philosophy is unfolded in the Hebrew Bible; indeed, statements need not be wrenched from their context in order to prove

---

[52] These were enumerated in a speech of Jan. 6, 1941: "Freedom of speech and expression . . . freedom of every person to worship God in his own way . . . freedom from want . . . freedom from fear . . . anywhere in the world."

that "Moses was the first Socialist" or that "the first Christians were the first Communists." Their concern for the building of a more just social order certainly made the Prophets speak in revolutionary terms, but the Socialism which modern ideologists have sometimes discovered in the Bible was not the materialistic doctrine with which we are nowadays familiar; it was rather an intensely religious conviction that human society must respond to the moral imperatives of a benevolent Creator.

With this reservation, it is still true that egalitarian demands for a fairer redistribution of the good things in life have often found direct inspiration in the Biblical word. One reason for Protestantism's immense appeal and doctrinal triumph in Northern Europe was its protest against the landowning interests of the Catholic Church, and the eventual parceling-out of monastic properties seized by the English crown helped to change economic horizons. The Counter-Reformation drove industrious merchants and artisans away from Catholic lands, but modern capitalism (despite the claims of some 20th-century theorists) was no invention of the Calvinists. Indeed, Calvin himself severely limited the taking of interest and explicitly condemned economic exploitation of the poor. More than any other Christian denomination, the Calvinists and Puritans developed a stern religious conscience in social matters and it was from their ranks that some of the outstanding modern social reformers actually emerged.

During World War II, a former editor of *The Church Times* published an anthology of Biblical and New Testament passages tending to confirm the Scriptural roots of humanitarian Socialism.[53] Such statements can be shown to denounce the evils of unfettered capitalism (Ex. 22:24–26; Lev. 25:35–37; Ezek. 18:5–9; Neh. 5:1ff.); to set forth the deceitfulness of wealth (Isa. 5:8–10; Ps. 73:1–12; Job 27:13–23; Ben Sira 21.8; Matthew 6:19–34; Mark 10:23–27; Luke 16:19–31; James 2:1–9); and to champion the cause of the poor (Deut. 15:7–11; 1 Sam. 2:1–9; 2 Sam. 12:1–15; Jer. 5:20–29; Zech. 7:8–9; Ps. 72:1–14, 146; Prov. 22, 28; Job 20; Eccl. 5:7–19). Similar authority can be invoked for the doctrines of human brotherhood and the dignity of labor (Lev. 19:13; Deut. 24:14–15; Jer. 22:13–16; Prov. 29:18–21; Ben Sira 33.30–31; Matthew 25:14–23; John 15:9–15; Ephesians 6:1–9; Colossians 4:1) and for true justice and equity in human relations (Deut. 1:16–17, 27:19; Isa. 10:1–2; Ps. 82:1–4, 145:8–9; Prov. 1:1–4;

[53] Sidney Dark, *The Red Bible* (London, 1942).

Luke 18:1–8; James 2:12–13). Among other texts beloved of religiously motivated Socialists are: "Cast in thy lot among us; let us all have one purse" (Prov. 1:14), "Woe to him that increaseth that which is not his!" (Hab. 2:6), "Sell whatsoever thou hast, and give to the poor" (Mark 10:21), and "It is easier for a camel to go through the eye of a needle, than for a rich man to enter into the kingdom of God" (Matthew 19:24). Many more Jewish and Christian sources can also be made to yield "Socialistic" teachings.

However one may view such interpretation, or exploitation, of Holy Writ, the Bible undoubtedly played an important part in the shaping of modern political attitudes toward social inequality. Saint-Simon, a French aristocrat who fought with Lafayette in the American War of Independence and later supported the French Revolution, was deeply influenced by Jewish Messianism and the Biblical concept of human brotherhood. One of the fathers of humanitarian Socialism, Saint-Simon tried to alleviate the plight of the underprivileged by advocating the redistribution of wealth and power in the interests of all mankind. Prosper Enfantin and other Saint-Simonians believed that Hebrew monotheism foreshadowed the future unity of humanity and their doctrines attracted Jewish supporters as well, including the exiled poet Heinrich Heine, who wrote that "Moses was such a Socialist, though as a practical man he only sought to remodel existing institutions . . . instead of hotheadedly decreeing the abolition of property, Moses only strove for its moral reform," particularly through his introduction of the Jubilee Year (when every alienated heritage reverted to the original owner). "Moses did not want to abolish property. Rather, he wanted everybody to own some, so that poverty should make no man a serf with servile thoughts. Freedom was always the great emancipator's final idea; it flames and breathes in all his laws on pauperism . . ." (*Geständnisse*, 1854).

In Britain, the first practical steps toward the implementation of Socialism were taken by the Welsh reformer Robert Owen, who ran cooperative industrial enterprises during the early 19th century. Though motivated by ideals akin to those of the Continental radicals, British pioneers of the Socialist philosophy were more pragmatic and less doctrinaire. More than any kindred political movement, the Labour Party which first came to power after World War I gave evidence of a strongly religious and Messianic vision, and Britain's first Labour prime minister, James Ramsay MacDonald, paid notable tribute to the Biblical ideal of social justice: "Perhaps no code of national law and custom has observed the balance between group life and individual life more successfully than that of Israel" (*The Socialist Movement*, 1911).

THE QUEST FOR PEACE

Some 3,500 years ago, Israel was compelled to face the realities and implications of man's apparently congenital inability to live at peace with his neighbor. Egypt's new Pharaoh, who "knew not Joseph," suspected that the Hebrews might constitute a "fifth column" for some ambitious foe and therefore resolved to enslave them (Ex. 1:8ff.). The idea that war is "one of the facts of life" certainly dominated Hebrew thinking—there are later echoes of this in the New Testament (Luke 14:31)—but the Bible never romanticizes war's basic inhumanity and disastrous consequences. Indeed, although "all the hosts of the Lord" that left Egypt at the time of the Exodus included 600,000 adult males (Ex. 12:37, 41), God did not lead them directly to the Promised Land through the battlefields of Philistia for fear that the sight of war might create havoc among the newly emancipated slave-people (Ex. 13:17). In fact, it took 40 years of wandering in the desert to prepare the Israelites for the ordeal they would have to face in Canaan and to train a generation capable of overcoming their sworn enemies.

Their successful revolt against the "natural" institution of slavery pitchforked the Israelites into another "natural" state of affairs— perpetual warfare. Since they were obliged to recover the land promised to the Patriarchs, the invading Israelites under Joshua had to fight relentless enemies such as Amalek (Ex. 17:8–16) and wage God's battles against peoples committed to the extinction of the Hebrews. Under the Judges, Saul, and David, new wars of survival were waged against nations who periodically subdued and oppressed the Israelites —from the Philistines and Edomites to the Arameans and desert nomadic tribes (1 Sam. 14:52, 30:1ff., etc.). The Bible subsequently records the many other wars of survival to which Israel was committed in defiance of tyrants whom far more powerful nations could not resist— Shalmaneser, Sennacherib, Nebuchadnezzar—while the Jews of the post-Biblical era braved the Seleucid emperor Antiochus and the war-machine of mighty Rome. From the first, all the odds were against Israel: Gideon and a mere 300 men surprised the hosts of Midian and

Amalek (Judges 7:7); Samson fought the Philistines single-handed (Judges 15:8, 15, 16:30); and David too made light of the overwhelming superiority of Goliath (1 Sam. 17:45–51) when he slew the first of his "ten thousands." Despite the later terms of his lament over Saul and Jonathan, "How are the mighty fallen, and the weapons of war perished!" (2 Sam. 1:27), David knew that it was not his own strength and skill so much as the guiding hand of the Lord that would deliver him from his enemies (1 Sam. 17:37, 45–6). And it was the fact that their battles had Divine sanction and a moral basis which (to the Hebrew mind) alone justified the resort to arms. This was true not only of the wars against Amalek and the Canaanites, but also of those in defense of the Gibeonites (Josh. 10:6–11) and in punishment of Benjamin (Judges 20:8ff.) and Ammon (2 Sam. 10:6–14).

In general, the Biblical view is that war is a judgment, bringing the miseries called forth by sin. King David himself was thus barred from constructing the Temple because he was "a man of war" who shed blood (1 Chron. 28:3; cf. 1 Chron. 22:8). While the Preacher, Koheleth, maintained that there was a time for war as well as a time for peace (Eccl. 3:8), the Psalmist stressed God's hatred for warlike pursuits: "He hath scattered the peoples that delight in war!" (Ps. 68:31). The Hebrew Prophets, above all, looked forward to war's final and total suppression (Isa. 2:4, etc.), and the collapse of Assyria's invading host during the reign of Hezekiah lent weight to the belief that God would make "wars to cease unto the ends of the earth" (Ps. 46:10). Philo observed how "the wars of the Greeks and the barbarians . . . have all flowed from one destructive source—greed, the desire for money, glory, or pleasure"; and, during the Middle Ages, the Spanish Bible commentator Naḥmanides (Moses ben Naḥman) declared that "the self-restraint which Scripture imposed on the children of Israel in regard to Ammon, Moab, and Seir [Deut. 2:5, 9, 19] carries a prohibition against all aggressive war." Thus, while not pacifists, the Jews would never have accepted the cynical Prussian view of Karl von Clausewitz that "war is nothing more than the continuation of politics by other means";[54] they would have agreed with the Union's General Sherman that "its glory is all moonshine" and that "war is hell."

---

[54] Cf. Mao Tse-tung's saying, "Politics is war without bloodshed, while war is politics with bloodshed."

THE MEANING OF *SHALOM*

In Hebrew, the word for "peace" is *shalom*, a term that signifies wholeness and completeness. In this lies more than a suggestion that peace, unlike war, constitutes *the* natural state of affairs and that the "complete" man can only flourish in a "whole(some)" society. The word *shalom* occurs frequently in Scripture, not always in the plain sense of "peace," since it has various nuances. Israel's proclamation of "peace" to a hostile city (Deut. 20:10) was thus a demand for its capitulation. The term can signify the mere absence or cessation of war (2 Kings 20:19; Prov. 16:7; Oba. 1:7); public tranquillity (Ps. 122:7); or a political alliance, as between Jabin and the Kenites (Judges 4:17) and Hiram and Solomon (1 Kings 5:26). "Peace" sometimes also means submission to God's will (Job 22.21), receipt of His grace, as in the Priestly Benediction (Num. 6:26) and the "covenant of peace" with Phinehas (Num. 25:12) and the divided and dispersed Israelites (Ezek. 34:25, 37:26); or a state of "wholeness" or integrity with God and man (Ps. 34:15, 37:37, 119:165, 122:6–8). The Prophets nevertheless warned that unscrupulous men could exploit the term *shalom* in pursuit of their own selfish ends, "saying: 'Peace, peace,' when there is no peace" (Jer. 6:14, 8:11; cf. Ezek. 13:10 and Micah 3:5), for "there is no peace . . . concerning the wicked" (Isa. 48:22).

As an ideal state of human affairs, *shalom* inspired many sublime Prophetic affirmations as to the course of human events. Isaiah foresaw a time "in the end of days" when Torah would "go forth out of Zion" and the peoples of the earth would turn to peaceful pursuits: "Nation shall not lift up sword against nation, neither shall they learn war any more" (2:3–4). This unparalleled vision was explicitly shared by Micah (4:2–3). Isaiah's famous evocation of the Messianic era, when universal peace would govern beasts as well as men (11:6–9), does not employ the term *shalom*; but this word does occur in the prophecy concerning a "Ruler of peace" (9:5–6) and in the portrayal of the state of God's "saints" (57:2). More mundane, Jeremiah bade the Jews "seek the peace of the city" to which they had been transported by their conquerors and pray for it, "for in the peace thereof shall ye have peace" (29:7). The Psalmist related the calm ensuing after a storm to the blessing of *shalom* which the Lord would finally bestow on His people (29:11);[55]

---

[55] The fact that this Psalm is included in the liturgy of the Sabbath also suggests that the Day of Rest brings a spirit of calm after the workaday stress of the week.

and in the pilgrim-songs (or Songs of Ascents) he urges that one "pray for the peace of Jerusalem"—for the prosperity and welfare of its inhabitants and well-wishers (122:6–8)—and himself prays: *Shalom al-Yisra'el* ("Peace be upon Israel," 125:5, 128:6). In the word-play of Ps. 122:6, Jerusalem's very name (*Yerushalayim*, formerly Salem, cf. Gen. 14:18) is emphasized as "the city of Peace." Even Bildad's short speech in the Book of Job reflects the Psalmist's idea of God's transformation of a stormy atmosphere into one of calm and serenity (and also, perhaps, of His pacification of the warring heavenly hosts, cf. Job 21:22, 40:9ff.; Isa. 24:21), since "He maketh peace in His high places" (25:2). *Shalom* also serves as a Biblical greeting or farewell (Gen. 43:23; Ex. 4:18), while it is frequently invoked (in a general sense) by the Psalmist and by Isaiah ("Peace, peace, to him that is far off and to him that is near," 57:19; and in 32:17, 52:7).

For the Rabbis, peace was not only a personal, but also a national ideal. The pursuit of peace was exemplified in the lives of the Patriarchs; Aaron was regarded as the supreme peacemaker; and, in the early part of his reign at least, Solomon lived up to his name (*Shelomo*, "the perfect" or "peaceable one"). The Mishnah records Hillel's famous universalist injunction: "Be of the disciples of Aaron, loving peace and pursuing peace, loving one's fellow men, and drawing them near to the Torah" (*Avot*, 1.12). Two other important Mishnaic statements were that of Rabban Simeon ben Gamaliel, "By three things the world is preserved: by truth, by judgment, and by peace" (*Avot*, 1.18), and one to the effect that "making peace between man and his neighbor" is an act whose "fruits one enjoys in this world" as a prelude to eternal bliss (*Pe'ah*, 1.1). These declarations on peace were no mere pious or conventional generalities, but heartfelt expressions of the Rabbis, longing for concord and security in an era of Roman cruelty, persecution, and military repression. Sectarian conflict heightened this desire for harmony, whether between one nation and another, one city and its neighbor, or between members of the same group or family. "It is written, 'Seek peace and pursue it' [Ps. 34:14]. The Torah does not order you to run after, or pursue, the commandments, but only to fulfill them when the appropriate occasion arises . . . But peace you must seek in your own place, and run after it to another" (Numbers Rabbah, *Ḥukkat*, 19.16). The Rabbis also maintained that, "for the sake of domestic peace, Scripture misquotes" (*Yevamot*, 65b, etc.), and believed that it was the role of the scholar to "increase peace in the world" (*Berakhot*, 64a). Peace is "the essence of all prophecies" and "the climax of all blessings" (*Sifre* to Num. 6:26); "the blessing of the Holy One is peace" (*Megillah*, 18a); and it is even enshrined in the Divine name: "Rabbi Yudan ben Rabbi Yose said: Great is peace, for God's name is peace, as it is said, 'And he called it YHVH-Shalom' [i.e., "the Lord is peace," Judges 6:24] . . . " (Leviticus Rabbah, Zav, ix, 9).[56]

Since the Biblical period, *shalom* has been the salutation used by one Jew to another;[57] today it is a standard greeting in the State of Israel. The term constantly recurs in Jewish liturgy, the Grace after Meals, and in the memorial prayer for the dead (*Kaddish*) as "He who maketh peace in His high places, may He make peace for us and for all Israel; and say ye, Amen."[58] The importance of peace in domestic and communal life was constantly emphasized by the medieval Jewish philosophers; the kabbalists related it to the process whereby man could act as a partner with God in the restoration (*tikkun*) of supernal Harmony (see, for example, Zohar, Lev. 10b); and the 19th-century Hasidic leader Naḥman of Bratslav wrote that "Jerusalem will be rebuilt only through peace" and that, without it, prayers are of no avail (*Sefer ha-Middot*, 1821). Jewish abhorrence of war is reflected in a commentary on Deut. 20:2–4 by Abraham Isaac ha-Kohen Kook, the first Ashkenazi Chief Rabbi of the Holy Land and a notable mystic and Zionist. The office of the priest "anointed for war" was not hereditary, because only peace confers the right to permanence. Thus no priest who functioned in time of war could be granted a hereditary status. In his own career, too, Rabbi Kook was an exemplary "disciple of Aaron," striving to promote good relations between Jews and Gentiles and between opposing Jewish political groups.

"PEACE ON EARTH"

Many of these Prophetic and Rabbinic sentiments about peace were adopted or modified by the early Christians. In his Sermon on the Mount, Jesus (who was later seen as the "Prince of Peace") said: "Blessed are

[56] The Midrash translates Gideon's phrase as "he called the Lord, peace."
[57] Islam borrowed the greeting as *salām,* and this has entered English both as "salaam" and as the popular corruption, "so long!"
[58] An elaboration of Job 25:2.

the peacemakers: for they shall be called the children of God" (Matthew 5:9); and the "good tidings of great joy" which the angel brings at the nativity conclude with two phrases sung by a heavenly chorus: "Glory to God in the highest, and on earth peace, good will toward men" (Luke 2:14). The words are based both on the *Kedushah* ("Sanctification") recited by Levites in the Temple and by cantor and congregation in the synagogue (from Isa. 6:3; cf. Ezek. 3:12) and on the ancient meditation from Job mentioned above. There is an echo of this in "Blessed be the King that cometh in the name of the Lord: peace in heaven, and glory in the highest" (Luke 19:38; cf. Ps. 118:26 and Matthew 21:9, 23:39, Mark 11:9, Luke 13:35). Spiritual peace is a central theme in the later books of the New Testament. Paul stressed that "justification by faith" in Jesus leads man to peace with God (Romans 5:1; cf. 14:17) and in his Epistle to the Philippians he wrote of "the peace of God, which passeth all understanding" (4:7). As opposed to "the works of the flesh," Paul also declared that "the fruit of the Spirit is love, joy, peace, longsuffering, gentleness, goodness, faith . . ." (Galatians 5:22). A close parallel is also drawn between Melchizedek (Gen. 14:18–20) and Jesus himself, that other "king of Salem" (i.e., ruler of peace) and high priest, "a minister of the sanctuary, and of the true tabernacle" (Hebrews 5:6ff., 6:20, 7:1–8:6).[59]

However, whereas Rabbinic and Jewish opinion was unanimous in regard to the virtue of a just peace, Jesus expressed himself in a paradoxical manner. Though adamant in his doctrine of non-resistance to civil authority, he proclaimed the divisive nature of his religious message: "Think not that I am come to send peace on earth: I am come not to send peace, but a sword. For I am come to set a man at variance against his father, and the daughter against her mother . . . And a man's foes shall be they of his own household" (Matthew 10:34–36; cf. Luke 12:51–53 and Micah 7:6). To the Jews, whom the Prophets imbued with hope for a Messiah of peace, this doctrine of dissension was unacceptable; but, for the disciples of Jesus, it meant "bearing witness" before the authorities and not denying their master, perilous though this might be (Matthew 10:32–33, 26:69–75). As a missionary faith, Christianity made the edge of that sword highly tangible. Yet, though this had the gravest consequences during the Middle Ages (with the crusade against

[59] In Melchizedek Philo saw a prefiguration of his Logos, which (through the Gospel of John) entered the theology of the Church; see also Chapter 1.

the Albigenses and other persecutions) and in later times (with the religious wars between Catholics and Protestants), all sections of Christendom continued to pay homage to the fundamental concept of peace as a lofty ideal. *The Book of Common Prayer* thus includes "Give peace in our time, O Lord" in its "Versicles and Responses" and its Litany offers a prayer for "unity, peace, and concord."

From the 17th century onward, most European thinkers tended to relate their views on war and peace to those of the Hebrew Bible. In his *Leviathan* (1650), the English absolutist philosopher Thomas Hobbes made a social contract, or treaty of peace, the basis of the State: "The first and fundamental law of Nature" was *"to seek peace and follow it."* Shakespeare, too, evoked the Biblical ideal in *Henry VIII*, especially at the end of the play (Act 5, Scene 5), where his Protestant hero, Archbishop Cranmer, hails the infant Elizabeth at her christening·

> She shall be lov'd and fear'd. Her own shall bless her:
>   Her foes shake like a field of beaten corn,
> And hang their heads with sorrow. Good grows with her;
>   In her days every man shall eat in safety
>   Under his own vine what he plants, and sing
> The merry songs of peace to all his neighbours.
>   God shall be truly known . . . .[60]

Though devoted to the military, as well as civil, implications of the Puritan experiment, Milton clearly distinguished between the "righteous war"[61] of England's Parliament and the imperialism of less "godly" regimes—depicted in the infernal hosts of *Paradise Lost* (1667). A generation later, John Ray's proverb, "He that preaches war is the Devil's chaplain," anticipated the pacifism of 18th-century philosophers such as Voltaire, whose *Candide* (1759) introduced two warring kings who had the *Te Deum* hymn sung in their camps before battle commenced. Voltaire was, of course, aiming his satire at the moral arrogance of rulers who claimed that "God and the Right" were on their particular imperialistic side.

In a study of the Bible and human progress, Woodrow Wilson declared:

[60] Cf. 1 Kings 5:5, Micah 4:4.
[61] This has a Rabbinic parallel in the *milḥemet miẓvah* ("mandatory war") which the Israelites were enjoined to wage on Amalek and other sworn enemies (see above).

"I will not cry 'peace' so long as there is sin and wrong in the world. And this great book does not teach any doctrine of peace so long as there is sin to be combated and overcome in one's own heart and in the great moving force of human society .... Parties are reformed and governments are corrected by the impulses coming out of the hearts of those who never exercised authority and never organized parties." The Biblical background to 20th-century internationalism was proclaimed by South Africa's premier, Jan Christiaan Smuts, when the first world body was inaugurated in 1920: "I do not know whether you are aware that the League of Nations was first of all the vision of a great Jew—almost 3,000 years ago—the prophet Isaiah." One of the first acts of the League was to grant Britain the Palestine Mandate for the establishment of a Jewish National Home. During the 1930s, the text of Ex. 12:49 ("One law shall be to him that is home-born, and unto the stranger that sojourneth among you") was actually selected as the motto of the Congress for the Protection of Minority Populations in European Countries, and the British Broadcasting Corporation (BBC) adopted a modification of Isa. 2:4 (as "Nation shall speak peace unto nation") for its own crest.

In recent times, there have been many attempts to eliminate the sources of conflict between the peoples of the world—through the promotion of one universal language or another (although no man-made tongue has even begun to rival English in this respect) and through the establishment of the League of Nations and its present-day successor, the United Nations Organization. The Council of Europe and various supranational political and economic groupings have been important steps toward an age-old ideal. The UN has its own "peace-keeping force" and the late President John F. Kennedy made a positive contribution with the Peace Corps which he brought into being as a means of assisting underdeveloped nations to become self-reliant. Man's innate tendency to blame the foreigner for his own vexations and failings is one of the greatest obstacles to international friendship and understanding. "Peace, peace, to him that is far off and to him that is near" (Isa. 57:19) is an ideal to which peoples and governments pay lip service, while their actual policies often run counter to the vision of the Prophets. Yet if man is to work out his own salvation, the discipline which society maintains over the individual must be extended into the national and international spheres. "He maketh wars to cease unto the end of the earth" (Ps. 46:10) may then become something more than a pious hope.

Part Two

THE BIBLE'S ROLE IN LANGUAGE AND LETTERS

3

THE TESTIMONY OF
EVERYDAY SPEECH

To every people after their language (Esther 1:22)

No development in the entire linguistic history of the West is more astonishing or profound than that of the Hebrew Bible's impact on the vocabulary and thought processes of the nations. Through the translation of the Scriptures into the vernacular, revolutionary changes took place within many European languages, affecting not merely their choice of word and phrase but, even more, the whole psychology and outlook of the peoples concerned. This process, which took hold during the Middle Ages, received its most powerful impetus at the onset of the Reformation in the early 16th century when the leaders of Protestantism made the spoken word the basis of their teaching.[1] The far-reaching result of this evangelical approach was, as Ralph Waldo Emerson has pointed out, that "our Jewish Bible has implanted itself in the table-talk and household life of every man and woman in the European and American nations" (*Representative Men*, 1845).

The pioneer translators of the Bible into English were John Wycliffe (born two centuries before the Reformation) and William Tyndale, who was one of the earliest martyrs for the Protestant cause. In his *Obedience of a Christian Man* (1528), Tyndale first drew attention to the fact that "the properties of the hebrue tonge agreth a thousande tymes moare with the english then with the latyne. The maner of speakynge is both one so that in a thousande places thou neadest not but to translate it in to english worde for worde. . ." This coincidence was not lost on some Puritans, nor on the 19th-century author and historian Macaulay, who called the English Bible "a book which, if everything else in our language should perish, would alone suffice to show the whole extent of its beauty and power" (*On John Dryden*, 1828).

Luther's German Bible (1534) was another great monument of the

---

[1] For further discussion of these translations and their literary importance, see Chapter 4.

Reformation, second only in importance to the *King James* or *Authorized Version* (1611), which it partly inspired. Both the English and the German Bibles paid such deference to the Hebraic word of God—the Hebrew language being widely regarded as the "mother of all tongues" (*matrix linguarum*)—that entire phrases and expressions were translated quite literally into the vernacular. This explains why original Biblical idioms ("My brother's keeper"—*"meines Bruders Hüter,"* Gen. 4:9; "scapegoat"—*"Sündenbock,"* Lev.16) have become naturalized in English and German, as have scores of other terms and proverbs for which no equivalents previously existed. The Bible's linguistic impact on Europe has received a telling assessment by George Adam Smith (in *The Legacy of Israel*, 1927): "The vivid simplicity of Hebrew narrative and the majestic eloquence of the prophets did much to mould the youth of our own and of the German language and the styles of our earliest writers."

Any detailed study of the Biblical sources of our modern languages must take account of both direct and indirect borrowings and of the Scriptural idiom's assimilation and absorption in current speech. However, a certain degree of caution must be exercised, since one or two over-enthusiastic writers have mistakenly attributed all or most Semitic words in our vocabulary to the pervasive influence of the Hebrew Bible. In some cases the Biblical Hebrew has given us a basic word like *sak* ("sack, sackcloth") or else it has merely transmitted non-Semitic (e.g. Sanskrit and Persian) words from Asia to Europe ("sapphire," Gen. 24:10; "[spike] nard," Song of Songs 1:12). A further group of Hebrew terms familiar to us is of post-Biblical (New Testament or Rabbinic) origin, while other words again (relating to Biblical localities) probably entered the European vocabulary no earlier than the Middle Ages.[2]

HEBREW LOANWORDS OF BIBLICAL ORIGIN

A fairly large number of Hebrew terms have passed directly into English and other languages, mostly in a religious context. They include *amen* ("so be it"), *Baal* (the name of a Phoenician god, and hence of any idol), *behemoth* (plural of *behemah*, "beast"; perhaps applied to the hippopotamus but now signifying any huge creature), *cherub* (an angelic being, later interpreted to mean a beautiful and innocent child), *ephod*

---

[2] Some instances are considered below.

(a priestly vestment), *Hallelujah!* (or *Alleluia;* "praise ye the Lord!" and, by extension, any song of praise to God), *Ichabod!* ("the glory has departed," see 1 Sam. 4:21), *jubilee* (Hebrew *Yovel,* twelve months of emancipation and restoration observed every fifty years and proclaimed by a *yovel* or ram's horn; whence any fiftieth anniversary or joyous season), *leviathan* (a sea monster or whale), *manna* (food which God provided for the Israelites in the wilderness, and hence any sweet and refreshing substance), *Messiah* ("the anointed one" or promised deliverer), *paschal* (relating to the Jewish Passover or to Easter), *Sabbath* (the seventh day of rest), *Satan* ("adversary," a name for the Devil), *selah* (perhaps a musical direction), and *seraph* (a celestial being). Some of these have provided us with familiar adjectives (cherubic, jubilant, messianic, sabbatical, satanic, seraphic) and verbs (jubilate, sabbatize, satanize).

Other Biblical words that have been absorbed by English include *Babel, bal(sa)m* (from the Hebrew *bosem*), *camel* (from *gamal*), *cane* (from *kaneh*), *cinnamon* (from *kinnamon*), *myrrh* (from *mor*), *shekel,* and *shibboleth.* Some of these have had an interesting linguistic history. *Babel* or *Babylon* (from the Akkadian *Bāb-ilu,* "the gate of the god") recalls the attempt by the inhabitants of Mesopotamia to storm Heaven in their famous tower, a scheme that God foiled by "confounding their language" (Gen. 11:9). Popular Biblical etymology ironically associates the name *Babel* with the Hebrew root *b-l-l* ("to confuse"), and the modern sense of the term is "a confusion of sounds or voices" or "a scene of noise and confusion." This in turn has given rise to the imitative verb "to babble" (French *babiller,* "to chatter, gossip"), meaning "to prattle, talk foolishly, utter meaningless sounds." In Calvinist and Puritan theology and polemics "Babylon" was the proverbial "wicked city" (Jer. 50, 51; cf. Revelation 17:5, etc., in the New Testament). *Cane* (from *kaneh,* "reed," Isa. 43:24) has given rise to such everyday terms as "sugar cane," "canal," "channel," "canister," "canon," and "cannon." *Shekel,* though in itself an innocuous term, has acquired pejorative overtones in the familiar expression "to rake in the shekels." According to the Biblical narrative (Judges 12:6), it was the mispronunciation of *shibboleth* (Hebrew *shibbolet,* "a flowing stream, brook" or "ear of grain") by the fugitive Ephraimites that led to their detection by Jephthah's followers when they tried to ford the Jordan. In modern Hebrew, as in English, French, German, and other languages, a *shibboleth* ˙ has come to mean any catchword or slogan indicating a sect or party, or any custom or speech peculiarity distinguishing the members of a group.

Further examples of Biblical "infiltration" into our everyday language deserve mention here. *Bedlam,* a corruption of "Bethlehem," derives from St. Mary of Bethlehem, a notorious "hospital" or insane asylum that was once one of London's popular sights. By extension, *bedlam* now means a "scene of uproar and confusion." *Gehenna,* another term with unpleasant associations, is actually the Greek form of two Hebrew words, *Gei* [*ben-*] *Hinnom* ("the Valley of [the son of hair] Hinnom"), signifying a place near ancient Jerusalem which was disfigured by human sacrifice and idolatrous rites. In modern parlance *Gehenna* is synonymous with "Hell" or "misery." During the later Middle Ages, the French form of this word, *Géhenne,* became confused with a Germanic root, *gehiner* ("to torture"), thus giving rise to the modern French *gêne(r),* which has the sense of "bother, torment." Another synonym for chaos or disorder is the French *tohu-bohu,* deriving from the Hebrew *Tohu va-Vohu* ("unformed and void," Gen. 1:2). The "writing on the wall" — *Mene Mene Tekel Upharsin* (Dan. 5:25) — which Daniel successfully interpreted to Belshazzar has, in its abbreviated form *Mene Tekel,* acquired the meaning "alarm, alert, warning cry" in modern German.

In some instances, Hebrew or Aramaic terms entered the vernacular from later sources as well, such as the New Testament and Rabbinic literature. *Hosanna* (Hebrew *Hosha-na* or *Hoshi'a-na,* "Save, we beseech Thee!"), though solidly rooted in the Hebrew Bible (Ps. 118:25, etc.), became more familiar in the New Testament context ("Hosanna in the highest," Matthew 21:9, Mark 11:10) and now serves as a cry of religious adoration. *Mammon* (Aramaic for "wealth" or "profit"), an early Rabbinic term, is best known for its use in the Gospels ("Ye cannot serve God and mammon," Matthew 6:24, Luke 16:13), from which source it has acquired the sense of "material riches" or "tainted money." Though strictly post-Biblical, *Rabbi* (Hebrew for "my master") originally meant "a teacher" and this meaning is preserved in the New Testament (Matthew 23:7–8, John 3:2, 26). In English and other modern languages, *Rabbi* (or *rabbin, Rabbiner,* etc.) is exclusively reserved for ordained teachers of Judaism. *Abba* (Aramaic for "father," akin to the Hebrew *av*) was chiefly used in prayer during the Rabbinic period and in this sense occurs in the New Testament ("Abba, Father," Mark 14:36, Romans 8:15, Galatians 4:6). Through Greek and Latin, *abba* is the source of the English *abbot,* French *abbé,* and German *Abt* and probably inspired the term "reverend father" in Catholic usage.[3] The strictly Jewish term *Kabbalah* ("tradition"), from the Biblical root *k-b-l* ("to receive"), was originally a general definition for Jewish oral teaching, but in time became synonymous with the whole range of Jewish mystical lore. Through the medieval Latin *Cabbala*, this word became *cabale* in French and from there passed into English usage with the added sense of "intrigue" or "conspiracy."[4] Thus, *Kabbalah* itself (also spelled *Kabala*, *Kabbala*, *Cabala*, *Cabbala*, *Cabbalah*, and even *Qabbala*) now means both "Jewish mystical doctrine" and "any esoteric or occult matter" or "any secret doctrine or mysterious art," while *cabal* signifies "a private group or party engaged in intrigue, seeking to overthrow the government and assume control; or the intrigue itself," whence the verb "to cabal."

Another group of words of Hebrew or Semitic origin relating to places mentioned in the Bible apparently reached Europe even later, perhaps during or after the Crusades. The lustrous fabric known as *damask* takes its name from the city of Damascus in Syria, and *gauze,* another, more loosely woven fabric, originates through the Middle French *gaze* in the name of the Palestinian town of Gaza. The vegetable called *scallion* in the United States and *shallot* in England owes its designation to Gaza's neighbor, Ashkelon. The scallion, native to Syria and Palestine, grew plentifully in the region of Ashkelon and the "Ascalon onion" as it was called (*scaloun* in 13th-century English) was relished by the Crusaders and soon imported to Europe.

PROPER NAMES DERIVED FROM THE BIBLE

An entire book could be written about the absorption of Biblical proper names in the languages and usage of the world's peoples. In general, the current form of these names has been influenced by the phonetic changes necessitated by their transfer and transliteration from Hebrew and Aramaic into Greek (notably the Septuagint) and Latin, from which

---

[3] The linguistic development of another such word, *Pharisee,* is discussed separately below.

[4] *Cabal* gained a curious place in English history as a description for Charles II's secret cabinets or committees. One powerful factor leading to the adoption of this new meaning was a rather odd coincidence: the initial letters of the surnames borne by five ministers of state who served the king actually spelled C-A-B-A-L!

sources English and other languages borrowed them in their turn. Since Latin could not convey the guttural sound of the Hebrew letter *het*, *Havvah* and *Hannah* evolved as Eve and Anna (Anne, more rarely Hannah), *No'ah* as Noah and *Rahel* as Rachel. The absence of an equivalent for the Hebrew *shin* in Greek and Latin modified *Shim'on* to Simon (or Simeon) and *Shoshannah* to Susan(nah). Nor are these the only changes that have taken place in the course of such transliteration.

A comparatively large number of modern "Christian" (given or first) names—perhaps as many as half—are of Biblical origin, and of these many are quite obviously Hebraic: *Adam* ("man"), *Benjamin* ("son of the right hand"), *David* ("beloved"), *Gabriel* ("man of God" or "God's champion"), *Jonathan* ("God has given"), *Joseph* ("he shall add"), *Michael* ("who is like God?"), *Saul* ("asked for"); and *Abigail* ("my father rejoices"), *Dinah* (perhaps "judges, vindicates"), *Judith* ("Jewess"), *Mary* (from *Miriam*, open to several interpretations), *Naomi* ("pleasant"), *Ruth* (perhaps "friendship"), and *Sarah* ("princess"). Apart from these names, however, there are dozens more in most European languages whose Biblical origin is not so easily recognizable, including diminutive forms such as Danny (for Daniel, "God has judged"), Joe and Jo (for Joseph and Josephine), Rae (for Rachel), Sam(uel), and so forth. *Jacob* (Hebrew *Ya'akov*, popularly interpreted to mean "he will supplant, overreach") is the source of *James* (Jim, Jimmy) and of the French *Jacques*, Italian *Giacopo*, Spanish *Iago*, etc., and *Joseph* that of the Italian *Giuseppe* and Spanish *José*. *John* (Hebrew *Yohanan* or *Yehohanan*, "God has been gracious") has given rise to an even greater variety of names: the popular English *Jack*, the Scots Gaelic *Ian*, the Erse (Irish Gaelic) *Sean*, and the French *Jean*, Italian *Giovanni*, Spanish *Juan*, German *Johann(es)* and *Hans*, and Russian *Ivan*. Some other Biblical names for men are *Ethan* (Hebrew *Eitan*, "long-lived, permanent"), *Ira* (the meaning of which is uncertain), and *Jeremy* (from *Jeremiah*; Hebrew *Yirmiyahu*, "May God exalt").

As their Biblical context indicates, *Hiram* (or *Ahiram*, "brother of the exalted one") is of Phoenician origin and Cyrus and Esther derive from Old Persian. Even the name of the apostle *Thomas* derives from the Aramaic *Te'oma* ("twin," akin to the Hebrew *Te'om*), although it was in origin apparently an epithet, the apostle's real name being Judas. Many familiar women's names also have interesting Biblical roots: *Adah* ("ornament"), *Beulah* ("married"), *Debra* (a form of *Deborah;*

Hebrew *Devorah,* "bee"), *Edna* ("delight"), *Elizabeth* ("God has sworn," or "God's oath"), *Jacqueline* (from *Jacob*), *Madel(e)ine* (or *Magdalene, Marlene,* etc.; from *Magdala* or *Migdal,* a town near Lake Tiberias), and *Shar(r)on* ("plain," relating to part of the coastal lowland of Palestine). Some of the derivatives from these women's names are extensive: from *Ann* we have *Nan, Nancy, Nan(n)ette,* and *Nina;* from *Mary* forms ranging from *Maria* and *Marie* to *Mae, Marian(ne), Marietta, Marion, May, Minnie, Molly,* and *Mollie;* from *Sarah* come *Sadie* and *Sally;* and from *Susanna* the forms *Sue, Susie,* and *Suzanne.* An even lengthier train of names follows *Elizabeth—Bessie, Beth, Bets(e)y, Betty, Elisa, Elisabeth, Eliza, Elsa, Elsie, Elspeth, Isabel(le), Libby, Lillian,* and *Lisa* or *Liza.*[5]

Several of these Biblical proper names have acquired lasting significance in some memorable phrase—"the old Adam," "to raise Cain," "David and Jonathan," "a Jezebel," "Job's comforters" and "the patience of a Job," "as old as Methuselah," etc. "The old Adam" alludes to his unregenerate condition (and "Adam's ale" to his only drink—water!); "raising Cain" means making a disturbance" (a reference to Cain's murder of Abel); inseparable friends are like "David and Jonathan"; a loose woman is often compared to the idolatrous wife of Ahab ("shameless Jezebel"); "Job's comforters" bring one little solace indeed and his trials certainly demanded infinite patience; while the 969 years of Methuselah's life have made his age proverbial. In many languages a *jeremiad* means a lament (recalling the Lamentations of Jeremiah) and a "judgment of Solomon" a subtle decision. The ark of bulrushes in which Moses was placed (Ex. 2:3) has inspired *moïse,* the modern French term for a wicker cradle, while the German rallying cry and motto, *Gott mit uns!* ("God with us!"), was literally inspired by the Hebrew *Immanuel* (Isa. 7:14). Other terms and expressions involving Biblical proper names include "Aaron's rod," "a Garden of Eden," "Naboth's vineyard," "the wisdom of Solomon," and Shylock's delighted call, "A Daniel come to judgment!" (in Shakespeare's *The Merchant of Venice*).[6]

---

[5] Many Jews fleeing Spain after the Expulsion of 1492 satirically nicknamed Queen Isabella *Izevel* (Jezebel).

[6] For other Biblical expressions in current use, see below.

INDIRECT BORROWINGS

At least as many Biblical terms have passed into general usage by way of translation into Greek and Latin. When the Hellenistic Jews of Alexandria produced their Septuagint version of the Hebrew Bible in the third century B.C.E., they had to make allowance for the fact that the reader for whom they catered, though loyal to the Jewish faith, was so assimilated to the prevailing Greek culture that vernacular equivalents had to be found for all but a few technical terms that could not be translated at all (*Amen, ephod, Gehenna, Hallelujah!, manna, Sabbath, Selah*, etc.), among which proper names were obviously predominant. And, since so many Biblical words and concepts were molded by the religious psychology of Jewish monotheism, the authentic Greek terms actually employed in the Septuagint underwent a profound semantic change. In short, Greek received a Hebraic injection, so that the vernacular translation of the Bible was in fact Jewish thought presented in Greek dress. Jerome's Latin Vulgate later followed the Septuagint's lead in this respect, even though the Christian translator had both the Greek and the Hebrew texts of the Scriptures in front of him when he set to work on his own Latin version. This need to convey the original sense of the Biblical word became even more critical after the "parting of the ways" between Rabbinic Judaism and Gentile Christianity led to a widespread ignorance of the Hebrew language in the lands of the West. The same process continued throughout the medieval period, when the earliest attempts were made to produce translations of the whole Bible or of the Psalms and other Biblical books in English, French, German, and other languages.

The precise workings of this semantic development call for detailed discussion and illustration. In the Hebrew Bible, the Ineffable Name of God is written YHVH (or YHWH),[7] without vowel points, in order to prevent the idle use or profanation of its true, original pronunciation.

---

[7] Some Jewish editions of the Bible still omit even YHVH's substituted (Masoretic) pointing. Since Hebrew is a consonantal language, the vowel sounds were originally supplied by the reader and were only fixed as late as 800 C.E. To this day, an unpointed (unvocalized), handwritten text of the *Torah* is used for public reading in the service of the synagogue. Because of the [*Adonai*] pointing chosen by the Masoretes for the Divine Name, many Christian scholars (perhaps beginning with Pietro Columna Galatinus in the early

Out of reverence for the Divine Name, the Masoretes substituted the vocalization of *Adonai* ("my Lord") so as to indicate that such was the proper and respectful pronunciation of the Tetragrammaton (Four-letter Name of God). However, the authors of the Septuagint—bypassing YHVH—chose the Greek word *Kyrios* ("lord, master") to translate the Ineffable Name, thus infusing the vernacular term with a religious sense that it had never possessed in its earlier history. Later, in the Vulgate, *(ho) Kyrios* was replaced by the Latin *Dominus* ("Lord") which, in medieval French, survived for a time in the combination *Damned(i)eu* ("Lord God," equivalent to the Latin *Dominus Deus*). The translators of the later Middle Ages and the Reformation found new vernacular equivalents for the original Hebrew in the French *Seigneur*, English *Lord*, German *Herr*, etc., thus maintaining the Jewish avoidance of the Tetragrammaton's true pronunciation.

The semantic changes referred to above have characterized the emergence of words such as "angel," "devil," "holocaust," "idol," "paradise," "priest," "prophet," "psalm," "temple," "bless," "curse," "charity," "righteousness," and "sanctify." In their search for a suitable equivalent for the Hebrew *mal'akh* ("messenger, "angel"), the early translators hit upon the Greek word *angelos* ("messenger"), which was hitherto devoid of *mal'akh's* Biblical sense and would almost certainly never have passed into other languages, had it not been for the demands of Bible translation. Because *mal'akh (YHVH)* was the equivalent for the Hebrew *mal'akh* ("messenger, angel"), the early *angelos*) in the Septuagint, acquiring a new, Biblical-Hebraic significance. The Vulgate thus had no need to infuse the Latin word *nuntius* ("messenger") with the sense of *mal'akh*, since this was already present in *angelos;* this Greek term was readily adopted in the Latinized form of *angelus*, which later translators borrowed in the modified forms of the French *ange*, English *angel*, German *Engel*, etc., the semantic essence remaining, as ever, entirely Hebraic.

The transformation of the Hebrew term *Satan* ("opponent, adversary") has an even more intriguing history. As previously indicated, *Satan* entered English and other languages in its original form as a

16th century) read YHVH as "Jehovah," an artificial pronunciation which has entered Protestant hymnology and is still widely, though mistakenly, honored. It is believed that the interjection "by Jove!" was never a pagan oath transferred to English, but a disguised form of "by [the great] Jehovah!"

proper noun, but the fact that other malignant spirits (e.g., Belial and Beelzebub) made their appearance in later Hebraic and in Christian tradition led translators to seek some Greek equivalent for the "angel of darkness" who takes on a personalized character in the Book of Job. So it was that, alongside *Satanas*, the Greek word *diabolos* ("slanderer") was eventually supplied—an obscure term that only rose to prominence because of the Devil's role in Christian tradition. This Greco-Hebraic fusion provided Latin with the modification *diabolus*, from which French derived *diable*, English *devil*, and German *Teufel*. This coexistence of *Satan* and *devil* is not, however, the end of the story. From early Rabbinic times, popular imagination conceived the idea of innumerable evil, unclean spirits (Hebrew *shedim, mazikim*) that assume particular importance in the New Testament. To these arch-enemies of God's angels a new Greek term, *daimon(ion)*, was applied, the plural form of which, *daimonia*, became a counterpart to the angels as "messengers of the Devil." *Daimonia* passed into Latin as *daemones* and, in time, *diabolus* and *daemon* became confused, to the extent that our modern "devil" has acquired two senses—one from the Greek Septuagint (*the* Devil, i.e. Satan) and another from the Latin Vulgate (devils, i.e. demons).

Gan Eden ("the Garden of Eden," Gen. 2:8) involved the authors of the Septuagint in some linguistic acrobatics when they tried to find an equivalent for *gan* ("garden"), which obviously here implies a far vaster region than the plain Hebrew would lead the reader to understand. From an Old Persian word, *pairi-daēza* ("enclosure")—indicating some sort of extensive royal "park" in which wild beasts were preserved for hunting—the Greeks borrowed *paradeisos* to describe the idyllic surroundings of the first human couple. This word (which Hebrew, incidentally, has also appropriated as *pardes*, "orchard, park"; see Song of Songs 4:13, Eccl. 2:5, Neh. 2:8) passed into Latin (as *paradisus*) and from there into French *(paradis)*, English *(Paradise)*, and other languages in the restricted sense of the Biblical "Garden of Eden."

On the whole, the semantic development of most other Biblical terms of this kind was more straightforward. For the Hebrew *elil* ("idol")—a concept obviously foreign to the Greeks and Romans—the Septuagint supplied *eidolon* ("phantom"), whence *idol's* Hebraic idea of a false god, its cultic representation, or (in the modern sense) anything insubstantial or fallacious. Aaron's priestly descendants, the *kohanim* (plural of *kohen;* a term from which the Jewish surname "Cohen" ultimately derives), were given a rather obscure Greek designation: the *kohen* was made a *presbyteros* ("elder"), one chosen to perform sacred rites, a word which in Late Latin became *presbyter,* whence the French *prêtre,* English *priest,* and such interesting derivatives as "Presbyterian" and the legendary Prester John (in Old French, *prestre Jehan*). The Old Testament *navi,* who admonished the erring and foretold the reward of the righteous and the punishment of the wicked, was described in an invented Greek term as a *prophētēs* ("one who speaks before, or for"); through the Latin *propheta* and the English *prophet,* the full significance of the Hebrew has been retained. The word *mashi'ah* presents another interesting example of parallel development, since (as "Messiah," i.e. "the anointed one") it was absorbed through Latin *(Messias)* by the various modern languages, yet gave rise to an alternative expression in response to the demands of Christian theology. Because Jesus of Nazareth was, for his followers, *the* "Anointed One," *mashi'ah* was literally translated into Greek as *Christos,* a term which—combined with "Jesus"—reappeared as a proper name in Latin and German *(Jesus Christus),* as well as other European tongues.

Abstract concepts of Biblical origin constitute another important group of indirect borrowings from the Hebrew language. Since there was no handy equivalent for the verbal root *b-r-kh* ("to bless"), the Septuagint translated this word as *eu-logo* ("to commend, praise"), a term which has given rise to our modern "eulogy." In Latin, *eu-logo* was rendered *benedico* ("to speak well of"), from which certain words in English *(benediction, benison)* and French (*bénir,* "to bless"), as well as the name *Benedict* (Hebrew *Barukh*), immediately derive. In this case, however, English and German found equivalent forms elsewhere: "to pronounce a formula conveying spiritual beneficence" became *segnen* in German and *bless* (from an Anglo-Saxon word meaning "to consecrate with blood") in English. Thus the Hebrew *berakhah* is both a "benediction" and a "blessing" in the English language, while the sense of the Biblical verb has once more been preserved.

This is also true of other specialized and abstract ideas—"holy, holiness" (and the verbs "to hallow, sanctify"), "charity," "righteousness," "mercy" (or, as the English Bible translated *hesed,* "loving-kindness"), and even "justice" and "peace." Often, however, these familiar renderings do *less* than justice to the original Hebrew. "Charity" (Latin *caritas,* "dearness") conveys the idea of institutionalized assistance to the poor which *zedakah* (with its notion of the individual donor's obligation to give) does not imply in the Bible, and it is significant that the same Hebrew root furnishes the word *ẓedek* ("justice"). The somewhat negative overtones of "Law" and "Commandment" are also alien to *Torah* ("teaching, instruction," i.e. the Pentateuch, or the entire Written and Oral Law in a generalized sense) and *miẓvah* (which contains the idea of a commandment eagerly performed). *Shalom,* too, conveys far more than the absence of war implicit in *pax, paix, peace, Frieden,* etc. From its verbal root the Hebrew term derives the highly positive concepts of health, wholesomeness, and harmony which make the modern Israeli's everyday greeting, *Shalom!,* so distinctive. Despite these reservations, however, there is no disputing the Bible's seminal role in the development of many such terms and concepts in the language of modern man, which—from that source—has "caught some gleam of Hebrew meaning."

BIBLICAL PHRASES AND IDIOMS

Our main concern has so far been with those elements in our daily vocabulary that are, in one way or another, traceable to the Hebrew Bible. In several European languages—notably English—Biblical phraseology is an even more pervasive and important factor in the average person's thinking and expression. "Great consequences have flown from the fact that the first truly popular literature in England—the first which stirred the hearts of all classes of people and filled their minds with ideal pictures and their everyday speech with apt and telling phrases—was the literature comprised within the Bible" (John Fiske, *The Beginnings of New England,* 1889). The English Reformation's injection of the Biblical idiom into the language of ordinary men and women was vigorously promoted by Tyndale, who is reputed to have foretold the coming of a day when "a boy that driveth the plow" would be more familiar with the Scriptures than many a scholar of the Reformer's own time. Tyndale's work was continued by Miles Coverdale and the editors of the *"Great" Bible,* public readings of which (from copies that Henry VIII had installed in every parish church) were commonplace by 1540.

From that time onward, the English may be described as "a Bible-reading people." The language of the Hebrew Prophets became as familiar to the common man as that of the Psalms and it had an enormous

Title-page of the *"Great" Bible* (1539). King Henry VIII is shown handing copies to Archbishop Cranmer and Lord Chancellor Thomas Cromwell for distribution to the people.

impact on his imagination and outlook. "Bloody" Mary Tudor's
accession to the throne and her short, fanatically Catholic reign (1553–58)
scarcely impeded this momentous process, merely spurring the more
determined Protestant exiles to publish their *Geneva Bible* (1557), the
Scriptural text which Shakespeare is known to have consulted. Once
Queen Elizabeth I succeeded her half-sister and reestablished
Protestantism, England, to quote the historian John Richard Green,
"became the people of a book, and that book was the Bible. It was read
in churches, and it was read at home, and everywhere its words, as they
fell on ears which custom had not deadened to their force and beauty,
kindled a startling enthusiasm. As a mere literary monument, the English
Version of the Bible remains the noblest example of the English tongue,
while its perpetual use made it from the instant of its appearance the
standard of our language" (*A Short History of the English People*, 1874).
The *"Great" Bible* and its Geneva companion paved the way for the

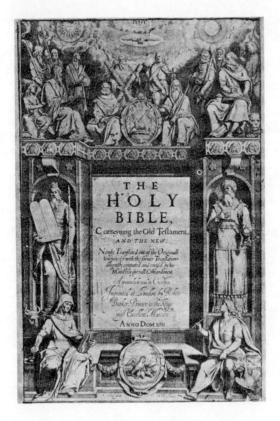

Title-page of the first
edition of the *Autho-
rized* or *King James
Version* of the Bible
(1611).

King James (Authorized) Version (1611), the editors of which revised the English text of the "Old" Testament on the basis of the original Hebrew. Despite its already obsolescent language, the *Authorized Version* became, and has to a large extent remained, the classic English translation of the Holy Scriptures, outstanding for its far-reaching influence on the Englishman's (and American's) mind.

Some idea of the Bible's diffusion throughout the English language can be gained by referring to a few selected portions of the "Old" Testament, beginning with the Pentateuch. We speak of someone behaving like "the great I Am" (Ex.3:14) or bearing "the mark of Cain" (Gen. 4:15), of people constituting "a plague" (Ex. 9:14), making "their exodus" (Ex. 13), and "worshiping the Golden Calf" (Ex. 32:4). The list of proverbial expressions is even more imposing. A man earns his living "by the sweat of his brow" (Gen. 3:19), may "eat forbidden fruit" (Gen. 2:17), crave the "fleshpots of Egypt" (Ex. 16:3), and sacrifice something worthwhile for "a mess of pottage" (Gen. 25:34), yet "man does not live by bread alone" (Deut. 8:3), since in the end he must go "the way of all flesh" (Gen. 6:12) and "return to the dust" (Gen. 3:19). Evildoers who dwell in "the cities of the plain" (Gen. 13:12) often look for "a scapegoat" (Lev. 16) and "make war" rather than peace (Deut. 20:12), but they will discover that the penalty is "an eye for an eye and a tooth for a tooth" (Ex. 21:24; Lev. 24:20).

As one proceeds through the Prophetical books and later Writings, such wealth of Biblical expression—whether literal or in some popular modification—becomes even more dazzling. In this "vale of tears" (Ps. 84:7) the appeal to man's conscience can be like "a voice crying in the wilderness" (Isa. 40:3) and, when disaster threatens, only the wise man will know how to "escape by the skin of his teeth" (Job 19:20); even then, he may not be permitted to enjoy "the sleep of the just" (Eccl. 5:11). The wicked, on the other hand, "sow the wind and reap the whirlwind" (Hos. 8:7), since they are unable to see "the writing on the wall" (Dan. 5:25) and are fated to "lick the dust" (Ps. 72:9). Thus "pride goes before a fall" (Prov. 16:18), for "can a leopard change its spots?" (Jer. 13:23). Those who are adventurous may "arise as one man" (Judges 20:8), then "go down to the sea in ships" (Ps. 107:23), cast themselves on the mercy of "the four winds of the heaven" (Dan. 7:2), and sail into "the Great Unknown" (Job 36:26). The more cautious, remembering that man's lifespan is "but threescore years and ten" (Ps. 90:10), teach their children "the good and the right way"

(I Sam. 12:23). They take care not to "spare the rod and spoil the child" Prov. 10:12), *een Uriasbrief* (cf. 2 Sam. 11:14ff.), *hemel en aarde bewegen* "you can't take it with you" (Eccl. 5:14), since "man proposes, God disposes" (Prov. 16:9) and "there is nothing new under the sun" (Eccl. 1:9)![8]

Elsewhere in Europe, other Protestant translations of the Bible molded everyday speech and left their imprint on modern expression. This was especially the case with those that appeared in France, Germany, the Netherlands, Scandinavia, Poland, and Hungary. The Dutch *Statenbijbel* (1627–37) introduced phrases and expressions such as *zo oud als Methusalem* ("as old as Methuselah," cf. Gen. 5:27), *met de mantel der liefde bedekken* ("to cover with the cloak of charity," cf. Gen. 9:23, Prov. 10:12), *een Uriasbrief* (cf. 2 Sam. 11:14ff.), *hemel en aarde bewegen* ("to move heaven and earth," cf. Isa. 13.13, Haggai 2:6), and *Poerem hebben* ("to make Purim," i.e. to make merry, cf. Esther 8:16–17, 9:20–28). In France, two 13th-century Bibles also the pioneering translations of Jacques Lefèvre d'Etaples (1528) and Robert Olivetan (1535) enriched spoken French both with direct loanwords (several of which were colorfully exploited by Rabelais) and with phrases such as *les amis de Job* ("Job's friends," i.e. his "comforters"), *bouc émissaire* ("scapegoat"), and *trouver grâce* ("to find favor"). Other Biblical terms and proverbs absorbed by the French language include *une brebis égarée* ("a lost sheep," Ps. 119:176), *l'arbre de vie* ("the Tree of Life," Gen. 2:9; Prov. 3:18), *l'orgueil précède la chute* ("pride goes before a fall," Prov. 16:18), and *ne pas entrer dans la terre promise* ("not to enter the Promised Land").

---

[8]   Some other everyday phrases and expressions that originate in the Pentateuch are "Am I my brother's keeper?" (Gen. 4:9), "a good old age" (Gen. 15:15), "the fat of the land" (Gen. 45:18), "spoiling the Egyptians" (Ex. 12:36), "be sure your sin will find you out" (Num. 32:23), and "the apple of his eye" (Deut. 32:10). From the later Biblical books English has acquired "hewers of wood and drawers of water" (Josh. 9:21), "to draw a bow at a venture" (1 Kings 22:34), "a word in season" (Prov. 15:23), "no peace for the wicked" (Isa. 48:22), "see eye to eye" (Isa. 52:8), and "a brand plucked from the burning" (Amos 4:11). Like Proverbs, the Book of Psalms is a major source of such figures of speech: "out of the mouths of babes and sucklings" (Ps. 8:3), "a little lower than the angels" (8:6), "the land of the living" (27:13), "to go from strength to strength" (84:8), "at death's door" (107:18), "at their wits' end" (107:27), and "put not your trust in princes" (146:3).

The opening page of
Luther's German Bible,
*Die gantze Heilige
Schrifft Deudsch* (Wit-
tenberg, 1534).

An achievement of even greater significance was the German Bible of
Martin Luther (1534), which—paradoxically enough—made the New
High German dialect of the Catholic South the accepted vehicle for
Protestant theology, preaching, and worship. Heine called "this old
book" the German language's "fountain of rejuvenation" and pointed
out that "all expressions and idioms to be found in the Lutheran Bible
are German. The writer must go on using them . . ." Though no great
Hebraist, Luther had an extraordinarily acute ear and managed to
capture much of the Hebrew text's tautness and simplicity in his remarkable German translation. Nietzsche, who preferred the "Old" Testament
to the New, declared that, "compared with Luther's Bible, almost
everything else is merely 'literature'—something which has not grown in
Germany, and therefore has not taken and does not take root in German
hearts, as the Bible has done" (*Jenseits von Gut und Böse,* 1886).

Luther's text brought a vast number of Biblical terms and phrases into ordinary German usage—*im Schweisse deines Angesichts* ("in the sweat of thy brow," Gen. 3:19), *das Kainszeichen* ("the mark of Cain," Gen. 4:15), *die verbotene Frucht* ("forbidden fruit," Gen. 2:17), *Anbetung des goldenen Kalbes* ("worshiping the Golden Calf," Ex. 32), *der Tau des Himmels* ("the dew of Heaven," Gen. 27:28), *das Jammertal* ("the valley of Baca" or "vale of tears," Ps. 84:7), and dozens more. As in English, everyday speech was immeasurably enriched by Biblical proverbs that have become standard German, such as *den Weg alles Fleisches gehen* ("to go the way of all flesh," Gen. 6:13), *der Mensch lebt nicht vom Brot allein* ("man does not live by bread only," Deut. 8:3), *säen Wind und Ungewitter ernten* ("to sow the wind and reap the whirlwind," Hos. 8:7), *der Mensch denkt, Gott lenkt* ("man proposes, God disposes," Prov. 16:9), and *der Hochmut kommt vor dem Fall* ("pride goes before a fall," Prov. 16:18).

SOME LINGUISTIC CURIOSITIES

Through the Latin of the Vulgate a number of Biblical quotations have become familiar tags and mottoes in the Western world. *Fiat lux* ("Let there be light," Gen. 1:10) is a popular inscription on college, municipal, and similar crests, while *Dominus illuminatio mea* ("The Lord is my light," Ps. 27:1) adorns the arms of the University of Oxford. In the United States, Yale University provides a rare instance of a non-Jewish institution's adoption of such a Biblical motto *in the original Hebrew:* Yale's choice of *Urim ve-Tummim,* those oracular media borne by the Israelite high priest, is peculiarly significant in the socio-religious context of Puritan New England. Other citations of the Bible have interesting literary associations. *De profundis* ("Out of the depths," Ps. 130:1) was extracted from the Catholic liturgy to become Luther's hymn, *Aus tiefer Not;* Goethe's *Faust* includes the dramatic *Dies irae* ("Day of Wrath," Zeph. 1:15); and *Non plus ultra* ("Thus far and no further," Job 38:11), a standard expression in several modern languages and a favorite among politicians, was exploited (as *bis hierher und nicht weiter*) in Schiller's *Die Räuber.*

The history of the name *Lucifer* is especially intriguing. The Book of Isaiah tells of an archangel's rebellion against God's rule and of his subsequent downfall and exile to Hell:

How you are fallen from heaven,
  O Day Star, son of Dawn!
How you are cut down to the ground,
  you who laid the nations low!
You said in your heart
  "I will ascend to heaven;
Above the stars of God
  I will set my throne on high . . .
I will make myself like the Most High."
But you are brought down to Sheol,
  to the depths of the Pit . . . (Isa. 14:12–15).[9]

In the original Hebrew, "Day Star" is *Heilel,* for which the Vulgate invented the word *luci-fer* ("light-bearer"). Since the rebel angel became identified in later Hebrew and Christian mythology with Satan, the "Master of Evil" (whence Milton's "superior fiend" in *Paradise Lost*), *Lucifer* as a name assumed an identity of its own. For obvious reasons, "lucifer" also came to mean a safety match and this term was popularized by British troops enjoying their cigarette ration in the trenches of World War I.

Several more Biblical terms have had very odd reincarnations. "Canaanite" in Hebrew (*Kena'ani*) means both an inhabitant of the land of Canaan and a merchant or trader, in which sense *am Kena'an* (literally, "the people of Canaan") is translated as "merchant folk" in Zephaniah 1:11. Samuel Adams, who is said to have used a kindred term in a speech at Philadelphia in 1776, probably borrowed it from a book that had just appeared, Adam Smith's classic *The Wealth of Nations,* which maintained that "a nation governed by shopkeepers" might well assume a dominant economic position in world affairs. Smith's book was widely read and provided the Emperor Napoleon with his famous and scornful dismissal of the English as "a nation of shopkeepers." An even stranger tale originates in an obscure German student's death in a brawl with a citizen of Jena in 1624. The pastor who officiated at his interment took as his text a passage from the Book of Judges relating Delilah's betrayal

[9] Isaiah's "taunt song" is also considered to have more straightforward, political implications, the overweening Lucifer being interpreted to represent Sargon, the ambitious king of Babylon, whose power and splendor were—like the sun's—then ascending in the East.

of Samson, and injected all the pathos he could muster into the traitress'
cry, *Die Philister über dir, Simson!* ("The Philistines be upon thee,
Samson," Judges 16:9). The peculiar circumstances surrounding the use
of this Biblical quotation soon led German students to call burghers,
merchants, and all other "unenlightened" people *Philister,* and the term
became popular among Germany's intellectuals. Aristocrats were oddly
designated "Barbarians," the middle classes "Philistines," and the
ignorant masses "Populace." Heine made much sardonic use of the term
"Philistine" and it was as a result of Matthew Arnold's close and
sympathetic study of Heine's writings that the expression finally reached
England as a synonym for the Nonconformist middle classes — watch-
dogs of respectability who lacked "sweetness and light" (*Culture and
Anarchy,* 1869). In this way, "Philistinism" now conveys the idea of
smugness and unthinking materialism.

In the "square" Hebrew script that came into general use at about the
end of the first century B.C.E., the smallest letter was *yod* or *yud* [ˈ], a
Semitic term and symbol from which the Greeks derived the smallest
letter of their own alphabet, *iota* [ι]. This process has interesting
associations with the New Testament and with present-day speech. In the
course of his Sermon on the Mount Jesus declares: "Think not that I am
come to destroy the law, or the prophets: I am not come to destroy, but
to fulfil. For verily I say unto you. Till heaven and earth pass, one jot or
one tittle shall in no wise pass from the law, till all be fulfilled. . . "
(Matthew 5:17–18). Here, "jot" represents the end of a linguistic chain
that leads from the Hebrew *yod* to the Greek *iota* and the *iota unam* of the
Latin Vulgate, and from there to the "one iott" of Tyndale's Bible and the
"one jot" of the *Authorized Version.* From this source English has
derived the word *jot* in the sense of "a very small amount" and the
verb "to jot (down)," meaning "to write briefly or hastily, or to set down
in the form of a short note," as well as the familiar expression, "not
one jot." Similarly, "tittle" (a modification of "title" in the Bible translations of Wycliffe and Tyndale) derives from the Vulgate's *titulus,* which
was in turn borrowed from a Greek term meaning "apex of a letter." This
makes good sense, if, by a process of detection, we relate "tittle" or
titulus to the Hebrew word *tag,* meaning "the crownlet on a letter." In
the handwritten text of a *Torah* scroll, certain Hebrew letters are traditionally "crowned" with a small decorative flourish of approximately the
same size as the letter *yod.* Hence "jot or tittle" originally meant "the
smallest particle" and the word "tittle" itself is now used in the sense of

"any small sign employed as a diacritical or punctuation mark; or the least possible amount." The expressions "one jot" and "one jot or tittle" are widely used by many who scarcely suspect their true origin.[10]

The Pharisees (Hebrew: *Perushim*, "separatists") were a Jewish religious and political party originating in the second century B.C.E. who, in opposition to the aristocratic and literalist Sadducees, maintained a belief in the afterlife and the validity of the Oral as well as the Written Law. It is the Pharisaic stream in Judaism which flowed into the great Rabbinical schools of Hillel and Shammai and which fed the normative traditions of post-Biblical Israel. The religious approach of the Pharisees also influenced the teachings of early Christianity and Paul himself, the Apostle to the Gentiles, gloried in the fact that he had sat "at the feet of Gamaliel" (Acts 22:3), probably Rabban Gamaliel, one of the greatest of the Pharisee leaders. The term *Perushim* is first said to have been applied to the opponents of Hellenizing (Saducean) tendencies who were expelled from the Sanhedrin under John Hyrcanus. These "separated ones" made the name with which they were branded a title of honor by giving it the alternative interpretation of "exponents of the Law." The polemical approach of the New Testament transformed "Pharisee" into a term of reproach and abuse, although certain textual references make it clear that not all the adherents of Pharisaism were condemned (Matthew 23), only the hypocrites whom the Talmud also reproved. In modern parlance "Pharisee" and its derivatives, "pharisaical" and "pharisaism," have thus undeservedly acquired the extra connotation of "formalism, self-righteousness, sanctimoniousness, and hypocrisy."

Schlemiel, a comic Yiddish word meaning "bungler" or "chump," seems at first glance to be quite remote from any discussion of the Bible's impact on our daily language. Like a number of other Yiddish terms (e.g., *ganfen,* "to steal," and *koscher,* "ritually fit, or respectable"), *Schlemiel* entered German by way of *Rotwelsch* (thieves' slang) and first made its mark in literature when it inspired the title of Adelbert von Chamisso's famous tale about the man who lost his shadow (*Peter Schlemihls wundersame Geschichte,* 1814). Although the Hebrew phrase *she-lo mo'il* ("useless, of no benefit") has been suggested as a possible origin for *Schlemiel,* it is most probably based on the name of a person mentioned in the Bible, Shelumiel the son of Zurishaddai, prince of

---

[10] For Matthew 5:18 the *Revised Version* supplies the phrase, "Not an iota, not a dot."

Simeon (Num. 1:6). In the last section of *"Jehuda Ben Halevy,"* one of his *Hebräische Melodien* (1851), Heine comically describes his quest for the source of this term and then sets forth the curious solution proposed by a converted Jew, the Berlin police director Julius Hitzig:

> Phineas, blind with fury,
> In the sinner's place, by ill-luck
> Chanced to kill a guiltless person,
> Named Schlemihl ben Zuri Schadday.
> He, then, this Schlemihl the First,
> Was the ancestor of all the
> Race Schlemihl. . . .[11]

Whatever the basis for this "popular oral tradition" (for so Hitzig describes it), *Schlemiel*—like many other Yiddish modifications of Hebrew words and expressions—has since passed into everyday English and American usage.

Shabbat ("Sabbath"), from the Hebrew root meaning "to rest" (Gen. 2:3), has acquired a sinister, non-Hebraic meaning through the medieval French *sabbat*—a synonym for "tumult or uproar" (cf. *tohu-bohu*). During the Middle Ages and Renaissance, a *sabbat* was a midnight assembly of witches, warlocks, and sorcerers who sometimes performed a "black Mass" in honor of the Devil, to whom they declared allegiance through various orgiastic rites. A more familiar form of this term in English is "witches' Sabbath." Why and how the sober Biblical day of rest came to mean anything of the sort is puzzling, unless the original sense of "uproar" was a derisive reference to Jewish home observances and synagogue services, with their attendant chanting and Sabbath songs.

The last of these linguistic curiosities has its roots in the Apocrypha. From the story of Hannah and her seven sons, all of whom preferred martyrdom to apostasy (2 Maccabees 7), the early Church established a cult of the "Seven Maccabee Brothers" or "Seven Martyrs," whose tragedy was thought to prefigure the self-sacrifice of later Christian saints. This association with a gruesome death led to the medieval French *Macchabée* or *Macabré* becoming a synonym for "corpse" and to the modified adjectival form of *macabre,* signifying anything ghastly

[11] For the Biblical episode that forms a background to this legend, see Num. 25:6–18.

or funereal. From the Middle Ages onward, the *"Danse Macabre"* was a widespread theme in art and music, taking the form of an eerie procession of corpses and living people who are led toward the grave by a grisly skeleton. Thus, from the heroic saga of the Maccabees has come the incidental association of *macabre*, meaning "concerned with death, designed to produce a horrifying effect, or tending to distress".[12]

A final word must be said about some of the extravagant claims that have been made in support of the idea that Hebrew (once mystically regarded as the source of all tongues) was virtually the basis of English and French. In the 16th century, an eccentric genius named Guillaume Postel tried to establish a connection between the Semitic and Celtic languages which would lend weight to his belief that the remote ancestors of the French were, with the ancient Hebrews and Chaldeans, cofounders of Western civilization. These ideas were popularized by "Postellians" such as the mystical poet Guy Le Fèvre de la Boderie,[13] who playfully derived *Gallia* (Gaul, i.e. France) from the Hebrew *gal* ("wave"), Paris from *pe'er Ish* ("glory of man"), and countless other French terms from Semitic roots. Although such "etymology" never amounted to more than an intellectual fad, it contributed to French prestige and to the notions of a glorious national destiny fostered during the reign of Louis XIV (the "Sun King"). The "Hebrew madness" soon spread to England, where certain Puritans conceived the Anglo-Israel doctrine which, to this day, continues to lay great emphasis on the (accidental) similarity of some Hebrew and English words: *sekhel* ("understanding") and *skill, kol* ("voice") and *call, semel* "symbol" and *simile, dumah* ("silence") and *dumb*, and so forth.[14] A very small percentage of our modern vocabulary and a much larger proportion of our imagery and standard expression can certainly be traced to the Bible and the Hebrew language, but there the matter ends. No amount of fanciful and reckless speculation can substitute for objective and scientific analysis of a word or idiom, since—as we have seen—it is more the vital essence of the Biblical phrase than its mere shell that has lent a Hebraic color to the English language.

[12] According to one wild theory, *macabre* is related to the Hebrew root *k-v-r* ("to bury").

[13] La Boderie's work is also discussed in Chapters 1, 4, and 5.

[14] These odd currents in England and France are also alluded to in Chapter 4. Victor Hugo's tutor in Kabbalah, Alexandre Weill, toyed with such ideas in his *Étude Comparative de la Langue Française avec l'Hébreu*. . . (Paris, 1898).

PATTERNS OF SPEECH

As the next chapter will demonstrate, the Bible's influence on the spoken word has extended to the written word as well. Alone among the Italian writers of his time, Dante shook off the bonds of Classical style and imbued his native tongue with a vigorous new Biblical imagery and expression. The trend that he largely inaugurated has continued ever since, together with the pervasive influence of the vernacular Bible. Its effects may be seen most clearly in England, France, Germany, and America; in the works of Milton, Blake, and Bridie, of Du Bartas and Hugo, and of Goethe, Heine, and Mann. Taine, the great French historian and philosopher, paid lyrical tribute to the Bible's impact on his neighbors across the Channel when he wrote: "Hence have sprung much of the English language and half of the English names. To this day the country is biblical" (*Histoire de la littérature anglaise,* 1864). And when Hitler sought to "purge" German culture of its Biblical-Hebraic components, Cardinal Faulhaber of Munich delivered a trenchant and memorable retort: "If we are to repudiate the Old Testament and banish it from our schools and national libraries, then we must disown our German classics. We must cancel many phrases from the German language . . . We must disown the intellectual history of our nation" (*Judentum, Christentum, Germanentum,* 1934).

Emblem of the British Broadcasting Corporation: the motto incorporated takes its inspiration from Isaiah 2:4.

Although rhetoric as such is foreign to the Biblical spirit, several of the English-speaking world's greatest public figures have made notable use of the Scriptural phrase in their books and speeches. A significant example of Winston Churchill's Biblicism may be found in a BBC broadcast that he made (echoing a passage in the Song of Deborah, Judges 5:20) on June 16, 1941: "Ah no, this is not the end of the tale. The stars in their courses proclaim the deliverance of mankind . . . !"

Nor, to quote Britain's wartime statesman, is this "the end of the tale." The language of the Hebrew Bible has become part of the cultural heritage of the English and American peoples, a vital and indelible characteristic of their entire thinking and mode of expression.

BIBLICAL THEMES AND ECHOES
IN WORLD LITERATURE

My tongue is the pen of a ready writer

(Psalms 45:2)

Since the dawn of civilization no book has inspired as much creative endeavor among writers as the "Old" Testament, the Hebrew Bible. In poetry, drama, and fiction its literary influence has been unrivaled. The German poet Heinrich Heine, writing in 1830, described its significance in lyrical terms: "Sunrise and sunset, promise and fulfillment, birth and death, the whole human drama, everything is in this book . . . It is the Book of Books, *Biblia*." With varying insight, but unvarying consistency, writers in almost every land and culture have for more than a millennium found a matchless treasure house of themes and characters in the Bible. These they have reworked and reinterpreted in the portrayal of eternal motifs—as, for example, God and Man, the conflict of Good and Evil, love, jealousy, and man's struggle for freedom, truth, and justice.

From what might be called the unconscious artistry of the Scriptures attempts have been made to trace the basic elements of the literary genres. A complete drama can certainly be found in the Book of Job (which contains the essentials of dialogue, character delineation, and dramatic incident) and dramatic episodes in the Songs of Moses and Deborah. The Bible also offers many examples of poetic composition: meditative verse in Psalms, love poems in the Song of Songs, the elegy or dirge in David's lines bewailing Saul and Jonathan and in the Book of Lamentations. Complementing these are prose forms such as the novel in the stories of Joseph, Samson, and Esther and the short story in those about Gideon, Jephthah, and Jonah.

Probably the earliest literary adaptation of the Hebrew Bible was the work of Ezekiel the Poet, a Hellenistic Jew of Alexandria who lived in the second century B.C.E. His Greek dramatic poem, *Exagoge* ("The Exodus from Egypt"), which has survived only as a fragment, closely follows the Biblical story. It constitutes the only link between the Biblical drama of the Classical world and that of the Christian Middle Ages, and between

218

the secular Jewish literature of the pre-Christian era and that of medieval Spain and Italy.

It was only after the Church, having closed all theaters in the sixth century, eventually decided to permit the revival of drama as a religious vehicle and under its own strict control some time in the 11th century that themes drawn from the Bible reappeared in the literature of the West.[1] Church performances of plays relating the events of the Nativity (at Christmas) and the Passion (at Easter) were accompanied by sermons invoking the Biblical prophecies which, according to Christian theology, foretold the advent of the Messiah in the birth of Jesus. Once actors began representing the Prophets and declaiming their words, the stage was set for the writing of Old Testament Mystery and Miracle Plays side by side with the Nativity and Passion Plays based on the Gospels. And once Latin dialogue was replaced by the vernacular, these plays enjoyed a tremendous success throughout Western Europe. Some of the new dramas were written in France and Italy, others (often entire cycles) were produced in England.

Theological considerations at first dominated the choice of subjects and their interpretation: the binding of Isaac, the sacrifice of Jephthah, and the death of Absalom were seen as prefigurations of the Crucifixion; the Apocryphal figures of Judith and Susanna represented the triumph of Virtue (and hence of the Virgin) over Vice (or Satan); and, in Christian typology, David, Isaac, Job, Joseph, Joshua (a name akin to Jesus, or Yeshu), Moses, Noah, and Solomon were thought to prefigure the Savior. Belshazzar stood for the Antichrist, Elijah for John the Baptist, Jonah for the Resurrection. In time, however, Biblical drama moved out of the confines of the Church and became the concern of English merchant guilds, French fraternities, and other lay groups elsewhere. With the decline of these medieval plays toward the end of the 15th century, writers sought to broaden their scope by exploiting the farcical and comic potentials of stock episodes such as the drunkenness of Lot and Balaam and his ass.

Meanwhile another process—less familiar, but hardly less significant —had been taking place. During the 12th and 13th centuries, Anglo-Norman writers of "romance" were busy refurbishing the old Celtic legends, notably those involving King Arthur and his Knights of the Round Table. Some of these writers were clerics familiar not only with

[1] Early Jewish and Islamic treatments are dealt with separately below.

the Bible but also with Jewish legendary material from the Midrash, to which they had been introduced by Jewish scholars and translators with whom they had contact. As a result of this exchange of information and ideas many of the Arthurian motifs have their source in Hebrew literature, King Arthur himself embodying some features of the virtuous Joseph and the noble David. In this way a fresh Biblical stream now flowed into the epic poetry and prose of the West.

It was only with the Reformation that Biblical drama could be rejuvenated through a more imaginative treatment of the well-known Bible stories. Luther's German Bible (1534), the various English translations culminating in the *Authorized Version* (1611), and the French Bibles of Olivetan (1535) and Diodati (1644) together ensured the supremacy of the Protestant Old Testament in the vernacular and, with it, a growing readership for works of Biblical inspiration wherever the Christian Reformers gained the upper hand. In Germany, Luther encouraged his supporters to write plays on themes such as Judith and Tobit which were drawn from the Apocrypha, although the Hebrew Bible itself was not neglected. Biblical drama now took root with the spread of the Reformation itself—in England, Holland, and Scandinavia—and Biblical epics were written in England, France, Hungary, and Poland. The epic genre also attracted Catholic poets, although few of these could compete with Protestants such as Du Bartas and Milton. The "open Bible of the Reformation" alone provided the insights relating to God, Man, and Nature which writers of the new age sought overtly in their doctrines, and obliquely in their style and imagery.[2] By the 17th century, the Biblical drama and epic had been joined by the Biblical novel and the process of development was virtually complete.

There were, too, other significant consequences arising from the triumph of the Protestant Bible, particularly in England and Germany. Here the new translations had an incalculable influence on the everyday language of the people, helping to mold their very way of thinking.[3] Furthermore, many of the Biblical epics expressed the yearning of oppressed nations for their lost independence (as in Poland and Hungary), or of persecuted dissenters for freedom of conscience (as in England and France). From the Renaissance era onward, works on Biblical themes increasingly took on social and political overtones and this process

[2] Harold Fisch, *Jerusalem and Albion* (1964), p. 55.
[3] These linguistic considerations are more fully discussed in Chapter 3.

gained momentum during the upsurge of nationalism in 19th-century Europe.

Another important factor has been the contribution which Jews have made since the beginnings of Jewish emancipation in the 18th century. General literature has been enriched by the insight into the Bible afforded by their distinctive background and heritage; and Biblical themes have played a major role in Modern Hebrew and in Yiddish literature.

ENGLAND

The early impact of the Hebrew Bible on English literature may be traced as far back as the first Anglo-Saxon paraphrases of Biblical books and passages in the seventh century. They include three by the poet Caedmon (c. 670), covering the Books of Daniel, Exodus, and Genesis—where Abraham takes on the character of an Anglo-Saxon chief leading his thanes into battle. Other old English poems paraphrase Psalms, give an epic treatment to Judith, or rework familiar Bible stories: two examples are the 13th-century *Iacob and Iosep,* a lively poem in the Midlands dialect, and the 14th-century version of Jonah entitled *Patience.* Medieval England produced a wide selection of plays dealing with Old Testament subjects, such as the *Ordo de Ysaac et Rebecca et Filiis Eorum* ("Of Isaac, Rebekah, and Their Sons"), the *Histories of Lot and Abraham,* and the *Mactatio Abel* ("Sacrifice of Abel"), which draws a sympathetic picture of Cain that contrasts markedly with that of the avaricious peasant presented in the Anglo-Norman *Jeu d'Adam* ("Adam Play").

Many Biblical dramas were gathered together in cycles of plays performed over a period of hours or even days in major towns such as Chester, Dublin, Lincoln, Wakefield, and York. Appropriately enough, one old drama—*Noah's Ark*—was presented by the shipwrights' guild of Newcastle upon Tyne. A number of these plays continued to draw audiences well into the 16th century, especially those that dealt humorously with figures such as Noah and Balaam.[4]

Although *Yefthae* ("Jephthah," 1544), a politically motivated Greek academic play by the Catholic John Christopherson, was a work in the

---

[4] For some of the details contained in this section I am indebted to Murray Roston's *Biblical Drama in England* (1968).

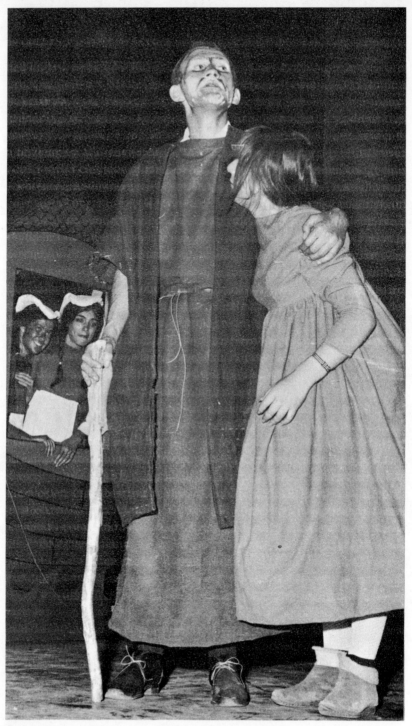

The Deluge, an English Mystery Play performed by students of the Hebrew University, Jerusalem.

spirit of the Renaissance, it was the English Reformation that gave the main impetus to religious drama. The same Biblical theme recurs in *Jephthes sive votum* ("Jephthah or the Vow," staged in 1542 and published in 1554), a neo-Latin play by the Scottish poet George Buchanan, who also wrote a paraphrase of Psalms (1566); and in "Jephthah Judge of Israel," an old English ballad quoted by Shakespeare (*Hamlet,* Act 2, Scene 2). Another Old Testament drama of the period, Nicholas Udall's *Ezechias,* was performed before Queen Elizabeth I at King's College Chapel, Cambridge, in 1564. Udall is also the reputed author of *The Historie of Jacob and Esau,* written some ten years before its publication in 1568, which underscores with lively comedy the religious conflicts of the age by portraying Jacob, the righteous Hebrew, as an obvious Protestant and Esau, the graceless pagan, as an equally obvious Catholic.

The religious and political climate strongly influenced later Biblical plays in 16th-century England. The anonymous *New Enterlude of Godly Queene Hester* (1561), based on the Book of Esther and its tale of intrigue at the Persian court, contained undertones of popular discontent with Henry VIII and his ministers of state; while *A Looking Glass for London and England* (1594), a play by Robert Greene and Thomas Lodge, combined Elizabethan satire and the Reformation spirit in weaving the story of Jonah into an account of the Israelite kingdom after Jeroboam's overthrow. Here Nineveh clearly represents the emerging Puritan view of the "sinful" city of London. The same kind of moralistic treatment characterized contemporary dramas about Joseph and others about Susanna, notably Thomas Garter's *The Commody of the Moste Vertuous and Godlye Susanna* (1578). However, George Peele's *The Love of King David and Fair Bethsabe* (1599), which blamed Absalom's revolt on David's illicit romance, pandered to the Elizabethan taste for gory spectacle by staging Joab's execution of the rebellious prince as he hung suspended by his hair from a tree.

Side by side with this moralistic handling of Biblical motifs went a less serious approach evident in many of the plays written in the 17th century, which to some extent form a continuation of the late Elizabethan tradition. Among these are Samuel Rowley's *Joshua,* and two other dramas which he wrote in collaboration with a certain Jewby, *Absalom* and *Sampson,* all of which were staged in London in 1602. Like Peele, Rowley and Jewby were alive to the uses of the stage, *Sampson* including one scene in which the Hebrew judge appears carrying the town gates on his shoulders, to the great delight of the audience. A new Apocryphal theme, probably the first English dramatization of the subject, was William Houghton's *Judas Maccabaeus* (c. 1601), while other playwrights continued to deal with the stories of Judith and Holofernes, Jephthah, and Noah. One of the most entertaining spectacles of the early 17th century, according to contemporary accounts, must have been *Solomon and the Queen of Sheba,* a masque performed at Theobalds Inn before James I and the King of Denmark in July 1607. This "ended in bacchanalian revelry . . . in which His Danish Majesty sought to dance with Sheba's tipsy queen but could not keep his footing"!

The influence of the English Bible is already apparent in Peele's drama about David and Bath-Sheba, the 16th century having seen the hastening of that momentous process of Bible translation which began with John Wycliffe in the 1380s and gathered speed with the appearance of Bibles by William Tyndale and Miles Coverdale in the 1530s. The subsequent publication of the *"Great" Bible* (1539) and the *Bishop's Bible* (1568), among others, prepared the way for the *King James (Authorized) Version* of 1611, the characteristic language and style of which left an indelible stamp on English prose.[5] Poetry, too, became charged with Biblical idiom through the various translations of the Book of Psalms, most notably *The Whole Booke of Psalmes; collected into Englysh metre . . . conferred with the Ebrue . . .* (1551), which a team of scholars headed by Thomas Sternhold successfully launched through hundreds of editions. This English Psalter was the basis for the Church of Scotland's *Psalms of David,* still in wide use among English-speaking Protestants.

Although the dramas and comedies of William Shakespeare (1564–1616) are not specifically concerned with Biblical themes, their English phraseology is rich in Scriptural echoes. Shakespeare was steeped in the Bible, which he mainly knew from the translations of Coverdale and from the Calvinist Geneva edition of 1560. Modern scholarship has also emphasized the many linguistic parallels between the *King James Version* and the choice of phrase evident in Shakespeare's plays. Indeed, the modern reader is sometimes apt to confuse quotations from these two sources. Even a brief examination of Shakespeare's works will indicate how much the great dramatist owed to the Hebrew Bible. Some notable examples of his Biblicism are "Woe to that land that's govern'd by a child" (*Richard III*, Act 2, Scene 3; cf. Eccl. 10:16); "A Daniel come to judgment!" (*The Merchant of Venice*, Act 4, Scene 1); "We'll set thee to

---

[5] See Chapter 3 and below.

school to an ant, to teach thee there's no labouring i' th' winter" (*King Lear*, Act 2, Scene 4; cf. Prov. 6:6ff., 30:25); and "Who, like a boar too savage, doth root up/His country's peace" (*Timon of Athens*, Act 5, Scene 1; cf. Ps. 80: 13–14). There are unmistakable echoes of the Tenth Commandment (Ex. 20:14, Deut. 5:18) in the lines: "I will be master of what is mine own—/She is my goods, my chattels, she is my house,/My household stuff, my field, my barn,/My horse, my ox, my ass, my any thing . . ." (*The Taming of the Shrew*, Act 3, Scene 2). And in *Henry VIII*, first staged two years after the appearance of the *King James Version* (i.e., in 1613), the Biblical note reaches a crescendo. Broken by his disgrace, Cardinal Wolsey (Act 3, Scene 2) laments: "O, how wretched/ Is that poor man that hangs on princes' favours!" (cf. Ps. 146:3), and concludes that, "when he falls, he falls like Lucifer,/Never to hope again" (cf. Isa. 14:12ff.). This dramatic presentation of the religious and political clashes in 16th-century England ends with a paean of praise to the infant princess (later Queen Elizabeth I or "Gloriana"), whose predicted wisdom is likened to that of Saba (the Queen of Sheba) and whose future reign is pictured in glowing Scriptural terms (cf. Micah 4:4). Here, the Biblical imagery of the vine and cedar are especially prominent (Act 5, Scene 5). The genius of Shakespeare thus helped to naturalize the English Bible in the everyday speech of Elizabethan England.

With the rise of Puritanism, which frowned on the theater as a godless frivolity, Biblical drama underwent an eclipse during the years 1610– 1660. Instead, prose and poetry (sometimes attaining epic dimensions) were the media used to reinterpret Old Testament subjects in the light of current religious and political issues. This is true even of a royalist like Francis Quarles who chose to write a verse paraphrase, rather than a drama, about the Book of Jonah in *A Feaste for Wormes* (1620), a theme which he later also developed in his *Divine Poems* (1630). It is interesting to note that the Puritans, though great Psalm singers, were less inclined than the moderate Anglicans to use the Bible as a model for their own works. Thus, while the Puritans flattened Biblical poetry into prose, the "Hebraic" moderates managed—even in their prose—to preserve the poetic vibrations of the Hebrew.[6] The influence of the Book of Psalms pervades the meditative works of George Herbert (*The Temple*, 1633), that of Job the writings of John Donne (whose

[6] Fisch, *op. cit.*, pp. 53–55.

sermons are suffused with Biblical Hebrew's parallelism), while some of the philosophical works of Sir Thomas Browne (*Religio Medici,* 1643) and of the navigator and poet Sir Walter Raleigh (*Instructions to his Son,* 1632) also owe much to the Hebraic spirit.

The Puritans were especially attracted to the Judges of Israel, with whom they tended to identify themselves, and their doctrine of Election and Covenant (the latter constituting a central feature of their theology and social life) derived to a great extent from Hebrew sources, such as the Book of Genesis. In an extreme and reckless form, this Covenant idea inspired John Sadler, a Puritan Member of Parliament, to publish his *Rights of the Kingdom* (1649)—an early manifesto of the British Israelites, who still maintain that the English and their ethnic kinfolk throughout the world are descended from the Lost Ten Tribes of Israel. [7]

The works of John Milton (1608–1674), the outstanding representative of the Puritans, contain an unusual concentration of Biblical and Hebraic notions and sentiments. Milton certainly knew enough Hebrew to enable him in later years to study the Hebrew Bible and, perhaps also, the classical Jewish commentators. Faithful to his idea that God had chosen England as the Messiah-Nation and himself as the prophet and poet of the English Reformation, Milton injected all his powers of moral passion and prophetic rebuke into writings as varied as the pamphlet *Areopagitica* (1644) and the sonnets "To the Lord General Cromwell" (1652) and "On the Late Massacre in Piedmont" (1655). The eloquence of the latter poem led the Great Protector to take effective steps in defense of the persecuted Waldensian Protestants:

> Avenge, O Lord, thy slaughter'd saints, whose bones
> Lie scatter'd on the Alpine mountains cold;
> Ev'n them who kept thy truth so pure of old,
> When all our fathers worshipp'd stocks and stones,
> Forget not! . . .

Milton's greatest epic, *Paradise Lost* (1667), explicitly seeks to "justify the ways of God to men" in relating the Creation story and the Fall

---

[7] Anglo-Israelism, which gathered force as a movement in the late 18th century, bases its claims on bizarre theological and linguistic assumptions (e.g., that the Saxons were really "Isaac's Sons" and the British the *Berit-Ish,* or "Covenant Men," an invented Hebrew term).

of Man within the framework of the Christian tradition. The fundamental stress is, however, on human freedom and individual responsibility, Adam remaining a free agent sustained by his belief in ultimate redemption, and from this it is clear that Milton himself came closer than most of his fellow-Puritans to Hebraic norms. The conflict, developed in the Book of Job, between man's faith in God's ultimate justice and the feeling that the punishment meted out to a particular individual is excessive dominates the one great Biblical drama in the English language, Milton's *Samson Agonistes* (1671). Here the Hebrew Judge (Samson), "Eyeless in Gaza at the mill with slaves," is both an idealization of the Biblical figure and, undisguisedly, a portrait of the writer himself, blind and abandoned after the return of the Stuarts.

During the late Commonwealth and early Restoration period, themes drawn from the Hebrew Bible were very often exploited for political ends. Abraham Cowley's verse epic, *Davideis* (1656), expresses through the mouth of Samuel the antagonism which the author felt—under Cromwell's rule, at any rate—toward the concept of monarchical government. Similarly, John Dryden made his near-blasphemous *Absalom and Achitophel* (1681) the vehicle for some powerful satirical comment on the intrigues of the Restoration court ("During his office, treason was no crime./The sons of Belial had a glorious time"). Here, Dryden thinly disguised Charles II as David, Charles' illegitimate son (the Duke of Monmouth) as Absalom, and Lord Shaftesbury as the false counselor Achitophel. During the last decades of the century some attempts were made to revive Biblical drama. The legacy of Puritanism and other religious scruples nevertheless discouraged the presentation of Biblical themes on the 17th- and 18th-century stage, except in the form of the "sacred drama" or oratorio. Some playwrights tried to circumvent official objections by using Josephus' *Jewish War* and *Antiquities of the Jews* as source material for their works on heroic, semi-Biblical themes such as the revolt of the Maccabees, Herod and Mariamne, and the Roman destruction of Jerusalem. However, the dramatization of these subjects proved less successful in England than in Germany and elsewhere.

On the whole, most English Biblical works of the 18th century took the form of the oratorio. Like Charles Jennens' *Israel in Egypt* (c. 1738), Thomas Morell's *Joshua, A Sacred Drama* (1748) is best remembered as one of the texts which, enhanced by the music of Handel, appealed to English patriotism at a time when Biblical themes were banned from the theater. They created a vogue that Oliver Goldsmith was quick to exploit with his oratorio, *The Captivity* (1764), which portrays the Hebrews freed by Cyrus as dignified and uncorrupted in their Babylonian exile. In fiction, the novelist Henry Fielding displayed a strongly Hebraic background in his satirical *Joseph Andrews* (1742), which was intended to recall the lives of Joseph and Abraham. A further contribution was made by the English Hebraist Robert Lowth, Professor of Poetry at Oxford from 1741, who published first in Latin (1753) and then in English his *Lectures on the Sacred Poetry of the Hebrews* (1787), an original and pioneering study of Hebrew poetry in the Bible.

There was a significant revival of literary interest in Biblical themes from the second decade of the 19th century, with the dominant genre now that of poetry. Lord Byron (1788–1824) first broached the subject with his *Hebrew Melodies,* which were published with musical settings by Isaac Nathan as *A Selection of Hebrew Melodies, Ancient and Modern* . . . (1815). Among these are the "Vision of Belshazzar," said to have inspired one of Heine's early German poems; "Jephthah's Daughter"; the moving "Weep for those that wept by Babel's Stream"; and "The Destruction of Sennacherib," which opens with the well-known lines:

> The Assyrian came down like the wolf on the fold,
> And his cohorts were gleaming in purple and gold;
> And the sheen of their spears was like stars on the sea,
> When the blue wave rolls nightly on deep Galilee . . .

One of the most memorable Biblical allusions in English Romantic poetry occurs in John Keats's "Ode to a Nightingale" (1819): "Perhaps the self-same song that found a path/Through the sad heart of Ruth, when, sick for home,/She stood in tears amid the alien corn . . ." Biblical echoes also abound in the works of the great Scottish poet Robert Burns (1759–1796), while Thomas Moore's *Sacred Songs* (1816–20) include a poem about the Exodus which contains the well-known lines, "Sound the loud timbrel o'er Egypt's dark sea!/Jehovah has triumphed—His people are free! . . ."

The figure of Cain was at the center of much literary controversy in the late 18th and early 19th centuries following the appearance in 1761 of an English translation of Salomon Gessner's German prose epic, *Der Tod Abels* ("The Death of Abel," 1758). Samuel Taylor Coleridge inaugurated the new trend with his "Gothic" poem, *The Wanderings of*

Cain (1798), but the storm broke with Byron's romantic verse play, *Cain* (1821), which clearly challenged Divine benevolence by attempting to make a hero of the first murderer. Indeed, Cain and Lucifer—shattering all religious and literary convention—boldly deny the benevolence of God, describing themselves as "Souls who dare look the Omnipotent tyrant in/His everlasting face, and tell him that/His evil is not good." The poem—which reflects Byron's own religious skepticism—was widely condemned as blasphemous, the principal riposte which it drew being *The Ghost of Abel* (1822) by another Romantic, William Blake (1757–1827). A strong Biblical and Hebraic color is visible in the works of Blake, from the verse on Samson in his early *Poetical Sketches* (1783) through *The Four Zoas* (1795–1804) and *Milton* (1804) to *Jerusalem* (1804–18). An engraver as well as a poet, Blake produced some outstanding *Inventions to the Book of Job* (1820–26). His religious mystique, influenced by ideas drawn from British Israelite sources, occult circles, and, perhaps also, from the Jewish Kabbalah, is revealed in his notion of the Giant Albion whose limbs contain Heaven and Earth, and in the recurring Jerusalem motif expressed, for example, in the last quatrain of his preface to *Milton:*

I will not cease from mental fight,
Nor shall my sword sleep in my hand,
Till we have built Jerusalem
In England's green and pleasant land.

Sharply contrasting with the inspiration of these poets were two Biblical plays, both in their way curiosities of the time. *Esther the Royal Jewess; or the Death of Haman,* a lavishly produced melodrama staged in London in 1835, was the work of Elisabeth Polack, an Anglo-Jewish writer, and was practically the only 19th-century drama on a Biblical theme to escape censorship. Another religious melodrama, Robert Jameson's *Nimrod* (1848), the title of which disguised the leitmotiv of the Fall of Man, is remembered as an outstanding example of the Victorian theater at its worst. Scarcely an improvement on Jameson's play—with which it shared the central theme—was *The Tower of Babel* (1874), a somewhat absurd drama by Alfred Austin, who succeeded Alfred Lord Tennyson as Poet Laureate. The Bible was not, however, neglected by English poets such as William Wordsworth, whose "Michael" (1880) renews the old Puritan symbolism of the covenant, and Robert

Job and his "comforters" by William Blake, from his *Inventions to the Book of Job* (1820–26).

Browning (1812–1889), who studied Hebrew and knew something of Rabbinic lore. Browning, whose many poems on Jewish themes expressed unusual sympathy for the Jews of his day, dealt with Biblical subjects in "Saul" (1845) and "Solomon and Balkis" (1883). His wife, the poetess Elizabeth Barrett Browning, retold the story of Adam and Eve in her *Drama of Exile* (1844). There is a remarkable instance of the Hebrew Bible's powerful hold on English writing in Browning's sardonic poem, "Holy Cross Day" (1855), where a Jew of Rome— forced to attend one of the Church's conversionist sermons at Easter —optimistically recalls:

> The Lord will have mercy on Jacob yet,
> And again in his border see Israel set.
> When Judah beholds Jerusalem,
> The stranger-seed shall be joined to them:
> To Jacob's House shall the Gentiles cleave.
> So the Prophet saith and his sons believe . . .

An important cultural influence was exerted in the mid-19th century by the eminent poet and critic Matthew Arnold, whose ideas on Hebraism and Hellenism and on the pursuit of "sweetness and light" were set out in *Culture and Anarchy* (1869). Throughout the Victorian era, reverence for the Scriptural word was expressed by leading writers such as Thomas Carlyle, who maintained that the Psalms of David "struck tones that were an echo of the sphere-harmonies," and also by the British statesman William Ewart Gladstone, who claimed that "all the wonders of the Greek civilization heaped together are less wonderful than the single Book of Psalms" (*The Place of Ancient Greece*, 1865). A similar tribute was paid by the novelist Israel Zangwill, who, noting the Bible's impact on state and society, wrote that "its Psalms are more popular in every country than the poems of the nation's own poets. Beside this one book with its infinite editions . . . all other literatures seem 'trifles light as air'" (*The Voice of Jerusalem*, 1895).

Special reference should be made to the literary expression of patriotic sentiment, in which the imagery and cadences of the Bible have been dominant ever since Elizabethan times. The near-religious mystique of British imperialism in its benevolent, late Victorian form rings through "Recessional," a poem by Rudyard Kipling (1865–1936) which appeared in *The Times* (July 17, 1897) on the occasion of Queen Victoria's diamond Jubilee:

God of our fathers, known of old,
  Lord of our far-flung battle-line,
Beneath whose awful Hand we hold
  Dominion over palm and pine—
Lord God of Hosts, be with us yet,
Lest we forget—lest we forget! . . .

If, drunk with sight of power, we loose
  Wild tongues that have not Thee in awe,
Such boastings as the Gentiles use,
  Or lesser breeds without the Law—
Lord God of Hosts, be with us yet,
Lest we forget—lest we forget! . . .

The new rationalism of the 20th century demanded the removal of such paraphernalia as angels and miracles and the reassessment of Old Testament personalities, suspicious iconoclasts arbitrarily changing villains into heroes and heroes into villains—all in the "spirit of the age." The process was at first gradual for, after Gwen Lally's *Jezebel* overcame the Lord Chamberlain's objections to the staging of Biblical drama in 1912, the Apocryphal heroine Judith was the center of attention. A play by Thomas Sturge Moore staged in 1916 suggested that she had become the mistress of Holofernes before killing him and Judith and Vashti, the heroines of two Biblical verse plays in Lascelles Abercrombie's *Emblems of Love* (1912), were militant suffragettes. The break with tradition was in fact heralded by Isaac Rosenberg's short drama, *Moses* (1916), which in its attempt to strip the "real man" of his Lawgiver's trappings transformed him into a Nietzschean superman. The same approach characterized the new treatment of the classic villainess Jezebel in Clemence Dane's play, *Naboth's Vineyard* (1925), which made her a kindly, reasonable woman, and in John Masefield's more deliberately iconoclastic drama, *A King's Daughter* (1923), where the story was entirely rewritten in order to whitewash Ahab and his queen. From here the road leads straight to Laurence Housman's frankly anti-Biblical *Old Testament Plays* (1950)—*Abraham and Isaac, Jacob's Ladder, The Burden of Nineveh,* and *Samuel the Kingmaker*—the aim of which was to denigrate the traditional heroes and debunk the Bible, or rather the "Old" Testament, scarcely any attempts having been made to demythologize the "New."

Most 20th-century English works on Biblical themes have, however, pursued a more moderate path. This is less true of George Bernard Shaw in *Back to Methuselah* (1921), than of D. H. Lawrence (*David,* 1926) and Sir James Barrie (*The Boy David,* 1936). One of the more welcome aspects of recent English treatment of Biblical subjects has been the element of humor first introduced by A. P. Herbert in his short play, *The Book of Jonah (As almost any modern Irishman would have written it)* (1921), and which, though utilized by Arnold Bennett in his *Judith* (1919), was lost in the uproar over that drama's heroine appearing on the stage in a daringly revealing costume. And, rather than vilify his wonder-working Prophets, the Scots dramatist James Bridie makes them slightly ridiculous little men whose miracles, instead of being ignored, are consigned to a world of fantasy on the stage. Bridie's major Biblical plays are *Tobias and the Angel* (1931), notable for its lively humor and realism; *Jonah and the Whale* (1932; revised as *Jonah 3* in *Plays for Plain People,* 1944), where superficial frivolity disguises a serious approach to the central theme; and *Susannah and the Elders* (1937), the heroine of which is an incorrigible flirt who deserves far less sympathy than the sorely provoked old men who stoically accept their unjust fate.

Biblical motifs have attracted few English novelists and poets of the 20th century. On the other hand, some interesting Biblical plays were written after World War II. Norman Nicholson's *The Old Man of the Mountains* (1946) transposed the Prophet Elijah to a setting in the North of England, where he becomes a champion of the working classes, while his other verse play, *A Match for the Devil* (1955), produced at the Edinburgh Festival in 1953, retold the story of Hosea and his "wife of harlotry" in a Christian spirit. The Nietzschean element reappears in Christopher Fry's drama, *The Firstborn* (1946), a reworking of the Moses story in the form of a tragedy, where Moses—divested of his Biblical qualities and torn between idealism and reality—provides the impetus for the Hebrew nation's redemption. An interesting sidelight on literary activity in post-World War II England is the fact that so few of the Jewish writers who rose to eminence showed any interest in Biblical subjects. Wolf Mankowitz's *It Should Happen to a Dog* (1956), a one-act play on the Jonah theme, exploited the humor and idiom of London's East End; while Dan Jacobson, a South African immigrant, roused wide attention with his secularized romance, *The Rape of Tamar* (1970). In their choice of theme these two stood alone. Thus, in the most recent—

as in the earliest—period of English literary creativity, the Bible still retains its perennial fascination for British dramatists.

THE CELTIC REGION

In common with the English and other peoples, the Celts wrote paraphrases of the Hebrew Bible which form some of the earliest documents in their literary history. During the Middle Ages, a number of Mystery Plays on Biblical themes also made their appearance. The mainly Protestant translations of the Bible inspired by the Reformation have, however, had little direct influence on the prose and poetry of the two major surviving literatures (Irish Gaelic and Welsh). Probably the first Celtic literary work of Biblical inspiration was the tenth-century *Saltair na Rann* ("Verse Psalter"), an Erse (Irish Gaelic) Bible history in 150

Pages from *The Proverbs of Solomon, in Hebrew, in Irish, and in English* (Dublin, 1823).

cantos. The earliest complete editions of the Bible in Scots and Irish Gaelic appeared only in the 1680s. A strongly Christian spirit permeates Welsh literature from its earliest beginnings and there were several pre-Norman Welsh poems on Biblical themes, such as "The Plagues of Egypt" and "The Rod of Moses," in the tenth and 11th centuries. From the first known attempt to translate part of the Bible into Welsh in 1346, the Scriptures have exerted a profound influence on the Welsh people, among whom Puritan and Nonconformist preachers and writers found a warm response, but there have been practically no important literary works on Biblical subjects in the Welsh language.

Paradoxically enough, it was in the remote Celtic outpost of Cornwall that the outstanding literary treatment of a Biblical subject was written —and in a language that became extinct in the late 18th century. The *Origo Mundi* ("Beginning of the World"), as it is entitled in Latin, comprises the first part of a 15th-century Cornish trilogy known as the *Ordinalia*. An epic of slightly less than 3,000 lines, the *Origo Mundi* is an account of the main events of Bible history up to the building of Solomon's Temple. Its influence may be seen in *Gwreans an Bys* ("The Creation of the World"), another Cornish work of the pre-Reformation period, extant as a manuscript (dated 1611) in the Bodleian Library, Oxford, the text of which, together with an English translation, appeared in 1864.

A much earlier and far more significant factor was the Biblical and Midrashic element which revitalized the old Celtic Arthurian legends during the Middle Ages—that "matter of Britain" which was to enrich the literature of chivalry in England, France, and Germany. A fragmentary Hebrew adaptation of the King Arthur cycle (dated 1279) has also survived, testifying to the fruitful literary exchanges between Jewish and Christian scribes and exegetes of that era. The curious, but unsubstantiated, belief that *Excalibur,* the name of Arthur's sword, was some kind of magical Hebraic term seems to have originated with a 15th-century author, Henry Lovelich. Writing about the sword in his romance, *Merlin* (c. 1450), he notes: "The right name was cleped Escalibourc, which is a name in ebrewe, that is to sey in englissh, kyttinge iren, tymber, and steill." The fact that *Excalibur* is almost certainly of Celtic origin would, of course, only have reinforced British Israelite impressions that the religion and cultures of ancient Israel and Britain were closely related, if not one and the same.

THE UNITED STATES AND CANADA

No Christian community in history identified more with the People of the Book than did the early settlers of the Massachusetts Bay Colony, who believed their own lives to be a literal reenactment of the Biblical drama of the Hebrew nation. They themselves were the Children of Israel; America was their Promised Land; the Atlantic Ocean their Red Sea; the kings of England were the Egyptian pharaohs; the American Indians were the Canaanites (or the Lost Ten Tribes of Israel); the pact of Plymouth Rock was God's holy Covenant; and the ordinances by which they lived were the Divine Law. Like the Huguenots and other Protestant victims of Old World oppression, these émigré Puritans dramatized their own situation as the righteous remnant of a Church corrupted by the "Babylonian woe" and saw themselves as instruments of Divine Providence, a people chosen to build their new commonwealth on the Covenant entered into at Mount Sinai.

The cornerstone of the "New Jerusalem" which the Puritans yearned to establish in the American wilderness was, of course, the Bible, which deserved to be studied in "that most ancient language and holy tongue in which the law and oracle of God were written; and in which God and angels spoke to the holy patriarchs of old time," to quote the phrase of William Bradford (1590–1657), a founder of the Plymouth Colony and its governor from 1621 to 1656. When the Pilgrim Fathers left England to settle in the New World, they took with them the Psalter (1612) of Henry Ainsworth (1571–c. 1623), the Brownist leader, who was a noted Biblical and Rabbinic scholar. The Puritans of New England encouraged Hebrew studies and those who acquired even a superficial knowledge of the language loved to air their Hebrew in sermons, lectures, and everyday conversation. They preferred to give their children Hebrew names culled from the Bible and many of their towns and villages were named after ancient Hebrew settlements (Bethlehem, Salem, Shiloh, Zion). Indeed, the break with England in 1776 seems to have prompted some of the American revolutionaries to suggest the adoption of Hebrew as the official language of the new republic. The first important work printed in North America was the *Bay Psalm Book* (1640), a highly literal translation of Psalms based directly on the Hebrew text; stylistic considerations were subordinated to accuracy, since (as Richard Mather indicated in the book's preface) "God's altar needs not our polishings" and the word of God was meant only for those who wished to "sing in

Seal of Columbia University, New York, first adopted in 1755. Over the head of the seated woman is the (Hebrew) Tetragrammaton, YHVH ("Jehovah"); the Latin motto around her head means "In Thy light do we see light" (Ps. 36:10); the Hebrew phrase on the ribbon is *Uri El* ("God is my light"), a modification of Ps. 27:1.

Sion the Lord's songs of prayse according to his own wille." Generations of students at Harvard and Yale were required to learn Hebrew as the prime key to the Old Testament, Yale's official seal including the Hebrew legend: *Urim ve-Tummim*. This tradition was maintained to some extent by other colleges founded during the Colonial Period (Columbia, Dartmouth, Princeton, and Brown).

One curious aspect of early American Biblicism was the long and earnest attempt to identify the Indians with the Lost Tribes of Israel, an interesting variation on a theme familiar among Puritan circles in England.[8] John Eliot (1604–1690), the "Apostle of the Indians," engaged in missionary work among the Algonquins, for whom he translated the entire Bible (1661–63), his text constituting the first edition of the Scriptures printed in North America. Eliot claimed that the members of this tribe spoke in parables like the Biblical Israelites, anointed their

[8] For details of the "British Israelites," see above (England).

heads, abhorred the pig, and followed many other Hebraic practices. Anne Bradstreet (c. 1612-1672), America's first poetess of note, speculated in her epic, *The Four Monarchies,* as to whether the descendants of the Lost Ten Tribes were to be found among the Indians of the East or the West; and William Penn (1644-1718), founder of the Quaker colony of Pennsylvania, was sure that the Indians living within his territory (who, to his great joy, adopted him as their brother) ultimately descended from the Israelites of old. Yale's president, Ezra Stiles (1727-1795), also shared these views at one time, but later turned his missionary attention to the post-Biblical Jews, whose religious integrity he was eventually forced to respect. Stiles learned Hebrew and acquired a knowledge of other Semitic languages together with some Talmud and Kabbalah. He believed that a knowledge of the Hebrew language and culture was essential to a liberal education and sound grasp of the Bible and delivered a Hebrew oration at the Yale commencement exercises in 1781. As late as 1827, the playwright and politician Mordecai Manuel Noah (1785-1851), probably the most influential American Jew of his time, wrote a *Discourse on the Evidences of the American Indians Being the Descendants of the Lost Tribes of Israel.* Two years earlier, Noah had set himself up as "ruler" of Ararat, a tract of land on Grand Island in the Niagara River near Buffalo which he designated as a Jewish colony. When it was clear that the project had failed, Noah turned his proto-Zionist attention to the Holy Land.

The fact that the New England Puritans restricted their literary activity to the writing of sermons and tracts shows how closely they adhered to Judaic modes of thought—traditionally hostile to secular and imaginative works. This Puritan outlook probably accounts for the virtual absence of Biblical poetry and drama in American literature before the 19th century. Two rare exceptions were Thomas Ellwood's sacred poem, *Davideis* (1712), and *The Conquest of Canaan* (1785), an epic by Timothy Dwight (1752-1817), who was a leading Calvinist preacher and "Connecticut Wit." Drafted between 1771 and 1773, Dwight's poem has fervently patriotic undertones, allegorizing Joshua's military campaign in terms of George Washington's struggle against the British. Half a century later, the same theme inspired "The Battles of Joshua" (1843), an anonymous ballad, generally attributed to the New York Sephardi writer Samuel B. H. Judah (1799-1876), which portrayed the Israelite general as a cruel invader. This iconoclasm, so much at variance with the respectful Jewish and Christian approach to Biblical subjects in 19th-century American literature, also dominates Judah's tragedy, *The Maid of Midian*. Here, the plot was "founded on the massacre of the Midian captives by order of Moses" (Numbers 31:2–18) and, because of its sacrilegious nature, the play was never performed. The decade before the Civil War also saw the beginnings of the Biblical novel with *The First of the Maccabees* (1860) by Isaac Mayer Wise (1819–1900), the pioneer of Reform Judaism in the United States, and *The Pillar of Fire* (1859) and *The Throne of David* (1860), two romances by the author and preacher Joseph Holt Ingraham (1809–1860), the first of which became an early bestseller.

The Bible continued to maintain its literary ascendancy over the American mind throughout the 19th century. Though not tied to any denominational creed, President Abraham Lincoln (1809–1865) was a tireless reader of the Scriptures, which rang through some of his most memorable speeches. Quoting John Wycliffe's Prologue to the English Bible (1384), Lincoln in his Gettysburg Address (Nov. 19, 1863) asserted "that this nation, under God, shall have a new birth of freedom; and that government of the people, by the people, for the people, shall not perish from the earth." At about the same time, Julia Ward Howe (1819–1910) wrote her "Battle Hymn of the American Republic" as an expression of her reformist zeal; during the Civil War, it was one of the great marching songs of the Union army and it has since become familiar throughout the English-speaking world:

Mine eyes have seen the glory of the coming of the Lord:
He is trampling out the vintage where the grapes of wrath are stored;
He has loosed the fateful lightning of his terrible swift sword:
His truth is marching on! . . .

The "Battle Hymn of the Republic," with its well-known refrain ("Glory, glory, Hallelujah!"), was set to a tune that was borrowed for another song of the North—"John Brown's body lies a-mould'ring in the grave" —commemorating the famous abolitionist.

Nowhere was this Biblical current more apparent than in American poetry of the era, especially that of John Greenleaf Whittier (1807–1892), Henry Wadsworth Longfellow (1807–1882), and Walt Whitman (1819–1892). There are conscious echoes of the Bible in Whitman's *Leaves of Grass* (1855–92) and several evocations of Biblical figures in the poems of Whittier: "Judith at the Tent of Holofernes" (1829), "Palestine"

(1837), "Ezekiel" (1844), "The Wife of Manoah to her Husband" (1847), and "King Solomon and the Ants" (1877). Indeed, Whittier— a fervent Quaker—explicitly acknowledged his debt to the English Bible in "Miriam," a poem written in 1870:

> We search the world for truth; we cull
> The good, the pure, the beautiful
> From graven stone and written scroll,
> From all old flower-fields of the soul;
> And, weary seekers of the best,
> We come back laden from our quest,
> To find that all the sages said
> Is in the Book our mothers read.

Longfellow seems to have had some knowledge of Hebrew and was, in any case, greatly attracted to the Bible and Rabbinic lore. As a professor of languages, he went to unusual lengths in stressing his preference for the "beauty and simplicity, power and majesty" of the Scriptures over the Classics. Biblical and other Judaic motifs recur throughout Longfellow's poetry—from "A Psalm of Life" (1838) to his verse tragedy, *Judas Maccabaeus* (1871). Few writers of the 19th century made more effective use of the Bible's humanitarian appeal than Longfellow in his *Poems on Slavery* (1842). "The Slave Singing at Midnight" tells of a Negro who "sang of Zion, bright and free . . . songs of triumph, and ascriptions,/Such as reached the swart Egyptians,/When upon the Red Sea coast/Perished Pharaoh and his host . . ." Prophetic insight and moral indignation combine in "The Warning," which in Miltonic tones recalls Samson's last act of vengeance, and draws this conclusion:

> There is a poor, blind Samson in this land,
> Shorn of his strength and bound in bonds of steel,
> Who may, in some grim revel, raise his hand,
> And shake the pillars of this Commonweal,
> Till the vast Temple of our liberties
> A shapeless mass of wreck and rubbish lies.

There are also other echoes of the Bible in poems such as *The Courtship of Miles Standish* (1858), which refers to "the hundredth Psalm, the grand old Puritan anthem,/Music that Luther sang to the sacred words of the Psalmist."

A more distinctly Judaic note is struck in Longfellow's "Sandalphon" (1857), a reworking of the Rabbinic legend about the Angel of Prayer, and in the Spanish Jew Edrehi's first and third stories in *Tales of a Wayside Inn* (1863–73). These are "The Legend of Rabbi Ben Levi," a tale from the Talmud ("That book of gems, that book of gold,/Of wonders many and manifold") about the sage who tried to storm Heaven and overcome the Angel of Death, and "Azrael," on that Angel's encounter with King Solomon. In the Preface to these *Tales*, Edrehi is himself a near-Biblical figure: "Like an old Patriarch he appeared,/Abraham or Isaac, or at least/Some later Prophet or High-Priest . . . Well versed was he in Hebrew books,/Talmud and Targum, and the lore/Of Kabala; and evermore/There was a mystery in his looks . . ." One of Longfellow's best-known poems is "The Jewish Cemetery at Newport" (1852), which speaks of "these Hebrews in their graves" keeping "the long, mysterious Exodus of Death," their tombstones resembling "the tablets of the Law, thrown down/And broken by Moses at the mountain's base." Despite its unfortunate conclusion—that "the dead nations never rise again"—this poem, too, reflects Longfellow's compassion for "these Ishmaels and Hagars of mankind" among other oppressed peoples. *Judas Maccabaeus,* a drama about the "collision of Judaism and Hellenism," was written in little more than ten days. Based mainly on the Books of the Maccabees and on Josephus' *Antiquities of the Jews,* this tragedy does less justice to Longfellow's real ability than his more masterly poems.

Biblical motifs also figured prominently in the works of two Jewish poetesses of the 19th century, Adah Isaacs Menken (1835–1868) and Emma Lazarus (1849–1887). An actress and controversial bohemian, Adah Menken contributed some of her earliest poems to Isaac M. Wise's *Israelite* during the years 1857–59, associating Biblical motifs with the Messianic role of her people. Her verse collections, *Memoirs* (1856) and *Infelicia* (1868), teem with allusions to the Hebrew Bible, which she is said to have kept under her pillow. Two of the poems included in *Infelicia* were "Hear O Israel!" (which betrays the influence of Walt Whitman) and "Judith," where the sensual portrayal of the Apocryphal heroine foreshadows Oscar Wilde's treatment of Salome. An even greater degree of artistic inspiration may be seen in the Biblical and Jewish poems of Emma Lazarus, whose sonnet, "The New Colossus" (1883), dedicated to the Old World's "huddled masses yearning to breathe free," was engraved at the foot of the Statue of Liberty. Unlike her fellow-

Sephardi, S. B. H. Judah, Emma Lazarus was devoted to her people and to her Biblical heritage. She translated Hebrew poems by Judah Halevi and Solomon Ibn Gabirol (1879) and displayed prophetic insight in *Songs of a Semite* (1882) and the prose poetry of *By the Waters of Babylon* (1887), which expressed her belief that the Jewish people must recover its national identity and homeland in order to fulfill its mission to humanity. "The New Ezekiel" predicted this renewal of Jewish national existence on ancestral soil: "I ope your graves, my people, saith the Lord, / And I shall place you in your promised land," while "The Banner of the Jew" (another of the *Songs of a Semite*) issued a Zionist call for the reawakening of Israel in the spirit of the Maccabees:

> Oh, deem not dead that martial fire,
> Say not the mystic flame is spent!
> With Moses' law and David's lyre,
> Your ancient strength remains unbent.
> Let but an Ezra rise anew,

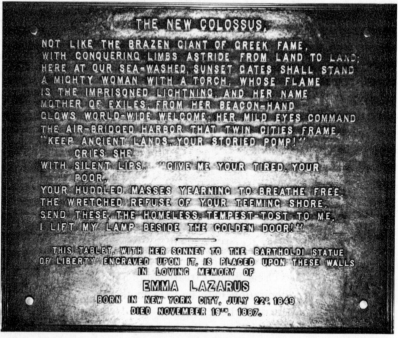

Sonnet by Emma Lazarus at the foot of the Statue of Liberty.

To lift the Banner of the Jew! . . .
Strike! for the brave revere the brave!

Emma Lazarus thus pointed to the beauty and grandeur of the Hebraic past and to the universal significance of the Jewish future, which she saw rooted in two great centers—Palestine and America. Her ideal provoked more response abroad than at home, but within half a century its actual realization was in full swing.

As in Western Europe, American literature of the 20th century saw an important and dramatic upsurge of interest in the Bible, under the twin impacts of religious revivalism and political developments such as the rise of Hitlerism. The Biblical novel enjoyed special popularity, although the quality of writing in this genre varied considerably. Louis Pendleton's *Lost Prince Almon* (1898), based on the survival of Joash after the massacre instigated by Athaliah, was a pioneer of the new trend and even appeared in a Hebrew edition in 1907. Those that followed often presented Biblical situations in a modern setting. A combination of romance and occasional religious earnestness linked some of these works of fiction with certain Hollywood motion picture "epics" that were lavishly produced by leading film-makers of the 20th century.[9] A more impressive achievement was, however, an anthology edited by Armin L. Robinson during World War II—*The Ten Commandments. Ten Short Novels of Hitler's War against the Moral Code* (1944), to which the German anti-Nazi Hermann R. Rauschning contributed a preface. Stories relating to each of the Commandments were prepared by leading American writers (Louis Bromfield, John Erskine, and Hendrik Willem Van Loon), as well as by European authors such as Thomas Mann, Franz Werfel, André Maurois, Jules Romains, and Rebecca West.

Modern American verse and drama on Biblical themes has generally attained a higher standard. "King Solomon and the Queen of Sheba" was included in *The Chinese Nightingale and Other Poems* (1917), the outstanding work of Vachel Lindsay (1879–1931), who also imitated the dramatic sermons of the Afro-American church in the title poem of his collection, *The Daniel Jazz* (1920). *The Green Pastures* (1930), a Pulitzer Prizewinning play by Marc Connelly (1890–   ) based on Roark Brad-

---

[9] These transpositions of the Old Testament to the motion picture screen include Cecil B. DeMille's *The Ten Commandments* (1923; new version 1956) and Dino de Laurentiis' equally spectacular *The Bible* (1966). See also Chapter 5.

A. Friberg's painting of Moses receiving the Law on Sinai, on which Cecil B. de Mille based a scene in his film *The Ten Commandments*.

ford's *Ol' Man Adam an' His Children* (1928), dramatized Old Testament history in terms of the Negro's anthropomorphic conception of God and of Negro life in the Southern States ("One thing we do know an' dat was dis boy Cain was a mean rascal").[10] Stephen Vincent Benét (1898–1943) wrote *King David* (1923), and T. S. Eliot (1888–1965), though hostile to "modern freethinking Jews," was clearly steeped in their Scriptures. In his religious pageant, *The Rock* (1934), Eliot refers rather significantly to Nehemiah's Samaritan and other opponents at the time when efforts were being made to restore and fortify Jerusalem after the Return from Babylon. Even Nehemiah's belief in the need to combine building with self-defense is vividly conveyed in the colloquial phrase: "the trowel in hand, and the gun rather loose in the holster."

Interesting and substantial were the Biblical dramas of Archibald MacLeish (1892–   ) and Robert Frost (1874–1963). In his verse play, *Nobodaddy* (1926), MacLeish used the disobedience of Adam and Eve

---

[10] An English parallel to this White view of the Black interpretation of the Bible is the well-known street corner song, "Darkies' Sunday School," which promises to "tell you Bible stories that you've never heard before" about the Patriarchs, Kings, and Prophets of Israel, who are presented in a good-humored, somewhat irreverent light.

to vindicate the Creator whom G. B. Shaw (in his preface to *Back to Methuselah*) had tried to dismiss as a mere superstition; God's punishment is manifested not as some heavenly thunderbolt, but in His withdrawal from intimacy with Man. The successful *J. B.* (1958), a modern Midrash on the Book of Job which won MacLeish the Pulitzer Prize, makes its hero a prosperous business executive whose life is shattered by a series of calamities. Reversing the Bible's arguments, J. B.'s comforters (a clergyman, a scientist, and a Marxist) exonerate him, while he insists on his own guilt. MacLeish's originality thus consists in his reappraisal of the conventional arguments of the Biblical age and of the 20th century. The Job theme also figured in Frost's verse drama, *A Masque of Reason* (1945), which purported to be the missing forty-third chapter of the Biblical book. Like the Scots playwright James Bridie, Frost concealed his serious exploration of the story in superficial humor and parody, humanizing the narrative without robbing it of its essential dignity. In *A Masque of Mercy* (1947), he presented the Book of Jonah's theme of Man's relationship with God in terms of Christian forgiveness. Frost and MacLeish exemplified

Raymond Massey (top) as Mr. Zuss, representing God, and Christopher Plummer as Nickles (the Devil) in a 1958 New York production of Archibald MacLeish's play *J.B.*, which is based on the Book of Job.

the mid-20th-century writer's preoccupation with the purpose of existence in the shadow of the bestialities perpetrated during World War II.

The American Jewish diaspora's new cultural importance in the modern era finds reflection in this Biblical current. As in Germany and Austria, Jewish writers in the United States (including some of the outstanding figures on the American literary scene) have mainly concerned themselves with the Hebrew Bible's significance in the light of contemporary Jewish experience. In "Hebrews" (from *The Sea,* 1924), James Oppenheim (1882–1923) proudly acknowledged his descent from the "mighty race" of Moses, David, and Isaiah ("I am of the terrible people, I am of the strange Hebrews . . ."), ironically observing that "our twenty centuries in Europe have the shape of a Cross/On which we have hung in disaster and glory." Louis Untermeyer (1885–   ), three of whose early verse collections were entitled *The New Adam* (1920), *Roast Leviathan* (1922), and *Burning Bush* (1928), revealed an original approach to Biblical subjects in his fiction and in various poems, such as "Koheleth," a rhymed résumé of Ecclesiastes, and "Goliath and David" (both in *Selected Poems and Parodies,* 1935). In the second of these, Goliath–who describes himself as "destruction's demon"—yearns to change places with his youthful opponent and shatter "this hugely rotting shell," while David—far from certain of the Philistine's villainy— asks God to "take this madness out of me" and casually flings away his pebble, asking Goliath to "come and play!" A more somber note was struck by Robert Nathan (1894–   ) in the poems "Moses on Nebo" (*A Winter Tide,* 1940), which presents the sad vision of Israel's age-old wanderings, and "These are the Chosen People" (*The Green Leaf,* 1950), an evocation of the martyred Jews, "upon their brow the diadem of thorn, / The one imperishable coronet," whom God has selected for a special fate:

> His is the voice of ages in their souls,
> The burning bush, the pillar in the night.
> These are the chosen; He has named them all.
> None can escape the poison of His grace,
> Or ever ease the everlasting smart.
> It is for them, the honey and the gall,
> To be the wakeful, the abiding race,
> And guard the wells of pity of the heart.

A more intensely Jewish strain can be detected in the works of the Canadian poet Abraham M. Klein (1909–72), whose versatility was expressed in several languages and in themes ranging from the reservation Indian to the prayers of the synagogue. In "Job Reviles" (*Hath Not a Jew*, 1940), Klein applies the MacLeish-Frost problem to the particular situation of his people during the long night of Nazism:

How Long, O Lord, will Israel's heart be riven?
How long will ye cry to a dotard God
To let us keep the breath that He has given?
How long will you sit on your throne, and nod?

In drama, on the other hand, the treatment of Biblical subjects by American Jewish writers has been rather less distinguished. Interest is attached to two plays of Biblical inspiration by Clifford Odets (1906–63) and Paddy Chayefsky (1923–   ), who were both raised in the Bronx. Odets' *The Flowering Peach* (1954), a retelling of the story of Noah, had a modern Jewish family setting, while Chayefsky's *Gideon* (1962) followed the colloquial style and humorous approach of Bridie in its dramatization of Man's alternate dependence on and rebellion against God. Despite the Angel's eloquent evocation of Moses, "a monumentally impassioned man," there is surprisingly little fire in Gideon himself, who uses the conventional jargon of economics and psychology to account for his triumph over the enemy.

With the Biblical novel, 20th-century Jewish writers have had greater impact on American literature, beginning with Robert Nathan's witty *Jonah; or The Withering Vine* (1925), which appeared in Britain as *The Son of Amittai,* and Louis Untermeyer's *Moses* (1928), originally planned as a study in verse of a divided soul—half realist and half philosophical anarchist. Adele Wiseman (1928–   ) made a Jewish home on the Canadian prairie the setting for her modern interpretation of the story of Abraham and Isaac (*The Sacrifice,* 1956). Another Canadian novelist, Charles Israel, made the comparatively obscure concubine of King Saul the heroine of his imaginative *Rizpah* (1961). Although Howard Fast (1914–   ) planned his Nietzschean *Moses, Prince of Egypt* (1958) as the first of a series of works about the Lawgiver, it was his better-known romance, *My Glorious Brothers* (1948), which—with his *Spartacus* (1952)—most powerfully conveyed the epic of humanity's struggle for freedom. Based on the revolt of the Maccabees, *My Glorious*

Brothers was also written against the background of the State of Israel's desperate fight for survival against the invading Arab armies in May 1948, and was in some ways the forerunner of other American bestsellers about the People and the Land of the Book—Leon Uris' *Exodus* (1958) and James Michener's *The Source* (1963). Thus, from its earliest years, the American nation set a literary seal on its Biblical heritage; and, even in the present age of diminished religious certainty, the moral concerns and issues that emanate from the Bible continue to inspire the American writer.

FRANCE

The impact of the Hebrew Bible was far less apparent in French religious literature of the Middle Ages than it was among the English. The 12th-century *Jeu* (or *Représentation*) *d'Adam* ("Adam Play"), the first play written entirely in French, was also important for some of its dramatic innovations (such as the use of an actor to play the part of God); but this drama of the Fall of Man has as many associations with England as it has with France. The one outstanding medieval French work on Old Testament themes was the late 15th-century *Mistère du Viel Testament* comprising 48 dramas on subjects drawn from the Hebrew Bible, including the Creation story, the life of Abraham, Moses and the Exodus, King David, and the Jewish redemption under Esther. Other French Mysteries and all the Miracle Plays are concerned with New Testament and later Christian themes, and in these post-Biblical Jews invariably appear as deicides and agents of the Devil. As elsewhere in Western Europe, Rabbinic sources enriched popular literature (particularly the *fabliaux*), and Hebrew terms and Biblical idioms and proverbs found their way into the French language from the late Middle Ages until the 17th century. The absorption of these expressions was aided by the appearance of two 13th-century French Bibles—the *Bible Complète* of the University of Paris and the *Bible Historiale* of Guyart des Moulins. The influence of Hebrew scholarship, particularly of the great medieval Jewish commentator Rashi (Solomon ben Isaac of Troyes, 1040–1105), may be seen in the exegetical works of Nicholas de Lyre (c. 1270–1349), to whom the early Christian Reformers were so indebted that a Latin jingle ran: *Si Lyra non lyrasset, Luther non lutasset* ("Had De Lyre not lyred, Luther would not have luted").

Biblical subjects first assumed significance in 16th-century French literature under the combined impact of the Renaissance and the Reformation. The new interest in Hebrew studies, promoted by François I's establishment in Paris of a "College of the Three Languages" (i.e., Latin, Greek, and Hebrew), was reflected in François Rabelais' *Pantagruel* (1532), where the giant Gargantua urges his son to master Hebrew, "Chaldean" (Aramaic), and Arabic, to read the Bible in the original tongues, and "not to despise the Talmudists and Kabbalists." Although Rabelais himself probably knew little or no Hebrew, his works contain many Hebrew terms and even a complete passage in (corrupt) Hebrew citing the Scriptures (*Pantagruel,* chap. 9) — clear evidence of the aspirations of his age. Years later, the eminent Neoplatonist poet and scholar Pontus de Tyard was to poke fun at the "arch-scoffer Rabelais" by hebraizing his name as *Rab-lez, "un maistre moqueur"* (*De Recta Nominum Impositione,* 1603, p. 27)!

A more serious pursuit of Hebraism was, however, evident in the activity of 16th-century French Bible translators and poets. The "return to the sources" inspired the Psalter (1509) of Jacques Lefèvre d'Étaples, whose French Bible (1528), revised in 1550, ran to over 200 editions and betrayed Protestant influences. A more radical approach was apparent in the Bibles prepared by Robert Olivetan (1535) and Sébastien Châteillon, or Castellio (1551), the latter's translation making a bold attempt to convey the flavor of the original Hebrew. A fresh religious current now swept French poetry. Clément Marot, whose sympathies with Reform twice led him into exile, published *Trente Pseaulmes de David mis en françoys* (1541) and *Cinquante Pseaulmes de David* (1543), which made the singing and translation of the Psalms fashionable at the French court. However, the religious effect of Marot's version, with its "sober, solemn music," transcended mere fashion, his Psalms becoming an integral part of the Calvinist liturgy of Geneva, where the poet was temporarily forced to take refuge in 1542.

Resurgent nationalism and the French Wars of Religion gave a great impetus to the writing of Biblical poetry, in which epic themes were prominent. The erudite Guy Le Fèvre de la Boderie (1541–1598) based his metrical versions of Psalms and the Biblical Songs on the Hebrew text, even following the idiom of the Hebrew Bible in his paraphrase of the Song of Moses (Exodus 15:1): "Ores je chanteray à l'Eternel unique, / Car magnifiquement son oeuvre est magnifique;/ Il a precipité et a fait abismer / Cheval et chevaucheur en la profonde Mer . . ." (*L'Encyclie des secrets de l'éternité,* 1571). The same technique is displayed in La Boderie's version of the Song of Deborah, where he plays on the meaning of the Prophetess' Hebrew name (Deborah = bee): "Debora gente Abeille / Reveille et leve toy, / Reveille toy reveille / Chante un Hymne au grand Roy . . ." (*Hymnes Ecclésiastiques,* 1578). There are many other Biblical paraphrases in the *Encyclie,* where David, together with Orpheus and Virgil, is eulogized as a creator of the poetic art, and in La Boderie's patriotic epic, *La Galliade* (1578), which endeavored to recreate French cultural history on the basis of theories that foreshadow those of the British Israelites.[11]

Some interesting parallels exist between the works and conceptions of La Boderie and those of his contemporary, the Gascon Protestant Guillaume de Salluste Du Bartas (1544–1590), who wrote the epics *Judith* (1573) and *La Semaine ou Creation du Monde* (1578). This first *Semaine,* an ambitious reworking of the Biblical account of Creation, presented a broad spectrum of contemporary scientific knowledge and had a sequel in the unfinished *Seconde Semaine* (1584–93), which contains a lengthy *"Hommage au langage hebrieu"* and aimed to unfold the later history of mankind up to the Christian era. Though outstanding for their lofty tone and moral purpose, these epic poems are often marred by pedantic detail and grotesque imagery. Du Bartas made a powerful impression in his time and, through translations such as Joshua Sylvester's *Divine Weekes and Workes* (1605), influenced Milton and Goethe.

There are especially vibrant echoes of Psalms and Lamentations in *Les Tragiques,* an anguished epic of the Huguenot cause written by Agrippa d'Aubigné (1552–1630) during the years 1577–94, but published in 1616, long after his retirement from French military and political affairs. Here, particularly in the section entitled *"Prière à Dieu pour venger les Protestants,"* D'Aubigné conjures up a series of apocalyptic visions in which he calls on God to defend "Zion" (the oppressed Calvinists) and chastize "Babel" (the tyrannical Catholic Church), likening the Huguenots to the Biblical House of Israel:

> Veux-tu long-temps laisser en cette terre ronde
> Regner ton ennemy? N'es-tu Seigneur du Monde,
> Toy, Seigneur, qui abbas, qui blesses, qui guéris,
> Qui donnes vie et mort, qui tüe et qui nourris? . . .

[11] See above.

Les Temples du Payen, du Turc, de l'idolastre,
Haussent au Ciel l'orgueil du marbre et de l'albastre,
Et Dieu seul, au desert pauvrement hebergé,
A basti tout le monde et n'y est pas logé!

(Will you allow your enemy to reign for long on this round earth? Are you not Lord of the world—you, Lord,—who cast down, who smite, who heal, who give life and death, who slay, and who feed? ... The temples of the heathen, of the Turk, of the idolater, raise to Heaven the pomp of marble and alabaster; and God alone, poorly lodged in the wilderness, has built the whole world and has no dwelling in it!).

The 16th century also saw the emergence of French Biblical drama, a genre in which Protestant writers were again prominent. *Abraham sacrifiant* (1550), a mystery play with revolutionary undertones by the Genevan Reformer Théodore de Bèze (1519–1605), made Abraham a stern Huguenot humanized by his love for the son whom God asks him to sacrifice. The Psalmist as a man of action figures in a dramatic trilogy by Loys Desmasures, *David Combattant; David Triomphant; David Fugitif* (1566), which alludes to the persecution of the Calvinists. The two most important Biblical dramas of the period were, however, *Saül le Furieux* (1572) by Jean de la Taille (1535–1617) and *Sédécie, ou les Juives* (1583) by Robert Garnier (1534–1590). La Taille's tragedy, which laid the foundations of French classical drama with its insistence on the unities of time and place, reflects the career and outlook of a militant Huguenot. Garnier's *Sédécie,* the first outstanding tragedy in the French language, portrays the cruel fate of Zedekiah and the royal house of Judah after Nebuchadnezzar's conquest of Jerusalem. As in La Taille's *Saül*—where the king's failure to obey God's command necessitates his punishment—so here, too, Zedekiah, ignoring Jeremiah's warning, allies himself with Egypt and brings about his own downfall. Although Greek influence shows itself in the prevailing concept of tragic destiny, the chorus which Garnier introduces in his drama clearly echoes the elegiac pathos of the Book of Lamentations.

During the French classical age ushered in by the 17th century, the Protestant element vanished with the subjection or enforced flight of the Huguenots, and works on Biblical themes now took their complexion from the austere religious views of the Jansenists of Port-Royal. Several religious and philosophical writers of the era showed a keen awareness of their Biblical heritage. The Jansenist Blaise Pascal (1623–1662), a great student of the Bible and of Rabbinic literature (which he read through various translations), showed unusual sympathy for the post-Biblical Jews. This attitude is very apparent in his "Thoughts" about religion (*Les Pensées,* 1670), from which it is clear that Pascal held the Midrash to be an important key to the understanding of the Scriptures. Though educated by the Jesuits, Jacques-Bénigne Bossuet (1627–1704) also inclined toward Jansenism and held Israel, the people chosen by God, to be the spiritual cornerstone of world history. This view found clear expression in his *Discours sur l'Histoire Universelle* (1681), where he noted that "the Jews were the only ones whose sacred Scriptures were held in ever greater veneration as they became better known." Bossuet's Biblical leanings are evident in the lyrical and grandiose eloquence of

A scene from Racine's classic French drama, *Athalie,* as staged by the Comédie Française.

his style, particularly in the Old Testament rhythm and imagery of his sermons and of his famous *Oraisons funèbres* (1663), funeral orations on great French personalities of the day. Both the Bible and Judaism also received the close attention of Richard Simon (1638–1721), a leading French Hebraist, who asserted that "one cannot understand the Christian religion if one is not instructed in that of the Jews, whose faith was its pattern" (1674).

The Bible-reading, puritanical approach of the Jansenists left a deep imprint on the works of the greatest French playwright of the age, Jean Racine (1639–1699), whose two Biblical tragedies, *Esther* (1689) and *Athalie* (1691), are among the masterpieces of French drama. Racine sought fresh material in Rabbinic lore (gleaned from the works of Richard Simon and other Christian Hebraists) in order to shed light on the later episodes of the Bible story dramatized in his *Esther*. There are many common dramatic features in *Esther* and *Athalie*: heroic central characters (Mordecai and Esther; Joad) and powerfully drawn, not unattractive villains (Haman; Athaliah); the central importance of a dream (as with Ahasuerus and Athaliah); the suppression of super-natural elements; and many Biblical echoes in the text. While the chorus in both of these dramas invokes the pathos and lyricism of the Psalms and Prophets, it is the high priest Joad, in the third act of *Athalie,* who paints the most glowing picture of that "New Jerusalem" foretold in the Scriptures:

> Peuples de la terre, chantez:
> Jérusalem renaît plus charmante et plus belle.
>   D'où lui viennent de tous côtés
> Ces enfants qu'en son sein elle n'a point portés?[12]
> Lève, Jérusalem, lève ta tête altière;
> Regarde tous ces rois de ta gloire étonnés. . . .
> Les peuples à l'envi marchent à ta lumière . . .[13]

(Sing, O nations of the earth: / Jerusalem reborn is more delightful yet and fair. / Whence come to her from every side / These children whom she bore not in her womb? / Raise your proud head, O Jerusalem; / And see all these kings astonished by your glory . . . / The nations vie with each other in walking in your light . . .).

[12] Cf. Isaiah 49:21.
[13] Cf. Isaiah 60:3.

As in England, the 18th century was a transitional period in French literary development of Biblical motifs and, once again, the drama was the dominant genre. For many of the great figures in the French "Age of Enlightenment" the Bible—and Jewish history—provided an indirect means of attacking Christianity itself, a technique employed by both Denis Diderot (1713–1784) and Voltaire (1694–1778). Diderot often parodied Biblical history, while Voltaire (in his *Dictionnaire Philosophique, 1764*) vilified both the Bible and the Jews, showing himself to be far from the preacher of toleration and enlightenment which he claimed to be. It was this subversive approach which characterized Voltaire's mocking tragedy, *Saül* (1763). A more conventional work, inspired by the figure of Jeremiah, was *Les Lamentations de Jérémie* (1752), a religious poem by François-Thomas de Baculard d'Arnaud (1718–1805) best known for the satirical epigram which it drew from the malicious Voltaire:

Savez-vous pourquoi Jérémie	(Do you know why Jeremiah
A tant pleuré pendant sa vie?	Wept so sorely during his life?
C'est qu'en prophète il prévoyait	As a prophet he then foresaw
Que Baculard le traduirait	That Baculard would translate him).

The Romantic movement of the 19th century brought with it a strong reaction against the skepticism of the previous age and a revival of interest in and sympathy for religion. Reverence for the Bible was expressed by many leading Romantic poets and playwrights. In his *Génie du Christianisme* (1802) François René de Chateaubriand (1768–1848) praised the unique and universal qualities of the Old Testament, a theme which he extended in his travel book, *Itinéraire de Paris à Jérusalem* (1811), and dramatized in his verse tragedy, *Moïse* (1836). Alphonse de Lamartine (1790–1869), who wrote the tragedy *Saül* (1818), acknowledged his debt to the Psalms and, after making a grand tour of Greece, Syria, and Palestine in the steps of Chateaubriand, recorded his *Souvenirs, Impressions, Pensées et Paysages pendant un voyage en Orient* (1835). Here this poet-statesman showed prophetic insight when he surveyed the Palestine of his day: "Such a land, resettled by a new Jewish nation, tilled and watered by intelligent hands . . . would still be the Promised Land of our day, if only Providence were to give it back its people, and the tide of world events bring it peace and liberty." Alfred de Vigny (1797–1863), who knew the Bible almost by heart, used Biblical themes in many of his verse collections, which are full of Hebraic imagery and diction. His *Poèmes antiques et modernes* (1826) include *"La fille de Jephté"* and *"Moïse,"* the latter portraying Moses as a man of genius whose greatness condemns him, like all of Vigny's heroes, to eternal solitude. *"La colère de Samson"* (in *Les Destinées,* 1864), a poem in which Vigny—like Milton—identifies himself with the betrayed and outraged Hebrew judge (Samson), also makes its hero a universal symbol of stoical resignation and fortitude. As in 19th-century England, the figure of Cain engaged literary attention, with works such as Charles Baudelaire's anti-bourgeois poem, *"Abel et Caïn"* (in *Les Fleurs du Mal,* 1857), and Leconte de Lisle's *"Quaïn"* (in *Poèmes barbares,* 1862), a miniature epic abounding in Hebraisms ("Ta victime, Iahvèh! celui qui fut Qaïn . . . La soif de la justice, o Khéroub, me dévore . . . "), which reflects that writer's bitterness and atheism.

The French Romantics' attachment to the Bible reached its zenith in the poems of Victor Hugo (1802–1885) who, in the preface to his *Odes et Ballades* (1826), maintained that, for the poet, "only two books need to be studied, Homer and the Bible . . . in a way these contain the whole creation in its dual aspect—in Homer through the genius of man, in the Bible through the spirit of God." Despite his gradual abandonment of orthodox Christianity, Hugo constantly turned to themes drawn from the Bible. What particularly distinguishes Hugo's treatment of these Biblical themes in *La Légende des Siècles* (1859–83) is the mingling of imaginative insight with lyrical or epic power. Thus, in *"La Conscience,"* Cain is pursued by an ominous eye even into the bowels of the earth, while *"Booz endormi"* draws a fine portrait of King David's progenitor:

> Booz était bon maître et fidèle parent;
> Il était généreux, quoiqu'il fût économe;
> Les femmes regardaient Booz plus qu'un jeune homme,
> Car le jeune homme est beau, mais le vieillard est grand

(Boaz was a good master and a loyal kinsman; / And, though thrifty, he was generous. / Women were more attracted to Boaz than to younger men, / for, while a youth has manly beauty, an old man has grandeur). Some other aspects of Hugo's Biblicism are the eulogies of Isaiah and Ezekiel in *William Shakespeare* (1864), and the kabbalism of poems like *"Ce que dit la Bouche d'Ombre"* in *Les Contemplations* (1856).

An important cultural influence in the post-Romantic era was exerted by the eminent French Bible scholar and Hebraist Ernest Renan (1823–1892). Apart from annotated translations of Job (1859), the Song of Songs (1869), and Ecclesiastes (1882), Renan published a monumental *Histoire du peuple d'Israël* (1887–93), in which he wrote that "the Bible in its various transformations is the great book of consolation for humanity." Some French writers associated with the modern Catholic Revival combined devotion to the Bible with admiration and warm sympathy for the People of the Book. Among them were Léon Bloy (1846–1917), Jacques Maritain (1882–1973), Charles Péguy (1873–1914), and Paul Claudel (1868–1955). Péguy, a Christian Socialist who asserted that "the Catholics have read only for two centuries, the Protestants only since Calvin, but the Jews for two thousand years," believed that Israel's prophetic mission had not ended with the Christian revelation (*Notre jeunesse,* 1910). This religious current runs deep in the works of Claudel, some of whose plays (such as *Le Pain dur,* 1918) portray Christianity's confrontation with Judaism. After 1948, he even advocated the State of Israel's official appointment as guardian of the Christian holy places and hoped that the Jews might there "reconstruct the Temple at the crossroads of three continents and of three religions. . ."

Biblical drama has undergone a significant revival in the 20th century, its themes attracting the attention of some outstanding modern French playwrights. André Gide (1869–1951), a solitary Protestant among the exponents of this genre, made the hero of his *Saül* (1922) an old man consumed by the gratification of his lusts. In another play, *Bethsabé* (1908), Gide retold the story of David and Bath-Sheba. André Obey (1892–) in his *Noé* (1931), translated into English as *Noah* (1935), drives home the idea that man's perversity—not some inexorable Divine plan—is responsible for the evil in the world. Like some of his English contemporaries, Obey demythologized the Bible by making God a benevolent, but harassed, figure who communicates with Noah by means of telephonic conversations. The new critical spirit also dominated *Judith* (1931), a psychological tragedy by Jean Giraudoux (1882–1944), where the Apocryphal story is reduced to a myth, Judith appearing as a courtesan and Holofernes as her not unlikeable victim. In Giraudoux's brilliant *Sodome et Gomorrhe* (1943), the Biblical quorum of ten righteous persons needed to avert disaster is reduced to a single couple whose inability to maintain sexual harmony brings about the final catastrophe. A fresh, Jewish stimulus has also been provided by writers such as Henry Bernstein (1876–1953), whose dramas of violent—often morbid—passion include *Judith* (1922) and *Samson* (1907), where Delilah—one of Bernstein's typical anti-heroines—is portrayed as a golddigger; and by Albert Cohen (1895–   ), whose *Ézechiel* (1956), first staged at the Comédie Française in 1933, represents the struggle between prophetic vision and harsh reality.

In poetry, too, the Biblical element has been prominent, beginning with Remy de Gourmont's Rabbinically inspired handling of the "Paradise Lost" motif in *Lilith* (1892). French verse treatment of Biblical subjects in the 20th century has, however, been dominated by poets of Jewish origin. The mystical Oscar Milosz (1877–1939), a half-Jew who wrote the Biblical play *Méphiboseth* (1913), used kabbalistic elements in his verse collections (*Ars magna,* 1924; *Le Poème des Arcanes,* 1927) and attempted to prove that the ancient Hebrews emigrated to Palestine from Spain. Max Jacob (1876–1944), a convert to Catholicism who died in a Nazi concentration camp, wrote many poems mingling religious yearning with sardonic humor, as in his *"Vantardises d'un marin breton ivre"* ("Boastings of a Drunken Breton Sailor"): *"C'est moi, c'est moi qui suis Moïse / Venez à la Terre promise / Rien à payer pour le passage. . . / C'est moi, c'est moi qui suis Samson / Je suis le patron des coiffeurs. / J'aurais bien dû rester garçon / ma femme a causé mon malheur . . ."* (It is I, it is I who am Moses. / Come to the Promised Land. / Nothing to pay for the trip. . . / It is I, it is I who am Samson. / I am the patron of hairdressers. / I should have stayed a bachelor; / my wife was the cause of my misfortune. . .).

A more authentically Jewish spirit may be seen in the works of Édmond Fleg (1874–1963), André Spire (1868–1966), and Gustave Kahn (1856–1936), all three of whom became enthusiastic Zionists. A prolific poet, playwright, and essayist, Fleg modeled his great verse cycle, *Écoute Israël* ("Hear, O Israel," 1954), on Hugo's *Légende des Siècles.* The titles of its four parts—*Écoute Israël* (1913–21), *L'Éternel est Notre Dieu* (1940), *L'Éternel est Un* (1945), and *Et Tu aimeras l'Éternel* (1948)—were taken from Deuteronomy 6:4–5, and its lyrical themes include the Jewish people's mission, Messianic yearnings, and unswerving faith in humanity despite massacre and degradation. For his legendary biographies— *Moïse raconté par les Sages* (1925; *The Life of Moses,* 1928) and *Salomon* (1929; *The Life of Solomon,* 1930)—Fleg drew his material from the Midrash. His use of the Biblical motif to dramatize a contemporary theme is well seen in *Nous de l'Espérance* (1949), where the infant Jewish State, menaced by the "Arch-wizard's armies of night," is rescued by

Elijah the Prophet and the heroes of modern and ancient Israel. Spire, who was both an important literary innovator and the inspiration of this Jewish revival, wrote some revolutionary *Poèmes juifs* (1919) on Biblical and other themes and *Samaël* (1921), a dramatic vision of the conflict between good and evil. Kahn, one of the leaders of the Symbolist movement, published a collection of *Images bibliques* (1929).

Since the end of World War II, other Jewish writers have found inspiration in the Bible, often as a means of portraying the grandeur and despair of their national history. The quest for the Biblical and Judaic roots of Western civilization is expressed in the poems and prose writings of Claude Vigée (1921–), a French scholar who settled in Israel (*Moisson de Canaan,* 1967; *La lune d'hiver,* 1970). Thus by the 1970s, French literature's return to the Biblical sources had been matched by a new and creative French presence in the Land of the Bible itself.

ITALY

While the Latin (Vulgate) Bible of Jerome was widely studied in medieval times and, to some extent, during the Renaissance as well, it never exercised the degree of influence on Italian culture that it did in other European lands such as England, France, and Germany. The earliest translations of the Bible into Italian were those of the heretical Waldenses (Vaudois), whose later descendants embraced Protestantism; a 13th-century Judeo-Italian[14] version of the Song of Songs; and the early 13th-century *Splanamento de li Proverbi di Salomone* by Gherardo Pateg. The first document of authentic Italian poetry is the *Cantico delle creature* ("Canticle of All Created Things"), a free adaption of Psalm 148 by San Francesco (St. Francis of Assisi, 1182–1226), which begins:

Altissimu, onnipotente, bon Signore
tue so le laude la gloria e l'honore
et onne benedictione. . .
Laudato sie, mi Signore, cu tutte le tue creature
spetialmente messor lo frate sole
lo qual jorna et allumini noi per loi. . .

[14] Judeo-Italian is a Jewish dialect of medieval origin (basically an archaic Italian written in Hebrew characters), the one surviving form of which is still spoken in Rome.

(Lord, most high, almighty, good, / yours are the praises, the glory, and the honor / and every blessing. . . / Be praised, my Lord, with all your creatures, / especially master brother sun / who brings day, and you give us light by him. . .).

The vernacular translations collected under the title *Biblia volgare* in the late 14th century gave rise to two Italian Bibles published in Venice in 1471, to the Reformist edition of Antonio Brucioli (1532) which, in turn, inspired an Italian Protestant Bible (Geneva, 1562), and to G. Marmochini's Bible (1562), the Old Testament section of which was based on the original Hebrew. As a result of the Counter-Reformation, translation and study of the vernacular Bible was limited to Italian-speaking Protestants such as Giovanni Diodati, whose edition (1607) enjoyed an unparalleled success. It was not until 150 years later that an Italian Bible under Catholic auspices (Archbishop Antonio Martini's edition of 1776–81) was officially countenanced. However, Italian Jews were active as Bible translators in the Renaissance era, notably David de Pomis (Ecclesiastes, 1571) and Ezechia da Rieti (Proverbs, 1617), both of whose works were printed in Venice.

Prior to the 15th century, the dominant Greco-Roman culture left little scope for the development of an Italian literary tradition nourished by the Bible. Only Dante Alighieri (1265–1321), Italy's greatest poet, made the Bible—with Virgil's *Aeneid*—the principal source and inspiration of his works. His "Divine Comedy" (*La Divina Commedia,* 1307–21), comprising *L'Inferno, Il Purgatorio,* and *Il Paradiso,* abounds in Biblical expressions, images, and linguistic traits derived from his reading of the Vulgate. From the very outset of his poem—*Nel mezzo del cammin di nostra vita* ("Midway upon the journey of our life")— Dante consciously imitates Jeremiah and he later reserves a place in Heaven for the patriarchs, kings, prophets, and other heroes of Israel, who symbolize faith, valor, and humility: ". . . righteous Abel, Noah who built the ark, / Moses who gave and who obeyed the Law, / King David, Abraham the Patriarch, Israel with his father and generation, Rachel. . . / These did He bless. . . " (*L'Inferno,* Canto 4). Dante influenced the poet Immanuel of Rome ("Manoello Giudeo," c. 1261– c. 1330), whose Hebrew account of a journey through hell and paradise (1491) closely followed the *Commedia.*

Although the influence of Psalms, Proverbs, and Ecclesiastes may be detected in many of the moral and didactic tales of 14th-century Italy, Biblical themes first achieved prominence with the religious Mystery

Plays *(sacre rappresentazioni)* that became popular a century later. As elsewhere in Western Europe, the older dramatic tradition persisted in the 16th century, which saw the composition and performance of many Old Testament "representations," which were often reworked in response to popular demand. Simultaneously, however, the Old Testament drama received a new lease of life as Renaissance playwrights injected a more realistic spirit into the familiar stories. This process may owe something to the Purim plays staged by Italian Jews in commemoration of Esther's triumph over Haman. This theatrical tradition actually dates back to the late 15th century, since a play about Judith and Holofernes was staged by the Jews of Pesaro at the wedding festivities of Giovanni Sforza in 1489, and Jewish playwrights and actors were subsequently much in demand at Italian Renaissance courts. A drama about Job, written toward the end of the century, is one of the oldest surviving literary works in Raeto-Romansch, a Romance language still spoken in parts of Switzerland and Northern Italy.

Biblical themes continued to engage the attention of Italian writers during the Baroque period and the era of the Counter-Reformation. The Italian Baroque writers tended to express their religious emotions in drama or music, for which the Bible provided suitable literary material, and it was the Italian Biblical drama of the 17th century which served as a model for some of the works of the French tragedian Racine. The outstanding exponents of Italian Biblical drama were Giambattista Andreini (1578–1654), whose *Adamo* (1613) is thought to have influenced the portrait of Satan in Milton's *Paradise Lost,* and Federico della Valle (c. 1560–1628), whose tragedies — *Judith* (1628) and *Esther* (1628) — inspired many imitations among writers seeking to promote the didactic aim of the Jesuits. Until the late 18th century there was no significant change in the treatment of Biblical subjects, and David, Saul, Jonathan, Joash, and Judith remained in favor among Italian dramatists.

A fundamental turning point in the history of the Italian Biblical drama came with the *Saul* (1782) of Vittorio Alfieri (1749–1803), who invested Saul's battles and death with the defiant grandeur of a man who endeavors to impose his will on friend and foe alike, even when his own doom has been sealed by Divine degree. Alfieri, the greatest Italian dramatist of the 18th century, also wrote a ponderous tragedy, *Abele* (1796), and another entitled *La figlia di Giefte* ("Jephthah's Daughter"). His plays, which constantly demonstrate longing for freedom and hatred of tyranny, did much to promote the rise of national feeling in Italy and thus, for the first time, made the Bible a vehicle of Italian patriotic expression. This tendency was also evident in T. Solera's libretto, *Nabucodonosor,* which was the basis for Giuseppe Verdi's famous opera, *Nabucco* (1842), where the Hebrew captives' prayer for deliverance was widely interpreted as a comment on Italy's subjugation to Austria. Tragic episodes in the Bible were now associated with the historic tragedy of the Jewish people and Israel's fate was identified with that of the Italian nation, oppressed and downtrodden through its reluctance to seek freedom through revolt. Thus, *La terra dei morti* ("The Land of the Dead"), a poem by Giuseppe Giusti (1809–1850), related Ezekiel's vision of the valley of dry bones to the plight of contemporary Italy. Another work in this spirit was *Il Profeta o La Passione di un popolo* (1866–84), an allegorical drama about the life of Jeremiah by Graziadio David Levi (1816–1898). Levi, an eminent poet and patriot who joined Mazzini in the *Risorgimento* revolt of 1848, wrote war songs for Garibaldi's brigades and identified the ethical values of Judaism with the liberal aspirations of his country. His poem, "The Bible" (1846), called on Zion (the Jewish people), that "immortal witness for truth," to make its eternal Book a rallying point for all lovers of freedom:

> Listen! the world is rising,
> Seeking, unquiet, thrilling,
> Awakens the new Century
> To new hopes and new visions . . .
> And from that Book the signal
> For the new day shall come .

Once the Italians had achieved their aim with the reunification of Italy, however, the Bible—a source of literary inspiration for many centuries— no longer influenced Italian writers to any significant extent. With a few exceptions, Biblical subjects have also been neglected by Italian Jewish writers of the 20th century. The legacy of the Bible is mainly apparent in the cultivation of a "Biblical" style and of a richly evocative lyricism involving the use of prophetic pathos and the avoidance of rhetoric.

SPAIN, PORTUGAL, and LATIN AMERICA

The marked influence of the Bible on Hispanic literature from medieval times until the 16th century stemmed both from the intense religious spirit that dominated Spanish and Portuguese writing and from the fruitful interplay of the Christian, Muslim, and Jewish cultures in the Iberian peninsula. Translations of the Bible were undertaken in the 13th century, Jews and Christians collaborating in the task of preparing a Spanish version of the Old Testament, taken directly from the Hebrew, in renderings that antedate 1250. Thus, although Juan I of Aragon prohibited such activities in 1233—suspecting that they had heretical tendencies—the more tolerant Alfonso the Wise (Alfonso X of Castile, 1221–1284) encouraged the translation of the Bible into the vernacular and, in his *General e grande Estoria,* linked the history of the world, as known in his day, with the Hebraic history of the Bible. During the 15th century, many Spanish Bible projects, based either on the Vulgate or on the original Hebrew, were undertaken by Jews or *Conversos* (Jews who embraced Christianity). The most important of these projects was the *Alba Bible* (1422–33), which Moses Arragel of Guadalajara produced at the command of Don Luis de Guzmán, Grand Master of the Order of Calatrava. After the Jewish expulsion from Spain in 1492, Abraham Usque, a Portuguese *Marrano* (crypto-Jew) who fled to Italy from the Inquisition, followed Arragel in the *Ferrara Bible* (1553), which he issued in two forms: one for his fellow-Jews and another for Spanish Christians. The Jewish edition later inspired translations into Ladino (Judeo-Spanish), the language which the exiled Jews took with them after their expulsion from Spain.[15] During the 16th-18th centuries, Catholic translations were mainly confined to Psalms, the Biblical "Songs," and the Wisdom Books, but complete Protestant Bibles (based on the Hebrew text) were published by Cassiodoro de Reina (Basle, 1567–69) and Cipriano de Valera (Amsterdam, 1602). Once the Catholic Church banned the translation of the Scriptures into Spanish, the printing of vernacular Bibles became a Jewish monopoly and, after 1600, Spain ceased to be a Bible-reading country for almost two centuries.

There are significant traces of the Bible's influence in medieval Spanish verse. Two poetic works of the early 15th century, both dealing with the story of Joseph, were the anonymous Muslim *Poema de Yuçuf,* composed in Spanish but written in Arabic characters, and the *Poema de Yoçef,* a Jewish adaptation of the Biblical tale expanded with material

[15] Like Judeo-Italian and Judeo-Provençal, Ladino is a Romance dialect written in Hebrew characters. Until World War II it was a *lingua franca* among Jews in parts of the eastern Mediterranean region, and now largely survives in Israel.

drawn from the Midrash and the 13th-century *Sefer Ha-Yashar* ("Book of the Righteous"), which runs to some 1200 lines. There are some interesting, characteristically Spanish aspects in this "Poem on Joseph," which was probably recited or sung on the Purim festival:

> . . . They drew him from the pit and sold him to the Moors
> For a price that was poor, for he was drawn and pale,
> With fear of the pit and the snakes on its floor,
> To Egypt went the Moors and with them went Joseph . . . (stanza 15)
>
> When Pharaoh heard about Joseph's brethren
> And about the honor that was done to them,
> Well pleased was the king with these pagans.
> Great good he desired them for the sake of Joseph. . . (stanza 233)[16]

Together with the *Poema de Yoçef*, a number of Ladino "romances" (popular Spanish ballads) accompanied the Jewish exiles into the Sephardi[17] Diaspora. Apart from those dealing with stories of love and adventure, chivalrous exploits, and historical and legendary episodes, there are several ballads on Biblical themes, such as "The Seduction of Dinah," "The Crossing of the Red Sea," "David and Goliath," and "The Song of Death," a versification of the tragic Apocryphal story of Hannah and her Seven Sons.

Little is known of Spanish Biblical drama before the 16th century. One of the first to write plays on themes drawn from the Bible was Diego Sánchez in the 1530s. The Binding of Isaac and the stories of Joseph and of Saul were other popular subjects. The massive *Madrid Codex* (1550–75) of 96 religious plays (*autos*) includes no less than 26 on Old Testament themes.

A Hebrew poet best known for his Spanish verse was Rabbi Santob de Carrión (Shem Tov ben Isaac Ardutiel), whose didactic and Biblical *Proverbios morales* or *Consejos y documentos al rey don Pedro* (c. 1355–60) were as popular among Christians as among Jews. Even after the Expulsion of the Jews in 1492, Hebraic influences remained strong in Spanish

---

[16] See *The Sephardic Tradition. Ladino and Spanish-Jewish Literature*, edited by Moshe Lazar, texts translated by David Herman (New York, 1972), p. 77ff.

[17] "Sephardi" is the term used to describe those Jews whose ancestors lived in or emigrated from Spain and Portugal, Sepharad being a Biblical locality (Obadiah 1:20) traditionally identified with the Iberian peninsula.

Renaissance culture. No discrimination against *Converso* scholars was tolerated by Archbishop Francisco Jiménez de Cisneros (1436–1517) at the University of Alcalá de Henares (Latin, Complutus), which he founded in 1500 and where, under his patronage, the first great Polyglot ("Complutensian") Bible was prepared and published (1514–17), with parallel texts in Hebrew, Greek, Latin, and Aramaic. The Kabbalah, reaching its literary zenith in Spain with the appearance of the Zohar (c. 1300), which has been attributed to Moses ben Shem Tov de León (c.1240–1305), was promoted by Jews and Jewish apostates. As in Renaissance Italy and France, kabbalistic lore captured the imagination of many leading Christian Hebraists, including Benito Arias Montano (1527–1598), chief editor of the Antwerp Polyglot Bible (1568–72), who also produced rhymed translations of Psalms and Prophets (in Latin) and of the Song of Songs (in Spanish). Arias' exceptional interest in Jewish studies antagonized narrow-minded priests, who engineered a prolonged campaign and trial on the grounds that he was a "Judaizer." Spanish poetry of the late 16th century to some extent reflects these Biblical and Hebraic currents. In the "State Poems" of Fernando de Herrera (1534–1597), Spain's new role as the nation chosen to dominate world affairs was stressed. Alluding to a Spanish victory, Herrera wrote that "the Holy One of Israel (*El Santo d'Israel*) opened His hand and let chariot, horse, and rider fall into the abyss."

Biblical influences are also evident in the religious poems of two churchmen, Fray Luis de León (1527–1591) and San Juan de la Cruz (St. John of the Cross, 1542–1591), the first a philosophical writer, the second a mystic. A distinguished humanist, Luis de León was the author of a commentary on Job and of Spanish translations of Psalms and the Song of Songs (*El cantar de los cantares,* c. 1561), The fact that Luis did not rely on the Vulgate, but consulted the Hebrew Bible, and the revelation by malicious rivals that he was of *Converso* origin (his great-grandmother had been burned at the stake as a relapsed Jewess) led to yet another "Judaizing" charge, which resulted in his imprisonment for five years.

The great age of Spanish Biblical drama was the 17th century, when both Christians and Jews distinguished themselves in this genre. The *auto*'s development had, in fact, been anticipated to a great extent by the religious plays and moralities of a Portuguese court dramatist, Gil Vicente (c. 1465–1536), many of whose works were written in Spanish. In Spain, the prolific Tirso de Molina (Gabriel Telléz, c.

1584–1648) was the author of two Biblical dramas, and Old Testament themes figured in the works of Pedro Calderón de la Barca (1600–1682), who wrote some 200 dramas and comedies in all. Calderón's *La Cena de Baltasar* ("Belshazzar's Feast," c. 1634) combined fine poetry with excellent stagecraft. Toward the end of the century, an anonymous *Sacrificio de Isaac* (1678) in the Aztec language appeared in Mexico.

An important contribution to the Spanish theater was made by several writers of Jewish origin, foremost among them Felipe Godínez (c.1588–c. 1639), a "New Christian" preacher of Seville, who was one of the few dramatists of the Spanish Golden Age to appear in person at an auto-da-fé. His Biblical plays include *Los trabajos de Job* ("The Trials of Job," 1638), memorable for the pathos with which Godínez evokes the sufferings of its hero. The prolific and very popular Antonio Enríquez Gómez (Enrique Enriquez de Paz, c. 1600–c. 1662) abandoned his career as a Spanish army officer to settle in Holland, where he reverted to Judaism. About half of his 22 dramas were devoted to Biblical subjects. A *Comedia famosa de Aman y Mordochay* (1699) was published in Leiden by Isaac Cohen de Lara (c. 1700), a Dutch Sephardi writer and book-dealer who included his own Spanish ballad, *"La Fuga de Jaacob de Barsheva"* ("Jacob's Flight from Beersheba") in the same volume. The *Comedia,* a graceful composition, was inspired by the Book of Esther and Midrashic commentaries on the Biblical story.

Epic poetry was another important vehicle of Spanish Biblical expression in the 17th century. Once again, the genre was dominated by *Marrano* and Jewish writers, although an early lead was taken by the anti-Semitic "Old Christian" Quevedo (Francisco Gómez de Quevedo y Villegas, 1580–1645), whose *Lágrimas de Hieremias castellanas* (1613) echoed the Book of Lamentations. João Pinto Delgado (died 1653), a Portuguese exile who reverted to Judaism in Amsterdam, dedicated his *Poema de la Reyna Ester, Lamentaciones del Propheta Jeremias y Historia de Ruth y varias poesias* (Rouen, 1627) to Cardinal Richelieu. Spanish and Portuguese culture found a congenial home in Amsterdam, the "Dutch Jerusalem," which attracted many refugee writers and scholars. Among the works that appeared there were the religious poems of Daniel Levi (Miguel) de Barrios (1635–1702), who for many years (1662–74) led a double life as a Spanish captain in Brussels and as a Jew in Amsterdam. Barrios' unfinished *Imperio de Dios en la harmonia del mundo* (1673?) was a verse adaptation of the Pentateuch. David Abenatar Melo (died c. 1646), who had once been tortured by the Spanish inquisitors, injected many references to current events in his paraphrase of the Psalter, *Los CL. Psalmos de David: in lengua española en uarias rimas* (1626), the prologue of which contained an account of his sufferings. One outstanding epic of the age was *El Macabeo* ("The Maccabee," 1638), a Baroque masterpiece by another Portuguese *Marrano*, Miguel de Silveyra (c. 1578–1638). Printed in Naples at the king's expense, this relates the exploits of Judah Maccabee up to the restoration of the Temple and, though now generally considered rather bombastic, had a great vogue in its time. It enjoys the distinction of being the oldest surviving literary treatment of this Apocryphal theme.

The declining importance of Biblical subjects in Spanish and Portuguese literature after the Golden Age affected the output of Jews and Christians alike. One work of interest and significance in the early 18th century was *Espejo fiel de Vidas que contiene los Psalmos de David in Verso* ("A True Mirror of Life Containing the Psalms of David in Verse," London, 1720) by Daniel Israel López Laguna (c. 1653–c. 1730), a refugee *Marrano* who settled in Jamaica. Like Abenatar Melo, almost a century before him, López Laguna often refers to the tortures and persecutions of the Inquisition in his book, which took 23 years to complete. The Sephardi diaspora produced *Coplas de Yoçef Ha-Tzaddik* ("Stanzas of Joseph the Righteous," 1732), a Ladino poem in 400 quatrains by Abraham de Toledo, first published in Constantinople, which became very popular and was widely distributed.

From the 19th century onward, Biblical subjects periodically inspired Portuguese and Latin American—as well as Spanish—poets, playwrights, and novelists. The Bible has had a muted role in 20th-century Spanish literature. A remarkable and fascinating exception to this tale of decline was the "ultraist" writer and critic Rafael Cansinos-Assens (1883–1964) who, after discovering his *Marrano* ancestry, reverted to Judaism and devoted much of his work to Biblical and Spanish-Jewish motifs. His *Psalmos. El Candelabro de los siete brazos* ("Psalms. The Seven-branched Candlestick," 1914), a collection of love poems and other verse in Biblical style, was the prelude to many other works of the type, culminating in *El amor en el Cantar de los Cantares* ("Love in the Song of Songs," 1930), which presented the Hebrew text of the Biblical book side by side with an original Spanish translation. The influence of Cansinos-Assens has been acknowledged by the foremost Argentine writer, Jorge Luis Borges (1899–   ), who uses kabbalistic and other Jewish elements in many of his narrative works, notably *El Aleph* (1949; *The Aleph and Other Stories 1933–1969*, 1970). The Biblical and Hebraic element in Spanish literature, though dormant, is thus far from dead; and the vital current that fed the *Marrano* literature of the 17th century can, quite visibly, again flow deep in the Ibero-American culture of the present day.

GERMANY AND AUSTRIA

For the past 15 centuries, writers in the German language have devoted an enormous amount of interest and attention to subjects drawn from the Bible and, in terms of their volume of output, they have no close rivals. It is, nevertheless, a grim and ironical fact that German reverence for the Scriptures often went hand in hand with scorn and hatred for the People of the Book.

The impact of the Bible on Germanic culture has been traced to the earliest encounter of the Teutons with missionary Christianity. In the fourth century, a Gothic bishop, Ulfilas or Wulfila (311–383), worked on a translation of the Bible: of its Old Testament portion only a few verses (from Ezra and Nehemiah) now survive. Ulfilas, who—according to an old Church tradition—invented the Gothic alphabet, is said to have omitted 1 and 2 Kings from his Bible because of the warlike disposition of the Goths! Later translations included a versified Old Saxon Genesis (the extant portion of which covers the Biblical narrative from Adam to the destruction of Sodom), and a tenth-century version of Psalms in Old High German. Early in the 11th century, the Book of Psalms and the Song of Songs were translated by Notker Labeo ("the German"), a monk of St. Gallen (c. 950–1022), who also produced a version of Job which has not survived.

A German commentary on the Song of Songs by Williram of Ebersberg (c. 1065) helped to popularize the figure of King Solomon, whose legendary wisdom—fortified by tales brought back to Europe by the Crusaders—became one of the stock literary themes of the later Middle Ages. Prominent in the 12th century were several German poems dealing with Moses and the Exodus, Judith, the Maccabees, and other subjects. The so-called *Wenzel Bible* (c. 1390), a version of the Old Testament, was notable for its style, and the first printed edition of the Bible in German by Johann Mentel (Strasbourg, 1466) was probably written in the mid-14th century. This translation, based on the Vulgate, was the model for 13 subsequent pre-Lutheran editions.

By contrast with England, France, and other Western countries, medieval Germany and Austria produced few Old Testament plays. The demonic portrayal of the post-Biblical Jew in German Miracle and Passion Plays, on the other hand, created a feeling of abhorrence that was later to have serious popular repercussions.[18] Old Testament themes are also largely absent from German poetry of the Middle Ages. It was the Middle High German of the 14th century that gave rise to a specifically Jewish literary culture which spread far beyond the Germanic world and assumed an independent history as Yiddish (i.e., *Jüdisch-Deutsch*, or Judeo-German).[19]

Biblical and Hebraic elements assumed a new and vital importance first with the Renaissance in the late 15th century, and later at the time of the Reformation. Hebrew studies were defended against "obscurantist" attacks by the great humanist Johann Reuchlin (1455–1522) during the famous "Battle of the Books" (1510–20), as a result of which German intellectuals won a fair measure of independence from oppressive and bigoted supervision. No less important was Reuchlin's pioneering work in the Christian interpretation of the Kabbalah, which helped to promote an even wider interest in Hebrew scholarship (*De Verbo mirifico*, 1494; *De arte Cabalistica*, 1517). It was in *De Verbo mirifico* ("On the Wonder-working Word") that he called Hebrew "the language in which God, angels, and men spoke together, not through the ambiguous murmur of a Castilian spring, Typhonian cave, or Dorian wood, but as friends talk face to face." Reuchlin's lead was followed by an impressive array of German Hebraists, including Sebastian Münster (1489–1552).

What Reuchlin—a loyal Catholic until his death—had unwittingly set in motion was a fundamental questioning of Papal authority and of the traditional text of the Bible presented in the Latin Vulgate. The religious and national awakening of Germany was to find its great advocate in Martin Luther (1483–1546), the leading spirit of the Reformation. Although he was not one of the most competent Hebraists of his time, Luther based his translation of the Old Testament on the Hebrew text

---

[18] Much controversy is still aroused by the famous Passion Play of Oberammergau, Bavaria, which (with lapses during the 18th century) has been performed about once every ten years since 1634.

[19] See below.

and published the first complete German edition, *Biblia: das ist: die gantze Heilige Schrifft Deudsch* (6 vols., 1534). This was the basis of all subsequent German editions and of most other Protestant Bibles. Its appearance created a sensation among the German middle classes (the chosen target of Luther's missionary endeavors), and it had a greater influence on the language and thinking of its readers than any other comparable work, apart from the English *Authorized Version*.[20] Luther's Bible soon became the most widely read book in the German tongue, constituting Germany's greatest literary achievement of the 16th century and one of the most significant translations in the history of literature. Here, for the first time, ordinary Germans could ponder the Biblical accounts of Creation, the Patriarchs, Joseph, and of the Israelites' liberation from their enslavement in Egypt. Luther simultaneously drew powerful portraits of Biblical figures in other vernacular works, such as the *Tischreden* ("Table-Talks") which he published during the 1530s: "Moses with his Law is most terrible; there never was any equal to him in perplexing, affrighting, tyrannizing, threatening, preaching, and thundering"—a picture which, in many ways, corresponds to that of the embattled and crusading Reformer himself. On the other hand, it was Luther's disenchantment with the post-Biblical Jews—whom he first saw as allies in his war with Rome—which eventually led to his violent polemic, "On the Jews and their Lies" (*Von den Jüden und jren Lügen,* 1543). As a result, the Lutheran Church (unlike those Protestant movements founded by Calvin, Zwingli, and other Reformers) retained all the superstitious antipathy toward the People of the Book which had its roots in the Christian Middle Ages.

On the purely literary level, however, Luther promoted a new emphasis and evaluation of the Book of Psalms which, as in England and France, became an integral part of the Protestant liturgy. His feeling for the Hebrew poetry of the Bible created a new and brilliant religious verse tradition in Germany, and his famous hymn, "Ein' feste Burg ist unser Gott,/ Ein gute Wehr und Waffen" ("A safe stronghold our God is still,/ A trusty shield and weapon," cf. Psalms 46:2), serves as a counterpart to the Hebraic prose of his Pentateuch ("Am anfang schuff Gott himel und erden...," Gen. 1:1). The impact of the Bible may also be seen in a poem by Luther's Swiss fellow-Reformer, Huldrych (Ulrich) Zwingli (1484–1531), who invokes the poetic pathos of Psalms, Isaiah,

[20] See Chapter 3.

and Jeremiah in his three-part *"Gebetslied in der Pest"* ("Prayer during the Plague"):

Hilf, herr got, hilf	(Help, Lord God, help me
in diser not!	In this extremity!
Ich mein, der tod	I think death
si an der tür. . .	Is at the door. . .
Tröst, herr got, tröst!	Comfort me, Lord God, comfort me!
Die krankheit wachst	The sickness grows,
We und angst fasst	Pain and fear seize upon
min sel und lib. . .	My soul and body. . .).

The dominant genre in 16th-century Germany was, however, Biblical drama. Luther and his fellow-Reformers fostered the writing of plays in both Latin and German on themes drawn from the Bible, Luther himself particularly recommending the Apocryphal stories of Judith (an illustration of Virtue's triumph over Wickedness) and Tobit (which also conveyed a laudable ethical message). This very emphasis on moral, rather than specifically religious, issues distinguished German Biblical drama from its counterparts in Catholic lands such as Spain. German playwrights of the Reformation era mainly resorted to the "Old" Testament, where they found all the dramatic and human elements that appealed to them, and the Hebrew Bible was thus transformed into secular literature.

The two leading German exponents of Biblical drama immediately after the Reformation were Sixtus Birck (1501–1554) and the celebrated Nuremberg Mastersinger Hans Sachs (1494–1576). Birck's humanist plays on Biblical themes—notably *Eva, Zorobabel* (1538), *Ezechias* (1538) and *Joseph* (1539)—all dealt with Old Testament subjects, while others dramatized Apocryphal themes, such as *Susanna* (1532), a vindication of innocence and virtue, which was notable for some unusual stage effects, the chorus singing appropriate Old Testament passages at certain points in the action. An English adaptation of Birck's *Wisdom of Solomon* was performed before Queen Elizabeth I by boys of the Westminster School in 1565. Hans Sachs, an amazingly prolific writer (his output includes about 200 plays, 1,800 poems, and over 4,000 songs!), devoted an even greater number of plays to Biblical and Apocryphal themes.

Biblical subjects roused the interest of poets and narrative writers, as well as dramatists, during the 17th century. Martin Opitz (1597–1639), a leading poet of the German Baroque, wrote *Jonas* ("Jonah"), the opera text *Judith* (1635), and a translation of Psalms (1637). There are Biblical echoes in *"Komm Trost der Nacht"* ("Come Solace of the Night"), an ode to the nightingale by Johann Jakob Christoffel von Grimmelshausen (c. 1622–1676), who compared the birds' songs of praise to God with the homage paid by the stars in the sky. In Christian Knorr von Rosenroth (1636–1689)—a Silesian Protestant who studied Hebrew under Dutch rabbis and became the outstanding Christian kabbalist of the age (*Kabbala Denudata*,1677–84)—a mystical tendency looms large, especially in his religious poem, *"Morgenandacht"* ("Morning Prayer"):

Morgenglanz der Ewigkeit,	(Morning splendor of eternity,
Licht vom unerschöpften Lichte,	Light of inexhaustible light,
Schick uns diese Morgenzeit	Send this morning
Deine Strahlen zu Gesichte	Thy rays to our eyes
Und vertreib durch deine Macht	And with thy power drive away
Unsre Nacht.	Our night.
Die bewölkte Finsternis	May the cloudy darkness
Müsse deinem Glanz entfliegen,	Flee before Thy glory,
Die durch Adams Apfelbiss	Which through Adam's bite of the apple
Uns, die kleine Welt, bestiegen,	Overpowered us, the microcosm,
Dass wir, Herr, durch deinen Schein	So that we, Lord, through Thy light
Selig sein. . .	May be blessed. . .)

The Biblical drama which, for over a century, had declined in importance, underwent a revival with Christian Weise (1642–1708), all of whose religious plays were inspired by the Old Testament. From the mid-18th century, the new social philosophy of Rousseau (which promoted a "Return to Nature" in literature) moved German Protestant writers toward an even more adventurous reinterpretation of the Hebrew Bible, which they now saw less as a religious document than as an authentic monument of pure literature. Germany's first important modern poet, Friedrich Gottlieb Klopstock (1720–1803) wrote *Der Tod Adams* ("The Death of Adam," 1755), a tragedy notable for its Rousseauesque yearning for an imagined Golden Age, and two other Biblical dramas, *Salomo* (1764) and *David* (1772). The Biblical vogue was particularly apparent in Switzerland, where Johann Jacob Bodmer (1697–1783), Salomon Gessner (1730–1788), and Johann Kaspar Lavater (1741–1801) all made important contributions. Gessner roused interest in the Cain theme with his sentimental prose epic, *Der Tod Abels* ("The Death of Abel," 1758), which in translation had important repercussions among English writers.[21] After publishing a German prose translation of Milton's *Paradise Lost* in 1732, Bodmer paid much attention to the Bible, from which he drew many of his themes, for instance in his epics *Noah ein Heldengedicht* (1750; revised as *Die Noachide*, 1765) and *Die Synd-Flut* ("The Deluge," 1751).

The Age of Enlightenment (*Aufklärung*) in Germany inspired a new rationalism (the *Haskalah* movement) among the Jews. Their leading spirit, Moses Mendelssohn (1729–1786), wrote aesthetic and philosophical works that displayed his mastery of the German language, and also directed the first German translation of the Bible under Jewish auspices, which was printed in Hebrew characters. His own contributions included the Pentateuch (1783), Psalms (1785–91), Ecclesiastes (1770), and the Song of Songs (1788). Mendelssohn's personal qualities inspired the classic portrait of the hero in *Nathan der Weise* ("Nathan the Wise," 1779), a drama about religious toleration by his friend Gotthold Ephraim Lessing (1729–1781). However, while Lessing—like the benevolent Nathan—preached brotherhood and "enlightenment," he considered the "Old" Testament to be morally and aesthetically inferior to the "New" and believed that, just as Judaism had given way to Christianity, Christianity in its turn would be superseded by a new "religion of humanity" (*Die Erziehung des Menschengeschlechts*, 1780). Friedrich Schiller (1759–1805) wrote essays on Biblical subjects, such as *Die Sendung Mosis* ("The Mission of Moses," 1783), and was not unaffected by Voltaire's hostility toward the Bible.

The Bible and Hebraic culture evoked a far more positive and significant response from Johann Gottfried Herder (1744–1803), who was virtually the first Protestant theologian to devote admiring attention to the Old Testament at the expense of the New, and to consider the Bible and the Jewish people with remarkable objectivity. A close friend of Moses Mendelssohn, Herder mastered Hebrew and Rabbinics and paid tribute to the Hebrew genius in his Song of Songs translation and

---

[21] See above.

commentary, *Salomons Lieder der Liebe* (1771–78). He is reputed to have affirmed that "it is worth studying the Hebrew language for ten years in order to read Psalm 104 in the original." Herder also wrote various "Jewish Parables" inspired by the Midrash and in his incomplete study, *Vom Geist der Ebräischen Poesie* (1782–83; *The Spirit of Hebrew Poetry*, 1833), maintained that the whole of Hebrew literature—from Genesis to Rabbinic times—was a single unit, endowed with unique quality and power, and Hebrew poetry, in its various categories, "the oldest, simplest, and sincerest in the world."

Herder's outstanding disciple was Germany's greatest writer, Johann Wolfgang von Goethe (1749–1832), who once confessed that "it is a belief in the Bible, the fruit of deep meditation, which has served me as the guide of my moral and literary life." As a boy, Goethe immersed himself in Luther's Bible translation and then wrestled with Hebrew and the Frankfurt Jews' Yiddish dialect. His youthful projects included a "Biblical, prose-epic poem" about Joseph, a verse tragedy about Belshazzar, and a drama about Jezebel. Although Goethe never wrote a major Biblical work, realizing the difficulties he would have to face in competing with the original text and in reconciling religious and aesthetic requirements, he often acknowledged his debt to the Hebrew Bible in later works, such as *Wilhelm Meisters Lehrjahre* (1795–6) and the autobiographical *Dichtung und Wahrheit* ("Poetry and Truth," 1811–22). The impact of the Bible on Goethe's work is most apparent in his dramatic masterpiece, *Faust* (1808), which contains nearly 200 passages with Old Testament parallels, beginning with the "Prologue in Heaven," for which the early chapters of Job served as a model, and ending with the scene of Faust's death and ascension, which was inspired by the Biblical and Rabbinic accounts of the death of Moses.

Although German literature of the 19th century was less rich in Biblical associations than its English and French counterparts, there were some important achievements in the field of drama. Ludwig Robert's *Die Tochter Jephthas* ("Jephthah's Daughter," 1813) was the first play of Jewish authorship staged in Germany. Austria's greatest dramatist, Franz Grillparzer (1791–1872), never completed his fine Romantic tragedy, *Esther* (1877), a fragment of little more than two acts. Three notable dramas were based on the Apocrypha: *Die Mutter der Makkäbaer* ("The Mother of the Maccabees," 1820), a Romantic tragedy by the mystical Zacharias Werner (1768–1823); *Judith* (1841), the first major work of Friedrich Hebbel (1813–1863); and *Die Makkabäer*

(1854), a tragedy by Otto Ludwig (1813–1865) which, though not entirely successful in its attempt to combine the saga of the Maccabees with the harrowing story of Hannah and her Seven Sons, contains some gripping and memorable scenes. Hebbel's outstanding tragedy, which established his reputation as a dramatist, made Judith a passionate woman dedicated to the destruction of Holofernes, a not unattractive, philosophizing superman. The play's powerful characterization and dialogue foreshadow the qualities of Hebbel's masterpiece, *Herodes und Mariamne* (1850).

Biblical influences are most evident in the poems and prose writings of Germany's greatest lyric poet, Heinrich Heine (1797–1856). Whether before or after his formal baptism, during his "Hellenist" period, or in the course of his "mattress grave" rapprochement with the faith of his fathers, Heine read and reread the Bible, "that great medicine chest of humanity," and "imperishable treasure" with which the Jews "trudged around throughout the Middle Ages as with a portable fatherland." It directly inspired poems such as *"Belsazar"* (c. 1820), a masterly ballad in his *Buch der Lieder* (1827), and *"Das Goldne Kalb," "König David,"* and *"Salomo"* (in *Romanzero,* 1851). There are also powerful Biblical overtones in "Halleluja" (*Letzte Gedichte,* 1869), and in *"Prinzessin Sabbat"* and *"Jehuda ben Halevy,"* two of the *Romanzero's* "Hebräische Melodien"—a title inspired by Lord Byron's *Hebrew Melodies* (1815). Biblical echoes resound throughout Heine's tribute to Judah Halevi, the great medieval Spanish poet and philosopher:

"Bei den Wassern Babels sassen	("By the Babylonian waters
Wir und weinten, unsre Harfen	We sat down and wept for Zion,
Lehnten an den Trauerweiden"—	Hung our harps upon the willows"—
Kennst du noch das alte Lied? . . .	Dost remember the old song? . . .
Lange schon, jahrtausendlange	Long—a thousand years already—
Kocht's in mir. Ein dunkles Wehe!	It has boiled in me—dark sorrow!
Und die Zeit leckt meine Wunde,	And Time licks my wounds in passing
Wie der Hund die Schwären Hiobs . . .	As the dog the boils of Job . . .

Auf der edlen Höhe Zions,	On the noble heights of Zion,
Wo die goldne Feste ragte,	Where the golden fortress towered,
Deren Herrlichkeiten zeugten	Bearing witness, in its splendor,
Von der Pracht des grossen Königs:	To a mighty monarch's glory,
Dort, von Unkraut überwuchert,	There is nothing left but ruins,
Liegen nur noch graue Trümmer,	Grey and overgrown with weeds,
Die uns ansehn schmerzhaft traurig,	And they gaze on one so sadly
Dass man glauben muss, sie weinten...	That one fancies they are weeping...)[22]

In his essays, too, beginning with *Ludwig Börne* (1830), Heine created many memorable images linking the Bible with the People of the Book, as in his evocation of the Hebrew Lawgiver, a famous passage in his "Confessions" (*Geständnisse,* 1854):

How small Sinai appears when Moses stands upon it! This mountain is only the pedestal for the feet of the man whose head reaches up to the heavens, where he speaks with God... There was a time when I could not forgive the legislator of the Jews his hatred against the plastic arts. I failed to see that, despite his hostility to art, Moses was himself a great artist; but his artistic spirit, like that of his Egyptian compatriots, was directed solely toward colossal and indestructible undertakings. He built human pyramids and carved human obelisks, took a poor shepherd tribe and transformed it into a people that would defy the centuries—a great, eternal, holy people, a people of God... Israel!

With the notable exception of Heine, the legacy of the Bible in 19th-century German poetry and prose is not impressive. Although his enigmatic philosophy and its attendant slogans ("The Superman," "The Will to Power") were later adopted by racist and totalitarian movements Friedrich Nietzsche (1844–1900) greatly admired the uncompromising morality and majesty of the "Old" Testament and reserved more praise

[22] Translation by Charles Godfrey Leland, in Nathan Ausubel's *A Treasury of Jewish Poetry* (New York, 1957), pp. 110–112.

for the modern Jews than for the modern Germans. His view of the Bible was expressed in *Jenseits von Gut und Böse* ("Beyond Good and Evil," 1886): "In the Old Testament of the Jews, the book of Divine righteousness, there are men, events, and words so great that there is nothing in Greek or Indian literature to compare with it."

During the three decades before the Nazi seizure of power in Germany, and for several years afterwards, there was an extraordinary and unique flowering of Biblical drama, partly in response to the social and political upheaval generated by World War I. The Job theme attracted Oskar Kokoschka (*Sphinx und Strohmann,* 1907), a Czech whose interest in the Bible later inspired *Der brennende Dornbusch* ("The Burning Bush," 1911), a drama about Moses. Georg Kaiser (1878–1945) began his dramatic career with *Die jüdische Witwe* ("The Jewish Widow," 1911), which—unlike most treatments of the Judith story—was a comedy. Herbert Eulenberg's tragedy, *Simson* (1910), anticipated the plays of Frank Wedekind (1864–1918), a prominent Naturalist (*Simson oder Scham und Eifersucht,* 1914), and of Hermann Burte (1917) and Karl Röttger (1921). Many Biblical themes were also exploited by the great Czech-born poet Rainer Maria Rilke (1875–1926).

Special interest was roused by two Biblical dramas that appeared toward the end of the First World War—*Jeremias* (1918; *Jeremiah,* 1922) by Stefan Zweig (1881–1943) and *Jaakobs Traum* (1918; *Jacob's Dream,* 1947), the first part of a dramatic trilogy by Richard Beer-Hofmann (1866–1945). *Jeremias,* a powerful pacifist work, was first performed in Zurich in 1917 while Zweig was attached to the Austrian war archives in Vienna. Exultant voices join the prophet Jeremiah in recalling the Biblical history of the Israelites, from their enslavement in Egypt to their entry into the Promised Land ("Trumpets blew, walls fell down; / Moab was overthrown, and Amalek. / With the sword we carved ways / Through the anger of the peoples and the times. . ."); and the ultimate deliverance promised by God to His exiled people receives a more universal significance and application. Equally dramatic, though more strictly relevant to the modern situation of the Jews, is the dialogue between Jacob, Samael, and the four archangels in Beer-Hofmann's mystical verse play, where the patriarch Jacob, during his night at Bethel, accepts the blessing and the burden which God offers both him and his descendants. Michael predicts: "The mighty Coastland kings—they all must end, / Mizraim vanish, Babel tottering fall! / Thou only — His eternal people—shalt forever wander— / An eternal wonder in

His eternal world!"; but Samael, with bitter sarcasm, warns Jacob of the penalties awaiting the "Chosen" People:

The mangy beggar turns to sneer and scoff
And prides himself that he's not of thy race. . .
Each folk to whom thou cling'st with love
Shall burn thee out like ulcer—to the root!
Beloved of God, by all the world more hated
Than plague or poisonous weed or raving brute!
Who bore and who begot thee burns to ashes,
Thy wife dies bleeding, shamed and lacerated,
They blot thee out!—Thine unborn child is torn—
Nay, trodden from its mother's womb—unborn. . .
Such—is His blessing![23]

Der junge David ("Young David," 1933), the trilogy's second part, expounds Beer-Hofmann's belief that individuals and nations are important only to the extent that they contribute to the welfare of humanity at large; the third part, *Vorspiel auf dem Theater zu König David* ("Prologue to King David," 1936), remained only a fragment. In his earliest lyric, *Schlaflied für Miriam* ("Lullaby for Miriam," 1898), Beer-Hofmann proclaimed God's mysterious purpose behind the apparently chaotic structure of the universe.

Biblical subjects also achieved new importance in German fiction. The downfall of Sennacherib forms the background to Arnold Zweig's story, "Jerusalem Delivered" (1910), and the Messianic significance of Judaism's oldest symbol, which "will give light to the children of Israel when they have found their way back to their homeland," inspired Stefan Zweig's ambitious tale, *Der begrabene Leuchter* (1937; *The Buried Candelabrum*, 1937).

With the disintegration of the Weimar Republic and Hitler's inauguration of the Third Reich in 1933, Biblical themes assumed a special poignancy and topical significance. Thomas Mann (1875–1955), the outstanding German novelist of the 20th century, started work on his prose epic about Joseph, which began to appear in the year of the Nazi rise to power. For Mann, the choice of an Old Testament subject was "certainly no mere accident," but a defiant conclusion that "to write a

[23] Translation by Ida Bension Wynn, in Ausubel, *op. cit.,* p. 199.

novel of the Jewish spirit was timely; because it seemed untimely." So it was that the non-Jewish leader of Germany's anti-Nazi intellectuals devoted all his imaginative resources to the writing of a kind of Midrash on a motif current in every genre of European literature since the Middle Ages. Mann's great novel cycle, *Joseph und seine Brüder* (1933–42; *Joseph and His Brothers*, 1934–44), which has been translated into many languages, consists of *Die Geschichten Jaakobs* (1933; *The Tales of Jacob*, 1934), *Der junge Joseph* (1934; *Young Joseph*, 1935), *Joseph in Aegypten* (1936; *Joseph in Egypt*, 1938), and *Joseph, der Ernährer* (1942; *Joseph the Provider*, 1944). The tetralogy is remarkable for its subtle blending of Biblical history, legend, and psychological characterization. Toward the end of World War II, Thomas Mann also published *Das Gesetz* (1944; *The Tables of the Law*, 1945), which appeared with nine other contributions by eminent modern writers in *The Ten Commandments. Ten Short Novels of Hitler's War against the Moral Code* (1944).[24]

While Hitler was busy destroying independent German thought and planning his campaign of expansion and the "Final Solution of the Jewish Question," other voices of protest took on a prophetic tone. Franz Werfel (1890–1945), a friend of Kafka, expressed his feeling of spiritual homelessness in *Der Weg der Verheissung* (1935; *The Eternal Road*, 1937), a Biblical play set to music by Kurk Weill and staged in New York by another prominent Jewish exile, Max Reinhardt. Werfel also wrote the novel, *Höret die Stimme* (1937; *Hearken unto the Voice*, 1938), which later reappeared under the title *Jeremias* (1956), and several later works in which he used Biblical themes and echoes to convey the tragedy of the age. In poetry, too, the Bible left its imprint on the works of many Jewish writers, notably Max Brod (1884–1968), Hugo Salus (1866–1929), Franz Werfel, and two distinguished poetesses—Else Lasker-Schüler (1869–1945) and Gertrud Kolmar (1894–1943). A victim of the European Holocaust, Gertrud Kolmar turned to themes like Moses and Judith, while Else Lasker-Schüler (who spent her last years in Jerusalem) was deeply affected by the heroic figures of the Hebrew Bible *(Hebräische Balladen*, 1913) and by the Palestinian scene (*Das Hebräerland*, 1937). One of her poems relates that.

The rock crumbles
From which I spring

[24] See above (United States).

Singing my songs to the Lord. . .
Steep from the path I fall
And all within me I flow
Down, slowly down, alone over rocks of lamentation,
To the sea. . . [25]

With the outbreak of World War II, this German enthusiasm for the
Bible went into lonely exile. Sammy Gronemann (1875–1952), who had
published his Purim play, *Hamans Flucht* ("Haman's Flight"), in 1926,
settled in Tel Aviv, where he wrote *Der Weise und der Narr: König
Salomo und der Schuster* ("The Wise Man and the Fool: King Solomon
and the Cobbler," 1942), a comedy with a legendary Biblical setting, and
Die Königin von Saba ("The Queen of Sheba," 1952). Translated by
Nathan Alterman, "The King and the Cobbler" became the first Hebrew
musical comedy success (1965). Another product of the war years was
Karl Boxler's Swiss-German novel, *Judas Makkabäus: ein Kleinvolk
kämpft um Glaube und Heimat* ("Judah Maccabee: A Small Nation
Fights for its Faith and Homeland," 1943), which made it clear that
Swiss democrats then drew a parallel between their own struggle for
independence and survival under William Tell and that of Jewish
freedom-fighters ever since the days of Judah "the Hammer." The last
glimmers of this Biblical tradition could still be seen in the dying "literature of exile" that survived the Nazis. In the United States, Lion Feucht-
wanger published *Jefta und seine Tochter,* his last novel, in 1957, while
two refugee writers in Israel, Max Zweig (*Saul,* 1961) and Martin Buber
(1878–1965), the author of *Elija; ein Mysterienspiel* (1963), contributed
plays on Biblical themes. Buber, a philosopher, theologian, Biblical
scholar, and Zionist thinker, had years earlier collaborated with another
great Jewish philosopher, Franz Rosenzweig (1886–1929), in the preparation of a 15-volume German translation of the Bible (*Die Schrift und ihre
Verdeutschung,* 1935–61), which strove to preserve the character of the
Hebrew text.

Since 1945, attempts have been made to revive the Biblical novel in
Federal Germany and Austria. A prominent part in this movement has
been played by Stefan Andres (1906–), a Catholic writer and anti-Nazi
who spent the years 1937–49 in Italy. Andres wrote several Biblically
inspired works, including *Der Mann im Fisch* (1963), a treatment of the

[25] Translation by Ralph Manheim, in Ausubel, *op. cit.,* p. 92.

Jonah story. The wish to atone for the monstrous evils of Hitlerism is undoubtedly a powerful factor in this return to the Bible, but it seems doubtful whether any new literary generation in the German-speaking world will succeed in recapturing the inspiration of the past.

THE SLAV LANDS

The Bible and the Hebrew language together occupy a unique place in the annals of early Slavic literature. In the ninth century, as part of his proselytizing campaign in the Balkans, the missionary monk Cyril of Salonika (known also as Constantine the Philosopher) created a basic alphabet for the Slavs. Since the Greek symbols on which this was based could not cope with all of the Slavonic sounds, Cyril had recourse to Hebrew for five of his consonantal symbols (Б,Ц,Ч,Ш,Щ—the phonetic equivalents of *b, ts, ch, sh, and shch*), and this new alphabet—modified in time as "Cyrillic"—facilitated the translation of the Bible and other religious works into Old Bulgarian (Church Slavonic). Cyril reputedly consulted the Hebrew text of the Old Testament, having learned Hebrew from Greek Jews or from the Judaizing Khazars of southern Russia, whose kingdom he visited on one of his missionary journeys.

RUSSIA

The Biblical and Hebraic impact on Russian literature far antedates the Mongol invasion in 1223, the few surviving fragments of the Old Testament mainly comprising Church Slavonic renderings of Psalms. In time the Russians, Ukrainians, and Belorussians developed their own separate languages and literatures from a common religious culture. Anonymous authors of the 11th century composed the "Primary Chronicle," which opens with the Biblical story of the Tower of Babel, and an East Slavonic translation of Josephus' *Jewish War*, which became very popular during the Middle Ages, influencing the style and imagery of Russian literary works, particularly martial tales. As Russia began to emerge from the long night of Mongol domination, the strongest impetus favoring the Bible's codification was the theological threat to the Church posed by the "Judaizing heresy" that appeared in the cities of Novgorod and Moscow during the 15th century. The "Judaizers" *(Zhidovstvuyushchiye)*, who rejected fundamental Christian tenets such as the Trinity and the Virgin

Birth, had a particularly high regard for the Old Testament (the importance of which Russian Orthodoxy has traditionally minimized) and based their translations of the Bible—notably Psalms, Daniel, and Esther—on the original Hebrew. The great achievement of the Novgorod Archbishop Gennady's Church Slavonic Bible (1499), a creative reaction to this heretical activity, was that it produced a unified text of the Bible independent of the Orthodox liturgy. Gennady's text was followed by the first complete Ukrainian Bible, commissioned by Prince Constantine of Ostrog (1581), and by the Moscow Bible of 1663.

The 15th century also marks the beginning of Russian popular literature dealing with themes drawn from the Bible. Apart from the *Skazaniye, kak sotvoril Bog Adama* ("The Story of God's Creation of Adam") and various apocryphal prose works about Solomon such as the "Tale of the Centaur" (on Solomon's construction of the Temple without recourse to iron), the Biblical account of Joseph proved attractive, particularly to poets. The *Dukhovnye Stikhi* (oral religious poems), of the 15th–17th centuries include *"Plach Iosifa"* ("Joseph's Lament"), which movingly conveys the misery of the young captive:

Kto by mne dal golubitsu	(Who will give me a dove
veshchayushchu besedami?	That can speak?
Poslal by ya ko Iyakovu,	I would send it to Jacob,
Ottsu moyemu Izrailyu:	To my father Israel:
Otche, otche Iyakove,	Father, father Jacob
Svyaty muzh Izrailev!	O holy man of Israel!
Proley slezy ko Gospodu	Shed tears to the Lord
O svoyom syne Iosife!	For your son Joseph!
Tvoi deti, moya bratiya,	Your children, my brethren,
Prodazha mene vo inu zemlyu. . .	Have sold me into a foreign land. . .
Zemle, zemle,	Earth, O Earth,
Vozopivshaya ko Gospodu za Avelya,	You who cried out to the Lord on Abel's behalf,
Vozopi nyne ko Iyakovu,	Cry out now to Jacob, to my
Ottsu moyemu Izrailyu!	father Israel!)

This pathetic and loving image of the ancient Hebrews contrasts with the hostile treatment of the post-Biblical Jew ("Christ-killer") in another of these religious poems, *"Son Presvyatyya Bogoroditsy"* ("The Dream of The Most Holy Mother of God").

Russian theater was inaugurated by a German adaptation of the Book of Esther, performed in Moscow in 1672. Some of the earliest Russian dramas were written by Johann Gottfried Grigori, a German Lutheran pastor who reworked the story of Adam and Eve as a morality play, and by Semyon Polotsky, whose *Komediya ob Yudifi* ("Judith") was also produced in the 1670s. The vogue for Biblical drama was maintained in the 18th century. Heights of artistry were attained by Mikhail Vasilyevich Lomonosov (1711–1765), one of the architects of the Russian literary language, and Gavrila Romanovich Derzhavin (1743–1816), the greatest Russian poet of the age. Lomonosov produced a lyrical translation of Psalms and an ode inspired by the Book of Job (c. 1742), while Derzhavin —whose work shows an obsession with death and the transience of life—wrote various poems of Biblical inspiration, among which *"Vlastitelyam i sudiyam"* ("To Rulers and Judges"), an adaptation of Psalm 82, is outstanding.

Conventional imagery and allusions drawn from the Bible were frequent in Russian works of the 19th century, such as *"Prorok"* ("The Prophet," 1826), a magnificent statement of the poet's mission by Aleksandr Pushkin (1799–1837), which concludes:

I Boga glas ko mne vozzval:	(And the voice of God called out to me:
'Vosstan, prorok, i vizhd, i vnemli,	'Arise, O prophet, see and hear,
Ispolnis voleyu Moyey,	Be filled with My will,
I, obkhodya morya i zemli,	Go forth over land and sea,
Glagolom zhgi serdtsa lyudey.'	And set the hearts of men on fire with your word.')

Pushkin, whose Russian poetry has never been surpassed, was an iconoclast with a taste for parodying the Scriptures. Biblical motifs and epigraphs also distinguish the works of such great writers as Count Lev (Leo) Tolstoy (1828–1910) and Fyodor Mikhailovich Dostoyevsky (1821–1881). During the last decades of the Czarist regime, Biblical subjects also figured in Russian prose and drama. Aleksandr Ivanovich Kuprin (1870–1938) published *Sulamif* (1908; *Sulamith*, 1923), a stylized romance about Solomon which has been acclaimed as a hymn to love, while *Samson v okovakh* (1925; *Samson in Chains,* 1923), a five-act tragedy, was one of the last works of Leonid Nikolayevich Andreyev (1871–1919), a staunch anti-Bolshevik who died an exile in Finland.

One significant reason for the upsurge of literary interest in the Bible during the years preceding the Bolshevik Revolution was the fact that many of the founding fathers of modern Hebrew literature, such as H. N. Bialik, were then still living in Russia, where they redirected attention to Biblical and Hebraic subjects. Through the translations of Vladimir (Ze'ev) Jabotinsky (1880–1940), Bialik's poems reached a wider public, winning the admiration of Maksim Gorky (1868–1936), whose explicit sympathy both for the Hebrew revival and for Zionist aspirations in Palestine was later obscured by the Soviet regime. Jabotinsky's fame as a soldier and as the leader of Zionism's activist wing has unduly overshadowed his significance as a Russian writer and translator. His literary masterpiece, the biblical novel *Samson nazorey* (1927; *Samson the Nazirite,* 1930), reflects much of his philosophical thinking on Jewish and general affairs and is remarkable for its insight into character. In answer to a visitor's request for some message to give the awaiting Hebrews, the captive Samson first recommends two acquisitions: iron and a king, for "there is nothing more valuable in the world than iron," while the Philistines' political organization makes them lords of Canaan. Then he corrects himself: "Tell them three things in my name, and not two: they must get iron; they must choose a king; and they must learn to laugh."

After the Bolshevik Revolution, Biblical subjects were either completely avoided or given an anti-religious, Marxist slant, belittling the "reactionary believer" and his holy writ.[26] Outside of the Soviet Union, Aleksey Mikhailovich Remizov's *Krug schastya: legendy o tsare Solomone* ("The Wheel of Fortune: Legends of King Solomon," 1957) appeared in Paris, as did Nikolai Otsup's dramatic sketches of Saul, David, and Solomon—*Tri tsarya* ("Three Kings," 1958). Perhaps it was no accident that these émigré writers concentrated their attention on the royalist issue in ancient Israel, which must have awakened poignant memories of the vanished dynasty of the Romanovs. During the cultural "thaw"

---

[26] According to a recent literary critic in the USSR, "the Bible and Biblical figures serve the cause of religious propaganda and continue to play a reactionary role in the realms of ideology and art" (*Kratkaya Literaturnaya Entsiklopediya,* Vol. 1, col. 612, Moscow, 1962). See Epilogue.

that followed the death of Stalin, two Soviet Jewish writers returned to the Bible, partly as a protest against the prevailing social system. Semyon Isaakovich Kirsanov (1906–   ) displayed a notable fondness for Biblical imagery traceable to his early years in the intensely Jewish milieu of Odessa. A poem which he wrote in the late 1940s had the Biblical title, *"Edem"* ("Paradise"), while his best-known work, *"Sem dney nedeli"* ("The Seven Days of the Week," 1957), was a long narrative poem inspired by the first chapter of Genesis. Kirsanov's bold assertion that the Socialist society had proved successful only in the material sphere, neglecting human values, encountered a storm of angry criticism. Harsher treatment was meted out to the underground writer and translator Iosif Brodsky (1940–   ), whose poems were denied publication in the Soviet Union and had to appear in the West (*Stikhotvoreniya i poemy,* 1965) and in Hebrew translation (1969). Brodsky, too, wrote an original Biblical poem, *"Isaak i Avraam,"* which—with expanded dialogue and linguistic embroidery—retells the story of Abraham's intended sacrifice of his son in obedience to God's command. As a "social parasite" and literary nonconformist, Brodsky figured in a show trial (1964) and was sentenced to a period of hard labor. Perhaps it is significant that two of his defenders, Samuil Marshak (1887–1964) and Anna Akhmatova (1888–1966), had in their own day found inspiration in the lyricism and drama of the Book of Books.

POLAND

As in other parts of Europe, translations of the Bible furthered the development of Poland's literary language, while the Psalms were a major source of poetical inspiration. The *Queen Margaret Psalter* and the *Queen Sophia (Szaros Patak) Bible* made their appearance toward the end of the 13th century. By the beginning of the Reformation, Poland had become an important center of humanist culture and scholarship: during the years 1503—1536, more books were printed in Cracow alone than in the whole of England. Italian influence among educated Poles proved an obstacle to the penetration of Lutheranism (another factor being the Slavs' grim experience of Germanic colonization under the Teutonic Knights), but Calvinism made swifter headway, as did the radical anti-Trinitarianism of Szymon Budny (died 1595). Most 16th-century Polish Bibles were the product of Protestant scholarship: Jan Leopolita's *Cracow Bible* (1561), the first complete text in the

Polish language; the Calvinist *Brześć (Radziwill) Bible* (1563); and Budny's Socinian (Unitarian) *Nieśwież Bible* (1572), the most famous of these three. However, it was the Polish Catholic Bible of Jakub Wujek (1593–99) that exerted the greatest literary influence, injecting an enormous concentration of Biblical imagery and expression into the Polish language.

The era of the Reformation and of the Jesuit-inspired Polish Counter-Reformation gave a powerful impetus to the versification and paraphrasing of the Book of Psalms. Here, the two pioneers were the Calvinist "father of Polish literature," Mikołaj Rej (1505–1569), who published his *Psałterz Dawidów* in 1546, and Jan Kochanowski (1530–1584), the outstanding Polish poet of the age, who issued his version under the same title in 1578. The latter's sensitive and beautiful Psalter was the finest poetical work of the time and served as a literary model until the 19th century. He also produced a whole series of verse epics on themes drawn from the Bible, but subsequently there was an abrupt decline in this type of literature.

With the resurgence of Polish nationalism in the early years of the 19th century, literary interest in Old Testament themes suddenly revived. Biblical imagery and expression constantly recur in the works of Poland's greatest modern writers, particularly in the Romantic era. Two notable examples are the *Księgi narodu polskiego i pielgrzymstwa polskiego* ("The Books of the Polish Nation and Pilgrimage," 1832) of the great poet and patriot Adam Mickiewicz (1798–1855), and the *Psalmy przyszłości* ("Psalms of the Future," 1845) of Count Zygmunt Krasiński (1812–1859), who was for much of his life a political exile. Kabbalistic notions played an important part in the thinking of Mickiewicz, who came to regard the French, the Jews, and the Poles as "chosen nations" that would determine the course of history. Similar ideas appear in *Żydowie Polscy* ("Polish Jews"), a work by the last great Polish Romantic, Cyprian Kamil Norwid (1821–1883), who summarized the history of the Jewish people from the time of Moses until the era of the struggle of both Poles and Jews ("Maccabees") against their common oppressors.

After Poland's subjugation to Russia in 1815 and the unsuccessful insurrection of 1863–64, Biblical themes served as a literary disguise for the discussion of contemporary events and conditions. Thus Kornel Ujejski (1823–1897), in his *Skargi Jeremiego* ("Lamentations of Jeremiah," 1893), set down in 1847–8, commemorated the heroism of Mickiewicz and the sufferings of his fellow-Poles, while *Faraon* ("The

Pharaoh," 1895–96), a major historical novel by Boleslaw Prus (1847–1912), made ancient Egypt the setting for some telling comments on the plight of the Jews in the writer's native land. Polish poets found in the Bible the moral values required by a people subjected to contempt, humiliation, and slavery. A more detached note first appeared in *Daniel* (1907), a drama by Stanisław Wyspianski (1809–1907), for whom Biblical and other Jewish figures performed the same function as those drawn from Greek and Roman mythology.

One of the most extraordinary phenomena of the post-Hitler period in Poland was the sudden and fruitful blossoming of religiously inspired literature under the new Communist regime. This trend was inaugurated by the Catholic writer Zofia Kossak-Szczucka, who survived several years in a Nazi concentration camp to write *Przymierze* (1946; *The Covenant, A Novel of the Life of Abraham the Prophet*, 1951). Another Catholic novelist, Jan Dobraczyński, published *Wybrańcy gwiazd* ("Chosen by the Stars," 1948), a story about Jeremiah, and *Pustynia* ("The Desert," 1957), a narrative work about Moses. Julian Tuwim (1894–1953), one of the outstanding Polish poets of the 20th century, retained a deep, almost religious, interest in Hebraic themes, and the conflict between his Jewish and Polish loyalties often expressed itself in Biblical terms.

CZECHOSLOVAKIA

The Biblical element in the literature of the Slav peoples inhabiting the area of present-day Czechoslovakia is largely confined to the development of Czech culture in the Bohemian region. Some books of the Hebrew Bible were translated into Czech in the 13th century, but it was under the impact of the Hussite movement that the entire Bible first appeared in that language when the Bohemian Reformer John Huss (c. 1369–1415) systematically revised earlier Czech versions at the beginning of the 15th century. The Hussite heresy had close parallels in contemporary Bible-reading sects elsewhere in Europe—notably the English Lollards and the Italian Waldenses—and, through the many foreign workers who found temporary employment in the Bohemian mines, its influence spread far and wide. Two classic Czech translations of the Scriptures were Jan Blahoslav's impressive *Kralice Bible* (1579–93), which was based less on the Vulgate than on the original Greek and Hebrew texts, and the Catholic *Wenceslas Bible* (1677–1715).

However, the Reformation did not inspire a single major Czech epic or drama on a Biblical theme. It was, in fact, not until the late 19th century that Old Testament subjects made any significant appearance in Czechoslovak literature. Most of the imaginative Czech writing on Biblical motifs came from the pens of Julius Zeyer (1841–1901) and Jaroslav Vrchlický (1853–1912). Zeyer, the son of a converted Jewess, learned Hebrew and yearned to visit the Holy Land. Biblical episodes form the basis of two of his dramas, *Sulamit* (1883), an adaptation of the Song of Songs, and *Z dob růžového jitra* ("From the Times of the Rosy Dawn," 1888), which deals with Isaac's stay in Gerar (Gen. 26:1–12). Zeyer also wrote a poem about Moses and *Asenat* (1895), a story dealing with Joseph's life in Egypt. Vrchlický, an outstanding Czech writer of the 19th century and probably the greatest Czech poet, displayed a notable interest in Judaism and Jewish literature from early youth, devoting about 100 poems and three of his dramas to Jewish subjects. In addition to these, he wrote *Trilogie o Samsonovi* (1900), a three-part novel about the Hebrew judge Samson, and translations of Lord Byron's *Hebrew Melodies* and of Hebrew and Yiddish poetry.

YUGOSLAVIA

The earliest literary activity in the "land of the southern Slavs" dates from the educational and missionary work of Cyril and Methodius in the ninth century, when their translation of the Old Testament—traditionally based on the Hebrew text—was dedicated to the Slavs of Macedonia.[27] A milestone in the Reformation's shortlived success in this region was the complete Slovenian Old Testament produced by the Reformer Primož Trubar (1508–1586) in the latter half of the 16th century. Trubar, the virtual architect of Slovenian literature, also published an important vernacular edition of the Psalms (*Ta celi psalter Davidov,* 1566). His close collaborator, Jurij Dalmatin (c. 1547–1589), published several translations from Biblical and Apocryphal literature, notably his Slovenian Protestant Bible (1584), together with a volume of "Tales about Solomon" (*Solomonove pripovisti,* 1580). While the Serbs remained faithful to the Orthodox Church and retained the literary use of Church Slavonic until the mid-19th century, Lutheranism made early inroads in Croatia and a Lutheran Bible in the Croatian language was printed in

[27] See above.

1563. Croatian humanism produced an outstanding scholar and Hebraist in Matthias Flacius Illyricus (Matija Vlačić, 1520–1575), a fanatical anti-Catholic, whose works include a linguistic dictionary of the Bible in Latin (1567). After the Counter-Reformation, however, Croatia became a bastion of Catholicism.

The Bible's first really significant impact on the literature of the southern Slavs has been traced to the works of the Croatian humanist Marko Marulić (1450–1524), who was greatly influenced by the Italian Renaissance, then an important factor in his native Split (Spalato). Marulić wrote a long allegorical neo-Latin poem about King David, and *Judita* (1521), the first religious epic in the Croatian language, which adopted some of the stylistic features of Petrarch's Italian poetry. *Judita*, written in 1501, kept fairly close to the original tale of the Apocrypha, but was intended to arouse national feelings against the Turkish oppressor. The atrocities perpetrated by the army of Holofernes thus form a parallel with those of the Muslim invader and the heroic example of Judith was meant to sustain the faith of the Croats in an eventual deliverance from their oppressors. Marulić's near-contemporary, the Montenegrin poet Mavro-Nikolo Vetranović of Ragusa (c. 1482–1576), followed the Croatian tradition of sacred drama, but his verse play, *Posvetilište Abraamovo* ("The Sacrifice of Abraham"), and his Apocryphal drama, *Suzana čista* ("The Chaste Susanna"), were more concise and vivid.

It was not until the early 19th century that the Biblical epic revived among Serbian and Croatian writers. For this much credit is due to Milovan Vidaković (1788–1841), a Serb who stood midway between the eras of Enlightenment and Romanticism and whose religious works starkly dramatized the conflict between good and evil. His *Istorija o prekrasnom Josifje* ("The Handsome Joseph," 1805) and *Mladi Tovija* ("Young Tobias," 1825) were followed by another epic, *Putešestvije u Jerusalim* ("Journey to Jerusalem," 1834), and these inspired several other poets, notably Petar Petrović Njegoš (1813–1851), prince-bishop of Montenegro and the greatest Montenegrin writer. The influence of Dante, Milton, Byron, and Lamartine has been traced in Njegoš' *Luča mikrokozma* (1845; *The Rays of the Microcosm,* 1953), a philosophical epic about Man's first revolt against God and eventual reconciliation with his place in Creation. While themes drawn from the Bible have not, on the whole, inspired great literature in modern Yugoslavia, there have been some interesting reinterpretations of

Biblical personalities and episodes. Thus, Borislav Pekić recently made use of Biblical legends in his book, *Vreme čuda* ("Time of Wonders," 1965).

OTHER COUNTRIES

Biblical subjects have also played a major role in the literatures of several other European nations, both in the West and the East, and in those of certain Muslim states. Although the works which the Bible, in these instances, inspired were only rarely of the first rank, the overall impact of the Old Testament on the poetry, drama, and fiction of some of these countries deserves mention in this survey.

THE NETHERLANDS

Although there were some medieval Dutch versions of Biblical books, including a Flemish translation of the whole Bible except for Psalms (c. 1300), Dutch literature first came under Biblical influence during the Renaissance. A Dutch edition of Luther's Bible (1526) was printed in Antwerp, a city that rallied Protestant—and especially Calvinist—support in the Low Countries until the "Spanish Fury" of 1576. Humanists and Reformers alike promoted the study of Hebrew during the 16th–17th centuries, particularly in the circle of the printer Christophe Plantin (c. 1520–1589), whose eight-volume "Antwerp Polyglot Bible" (1568–72) was one of the great publishing achievements of the age. The Reformation and Holland's 80-year War of Liberation (1568–1648) led to a new and powerful interest in the Bible: the conflict with Spain was likened to the Israelites' war against their enemies and, in the Dutch national anthem, *Wilhelmus van Nassouwe,* the Dutch champion, Prince William of Orange, was compared to King David. The first Dutch versions of the Old Testament based on the original Hebrew appeared only in the early 17th century (1614, 1623); they were followed by the famous *Statenbijel* (Leiden, 1627–37), commissioned by the Dutch States General, which (with modifications) remained the classic Dutch Protestant text until the mid-20th century.

The real pioneers of Dutch Biblical drama were the humanist Georgius Macropedius (Joris van Langhveldt, c. 1475–1558), who devoted some of his dozen neo-Latin plays to Biblical themes, and Carel van Mander (1548–1606) and Dirck Volkertszoon Coornhert (1522–1590), whose plays were written in Dutch. Two other neo-Latin dramas were written by the great Dutch jurist and statesman Hugo Grotius (Huig de Groot, 1583–1645)—*Adamus Exul* (1601) and *Sophomopaneas* (English translation, 1652). The latter work, a verse tragedy about Joseph (whose Egyptian name was Zafenat-Pane'ah, see Gen. 41:45), to some extent reflects Grotius' career as Sweden's ambassador to France (1634–45). A number of Biblical poems and plays were also published by Spanish and Portuguese Jews who found refuge in the Netherlands from the 16th century, but these were not written in Dutch and had no direct impact on the native literature.[28] Biblical drama reached its peak in Holland with Joost van den Vondel (1587–1679), who wrote numerous Biblical plays, including a trilogy about Joseph.

The 18th and 19th centuries saw a sharp decline in Dutch literary attention to Biblical subjects. The modern spirit of scientific enquiry found a curious reflection in *De Schepping* ("The Creation," 1866), a poem by Jan Jacob Lodewijk ten Kate (1819–1888), who combined religious faith with geological evidence in his treatment of this theme! The Sephardi poet, Isaac da Costa (1798–1860), who first championed Jewish emancipation, then embraced Calvinism under the influence of the writer Willem Bilderdijk (1822), retained a deep interest in Jewish and Biblical subjects. Hagar's return to Abraham's tent in Da Costa's dramatic poem, *Hagar* (1848), was intended to symbolize Islam's ultimate reconciliation with Christianity.

A revival of interest in the Bible has characterized Dutch literature of the 20th century. A fresh, Jewish element entered with the religious poems of Jacob Israël de Haan (1881–1924), who wrote the two-volume verse collection, *Het Joodsche Lied* ("The Jewish Song," 1915–21), and the travel sketches, *Palestina* and *Jerusalem* (1921). De Haan, who abandoned Socialism for Zionism, and Zionism for the most uncompromising Jewish Orthodoxy was a controversial writer and politician who spent his last years in Jerusalem, where he was finally assassinated. Interest in the Bible was reinforced after Holland's traumatic experiences during the Nazi occupation of World War II. The Catholic poet Bertus Aafjes (1914–) wrote *In den Beginne* (1949), an epic about the Creation, and several prose works on Biblical themes and the Land of the Bible. An original account of Susanna's life and experiences was given in *Het boek van Joachim van Babylon* (1947; *The Book of Joachim of*

---

[28] See above (Spain, Portugal, and Latin America).

Babylon, 1951), a bestselling Flemish novel by the Antwerp poet Marnix Gijsen (Jan-Albert Goris, 1899–   ) which ran to four editions within a year. Gijsen, a scholar and diplomat who often wrote on Jewish historical themes, ironically portrays the abandonment of religion and morality in his pseudo-historical tale. Other writers who found inspiration in heroic Biblical subjects after the defeat of the Nazis included the psycho-therapist Manuel van Loggem (1916–   ) with his novel, *Mozes* (1957), and Abel Jacob Herzberg (1898–   ), a concentration camp survivor, whose play, *Sauls dood* ("The Death of Saul"), appeared in 1959.

Afrikaans, a simplified variant of Dutch, is spoken widely in South Africa, where many Dutch Calvinists and French Huguenots found refuge from the 17th century onward. Their intensely religious up-bringing made the Afrikaners (or Boers) deeply conscious of the Bible, which became their guide and inspiration during their wanderings in the African interior. Like many other Protestants, the Afrikaners saw themselves as new Israelites charged with a Divine mission among barbarous races. Biblical themes, emphasizing the prophets and warriors of Israel, are common in Afrikaans poetry and fiction, the style of Afrikaans verse especially showing the influence of Psalms and Ecclesiastes, as in the poems of Totius (Jacob Daniel du Toit, 1877–1953). The Biblical element has also been prominent in South African drama, with *Silo is krank. . .* (1956), a play about Samuel by the leading Afrikaner writer Daniel François Malherbe (1881–   ), some of whose novels (*Die hart van Moab,* 1933; *Die profeet,* 1937) also have a familiar Biblical ring.

SCANDINAVIA

In two notable instances, Biblical and Hebraic influences can be detected in medieval Scandinavian literature. Anders Sunesøn (1164–1228), a Danish archbishop who studied in Oxford, Bologna, and Paris, wrote *Hexaëmeron* ("Six Days"), an 8,000–line neo-Latin poem on the Creation while the *Stjórn* ("Guidance"), an Icelandic paraphrase of some sections of the Old Testament, was also a product of the Middle Ages. However, the impact of the Bible really dates from the beginning of the 16th century, when Luther's German translation inspired similar undertakings by Scandinavian Reformers. In Denmark, a Pentateuch (1535) was issued by the "Danish Luther," Hans Tausen (1494–1561), but the oldest complete Danish text was Christiern Pedersen's *Christian III Bible* (1550), a literary monument which had a significant influence on the

Danish language. In its various revisions, the *Christian III Bible* remained in use until the 20th century and was, for at least three centuries, the main cultural inspiration of the Danish people. Their language and outlook were profoundly influenced by idioms, stories, and ideas drawn from the Bible, and more than 300 familiar Danish quotations are of Biblical origin. The Icelandic *Stjórn* was the first Biblical work current in Norway, where Lutheranism met early resistance because of its association with the conquering Danes. Later, however, the Danish Lutheran Bible gained acceptance and held sway until the late 19th century. Biblical terms and phrases enriched the literary Danish *(Riksmål)* spoken in educated circles, but themes drawn from the Bible are comparatively rare in Norwegian literature.

In Sweden, individual Biblical books were translated during the 14th–15th centuries, but it was not until the emergence of a firmly Protestant monarchy under Gustavus Vasa (who reigned 1523–60) that the Bible became a significant cultural factor. Biblical authority for his program of Church reform was invoked by Laurentius Andreae (c. 1475–1552) who, together with Ola(v)us Petri (1493–1552), produced the first complete Bible in Swedish, which was again based on Luther's German text. Their *Gustavus I (Gustaf Vasa) Bible* (1541) remained Sweden's "authorized version" until a new translation received royal sanction in 1917. Protestantism's triumph in Sweden had important repercussions, since the translation of the Bible laid the foundations of Swedish literature. The same process also took effect in remote Finland, a political dependency of Sweden. There, Archbishop Mikael Agricola (c. 1510–1557), another staunch Lutheran, published a version of Psalms (1551) and other Biblically inspired writings which molded Finnish, a language totally unrelated to the neighboring Teutonic sister-tongues — Danish, Norwegian, and Swedish.

As in Germany, Biblical and Apocryphal themes dominated Scandinavian drama and poetry of the 16th and 17th centuries in the wake of the Reformation. This trend was particularly evident in Sweden, where one of the earliest plays was the Bible translator Olaus Petri's *Tobiae Commedia* (1550), a dramatization of the Book of Tobit. Petri's version of Psalms illustrates the important influence of this portion of the Hebrew Bible: many hymns of the Swedish church are really paraphrases of the Psalter, retaining much of the phraseology of the Bible.

The age of Voltaire encouraged Sweden's "enlightened" skeptics to launch an indirect attack on Christianity by abusing the Old Testament.

On the other hand, one of the greatest 18th-century Swedish authors adopted a very different attitude toward the Bible. The mystic and visionary Emanuel Swedenborg (1688–1772) employed kabbalistic symbolism in his construction of the spiritual world and, in *De cultu et amore Dei* ("On the Worship and Love of God," 1745), produced a highly subjective paraphrase of the Genesis and Eden stories.

The works of Sweden's preeminent dramatist, August Strindberg (1849–1912), were steeped in the language of the Bible. The Scriptural motifs which he exploited to develop his favorite themes include the struggle between the sexes (the Fall of Man, Samson and Delilah), Man's eternal struggle with God (one part of Strindberg's *Legender* (1898) is entitled "Jacob Wrestles"), and the class struggle, illustrated by the story of Hagar and Ishmael, to which Strindberg alludes in his autobiographical *Tjänstekvinnans son* ("The Bondwoman's Son," 1886). In his latter years, Strindberg studied Hebrew and speculated about its origin and relationship to other languages.

Interest in Biblical subjects has been maintained in 20th-century Scandinavia. *De udvalgte* ("The Chosen One," 1933), a drama about King David, was the work of Kaj Munk (Harald Leininger, 1898–1944), a Danish pastor who fell victim to the Nazis, while the Book of Job inspired the Swedish poet Karin Maria Boye's *De sju dödssynderna* ("The Seven Deadly Sins," 1941), an unfinished cantata involving the theodicy problem. The same issues are raised in *Kains memoaren* (English edition: *Testament of Cain,* 1967) by another Swede, Lars Johan Wictor Gyllensten (1921–   ), who displays his knowledge of Midrashic lore, as well as of the Bible. An amusing product of amateur Bible research may be seen in *Jahves eld* ("Jehovah's Fire," 1918), a tale about Moses by the Swedish skeptic Hjalmar Emil Fredrik Söderberg (1869–1941). The story of Jonah has proved extremely attractive to modern Scandinavian writers, possibly because of its nautical interest. It has inspired two modern novels—Haakon B. Mahrt's Norwegian *Jonas* (1935) and *Profeten Jonas privat* (1937; *Jonah and the Voice,* 1937), a Danish work by Harald Tandrup—as well as Olov Hartman's modern Swedish Miracle Play, *Profet och timmerman* ("Prophet and Shipwright," 1954).

HUNGARY

The text of the oldest surviving document in Magyar (the Hungarian language)—a funeral oration entitled *Halotti beszéd* (c. 1200)—was based on the Biblical account of the Fall of Man, and some of the earliest Hungarian poetry was interwoven with imagery and phrases culled from the Bible. During the 15th century, Hussite preachers anxious to make the Bible familiar to the people produced versions of the Psalms and various Prophetical books. This concern for the Bible's translation into the vernacular became even more apparent during the Reformation, when Calvinist missionaries produced Bible translations that referred directly to the Hebrew text of the Old Testament. The first complete Hungarian Bible—by the Calvinist preacher Gáspár Károlyi (1590)—became the official text of the Hungarian Protestants. As elsewhere, the Calvinists of Hungary saw themselves as new Israelites thirsting for liberation from their (Catholic and Turkish) oppressors. In his poem, *Cantilena* (c. 1523), Ferenc Apáti made Samson a dramatic symbol of the Hungarian peasant revolt, while Andras Farkas drew a parallel between "God's two chosen peoples" in *Az zsidó és a magyar nemzetről* ("On the Jewish and Hungarian Nations," 1538). The Lamentations of Jeremiah were often quoted to describe the miseries inflicted on the Hungarian nation after the Turkish victory at Mohács in 1526, and many Reformation epics drew their inspiration from Biblical figures and episodes.

The religious turmoil of the early 17th century provided a new incentive for writing in the Biblical vein. A. Molnár's *Psalterium Ungaricum* (1608), the first complete verse translation of the Psalms in the Hungarian language, was a triumph of the Protestant spirit. Stylistically elegant and faithful to the original, it ran to over 100 editions and is still popular. Perhaps the most extraordinary episode in Hungary's religious and literary history concerns Simon Péchi (c. 1567–c. 1639), who became chancellor of Transylvania in 1613. Acquiring a knowledge of Hebrew during his diplomatic missions abroad, Péchi turned heretic and proceeded to organize Transylvania's Sabbatarians, who observed many Jewish practices. His translation of Psalms and his Bible (1624–29) adhered strictly to the original Hebrew, and he also produced a Hungarian version of the Jewish prayer book for the *Szombatos* (Sabbatarian) sect, which reached the peak of its success in 1635. As a result of the Counter-Reformation, the Hungarian Catholics regained strength and, in their polemics, made extensive use of Biblical quotation, attributing the country's distress to the evil effects of Calvinism. Miklós Zrinyi (1620–1664), an aristocratic Catholic, wrote a baroque poem, *Obsidio Szigetiana*, or, as it appeared in Hungarian, *Szigeti veszedelem* ("The

Siege of Szigetvár," 1651). The hero of this epic is motivated by Scriptural morality and his military science owes much to Biblical history.

Following the revival of Magyar nationalism in the early 19th century, the Bible recovered its literary importance. Patriotism became a religious leitmotiv in the writings of Ferenc Kölcsey (1790–1838), a Protestant nobleman whose *Hymnus* (1823), textually related to Jeremiah 32:21–29, became the Hungarian national anthem:

Őseinket felhozád	(You led our ancestors
Kárpát szént bérézére...	To the holy peak of the Carpathians.
Tókaj szölövesszein	On the vineyards of Tokay
Nektárt csepegtettél.	You poured nectar.
Zászlónk gyakran plántálád	Ever anew You placed our banner
Vad török sáncába,	Over the trench of the savage Turk,
S nyögte Mátyás bús hadát	And under the somber army of Matthias
Bécsnek büszke vára.	The proud fortress of Vienna suffered.
Jaj de bűneink miatt	Yet, alas, because of our sins
Gyúlt harag kebledben...	Your anger was inflamed in Your bosom...
Szándd meg Isten a magyart,	O God, have mercy on the Hungarian
Kit vészek hányának	Who is tormented by disaster.
Nyujts feléje védő kart	Stretch out Your shielding arm
Tengerén kínjának...	Over the ocean of his sufferings...)[29]

It was in drama that the Biblical current achieved its greatest impact in 19th-century Hungary. With his *Mózes* (1860), Imre Madách (1823–1864) dramatically reinterpreted the Israelite Exodus in terms of the Magyar struggle for national liberation. *Az ember tragédiája* ("The Tragedy of Man," 1862), Madách's Faustian masterpiece, made the stories of Adam and Eve and the trials of Job a framework for its philosophical analysis of Man's eternal conflict with the forces of Satan and his own shortcomings.

The Bible remained an important source of expression and style in 20th-century Hungarian literature. Endre Ady (1877–1919), a revolution-

---

[29] For this text I am indebted to Mrs. Eva Kondor of Jerusalem.

ary poet who—like many other Hungarian liberals—was raised as a Protestant, drew much linguistic and spiritual inspiration from the Old Testament, as did Attila József (1905–1937), some of whose mystical ballads exploited Jewish legendary material. Under the shadow of Hitlerism, Biblical drama flourished briefly in wartime Budapast, where Lajos Bálint's *Támár* (1942) and Károly Pap's *Batséba* (1940) and *Mózes* (1944) were staged by a Jewish theater group. There was a sudden flowering of Biblical poetry and fiction in postwar, Communist Hungary during the 1950s, when János Kodolányi (1899–) wrote *Az égö csipkebokor* ("The Burning Bush," 1957), a novel about Moses, and József Fodor published *A tékoai pásztor* ("The Shepherd of Tekoa," 1958), a dramatic poem about Amos.

RUMANIA

Under the impact of the Hussite movement in the 15th century and of Calvinism in neighboring Hungary and Transylvania a century later, attempts were made to replace the dominant Church Slavonic liturgy with services in the vernacular and to translate the Bible into Rumanian, a Romance language related to Italian and Spanish. As in many other countries, the Book of Psalms figured prominently in the religious awakening of the Reformation era. The "Psalters of Coresi" (1568, 1578) published by Diaconul Coresi (c. 1530–1590), a friar-printer of Braşov who helped to mold the literary language of his people, were probably the first texts printed in Rumanian. The first complete Rumanian Bible— named in honor of its patron, Prince Şerban Cantacuzino *(Biblia lui Şerban)*—appeared in 1688. Based on the Septuagint, this inspired all the later Rumanian editions of the Bible and had a decisive impact on the Rumanian language.

Rumania's national resurgence in the early decades of the 19th century was accompanied by the revival of Rumanian literature. Ion Eliade Radulescu (1802–1872), one of its leading pioneers, wrote many religious and philosophical commentaries on the Scriptures (*Biblice. . .*, 1858) and also translated the Bible and Lord Byron's *Hebrew Melodies* (1834). His successors applied themselves more directly to Biblical subjects. Rumanian poetry attained new heights of artistry with the many "psalms" of the radical poet Tudor Arghezi (1880–1967), whose alternating piety and blasphemy reflected the inner turmoil of a renegade monk. References to Biblical characters and episodes and to the landscape of the Holy Land abound in the poems of George Călinescu (1899–1965), an outspoken democrat whose books were burned by Fascist mobs. Another outstanding modern writer, Gala Galaction (1879–1961), exerted an incalculable influence on Rumanian culture through his remarkable translation of the Bible (in collaboration with Vasile Radu, 1938). The Hebrew Bible inspired his mystical prose and the themes of several of his novels, such as *Roxana* (1930). Unlike many other modern Rumanian writers, Galaction was a devoted friend of the Jews, whose cause he bravely championed during the Nazi era, and a prominent Christian Zionist.

GREECE

The Hebrew Bible's impact on Greek civilization dates from the Septuagint's completion in the third century B.C.E. , and it seems probable that no other work did more to promote a harmonious relationship between the Hellenic and the Judaic traditions. An early instance of the Septuagint's appeal to Hellenistic Jews is provided by the "Exodus" of Ezekiel the Poet, who lived in Alexandria.[30] The discriminatory decrees of the Byzantine rulers forced the Jews to look inward and to develop a new culture in Judeo-Greek,[31] which in medieval times was the medium for a number of interesting Bible translations. The most extensive work of this type intended for Greek-speaking Jews of the Balkans was the anonymous Polyglot Pentateuch of Constantinople (1547), which may have been written in the 14th century. Christian drama of the Middle Ages had meanwhile inspired a Cretan Miracle Play about the Sacrifice of Isaac (1159) which was the forerunner of several Greek treatments of this popular theme, notably the play entitled *Hé Thysía tou Abraam* ("The Sacrifice of Abraham," 1696) by another Cretan, Vitzentzos Kornaros (died 1677), who probably wrote his drama in 1635. This early masterpiece, still regularly staged in Greece, may have been based on an Italian play. Kornaros portrays Abraham as a distraught father torn between love for his son and devotion to his God.

[30] See the beginning of this chapter.

[31] Like its Romance counterparts (Judeo-Italian, Judeo-Provençal, and Ladino), Judeo-Greek is basically the medieval dialect written in Hebrew characters; but the language employed is nearer to ancient Greek than that preserved in any other relic of Byzantine literature.

It was not until long after the Greeks had regained their independence that subjects drawn from the Bible reappeared in their national literature. Constantine Cavafy (Konstantinos P. Kavafis, 1863–1933), an Alexandrian poet who spent some of his early years in London and Constantinople, showed considerable empathy for the zealous Jews of old in his poems, "One of the Hebrews (50 A. D.)" and "Alexander Jannai." With savage irony, Cavafy castigates Jewish assimilation, describing the "progress" of the Maccabees' hellenizing descendant in the second of these historical scenes:

> Proud with success, richly pleased,
> King Alexander Jannai
> and his royal consort, Alexandra the Queen,
> walk to the sound of escorting music,
> in motley pomp and luxury
> pass through the markets of Jerusalem. . .
> every bit the peers of Seleucid monarchs
> and yet good Jews, kosher Jews, pious Jews!
> But should circumstances ask it,
> skilful with the lingo of the Greeks
> they can hobnob with Greek and would-be-Greek
> rulers as their equals—no ifs and buts!
> Well done indeed, brilliantly done,
> accomplished for all men to see,
> the work begun by great Judas Maccabeus
> and his four brothers, all men of renown. . . [32]

Ironical, too, is the fact that it was Cavafy—a Gentile of the modern Greek diaspora—who anticipated Jews of mainland Greece in the expression of such sentiments. Something akin to Cavafy's approach may be seen in *Esther* (1967), a modern verse drama by Ioanna Dhriva Maravelidhou, who pays homage to those Jews in the Persian Empire who were ready to make any sacrifice necessary to preserve the worship of one God.

A more intense interest in the Bible and the People of the Book was displayed by the poet, playwright, and novelist Nikos Kazantzakis

---

[32] Translation by Simon Chasen, in Ausubel, *op. cit.,* p. 63. Cavafy's inclusion in this anthology suggests—mistakenly—that he was a Jew.

(1882–1957), whose drama, *Sodhoma kye Ghomorra* (1956), relates the age of the Bible to the modern world which, in his view, has reverted to the corruption of the past. Kazantzakis' attitude is complex and often contradictory; though opposed to Zionism, he praised the modern revival of Hebrew and even gave one of his novels (*Todah Rabbah,* 1934), a Hebrew title. And while he expressed a longing to hear the voice of the Old Testament God while on a visit to Mount Sinai, Kazantzakis tended to distort Rabbinic Judaism and the outlook of his Jewish contemporaries.

THE ORIENT

The literary treatment of Biblical subjects in the Oriental countries has, not unnaturally, been confined for the most part to the Islamic world. However, it was a Jewish warrior-poet of the Hejaz (northern Arabia) who lived about a generation before the birth of Muhammad— Samuel ibn 'Adiyā (c. 550)—who first glorified Biblical events in Arabic verse. Still famed for his chivalry among the Arabs, Samuel wrote a number of heroic poems, one of which alludes to the Exodus and later episodes in Israel's Biblical history:

> Are we not the children of Egypt, the chastised one, we for
>   whose sake Egypt was struck by ten plagues?
> Are we not the children of the split sea, we for whose sake
>   Pharaoh was drowned on the day of his charge? . . .
> Are we not the people of the quails and the manna, and they
>   to whom the rock poured forth sweet water? . . .
> Are we not the people of the holy mount which crumbled to dust
>   on the day of the earthquakes?
> Did not the mighty one humble itself? But God extolled it
>   above every high mountain.
> Upon it His servant and interlocutor prayed. .[33]

One of the favorite themes of Islamic literature is the Biblical story of Joseph, as presented in the 12th Sura of the Koran. One version, the *Poema de Yuçuf,* became popular in Muslim Spain[34] and provided the basis for later Christian adaptations of the Biblical account. Joseph's

[33] Translation by Hartwig Hirschfeld, in Ausubel, *op. cit.,* pp. 102–3.
[34] See above (Spain, Portugal, and Latin America).

Illustration from a 16th-century manuscript of *Yusuf o Zuleikha*, a romance by the Persian poet Jami, based on the Islamic version of the story of Joseph. Joseph is shown arriving at a feast arranged by Potiphar's wife, Zulayka.

encounter with the wife of Potiphar attracted particular attention, inspiring *Yūsuf o Zuleikhā* (c. 1490), the best known romance of the Persian poet Jāmī (Maulānā Nūreddin Abd'er-Raḥmān Jāmī, 1414–1492). A Jewish parallel to the Islamic *Yuçuf* was the Judeo-Spanish *Poema de Yoçef*, which moved to North Africa and the Near East with the Sephardi refugees forced out of Spain in and after 1492. It is probably one of the sources of the Judeo-Arabic *Ma'aseh Yosef Ha-Zaddik* ("Story of the Righteous Joseph"), versions of which still survive in the 20th century.

In the Far East, Biblical themes occasionally figure in the works of Bene Israel (native Indian Jewish) authors, outstanding among whom was the modern Bombay playwright Joseph (Penker) David (1876–1948), who wrote in four languages. Three of David's dramas in Marathi were *The Maccabeans* (1921), *The Assyrian Captive* (1922), and *Abigail* (1923). The Bible's penetration even into modern Japan has found reflection in dramas about Saul (1918) and Absalom (1920) by Torahiko Khori.

THE YIDDISH-SPEAKING WORLD

For the 1,000 years up to World War II, Jews in Central and Eastern Europe and Jewish immigrants in the New World made Yiddish (*Jüdisch-Deutsch,* or *"Teitsch")* their most widely used cultural medium. Originally a Middle High German dialect heavily infused with Hebraic terms and idioms and written in Hebrew characters, Yiddish acquired new Slavonic and Romance elements as it moved further afield with those for whom it was the language of everyday life. From the outset, Yiddish literature was mainly based on the Bible and its traditional Jewish interpretation and on Talmudic and Midrashic lore. Yiddish glosses from the 12th and 13th centuries reveal an early concern for the dissemination of the Bible in this Jewish *lingua franca,* and translations of individual Biblical books—both in prose and in rhyme—made their appearance from the 14th century onward. Among the best-known translations of this type was the anonymous *Shemuel Bukh,* a rhymed paraphrase of 1 and 2 Samuel (c. 1400), which was followed by many other versions of Biblical books by authors of the 15th—17th centuries. Two interesting examples of this literature are the late 16th-century *Ẓe'enah u-Re'enah,* popularly corrupted to *Tsenerene* ("Go Out and Behold," cf. Song of Songs 3:11), of Jacob ben Isaac Ashkenazi (published 1616), who reworked the Pentateuch with additional material drawn from the Talmud, Midrash, and other sources; and the *Teitsch-Hallel,* an anonymous 17th-century version of Psalms. Some outstanding translations of the Bible have been produced by leading Yiddish writers of the modern period.

Yiddish drama mainly owes its development to the *Purim-Shpil* ("Purim Play") in honor of Queen Esther, which was traditionally performed on the Purim festival in Central and Eastern Europe. Poems and parodies on the theme circulated in manuscript from about the 15th century and printed versions also appeared soon afterward. In time, these early poetic monologues were expanded into playlets and then into fullfledged dramas—such as the anonymous *Akhashverosh-Shpil* ("Ahasuerus Play," 1697)—closely resembling the German *Fastnachts-spiele* (comedies) of the Renaissance era. The comparatively late appearance of Yiddish drama probably resulted from Rabbinical opposition to Jewish involvement in an art which had remained under the sway of the Church from the Middle Ages. The secularization of the German theater in the 17th century, when professional troupes were first established on an independent basis, led to a relaxation of this ban. Apart from the story of Esther, there were dramatizations of other Biblical episodes in works such as the anonymous *Mekhiras Yosef* ("The Selling of Joseph," c. 1710), *Dovid un Golias* ("David and Goliath," 1717), and *Moshe Rabeynu Beshraybung* ("The Story of Moses, Our Teacher," c. 1750).[35] These pioneering Biblical dramas betray the influence of contemporary European theater, particularly in the introduction of comic characters; but although some non-Jewish plays may have served as models for Yiddish dramas on identical subjects, any elements or motifs that were alien to the Jewish spirit were rigorously excluded, to be replaced by Midrashic and other authentically Jewish material.

Biblical subjects attained a new significance with Abraham Goldfaden (1840–1908), the "father of the Yiddish theater," whose romantic operetta about the Song of Songs, *Shulamis* ("The Shulammite," 1880), adapted the old musical tradition of the Purim plays to suit the taste of the modern theater-going public. The Biblical operetta was, however, only one peripheral aspect of the "Old" Testament's impact on modern Yiddish drama. The last, Zionist period of the Hebrew writer Moses Leib Lilienblum (1843–1910) finds reflection in his Yiddish *Zerubbavel* (1887), which emphasized the need for a restoration of Jewish national independence in the Holy Land, and some Yiddish plays of the 20th century have sometimes discussed issues in contemporary Jewry against the background of the Bible.

In fiction, too, Biblical themes have attracted the attention of Yiddish writers, notably the internationally celebrated Sholem Asch (1880–1957). Asch first treated Biblical themes in two plays, *Yiftakhs Tokhter* (1914; *Jephthah's Daughter,* 1915) and *Yosef-Shpil* ("The Joseph Play," 1924), but—after arousing violent controversy with his New Testament fiction (*The Nazarene,* 1939, etc.)— he proceeded to write his Biblical novels, *Moyshe* (1951; *Moses,* 1951) and *Der Novi* (1955; *The Prophet,* 1955), the latter of which dealt with Deutero-Isaiah. In *Moses* and *The Prophet,* as in his other works, Asch revealed his extraordinary talent as a storyteller, stressing the individuality of his characters and depicting their environment and religio-moral conflicts and aspirations.

The influence of the Hebrew Bible on Yiddish poetry of the 20th

---

[35] A collection of these old Purim Plays, including dramatizations of the Sacrifice of Isaac and the Wisdom of Solomon, was published by Noah Prylucki in 1912.

century has been as important and, in many ways, even more interesting. Here, two vitally important factors were Bible translations of outstanding artistic and literary value by the poets Isaac Leib Peretz (1852–1915) and Yehoash (Yehoash Solomon Bloomgarden, 1872–1927). Peretz, who wrote in Hebrew as well as Yiddish, produced a new version of the "Five Scrolls" (Song of Songs, Ruth, Lamentations, Ecclesiastes, and Esther) which appeared posthumously in 1925, while Yehoash published Isaiah, Job, and some other Biblical books in 1910. Yehoash later began work on a complete Yiddish Bible, beginning with Genesis in 1922 and completing the Pentateuch by the time of his death. The Prophetical and other Biblical books were subsequently printed from his manuscripts. The Yehoash Bible has been called the greatest literary achievement in the Yiddish language and, with the original Hebrew text printed alongside the translation, it became the version most used in Yiddish-speaking homes throughout Eastern Europe and the New World. In his original poetry, too, first collected in *Gezamelte Lider* (1907; *Poems of Yehoash,* 1952), this writer devoted much attention to the Bible, expressing an awareness of the Divine force permeating the universe. The stylistic and thematic characteristics of the Bible are powerfully reproduced in poems such as "Jephthah's Daughter," "Psalm," and "The Harp of David," which describes how,

When the night her visions is weaving
With moonlight and starlight for warp,
The King in his chamber arises
And wakens the voice of his harp.

He sees not the hands of his playing,
He hears but a melody sweet;
He hears but the heart of him beating
With a musical, magical beat. . .

Then pours he his soul on the harp-strings,
Forgetful of sorrow and pain,
The old, gray monarch of Judah
Is a youthful Poet again![36]

---

[36] Translation by Alter Brody, in Ausubel, *op. cit.,* p. 233.

Biblical themes are also prominent in "Sodom" and other poems by Chaim Grade (1910–   ); in Moses Schulstein's dramatic poem, *"Yehudah Hamakkabi"* ("Judah Maccabee," in *A Layter tsu der Zun*, 1954); in verse and plays about the suffering of the individual by H. Leivick (Leivick Halpern, 1886–1962), especially the dramatic poem, *In di Teg fun Iyov* ("The Days of Job," 1953); and in the poetry of Itzik Manger (1901–1969). The delicate vein of satire apparent in "Jealous Adam" and "Adam and Eve" ("What did you do in the apple-tree row, / My child with the golden skin?" / "I have been gossiping with the snake / About the Commandment of Sin. . . ") was expanded in Manger's imaginative novel, *Dos Bukh fun Gan-Eydn* (1939; *The Book of Paradise*, 1965), which satirically contrasted the Eden of popular imagination with the reality of Jewish life in the pre-Hitler world of Eastern Europe.

Manger is, however, best remembered for his two lyrical works, *Khumesh Lider* ("Pentateuch Songs," 1935), in which Biblical figures assume the garb and mental characteristics of modern Yiddish-speaking Jews, and *Megile-Lider* ("Scroll Songs," 1936), a fascinating recreation of the old Purim Play tradition. Manger's original treatment of the Esther story in his *Megile* enjoyed a tremendous success when it was staged as a musical in Israel in 1967 and, soon after, in the U.S.A. It is no exaggeration to say that the revival of interest in Yiddish poetry and drama during the later 1960s owes as much to Manger's appealing treatment of familiar Biblical subjects as to a sentimental regard for the vanished world of East European *Yidishkayt*.

The Burstein family (Pesach, his wife Lilian Lux, and their son Mike) in a 1968 Israel production of Itzik Manger's *Megile*.

THE REALM OF HEBREW

The Bible's impact on the style, idiom, and thematic content of medieval and modern Hebrew literature is so demonstrable as to make any detailed discussion seem almost superfluous. Although Hebrew drama was, as a genre, virtually unknown before the 17th century, Hebrew poetry and fiction have older roots and in these the Biblical current was always strong. The influence of the Bible can be traced through the whole of Rabbinic literature, from the Midrash and Talmud with their rich narrative content, through the Biblical legends of the Middle Ages (a storehouse of imaginative short stories), to the Kabbalah, seen at its zenith in the *Sefer Ha-Zohar* ("Book of Splendor," c. 1300). In poetry, Biblical diction and echoes naturally suffuse the medieval *piyyutim* (liturgical poems) recited on solemn occasions and the religious and secular verse of the great Hebrew poets of medieval Spain, who revived the use of Biblical (rather than Mishnaic and Talmudic) Hebrew as a bastion against the Islamic world's much-vaunted reverence for the language of the Koran.

The outstanding exponent of Hebrew secular verse was Yehudah (Judah) Halevi (c. 1075–1141), the "sweet singer of Zion" and the greatest Jewish poet since the Bible, whose life and works have been a source of perennial fascination to writers like Heine, one of his most notable admirers. The Biblical element is especially vivid in his religious lyrics, in the *Shirei Ha-Galut* ("Poems of the Diaspora") and *Shirei Ziyyon* ("Songs of Zion"). The "Poems of the Diaspora" resound with the accents of the Book of Psalms and with the elegiac pathos of Job and Lamentations, or—like some of his lyrics—with a near-mystical evocation of love and Spring in the tradition of the Song of Songs. Yehudah Halevi's yearning for his ancient homeland finds memorable expression in his "Songs of Zion," which inaugurated a new genre in Hebrew literature—Biblically inspired and structured poems of love and longing for the Land of Israel. Of these, the most famous are *"Yefeh Nof"* ("Beautiful Bower"), *"Libbi be-Mizrah "* ("My heart is in the East, / And I dwell in the West"), and the splendid "Ode to Zion" (*"Ziyyon Ha-lo Tish'ali"*) which Jews observing the Ashkenazi rite recite each year on the fast commemorating the destruction of the Temple:

Zion, wilt thou not ask if peace's wing
Shadows the captives that ensue thy peace,

Left lonely from thine ancient shepherding?
Lo! west and east and north and south—world-wide—
All those from far and near, without surcease,
Salute thee: Peace and Peace from every side . . .
To weep thy woe my cry is waxen strong:—
But dreaming of thine own restored anew
I am a harp to sound for thee thy song . . .
And who will make me wings that I may fly,
That I may hasten thither far away
Where my heart's ruins 'mid thy ruins lie? . . .
How shall it any more be sweet to me
To eat or drink, while dogs all unrestrained
Thy tender whelps devouring I must see? . . .
Shinar and Pathros—nay, can these compare
With thee in state? And can thy purity,
And can thy light be like the vain things there?
And thine anointed—who among their throng
Compareth? Likened unto whom shall be
Levites and seers and singers of thy song?
Lo! it shall pass, shall change, the heritage
Of vain-crowned kingdoms; not all time subdues
Thy strength—thy crown endures from age to age . . .[37]

Compared with Yehudah Halevi's sublime poetry, that produced by
other Hebrew writers of the 14th and 15th centuries who turned to the
Bible was uninspired versification. Only Immanuel of Rome[38]—whose

---

[37] Free translation by Nina Salaman (in *Selected Poems of Jehudah HaLevi*,
Philadelphia, 1924) of the original Hebrew:

צִיּוֹן, הֲלֹא תִשְׁאֲלִי לִשְׁלוֹם אֲסִירַיִךְ. דּוֹרְשֵׁי שְׁלוֹמֵךְ, וְהֵם יֶתֶר עֲדָרָיִךְ:

מִיָּם וּמִזְרָח וּמִצָּפוֹן וְתֵימָן, שְׁלוֹם רָחוֹק וְקָרוֹב, שְׂאִי מִכָּל־עֲבָרָיִךְ . . .

לְבְכּוֹת עֱנוּתֵךְ אֲנִי תַנִּים, וְעֵת אֶחֱלוֹם שִׁיבַת שְׁבוּתֵךְ, אֲנִי כִנּוֹר לְשִׁירָיִךְ . . .

מִי יַעֲשֶׂה־לִּי כְנָפַיִם וְאַרְחִיק נְדוֹד, אָנִיד לְבִתְרֵי לְבָבִי בֵּין בְּתָרָיִךְ . . .

אֵיךְ יֶעֱרַב לִי אֲכֹל וּשְׁתוֹת. בְּעֵת אֶחֱזֶה, כִּי יִסְחֲבוּ הַכְּלָבִים אֶת־כְּפִירָיִךְ . . .

שִׁנְעָר וּפַתְרוֹס הַיַעַרְכוּךְ בְּגָדְלָם, וְאִם הֶבְלָם יְדַמּוּ לְתֻמַּיִךְ וְאוּרָיִךְ:

אֶל־מִי יְדַמּוּ מְשִׁיחַיִךְ, וְאֶל־מִי נְבִיאַיִךְ, וְאֶל־מִי לְוִיַּיִךְ וְשָׁרָיִךְ:

יִשְׁנֶה וְיַחֲלֹף כְּלִיל, כָּל־מַמְלְכוֹת הָאֱלִיל, חָסְנֵךְ לְעוֹלָם. לְדוֹר וָדוֹר נְזָרָיִךְ . . .

[38] See above (Italy).

Maḥberet Ha-Tofet Ve-ha-Eden ("Hell and Paradise," 1491) followed Dante's *Divina Commedia*—brought lustre to Hebrew poetry after the Spanish Golden Age and before the modern Hebrew Revival. By the 17th century, secular writing had shifted its center of activity to both Italy and to the Sephardi community in Holland. Here, for the first time, poetry gave birth to Hebrew drama with *Yesod Olam* ("The Foundation of the World," c.1638), a legendary account of Abraham's conflict with Nimrod and the idolaters, written in conformity with the classical unities by the Dutch rabbi and kabbalist, Moses ben Mordecai Zacuto (c. 1620–1697). A kind of Hebrew Mystery Play, *Yesod Olam* was clearly influenced by the Biblical *auto* (sacred drama) of the Spanish Renaissance. Dramas relating more directly to Biblical themes were written by the Italian poet and kabbalist Moses Ḥayyim Luzzatto (1707–1746) and the Dutch Sephardi poet David Franco-Mendes (1713–1792). Luzzatto's early verse play, *Ma'aseh Shimshon* ("The Story of Samson," 1724), which invested its tragic hero with the author's Messianic notions, was little more than a monologue; but Franco-Mendes' drama, *Gemul Atalyah* ("Athaliah's Revenge," 1770), was a notable adaptation of Racine's classic French tragedy. Other Hebrew dramas based on those of Racine were to follow in the 19th century.

The German *Haskalah* ("Enlightenment") movement, ushered in by Moses Mendelssohn and his followers during the 1780s, marked the literary ascendancy of the Ashkenazi Jews and the decline of Sephardi and Italian Jewry's long domination of Hebrew culture. Since Mendelssohn's pioneering translation of the Hebrew Bible was a principal foundation of the *Haskalah,* it was natural for the Biblical element to play a preeminent role in literary works by members of the new movement. *Shirei Tif'eret* ("Poems of Glory," 1789–1802), the magnum opus of Naphtali Herz (Hartwig) Wessely (1725–1805), was an 18-canto epic about the life of Moses and the Exodus from Egypt extending as far as the Giving of the Law on Mount Sinai. Moses is portrayed as a devout philosopher campaigning against ignorance and fanaticism, and the mission, suffering, and destiny of the Jewish people provide the leitmotiv of the whole work. Despite its obvious didacticism, *Shirei Tif'eret* contains some fine lyrical passages; partial translations appeared in German (1795) and French (1815), and the poem inspired many imitations by later Hebrew writers impressed by its revival of the Biblical style. The vogue for Biblical poetry and drama which Wessely's work inspired lasted well into the first half of the 19th century.

Under the impact of the *Haskalah,* Hebrew playwrights also turned their attention to the Bible. First in the field was Joseph Ha-Efrati (Tropplowitz, c. 1770–1804), whose *Melukhat Sha'ul Ha-Melekh Ha-Rishon al-Yeshurun* ("The Reign of Saul, the First King of Israel," 1794), notable for its ingenious and dramatic qualities and for its egalitarian outlook, made Saul not merely a proud and jealous ruler but also a pitiable figure, torn by guilt, envy, and suspicion. It was followed by a host of lesser Biblical dramas. By the mid-19th century, however, the *Haskalah* had long since vanished from the German-Jewish literary scene—where Hebrew had been displaced by German—and had become a far more potent force in Poland and Russia.

Like David Franco-Mendes in Holland, many of the *Maskilim* (exponents of the *Haskalah*) in Eastern Europe (Galicia, Lithuania) produced Hebrew versions of Biblical epics and dramas by leading writers of the West. *She'erit Yehudah* ("The Remnant of Judah," 1827), a paraphrase of Racine's *Esther,* foreshadowed the more mature Bible scholarship of Solomon Judah Leib Rapoport (1790–1867), a Galician Talmudist who later became Chief Rabbi of Prague. His contemporary, Me'ir (Max) Ha-Levi Letteris (c. 1800–1871), translated Lord Byron's *Hebrew Melodies* (1824) and Racine's *Athalie* (*Geza Yishai,* 1835) and *Esther* (*Shelom Ester,* 1843). A pseudo-Biblical style colors the poems of Abraham Dov (Adam Ha-Kohen) Lebensohn (1794–1878) and of his more eminent son, Micah Joseph (Mikhal) Lebensohn (1828–1852), whose verse collection, *Shirei Bat Ziyyon* ("Poems of a Daughter of Zion," 1851), contains several epic treatments of Biblical themes. Some of these adopt a novel, often anti-traditional, approach: *"Ya'el ve-Sisera"* ("Jael and Sisera") portrays the enemy general as the victim of political exigencies; and in *"Moshe al Har Ha-Avarim"* ("Moses on Mount Abarim") the poet—doomed by tuberculosis—identifies with the Lawgiver who was also fated to die before reaching the Promised Land. Samuel Leib Gordon (1865–1933), another Lithuanian writer, published a secularized commentary on the Bible and *Shulamit; o Hokhmat Shelomo* ("Shulamith, or the Wisdom of Solomon," 1896), a translation of Paul Heyse's German play about the Song of Songs. Other works of this type also appeared in England: *Va-Yegaresh et Ha-Adam* ("So He Drove Out the Man," 1871) was a version of Milton's *Paradise Lost* by Isaac Edward (Eliezer) Salkinson (1820–1883), a Russian Hebraist who became a Christian missionary and produced the standard Hebrew translation of the New Testament (1883); while the Manchester

Zionist writer Joseph Massel based his *Shimshon Ha-Gibbor* (1890) on Milton's *Samson Agonistes*, and his *Yehudah Ha-Makkabi* (1900) on Longfellow's *Judas Maccabaeus*.

The outstanding contribution to the poetic revival was made by Judah Leib (Leon) Gordon (1831–1892), a fiery critic of established religious attitudes and Biblical and Rabbinic values. Yearning for a distant and enchanting Jewish past distinguishes Gordon's sentimental early epics on Biblical themes: *Ahavat David u-Mikhal* ("The Love of David and Michal," 1857), *David u-Varzillai* ("David and Barzillai," c. 1855), and *Asenat Bat Potifera* ("Asenath, the Daughter of Poti-phera," 1868). Gordon's rejection of Orthodoxy and of Yiddish (the "Ghetto jargon") long dominated his outlook and writing and led him to portray some of the Bible's traditional "villains" in a positive fashion. Thus, Zedekiah's criticism of Jeremiah's "unrealistic" stress of spiritual matters at a time of national crisis finds powerful support in *Zidkiyyahu be-Veit Ha-Pekuddot* ("Zedekiah in Prison," 1879), a Biblical epic that reflects Gordon's own banishment to a distant province for alleged anti-Czarist activities. The officially inspired anti-Jewish pogroms of 1881 brought about a dramatic change in the poet's outlook: *"Ahoti Ruhamah"* ("Ruhamah, My Sister," 1882), which presented contemporary outrages in the guise of Shechem's rape of Dinah, despaired of Russian liberalism and gave vent to Gordon's denunciatory wrath:

> Abel's blood marks Cain's forehead!
> And your blood, too, all shall behold:
> A mark of Cain, disgrace and eternal shame
> On the forehead of the murderous villains. . .

In *"Bi-Ne'areinu u-vi-Zekeneinu Nelekh"* ("We Will Go with Our Young and Our Old"; cf. Ex. 10:9), a poem of the same period, Gordon called on the Jews to leave Russia, and his prophetic use of the invocation, "O House of Jacob, come ye, and let us walk" (Isa. 2:5), became the watchword of the Bilu[39] pioneers who set out to build the first Zionist colonies in Palestine (1882). Gordon's Biblicism was extraordinary and his influence on later Hebrew poets, notably Bialik, readily acknowledged.

[39] An acronym of the cited phrase in Hebrew: *Beit Ya'akov Lekhu Ve-nelekhah* ("O House of Jacob . . .").

Meanwhile, an important development had also taken place in the realm of Hebrew prose. Abraham Mapu (1808–1867), another Lithuanian *Maskil,* had studied languages and made himself familiar with modern European literature, particularly the popular French social and historical novels of his day. *Ahavat Ziyyon* ("The Love of Zion," 1853), which took more than 20 years to write, was not only Mapu's masterpiece but also the first Hebrew novel and, indeed, the world's first novel with a Biblical setting. Inspired by *Haskalah* ideals and distinguished by its command and imaginative use of Biblical Hebrew, *Ahavat Ziyyon* recaptured the atmosphere of the Hebrew kingdoms during the lifetime of Isaiah when the Israelites still lived as free men in their own land. The novel had an immense appeal to a generation still exiled in the poverty-stricken villages and townships of Eastern Europe and was translated into many languages. The first modern Hebrew bestseller, it appeared in no less than three English translations. Other Biblical novels followed soon after and tried — unsuccessfully — to profit from the new vogue of Hebrew Biblical romance, but it was not until the 20th century that other works of fiction on Biblical motifs achieved anything like the same success and importance.

Biblical themes and expressions have retained — and at times even redoubled — their importance in Hebrew literature of the 20th century. A major impetus has inevitably been the modern return to Zion under the banner and inspiration of the Zionist movement. The youthful iconoclasm of J. L. Gordon was taken a stage further by David Frischmann (1859–1922), a versatile and influential writer who abandoned all adherence to traditional norms. This radical outlook was expressed in two of his early poems, *"Lo Elekh Immam"* ("I Will Not Go With Them") and *"Elilim"* ("Idols"): in the first, Frischmann repudiated the past ("Their prophets are not my prophets, their angels are not my angels") and, in the second, he berated Abraham for failing to smash the "greatest idols of all" which he, the poet, was now prepared to demolish. With *Ba-Midbar* ("In the Wilderness," 1923), Frischmann began a series of fictional tales on Biblical motifs, which dealt with the newly liberated Israelites' spiritual conflict — torn between their pagan instincts and the new demands of the Mosaic law.

Hayyim Nahman Bialik (1873–1934), the greatest Hebrew poet of the modern age, was more firmly rooted in the Biblical-Judaic tradition. While few of his poems relate directly to Biblical themes, the imagery and language of the Bible (freed from the old *Haskalah* rhetoric) are nevertheless essential to his writing. "Indeed," he once confessed, "I am not apt to dip pen in ink without first looking into the Book of Books." From the poem *"Birkat Am"* ("The Blessing of the People," 1894), with its vision of the new Palestinian settlers as priests and Temple-builders, to *Va-Yehi Ha-Yom* (*And It Came to Pass. . .* , 1938), a collection of Biblical legends, this element envelopes much of Bialik's verse and prose. In *"Metei Midbar"* ("The Dead in the Desert," 1902), he sees Israel's "last generation of slaves and first generation of freemen" rise from their age-old slumber and prepare to take up arms against their enemies, thus setting an example to the submissive Jews of the Russian "Pale of Settlement." This call to action was accompanied by a thunder of scorn and anguished reproach in *"Be-Ir Ha-Haregah"* ("In the City of Slaughter," 1904), an epic evocation (using Biblical invective) of the Kishinev pogrom that shook Russian Jewry in the previous year. Bialik denounced the inertia of his fellow-Jews no less than the outrage itself, and boldly made God question the misdirected piety of His people:

> For God called up the slaughter and the Spring together—
> The slayer slew, the blossom burst, and it was sunny weather! . . .
> Come, now, and I will bring thee to their lairs,
> The privies, jakes, and pigpens where the heirs
> Of Hasmoneans lay, with trembling knees,
> Concealed and cowering—the sons of the Maccabees!
> The seed of saints, the scions of the lions!
> Who, crammed by scores in all the sanctuaries of their shame,
> So sanctified My name! . . .
> Wherefore their cries imploring, their supplicating din?
> Speak to them, bid them rage!
> Let them against Me raise the outraged hand—
> Let them demand!
> Demand the retribution for the shamed
> Of all the centuries and every age!
> Let fists be flung like stone
> Against the heavens and the Heavenly Throne! . . .[40]

[40] Translation by Abraham M. Klein (in Ausubel, *op. cit.*, pp. 259–263) of the original Hebrew:

כִּי־קָרָא אֲדֹנָי לָאָבִיב וְלַטֶּבַח גַּם־יָחַד:

הַשֶּׁמֶשׁ זָרְחָה, הַשִּׁטָּה פָּרְחָה וְהַשּׁוֹחֵט שָׁחַט . . .

Few poems in history have had more immediate and dramatic effects: Jewish self-defense groups were swiftly organized and valiantly resisted the next wave of pogroms which Czarist officialdom unleashed in 1905. The miseries which "*Be-Ir Ha-Haregah*" and other works of Bialik evoked also served to promote mass emigration to Palestine (where the poet himself settled in 1924) and the free lands of the West—an extraordinary instance of a literary work's influence on the course of human events.

Three leading contemporaries of Bialik were Saul Tchernichowsky (1875–1943), Zalman Shneour (1887–1959), and Ya'akov Cahan (1881–1960), in all of whom the new Zionist impulse was wedded to a rejection of the Diaspora and of the traditional values which it had fostered (an attitude which Bialik himself never adopted). Although his style and imagery were consciously Biblical, Tchernichowsky was in revolt against Jewish "puritanism" and sought the pagan undercurrent which, in his view, Israel's religious teachers had suppressed after the period of the Bible. His love of nature and physical prowess is apparent in many of his poems, including "Saul's Dance with the Prophets." This approach amounted to bold eroticism in the works of Shneour, whose late verse cycle, *Luḥot Genazim* ("Hidden Tablets," 1948), presented Israel's early history in a manner alien to the Bible by reassessing the role of the "opposition" (Korah, the false prophets, and their like), and by putting forward the idea that archaeology might some time in the future unearth the suppressed, "profane" writings of various opponents of tradition. Less revolutionary than Tchernichowsky and Shneour, Ya'akov Cahan tried to fuse European humanism with Jewish national feeling in the

---

וְעַתָּה לֵךְ וַהֲבֵאתִיךָ אֶל־כָּל־הַמַּחֲבוֹאִים:

בָּתֵּי מָחֲרָאוֹת, מִכְלְאוֹת חֲזִירִים וּשְׁאָר מְקוֹמוֹת צוֹאִים.

וְרָאִיתָ בְּעֵינֶיךָ אֵיפֹה הָיוּ מִתְחַבְּאִים

אַחֶיךָ בְּנֵי עַמְּךָ וּבְנֵי בְנֵיהֶם שֶׁל־הַמַּכַּבִּים,

נִינֵי הָאֲרָיוֹת שֶׁבְּ"אַב הָרַחֲמִים" זֶרַע הַ"קְּדוֹשִׁים".

עֶשְׂרִים נֶפֶשׁ בְּחוֹר אֶחָד וּשְׁלֹשִׁים שְׁלֹשִׁים,

וַהִגְדִּלוּ כְבוֹדִי בָּעוֹלָם וַיְקַדְּשׁוּ שְׁמִי בָּרַבִּים . . .

וְלָמָּה זֶה יִתְחַנְּנוּ אֵלָי? – דַּבֵּר אֲלֵיהֶם וְיִרְעָמוּ!

יָרִימוּ־נָא אֶגְרֹף כְּנֶגְדִּי וְיִתְבְּעוּ אֶת עֶלְבּוֹנָם,

אֶת־עֶלְבּוֹן כָּל־הַדּוֹרוֹת מֵרֹאשָׁם וְעַד־סוֹפָם,

וִיפוֹצְצוּ הַשָּׁמַיִם וְכִסְאִי בְּאֶגְרוֹפָם . . .

spirit of the 19th-century *Haskalah* idealists. His trilogy about Solomon (1924–45) and other Biblical plays are really historical melodramas.

Between the two World Wars, Hebrew literature also had flourishing centers outside of Palestine, in Poland and the United States. Itzhak Katzenelson (1886–1944), a Lithuanian poet and playwright who died in Auschwitz, dealt with the ultimate purpose of existence in *Ha-Navi* ("The Prophet," 1922), where Gehazi is portrayed as Elisha's "shadow," and made the hero of another Biblical drama, *Amnon* (1938), no more than a tragic weakling. Mattityahu Shoham (1893–1937) is mainly remembered for his four verse dramas about the collision between Biblical and pagan morality: *Yeriho* ("Jericho," 1924), which promises universal redemption, *Bil'am* ("Balaam," 1928–29), where Moses represents the forces of light and Balaam those of darkness; *Zor vi-Yrushalayim* ("Tyre and Jerusalem," 1933), which marks a notable shift in Shoham's views, Jezebel heading the pagan opposition to Elijah and Elisha: and *Elohei Barzel Lo Ta'aseh Lakh* ("Thou Shalt Not Make Gods of Iron," 1937), an allegory about the conflict between Aryanism (Gog) and Judaism (Abraham).

Since the 1920s, however, the focal point of modern Hebrew Biblicism has been the Land of the Bible itself, whether during the British Mandate or after the Israel declaration of independence in 1948. Here, in the pastoral tranquillity of the kibbutzim and villages of the early Zionist pioneers, a new lyrical poetry came into being, typified by the verse of the poetess Rahel (Rachel Bluwstein, 1890–1931), which contains many Biblical echoes and the well-known allusion to her Biblical namesake, "Her voice sings in mine. . . " Other innovators included the poets Nathan Alterman (1910–1970), Lea Goldberg (1911–1970), Yonatan Ratosh (1908–   ), and Uri Zevi Greenberg (1894–   ). The notion of a lost Eden dominates much of Alterman's writing, in which the nationalist note became increasingly powerful during World War II and the struggle for Israel's independence and survival, as in "Saul" ("sevenfold does a people bud / that on its soil lies slain in defeat. . . "). *Shirei Makkot Mizrayim* ("The Plagues of Egypt," 1944) transformed the Biblical Ten Plagues into a prototype of mankind's cyclical history with its recurring wars and renewal. Typical of Alterman's method is the poem, "From All Peoples," which violently condemns the Gentile's indifference to the fate of the Jews:

When our children cried in the shadow of the gallows,
We never heard the world's anger;
For thou didst choose us from all peoples,
Thou didst love us and favor us. . .
How great the concern for paintings and sculptures,
Treasures of art, lest they be bombed;
While the art treasures of baby-skulls
Are dashed against walls and pavements. . .
And Thou dost gather our blood in buckets
For there is none else to gather it . . .
And Thou wilt seek it from the hands of them that murdered
And from the hands of those that kept silent.[41]

Alterman also displayed a lighter touch with his Hebrew translation of Sammy Gronemann's German comedy about King Solomon and the cobbler (*Shelomo Ha-Melekh ve-Shalmai Ha-Sandelar,* 1942), the basis for the first successful Hebrew musical.[42]

An important translator of European classics and a well-known children's writer, Lea Goldberg remained generally more aloof from contemporary themes even in a Biblical framework, and her poem, *"Ahavat Shimshon"* ("The Love of Samson," 1951–52), is characteristically bereft of political overtones. Ratosh, a disciple of Tchernichowsky and the anti-traditional radicals, delved into ancient Semitic mythology in order to fortify his view that the exiles restored to their homeland were no longer Jews but Hebrews. His "Canaanite" poetry was the subject of great controversy and his philosophy has been adopted by successive fringe-groups of both left and right. Uri Zevi Greenberg, one of the outstanding poets of his generation, differed from most other Hebrew authors in adopting an ultranationalist, religio-mystical position inspired by the "Revisionist" Zionism of Ze'ev (Vladimir) Jabotinsky. Biblical drama and pathos resound through the poetic expression of his philosophy, according to which the Jews court disaster by worshiping Europe's fraudulent civilization with its countless "isms" and by shrugging off their Divinely ordained vocation. "Jerusalem the Dismembered," part of a long poem entitled *Yerushalayim shel Matah* ("The Earthly

---

[41] Translation by Simon Halkin, in Ausubel, *op. cit.,* pp. 151–2.
[42] See above (Germany and Austria) and also Chapter 6.

Jerusalem" 1937), expresses Greenberg's sense of outrage at the city's alienation from his ideal:

> And I longed to bellow like an ox: "O Jerusalem! How endure you
>   the horror and the shame, the fears—and fall not
> Into the Valley of Jehoshaphat, as within a grave? . . .
> What shall I do for you, O City of my blood? To redeem you I
>   cannot—all the nation is buried in its aversion and I in mine. . .
> It grieves me that Jews go about within your borders, no psalms
>   upon their lips, nor hands upraised like menorahs. . .
> And this is my vision, like a goblet of glass shattered here upon
>   your knee. . . [43]

From *Sha'ul Melekh Yisra'el* ("Saul King of Israel," 1944), a tragedy of fate by Shin Shalom (Shalom Joseph Shapira, 1904–) and his refugee friend Max Brod, to *Massa le-Nin'veh* ("Journey to Nineveh," (1962), a retelling of the Jonah story by Yehudah Amichai (1924–), themes drawn from the Bible have continued to figure prominently in modern Hebrew drama. One of the most original recent treatments is Benjamin Galai's *Sippur Uriyyah* "The Story of Uriah," 1967–68), a tragicomedy depicting simultaneously the Davidic intrigue and an Inca tale on a similar theme. In prose, particularly since 1948, the Biblical influence has been no less apparent, as in writers such as Shemu'el Yosef Agnon (1888–1970), the first Hebrew author to gain the Nobel Prize for Literature, and Hayyim Hazaz (1898–1973). Although their Biblicism was more a matter of style and expression than of theme, Hazaz wrote a lyrical and masterly short story about Zipporah, the wife of Moses, entitled *"Hatan Damim"* ("Bridegroom of Blood," 1925), while Agnon, a religiously observant Jew, reworked Biblical and Rabbinic lore in the anthologies *Yamim Nora'im* (1938; *Days of Awe,* 1948) and *Attem Re'item* ("Ye Have Seen," 1959). Biblical fiction is naturally popular in Israel, where the stories and their settings are uniquely vivid and familiar. An outstanding exponent of the Biblical novel is Moshe Shamir (1921–), whose *Melekh Basar va-Dam* (1951; *A King of Flesh and Blood,* 1958), based on the life of Alexander Yannai, experimented with Biblical and Mishnaic language—a technique which he did not pursue

---

[43] Translation by Charles A. Cowen, in *Jerusalem* (New York, 1939).

in *Kivsat Ha-Rash* ("The Poor Man's Lamb," 1956), a tragic study of Uriah's destruction by King David. In poetry, drama, and fiction, the Bible thus retains—and, if anything, strengthens—its hold on the imagination of the modern Hebrew writer and of his readers in the Land of Israel.

SUMMARY

In this detailed survey of the countless adaptations of Biblical themes in the literature of the nations, an attempt has been made to provide some insight into the various ways in which the rhythm, imagery, and idiom of the Hebrew Bible have penetrated the expression of many poets, playwrights, and novelists—even in those cases where their subject matter was not in itself Biblical. It is interesting to note how the very titles of certain literary classics have undergone a Biblical transfusion. Milton's *Paradise Lost*, Lamartine's *La Chute d'un ange* (1838), Shaw's *Back to Methuselah*, and John Steinbeck's *East of Eden* (1952) all deal with subjects that are, to a greater or lesser extent, connected with themes drawn from the Bible. But this is not the case with the purely allusive titles of a host of modern works, such as Edith Wharton's *Valley of Decision* (1902; cf. Joel 4:14), Samuel Butler's *The Way of All Flesh* (1903; Gen. 6:12), Ernest Hemingway's *The Sun Also Rises* (1926; Eccl. 1:5), Pearl Buck's *The Good Earth* (1931; Deut. 6:18), Aldous Huxley's *Eyeless in Gaza* (1936; Judges 16:21), and Warwick Deeping's *The Strong Hand* (1912; Ex. 3:19, etc.) and *Corn in Egypt* (1942; Gen. 42:2). This is also true of other novels—Margaret Mitchell's *Gone With the Wind* (1936; cf. Ps. 78:39, 103:16), Steinbeck's *The Grapes of Wrath* (1939; Deut. 32:32), and Vladimir Dudintsev's *Nye khlebom yedinym* (*Not by Bread Alone,* 1956; Deut. 8:3)—and of Lillian Hellman's play, *The Little Foxes* (1939; Song of Songs 2:16). Further examples are legion.

When it was universally revered in an age of faith, the Bible provided a wealth of inspiration for epic poets and dramatists; and, when skepticism offered a more jaundiced view of the Bible, the very hostility of rationalist (or atheist or Communist) criticism redirected men's attention to the Scriptural word. As Bruce Barton has pointed out, "Voltaire spoke of the Bible as a short-lived book. He said that within a hundred years it would pass from common use. Not many people read Voltaire today, but his house has been packed with Bibles as a depot of a Bible society!"[44] At times, writers have tried to portray the Patriarchs and Prophets as they really were through the use of psychological motivation and other techniques; at others, they have retold the familiar stories within the framework of contemporary events and conditions, seeking new religious or socio-political insights for the reader's consideration and entertainment. Such reinterpretation of great Biblical personalities and episodes remains one of the most powerful impulses in literature, and the process is likely to continue as long as the Bible retains its position as the world's "Number One bestseller."

[44] See Solomon Goldman's *The Book of Books* (New York, 1948), p. 330.

Part Three

THE BIBLE
IN THE ARTS

5

PAINTING AND
SCULPTURE

In wisdom, in understanding, and in knowledge
... to work in gold, and in silver, and in
brass, and in cutting of stones for setting,
and in carving of wood, to work in all manner
of skilful workmanship (Exodus 35:31–33).

The development of representational art among the ancient Israelites was
subject to obvious limitations arising from the Second Commandment:
"Thou shalt not make unto thee a graven image, nor any manner of
likeness, of any thing that is in heaven above, or that is in the earth
beneath, or that is in the water under the earth ..." (Ex. 20:4; Deut. 5:8).
The idolatrous cults of the ancient Near East fostered the worship of
beasts and of deities conceived as part-man and part-beast, whence the
Torah's specific prohibition against the fashioning of "any figure, the
likeness of male or female, the likeness of any beast ... of any winged
fowl ... of any fish ... " (Deut. 4:16–18). Pagan art was religiously
motivated and the Mosaic ban on the manufacture of images implied
their prohibition not so much *per se* as for the purposes of worship.
From Abraham, the first great iconoclast, this detestation of images
passed down through his immediate descendants to the Hebrew nation
and from Israel to Islam and some sections of the Christian Church.
"When, at the very dawn of their history, the Children of Israel established
it as a law of their religion that no one should make the likeness of any
living thing for worship, they took an epoch-making decision ... The
Israelites therefore expressly forbade three-dimensional representations,
but even two-dimensional pictures ... were considered equally suspect.
The underlying fear of Israel, Islam, the iconoclastic Byzantines, and the
Reformation was that the semblance might become confused with the
reality, that the image might be worshipped for itself ... The famous
story of the Golden Calf is an obvious example of the struggle between
the Spirit that lives by the Word alone, and the erring flesh that clings to
imitations of familiar objects, perhaps because men are lacking in imag-

ination. The simultaneous receiving of the Word by Moses on Mount Sinai, in the midst of a devouring holy fire and, down on the plain, the graven image set up amid dancing and bonfires, is a symbol of eternal significance."[1]

This fundamental law against the worship of idols was restated throughout the Bible. Moses warned the Israelites not to follow the practices of the nations around them, who venerated images of wood, stone, silver, and gold (Deut. 29:16), and the Psalmist later mocked the pagans, whose "idols are silver and gold, the work of men's hands. They have mouths, but they speak not; eyes have they, but they see not . . . they that make them shall be like unto them; yea, every one that trusteth in them" (Ps. 115:4–8; cf. 135:15ff.). To identify God with any material thing—whether animal, tree, or the "host of heaven"—amounted to a confusion of the Creator with the work of His creation. Thus, any "higher" worship of astral bodies was rigorously suppressed. The Second Commandment impeded representational art among the Hebrews and led their feeling for beauty into other channels. As Heine pointed out, the artistic temperament of the lawgiver "was directed solely toward the colossal and indestructible," but unlike the Egyptians among whom he had grown up, Moses "built pyramids of men and carved obelisks out of human material," transforming the Hebrew tribes into a nation of eternity. It was this same Moses (who smashed the tablets of the Law when he witnessed the Golden Calf idolatry at the foot of Sinai) whose command led to the building of the Sanctuary—a place of "splendor and beauty"—in accordance with the word of God and "after the pattern shown in the mount" (Ex. 25–29; 31:1–11; 35:4–39:43). The lawgiver thus allowed certain forms of artistic expression to reflect the inner beauty of Israel's religious inspiration. A modern poetic version of this approach may be seen in Franz Werfel's affirmation that "religious is the everlasting dialogue between humanity and God. Art is its soliloquy" (*Zwischen Oben und Unten*, 1946). Initially, Hebrew artistry was directed toward the embellishment of the Sanctuary and of the Temple; in time, the synagogue and ritual objects were also decorated and beautified by "wise-hearted" and "skillful" men who established a tradition that spread from Judaism to its two "daughter faiths," Christianity and Islam.

[1] Marcel Brion, Introduction to *The Bible in Art* (London, 1956), pp. 7–8.

And so, paradoxically almost, much of the modern world's greatest artistic achievement owes something to the inspiration of an iconoclastic religion.[2]

ART IN ANCIENT ISRAEL

As Semites originating in Mesopotamia, the Hebrews must have absorbed much of the culture of their native environment and their weaving, pottery, weapons, and other artifacts no doubt reflected the fashions prevalent among peoples of kindred stock. The Exodus liberated them from physical enslavement, but slavishness in other respects was not immediately eradicated. Egyptian civilization presumably impressed itself on the taste and fashions of the Israelites who took the "jewels of silver, and jewels of gold, and raiment" which the terrified Egyptians willingly gave them on their departure (Ex. 12:35–36), and it was from the voluntary offerings of such precious materials that the Sanctuary and its appurtenances were constructed (Ex. 25ff.). In broad detail, the "fashion" of all these sacred objects was Divinely inspired, but when the Judahite Bezalel and the Danite Oholiab were placed in charge of the practical execution of God's plan, contemporary Egyptian and Canaanite designs were probably dominant. Two features of the Tabernacle are of outstanding interest and importance: the winged Cherubim of beaten gold that hovered over the Ark of the Testimony (Ex. 25:18–22, 37:7–9) and the pure golden Candlestick (Hebrew, *Menorah*; properly, "lampstand") whose seven branches were to give light within the Sanctuary (Ex. 25:31–40, 37:17–24). With the (human-faced) Cherubim we encounter both an enigma and a contradiction, since their exact appearance is a matter for dispute, while the prevalence of winged bulls and lions in the cults of the ancient Near East suggests that a foreign artistic influence here entered early Judaism. Furthermore, these Cherubim—forerunners of all the angelic images and pictures of later times—were clearly representational, requiring the devoted skill of an inspired artist rather than a mere craftsman. The plain fact is that, while Moses stood aghast at the fashioning of the Golden Calf, God specifically ordained the design and creation of a "graven image" for the Sanctuary in which His high priest was to be Aaron, who had given way to the people by

---

[2] At least three-quarters of European painting before 1500 (and much of it after that date) is concerned with Biblical and New Testament subjects.

designing the molten calf. Until the destruction of the First Temple in 586 B.C.E., the Cherubim remained part of Israel's artistic expression and, even later, they were still to figure in Jewish ceremonial art; Cherubim, Seraphim, and other angelic forms subsequently played an important part in the iconography of Christendom. Through the celebrated vision of the prophet Zechariah (4:1–14), the Menorah or Candlestick was to become the central and Messianic emblem of Judaism, a variation of the "Tree of Life" symbol found in many regions of the ancient Near East. Whether in the design of the synagogue or on the arms of the modern State of Israel, the Menorah has become a characteristically Jewish motif, overshadowing its later rival, the "Star (or Shield) of David."[3]

During the era of the First Temple, that built by Solomon, specifically Jewish art forms are not easy to find. Foreign influences are generally apparent: in the "molten sea" or laver, resting on twelve bronze oxen (which faced each compass direction in threes), whose base was decorated with lions, oxen, and Cherubim (1 Kings 7:23ff.; 2 Chron. 4:2ff.); in Solomon's ivory throne, flanked by statues of lions (1 Kings 10:18–20), for which an Assyrian origin has been traced; and in other works of art, such as the plaques from the "House of Ivory" which King Ahab built in his capital, Samaria, in the ninth century B.C.E., these betraying a Phoenician inspiration which may have been introduced by craftsmen from Jezebel's native Sidon. Egyptian or Assyrian elements have also been detected in Israelite scarab seals of the eighth century B.C.E. Even when Jewish national sentiment dramatically revived after the return from Babylon and the construction of the Second Temple, an authentic Jewish art did not immediately come into being. Persian influence was succeeded by that of Greece, Hellenization revealing itself in the cities, baths, and statues which Greek suzerainty imposed on Judea from the time of Alexander the Great (fourth century B.C.E.) onward. When the Seleucid tyrant Antiochus IV (Epiphanes) undertook a more militant and repressive policy toward the Jews and their culture after 168 B.C.E., the Temple itself did not escape his despotic attention and decorative statues and pagan images were placed in its precincts. The Hasmonean revolt led at first to renewed Jewish objection to representational art, reflected in the scrupulous cleansing and purification of the Temple, but Greek standards again prevailed under the later Hasmonean kings, inspiring the design of buildings and even the minting of the earliest

[3] The Cherub and Menorah designs are discussed in greater detail below.

Jewish coins. It is nevertheless significant that Hasmonean coins never bore the ruler's effigy—as was otherwise the custom among nations of the Classical age. "The Greeks stressed the holiness of beauty; the Jews emphasized the beauty of holiness" (Emil G. Hirsch). Though far from insensitive to art and beauty, the Jews were wary of subscribing to the spirit which pervaded their Hellenistic expression. And it is perhaps significant that the Hebrew alphabet (whatever pictorial meanings have been read into its individual letters) was distinctly abstract. "When the Hebrew spirit prevails over the Greek," the Anglo-Jewish artist Solomon J. Solomon once wrote, the Jew "strips art of its pagan sensuality so that its beauty stands revealed, untarnished by barbaric or ungodly association."

A new approach to figurative art became apparent after the Herodian dynasty replaced that of the Hasmoneans. On the whole, Herod the

Façade of the Second Temple from the model of Herodian Jerusalem designed by Professor Michael Avi-Yonah.

Great respected Jewish religious susceptibilities—at least within the limits of Judea—and his reconstructed Temple is said to have been one of the architectural wonders of the Roman world. Representations of the Herodian Temple are to be found in countless artifacts, and some idea of its size and beauty may be gathered from the model built by Professor Michael Avi-Yonah (and based on available authoritative sources), which now stands amid his larger reconstruction of Herodian Jerusalem in the grounds of the Holyland Hotel in present-day Jerusalem. By late Hasmonean times, Jewish opinion was sharply divided over the representational art and its halakhic permissibility: both the Greeks and the Romans had initiated a shift in emphasis and inspiration from the religious (and pagan) to the less objectionable secular portrayal. The painting and sculpting of contemporary likenesses, landscape and histori-cal scenes, and even of political topics clearly offered less of a threat to Judaism, and some Jewish teachers therefore adopted a more liberal, conciliatory attitude toward such manifestations. Thus, while Herod was careful not to adorn his desert palace at Masada with any three-dimensional image, he thought nothing of the public display of statues in places with a sparse Jewish population, while his relatives—even those who were more devoted to their faith—did not scruple to have their portraits painted. Likenesses of the later Herodians did not appear on the coinage of Judea, but they did figure on coins that circulated in predominantly non-Jewish regions of the kingdom. As ultra-nationalist feeling hardened, certain types of representational art became weapons in the hands of Jewish patriots, who invoked the literal interpretation of the Second Commandment. Political, rather than purely religious, con-siderations motivated those who agitated against the use of Roman coins bearing the Emperor's effigy; there was an outcry against the standards borne by Roman legionaries when they marched through Jerusalem; and the golden eagle which Herod placed over the Temple gate in deference to Rome led (as Josephus records toward the end of the first book of his *Jewish War*) to a minor insurrection.

On the whole, however, more tolerant attitudes prevailed until open war with Rome broke out in 66 C.E. Indeed, many of the leading Rabbis were remarkably open-minded, unlike Josephus the historian who, as a revolutionary general, demonstrated his iconoclastic zeal in Galilee at the outbreak of hostilities. According to the Jerusalem Talmud, various "likenesses" were to be found in Jerusalem prior to the destruction of the Temple (*Avodah Zarah*, 3.1, 42c); and, while the Jews naturally fought against the Sanctuary's profanation when a statue of the Emperor Caligula was introduced for the purpose of worship in 37 C.E., no such protests were heard when Babylonian synagogues had effigies of the ruler placed within them by local patriots in later Rabbinic times. Some reflection of this liberalism may be seen in a Midrashic source (*Tanḥuma to Tazri'a*, 7): "Tinnius Rufus asked, 'Which is more beautiful, God's work or man's?' Rabbi Akiva replied: 'Unquestionably, man's work; for nature supplies only the raw material, while human skill makes of it works of art and of good taste' . . . " And, from another early text (*Tosefta* to *Mishnah Berakhot,* 7.4), came the injunction, "When you see handsome people or fine trees, pronounce the benediction: Praised be He who created beautiful things," which pious Jews throughout the world still echo as a blessing. The violent campaign fomented by extremists immediately before and during the war with Rome seems to have stifled genuine artistic expression among Jews of the time, but attitudes changed once again after the destruction of the Second Temple.

Despite the ravages of time and of successive conquerors, archaeology has brought to light many important examples of early Hebrew craftsmanship (coins, seals, carved ivory, etc.) and of Hasmonean and Herodian architecture: the palaces at Masada (fully excavated in recent years by Professor Yigael Yadin); the enlarged seaport city of Caesarea with its theater and aqueduct; the funerary monuments in Jerusalem's Kidron Valley, notably the Tomb of Zechariah and the Pillar of Absalom the Western and Southern Walls. Of these, the Tomb of Zechariah is a rock-hewn Hasmonean monument of Hellenistic conception, as is the Pillar of Absalom, while the real dimensions and formidable masonry of the Temple structure have mainly been uncovered since Israeli archaeologists, led by Professor Benjamin Mazar, began work on the ancient western and southern enclosures in 1967. The fact that Jewish representational art effectively came into being during the Hasmonean period is proved by certain characteristic designs found on coins—ritual objects such as the Menorah and the *lulav* (palm branch) and *etrog* (citron) used on the festival of Tabernacles.

JEWISH ART AFTER THE TEMPLE'S DESTRUCTION

Following the abortive and tragic revolt under Bar Kokhba, which culminated in the fall of Bethar (135 C.E.), the Jews were forced to accept political realities and to make their peace with the Roman overlord. One outcome of this development was a renewed liberalism in the Second Commandment's interpretation, whether in regard to Roman imagery of the secular type or to Jewish artistic expression. Both the Palestinian (*Yerushalmi*) and the Babylonian (*Bavli*) recensions of the Talmudic tractate *Avodah Zarah* ("Idolatrous Worship") contain numerous references to Rabbinic Judaism's increasingly tolerant approach to aesthetic matters. The prestigious Rabban Gamaliel, who died some years before the Bar Kokhba rebellion, had no compunction in attending a bath at Acre (where a statue of the goddess Aphrodite was set up as an adornment), and this sophisticated attitude became a legal precedent wherever non-Jews distinguished between the worship of and the taste for statues (T.B. *Av. Zar.*, 41a, 44b). The painting of frescoes was first countenanced in the third century C.E., many Rabbis permitting the decoration of synagogues with murals and mosaics (T.J. *Av. Zar.*, 42d–43d). Archaeology has again shed light on this trend, proving that the Talmud merely consigns to writing what was already well established in practice. Carvings of the Menorah and other ritual symbols appear on Jewish sarcophagi of the second–third centuries found in catacombs at Rome; carved stone lions figure in the decoration of some remarkable third-century synagogues in Galilee (Baram, Capernaum, Chorazin); and representations of animals, birds, and even Greek mythological themes occur in the beautiful mosaic floors of fourth–sixth century synagogues uncovered in Palestine (Bet Alpha, Naarah) and Tunisia (Hammam Lif). Messianic yearning reveals itself in stylized representations of the Temple (often reduced to the potent Menorah emblem) in the synagogue mosaics of Bet-She'an and Jericho, the necropolis of Bet-She'arim, Jewish gold glass from Rome, and in frescoes painted on the walls of Roman catacombs. Perhaps the most famous reproduction of the Temple Menorah is that carved on the Arch of Titus in Rome by non-Jewish hands to celebrate the conquest of Jerusalem in 70 C.E.

Although this survey of Biblical influences on early Jewish art has overlapped the birth and consolidation of the Christian Church, the wider implications of Jewish artistic achievement for Western painting

The Sacrifice of Isaac (*Akedah*) in the 6th century floor mosaic of the synagogue at Bet Alpha, Israel.

and sculpture will soon be apparent. Marianos and his son Ḥanina, who executed the mosaics at Bet Alpha, and the anonymous Jewish artists who decorated the walls of the synagogue at Dura-Europos in Mesopotamia were, in a very real sense, the creative force behind all the painting and manuscript illumination that later Jewish and Christian artists devoted to Biblical themes. In fact, according to one theory, those subjects from the Bible which Jewish artists treated in the early centuries of the common era had been foreshadowed or suggested in chapters 44–50 of Ecclesiasticus (the Wisdom of Ben Sira) and in a *Seliḥah* (penitential prayer) based on a passage in the Mishnah (*Ta'anit*, 2.4). The latter text was well-known long before Jews began to illustrate Bible themes in synagogue mosaics and frescoes. An elaboration of the Mishnaic passage, as presented in the *Seliḥah*, reads: "He who answered our father Abraham on Mount Moriah . . . Isaac his son when he was bound on the altar . . . Jacob in Bethel . . . Joseph in prison . . . Moses at Horeb . . . Aaron with the censer . . . Joshua in Gilgal . . . Samuel in Mizpah . . . David and Solomon his son in Jerusalem . . . Elijah on Mount Carmel . . . Elisha in Jericho . . . Jonah in the belly of the fish . . . Hezekiah in his sickness . . . Daniel in the lions' den . . . Mordecai and Esther in Shushan the capital . . . Ezra in the Captivity—He shall answer us." With only

329

a few variations, this is substantially the same list of Biblical worthies as the one presented in Ben Sira's account, beginning with chapter 44 ("Let us now praise famous men, and our fathers that begat us . . . ").

A comprehensive Biblical tableau was discovered by a Franco-American team of excavators working on a Syrian site in 1928–32. Here they uncovered the remains of an ancient frontier city (Dura-Europos) ruled in turn by Assyria, Rome, and Parthia until its destruction by Sassanid invaders in 256 C.E. During the latter part of its history, Dura-Europos had a mixed population whose religious needs were met by a Roman temple to Mithras, a small Christian chapel, and two successive synagogues, the second of which was completed in about the year 245 C.E. The frescoed walls of this later synagogue constitute the most important artistic monument of Jewish antiquity, and they have remained in a remarkable state of preservation. Pagan figures and symbols appear among the vast array of Biblical murals decorating all the walls of this synagogue, reflecting the cultural assimilation of the local Jewish community. The worshipers' loyalty to Persia may be inferred from the sympathetic portrayal of King Ahasuerus seated on Solomon's lion throne (which the Rabbis believed no one but a Persian monarch was worthy to inherit); and traditional Jewish Messianism suffuses the detailed rendering of Ezekiel's "Vision of the Dry Bones," with the reunited tribes of Israel gathered under a resurrected King David. At least two artists painted these frescoes: one, influenced by Persian art, depicted some of the Biblical figures (Ezekiel, Mordecai, and others) as Parthian horsemen; the other, inspired by Western examples, portrayed Moses, Jacob, Joseph, and other major Biblical personalities as Romans. The

Haman is seen leading Mordecai through the streets of Shushan (left), while Ahasuerus and Esther are enthroned (right) in this west wall panel from the 3rd century synagogue of Dura Europos.

way in which these and other themes are presented shows the unmistakable impact of Rabbinic lore and legend; and here, for the first time, human images are represented by Jewish painters—in a synagogue. These frescoes (later transferred to the Damascus Museum) are the earliest concrete evidence of Hellenistic art of this type in a Jewish milieu; previously it had been known only from glimpses in the Christian wall-paintings of the Roman catacombs.

A number of the Dura-Europos frescoes are of special interest and importance. There are striking portrayals of the *Akedah* (Binding of Isaac), in which—by contrast with the text of Gen. 22:11—the hand of God stretches out to restrain Abraham from sacrificing his son; of Jacob's dream; of a Jew (Ezra?) reading the Torah from a scroll; of the anointing of David; of Elijah humiliating the prophets of Baal and reviving the Widow of Zarephath's son; and of scenes from the Book of Ezekiel. Because the paintings of Ahasuerus and Esther and of Mordecai's triumphal ride on a white horse could be seen quite clearly from the women's benches in the synagogue, it has been suggested that these frescoes were so placed for the convenience of women, who normally came to hear the reading of the *Megillah* (Esther Scroll) on the festival of Purim in accordance with a Talmudic ruling (*Megillah*, 4a). The first decorations in the Dura-Europos synagogue seem to have been those painted on a panel above the niche in the eastern wall which formerly housed the Torah scrolls: these murals depict the façade of the Temple (including representations of the Menorah and Ark of the Covenant), together with the palm branch and citron ceremonially blessed and waved on the Tabernacles festival. In this panel some have seen a reflection of the worshipers' anxiety to stress the unity of the Jewish people, as symbolized in the wistful motif of the House of God. Like the carved lions of the Galilean synagogues (ancestors of the painted or carved wooden lions that often adorn the Holy Ark in modern synagogues), the frescoed or mosaic Menorah has also survived in Jewish ritual art, two such "candelabra" frequently standing on either side of the Ark of the Law in contemporary Jewish places of worship.

The art of Dura-Europos was novel, but not unique. Many of its features later reappear in other early synagogues: pagan decorations such as the signs of the Zodiac (found on ceiling tiles at Dura) occur in the delightful floor mosaics of Bet Alpha, where there are also representations of the *Akedah* and of the Menorah, lion, *lulav*, and *etrog* motifs. Temple and Torah Ark designs similarly figure in numerous mosaics;

the Menorah almost everywhere (from synagogues to Roman and Palestinian funerary reliefs); and the *shofar* (ram's horn used to proclaim the Jewish New Year)—a symbol of the *Akedah*—in synagogue mosaics at Jericho and Bet Alpha. Jewish ritual art has its roots in these early depictions, from which the illuminated Bibles and prayer books of the Middle Ages, some modern Esther Scroll (*Megillah*) decorations, Ḥanukkah lamps, and traditional embroideries all take their inspiration. The fact that Jewish artists (such as those who produced the Dura-Europos murals) had no qualms about representing the human face and figure in scenes like the drowning of the Egyptians in the Red Sea strongly suggests that, if such portrayals could be tolerated in the synagogue, they could also be permitted in scrolls and Biblical texts prepared for use in the home. From such sources a Jewish book-art must have emerged, on which early Christian artists presumably drew for thematic and stylistic inspiration.[4]

Jewish art's retreat to more conventional designs, and its gradual abandonment of figure scenes during and after the sixth century C.E., evidently reflect both the deteriorating social status of the Jews under the Byzantine emperors and the growth of an iconoclastic spirit in the Eastern Church. When the rise of Islam swept away the representational art of Hellenistic Jewry, new non-figurative styles dominated the Orient and further development of Biblical portrayal was restricted to Western Europe. Even after idolatry ceased to offer any real threat to Judaism, some Rabbis continued to oppose representational art and the Responsa literature of medieval Jewry reflects the struggle of scholarly opinion. Rabbis in the Islamic world particularly condemned the painting or sculpture of human and animal forms as an unforgivable distraction from the worship of the synagogue and the main purpose of existence. Jewish art nevertheless attempted to steer a middle course between Muslim iconoclasm and Christian imagery, and the design of the synagogue itself contributed some important elements to Christian and Muslim architecture. It gave the mosque its *almimbar* (dais)—a relic of the *bimah* (platform) from which the Torah scroll was read[5]—and the *miḥrab* shrine housing the Koran (inspired by the *Aron ha-Kodesh* or Ark of the Law). For the Christian church the synagogue provided

---

[4] See below.

[5] In Ashkenazi usage, from the 12th century onward, the *bimah* was often styled *almemar*.

other features: the apse (based on the recess for the Torah scrolls), the raised altar structure (akin to the *bimah*), the bishop's throne (a relic of the seat reserved for the *gabbai* or synagogue warden), and the perpetual light in Catholic churches (inspired by the *ner tamid*, a synagogue memorial of the ancient Temple's oil lamp). Some authorities have even suggested that there may be a link between the Menorah and Islam's characteristic minaret (in Arabic, *manārah*, "lighthouse"), which gave rise to the tower structure in Europe (as in the Italian campaniles of Florence and Venice and church steeples and towers dating from the Middle Ages). Jewish art, whether religious or secular, continued its development throughout the centuries following the dispersal from Palestine and its characteristics were sometimes emulated by other cultures; to a great extent, however, its Biblical inspiration forms part of the general history of medieval and modern painting and sculpture and its themes enriched the general store of other (mainly Christian) artistic traditions.

THE BIBLE IN EARLY CHRISTIAN ART

The fact that a literal interpretation of the Second Commandment was dominant in the primitive Church is not always appreciated. The iconoclastic spirit which the prophet Muhammad injected into Islam is generally familiar, but the opposition which the Church Fathers Tertullian, Eusebius, and Jerome expressed toward representational art is not so well known. Under the Emperor Leo II (the Isaurian), a Syrian Christian who spoke Arabic and understood the Oriental mentality, a frenzied campaign against the use of imagery was waged throughout the Eastern Empire during the eighth century and, although it ultimately failed, iconoclasm of this sort was to reappear within Christendom from time to time, particularly during the Reformation.[6] The Church nevertheless found it necessary to harness the talent and energy of inspired artists *ad majorem Dei gloriam*, and this policy was eventually to prevail both in the East and the West for centuries to come. Doctrinal motives encouraged the leaders of Christianity to shake off "Judaic" prejudices

---

[6] The Cistercian Order's prohibition of stained-glass windows in churches (1134) was followed by a controversy over the same issue in the Cologne synagogue.

against non-abstract painting and sculpture and to seek inspiration in the artistic traditions of the ancient Hellenistic world.

Early Christian art's saturation in themes drawn from the Hebrew Bible rather than from the New Testament is not surprising, in view of widespread reverence for the Greek Septuagint. The popularization of "Old Testament" subjects throughout the Jewish Diaspora and the comparative obscurity of most New Testament figures during the Church's infancy contributed to this development. It was the Septuagint which inspired Christian artistic expression in Roman carvings and murals, Byzantine mosaics, ecclesiastical picture cycles, and medieval illuminations. The Jews, a highly literate minority soaked in the Bible, could manage without pictorial art in their synagogues when external pressures made this necessary; but the church or chapel had to provide some appealing and easily digestible means of education for the Christian masses. In religious paintings, carving, sculpture, and icons Christianity found the tools that it required. The Church was also at pains to show how the heroes and heroines of the Bible symbolized or predicted ideas and events recorded in the Gospels. Various Biblical figures and episodes thus make their appearance in Christian funerary art from early times. The sacrifice of Abel is depicted on a first-century sarcophagus (Sant' Agnese, Rome); the suffering Job in early Christian frescoes from the Roman catacombs and the graveyard of St. Peter and St. Marcellino; the stories of Jonah, Noah, and Susanna in Roman sarcophagi and catacombs; and the Sacrifice of Isaac (a central theme of early Christian art) in the third-century catacomb of Priscilla and in the Vatican grottoes. The art of the catacombs was dominated by the idea of Salvation— deliverance from sin and death—and appropriate Biblical episodes were used to make this doctrine comprehensible to the untutored masses. No fewer than 57 separate interpretations of the Jonah story have been found in the Roman catacombs and on various sarcophagi, and some of these may have been Jewish rather than Christian. The occurrence of this motif on one sarcophagus (now in the British Museum) is thought to represent a lost Jewish pictorial prototype of the Biblical theme's later Christological interpretation.

CHRISTIAN TYPOLOGY

The choice of Biblical subjects in early Christian art was largely determined by their appearance in the second-century prayers of the *Commen-*

datio Animae ("Recommendation for the Soul"), a document which may be seen as a parallel to the passages from Ben Sira and the Mishnah that influenced Hellenistic Jewish art development. Until the fifth century C.E., the *Commendatio Animae* seems to have dictated the scope of Christian painting and sculpture on Scriptural themes. Mention has already been made of symbolism as a factor in the choice of motifs and the whole question of artistic reinterpretation of the Bible under the aegis of the Church (what is generally known as Christian typology) calls for some further elaboration. Briefly, selected Biblical and Apocryphal figures and events were seen to represent prophetic glimpses or "prefigurations" of New Testament miracles, personalities, or episodes. The story of Adam and Eve and the Fall of Man (portrayed in the Christian chapel at Dura-Europos) symbolized the doctrine of Original Sin; Athaliah's murder of the children of the Davidic house foreshadowed the Massacre of the Innocents; the ascetic, desert-dwelling Elijah (often shown as emaciated and wearing a hair shirt) was a precursor of John the Baptist; the birth of Jesus had been predicted by Balaam (Num. 24:17), Isaiah (7:14, 11:1), and Micah (5:1–3), who were therefore associated with the cult of the Virgin; the "type" of Jesus was seen in Daniel, David (his reputed ancestor), Isaac (whom Abraham was ready to sacrifice to God), Job, the virtuous Joseph, Joshua (whose Hebrew name, *Yehoshu'ah,* was akin to *Yeshuah,* or Jesus), the lawgiver Moses, Samson, and Solomon; and the Crucifixion and Passion were prefigured in events like the death of Absalom. The three angels who visited Abraham represented the Trinity, their tidings about the birth of Isaac foreshadowed the Annunciation, and the dismissal of Hagar symbolized the rejection of the "Old Law." Jacob's struggle with the angel signified man's unending battle against Satan and the powers of darkness; the paschal feast which Moses commanded the Israelites to prepare before their Exodus from Egypt symbolized the Last Supper; the crossing of the Red Sea and, later, of the Jordan was linked with the baptism of Jesus (as the design of some baptismal fonts clearly shows); Samson, who overcame the lion, represented Jesus triumphing over Satan and breaking the jaws of Hell; Elijah's despair in the desert was compared to the Agony in the Garden, his revival of the widow's son to the resurrection of Lazarus, and his ascent in a fiery chariot to the Ascension of Jesus. Jonah's ordeal in the belly of the whale (a favorite theme of early Christian art) stood for the Entombment and Resurrection or for the life hereafter.

Further examples of Christian typology—one of the most vital and important elements in pre-Renaissance art—are legion. Belshazzar was the Antichrist; Daniel, the Three Hebrews, and Susanna represented the elect saved from hellfire and other perils; Bath-Sheba, Jael, Rebekah, Judith, and the beloved Shulammite of the Song of Songs variously figured as the Virgin or the Church Triumphant. Esther, too, was linked with the cult of the Virgin and, until the later Middle Ages, her intercession with Ahasuerus on behalf of the imperiled Jews was seen as a prefiguration of Mary's mediation on mankind's behalf. The Queen of Sheba (whose rich gifts to King Solomon were thought to foreshadow the Adoration of the Magi) symbolized the Gentile Church; and Hosea's marriage to the harlot Gomer stood for the union of Jesus with the Church or of God with His faithless people. Because of his name and the symbolic meaning attached to episodes such as the arrest of the sun's course in the heavens, Joshua became one of the Nine Worthies, Ezekiel, usually protrayed with a fiery chariot (the *Merkavah*), or with a double wheel (symbolizing the two Testaments), sometimes held a scroll bearing the legend: *Porta clausa est, non aperietur* ("This gate shall be shut, it shall not be opened," Ezek. 44:2); and a more subtle typology suffused the miracle of the fleece in the story of Gideon, where it was thought to represent the fate of the Jews—first chosen and favored (wet), then rejected (dry)! Noah in his Ark exemplified the Christian's hope of Salvation amid the Deluge of sin.

According to several modern scholars, Jewish influence on early Christian art and iconography was not restricted to the subjects which the Hebrew Bible offered to the Church. A pictorial tradition may also have had some impact on the actual technique and presentation of Biblical motifs. There are obvious analogies between the frescoes of Duro-Europos and those of the early Church[7] and it is now thought probable that the Jews of Alexandria and other parts of the Hellenistic world had artists who made illustrations for manuscript copies of the Bible. From such Jewish prototypes there evidently developed a specific art of pictorial embellishment, which Christians took over by about the second century C.E. It has therefore been suggested that all the early Christian illuminated texts of Scripture are traceable to Alexandrian Jewish models, which left their mark on the fifth-century Greek *Cotton Genesis* (British Museum, London; the earliest illustrated Bible extant),

[7] The early portrait of Jesus has some likenesses in the Dura-Europos paintings.

the sixth-century *Vienna Genesis* (National Library, Vienna), the *Codex Amiatinus*, and the tenth-century *Rotulus of Joshua* or *Joshua Roll* (Vatican Library). The last of these was originally a 30-foot-long frieze depicting the Israelites' entry into and conquest of the land of Canaan; just as the Dura-Europos murals portrayed the Hebrews as Persians or Romans, so here they figure as soldiers in Roman dress with Joshua as their *imperator*. It has been asserted that certain features of the prototype and its imitations (such as Pompeian landscapes and Hellenistic architecture) later influenced Byzantine painting of the 11th-12th centuries, the 13th-century Genesis mosaics of the Cathedral of S. Marco in Venice, the design of Russian icons, and even the technique of some later medieval Italian artists. There is certainly much evidence to show that Christian representations of the first five centuries of the common era found inspiration in earlier works of art on Scriptural themes: in the Dura-Europos murals, the Torah read by Moses is depicted not as a tablet (or tablets), but as a scroll, and this is the form in which the Ten Commandments are portrayed on the fifth-century wooden doors of Sta Sabina (Rome). In the fourth-century mosaics of the church of Sta Maria Maggiore, also in Rome, the scene in which the Israelites cross the Jordan is based on the triumph over the fall of Jerusalem on the Arch of Titus. At Dura-Europos, entire stories and linked episodes from the Bible were painted; in similar fashion, the Sta Maria Maggiore mosaics depict the life of Jacob as a continuous cycle, while the career of Samson receives much the same treatment in fourth-century marble bas-reliefs from Naples Cathedral.

Part of the 10th century Greek manuscript known as the *Joshua Roll*. The conquering Israelites are typically portrayed as Roman soldiers.

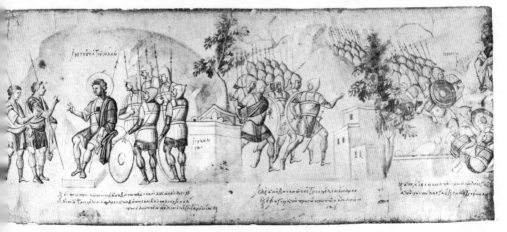

BIBLICAL THEMES IN THE ART OF THE CHURCH

Artists whose names have long been forgotten were, throughout the early Middle Ages, commissioned to produce works that would enthrall worshippers in churches, chapels, and the great Gothic cathedrals of the West. The icon, revered as a manifestation of the Divine, held sway among the Christian masses of the East. And from monasteries in all parts of Christendom came illuminated manuscripts intended to familiarize laymen with the great figures and episodes in the Hebrew Bible and the New Testament. The underlying purpose of all these endeavors was to promote a sense of awe and a desire for worship; after the invention of printing, the illustrated book fulfilled the same role. By the 15th century, however, most of the artists signed their works or could be identified; some, like Michelangelo, devoted their lives to the creation of beauty in the interests of the Church, while others produced paintings and sculpture for wealthy lay patrons. To a large degree, the Renaissance secularized European art, even though some masters (notably Rembrandt) paid great attention to the Bible. However, the Church retained its hold on artistic treatment of Scriptural themes for the best part of 1,500 years.

Perhaps the most ancient form of Christian art was the fresco or wall-painting, which was particularly developed during the later Middle Ages. Second-century examples from Naples depict Adam and Eve and others, dating from the eighth century (at the church of Sta Maria Antiqua, Rome), show Isaiah standing by the bed of the dying King Hezekiah, scenes from the life of Jacob, and episodes in the career of Joseph. Twelfth-century Romanesque examples from the church of Saint-Savin, France, treat Abraham, Joseph, Noah, and other Biblical figures, while portrayal of the prophets Ezekiel and Samuel was common in frescoes of the medieval period. Jacob's struggle with the angel provides the motif for some interesting wall-paintings in the Russian cathedral of Hagia Sophia, Kiev (11th century), and at Assisi in Italy (13th century); and there is a highly detailed, 14th-century Joseph cycle from Sopočani in Serbia. A fresco by the Italian Renaissance artist Pinturicchio, now in the Vatican, portrays the prophet Joel holding twelve scrolls—representing the gospel preached by the twelve Apostles in twelve languages—as a symbolic manifestation of the outpouring of the Holy Spirit. Wall-painting continued to develop in Italy, where it reached its culmination in the splendid Biblical frescoes which Michelangelo executed in the Vatican's Sistine Chapel; but when the Gothic architecture of Northern Europe eliminated wall-space in order to let in more light, frescoes were replaced by stained-glass windows. The latter genre was particularly suited to the "freezing" of dramatic incidents, such as Samson's rending of the lion; the destruction of Sodom and Gomorrah and the transformation of Lot's wife into a pillar of salt; and the coronation and Judgment of Solomon, his construction of the Temple, and meeting with the Queen of Sheba. A roundel of Moses and the burning bush (c. 1280) adorns a church at Mönchengladbach in the Rhineland and 13th-century stained-glass windows in La Sainte-Chapelle, Paris, portray the Creation, Judith's slaying of Holofernes, and other subjects. "Bible windows" were prominent in the Gothic art of the Middle Ages: examples are found in the Chapel of the Three Kings (1270–80) and in the Chapel of Stephen (c. 1290) at Cologne Cathedral.

Mosaics were one of the main vehicles of Biblical education, continuing a tradition that began in the fourth century, if not earlier. Some of the oldest, in the church of Sta Maria Maggiore (Rome), represent Abraham's meeting with Melchizedek and the life of Moses; sixth-century examples from Ravenna also treat the first of these themes, while others of the eighth century (at Rome) offer a cyclic portrayal of Joseph. The high point of Biblical art in mosaics was reached in the 12th century, particularly in the Sicilian cathedrals of Monreale and Palermo. Here, there are depictions of the Tower of Babel (a favorite moral story), the Cain and Abel drama, the Creation, the meeting of Eliezer and Rebekah, Jacob's dream at Bethel, Noah and the Flood, and the grim fate of Sodom and Gomorrah. The cathedral of S. Marco (Venice) possesses some outstanding mosaics of about the same period (12th–13th centuries) dealing with a variety of Biblical themes. The death of Absalom— a favorite typological subject—figures in the 15th-century pavement mosaic of Siena Cathedral. This genre was mainly confined to the Byzantine Empire and medieval Italy. Motifs drawn from the Bible were also exploited by craftsmen working in other fields. An ivory relief on the decorated binding of a prayer book written for the French king Charles the Bald (c. 870) shows David the Psalmist entering the House of the Lord (Swiss National Museum, Zurich). French artistry is also displayed in the *Tapestry of the Three Coronations* (Sens Cathedral), which makes Bath-Sheba sitting at the right hand of Solomon (1 Kings 2:19) a type of the coronation of the Virgin, and in the famous *Chaise-*

Dieu Tapestry (1510), where the representations include Athaliah, Elijah and the widow of Zarephath, and Gideon. In the Eastern Church, artists remained anonymous for longer than in the West: the beautiful Russian church of Yaroslavl on the Volga contains scenes from the life of the prophet Elijah (whose cult was fostered by the Carmelite Order), painted by an unknown master of the 17th century.

SCULPTURE

The finest expression of Biblical art in the medieval Church was in the realm of three-dimensional portrayal—sculpture and carving. From the ninth century onward, carved effigies of the Hebrew kings and prophets often decorated capitals and portals of Romanesque cathedrals and churches. These static figures later began to converge into groups as the separate art forms regained their freedom from architectural domination. The bronze door of the church of S. Zeno (Verona) depicts Abraham, Cain and Abel, the Creation, and other Scriptural motifs, while the one at the cathedral of St. Sophia, Novgorod (1155), takes up a favorite Carmelite subject—the ascension of Elijah. King David figures on portals and capitals of the 12th century at Bourges, Chartres, Moissac, Saint-Benoît-sur-Loire, and Vézelay, and at Amalfi in Italy; and Deborah, sword in hand, as one of the prophetesses on the 15th-century choir stall in Ulm Cathedral, Germany. Nebuchadnezzar's dream of the stone which shattered the mighty image with feet of clay (Dan. 2) is depicted in Gothic carvings from the French cathedrals of Amiens and Laon; scenes from the life of Noah appear in other carvings at Bourges and the English cathedrals of Salisbury and Wells; and there are cycles in this genre dating from the 13th century at Chartres and Rheims, which deal with the story of Job. This last subject also inspires a bas-relief of the same period at the cathedral of Notre-Dame, Paris. The Chartres carvings portray an ulcerated Job sitting on a dungheap and watched by his family; a demon places his right hand on Job's bald head and his left under Job's foot (see Job 2:7ff.).[8]

---

[8] This "dungheap" scene results from the Septuagint's translation of the Hebrew phrase, *be-tokh ha-efer* ("amid the ashes," Job 2:8), as *tēs koprias* ("on the dunghill"). In the Arab world, rubbish is consigned to a "city dump," where the accumulation is burned month by month. This dump or dungheap (*mazbalah*) becomes solidified in time and can reach a considerable height; as

The Apocryphal story of the "seven brethren" who suffered martyr-dom rather than deny their faith by eating swine's flesh (2 Macc. 7) greatly appealed to the early Christians and in medieval typology the "Maccabee Martyrs" were canonized, Hannah's children symbolizing the Church Militant and Antiochus the Antichrist. A church of the Seven Holy Maccabees once stood in Lyons, France, and the cathedral of Saint-Pierre, Geneva, contained a Chapel of the Maccabees. The church of St. Andreas in Cologne has both a shrine (1506–27) and an altar (c. 1717) commemorating the Apocryphal saints. These legendary martyrs—"Maccabees" only through their association with the Hasmo-nean revolt against the Syrian tyrant[9]—were often portrayed with amputated hands; the Virgin with seven swords sometimes appears next to the figure of their heroic mother, Hannah. Sculptors of the Middle Ages devoted much attention to great Biblical themes. The 12th-century Shrine of the Three Magi in Cologne Cathedral preserves a statuette of the prophet Joel; there is a 13th-century sculpture in Bamberg Cathedral showing the prophets Hosea and Jonah in animated conversation; Joshua, David, and Judah Maccabee figure among the Nine Worthies formerly arrayed in the Cologne Town Hall (c. 1370); and Micah is seen wearing a turban and holding a phylactery in a statue of the 16th century at Albi, in the South of France. Italian sculptors of the 14th century executed scenes from the Creation at the cathedral of Orvieto and in the Florence Campanile; a 17th-century statue in Antwerp Cathedral represents Gideon as a helmeted and armored knight with a broken pitcher in his hand; and the more striking episodes in the life of Solomon figure in the sculpture of various medieval cathedrals. The wise king's meeting with the Queen of Sheba inspires works of this kind at Amiens, Chartres, and Rheims.

Representations of the Tabernacle and Temple interiors, of the seven-branched Menorah, the Ark of the Covenant, and other appurtenances are fairly common in ecclesiastical art of the 11th–15th centuries, some

---

such, it often serves as a watchtower and, in ancient times, was the refuge of lepers and dogs. Some scholars have suggested that the Septuagint's Greek translators may have had in mind a scene in Homer's *Iliad* (xxii. 414) describing Priam's lament for Hector. In medieval art, Job's wife is often represented as a shrew, while his "comforters" sometimes mock him by playing musical instru-ments. An altarpiece by Dürer shows Job's wife dousing him with a pail of water.

[9] For a curious semantic development of the term *Maccabee*, see Chapter 3.

of the earlier examples allegorizing the Sanctuary as a "Temple of Wisdom." A baptismal font in the shape of a Bronze Sea (c. 1107–18) stands in the church of Saint Barthélemy, Liège, and other works of the same type seem to have been popular in the 12th century. Talmudic legislation prohibited the exact three-dimensional reproduction of the Temple Menorah by Jews (*Avodah Zarah,* 43b, etc.), but Christian artists were not bound by any such restrictions. Seven-branched candelabra (probably inspired by the Arch of Titus relief and by designs in early documents) ornament the cathedrals of Essen (c. 1000) and Brunswick (1170–80) and churches at Paderborn (c. 1300) and Vulturella (Mentorella) near Rome (14th century). A particularly large and ornate example (c. 1160) formerly stood in the church of Saint-Remi, Rheims. Though not strictly Biblical, the *Ecclesia et Synagoga* motif (contrasting the "enlightened" Church with the obstinately "blindfold" Synagogue) was prominent in Christian art of the Middle Ages: the theme appears in stained-glass windows and especially in church sculpture, two of the best-known examples being the twin figures from the cathedrals of Strasbourg (c. 1230) and Freiburg (c. 1300).

ILLUMINATED MANUSCRIPTS

The medieval Church extensively employed sculpture and carving to impress its interpretations of Biblical personalities and events on the unlettered Christian masses. Between the sixth and 15th centuries, however, an even more vivid artistic genre emerged from the monasteries of both East and West to rival three-dimensional representation in the sheer beauty and perfection of its technique: the illuminated manuscript. Though at first rather stylized, the illustrations in these Bibles, Psalters, breviaries, and Books of Hours were revitalized from the Carolingian period onward, when several recognized schools of illumination came into being. Whether from Dura-Europos or from some vanished pre-third-century illustrated scroll or codex, the influence of an earlier Jewish prototype is apparent in Christian illuminations of the Bible (both Greek and Latin), which occasionally depend on Midrashic interpretations of Scripture that the artists are unlikely to have borrowed from Jewish sources of their own time. The direct iconographic relationship between the Sta Maria Maggiore mosaics and the fragmentary Greek *Cotton Genesis* points to their mutual reliance on such a Jewish artistic prototype. In any case, the *Cotton Genesis* tradition subsequently influenced Biblical representation in both the Eastern and the Western Churches throughout the Middle Ages, although Byzantine portrayals also relied on the early Greek *Vienna Genesis*. A Jewish school of illumination (mainly decorative and non-representational) grew up in the Islamic world and a less inhibited Ashkenazi school developed in Christian Europe during the 13th century; in both cases, however, there is little evidence of direct continuity from any ancient Jewish model, the artists drawing their inspiration from earlier and contemporary Muslim and Christian book illustration.[10]

One of the oldest illuminated documents is that known as the *"Itala Fragments"* (fifth century; Berlin), which uses a Latin Bible translation earlier than Jerome's Vulgate to illustrate episodes from the First Book of Samuel. The *Cotton Genesis* (now in the British Museum), a work of the same period probably executed in Egypt, is the oldest surviving illustrated Bible. The themes with which it deals include a cycle depicting the story of Joseph. Illustrations to the incomplete text of the *Vienna Genesis* (sixth century; National Library, Vienna) appear at the bottom of each page, suggesting that they were based on a Classical scroll archetype. The miniatures cover a wide and colorful field: cyclic treatments of the Creation and Joseph stories; Noah and the Flood; Abraham's meeting with Melchizedek; the death of Isaac; Jacob's acquisition of Esau's birthright and his struggle with the angel; Lot's wife transformed into a pillar of salt; and the life of Moses prior to the Exodus. The *Cotton* and *Vienna Genesis* manuscripts are only two surviving examples of an important early Byzantine school of illumination which flourished in Alexandria, Antioch, and Constantinople (Byzantium). Typological considerations also led to the appearance of certain Hebrew prophets in other Greek works of the period, such as the *Rabbula Gospels* or *Codex* (sixth century; Florence), which portrays Ezekiel in conjunction with David and Jesus, and manuscript copies of the New Testament. Scenes from the life of David adorn the text of Samuel, Kings, and Psalms in Syrian Bibles of the seventh century.

During its pre-iconoclastic period (i.e., until the early eighth century), Byzantine illumination developed as a system of consecutive Biblical illustration. This pictorial technique was used in the *Christian Topography* written by an Egyptian monk, Kosmas Indikopleustes (c. 540), one copy of which is now in the Vatican Library. Anxious to substitute a Christian

---

[10] Jewish illumination is discussed separately below.

Part of the Joseph cycle from the 6th century Byzantine *Vienna Genesis.*

world-picture for the Ptolemaic one still prevalent in his time, Kosmas (or Cosmas) made the Tabernacle of Moses his symbol of the earth and this motif was to retain a mystical hold on the imagination of medieval illuminators. Other Biblical subjects prominent in the *Topography* include Daniel, Elijah, Habakkuk, Jeremiah, Jonah, and Moses. Isaiah is shown warning Hezekiah of the Babylonian invasion and captivity (2 Kings 20:16–18; Isa. 39:5–7) and standing by the sick monarch's bedside. Once the Isaurian campaign against imagery had died down and the iconoclastic bans had been lifted after the year 843, Biblical representation was revived on the basis of surviving antique models. Thus the Greek *Sermons of St. Gregory of Nazianzus* (c. 880; Bibliothèque Nationale, Paris) contains many illustrations from the Bible, including a narrative cycle on the vision of Ezekiel. The Book of Jonah was especially popular in the Eastern Church, the episodes most favored by illuminators being Jonah's "calling" (1:2), his embarkation at Joppa (1:3), and his preaching to the Ninevites and their king (3:4ff.). Examples are found in the *Rabbula Codex*, the *Topography* of Kosmas, the *Sermons of St. Gregory*, and in the 11th-century *Khlyudov Psalter* (Moscow).

From the mid-ninth century onward, the continuous (cyclic) treatment particularly characterized Psalters illustrating the life of David (as shepherd, lion-killer, musician, and anointed king), the Exodus from Egypt, and other episodes referred to in the text. "Aristocratic" Psalters contained full-page miniatures, while the "monastic" sort only had marginal illuminations. The tenth-century Greek *Joshua Roll* (Vatican Library) mentioned earlier is really one vast parchment tableau of the Israelite invasion and conquest of the Promised Land. Here, abbreviated captions are attached to the consecutive paintings on the scroll, illustrating episodes such as the battle of Ai and the fall of Jericho. The *Joshua Roll's* stylistic and iconographic features suggest that it probably had a second-century prototype in the Hellenistic world. Greek "Octateuchs" containing the Pentateuch, Joshua, Judges, and Ruth are among the best-known Byzantine manuscripts of the Bible; those of the 11th–13th centuries have their text adorned with miniature illuminated insertions. Copies of the 12th-century *Homilies of the Monk James* (Vatican Library; Bibliothèque Nationale) display miniatures illustrating the Song of Songs.

The first major illuminated Biblical text of the Western (Latin) school is the seventh-century *Ashburnham Pentateuch* (Bibliothèque Nationale); since many of its miniatures have been cut out, no full comparison with the *Cotton* and *Vienna Genesis* texts is possible, but the iconography of this enigmatic document differs markedly from the Eastern tradition. The full-page miniatures of the *Ashburnham Pentateuch* include a cycle on the Creation and also deal with the Ark of Noah after the Flood; Isaac, Rebekah, Jacob, and Esau; Jacob's appropriation of Laban's household idols; and the life of Moses. A stylized Jerusalem illuminates the opening page of this manuscript. After the reign of Charlemagne (Emperor of the West from 800 to 814), the French city of Tours was the leading center of Biblical illustration in northern Europe and it seems likely that the great Bibles produced there were inspired by an illuminated manuscript of the *Cotton Genesis* recension and also by the *Ashburnham Pentateuch*, which probably reached Tours in the ninth century. The eighth-century Spanish monk Beatus' illustrated commentary on the Apocalypse (Revelation of St. John) may also have been known to Frankish artists. Other Carolingian centers of manuscript illumination produced the ninth-century *Utrecht* and *Stuttgart Psalters*, which headed each of the Psalms with an appropriate illustration. The *Bible of Charles the Fat* and the *Grandval Bible* (c. 840; now in the British Museum), another product of Tours, were two other notable achievements of the era. While artists of the Spanish school, who were responsible for the Apocalypse commentary of Beatus, developed a system of Biblical text illustration deriving from antiquity (a forerunner of the tenth-13th-century Catalan method of illumination), those of the Carolingian Empire did not. In the case of the latter, Biblical illustrations were generally symbolic and the symbolic method was followed by the Anglo-Saxon, Franco-Saxon, and Italian regional schools. Accordingly, in Carolingian Psalters, Bibles, and other manuscripts dating from before the year 1000, David the Psalmist is often portrayed as a regal figure surrounded by his four musicians (Asaph, Heman, Ethan, and Jeduthun), symbolizing Jesus and the four Evangelists.

Illuminated heading to Psalm 18, in the 9th century *Stuttgart Psalter*. Here David is being pursued by Saul and his troops.

Typology and symbolism continue to dominate French, German, and Italian illuminations of the tenth and 11th centuries. An outstanding example of Carolingian artistry is the *Bible of S. Paolo fuori le mura*

(870–875; Rome), which was produced at Rheims.[11] Apart from cycles dealing with Balaam and Judith, this Bible contains some impressive illustrations of the Judgment of Solomon and of the erection of the Tabernacle and consecration of the Levites. This last illumination, in which the seven-branched Menorah and the Ark of the Covenant (incongruously surmounted by a cross) form a centerpiece, is notable for its typological overtones. The same considerations govern the method of portrayal in the tenth-century *Libri Maccabaeorum* (Leyden) and *Paris Psalter* (Bibliothèque Nationale), the second of which includes a significant full-page miniature of David enthralling men and beasts with the charm of his music. Church exposition of Zech. 14 similarly determined portrayals of Zechariah in the Temple presented by the German *Bernward-Evangeliar* (c. 1010; Hildesheim Cathedral) and *Maria Lyskirchen-Evangeliar* (c. 1120; Cologne) illuminations.

The cyclic treatment of Biblical stories owes its revival to the influence of Byzantine art in Western Europe during the 12th century. The illustrations in most French, German, and English Bibles of the period probably derived from Byzantine prototypes and the practice of adding a sequence of full-page illuminations to the Psalter may also have been inspired by "aristocratic" Byzantine texts of Psalms. In Spain, where a continuous cyclic tradition had survived, masterly illustrations in the *León Bible* (1162; Leon Archives) show the prophet Elisha watching the two bears that punish the boys who mocked his bald pate (2 Kings 2:23–24), and Jeremiah in mourning for Jerusalem. Another Latin Bible of León (1197; Amiens) depicts the zealous Phinehas in the act of running his spear through the coupled Zimri and Cozbi (Num. 25:6–8). There is no trace of Christian typology in these illuminations. Elsewhere in the West, contemporary techniques may be seen in two 12th-century English manuscripts—the *Winchester Bible* and the *Lambeth Bible*—and on the European continent in the *Admont Bible* (c. 1140; State Library, Vienna). The belated influence of the *Cotton Genesis* recension has been detected in the outstanding illuminated document of this period, the *Hortus Deliciarum* ("Garden of Delights," 1167–95; formerly in the Strasbourg City Library), which contains a vast improvement on the Tabernacle motif, here executed with much delicacy and attention to detail. There are also representations of the Tower of Babel, Isaac blessing Jacob, Jonah and the fish, and Solomon's Beloved (in the Song of Songs),

---

[11] This is also known as the *Bible of Charles the Bald*.

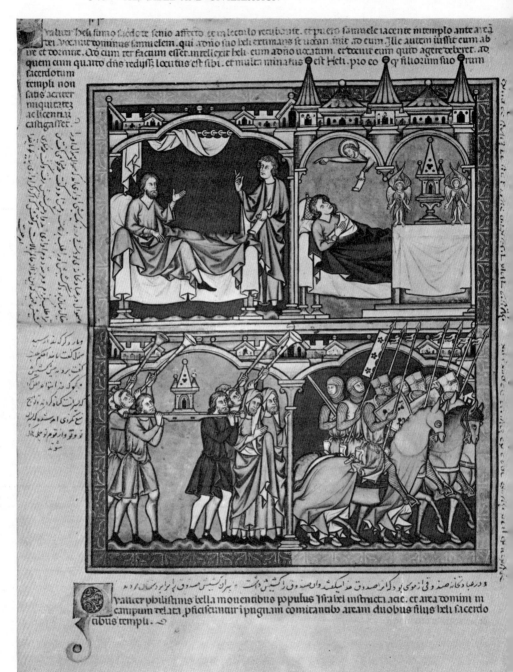

Scenes from the story of Samuel in the *Pierpont Morgan Picture Bible*, N. France (c. 1250).

symbolically portrayed as the Virgin flanked by monks and laymen.[12]

Alongside the development of the Gothic style in manuscript illumination came the spread of Biblical cycles attached to English and French Psalters of the 13th century. A complete series of such illustrations—from the Creation to the building of the Second Temple—was produced in France (mainly in Paris) during the reign (1226–70) of Louis IX (St. Louis). Two important examples of the new French book-art are the *Pierpont Morgan Picture Bible* (c. 1250; New York), known also as the *Maciejowski Psalter,* and the *Psalter of St. Louis* (c. 1256; Bibliothèque Nationale). The former contains episodic treatments of Biblical figures such as Samuel, Saul, Jonathan, David and Abigail, Amnon and Tamar, and Ruth and Naomi. Among scenes illustrated in the latter are the fate of Lot's wife, Jacob's dream, Deborah going into battle against Sisera, the story of Jephthah, and Samuel's presentation to Eli. Contemporary social conditions find reflection in the fact that both Joseph and the priests of Joshua's time are shown wearing the pointed hat (*Judenhut*) forced on Jews during the Middle Ages. Another illuminated manuscript of the same period and provenance, the *Psalter of King Wenceslas of Hungary and Bohemia* (c. 1260; Courtauld Institute of Art, London), works eight separate miniatures into one full-page illustration of the life of Jacob. The English *Rutland Psalter* represents King David playing the organ rather than the usual harp or lyre, while the Armenian *Bible of Erzwka* (1929; Armenian Patriarchate, Jerusalem) portrays Susanna and the lascivious Elders before Daniel on his seat of judgment. In the world of medieval Christendom, the Book of Psalms was the most popular section of the Hebrew Bible and it was therefore that most frequently and lavishly illustrated. Illuminations are often highly literal: Ps. 27:1 ("The Lord is my light . . . ") shows David turning to Jesus or the hand of God and pointing to his eyes; Ps. 53:2 ("The fool hath said in his heart . . . ") usually portrays a half-naked medieval jester with a bauble in his hand; and Ps. 137 ("By the rivers of Babylon . . . ") also inspired some very obvious representations.

The technique of illustrating Biblical texts with a continuous pictorial tableau quickly spread from France and, by the 14th century, it had

---

[12] Metaphors for the Beloved ("rose of Sharon," Songs of Songs 2:1, etc.) became stock attributes of the Virgin, and the "black madonnas" of medieval French and Spanish illumination owe their dusky faces to the phrase "black but comely" (Song of Songs 1:5).

oment le roi Cysera qüt il
vient de bataille busb œo q dame
delbola li wnasb.·.

oment dame Delbola oœlt le
Roy Cysera en dormaunt feraunt
vne closbe p mi sa restc.~

Jael and Sisera from an early 14th century English manuscript, the *Queen Mary Psalter*.

become familiar in other European lands and cultures. Apart from the French *Bible Moralisée* and *Histoire Universelle*, examples include the German *Biblia Pauperum* or *Armenbibel* (1330–31; National Library, Vienna) and *Weltchronik* of Rudolf von Ems and the often splendidly illustrated *Haggadot* (Passover liturgies for the *Seder* service) of Spanish Jewry.[13] The English *Queen Mary Psalter* (British Museum) deals with episodes such as the sacrifice of Jephthah's daughter, Jael's killing of Sisera, and the rape of Tamar. One unusual subject in the French *Bible of Jean de Papeleu* (1317; Bibliothèque de l'Arsénal, Paris) shows the prophet Hosea with his harlot wife, Gomer. Originally produced in Strasbourg in 1324, the *Speculum Humanae Salvationis* (an example in the Cologne Archives dates from 1370) mingles verse and illumination in its panorama of Passion and Salvation from the Fall of Man to the Last Judgment. A contemporary German work, the *Wenceslas Bible* (National

[13] See below.

Library, Vienna), contains several novel and interesting illustrations: Jezebel ordering the execution of the prophets and being eaten by dogs; Athaliah murdering the children of the House of David (a prefiguration of the Massacre of the Innocents); and Cyrus giving orders for the rebuilding of the Temple and having cedars of Lebanon cut down for the work of reconstruction. Another illumination in this Bible portrays Ezra expounding the law of Moses to the assembled Jews after their return from Babylon.

During the early part of the Italian Renaissance, there was a vogue for the illustration of Biblical texts with elaborate miniatures on the opening page of each Scriptural book. Some examples of this iconographical tradition are the 14th-century *Padua Bible* and the 15th-century *Bible of Borso d'Este*. The fashion took hold in England and France, where highly detailed and richly illuminated manuscripts were commissioned and produced in a dazzling array. One miniature in the early 15th-century *Très Riches Heures du Duc de Berry* (Musée Condé, Chantilly) shows Nebuchadnezzar complacently stoking the furnace into which Shadrach, Meshach, and Abed-nego have been thrown at his behest, while the miracle of the fleece in the story of Gideon appears in the *Petite Heures d'Anne de Bretagne*. The purification of the prophet Isaiah's lips with a burning coal (Isa. 6:5–7), a popular theme in early and medieval manuscripts, is illustrated in the 15th-century *Breviary of the Duke of Bedford* (Bibliothèque Nationale), while an illumination to Ps. 53:2 in the 16th-century *Henry VIII Psalter* (British Museum) magnanimously portrays Britain's "merry monarch" as King David and the fool as his court jester![14] The famous *Alba Bible* (1433; Duke of Alba Library, Madrid) which Don Luis de Guzmán, Grand Master of the Order of Calatrava, commissioned from a Jewish scholar, Moses Arragel, was an unusual blend of Jewish and Christian learning and both the text and the commentary that accompanies it are in Spanish. Although most of the illuminations which this Bible contains are based on Christian sources, they do include a certain amount of Midrashic inspiration. An even more curious example of Jewish-Christian collaboration—involuntary in this case—was the *Postillae perpetuae in Vetus et Novum Testamentum*, an exposition of the literal sense of the Scriptures by Nicholas de Lyre (died 1349), who relied heavily on the Jewish

---

[14] In other manuscripts the fool is David himself feigning madness before Abimelech.

Bible commentaries of Rashi (1040–1105). De Lyre's *Postillae* (1322–30), the first Christian commentary on the Bible to be printed (Rome, 1471–72), had a profound impact on the translations of Reformers such as Wycliffe and Luther.[15] The illustrations in the earliest known example (1440; City Library, Tours) duplicate the Ark of the Covenant with its Cherubim, the Table of Shewbread, and the Menorah according to both Rashi (*"secundum rabi salomon"*) and Christian theologians (*"secundum alois doctores"*). The Menorah illustrations eventually found their way into the *Schedelsche Weltchronik* (Nuremberg, 1493).

As in painting and sculpture, the early Renaissance preserves the name of one of the last great masters of manuscript illumination, the miniaturist Jean Fouquet (c. 1420–c. 1480). A native of Tours, that old center of French book-art, Fouquet has been acclaimed as one of the creators of French painting. His freshly colored miniatures for the *Antiquités judaïques* of Josephus (c. 1470; Bibliothèque Nationale) combine Italian artistry with the scenic background of his homeland. Fouquet's Biblical tableaux display a masterly grouping of his subjects and a keen sense of drama. Outstanding among these are the Tower of Babel, the revolt of Korah, David's grief over the death of Saul (shown in rending his garments before his massed troops), Solomon's construction of the Temple, the Return to Zion under Cyrus, Judah Maccabee's triumph over his enemies, and Pompey's entry into the Holy of Holies. In a separate work, the *Book of Hours of Étienne Chevalier* (Musée Condé, Chantilly), Fouquet also illustrated the story of Job. With the *Lübeck Bible* (1494), the art of Biblical manuscript illumination reached the end of the road in the Christian West—an inevitable outcome of competition from the new printed book. When the first printed Bibles rolled off the press, their design was a deliberate copy of the best-known Italian illuminated texts and some of Johann Gutenberg's pioneering editions, such as his 42-line Latin Bible (1455), were reproductions of such manuscripts, even imitating their lettering and decorative initials and borders. This practice was shortlived: although the art of illumination still survives, it caters for the needs of wealthy individuals and relies on specialized taste. Illustrated Bibles are printed for the million; the Biblical miniature or illumination is now only within reach of the collector.

---

[15] On Rashi, De Lyre, and the Reformers, see also Chapters 1 and 4.

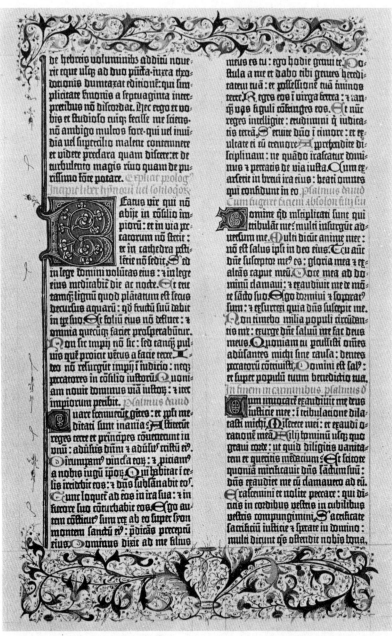

A page from Johann Gutenberg's Latin Bible (c. 1455), the printed text with its handsome illumination resembling a manuscript work.

THE BIBLE IN MUSLIM BOOK-ART

The prophet Muhammad is said to have declared that the portrayers are those who will incur the severest punishment on the Day of Judgment, and his hostility toward representational art has remained typical of Islam. Muslim craftsmen were thus compelled to channel their energy into other spheres: architecture, decorative lettering, and abstract ornamentation. For a time, this hatred of the image was also shared by the Eastern Church during its iconoclastic, Isaurian period. As sectarianism made its appearance in the Islamic world, however, new and more liberal currents began to flow East and more aesthetic considerations began to prevail. From about the tenth century, the influence of Christian art seems to have penetrated the lands of Islam, especially Persia. Here there was a mellowing of the sterner, puritanical features of the Faith: poetry took on a voluptuous accent (notably in the works of Omar Khayyām) and, by the 14th century, artists felt free to decorate manuscripts with pictures of men and beasts. The text of the Koran was sacrosanct, but religious susceptibilities were not outraged by the illustrating of secular works; and the Biblical traditions which Islam had absorbed soon made their appearance in illuminated manuscript histories, scientific treatises, and *Stories of the Prophets*.

Wherever the cultural influence of Persia was dominant, this type of art flourished during the 14th–17th centuries. The Biblical themes most favored were those drawn from the Book of Genesis (Adam and Eve, Cain and Abel, Noah and the Flood, and Joseph and Potiphar's wife), but some later figures also had a wide appeal, notably Moses the Lawgiver, the wise King Solomon, and the prophet Jonah. Changes in style reflect those governing the Persian secular miniature and the method of portrayal is typically sensuous and realistic. The story of Jonah, with its account of the Hebrew's miraculous survival in the belly of the whale, proved especially attractive. An illumination in *Jāmī at-Tawarikh* by Rashid ad-Din, a 14th–15th-century Persian manuscript (Metropolitan Museum of Art, New York), shows Jonah being spewed up by the great fish; and a 16th-century Turkish miniature from Ishaq al-Nishapuri's *Qisas al-Anbiya* (British Museum) portrays the same incident with the addition of an angel who benevolently contemplates the scene. Several major Biblical personalities figure in a Turkish illuminated manuscript of the 15th century, Luqman-i Ashuri's *Subdat al-Tawarikh* (copy dated c. 1583; Chester Beatty Library, Dublin). Here, there are representations of Jacob, Joseph in Egypt, David (portrayed as a turbaned Oriental potentate), Solomon, and Job. The story of Joseph, retold in the 12th Sura of the Koran, was extraordinarily popular in the Islamic world: an adaptation by the Persian poet Jāmī, his best-known romance, inspired numerous illustrations, probably because of the suggestive episode involving the wife of Potiphar ("Zuleika" in Muslim tradition). A 16th-century manuscript of Jāmī's *Yūsuf o Zuleikhā* (British Museum) depicts Joseph's arrival at a feast arranged by his would-be lover.

Even more than their counterparts in the lands of Christendom, Muslim artists relied on Midrashic lore for the elaboration of Biblical motifs. Such Jewish influence may not always have been restricted to the literary field: as in Europe, some outstanding Biblical illuminations were the work of Jewish artists, who may conceivably have found additional employment outside their own community. One of these artists presumably illustrated the *Sefer Sharḥ Shāhīn al ha-Torah* (1686; Israel Museum, Jerusalem), a Judeo-Persian paraphrase of stories from the Pentateuch by the great 14th-century Jewish poet Mawlānā Shāhīn Shirazi (Shāhīn of Shiraz). The illuminations in this manuscript deal with

Picture of Noah's Ark, fashioned from Kufic script and signed by the Turkish artist, Hafiz Othman (d. 1699).

episodes such as the finding of Moses in the bulrushes, the Israelites' battle with the Amalekites (where the opposing warriors are depicted as contemporary Persian soldiers), and the slaying of Zimri and Cozbi by Phinehas. The prevalence of Midrashic tradition may be seen in another illustration of the infant Moses challenging Pharaoh and undergoing an ordeal by fire. When Muslim religious austerity reasserted itself, illumination and figurative portrayal gave way to less objectionable forms of decoration. In one imaginative late 17th-century example, autographed by the artist (Hafiz Othman), the Ark of Noah is fashioned from Kufic script, a type of Arabic calligraphy (Boston Fine Arts Museum, Mass.).

BIBLICAL MOTIFS IN HEBREW ILLUMINATED MANUSCRIPTS

Apart from the conflict of interpretation relating to the Second Commandment, the Jews of post-Biblical times were also subject to a Talmudic prohibition against the ornamentation of Torah scrolls (*Shabbat*, 103b) which must have placed some initial restraint on manuscript illustration. On the other hand, the decorating of texts other than the Pentateuch or of Bible codices for use outside the synagogue was not specifically forbidden. The existence of a Jewish school of Biblical illumination in the Hellenistic period would bridge a vital gap between Dura-Europos and the Bet Alpha mosaics on the one hand and the earliest Christian frescoes, mosaics, and miniatures on the other. It has been pointed out that some of the oldest representations of Jesus bear an uncanny resemblance to that of a priest (Jeremiah?) in the Dura-Europos murals; and the Evangelist portrayed at the head of early Latin and Greek texts of the Gospels has a more definite Jewish prototype. However, no hard evidence has yet come to light of Hebrew illuminated manuscripts predating those of Christian origin: the oldest examples of Jewish book-art date only from the early tenth century. Yet if the ancient synagogue mosaics and murals are compared with illustrations in Greek, Latin, and Hebrew manuscripts of the early Middle Ages, it becomes clear that certain iconographical elements—the Temple, its best-known implements, and various characteristic "carpet" designs—persist and continue to dominate Biblical representation. The Temple motif was, of course, a symbol of Jewish Messianic aspiration and, as such, underwent a typological reinterpretation in Church theology; the

Jewish legendary material which was to enrich both Christian and Muslim art probably derived from a lost illustrated paraphrase of the Bible, rather than from the original text; and the geometrically patterned and decorated "carpet" pages of medieval Hebrew illuminated manuscripts (reminiscent of Oriental carpet design) may well point to a source older than the mosaic floors of Hellenistic synagogues.

Those illustrated Hebrew Bibles from the medieval period which still exist were the product of four regional schools (in the Orient, Spain, Northern Europe, and Italy), but all of these manuscripts (and others, such as prayer books and *Haggadot*, containing Biblical illuminations) have certain elements in common. The Oriental documents, mainly of Egyptian origin, are apparently the oldest and probably represent a foundation of Jewish book-art. As in manuscripts of the Koran dating from the same era, carpet pages decorated with geometrical motifs adorn the first and last few leaves of such Bibles, the earliest of which (895; Karaite synagogue, Cairo) has no figurative illustrations.[16] In Jewish art of the Roman period, the Temple façade and ritual implements such as the Menorah, Ark of the Covenant, and jar of manna were reproduced in synagogue murals and mosaics and in gold-leaf glass, coins, and oil lamps. Stylized representations of these motifs appear on two pages of the *First Leningrad Bible* (929; Leningrad Public Library) amid the usual carpet design, the seven-branched Candelabrum being especially prominent. Only a few of the surviving Hebrew Bibles from the Orient contain such illustrations in the text, notably two 11th–12th-century Persian Pentateuchs (now in the British Museum). One of these depicts the sacred vessels of the Tabernacle (illustrating Num. 7:1), while the other provides a picture of the two Tablets of the Law, inscribed with the opening words of each Commandment, next to the text of the Decalogue (Ex. 20:2ff.).

The influence of this Oriental style of decoration may be seen in Hebrew illumination of the Spanish and Provençal schools. Carpet pages, the Tabernacle motif, and the use of micrography are generally prominent. The *Perpignan Bible* (1299; Bibliothèque Nationale) resumes the elaborate exposition of the Menorah and other appurtenances of the Sanctuary, arranged in a somewhat arbitrary manner within frames,

---

[16] Although the origin of these carpet pages is unknown, similar designs have been found in eighth-century sacred manuscripts by Hiberno-Saxon and Northumbrian Christian artists, such as the *Lindisfarne Gospels*.

and a Bible of the same type (1277; Biblioteca Palatina, Parma) was produced in Toledo. A more Westernized taste is evident in the *Cervera Bible* (1300; National Library, Lisbon), where there are illuminations of the Menorah at the end of Exodus, of Jonah being thrown into the sea and swallowed by a whale, and a full-page miniature of the vision of Zechariah featuring a handsome golden Menorah flanked by green olive trees. A colophon at the end of this manuscript reveals the name of the artist, Joseph ha-Zarefati ["the Frenchman"]. Several plans of the Temple figure in medieval Hispano-Jewish illumination: a large fragment in the *First Ibn Merwas Bible* of Toledo (1306; British Museum) depicts all the implements and vessels of the Second Temple in ground-plan form; and the *Farḥi Bible* (1366–82; Sassoon Collection, formerly at Letchworth, England), which took Elisha ben Abraham ben Benveniste (Crescas) 17 years to copy and decorate, contains several pages illustrating these motifs, so frequent in Hebrew manuscript illumination. The *Farḥi Bible*, one of the most richly decorated books of the Spanish school, includes nine full-page miniatures among the 192 ornamented pages that precede the actual text; one of these miniatures is a plan of Noah's Ark, two others being devoted to the walls of Jericho and the tents of Jacob and his wives. Among the text illustrations in the margins and between the columns of the *First Joshua Ibn Gaon Bible* (1301; Bibliothèque Nationale) are the dove holding an olive branch, Abraham's sacrificial knife, the goblet of Pharaoh's butler, and David's sling with the sword of Goliath. The *Kennicott Bible* (1476; Bodleian Library, Oxford), a masterpiece of medieval Hispano-Jewish art, was illuminated by Joseph Ibn Ḥayyim, who drew much of his inspiration from the *Cervera Bible* of 1300. New elements were, however, added, including some fully decorated carpet pages illustrating the Tabernacle and its implements. The scene depicting Jonah's maritime adventure is based on the Cervera model, but there are also some original paintings, notably one of King David enthroned as the founder of a royal house at the beginning of 2 Samuel. Among other great achievements of this type are a sumptuous, late 15th-century Portuguese Bible (Hispanic Society of America, New York) and the elaborately decorated *Lisbon Bible* (1483; British Museum).

Examples of the Spanish school's Biblical illumination may also be seen in some splendid illustrated Passover *Haggadot* of the 14th century. The art of representation flourished in the Iberian peninsula once the Jewish communities there came under Christian rule. The *Golden Hag-*

gadah (c. 1320; British Museum) was decorated by two illuminators whose iconography followed that of the contemporary Latin school of Paris. Thus, one of the 14 full-page miniatures shows the haloed angel of Christian tradition appearing to Moses by the burning bush, while the return of Moses and his family to Egypt virtually reproduces the familiar Christian scene of the Holy Family's flight into Egypt! Jewish (Midrashic) lore inspires other miniatures, such as that portraying the angel rescuing Abraham from the fiery torture of the Chaldeans. Episodes from the Biblical books of Genesis and Exodus (ranging from the creation of Adam to the dance of Miriam and her maidens after the crossing of the Red Sea) figure among the illuminations of the *"Sister" to the Golden Haggadah* (British Museum), a later product of the 14th-century tradition; and Biblical motifs are prominent in the *Barcelona Haggadah* (British Museum), the *Rylands Spanish Haggadah* (John Rylands Library, Manchester), and the *Kaufmann Haggadah* (Library of the Hungarian Academy of Sciences, Budapest). The last of these contains an incomplete miniature cycle of the Book of Exodus, partly of Midrashic inspiration.

The *Sarajevo Haggadah* (c. 1350; Sarajevo National Museum, Yugoslavia) is the best-known Hebrew illuminated manuscript.[17] Its accidental discovery in 1894 revolutionized Jewish art history, making it clear that the Second Commandment had not suppressed figurative design among Jews of the Middle Ages. This manuscript was probably copied and illustrated in Barcelona or Perpignan and its miniatures (in the prevalent Italian-Gothic style) derive from the Latin Bible illumination of the Franco-Spanish school. A specifically Jewish element is, however, evident in the artist's avoidance of Divine representation: the miniature of the Seventh Day of Creation substitutes the figure of a Jew piously resting on the Sabbath for the seated Christian motif of God the Creator. The full-page miniatures preceding the decorated text of the *Haggadah* begin with the Creation, depict the major events of Genesis and Exodus (from Adam and Eve in the Garden of Eden to the giving of the Ten Commandments), show Moses in the act of blessing the assembled Israelites and laying his hands on Joshua, and conclude with illustrations

[17] A handsome reproduction of the *Sarajevo Haggadah* (London, 1963) was published with a detailed introduction by the late Cecil Roth. A facsimile edition of the *Kaufmann Haggadah* (1954), published in Budapest, follows the incorrect pagination of the original. Some of the old printed *Haggadot* (e.g., the Prague edition of 1527) are often resurrected for a wider market.

of the Tabernacle and of a medieval synagogue interior. Outstanding among these scenes is the full-page treatment of Moses receiving the Law on Sinai while the voice of God reverberates through the ram's horn and the people at the mountain's base stand awed and intent. It seems likely that this impressive manuscript was brought to Italy by a Sephardi refugee when the Jews were expelled from Spain in 1492; it was still in Italy over a century later, but eventually found its way to Bosnia, where its Jewish owners showed scant awareness of its value and importance.

The Ashkenazi Bibles and religious texts of Northern Europe are illuminated in a style very different from that of the Oriental and Spanish traditions. Carpet pages are absent and the Temple–Tabernacle motif is fairly rare; micrography and pen-drawing are common. In 13th–14th-century Germany, animal heads (borrowed from Christian and Muslim art) often characterize the portrayal of the Righteous, as in one early example, the *Ambrosian Bible* of Ulm (1236–38; Biblioteca Ambrosiana, Milan). The *British Museum Miscellany* (c. 1280), one of the richest illuminated manuscripts of Franco-German provenance, illustrates a number of Biblical subjects: three of its full-page miniatures show Aaron pouring oil into the lamps of the Menorah, Samson rending the lion, and Solomon passing judgment on the two harlots. Biblical text illustrations in the 13th-century French *Dragon Haggadah* (Staats- und Universitätsbibliothek, Hamburg), originally part of a prayer book ornamented with dragons and grotesques, include scenes from the Israelite bondage and the Ten Plagues visited on the Egyptians.

A large number of Ashkenazi illuminated manuscripts were produced in or about the year 1300. The *Regensburg Pentateuch* (Israel Museum, Jerusalem) contains six full-page miniatures depicting various Biblical and Midrashic episodes such as the Binding of Isaac, Moses receiving the Law, Esther before Ahasuerus, and Job with his friends. Moses and the Israelites at Sinai wear the infamous Jew's hat and their portrayal in profile is almost a caricature. This Pentateuch is notable for its detailed treatment of the Tabernacle theme (rare in Ashkenazi manuscript works), which here betrays the influence of earlier full-page expositions in Hebrew Bibles from Spain. Standing to one side of the sacred implements, Aaron (whose priestly garb features headgear resembling a bishop's miter) stretches one arm out to light the giant Menorah depicted on the opposite page. Another full-page Menorah scene figures in a Pentateuch (1300; Bibliothèque Nationale) illuminated by Joseph the Scribe at Poligny, near the Franco-Swiss border. Below the branches of the

In this portrayal of the Giving of the Law at Sinai from the *Regensburg Pentateuch* (c. 1300), Moses and the assembled Israelites are shown wearing the German Jewish hat.

Candelabrum there are vertically arranged illustrations of the Judgment of Solomon and of the Binding of Isaac; a lion and a dragon crouch between the tripod legs of the Menorah. A gold-tooled coat of arms on the binding of this manuscript indicates that it was once the property of Cardinal Richelieu. A German Bible of the same date (British Museum) offers some interesting examples of illustrated micrography: Pharaoh's baker carrying a triple basket on his head, Joseph riding on a horse, the four beasts of Ezekiel's vision, and Jonah being spewed from the mouth of the whale. In the German *Schocken Bible* (c. 1300; Schocken Library, Jerusalem), 35 initial-word panels precede the various Biblical books. The full-page illumination before Genesis comprises 46 Biblical illustrations in the form of medallions or roundels; their arrangement closely resembles that of 13th-century stained-glass windows and it is known that such windows decorated synagogues as well as churches of the period. These illustrations cover a wide field—from the first couple to Balaam, his ass, and the angel. Appropriate Biblical illuminations accompany the narrative of the *Birds' Head Haggadah* (Israel Museum, Jerusalem), the oldest surviving Ashkenazi manuscript of its type, where the Jewish figures are depicted with birds' heads and similar distortions so as not to offend religious susceptibilities. Another of these illuminated manuscripts from southern Germany, the *Duke of Sussex Pentateuch* (c. 1300; British Museum), is mainly ornamented with grotesques and dragons, but the full-page illumination to the Book of Numbers portrays four knights holding the emblematic banners of Judah, Reuben, Ephraim, and Dan, while the initial-word panel to Ecclesiastes shows David playing the harp. Before its acquisition by the British Museum, this Pentateuch belonged to a noted Hebraist of the British royal family, the Duke of Sussex (1773–1843).

Slightly later than these manuscripts is the *Tripartite Maḥzor* (c. 1320), a Jewish liturgical work. Its first volume (now in Budapest) contains an interesting depiction of the Judgment of Solomon, in which two pleading women are painted with dogs' heads; the second volume (now in the British Museum) illustrates the story of Ruth and the giving of the Law, which a beardless Moses is seen kneeling to receive on a hillside, backed by a mitered Aaron and the men of Israel (who wear the familiar *Judenhut*). The German school of Hebrew illumination remained active in the 15th century. A miniature illustrating a liturgical poem composed for the Ḥanukkah festival and painted in a liturgical miscellany from Mainz (c. 1427; Staats- und Universitätsbibliothek, Hamburg) departs from the usual practice by making Hannah and her seven martyr sons its (Apocryphal) subject; the story of Judith is also illustrated. The *Second Nuremberg Haggadah* (c. 1450; Schocken Library, Jerusalem) includes three cycles of Biblical text illumination: the story of the Exodus from the birth of Moses to Miriam's dance of triumph; the Genesis narrative from Adam and Eve to Joseph's appointment as viceroy to Pharaoh; and later episodes from the Bible, beginning with Moses receiving the Tablets of the Law and ending with Job. This *Haggadah* also contains some eschatological motifs involving the prophet Elijah, who appears at the end of the manuscript leading the Israelites as he rides on a donkey.

An early example of Hebrew illumination from Italy is the *Bishop Bedell Bible* (1284; Emmanuel College, Cambridge), executed in Rome, which is decorative rather than representational. Watercolor pen drawings and painted illuminations adorn a two-volume Italian Hebrew Bible of slightly later date (c. 1300; British Museum), which has initial-word panels at the head of each Biblical book. The one next to Genesis contains seven medallions, five of which depict stages of the Creation, each showing the hand of God emerging from the sky. A delicate, full-page illumination of a Menorah, combined with grotesques and dragons, appears at the end of this volume. Among the small initial-word panels in a late 13th–century Hebrew Psalter (Biblioteca Palatina, Parma) are two illustrating Ps. 137 (weeping figures with their violins hung on willows) and Ps. 149 (a man conducting a choir). Hebrew illumination reached its zenith in Renaissance Italy, where wealthy Jewish loan-bankers gave their patronage to artists who produced masterpieces such as the sumptuous *Rothschild Miscellany* (c. 1470; Israel Museum, Jerusalem). Here, Sodom is depicted as a medieval city and a full-page miniature of a rural landscape serves as background to the "Wealth of Job." In the *Miscellany's* Psalter, there is a picture of David seated in a garden near a wood from which deer emerge, charmed by his playing. The illustration to Ps. 118 ("Out of my straits I called upon the Lord . . . ") shows David hiding from Saul in a rocky cleft. The *Rothschild Siddur* (1492; Jewish Theological Seminary, New York), an outstanding illuminated prayer book, includes an elaborate marginal illustration to the Mishnaic tractate *Avot* depicting Moses in the act of receiving the inscribed Tablets of the Law on Mount Sinai; behind a fence stand the Israelites, fashionably dressed as Italians of the late 15th century. An illumination at the beginning of the Song of Songs portrays King Solomon and a minstrel. In the *Aberdeen Bible* (1493; University of Aberdeen Library, Scotland) a fusion of Spanish and Italian styles characterizes the handwritten text, although the actual illumination is purely Italian. This Bible was probably completed in Naples by a Jewish refugee from Spain. A similar history is attached to the *Bibliothèque Nationale Portuguese Bible* (c. 1494–97; Paris), one of the world's most magnificent illuminated manuscripts. This was written and partly illustrated in Lisbon on the eve of the Jewish expulsion from Portugal, after which it was completed in Florence. Some artistic features suggest that Attavante degli Attavanti, the court illuminator to King Matthias Corvinus of Hungary, may later have had a hand in the illustrative work.

The invention of printing put an end to the Jewish illuminator's craft and, by about 1500, handwritten Hebrew Bibles and religious texts virtually ceased to be produced. This development, as we have seen, affected manuscript decoration throughout the Western world. A different form of ornamentation was applied to the printed Bible, where woodcuts and engravings replaced colored illustration until modern techniques made the printing of color reproductions possible. Within the Jewish community, however, one form of illumination survived and even gained greater prominence: the decorated *Megillah* or Scroll of Esther read in the synagogue on the festival of Purim. Whether printed or hand-illuminated, these *Megillot* evolved a special artistic tradition of their own in various parts of the Jewish world. Among the Midrashic legends that received pictorial treatment in illuminated *Haggadot* was the tale of the infant Moses who took the crown from Pharaoh's head and placed it on his own (Exodus Rabbah, 1.26). By some curious chance, this legend eventually found its way into Christian art of the Renaissance, where it inspired paintings by Giorgione (Florence) and Poussin (Louvre, Paris). The perennial motifs of the Tabernacle, Temple, and Menorah found their way into later Jewish ritual art, modified forms of the Menorah reemerging as the eight-branched Ḥanukkah lamp or as ornamental embellishments to the Ark of the Law in the synagogue. The two Tablets of the Law, inscribed with the Ten Commandments, decorated the inside of doors on the Holy Ark in Italian synagogues of the 15th century. Soon these tablets appeared, in diptych form (i.e., with rounded tops), above the Ark and this is now the prevalent custom, the twin tablets having since become a central artistic motif and symbol of Judaism.

PORTRAYALS BY THE GREAT MASTERS

The fresh currents that began to sweep through Western art during the 14th century did not at first constitute a revolt against the ecclesiastical tradition with its typological and static representation. That was not to come until the era of the High Renaissance, the final break with the old tradition occurring in 17th-century Protestant Holland. But a new warmth and realism entered painting when the creators of the Florentine school of art, rejecting the Middle Ages, found new inspiration in classical ideals. The true founder of this movement was Giotto (Ambrogio Bondone, c. 1266–1337), whose paintings achieved three-dimensional effects and foreshadowed the "modern" style in their ability to convey human emotion. Giotto's frescoes at Assisi, Rome, and Florence had an immense impact on contemporary and later painting: the landscape background was no longer stylized and the human figure assumed central importance. Symbolism made way for natural portrayal and Biblical subjects gave the artist an opportunity to study life in his own

Donatello's bronze
sculpture of Judith and
Holofernes (1455–57).

day, Giotto himself concentrated on New Testament themes, and his treatment of subjects from the Hebrew Bible was rare. A stone relief of Jubal, the traditional inventor of instrumental music (Gen. 4:21), was designed by Giotto for the Campanile at Florence (and executed by Andrea Pisano); while his visualization of the Temple as a cupola-surmounted, circular or octagonal structure resembling the Dome of the Rock at Jerusalem was to leave an imprint on subsequent Renaissance depiction. Realism was also the hallmark of sculpture in the wealthy and industrious duchy of Burgundy, where Philip the Bold made his capital, Dijon, one of the artistic centers of Northern Europe. Philip richly endowed the nearby Chartreuse of Champmol, where the Dutch sculptor Claus Sluter (died 1406) revealed his genius in the carvings he made for the portal and for the *Well of Moses* (or *Puits des Prophètes*, 1397–1402), which was surrounded by six life-sized Hebrew prophets, whose costumes were painted in a polychrome and gilded splendor. Sluter's Zechariah is portrayed as an old man of rugged grandeur and his Jeremiah is even more naturalistic, the prophet's nose having been adorned by the artist with a pair of spectacles![18] To Moses, the most remarkable of these figures, Sluter gives extraordinary vitality; with his forked beard and horns,[19] this Moses is the prototype of later representations and fore-shadows the style of Donatello. Sluter was thus one of those great artists who freed the statue from the domination of architecture.

Italian (and particularly Florentine) masters set the pace and tone of early Renaissance art in the 15th century. A goldsmith by training, Lorenzo Ghiberti (1378–1455) designed bronze doors (1403–24) for the church of St. John the Baptist in Florence and then won the competition for a second set, which took 27 years to complete (1425–52). Ghiberti utilized every resource of perspective and light and shade in his second doors for the Baptistery, lending realism to the Biblical scenes gleaming in high relief under a gold coating. His own portrait is twice reproduced in the decorative borders of these second doors, which Michelangelo was to deem worthy of standing at the entrance to Paradise. The ten magnifi-cent reliefs include representations of the Creation, Cain and Abel, Noah, Joseph, and Joshua, and of Solomon's welcoming of the Queen of Sheba. Biblical motifs such as these were prominent in works by the great Florentines: Paolo Uccello (1397–1475) painted Creation scenes

---

[18] A number of such artistic curiosities are discussed later in this chapter.
[19] The "horned Moses" was a phenomenon of the Middle Ages; see also below.

(c. 1431), *Four Prophets* (1443), and a fresco of the Deluge (c. 1445; Sta Maria Novella, Florence); Masaccio (Tommaso Guidi, 1401–1428) executed another fresco, *The Expulsion* (1427; Sta Maria del Carmine, Florence), showing Adam and Eve departing from the Garden of Eden with their faces overshadowed by despair; Antonio Pollaiuolo (c. 1432–1498) treated a favorite Italian Renaissance subject, *Tobias and the Angel Raphael* (Pinacoteca, Turin); and Andrea del Verrocchio (c. 1435–1488), Leonardo da Vinci's teacher, imitated Ghiberti and Donatello with his graceful sculpture of David (1476; Bargello, Florence).

The outstanding sculptor of the age was Donatello (Donato di Niccolò di Betto Bardi, c. 1386–1466), whose *David* was the first free-standing bronze nude modeled since Classical antiquity. Apart from this statue (1430–32; Bargello, Florence), Donatello executed studies of Moses, Joshua, Jeremiah, and Habakkuk (Campanile, Florence) and of Judith in the act of slaying Holofernes (Piazza della Signoria, Florence); the Habakkuk statue (1427–36) is known as *"Lo Zuccone"* ("the Bald One"). Donatello's ornate *Judith and Holofernes* (1455–57) was looted from the palace of the Medici in 1494, when rebel mobs removed it to the public square and set it up as a warning to tyrants! Two other Florentine masters who turned to the Bible were Benozzo Gozzoli (c. 1420–1497) and Sandro Botticelli (1444–1510). Gozzoli mainly worked for his Florentine patron, Cosimo de' Medici, but his Biblical frescoes (depicting the Tower of Babel, the birth of Jacob's twin sons, the story of Joseph, Moses, Solomon and the Queen of Sheba, etc.) were painted in the Campo Santo, Pisa. Although Botticelli expressed the neo-Platonism of Lorenzo de' Medici's humanist circle (in works like his famous *Birth of Venus*), he was chosen to paint a series of religious frescoes on the walls of the Sistine Chapel in the Vatican. In the execution of these portrayals—some Biblical, others from the New Testament—Botticelli was assisted by artists such as Perugino, Pinturicchio, and Signorelli. One scene, *The Punishment of Korah, Dathan, and Abiram* (1482), shows an irate Moses calling down God's wrath on the rebels, who are swallowed up elsewhere in the picture. This episode was specially commissioned because the Church saw Korah and his company as heretics and Aaron as a forerunner of the Popes. In the background stands the Arch of Constantine bearing a harsh Biblical warning against religious schism. Botticelli also painted subjects such as Esther, Tobias (Accademia, Florence), and Judith (Uffizi Gallery, Florence; Rijksmuseum, Amsterdam).

Themes from the Bible also attracted other Italian masters, notably the Venetians Andrea Mantegna (c. 1431–1506) and Giorgione (Barbarelli, 1477–1510). Indifferent to the softer effects of the painted picture, Mantegna combined realism of form with realism of matter and imitated the hard effects of sculpture. His *Samson and Delilah* (National Gallery, London) and portrayals of Judith (especially that of 1495; National Gallery of Art, Washington, D.C.) are interesting examples of his technique, as is the statuesque *Esther and Mordecai* (c. 1495; Cincinnati Art Museum). Giorgione, severe and Hellenic, stressed man's role not as the center of creation, but as part of the cosmos; his often allegorical figures seem lost in a dreamworld. Giorgione's Biblical subjects include the Judgment of Solomon and a study of Judith delicately trampling the head of a vanquished Holofernes (Hermitage, Leningrad). A painting of Susanna arraigned before Daniel (Glasgow Art Gallery) has also been attributed to this artist. The Apocryphal figure of Tobias attracted two Umbrian painters, Perugino (Pietro Vannucci, c. 1445–1523) 'and Pinturicchio (Bernardino di Betto, c. 1454–1513), both of whom worked with Boticelli on the Sistine Chapel frescoes, where Pinturicchio executed a *Moses* of his own. Eight scenes from the Book of Tobit (Berlin Museum) have been attributed to Pinturicchio, while there are round paintings of Isaiah and Jeremiah by Perugino (Nantes Museum, France). In a different genre, Paolo di Martino included Samson's dramatic slaughter of the Philistines with the jawbone of an ass in his marble-inlaid floor at Siena Cathedral (1426). From the time of Giotto onward, the Temple of Herod was often made the background to religious paintings, mainly on New Testament themes. An especially popular subject, *The Presentation of Jesus in the Temple*, illustrates this practice, and there are examples by the Florentine master Fra Angelico (Giovanni da Fiesole or Guido di Pietro, c. 1387–1455) and by two Venetians, Giovanni Bellini (c. 1430–1516) and Vittore Carpaccio (c. 1465–1526). Mantegna also treated this episode in the same fashion, repeating the Temple motif in his *Circumcision of Jesus*, which was likewise painted by Bellini. '

Meanwhile, the rays of the Renaissance sun were beginning to penetrate other parts of Western Europe. The Flemish painter Hugo van der Goes (c. 1440–1482), who astonished even the sophisticated Florentine public with his mastery of technique and portrayal, produced works on Adam and Eve and *The Meeting of Jacob and Rachel* (Christ Church, Oxford), while in Germany the Master of the Legend of St. Barbara painted *The Story of Job* (1480–83; Wallraf-Richartz Museum, Cologne). The spectral character of this last work was widely reflected in paintings by the Dutch master Hieronymus Bosch (c. 1450–1516) who, though unaffected by Italian developments, abandoned the traditions of the North and anticipated the new age with his disconcerting mixture of realism and fantasy. Bosch's Biblical subjects include Noah leaving the Ark (Bojmans Museum, Rotterdam), *The Garden of Eden* (in his triptych, *The Garden of Delights*), and a detail of Jerusalem from his *Adoration of the Magi* (Prado Museum, Madrid).

RAPHAEL, MICHELANGELO, AND THE *CINQUECENTO*

The great Italian masters of the 16th century (the *Cinquecento*) glorified man as man, abandoning the theological reservations that still lingered among many of their predecessors. The Middle Ages, with their symbolism and subordination of detail to the whole, had passed and the Renaissance, with its awakening of all the arts, had arrived. Since the aim of art was not truth, but beauty, the object of the artist and craftsman was to ensure the glorification of that inaccessible quality. Florence, now at the zenith of its fame and achievement, furthered the cult of Beauty in its Platonic Academy and witnessed the attainment of unparalleled artistic heights under its Medici rulers. Rejecting every *a priori* concept or system, Leonardo da Vinci (1452–1519) became the embodiment of the ideal Renaissance man—painter, sculptor, architect, anatomist, and engineer. Biblical motifs were extensively treated by the great Florentine master Raphael (Raffaelo Santi or Sanzio, 1483–1520), who studied under Perugino. The prophet Hosea is the subject of his fresco in the church of Sta Maria della Pace (Rome) and Isaiah figures in one in the church of Sant' Agostino, while a marble statue which he designed portrays Jonah as a naked youth with curly hair (Sta Maria del Popolo, Rome). Most of the Biblical figures and scenes which Raphael painted were for the Vatican *Logge,* where paintings by Piero della Francesca and Signorelli were ruthlessly plastered over to make way for his frescoes. The Loggia decorations, executed by Raphael's pupils under the direction of Giulio Romano and completed in 1519, provide one of the most important artistic tableaux of the Hebrew Bible. Scenes depicted include Isaac and Rebekah interrupted in their lovemaking by Abimelech (Gen. 26:8–11); Isaac's halfhearted blessing of Esau; Jacob at Bethel and his appropriation of Laban's idols, which Rachel subsequently hides; and episodes from the life of Solomon, notably the reception of the Queen of Sheba. In the sequence dealing with Jacob, Esau's fugitive brother is seen (in the dream of the ladder) sleeping at the foot of a monumental staircase—a standard Renaissance exaggeration of the Bible's simple description.

The unchallenged interpreter of the Bible among artists of the Renaissance was Michelangelo Buonarroti (1475–1564), whose painting and sculpture constitute some of the world's outstanding portrayals of Scriptural motifs. His colossal (16-foot-high) statue of *David* (1501–04; Accademia, Florence) was carved out of a gigantic block of marble which a minor sculptor had first tackled 70 years before, leaving his project unfinished. The torso of Michelangelo's *David* is one of the most perfect works of Renaissance art, equal to the finest statues of antiquity. In its uncompromising nudity, it states for the first time the essence of Michelangelo's ideal; and the heroic stance, symbolic perhaps of the artist's native Florence, gave a new force and vitality to its Classical conception. In 1508, Pope Julius II diverted Michelangelo from his prework on the liminary tomb which the pontiff had commissioned and—to the artist's considerable annoyance—asked him to decorate the ceiling of the Vatican's Sistine Chapel. Originally, this only called for representations of the twelve Apostles, but Michelangelo eventually depicted 13 subjects from the Bible, 12 sibyls and Prophets, and some other figures. The frescoes took four years to complete (1508–12) and are numbered among his masterpieces. "Unless you have seen the Sistine Chapel," wrote Goethe, "you can have no idea of what one man is capable of achieving." The ceiling is divided into compartments and the Genesis cycle begins above the altar with *God Creating* and ends with *The Drunkenness of Noah*. Michelangelo painted his Biblical frescoes in reverse order and increased the size of his figures as the work proceeded, in order to give greater effect to the height of the vault. *The Creation of Adam* is considered to be outstanding even among these superb paintings: here the newly created man reclines on a rock and springs to life as God, borne aloft by Cherubim, reaches out to touch his limp hand. This personification of the Creator, far from being an innovation, was very much part of Christianity's representational tradition until the era of Reform.[20] *The Flood*, though less satisfactory, is full of powerful and moving figures, and the Ark floating on the waters resembles a house.

[20] See below.

Michelangelo's *Creation of Adam* from the Sistine Chapel.

As in other Renaissance paintings, the sons of Noah in the last fresco of this series are oddly depicted in the nude. The prophets of Israel who surround these Biblical scenes are superhuman beings, endowed with Divine strength and wisdom. Jeremiah is a brooding, seated figure, Isaiah more youthful and contemplative, Joel reads a scroll. Below the Biblical scenes and the representations of the Prophets and sibyls (who in Christian tradition foretold the advent of Jesus to the Jews and Gentiles respectively) are four episodes illustrating God's intervention on His people's behalf. Exasperated by the artist's slow progress (to paint the ceiling he had to work on his back), Pope Julius is said to have clambered up to Michelangelo's perch on one occasion in order to whack him with his cane. It was only years later that Michelangelo heeded the pleas of Pope Paul III by returning to complete his Sistine Chapel masterpiece with a painting of *The Last Judgment* on the wall behind the altar (1535–41). In this, later events—such as the rise and spread of Protestantism and the sack of Rome (1527)—produced a gloomier and more violent atmosphere; the old exuberance and joy in man's perfection had vanished.

Although more than four centuries have passed since its completion, Michelangelo's huge statue of *Moses* (1513–16; S. Pietro in Vincoli, Rome) remains the most famous portrayal of the lawgiver by any artist or sculptor. It was intended as only one of 40 statues for the mausoleum of Julius II, who summoned Michelangelo to Rome in March 1505 and commissioned the design and execution of the greatest tomb in Christendom. The work was delayed by a quarrel between the two men and by the Pope's sudden demand for the Sistine Chapel frescoes three years later. "I've grown a goiter by dwelling in this den," Michelangelo complains at the beginning of one of his sonnets (published in an expurgated version after his death). Pope Julius never lived to see the completion of his funerary colossus and, after the statues of Rachel and Leah (flanking Moses) were finished, the much-reduced monument was finally set up—32 years after Julius had breathed his last—in 1545. Michelangelo himself sorrowfully declared: "I lost all my youth in bondage to this tomb." *Moses,* with its fierce stare, almost reflects the attitude of Julius II in the portrait by Raphael; and, with its traditionally horned face (a legacy of early Bible translation),[21] the statue has been termed Michelangelo's own vision of the "Old Covenant"—pitiless, omnipotent, and terrible. The Florentine painter Giorgio Vasari (1511–1574), who eulogized the artists of his native city, declared that Michelangelo's *Moses* was "unequalled by any modern or ancient work." The Tablets of the Law which the figure grasps are rectangular in shape, although the double-arched (diptych) form—current from the 15th century—was already in vogue and was later to replace all other artistic representations. Michelangelo died in his 90th year, leaving behind him masterpieces which, even singly, might still have assured him enduring fame. *David* and *Moses* are two monuments to his genius, for (as the sculptor himself predicted in another of his sonnets) "shapes that seem alive, / wrought in hard mountain marble, will survive / their maker, whom the years to dust return!"

In cosmopolitan Venice, with its splendid palaces, wealth born of jealously guarded mercantile links with the East, and stately pageants on the Grand Canal headed by the gondola of the Doge, art moved at a more leisurely pace than elsewhere. Giorgione, who lived into the *Cinquecento,* cultivated the decorative tradition of the late 15th century, as did others like Titian (Tiziano Vecello, c. 1477–1576) and Paolo Veronese (c. 1528–1588), two of the greatest Venetian masters. Titian painted a robustly sensual *Fall* depicting Adam and Eve (1570; Prado, Madrid) and studies of Cain and Abel and David and Goliath (1543–44), the first of which exemplifies his later grappling with the new "Manneristic" style. Veronese treated Esther, the meeting of Eliezer and Rebekah (Versailles), the destruction of Sodom and Gomorrah (Louvre), and the reception of the Queen of Sheba (Pinacoteca, Turin). Lyrical and anti-

---

[21] The "horned Moses" is discussed in the latter part of this chapter.

naturalistic, he often took liberties with "sacred" themes and in 1573 was disciplined by the Inquisition. Veronese was chosen to decorate the Palace of the Doges (1575–78) and his allegorical fresco, *The Triumph of Venice*, was painted on the ceiling of the Palace's Grand Council Chamber. He also executed an attractive *Judith* (Kunsthistorisches Museum, Vienna), at least three separate paintings of *The Finding* of *Moses* (Hermitage, Leningrad; Prado, Madrid; National Gallery of Art, Washington, D.C.), and portrayals of Susanna watched by the Elders as she bathes (Dresden Museum; Louvre; Prado, Madrid). In the Washington gallery's example of *The Finding of Moses*, Pharaoh's daughter and her retinue are dressed as contemporary Venetians and the figures depicted even include a court dwarf. The rustic style pioneered by Jacopo Bassano (c. 1518–1592) found expression in his paintings of Noah entering and leaving the Ark (Prado, Madrid) and of Jacob's return to Canaan (Doges' Palace, Venice). Bassano also executed a pastoral landscape with Jacob and Esau (Kunsthistorisches Museum, Vienna).

With Tintoretto (Jacopo Robusti, 1518–1594), the last of the great Venetian masters, a different note is struck in the portrayal of Biblical themes. Though briefly apprenticed to Titian, Tintoretto partly emulated Mantegna's sculpturesque technique, stressing contrasts of light and shade; dynamic and often violent, his subjects are dramatic or romantic moments captured by the mind's eye. In the spirit of the Counter-Reformation, Tintoretto turned mainly to religious themes and largely abandoned myth and allegory. Many of his paintings were commissioned for the Scuola di S. Rocco in Venice, including studies of Elijah, Ezekiel, and three murals illustrating scenes from Exodus: *The Rain of Manna*, *Moses Striking the Rock*, and *The Raising of the Serpent in the Wilderness*. Tintoretto's typical boldness and color effects are also apparent in *The Swooning of Esther* (1545), in paintings of Joseph and Potiphar's wife, Judith slaying Holofernes, and Solomon and the Queen of Sheba (all in the Prado, Madrid), and in one of Samson and Delilah (Duke of Devonshire Collection). Perhaps the most famous of Tintoretto's Biblical pictures is *Susanna and the Elders* (c. 1560; Kunsthistorisches Museum, Vienna), a voluptuous portrayal of a beautiful woman in the nude. Elsewhere in Italy, a few other artists handled Biblical motifs: the Lombard Bernardino Luini (c. 1480–c. 1547), a follower of Leonardo da Vinci, executed a series of paintings on the Exodus theme (Brera Gallery, Milan); the Tuscan Jacopo Pontormo (1494–1556) produced a

Job and His Wife, a painting
by Albrecht Dürer (c. 1504).

Joseph cycle, *Storia di Giuseppe Ebreo*; and the Florentine Giovanni
Battista Rosso (1494–1540), like Pontormo an ex-pupil of Andrea del
Sarto and a Mannerist, painted *Moses Defending the Daughters of Jethro*
(c. 1523; Uffizi Gallery, Florence), a study of violence and action.

   In Germany, Albrecht Dürer (1471–1528) was the outstanding interpreter of the Renaissance, his artistic and humanist studies having led
him as far afield as Venice (1494–95; 1505–07), Austria, and the Low
Countries. It was through Dürer that most of the new forms and ideas
were introduced into the North. German pessimism, the heritage of the
Middle Ages, and the pure and positive spirit of the Renaissance conflict
in his work, which includes some examples of Biblical representation.
He engraved *Samson slaying the Lion* and painted *Job and His*

Wife (c. 1504; Städelsche Kunstinstitut, Frankfurt am Main) and *Adam and Eve* (1508; Prado, Madrid). A painting of Lot's wife transformed into a pillar of salt (National Gallery of Art, Washington, D.C.) has also been attributed to the great German master. Lucas Cranach the Elder (1472–1553) retained certain features of the Gothic style, although charmingly executed nudes and other profane subjects of the Renaissance played an important part in his work. This latter tendency finds several notable illustrations: Bath-Sheba bathing under the eyes of David (1526; Kaiser Friedrichs-Museum, Berlin); Samson asleep in Delilah's lap against the background of a mountainous landscape (Augsburg Gallery); and Lot's elder daughter sitting on his knees while the younger plies him with wine (Pinakothek, Munich). Cranach also painted Adam, Jael, several representations of Judith (one in the Kunsthistorisches Museum, Vienna), the crossing of the Red Sea (Pinakothek, Munich), and Miriam's dance of triumph (Augsburg Gallery). Hans Holbein the Younger (c. 1497–1543) was a cosmopolitan painter, engraver, and miniaturist, the least typical of all the German masters. Born and trained in Augsburg, he moved first to Basle and then to London, where he specialized in portraits for the English court. Holbein painted Daniel together with the prophet Hosea (Basle) and a mural of Samuel slaying Agag (Basle Town Hall). He also executed a series of woodcut illustrations to Luther's Old Testament, including Jacob's blessing of Ephraim and Manasseh, Moses by the burning bush, and the Israelites gathering manna in the wilderness. His watercolor and ink drawing, *King Rehoboam* (1530; Kunstmuseum, Basle), shows Solomon's heir threatening the Elders with a lash worse than his father's; as Rehoboam storms at them, some of the Israelite spokesmen turn away in consternation. Another wood engraving of the same period, which Hans Lufft produced for Luther's Bible (1534), depicts the grim end of Jezebel.

Scenes from the Bible were also illustrated by some of the major 16th-century artists in the Low Countries. Bernard van Orley (c. 1488–1541) painted a crowded scene of the destruction of Job's children (Brussels Museum) and designed several tapestries on Biblical themes, while Lucas van Leyden (1494–1533), an admirer of Dürer, engraved Biblical episodes such as *Potiphar's Wife Accusing Joseph* (1521; National Gallery of Art, Washington, D.C.) and *David Playing before Saul*. The salacious theme of the elderly, drunken Lot making love to his daughters particularly appealed to artists in Northern Europe and Lucas van Leyden produced a painting of the subject (Louvre) as well as an en-

The Tower of Babel by Pieter Bruegel the Elder (1563).

graving. Other works by this Dutch artist portray *Moses Striking the Rock* (c. 1527, Nuremberg) and *Susanna before the Judges* (c. 1511, Berlin) he also engraved legendary episodes such as Adam and Eve lamenting the death of Abel and Cain's accidental death at the hands of Lamech. Pieter Bruegel the Elder (c. 1525–1569), the outstanding Flemish painter of the age, shared Bosch's fantastic vision of a world peopled by diabolical and spectral beings. In *The Tower of Babel* (1563; Kunsthistorisches Museum, Vienna) the scene is viewed from above, as if one were airborne and plunging earthward toward it. The Tower stands in a vast landscape near the banks of a river and, in the foreground, a king arrives to survey the progress of the work.

Apart from the famous *Chaise-Dieu* example (1518), several 16th-century tapestries treated Biblical subjects. One from Brussels (now in Vienna) represents the story of Joshua; another, of French origin (c. 1550; Sens Cathedral), portrays the Apocryphal heroine Judith. The *Story of the Virgin Tapestry* (Rheims Cathedral) represents Solomon's

Beloved as Mary in strict accordance with Church typology. Medieval overtones characterize the imagery of this craft during the Renaissance. The importance of ecclesiastical patronage later waned and a more objective treatment of Biblical themes became apparent in the following century, especially after the Gobelins "manufactory" was revived by Louis XIV. Renaissance artists, like their predecessors, often used a representation of the Temple as background for the discussion of scenes from the New Testament. Perugino's *Sposalizio* ("Marriage of the Virgin," c. 1503–04; Caen Museum) shows the Temple as an octagonal, domed structure and this picture is thought to have been the model for Raphael's painting of the same title (1504; Brera, Milan). In another *Sposalizio* (also 1504) by Donato Bramante (1444–1514), a distant cousin of Raphael, the Temple is a round building. A number of 16th-century masters also exploited the motif: Bosch, Dürer, and Veronese in their respective versions of *The Child Jesus Confuting the Doctors*, and *Jesus Casting the Money Changers out of the Temple* by Lucas Cranach, Bruegel, and the Spanish master El Greco (1541–1614).

THE AGE OF BAROQUE

Toward the end of the 16th century, a new realism, at war with the Classical and idealistic image of Renaissance painting, was introduced by Caravaggio (Michelangelo Merisi, 1573–1610), whose social conscience set him at odds with the society of aristocratic and Catholic Rome. Caravaggio's two important Biblical studies were one of David (c. 1605; Borghese Gallery, Rome) and a violent interpretation of the Judith and Holofernes drama (Naples Museum). This latter theme also inspired a painting by the Florentine artist Cristofano Allori (1577–1621), while Allori's compatriot, Lorenzo Lippi (1606–1665), found an original subject in his *Jacob by the Well*. (Pitti Palace, Florence). Among those associated with the Baroque decorative school created by the Caracci family at Bologna were Guido Reni (1575–1642), who ran a religious picture factory and painted *Samson's Victory* (1611–12; Bologna) and the recently discovered *Job* (1622–36; Notre Dame, Paris); Guercino (Giovanni Francesco Barbieri, 1591–1666), an amazing landscapist, who treated Joseph's sons receiving their blessing from Jacob; and Carlo Cignani (1628–1719), whose portrayal of Joseph and Potiphar's wife (Dresden Museum) shows a young woman throwing herself on the handsome youth, who reels back in virtuous horror. The Roman master Gian Lorenzo Bernini (1598–1680) excelled as a sculptor, architect, and painter. Invited to Paris by Louis XIV in 1665, he executed an equestrian statue of the king which (though it failed to please the French despot) still stands under the title *Marcus Curtius* at Versailles. Two Bernini sculptures inspired by the Bible are those of David (1623) and of Daniel and Habakkuk (1656; Sta Maria del Popolo, Rome). The magnificent and immense twisted columns which form part of Bernini's baldachino (1624–33) under Michelangelo's dome at St. Peter's, Rome, were based on pieces reputedly surviving from the Temple in Jerusalem. The columns were widely copied and even prompted an architectural treatise by F.J. Ricci favoring a new, "Solomonic" style.

As a product of the Counter-Reformation, the Baroque manner especially appealed to artists in staunchly Catholic Spain. José (or Jusepe) Ribera (1591–1652), an admirer of Caravaggio, worked in Naples and had much influence on Italian artists, among whom he was known as *il Spagnoletto* ("the little Spaniard"). He painted Job (Pinacoteca, Parma) and scenes from the life of Jacob, notably the impressive *Jacob's Dream* (c. 1646; Prado, Madrid). Though an aristocrat, Velasquez (Diego Rodriguez de Silva y Velázquez, 1599–1660) shared Caravaggio's individualism and democratic feeling. One of his few religious paintings deals with *Joseph's Coat Brought to Jacob* (Escorial). Flemish and Venetian influences have been detected in the work of Bartolomé Estebán Murillo (1617–1682), who expressed some of the piety of the Jesuits and dealt with far more Biblical motifs than either Ribera or Velasquez. Murillo executed studies of Eliezer and Rebekah (Prado, Madrid), Job (Pinacoteca, Parma), and the sale of Joseph to the Midianites (Wallace Collection, London). There are also paintings by this Spanish master of Esau selling his birthright (Harrach Gallery, Vienna), Isaac blessing Jacob (Hermitage, Leningrad), Jacob's dream (also in Leningrad), and Jacob appropriating Laban's teraphim (Duke of Westminister Collection).

After the rise of the Bourbons, France eclipsed Italy as the "Light of Europe," and French artists swiftly gained prominence in the 17th century. A new Classicism came into being—distinct from that of the Italian Renaissance and molded by the French predilection for order. Georges de la Tour (1593–1652) recalls the earlier style of the 15th-century miniaturist Jean Fouquet beneath the Caravaggian surface of paintings such as *Job and his Wife* (Épinal Museum); while Claude Vignon (1593–1670) was influenced by Rembrandt (*The Queen of Sheba*, Louvre).

The two outstanding French interpreters of the Bible in 17th-century art were Nicolas Poussin (1594–1665) and Claude Lorrain (Claude Gellée "le Lorrain," 1600–1682), who both spent many years in Rome. In the work of these artists naturalistic colors and settings gave rise to the landscape painting , and the Biblical subject was often only a pretext for the study of nature. A lover of ancient sculpture, of Raphael and Titian, Poussin rivaled the French dramatist Racine in his ability to charge a Classical scene with life and emotion. He painted *Eliezer and Rebekah* (Louvre) and *Four Seasons* for the Duc de Richelieu (1660–64, Louvre): Spring is represented by *Adam and Eve*, where the first couple appear in a peaceful landscape, rather like a vast park; Summer shows *Ruth among the Gleaners*; and Winter depicts *The Flood*. The sacrifice of Noah forms the subject of another painting in the Prado (Madrid), while *The Triumph of David* on his return from the battle with Goliath was portrayed at least twice by Poussin (c. 1626, Dulwich Gallery, London; 1627, Prado, Madrid). There is also a representation of Bath-Sheba dating from 1633–34, and one of the Judgment of Solomon (Louvre). Poussin was haunted by the figure of Moses and devoted many canvasses to almost a complete cycle of the lawgiver's life: *The Finding of Moses* (Louvre), *Moses and the Burning Bush* (Copenhagen Museum), *Moses Striking the Rock* (a subject he treated seven times), *The Spies Carrying the Cluster of Grapes* (Louvre), and *The Dance Around the Golden Calf* (1635; National Gallery, London). Less intellectual than Poussin, Claude Lorrain added much picturesque detail to his harmonious landscapes with their increasingly atmospheric horizons. Some examples are *The Expulsion of Hagar* (1668; Pinakothek, Munich) and *Hagar and the Angel* (National Gallery, London); and two versions of *The Mill* (1648; one in Rome, the other in the National Gallery, London), which set the marriage of Isaac and Rebekah in a characteristically spacious rural setting. Claude Lorrain also displayed his mastery of the idyllic scene in paintings of Jacob and Rachel (Hermitage, Leningrad); Jacob's struggle with the angel (Leningrad,) a landscape at night; and of Jacob and Laban (Dulwich Gallery, London). One of his best-known canvasses is *The Embarkation of the Queen of Sheba* (1648; National Gallery, London), where the setting sun produces interesting contrasts of light and shade on the peadeful harbor with its Classical architecture.

Gaspard Dughet (also known as Gaspard Le Guaspre, 1615–1675), a brother-in-law of Poussin, painted a stormy landscape showing the hapless Jonah being cast into the sea (Windsor Castle); while Charles Le Brun (or Lebrun; 1619–1690), for long the dictator of French art, executed a study of the sacrifice of Jephthah (Florence). This latter theme also attracted his rival, Pierre Mignard (1612–1695), who replaced Le Brun as Louis XIV's favorite artist after the death of Colbert (1683). Mignard's paintings of the homecoming of Jephthah and of the tragic fate of Jephthah's daughter are now in the Hermitage collection (Leningrad). Their successor, Antoine Coypel (1661–1722), showed similar interest in the Jephthah story (painting at Laon) and based his dramatic portrayal of Athaliah's downfall, *La chute d'Athalie* (1692; Louvre), on the classic literary interpretation of Racine. The Gobelin factory, revived in 1662 and energetically directed by Le Brun from 1664, produced some famous tapestries on subjects drawn from the Bible, mainly designed by Simon Vouet (1590–1649). These include cycles devoted to Jael and Esther.

FROM RUBENS TO REMBRANDT

Flemish art reflected the pious humanism and Baroque tendencies of the Counter-Reformation, displaying a fervor and a realism that owed more to late Gothic flamboyance than to the classicism of the Renaissance. Peter Paul Rubens (1577–1640) dominated Flemish art in all of its genres. His personal style reveals itself in his many religious paintings, a large number of which treat Biblical themes. With Jan Bruegel the Elder (1568–1625) he executed *Adam and Eve in Paradise* (Mauritshuis, The Hague), which depicts a peaceful woodland teeming with birds and beasts and shows Eve in the act of plucking an apple and offering it to Adam. Abraham's dismissal of Hagar inspires a domestic, emotional scene (Hermitage, Leningrad); the destruction of Sodom and Gomorrah provides a background for his portrayals of Lot's wife turned into a pillar of salt and of the father's incestuous relationship with his daughters (both in the Louvre); and the reconciliation of Jacob and Esau is the occasion for a swirling Baroque composition (Alte Pinakothek, Munich). Moses' raising of the brazen serpent in the wilderness is a typically dramatic and convoluted picture (National Gallery, London), while Samson and Delilah are similarly treated in another canvas (private collection). Rubens painted several episodes from the life of David: Abigail pleading before the offended warrior (Detroit Institute of Art); *Bath-Sheba at the Fountain* (c. 1635; State Art Collection, Dresden), an opulent study of a seated nude; and David as king and harpist (1610–15; Stadtmuseum, Frankfurt am Main). Other paintings show *The Judgment of Solomon* (Copenhagen State Museum); the ascension of Elijah; Jonah cast into the sea; Esther before Ahasuerus; and *Daniel in the Lion's Den* (National Gallery of Art, Washington) the last being an especially powerful and realistic canvas. A dramatic chiaroscuro (light and shade technique) is used to portray Judith in the act of slaying Holofernes (Brunswick Museum), while dogmatic considerations motivated the representation of Judah Maccabee praying for the dead Jewish warriors in a scene executed for the cathedral of Tournai (Nantes Museum).[22] Rubens also made several paintings of a favorite artistic motif, Susanna watched by the lascivious Elders as she bathes (Munich and Turin Art Galleries: Stockholm National Museum; Academia San Fernando, Madrid).

Formerly Rubens' right-hand man, Anthony van Dyck (1599–1641) broke away from his master to become a Romantic painter and portraitist of England's Stuart court, settling in London in 1632. He treated the alluring Samson and Delilah theme (Dulwich Gallery, London) and, like Rubens, executed a Baroque study of Moses and the brazen serpent (Prado, Madrid). Though a Fleming, Jacob Jordaens (1593–1678) was a sincere, even militant, Calvinist. The atmosphere in which he worked nevertheless compelled him to swim with the current, to the extent that many of his paintings were destined for Catholic churches. His *Judgment of Solomon* is now in the Prado collection (Madrid).

Protestantism's triumph in the northern Netherlands was secured by Spain's final recognition of the United Provinces in 1609. In Holland, as in some other lands where the Reformation vanquished Rome, the Puritan spirit discouraged religious art and practically outlawed sculpture, owing to a rigid interpretation of the Second Commandment. However, after Louis XIV's revocation of the Edict of Nantes in 1685, some 200,000 French Huguenots sought refuge in England, Holland, Germany, and Scandinavia; their industry and manifold talents enormously enriched states hostile to the French monarchy and also gave a new impetus to architectural technique and design—a permissible outlet for Protestant artists. Dutch painters were encouraged to observe

---

[22] For the background to this painting, see the end of this chapter.

and give reflection to the activities of the powerful new middle class, for which reason scenes from the Bible as well as from everyday life began to assume a new realism, divorced from theology or idealization. Joachim Uytewael (or Wtewael; 1566–1638), exceeded the bounds of Dutch propriety with his (if anything) over-realistic *Lot and His Daughters* (Francis Howard Collection). It was only in the next generation, with *The Jewish Cemetery* of Jacob van Ruisdael (c. 1628–1682) and the great Biblical and other portrayals of Rembrandt, that a more Romantic spirit was to emerge in Dutch art, revolting against an oppressive conformity. By then, Jan Steen (1626–1679) had developed a rather theatrical lyricism in order to defy such tyranny; Steen's Biblical themes include the perennial rejection of Hagar and Jacob appropriating Laban's idols, as well as *Moses Striking the Rock* (Johnson Collection, Philadelphia) and two more unusual subjects, *Esther Before Ahasuerus* and the spirited *Wrath of Ahasuerus* (1660).

In the grandeur of their conception and execution, Michelangelo's "Old Testament" statues and frescoes have no equal; in their insight and compassion, the Biblical paintings of Rembrandt Harmensz van Rijn (1606–1669) are unrivaled. Though typically independent in his religious views, Rembrandt was a Protestant in the full sense of that term. The Hebrew Bible, to which he constantly returned for inspiration, was the source from which he drew a vast array of subjects—whether in the oil paintings executed for wealthy patrons or in the etchings produced for a wider public. The Biblical episodes that he depicted served less to describe particular texts than to suggest them; in every case, it is the universal significance and individual merit of the subject which counts, not its traditional Christian interpretation. For some 20 years, Rembrandt lived in the St. Antonie Breestraat quarter of Amsterdam, close to the Jewish population, and even in his last years Jewish peddlers were his neighbors. Among the prosperous and cultured Sephardim and the impoverished Ashkenazim the artist discovered warm friends and something more: the subjects and exotic color which both Jewish elements provided. Not since the earliest beginnings of Christian art in Europe had Biblical portraits been based on contemporary Jewish models. Throughout the Dark Ages, the medieval period, and even the Renaissance, the heroes and heroines of the Hebrew Bible were either stylized figures, faithful portrayals of contemporary Italians, Frenchmen, Germans, or Spaniards, or products of the artist's own imagination. With Rembrandt came a profound change, for the Hebrews of old were visualized as modern Jewish types; transferred to his canvasses, they made the Bible a panorama of real life. There is abundant evidence of Rembrandt's Jewish contacts and interests in etchings and drawings such as *Jews in a Synagogue* (1648) and in his portraits of *Manasseh Ben Israel, The Jewish Doctor,* and *The Jewish Bride* (1668).

A significant proportion of Rembrandt's 650 paintings and 1,800 etchings and drawings is devoted to Biblical motifs. In some instances, the artist's treatment constitutes a "Midrash" deviating from traditional portrayals of specific subjects, and this again suggests that Rembrandt acquired useful background knowledge from Jewish scholars in Amsterdam. It is also of interest to note that some themes much favored by other artists—the Creation, Adam and Eve, Noah and the Flood, Solomon, and Judith—were neglected by the Dutch master. However, his penchant for the dramatic and the mysterious found ample scope in other subjects from the Bible and the Apocrypha, and these are best discussed in chronological order. Abraham, the founder of the Hebrew nation, is the archetype of hospitality and this finds illustration in one of Rembrandt's early paintings (1636; Hermitage, Leningrad). There is a drawing of *Hagar Expelled by Abraham* (Rijksmuseum, Amsterdam) and a painting of the same domestic and emotional scene (1640; Victoria and Albert Museum, London). An etching, *Abraham and Isaac* (1645; Pierpont-Morgan Library, New York), depicts the patriarch and his young son; and the *Akedah* (Binding of Isaac) theme inspires a painting, *The Sacrifice of Abraham* (1635; Hermitage, Leningrad), and etchings in which the angel is seen grasping the patriarch's arms as he prepares to offer up his son in obedience to God's command (1655; Metropolitan Museum of Art, New York, and Israel Museum, Jerusalem). *Isaac Blessing Jacob* is the title of an ink and wash drawing (Groningen Museum, Holland) and of a painting, while the story of Jacob, the third of the patriarchs, is portrayed in two ink drawings of Esau selling his birthright, a painting of the vision at Bethel (Dresden), and a remarkable canvas of *Jacob Wrestling with the Angel* (Berlin). It is thought that Rembrandt's famous *Danaë* nude (Hermitage) may have been intended to represent Jacob's unplanned marriage to Leah. The destruction of Sodom and Gomorrah, another episode from the patriarchal history, forms the background to pen and ink drawings of Lot's departure from the wicked city and the incest motif (Louvre), as well as of a chalk drawing of *The Drunken Lot* (1633; Städelsche Kunstinstitut, Frankfurt am Main).

An entire cycle of paintings is devoted to the story of Joseph, beginning with *Joseph's Dream* (1645; Berlin); and *Joseph Telling His Dreams* is also the subject of an early etching (1638; Israel Museum, Jerusalem). There are representations of Jacob being shown the bloodstained Coat of Many Colors (Hermitage; Earl of Derby's collection, Knowsley) and of the attempted seduction of the young Hebrew (Berlin; National Gallery of Art, Washington, D.C.). The Berlin example, *Joseph Accused by Potiphar's Wife* (1655), portrays the frustrated enticer sitting in bed and angrily denouncing Joseph to her husband. In *Jacob Blessing the Sons of Joseph* (1656; Staatliche Kunstsammlungen, Kassel), Joseph stands over the dying patriarch while the latter places a hand on each boy's head. Rembrandt's first illustration to the Book of Exodus is his version of the finding of Moses (Johnson Collection, Philadelphia). Next to Michelangelo's statue at Rome, the most famous portrayal of the lawgiver in art is probably the Dutch master's painting, *Moses Showing the Tablets of the Law* (1659; Kaiser Friedrichs-Museum, Berlin). There are several points of interest in this canvas, a product of Rembrandt's tragic later years. Because of the dramatic presentation—the tablets being held aloft over Moses' head—it has often been thought that this painting represents the breaking of the first Commandments (Ex. 32:19), whereas it in fact portrays the second return from Sinai (Ex. 34:29). A certain luminosity about the figure (suggestive of the "beams" that shone from the face of Moses) confirms this fact. The painting is only the fragmentary centerpiece of a much larger canvas, commissioned for a room in the Amsterdam Town Hall, which the city fathers rejected in favor of a work on the same theme by one of Rembrandt's ex-pupils.

A sepia pen-drawing of Jael in the act of killing Sisera (1659; Rijksmuseum) heads the illustrations to the Prophets. A minor cycle treats the epic story of Samson: *The Sacrifice of Manoah* (1641; Dresden), *Samson's Wedding Feast* (1638; State Gallery, Dresden), *Samson Threatening His Father-in-Law* (1635; Berlin), *Samson and Delilah* (1628; Berlin), and *The Blinding of Samson* (1636; Frankfurt am Main), an exuberantly Baroque tableau. *Samson's Wedding Feast* is a broad, richly detailed canvas notable for the beam of light which picks out the bride in the center and her husband, who is seen turning away to pose his famous riddle to the attentive Philistines. The woman who will subsequently betray Samson has an enigmatic expression on her face, while the wedding guests feasting or making love around the table are, as their faces reveal, low and sinister types. With *Rembrandt's Mother as the Prophetess*

Hannah (1631; Rijksmuseum) and the painting of Samuel's presentation to Eli (Bridgewater Collection, London) we enter the era of the Israelite kings. The realism and pathos with which Rembrandt portrayed the tragic career of Saul were unique and outstanding in his day, and the effect of these paintings is still very powerful. Saul and David inspired an early study (1631; Frankfurt) and, later, *David Playing the Harp Before Saul* (c. 1655; The Hague). In the second of these the angry king, moved to tears, hides his face behind a curtain as David plays on, absorbed in his music; the portrait of Saul in this picture is one of the alleged likenesses of the philosopher Baruch Spinoza. There is also a painting of the victorious David offering the vanquished Goliath's head to the Hebrew monarch (1628). David's infatuation with Bath-Sheba finds illustration in several canvasses: *Bathsheba at her Toilet* (1643; New York), and two versions of Uriah's wife taking her bath (1643; Metropolitan Museum of Art, New York; 1654, Louvre). In the Louvre painting, *Bathsheba* (for which Rembrandt's concubine, Hendrickje, served as model), the nude is depicted with unusual care and delicacy. The letter in Bath-Sheba's hand and the emotion so evident in her face both suggest the inner struggle which she experiences as she is torn between loyalty to her husband and obedience to the king's will. This is a remarkably apt and compelling treatment of the Biblical episode, which has a sequel in Rembrandt's pen and brush drawing, *Nathan Admonishing David* (Metropolitan Museum of Art, New York). Other events are depicted in *David's Farewell to Jonathan* (1642; Hermitage) and *The Reconciliation of David and Absalom* (1642). Rembrandt's taste for the exotic may be seen in the turbans which often deck his Biblical characters; the same headgear also appears in some of his New Testament etchings.

A more melancholy atmosphere is created in *Jeremiah Mourning the Destruction of Jerusalem* (1630; Rijksmuseum) and the pen and ink drawings of Job and of *Jonah Beside the Walls of Nineveh* (Graphische Sammlung Albertina, Vienna). The Book of Esther inspires an etching of Mordecai riding on the Persian king's horse and being led by his enemy, Haman (Rijksmuseum), and three paintings: *Mordecai Pleading with Esther* (1655), *Ahasuerus and Haman at Esther's Feast* (1666), and *Haman in Disgrace* (1660). Two final paintings based on the Bible are *The Vision of Daniel* (c. 1652; Staatliches Museum, Berlin) and *Belshazzar's Feast* (1634; National Gallery, London). The latter, an especially dramatic canvas, portrays the consternation of the Babylonian court

Belshazzar's Feast by Rembrandt (1634).

when the hand appears writing on the wall amid a blaze of mysterious light; the Hebrew warning, *Mene Mene, Tekel Upharsin*, is for some reason inscribed as five vertical columns, the last word being split.

Rembrandt also paid great attention to themes from the Apocrypha. There are two versions of *Susanna and the Elders* (1647, Berlin; The Hague) and a cycle dealing with episodes from the Book of Tobit: the blind Tobit and his wife (Moscow, Berlin, etc.); young Tobias setting out on his journey (Hermitage); the restoration of Tobits' sight (Brussels), a painting that has been widely admired for its accurate depiction of an operation for cataracts in the 17th century; and the departure of the angel at the end of the story (Louvre). The last of these tableaux, *The Angel Leaving Tobias and His Family* (1637), illustrates the moment of climax when Raphael (whose Hebrew name means "the healer of God"), having cured the blindness of Tobit and restored him to happiness and prosperity, reveals his supernatural identity as he departs.

This is an interesting "Midrashic" treatment of the incident, since the sudden transformation of Raphael into a winged being is not specifically mentioned in the original text. A blinding light breaks through the dark clouds hovering over the scene; Tobias falls to his knees, his wife gazes in terror at the apparition, and the young couple are awed and prayerful. Here, as in so many of his works, Rembrandt displays his genius. His handling of the sacred theme is masterly and unique.

LATER INTERPRETATIONS

The great themes first treated by the Renaissance masters were repainted or even copied by Velasquez, Rubens, Rembrandt, Goya, and other outstanding artists of the 17th and 18th centuries. And until Paris became the world's new capital of art in the late 19th century, the Renaissance tradition still continued to influence painters, who regularly made the pilgrimage to Italy. These great themes included Biblical figures and episodes made famous by masters like Raphael, Michelangelo, and Rembrandt, which retained their hold on the artistic imagination. Even amid the Rococo excesses that succeeded the Baroque style, painters dutifully produced works inspired by the Bible, although there was little evidence of genius in such canvasses. Giovanni Battista Tiepolo (1696–1770) executed representations of Abraham receiving the three angels, *The Sacrifice of Abraham* (c. 1715; Ospedaletto, Venice), and of Joshua arresting the course of the sun to ensure Israel's victory over the Amorites (Poldi-Pezzoli Museum, Milan). The murals which Tiepolo painted for the archbishop's palace at Udine (1725–28) include depictions of Rachel, Solomon, and Elijah in the desert. His *Gathering of the Manna* and *Sacrifice of Melchizedek* (c.1735–40; Verolanuova) are gigantic altarpieces. Francesco Guardi (1712–1793), another Venetian, was a disciple of Canaletto and a master of light and atmospheric effects; his works include a cycle of paintings illustrating *The Story of Tobias* (c. 1747; Church of the Angel Raphael, Venice).

Elsewhere in Europe, the 18th century produced symptoms of a decline in Biblical representation. Some isolated achievements were *Hagar in the Desert* (Österreichische Galerie, Vienna), a marble by the distinguished Austrian sculptor Georg Raphael Donner (1693–1741); *The Feast of Belshazzar* (Brussels), a painting by the Flemish artist Pieter Verhaeghen (1728–1811), who developed the historical manner of the 17th century; and a portrayal of Lot and his daughters by the Spanish master Goya (Francisco José de Goya y Lucientes, 1746–1828). In England, on the other hand, the ground was being laid for that quickening interest in Biblical subjects which was suddenly to explode in the works of Blake and which would gather force in the era of the Pre-Raphaelites. Though essentially a portraitist, Sir Joshua Reynolds (1723–1792) directed artistic attention to the Bible with his studies of Samuel as a child (Dulwich Gallery, London) and of the infant Samuel at prayer (National Gallery). In point of fact, the real pioneer of the genre in England was an immigrant Dutch artist, Aaron de Chaves (died 1705), known as the first Jewish painter to begin work in the country after the readmission of the Jews under Cromwell in 1656. A canvas by Chaves, *Moses and Aaron and the Ten Commandments*, must have created Jewish legal history when the elders of the Spanish and Portuguese synagogue in Creechurch Lane allowed it to be hung over the Ark of the Law; the painting has remained in the possession of the London Sephardi congregation. Related Biblical subjects were treated by the early American portrait painter John Singleton Copley (1738–1815), who emigrated to England on the eve of the War of Independence. Copley executed canvasses of *Samuel and Eli* (Wadsworth Atheneum, Hartford, Connecticut) and *Samuel Denouncing Saul* (Museum of Fine Arts, Boston).

The 19th century witnessed a significant revival of Biblical portrayal, particularly among leading artists in France and England. Jean-Baptiste Corot (1796–1875), famed for his landscapes, painted the moving *Hagar in the Wilderness* (1835; Metropolitan Museum of Art) and Théodore Chassériau (1819–1856), a pupil of Ingres, produced a charming and warmly colored nude, *The Toilet of Esther* (1841), while the great Impressionist Edgar Degas (1834–1917) portrayed the tragic meeting of Jephthah and his daughter (Smith College, Massachusetts). The theme of Lot and his daughters was treated by Gustave Courbet (1819–1877), who headed the French realist school. Eugène Delacroix (1798–1863), the outstanding French Romantic painter, showed more than a passing interest in the Bible. His fresco of Jacob wrestling with the angel (Saint-Sulpice, Paris) was meant to portray the artist's struggle to wrest Nature's secrets from her; and his canvasses include one of Daniel in the lions' den (1849) and another (Palais Bourbon, Paris) illustrating Ps. 137 ("By the waters of Babylon"). Perhaps the best-known interpreter of the Scriptures in 19th-century French art was the engraver Gustave Doré (1832–1883), who executed a whole series of illustrations on "Old Testament" themes. Doré's Biblical tableaux, notable for their dramatic effect, represent incidents such as Lot's flight from Sodom, Joseph revealing himself to his awestruck brethren, and Pharaoh, overwhelmed by the last, devastating plague, imploring Moses to leave Egypt with the enslaved Israelites. A number of the engravings which illustrate the events of the Exodus are still reproduced in popular editions of the Passover *Haggadah*.[23] Doré also treated subjects from the Apocrypha: Mattathias calling the Jews to arms against Antiochus, Judah Maccabee victoriously pursuing the shattered Syrian troops, and the heroic Eleazar sacrificing his life as he is crushed by the armored elephant which he has stabbed to death. Toward the end of the 19th century, Auguste Rodin (1840–1917) devoted some attention to the Garden of Eden motif. In 1880, he began work on the gigantic *Porte d'Enfer* ("Gate of Hell", completed in 1917) with the aim of challenging his opponents. This gave rise to his Adam and Eve (1881), to his marble *Eve on the Rock* (1881) and *Adam and Eve* (1884), and to an *Adam* that now stands in the Billy Rose Garden of the Israel Museum in Jerusalem.

It was the English revolutionary poet William Blake (1757–1827) who provided the greatest impetus for Biblical representation in his homeland.[24] Though close to the Hebraic spirit in his mysticism, he was almost anti-Judaic in his moral outlook. Yet for Blake, who wrote his poems as prophecies, the Hebrew Bible was "the great code of art." He himself executed a large number of etchings and watercolors on Biblical motifs and these display his originality and genius for the striking effect. He painted Adam and Eve, Ezekiel, Jacob, Moses, and other figures and engraved several more. The painting of Jacob shows the angels ascending and descending on a corkscrew staircase; the watercolor of *The Death of Moses* illustrates the legend that, when the lawgiver died, Satan tried to snatch his soul, only to be warded off by the archangel Michael's lance; and two other watercolors depict Naomi, Ruth, and Orpah in the land of Moab (Victoria and Albert Museum, London) and Samuel being conjured up for Saul by the witch of Endor (National Gallery of Art, Washington, D.C.). The important series of 21 watercolors which Blake produced as *Inventions to the Book of Job* (1826; Tate

---

[23] Doré's "Bible Gallery" has often been reissued (a recent edition appeared in Israel in 1962). Biblical engravings were popular in the 18th century and Le Club français du livre reprint has published a collection of 1665 (*La Bible en 503 scènes gravées*) as one of its curiosities (Paris, 1961).

[24] On Blake's literary output, see Chapter 4.

Gallery, London) includes remarkable portrayals of *The Afflicted Job* with his wife and three "friends," *Job Laughed to Scorn*, and *Job Cursing the Day he was Born*. The artist-poet also executed a striking color-printed drawing of *Nebuchadnezzar*, showing the shaggy wildeyed monarch crawling on all fours in fulfillment of Daniel's prophecy together with one of *Elijah in the Chariot of Fire*. The Job theme also appeared earlier in Blake's work, *The Marriage o' Heaven and Hell* (etched c. 1793), together with the caption: "One Law for the Lion and the Ox is oppression."

A near-contemporary of Blake, William Turner (1775–1851), portrayed the dramatic incident of the Tenth Plague (National Gallery), but the real interest and emphasis shifted to artists who associated themselves with the Pre-Raphaelite Brotherhood (1848), which aimed to restore the characteristics of Italian art before the advent of Raphael. Some of the leading Pre-Raphaelites now displayed their technique in treating various Biblical and historical themes. Dante Gabriel Rossetti (1828–1882), the son of an Italian political refugee, divided his talents between art and poetry and painted *David the Psalmist* (Llandaff Cathedral); it was mainly his personality that kept the uncohesive "movement" together for some 20 years. John Millais (1829–1896) portrayed Moses at the battle with the Amalekites, his hands supported by Aaron and Hur; Ford Madox Brown (1821–1893), a sympathizer if not strictly a member, executed a curious watercolor showing the prophet Elijah reviving the widow's son and *The Coat of Many Colours* (1866; Walker Art Gallery, Liverpool), a painting notable for its varied portrayal of Jewish types. The Pre-Raphaelites eventually went their separate ways: Millais gained fame and respectability at the Royal Academy and was knighted; William Holman Hunt (1827–1910), whose best-known religious paintings are *The Light of the World* and *The Finding of Christ in the Temple*, left England to find inspiration in the Holy Land; and Frederick Leighton (1830–1896) later developed a style of his own in *Elijah in the Wilderness* (1879; Walker Art Gallery, Liverpool) and other works.

One of the more complex personalities associated with the Pre-Raphaelite Brotherhood was the Jewish artist Simeon Solomon (1840–1905), who fell under the corrupting influence of the poet Swinburne and ended his career as a drug-addict and alcoholic. A child prodigy who entered the Royal Academy before the age of 15, Solomon created a stir with his portrayal of the infant Moses adrift on the Nile, *The Daughter of Pharaoh*, and other Biblical canvasses. Some interesting examples of his work are *The Song of Solomon* (1868; Municipal Gallery of Modern Art, Dublin), a drawing presented to Walter Pater, the eminent Victorian critic of the Renaissance; and two paintings, *King David* (1859; City Museum and Art Gallery, Birmingham) and *The Mother of Moses* (1860; private collection). *King David* already foreshadows the decadence and sexual ambiguity which were to characterize all of his later work and lead him to degradation and the workhouse. Solomon also designed a series of stained-glass windows on Biblical themes, executed wood engravings for "Dalziel's Bible Gallery," and produced illustrations of contemporary Jewish life which owe more to Rembrandt than to the Pre-Raphaelite school.

Despite their common surname, Simeon Solomon and the successful portraitist Solomon J. Solomon (1860–1927) were not related, the latter betraying certain Impressionist influences and moving in a higher social circle. Solomon J. Solomon revived the grand manner of Gainsborough and Reynolds and painted the portraits of Queen Victoria and other eminent contemporaries. His reputation was established by a series of Biblical subjects with backgrounds inspired by the artist's visit to the Middle East. These include *Isaiah Rebuking the Women of Jerusalem*

Samson, oil painting by the English artist Solomon J. Solomon (1887).

(an amusing canvas based on Isa. 3:16ff.) and *Samson* (1887; Walker Art Gallery, Liverpool), a dramatic oil painting in which the Hebrew judge is seen being captured by the Philistines while Delilah stands to one side, enjoying her triumph.

On the European continent, interpretation of Biblical episodes by leading 19th-century artists often had a Jewish flavor. In one case, however, the religious factor proved ambiguous: Johannes (1790–1854) and Philipp Veit (1793–1877), grandsons of the philosopher Moses Mendelssohn, joined the Nazarene Brotherhood, a German Christian art group working in Rome, and became Catholics. Philipp and three of his associates painted a series of murals depicting the story of Joseph for the Casa Bartholdy (Rome); these are now in Berlin. When the German Jewish artist Moritz David Oppenheim (1799–1882) also came to Rome, he fell under the influence of the Nazarenes and his later works include scenes from both the Hebrew Bible and the New Testament. After his return to Germany, however, Oppenheim largely specialized in Jewish subjects and the eminent patronage which his work received led to his being dubbed "the painter of the Rothschilds." Apart from his famous and historically important series of *Bilder aus dem altjüdischen Familienleben* (1865; issued in the U.S. as *Family Scenes from Jewish Life of Former Days*, 1866), Oppenheim produced a notable oil on wood painting, *The Return of Tobias* (1823; Thorvaldsens Museum, Copenhagen). Even more famous was the portraitist Eduard Julius Bendemann (1811–1889), who (after his conversion to Christianity) rose to become director of the Düsseldorf Academy of Art. Bendemann executed two Biblical canvasses, *The Exiles of Babylon in Mourning* (Wallraf-Richartz Museum, Cologne) and *Jeremiah at the Destruction of Jerusalem* (Berlin), and these are generally considered his best paintings. The leading Dutch artist of the 19th century was Jozef Israëls (1824–1911), who learned his craft by copying old masters at the Louvre and eventually gained renown as a painter of portraits and historical subjects, although fishermen and countryfolk became prominent in his later work. The influence of Courbet and Millet has been detected in the painting of Israëls, but his often somber atmosphere and his deep spirit of humanity are clearly traceable to the Dutch master, Rembrandt. *Saul and David* (Stedelijk Museum, Amsterdam), a portrayal of the future Psalmist playing before the king of Israel, is one of his most thoughtful compositions. Three-dimensional representation by Jewish artists encountered much opposition from the Rabbinate until recent decades and objections from ultra-Orthodox quarters are still far from uncommon. It was because of such explicit hostility that the Hungarian sculptor József Engel (1815–1901) abandoned his craft for a time in deference to his father's wishes. However, by the end of the century a more tolerant attitude encouraged the development of sculpture by Jews and Boris Schatz, Enrico Glicenstein, and Jacob Epstein were then able to display their genius without fear of constraint. The Biblical subjects which they and painters and etchers of the 20th century illustrated are the subject of a separate discussion.

CURIOSITIES OF BIBLICAL ART

For a variety of reasons—some theological, others more mundane and sociological—artists and craftsmen from the Middle Ages to the 18th century created or perpetuated strange legends in treating certain personalities and episodes from the Hebrew Bible. In some instances, these fantasies were restricted to a particular historical period, but in other cases they gave rise to motifs and traditions that have had a profound cultural influence over the centuries. A number of such Biblical curiosities deserve special consideration.

Anthropomorphism. The visualization of God as a Being endowed with human physical or psychological characteristics was a normal part of many primitive cultures and religions. Biblical anthropomorphism is not necessarily a contradiction of the Mosaic and Hebraic spirit, but rather a means whereby God and His attributes are made real or expressed allegorically in terms of man's limited experience and conception. Adam is created *be-zelem Elohim* ("in the image of God"); the Lord "speaks" directly to the Hebrew patriarchs and prophets; and Moses is privileged to know God "face to face." With His "mighty hand and outstretched arm" the Lord delivers His people from Egyptian bondage and, as "a man of war," casts Pharaoh's chariots into the Red Sea. Divine Providence iş referred to as "the eyes of the Lord"; the Psalmist calls Heaven "the work of Thy fingers"; and God is often said to "dwell in Zion," "sit on a lofty throne," and "make His face to shine upon" those who love Him. Yet such anthropomorphism is merely poetic; archaeology has produced no evidence of any systematic flouting of the Second Commandment by the ancient Hebrews. Clearly, as the Rabbis put it in a well-known phrase, "the Torah speaks in the language of men" (*Berakhot*, 31 b).

Relief from a tomb-
stone in Amsterdam
(1717), which shows
God appearing to the
young Samuel—a rare
instance of anthropo-
morphism in Jewish art.

In early Jewish art, however, the hand of God was represented stretch-
ing out to prevent Abraham from sacrificing Isaac (Dura-Europos
frescoes; Bet Alpha mosaics)—in contradiction to the original text of
the Bible (Gen. 22:11). And there is even more radical artistic treatment
in later documents, such as the *Sarajevo Haggadah* (where the figure of a
Jew resting on the Seventh Day of Creation is, according to one theory,
not a man but the Creator Himself). Nor was such representation
restricted to miniatures and engravings: an Amsterdam Jewish tombstone of 1717 depicts God (appearing to the young Samuel) as a three-
dimensional figure whose face sheds light on the scene. "Graven images"
of this type are very rare in Jewish art. On the other hand, God was
frequently represented by Christian painters and sculptors, usually as a
venerable, haloed figure. Some interesting examples are to be found in the
11th-century English *Aelfric Heptateuch* (British Museum; God making
His covenant with Abraham); the 12th-century *León Bible* (God handing
the Ten Commandments to Moses); the 14th-century *Queen Mary Psalter*
(God enthroned in Heaven while Lucifer reigns in Hell) and *Holkham Bi-*

ble (British Museum; God creating the world); Ghiberti's doors for the Florence Baptistery (the giving of the Law on Sinai); Michelangelo's Sistine Chapel fresco of *The Creation of Adam*; the *Alba Bible* (God condemning Cain); and a 16th-century Greek illuminated manuscript (Santa Katerina, Sinai; the Creation). One of Holbein's engravings shows God appearing to Moses amid the fires of the burning bush. The anxiety of the Church to imbue worshipers with a feeling of awe probably accounts for the anthropomorphic tradition in Christian art; but its occurrence in Jewish representation is less easily explained. Another type of personification may be seen in the Carolingian *Stuttgart Psalter* (c. 820; Württemberg State Library), where the River Jordan is depicted as a human being in accordance with a Talmudic interpretation of "Jordan" as *Ye'or-Dan* ("the river of Dan").

The Horned Moses. One of the most persistent curiosities in the art of the Church is the horned figure of Moses, which apparently derives both from early Bible translations and from the ancient belief that horns were a symbol of warlike prowess. Until the end of the Carolingian period, Moses was generally portrayed as a beardless youth holding a rod and, in the East, Byzantine iconography ignored any strange new image of the lawgiver that appeared in the Latin Church. The Hebrew text of Ex. 34:35 reads *ki karan or penei Moshe* ("the skin of Moses' face sent forth beams [of light]."), but because the verb *karan* (*qaran*) was associated with the familiar noun *keren* (*qeren*), meaning both "ray, beam" and "horn," another translation suggested itself. In his early Greek version of the Scriptures, Aquila the Proselyte (second century C.E.) first gave *karan* this "horn" significance and, in his Vulgate, Jerome later translated it as *"cornuta"* ("was horned"). In various cultures—from the "Sea Peoples" who invaded the coastal regions of ancient Egypt to the Norsemen and Anglo-Saxons two millennia after them—a horned headdress, which among the Germanic tribes represented the transfer of power and divinity from the god to his royal or priestly agent, was a common adornment. Whether the Church Father meant his interpretation to be taken literally by artists and sculptors is quite a different matter. In any case, it was not until several centuries had passed that Moses was visualized as a horned figure: possibly the first example may be found in the 11th-century *Aelfric Heptateuch*, which speaks of the lawgiver as "gehyrned" and so portrays him in its illustrations. Over the next few hundred years the "horned Moses" became traditional in Christian iconography: some notable examples are the statues by

Giovanni Pisano (c. 1300; Museo dell'Opera Metropolitana, Siena), Claus Sluter (Dijon), Donatello (Campanile, Florence), and Michelangelo (Rome). In these, Moses is a patriarchal, full-bearded figure with two horns projecting from his head; and it is Michelangelo's image that has persisted down the centuries in the mind of Christian artists. When later anti-Semitic fantasy transformed the Jews into agents of the Devil, the "horned Moses" acquired new and more sinister associations as the personification of the "Old Covenant"—a grim and terrifying figure whose head, like Satan's, sprouted the inevitable horns. Indeed, the image was transformed to the Jewish people in general and, until quite recently, many unenlightened folk even in the West still firmly believed that horns (and perhaps a tail) might be discovered on any Jew whom they encountered![25]

Syncretism. Most of these artistic phenomena have, however, less unsavory associations. In Christian typology, the priest-king Melchizedek prefigured the Eucharist by presenting Abraham with bread and wine after the patriarch had vanquished Chedorlaomer and his royal allies (Gen. 14:18). Medieval manuscripts accordingly portray him as an episcopal figure with appropriate vestments. In one strange instance this picture even penetrated a late Italian Hebrew work (the *Harrison Miscellany*), where Abraham, clad as a Roman warrior, is greeted by the king of Salem, who wears a bishop's miter. Another curious instance of Jewish-Christian "collaboration" may be found in the *Mantua Haggadah* (1560), which borrowed Michelangelo's Sistine Chapel portrayal of Jeremiah for one of the Rabbis of Bene Berak who, according to Jewish tradition, spent the entire night of the *Seder* discussing the events of the Exodus.[26]

The Golden Fleece, the Monastic Elijah, and the Bespectacled Jeremiah. The Book of Judges (6:36ff.) describes the miracle of the dry fleece which Gideon placed on a threshing-floor in order to ascertain God's intention: when he rose the next morning, a bowlful of water wrung out of it provided Gideon with the sign that he had demanded. During the

---

[25] For a full discussion of this subject, see Ruth Mellinkoff's *The Horned Moses in Medieval Art and Thought* (Berkeley, 1970).

[26] A woodcut from Holbein's *Lyons Bible* (1538) also found its way into the *Haggadah* as an illustration for the child "who is too small to ask a question" about the *Seder*. In both Jewish and Christian publishing, the "lifting" of such pictures was not so much plagiarism as printers' economy.

A striking example of anachronism—Abraham as a Roman general and Melchizedek wearing a miter. From the *Harrison Miscellany*, a 17th-18th-century Italian manuscript.

Middle Ages, a mingling of this Biblical episode with the Classical legend about Jason was to inspire the emblem of the Burgundian Order of the Golden Fleece, one of the supreme honors of chivalry. In medieval Christian art Jael was frequently represented as a heroine on the pattern of Judith, wielding a hammer in place of a sword. Misogynist tendencies sometimes made Jael, with Delilah, a symbol of feminine guile and duplicity, although artists of the Renaissance era in Northern Europe generally converted her into a symbol of force. In Greece, Elijah's name was associated with that of the sun-god Helios and a cult of the prophet thus spread to Byzantium and Russia, where he often figured in icons and Church art. Because of his triumph over the priests of Baal on Mount Carmel, Elijah became the patron of the Carmelite Order founded in the West, where his cult was fostered by the Carmelite monks. This odd association led artists to clothe Elijah in the characteristic white mantle of the Order. The bespectacled Jeremiah is an artistic freak that apparently derives from Jer. 8:22–23 ("Is there no balm in Gilead? Is there no physician there?... Oh that my head were waters, and mine eye a fountain of tears, that I might weep day and night... "). This text suggested that the Hebrew prophet suffered from an eye ailment and so Claus Sluter carefully placed a pair of spectacles in gilded leather on the nose of Jeremiah, whose figure ornaments the *Puits des Prophètes* near Dijon![27] On one occasion, Jeremiah was cast into a pit at the behest of King Zedekiah because of the demoralizing effect of a certain prophecy (Jer. 38:1–13). This episode led some artists to depict Jeremiah with a symbolic manticore—a legendary creature, thought to live in the bowels of the earth, which was often portrayed in medieval bestiaries.

Other Eccentricities: Two rather more sober motifs were the Biblical Judgment of Solomon and Daniel's vindication of the chaste Susanna in the Apocrypha. During the Middle Ages, these two events were widely regarded as exemplary instances of Justice and they were therefore represented in paintings and tapestries displayed in courts of law. According to another Apocryphal source (2 Macc. 12.39–48), Judah Maccabee discovered idolatrous charms on the bodies of some of his fallen troops and, for fear of Divine retribution, offered prayers and a propitiatory sacrifice for the men who had died in a "state of sin." For the Catholic Church, this incident proved a useful weapon during the Counter-Reformation, when it served to justify the doctrine of Purgatory. Hence the painting by Rubens of Judah Maccabee praying for the dead Jewish warriors, originally produced for the Chapel of the Dead in Tournai Cathedral. The "Seven Maccabean Martyrs" who defied the Syrian tyrant Antiochus were, in Christian typology, prefigurations of the saints and martyrs of the Church and they were accordingly canonized. In this lies one of the strangest ironies of history and art: for the heroism of Hannah's seven sons lay in their refusal to defile themselves with swine's flesh and in preferring death to the flouting of the Law.

Anachronism. The portrayal of Biblical subjects was characterized by a good deal of anachronism until the age of Rembrandt. This is hardly surprising in view of the fact that, throughout the Dark Ages, the medieval period, and even the Renaissance, there was scant documentary material relating to the dress and appearance of the ancient Israelites. Furthermore, anachronistic portrayal had ancient and honorable roots: the Dura-Europos murals of the third century C.E. transformed the heroes

27 On Sluter's *Well of Moses*, see above.

of the Bible into contemporary Persians or Romans and, since there was apparently some pictorial tradition linking these early Jewish representations with primitive Christian art, the tenth-century *Joshua Roll* naturally made Romans out of the Israelites. In *Moses Receiving and Proclaiming the Law*, a Carolingian miniature from the ninth-century French *Grandval Bible*, Moses and his people are also Romans clad in togas and the Ten Commandments are inscribed on a scroll rather than stone tablets. Some idea of how the ancient Romans actually appeared could be gathered from the monuments scattered over Italy, particularly in Rome itself, and the Arch of Titus provided at secondhand some crude notion of the Temple's sacred vessels; but until the 17th century Christian artists practically never identified "Old Testament" personalities *facially* with the Jews living in their midst. Only the stock villainous character of Judas was given recognizably Jewish features by a few artists, and Judas was a figure in the New Testament, not the Hebrew Bible. In some cases, however, the "Jewishness" of Biblical worthies was proclaimed by the infamous "Jew's hat", as in the 13th-century *St. Louis Psalter* and, strangely enough, in Jewish manuscript works such as the early 14th-century *Regensburg Pentateuch* and *Tripartite Maḥzor*. Medieval miniatures of German Jewish provenance often bestow a *Judenhut* on Biblical figures, whose appearance thus borders on the ridiculous. Illuminated Hebrew manuscripts from Spain and Italy generally portray Biblical heroes and heroines as Jews in contemporary (often fashionable) dress, but without such obvious incongruities. It is perhaps worth noting that in Christian art Cain sometimes wears the pointed *Judenhut*, unlike Abel—the "good shepherd"—who bears a lamb on his shoulders.

This convention was maintained throughout the 15th and 16th centuries and well into the 17th century as well. *The Book of Hours of the Duke of Bedford* makes the Tower of Babel an opportunity for the portrayal of contemporary building methods; Jean Fouquet visualizes the Temple as a Gothic cathedral; Claus Sluter's sculpted prophets are all late-medieval Europeans; and, in his painting of the grim punishment of Korah, Botticelli decks Aaron in a papal crown and makes a Roman triumphal arch serve as background. Both Jewish and Christian miniaturists represent Biblical heroes and heroines as men and women of their own day and Sodom, Jericho, and Jerusalem as walled and fortified cities of the medieval West. Painters and sculptors still recreated the Bible and the Apocrypha in the light of their own limited knowledge and conception of antiquity. And, although a more realistic picture began slowly to emerge in the 17th century, Claude Lorrain's painting of *The Embarkation of the Queen of Sheba*—far from calling any port of the ancient East to mind—depicts some French or Italian harbor of the Bourbon era.

The naturalistic portrayal which Rembrandt pioneered in Biblical painting and etching meant, most of all, that his characters looked like the "people of the Book" rather than typical Dutchmen, Frenchmen, Italians, or Germans. His choice of Jewish models caused a stir, but the technique was not widely copied until the 19th century. On the other hand, clothing and scenery in Rembrandt's canvasses were more remarkable for their atmospheric treatment than for authenticity: the "Oriental" color and style of these had to suffice. Rembrandt's Saul is a turbaned Eastern potentate, other Biblical characters are dressed in a mixture of Oriental and Western costume, and contemporary effects are particularly noticeable in *Joseph Telling His Dreams*. The antiquarian manner dominated representations of the 18th century, when the Age of Enlightenment fostered a keener feeling for history, but even then the artist's imagination was often the highest form of "reality."

During the Victorian era, the English Pre-Raphaelites (notably Holman Hunt and Ford Madox Brown) brought a genuine realism to the portrayal of the Bible. Yet older conventions were hard to dislodge: a 19th-century *Megillah* (formerly in the Cecil Roth Collection), executed for the vestigial Jewish community of Kai Feng-fu, reflects the vision of its decorator, who depicts Esther, Mordecai, Ahasuerus, and other figures as typically Chinese in a Chinese milieu; and Harold Copping's color plates for a present-day edition of *The Holy Bible* (London, 1958) perpetuate the artistic stereotype of the Hebrews as idealized Beduin. There is about as much truth in this pictorial misconception as there is in the once-popular idea that most Arabs resemble Rudolph Valentino's Sheikh of Araby. The whole nature and significance of 20th-century Biblical portrayal have made the issue of anachronism largely irrelevant. Contemporary artists tend to see the great figures of the Hebrew Bible in ageless, universal terms; both the concept and the execution are essentially Hebraic.

THE BIBLE AMONG ARTISTS
OF THE 20th CENTURY

Whereas many modern writers and musicians have constantly returned to the Bible in their search for themes of lasting relevance, few Christian artists of the 20th century have done likewise. Why this is so remains far from clear: perhaps a combination of religious skepticism, social and political involvement, or even sheer lack of inspiration accounts for this phenomenon. One of the rare exceptions was the Czech-born Expressionist Oskar Kokoschka, (1886–) who executed a series of 41 lithographs relating to Saul and David and a canvas depicting Susanna. Another was the German Expressionist painter Emil Nolde (1867–1956), whose *Joseph Telling his Dreams* (c. 1910; Kunsthistorisches Museum, Vienna), one of a series of Biblical groups, shows Joseph surrounded by his jeering and plotting brothers—crude, barbaric figures with wild eyes and gestures. For Nolde, the Bible stories illustrated basic human passions and in this painting color emphasizes the atmosphere of hatred. In 1937, over 1,000 of the artist's works were confiscated by the Nazis, who detested his "decadence." More recently, Salvador Dali (1904–)—a Communist turned Catholic—executed a series of 25 paintings (1967–68) about the rebirth of Israel, which evoke the grandeur and tragic aspects of Jewish history. These include symbolic interpretations of Biblical texts: Gen. 1:26 (the sea), Num. 13:30 (Caleb and Moses), Deut. 1:21 (Israel's return to the Land), Ps. 118:5 (the Nazi concentration camps), and Jer. 31:21 (the virgin of Israel). Practically all the remaining works of significance have been produced by artists and sculptors of Jewish origin, mainly in response to Zionism, the nightmare of Hitlerism, and the emergence of the independent State of Israel. However, even among Jews, this preoccupation has not always been common: Biblical subjects certainly attract Chagall and Epstein, but they hold no allurement for Modigliani or Pissarro and even the staunchly Zionist and religiously minded etcher Hermann Struck (1876–1944) made no serious forays into the Biblical terrain.

Max Liebermann (1847–1935), one of the most eminent German painters, was not the most likely artist to seek inspiration in the Bible. A celebrated portraitist, he detested photographic naturalism and developed a highly "Nordic" manner, avoiding bright color effects. He nevertheless executed a painting of Job and a violent and sensual study of Samson and Delilah, portraying both characters in the nude. Although

Mattathias, a late 19th–century sculpture by Boris Schatz.

he lived and worked in Berlin from 1886, Lesser Ury (1861–1931) only achieved success toward the end of his life. The most famous of all his Biblical canvases is *Jeremiah* (Tel Aviv Museum), in which the prophet reclines under a vast, starry night sky. Boris Schatz (1867–1932), who trained in Paris under Antokolski, founded the Bezalel School of Art in Jerusalem, where he settled in 1906. Mainly a painter with a "naturalistically romantic" style, Schatz sculpted a heroic *Mattathias* (formerly in Belgrade) and also produced an *Isaiah* and a cast metal relief of *Jeremiah* (1905–08). As a student in Munich, Enrico (Henryk) Glicenstein (1879–1942) twice won the Prix de Rome for his first efforts as a painter and sculptor. In later years he was to execute statues of Jeremiah and Jephthah's daughter. Glicenstein also made 60 plates for *The Book of Samuel*. Three men who were associated with Schatz during the Bezalel School's early years were the Austrian illustrator Ephraim M. Lilien (1874–1925) and the painters Abel Pann (1883–1963) and Jakob Steinhardt (1887–1968). Lilien developed an individualistic style, elegant and crisp in its sharp contrasts of black and white, for the etchings he devoted to Jewish, Zionist, and other subjects; a number of these became classics of their type (e.g., his *Vision of Jerusalem*). He drew *Abraham Looking at the Stars* (c. 1908) and illustrated *Juda* (1902), a book of German ballads on Biblical themes by the aristocratic Christian Zionist Börries Freiherr von Münchhausen. Pann, one of the Bezalel School's first teachers, used local Oriental models for his principal work, *The Bible in Pictures*, executing a series of near-Pre-Raphaelite pastels on Biblical motifs during the early 1940s. An international prizewinner, Steinhardt produced his own *Haggadah* (1923), the cover of which was decorated with some woodcuts of the Ten Plagues which became famous throughout Europe. Leaving Germany in 1933, Steinhardt settled in Jerusalem, where he enhanced his reputation with woodcuts of Samson and Delilah and others for *The Book of Jonah* (1953) and *The Book of Ruth* (1957).

Several of the more eminent Jewish artists who illustrated the Bible left Central and Eastern Europe to continue their work in Britain and the United States. Born in Lithuania and trained in Paris, Jacques Lipchitz (1891–1973) excelled as a sculptor and, from the early 1930's under the impact of Nazism, turned to Jewish and Biblical themes (*Jacob Wrestling with the Angel, David and Goliath*). *The Miracle,* inspired by the Israel declaration of independence in 1948, shows an exultant figure raising its arms as it faces the Tablets of the Law, from which a seven-branched Menorah shoots forth. The painter Ben Zion (B.Z. Weinman, 1897–) also settled in the U.S., where he became famous as an unconventional interpreter of Biblical subjects. Though originally a student for the Rabbinate, Ben Zion left his native Ukraine and became an artist in Vienna. His Orthodox background found expression in more than 150 paintings of Biblical inspiration, marked by a strong linear structure with a muting of color; in their technique these herald Ben Zion's etchings, a genre in which his main compositions were to be executed. Characteristic examples of Ben Zion's chunky figures may be seen in the oil painting *Prophet at Night* and the etching *Jeremiah* (both in New York). Unlike Lipchitz and Ben Zion, the Viennese poet and artist Uriel Birnbaum (1894–1956) spent many years of his life as an exile in Holland. The arresting nature of his style finds illustration in the scrawny figure of the prophet in *Das Buch Jona* (1921), a volume of lithographs. Birnbaum also produced a cycle of paintings entitled *Moses*

(1924). The world-ranking sculptor Jacob Epstein (1880–1959) was a migrant of a different sort, born in New York City and British by adoption. An uncompromising realist, Epstein was the center of controversy in the artistic world almost until the end of his life, shocking conventional opinion with his unambiguous male and female nudes. Despite its title, Epstein's *Genesis* (1931) was inspired by African motifs rather than by the Bible. His bronze *Burial of Abel* (1938) was followed by a heroic and deliberately primitive sculpture of *Adam* (1939) and by the monumental *Jacob and the Angel* (1941), where the two figures are locked in a passionate embrace. Epstein also made a series of drawings to illustrate the Hebrew Bible.

The medieval craft of manuscript illumination found a brilliant modern exponent in Arthur Szyk (1894–1951). Born in Poland, Szyk worked in Paris during the 1920s, illustrating *The Book of Esther* and other volumes before he moved to the U.S.A. He spent the years 1932–36 preparing his famous *Haggadah* (1940), a small masterpiece of refined calligraphy and exquisitely designed miniatures which is still in great demand. Szyk's elaborately decorated version of the State of Israel's Declaration of Independence (1948) portrays Moses, Aaron, and Joshua in the centerpiece of its lower border and Ezekiel and David the Psalmist (with short appropriate Biblical quotations) at either side. With its luminous colors (rather like Gothic stained glass) and superbly executed Hebrew lettering, this is an outstanding example of the illuminator's art. Another master of his craft was the German-born sculptor Benno Elkan (1877–1960), who left impressive public monuments in Mainz and Frankfurt before taking refuge in England after the advent of Hitler. Elkan's forte was the candelabrum: there are large examples, engraved with his Biblical figures, at King's College, Cambridge, and New College, Oxford, and twin candelabra of the same type in Westminster Abbey. The giant Menorah by Elkan which now stands on the esplanade facing Israel's Knesset building in Jerusalem was presented by the British Parliament in 1956. Among the reliefs on this Menorah depicting major events in Jewish history are many inspired by the Bible: the Tablets of the Law framed by the burning bush; Moses directing Joshua's battle with the Amalekites; Nadab and Abihu perishing in the fire; Ezekiel's vision of the dry bones; Job and his comforters; Ezra reading the Torah to the returned exiles; and the five embattled Hasmoneans.

Not since Rembrandt has the Hebrew Bible found a more brilliant or original artist as its interpreter than Marc Chagall (1887–). Biblical motifs are prominent in much of Chagall's work, which includes more than 40 paintings on themes drawn from the Bible: *The Creation, Paradise, The Expulsion from Eden*; *Noah's Ark*; scenes from the life of Abraham; *The Circumcision of Isaac*; Jacob's dream of the ladder and his struggle with the angel; scenes from the life of Moses; *David as King and Harpist*; themes inspired by the Song of Songs; and many others. These remarkable paintings, executed in iridescent colors, are now displayed in the Louvre and leading galleries and collections. Chagall also executed a series of 105 plates illustrating the Bible (1931–40), which were reworked and completed in 1956. The stained-glass windows for the synagogue at the Hadassah–Hebrew University Medical Center (1961) comprise a series of motifs on the Twelve Tribes of Israel. A Menorah forms the centerpiece of Chagall's mosaic wall at the Knesset, where his Gobelin tapestry features *King David's Entry into Jerusalem*. (1966).

The fresh, childlike quality which Chagall brought from his Russian Jewish milieu can also be detected in the Biblical paintings of Shalom

A detail from *King David's Entry into Jerusalem*, part of the tapestry designed by Marc Chagall for the Knesset in Jerusalem.

Moskowitz (1887–), who (as his Yiddish nickname, "Shalom *der Zeygermakher*," indicates) earned his living as a watchmaker in Safed, Israel. Turning to art when he was already 70, Moskowitz became an international celebrity on the strength of his primitive pictorial account of the Bible, designed as a series of consecutive pictures rather like a strip cartoon. Naïvely anachronistic, his narrative paintings mingle Biblical, kabbalistic, and Ḥasidic motifs with gay abandon. It is perhaps ironical that the 20th century, which has seen a widespread indifference (if not hostility) toward the Bible and its ethic, should also have witnessed a revolt against the figurative, representational tradition that dominated art over the past two millennia. This revolt, largely the creation of the French Impressionists, has brought abstract art into prominence, whether in the Biblical and religious or the general spheres.

EMBLEMS, MOTION PICTURES, AND POSTAGE STAMPS

A number of Biblical motifs have an iconographical history peripheral to the fine arts as such, but their importance in certain forms of representation deserves separate treatment.

The Dove and Olive-Leaf. According to the Biblical narrative (Gen. 8:8–12), Noah released a dove from the Ark "to see if the waters were abated from off the face of the ground," but the bird at first "found no rest for the sole of her foot." Only after another seven days was there any evidence that the Flood was nearing its end for, when the dove came back after again being released, "lo in her mouth an olive-leaf freshly plucked." When another week had passed and the bird was released for the third time, "she returned not again to him any more." This episode is closely followed by God's covenant of peace, symbolized by the rainbow betokening God's promise that "the waters shall no more become a flood to destroy all flesh" (Gen. 9:8–17). The dove holding an olive-twig (or leaf) in her mouth has become the best-known symbol of peace and the release of doves is a prelude to many ceremonial occasions, such as the International Olympic Games.

The Lion of Judah. Each of the Twelve Tribes of Israel acquired its own emblem, several being foreshadowed in the blessing of Jacob (Gen. 49:1–27); the emblem accompanied each Israelite clan as it journeyed in the wilderness, "every man with his own standard, according to the ensigns" (Num. 2:2). The lion which emblazoned the banner of Judah (Gen. 49:9) became a standard Jewish motif, figuring in the art of the synagogue. However, since the Semitic kings who invaded Ethiopia in the second century B.C.E. claimed that they were descended from Menelik—a legendary son of King Solomon and the Queen of Sheba— this Jewish banner entered the iconography of the ruling house. Solomon's throne was decorated with numerous lions (1 Kings 10:18–20), Sheba (Seba, the land of the Sabeans) and Ethiopia (Cush) are mentioned together in the Bible (Isa. 43:3, 45:14) as great sources of wealth, and the medieval chronicles of Christian Ethiopia tell of a supposed romance between Solomon and Sheba's queen, associating Jewish legends with the traditions of the Coptic Church. The Conquering Lion of Judah (used also as a synonym for the ruler) has long figured on the arms of the negus and also appears on the national flag of Ethiopia.

Cherubim. As we have seen, human-faced Cherubim formed part of the Ark of the Covenant's decoration (Ex. 25:18–20, 37:7–9). In Christian iconography, the four-winged Cherubim of Ezekiel's vision (1:5ff.) were often confused with the six-winged Seraphim of Isaiah (6:2), both types of angel being depicted with an assortment of heads—human, ox, lion, or eagle. Representations of Cherubim and Seraphim are common in medieval illuminated manuscripts, churches, and cathedrals. By the Renaissance era, "cherub" had come to denote something far less mystical and terrifying—the rosy-lipped child-angel which springs to the modern mind. Typical examples may be seen in a fresco (1597–1604) of the Farnese Gallery, Rome, in Domenichino's *Last Communion of St. Jerome* (1614; Vatican), and in François Boucher's *The Birth of Venus* (1754; Wallace Collection, London), where two delightful cherubs frolic in the waves. In Baroque and later art the original, Biblical significance of "Cherub" all but disappeared. For cultivated Europeans of the 18th century it was by no means odd that Beaumarchais should apply the name Chérubin to the amorous page in his *Mariage de Figaro* (1784) or that Mozart should introduce the same character as Cherubino in his operatic version of Beaumarchais' play (*Le Nozze di Figaro*, 1786).

Patriotic Motifs. The Renaissance mythology which was fostered by Guillaume Postel[28] and his followers in 16th-century France wove the Menorah, Lily, and Cockerel motifs into the iconography of the Christian

---

[28] On Postel and the Christian Kabbalah, see Chapter 1.

Kabbalah. Exploiting Biblical, Patristic, Rabbinic, and even spurious texts in which these symbols occurred, the "Postellians" endeavored to link the Gauls (and their modern French descendants) with the Jews of old. The Cockerel's association with France apparently derives from the dual significance of the Latin word *Gallus*, which means both "cockerel" and "Gaul," the *Coq Gaulois* having become a French national emblem toward the end of the Crusades, when the rules of heraldry were formulated. Since the Hebrew term *gever* can also mean either "man" or "cockerel," Postel was able to connect it with "the saying of the man" (Hebrew, *ne'um ha-gever*) Balaam, who gave voice to prophetic utterances about Israel (Num. 22:2ff. and especially 24:3ff.). Balaam, moreover, was an inspired heathen seer in Rabbinic tradition and—conveniently for Postel—one who, in Christian typology, predicted the advent of Jesus (Num. 24:17). The *Coq Gaulois* thus figures in the patriotic poetry of Postel's leading disciple, Guy Le Fèvre de la Boderie.[29]

The *Fleur-de-lys*, a conventionalized heraldic iris, is perhaps the most ancient emblem of the French monarchy, although a primitive form of this motif was current long before Christian times. The *fleur-de-lys* was associated with France from the Carolingian era, appears on a statute of Philip Augustus (1180), and thereafter adorns the "Lily Banner" of the French royal house. In 1376, Charles V reduced the number of lilies to three, in honor of the Trinity, a patriotic legend asserting that Clovis I (Emperor of the Franks, c. 466–511) received the *fleur-de-lys* from the Virgin Mary as a symbol of purity. There are numerous references to the lily in the Hebrew Bible: Solomon's Beloved calls herself "a rose of Sharon, a lily of the valleys" (Song of Songs 2:1) and Hosea likens Israel to a blossoming lily (14:6). *Shoshannah* ("lily") is, of course, the name of the virtuous, undefiled heroine of the Apocrypha (Susanna). A miniature in the *Speculum Humanae Salvationis* (c. 1370) shows two Levites bearing the Ark of the Covenant, which is prominently adorned with *fleurs-de-lys*, and Claus Sluter's figure of King David at Dijon (c. 1400) wears a crown decorated with the same lily device, in deference to prevailing sentiment. Here once again, Postel was able to link a symbol of the French monarchy (which he, as a reincarnation of the prophet Elijah, proclaimed as the "Universal Empire") with the Bible.

[29] La Boderie's injection of Hebraism into 16th-century French poetry is discussed in Chapter 4.

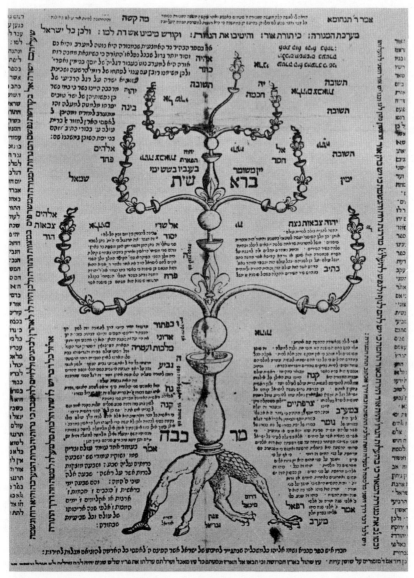

Representation of a Candelabrum (menorah) forming a centerpiece to *Or Nerot Ha-Menorah* (Venice, c. 1548), a Hebrew broadsheet by the French Christian kabbalist Guillaume Postel. One curious feature is the anti-clockwise arrangement of the surrounding text.

The Menorah, a central motif in his kabbalistic system,[30] was adorned with "flowers" (Ex. 25:31ff., 37:17ff.), for which the Aramaic of the Targum supplied "lilies" (*shoshannaha-peraheha*); and the same design also appeared in the "lily-work" (*ma'aseh shoshan*) and "lily flower" (*perah shoshan*) decorations which the Phoenician architect Hiram created for Solomon's Temple (1 Kings 7:22, 26; 2 Chron. 4:5). Pressing various passages from the Talmud, Midrash, and Zohar into support for his contentions, Postel demonstrated that the Menorah and its lily emblem united Biblical mystery and tradition with "Gallic" imperialism and iconography. However extraordinary such claims may seem to the modern rational mind, they were not so very odd in the context of Renaissance France, when the ground was being laid for the absolutist monarchy of Louis XIV with its theory of the Divine Right of Kings. The British-Israelites, led by John Sadler, were to speak in similar terms from the Puritan era onward.[31] La Boderie, for his part, chose to perpetuate the "Gallic" legend in French verse:

> Béselel dond le nom est en l'Ombre de Dieu
> Ensuyvant le desseing du grand Prophéte Hebrieu,
> Orna du beau Lis d'Or ornement des fleurs franches,
> Du Chandelier mystic la tige et les sept branches ...[32]

As previously indicated, the Menorah remained essentially a Jewish symbol, combining within itself a number of ideas which proclaim Judaism's Messianic hope. In funerary art, synagogue design, and (modified as the eight-branched Hanukkah lamp) domestic ritual, the "Candelabrum" engraved itself on the historical conscience of the Jew; and, inspired by the Arch of Titus model, it has latterly assumed a new importance on the arms of the State of Israel. In this connection it is perhaps worth mentioning that another incident in the Bible, the twelve spies' reconnaissance trip through the land of Canaan (Num. 13), is

---

[30] See François Secret's *Guillaume Postel (1510–1581) et son Interprétation du Candélabre de Moyse en hébreu, latin, italien et français* (Nieuwkoop, 1966).

[31] "Anglo-Israelism" is discussed in Chapter 4 (England).

[32] ("Bezalel, whose name means 'in the shadow of God,'/ following the design of the great Hebrew Prophet, / used the fair Golden Lily of the Franks / to adorn the mystical Candelabrum's trunk and seven branches" (*L'Encyclie des secrets de l'eternite,* 1571, p. 166).

the basis for a modern emblem of a different sort. Before they returned with their "evil report" of the land, the spies "came unto the valley of Eshcol, and cut down from thence a branch with one cluster of grapes, and they bore it upon a pole between two" (Num. 13:23). This motif of the two men bearing an outsize bunch of grapes between them has become an appropriate badge for the Israel Ministry of Tourism.

The Jesse Tree. Another iconographical theme with a long and interesting history is the Jesse Tree. This originates in the Christological interpretation of Isa. 11:1–10 ("And there shall come forth a shoot out of the stock of Jesse, and a twig shall grow forth out of his roots. And the spirit of the Lord shall rest upon him . . . "). In Christian iconography, Isaiah is sometimes represented wearing a phylactery inscribed with one of his prophecies about the Messiah's advent or, more often, in association with the Jesse Tree. Among the Church Fathers, Tertullian seems to have first linked the "shoot out of the stock of Jesse" with Jesus, whose descent the New Testament traces to King David. The earliest known pictorial interpretation is found in an illuminated manuscript from Bohemia (c. 1086; University Library, Prague), where the Tree grows out of the ground at the feet of Jesse, who is seated next to Isaiah. But the characteristic form of this motif only emerged later in the early 12th-century *Bible of Saint-Bénigne* (Municipal Library, Dijon); here the Tree grows out of Jesse's body, bearing the seven doves of the Holy Ghost in its seven medallions or branches.[33] A Cologne manuscript of roughly the same date (c. 1160; British Museum) oddly shows the Tree emerging from Jesse's corpse, presumably linking the father of David with the patriarch Adam who, according to pious legend, rose from the dead when Jesus was crucified above his grave. Developments of the Jesse Tree motif occur in a later German manuscript (c. 1220; Royal Library, Brussels) and in the *Hortus Deliciarum* (1167–95), where the design is steadily elaborated and Jesus finally appears at the top of the Tree. There are examples of the Jesse Tree theme in stained-glass windows (1150–55, Chartres Cathedral; 1220–35, church of St. Kunibert, Cologne), an altar carving (c. 1536; St. Viktor, Xanten), and an Augsburg monstrance of the late 17th century (Hauzenberg Parish Church, Lower Bavaria).

[33] This suggests a link with the seven-branched Menorah and certain other "Tree" motifs in Christian iconography (e.g., those of the "Old" and the "New" Adam).

The Temple of Jerusalem. Once or twice in the earlier part of this chapter we have referred to the way in which artists from Giotto onward visualized the Temple, which usually serves as a background to various episodes from the New Testament: the Marriage of the Virgin, Jesus Confuting the Doctors, and Jesus Casting out the Money Changers. Perugino's painting, *The Charge to Peter*, depicts a structure very similar to that shown in his *Sposalizio*. In early Christian art, the fourth-century rotunda of the Holy Sepulcher was the symbol of an idealized Jerusalem, but later the seventh-century Muslim Dome of the Rock replaced that shrine in Christian, as well as Muslim and Jewish, representation. One medieval Spanish painting, however, introduces an original touch: the Temple's interior is presented as that of a contemporary synagogue. Conventional anachronism dominated the work of artists from Jean Fouquet, who saw the Temple as a Gothic cathedral, to such a realist as Rembrandt, who followed his Italian predecessors in *The Circumcision of Jesus* and *The Presentation of Jesus in the Temple*. Rembrandt's painting of *The Woman Taken in Adultery* (National Gallery, London) evokes an exuberant, though dimly lit, Baroque image of the Temple interior. Something more closely approximating to the true design may be glimpsed in the engravings and paintings which a Dutch Rabbi and artist, Jacob Judah Leon "Templo" (1603–1675), executed on the basis of models which he had previously built and in which he relied on authoritative sources. He published a work in Spanish on the Temple of Jerusalem (*Retrato del Templo de Selomoh*, 1642), illustrated with his own copper engravings, which was reissued in French (1643), Hebrew (1650), and Dutch and Latin editions (1665); and other illustrated treatises on the Ark of the Covenant (1653), the Cherubim (1654), and the Tabernacle (1654). This subject proved very popular in Holland: an imaginative, but (by modern standards) not outlandish overall view of the Temple, the work of some unknown engraver, appeared in the *Amsterdam Haggadah* of 1695. The research which Judah "Templo" first undertook in the 17th century foreshadowed the painstaking reconstruction of Herodian Jerusalem which, as we have noted earlier, Michael Avi-Yonah has presented as his "Holyland Model" to the interested viewer of today.[34] Outside the limited sphere of religious art, representations of the Temple declined in importance after the 18th century. One important exception is the English Pre-Raphaelite William Holman

[34] See the beginning of the chapter.

Hunt's *The Finding of Christ in the Temple* (1862; Walker Art Gallery, Liverpool), which combines the Italianate technique of the artist's school with some inspired and realistic portrayals of priests, Levites, and Pharisees in a covered forecourt of the Second Temple. The color is rich, but naturalistic, and the attention to detail is quite astonishing.

Printers' Marks. The publications of early printing houses were first identified by special printers' marks and, though the fashion later declined, a number of these devices have been adopted by modern printers and publishers. Several printers' marks of the Renaissance era have Biblical associations. First in Italy and later in the Orient, the Soncino family pioneered Hebrew printing during the 15th–16th centuries. The fortified tower which they chose as their device may well have been the crest of Soncino, the city in Lombardy from which they originated; but it was given a new significance when surmounted by the Hebrew legend: "The name of the Lord is a strong tower: the righteous runneth into it, and is set up on high" (Prov. 18:10). This became the classic Hebrew printers' mark and was revived first by a German publisher and later by the present-day Soncino Press in London for their editions of Judaica. Me'ir Parenzo (died 1575) seems to have entered the printing trade at the famous press of the Christian humanist Daniel Bomberg in Venice. On a smaller scale, Parenzo was to emulate the fine Hebrew printing of his master; his device was a well-drawn seven-branched Menorah standing on a tripod base. A contemporary of Parenzo in Venice was the patrician Marc'Antonio Giustiniani, who was to gain notoriety for his commercial war with Alvise Bragadini—a conflict which led to the end of Hebrew printing in Renaissance Italy. Though a Christian, Giustiniani also chose a Biblical motif for his printers' mark—a conventionalized, octagonal figure of the Temple adorned with a scroll reading (in Hebrew): "The glory of this latter house shall be greater than that of the former" (Haggai 2:9). This inspired many copies and the device was soon pirated by the sons of Mordecai ben Gershom Kohen in late 16th-century Prague. Almost all the other Christian printers of Hebrew books—Estienne (Paris), Fagius (Isny), Froben (Basle), and Plantin (Antwerp)—used non-Biblical devices. Among Jewish printers, a family crest was sometimes adopted: that used by Tobias ben Eliezer Foà in the mid-16th century shows a palm tree flanked by two lions and surmounted by a Shield of David; the accompanying legend reads: "The righteous shall flourish like the palm-tree" (Ps. 92:13). Foà's choice of this text was more apt than he knew, for his descendants remained active in Italian printing and publishing until the 19th century.

Motion Pictures. Almost from the inception of the motion picture industry, stories from the Bible were adapted for the screen and, over the past 60 years, movies of this type have been produced by some of the leading film-makers. However, despite the fact that Biblical themes easily lend themselves to dramatic screen portrayal, few of the countless movies which they have inspired can be considered great landmarks in the history of cinema. During the early "silent" era, Gaumont released *Belshazzar's Feast* (1913), Eclectic *Esther* (1914), and Universal a movie entitled *Samson* (1914). The Dormet Film Corporation's *Joseph and His Brethren* (1915), "adapted from the $100,000 spectacular stage production" of the same title, remained exceptionally faithful to the Scriptural sources. The U.S. motion picture pioneer D.W. Griffith (1875–1948) based his *Judith of Bethulia* (1914) on the Apocryphal story and on a romance by Thomas Bailey Aldrich. This Biograph production, which had Lillian and Dorothy Gish among its stars, was reissued in 1917 as *Her Condoned Sin. The Fall of Babylon* (1919) was originally a long sequence in Griffith's mammoth film classic, *Intolerance.*

The "Biblical epic" owes more to the U.S. producer-director Cecil B. DeMille (1881–1959) than to any other mogul of the Hollywood film world. DeMille brought a missionary zeal to his motion picture work deriving from the Bible readings which were a feature of his home-life as a child: his father was an Episcopalian minister turned actor, his mother was by birth an English Jewess. One of DeMille's favorite sayings was: "You can take any 50 pages of the Bible and make a good picture." The Hebrew Bible inspired three of his most successful productions—the first (silent) version of *The Ten Commandments* (1923), *Samson and Delilah* (1949), and the remake of *The Ten Commandments* (1956). DeMille's earlier interpretation of the Exodus saga, filmed at the then staggering cost of $1,400,000, broke every attendance record and promoted many screen careers. *Samson and Delilah,* a Paramount production based on the "original treatments" of Harold Lamb and the Hebrew writer Vladimir (Ze'ev) Jabotinsky, starred Victor Mature and Hedy Lamarr in the title roles and had a musical score by Victor Young. DeMille's passion for authenticity was proverbial and, from the mass of documentation used in the Cinemascope remake of *The Ten Commandments,* his research-consultant (Henry Noerdlinger) was able to compile and publish a substantial work of reference entitled

Moses and Egypt. Arnold Friberg, a prominent American artist, was commissioned to execute a series of paintings for the movie and on these the various settings and costumes were carefully based. In their realism and detail, Friberg's paintings are a notable contribution to modern religious art and to contemporary representation of the Bible. Henry Wilcoxon, DeMille's associate producer, appeared in the film and the musical score was written by Elmer Bernstein. The star-studded cast was headed by Charlton Heston (as Moses), Anne Baxter (Princess Nefretiri), Yul Brynner (Rameses II), Yvonne De Carlo (Zipporah), John Derek (Joshua), Sir Cedric Hardwicke (Sethi I), and Edward G. Robinson (Dathan). However one may judge Cecil B. DeMille's claim that the Biblical "epics" which he brought to the screen "greatly influenced youth to better moral living" and "inspired a number of young men to become ministers, priests, and Rabbis," there is no denying the fact that *The Ten Commandments* made cinema history, if only because the two versions attracted hundreds of millions of moviegoers throughout the world.

The "epic" tradition which DeMille pioneered had important repercussions far beyond Hollywood. Thus, *Shulamith* (1931) was a Yiddish screen version of Abraham Goldfaden's 19th-century Jewish romance about King Solomon, while *The Queen of Sheba* (1953) was a spectacular Italian treatment of a related motif. Another Italian film-maker, Dino De Laurentiis, produced *The Bible . . . In the Beginning* (1966), a widescreen adaptation of the Genesis story from the Creation to the destruction of Sodom and Gomorrah. This Twentieth Century Fox movie, based on a script by Christopher Fry, starred John Huston (who also directed the film), Ava Gardner, and Peter O'Toole. It was clear that the center of Biblical motion picture endeavor still remained in Hollywood. *David and Bathsheba* (1951), another Twentieth Century Fox production (directed by Henry King), was a typical "epic" romance, starring Gregory Peck, Susan Hayward, Raymond Massey, and James Robertson Justice. So was United Artists' *Solomon and Sheba* (1959), a Cinemascope movie with Yul Brynner, Gina Lollobrigida, and George Sanders in the star roles. In most cases, the Biblical text was followed with varying degrees of faithfulness, but romantic interest was introduced to meet contemporary taste and demands. In *The Story of Ruth* (1960), a Twentieth Century Fox Cinemascope production by Sam Engels, the script by Norman Corwin made Ruth a heathen priestess whose love for Naomi's doomed son, Mahlon, results in her sincere conversion to Judaism. The Fox studios also released a less successful movie of the spectacular type, *The Song of Esther*, during the 1950s. Universal International's *The Private Lives of Adam and Eve* (1960), directed by Albert Zugsmith and Mickey Rooney, tried to "cash in" on the Biblical vogue, but with some unforeseen results. This film portrayed a group of couples, all bound for speedy divorce proceedings in Reno, who find themselves compelled to spend the night in a Nevada church; there the Eden story is retold in a dream sequence with all of the 20th-century characters doubling in Biblical roles. The picture was denounced as "blasphemous and sacrilegious" by the U.S. Legion of Decency, which condemned the film-makers' exploitation of "indecencies and pornography." Public sensitivity to the manner in which the Bible was brought to the screen curtailed such adventurous treatment and induced more restrained and limited film-making during the years that followed.

Outside the purely commercial sphere, a great deal of effort has also been devoted to the Hebrew Bible in movies of a religious or educational type. After World War II, Crusader Films produced a series of "Living Book" movies—*Exile from Eden, Noah and His Family, Hagar the Egyptian, Isaac and Rebekah, Jacob and Esau, Flight from Haran, The Story of Joseph*, and many others—which suppressed the Hollywood tendency to indulge in the romantic and the sensational. A Lutheran company, Cathedral Films, produced other religious movies such as *Queen Esther* (1947), which brought the Biblical story to life against a modern narrative setting in New York. Sacred Films provided similar fare for Jewish audiences, a standard technique being the issue of a Biblical movie in two versions—one for Christian and another (excluding Christological matter) for Jews. In Britain, J. Arthur Rank released short motion pictures like *Ruth* (1948), where the prime motive was educational. The Bible and Jewish history have not inspired much significant effort in Israel, although some film-makers there (notably Yehoshua Brandstatter) have produced short motion pictures relating modern observance of the Biblical festivals to their historical background. An interesting recent development has been the recreation of Bible stories on the screen through famous works of art. In 1966, Clifton Bible Classics issued *And There Was Light*, where the history and formation of the Scriptures were represented by 265 separate art masterpieces, while NBC's *The Law and the Prophets* (1967) portrayed "the wonders of the Old Testament" from Genesis to the latter Biblical books by means of the same technique.

Postage Stamps. Designs of Biblical interest and inspiration have figured on the postage stamps of many countries in recent decades. As a universal symbol of peace, the dove has appeared on a host of stamps (France, 1934; Vatican City, 1938; Switzerland, 1932, 1945; Israel, 1950; Portugal, 1951; Poland, 1952; Rumania, 1955, etc.), Communist states often modifying the religious aspects of this motif by omitting the olive-leaf. The vast majority of "Biblical" issues have, understandably, been restricted to Europe and the New World, although there are a few remarkable exceptions. A pioneer in this field of art was the Vatican City, which issued a stamp (1938) depicting the ascension of Elijah. On the 400th anniversary of the death of Michelangelo (1964), the Vatican printed a set of three postage stamps showing the Renaissance artist's Sistine Chapel frescoes of Isaiah, Jeremiah, and Joel. Michelangelo's Adam and Eve subsequently appeared on Vatican City pictorials issued to mark the 25th anniversary of the United Nations in 1970. A number of these frescoes (Isaiah, Daniel, Zechariah, Jonah, Jeremiah, Ezekiel, and Adam and Eve) also figure on an Italian pictorial series of 1961. Switzerland has reproduced some of its art treasures in a stamp depicting a church ceiling fresco of Joseph's dream (1966) and in another, from a stained-glass window in Berne Cathedral, which portrays "The People of Israel Drinking" (1969). Other national works of art appear in three Spanish pictorials: Murillo's *Rebecca and Eliezer* (1960), Ribera's *Jacob's Flock* (1963), and J.M. Sert's painting of *Jacob's Struggle with the Angel* (1966). In neighboring Portugal, commemorative stamps issued on the centenary of the death penalty's abolition (1967) depict the Sixth Commandment inscribed in Latin and Portuguese on two battered Tablets of the Law, which may also be intended to represent tombstones. A version of Michelangelo's *Adam* appears on a Belgian stamp (1962) issued in honor of the Universal Declaration of Human Rights, while a French pictorial of 1963 reproduces *Jacob's Struggle with the Angel* by Delacroix. In 1956, the Netherlands printed a series of stamps showing details from paintings by Rembrandt on the 350th anniversary of the Dutch master's birth; two of the works illustrated are *Old Blind Tobit* and *Young Tobias with the Angel.* More unusual than these are a Cyprus issue of 1971 depicting a sixth-century mosaic of the Creation and a stamp which Monaco printed in 1972 to mark the 50th anniversary of the death of Saint-Saëns: this shows, next to the composer's portrait, the final tragic scene in his opera, *Samson and Delilah.*

The famous cultural "thaw" that succeeded the Stalinist era in Eastern

Europe seems to have affected stamp design as well as other forms of art. Czechoslovakia greeted the 400th anniversary of Michelangelo's death with a pictorial (1964) illustrating various masterpieces by the artist, including the head of his *Moses*. Rumania included Rembrandt's *Haman Beseeching Esther* in a series depicting great paintings (1967), while M. Rocca's *Samson and Delilah* and G.B. Langetti's *Dream of Joseph* are two Italian Biblical studies (from paintings in the Budapest National Gallery) that appeared on Hungarian stamps of 1970. Among recent Polish issues are one of a folk sculpture by F. Czajkowski showing Adam, Eve, and the Tree of Knowledge (1969), "God, Adam, and Eve," a detail from the *Happiness in Paradise* tapestry in Wawel Castle (1970), and a reproduction of Jacob from a 14th-century stained-glass window (1971). A Yugoslav pictorial series of 1970 reproduces *The Sacrifice of Abraham* by Federiko Benkovic and *Jacob's Ladder* by Khristofor Zefarović. "Beating Swords into Plowshares," a classic Biblical motif (Isa. 2:4; Micah 4:3), has inspired two separate reproductions of a sculpture by E. Vuchetich: a Hungarian stamp in honor of the Moscow

"Let us beat our swords into plowshares!" is the Russian text on this stamp issued by the U.S.S.R. in 1970.

Michelangelo's statue of Moses on a Paraguayan Commemorative Stamp issued in 1970.

World Peace Congress (1962) and a commemorative of the U.S.S.R. to mark the 25th anniversary of the United Nations (1970).

By contrast, the United States has issued only one stamp on a Scriptural theme—a detail of two hands from Michelangelo's *Creation of Adam* for the 1957–58 Geophysical Year (1958). All the remaining American pictorials have come from south of the Rio Grande. In Brazil, an issue limited to use in lawcourts and portraying the Ten Commandments (inscribed in Hebrew) has been in circulation for some time. Another Brazilian stamp, issued in 1958, marked the bicentenary of the Basilica of the Bom Jesus do Matosinhos at Congonhas do Campo, where the Rococo sculptor Aleijandinho (Antonio Francisco Lisboa, 1738–1814) executed his famous Terrace of the Prophets. The sculpture of the prophet Joel is illustrated on this interesting pictorial. Two handsome stamps from Paraguay depict Michelangelo's great *Moses* and Titian's *Fall* (Adam and Eve), these having appeared to mark a national centenary in 1970. In the West Indies, Grenada commemorated Human Rights Year (1969) with a handsome, multicolored reproduction of *Belshazzar's Feast* by Rembrandt and produced another—of Titian's "Adam and Eve"—for Expo 70, the Osaka World Fair (1970). A striking pictorial of Noah's Ark, the Dove, and the Rainbow was printed by Trinidad and Tobago on the occasion of the UN's 25th anniversary (1970). The most elaborate series of "Biblical" stamps has been produced by the Republic of Nicaragua (1971)—the Ten Commandments illustrated by paintings of the great masters, with accompanying details printed on the reverse (gummed side) of each stamp. An "introduction to the Decalogue" is provided by Rembrandt's *Moses Showing the Tablets of the Law* (actually the First Commandment). This is followed by Botticelli's Sistine Chapel fresco of Moses before the burning bush ("First Commandment," though properly the Second); Degas' *The Daughter of Jethro* ("Second Commandment," actually the Third); Michelangelo's Sistine Chapel fresco of *The Drunkenness of Noah* ("Fourth Commandment," properly the Fifth); and Francesco Trevisani's *Cain and Abel* ("Fifth Commandment," actually the Sixth). After these come Rembrandt's painting of *Joseph Accused by Potiphar's Wife* ("Sixth Commandment," properly the Seventh); Gerbrand van den Eeckhout's *Isaac Blessing Jacob* ("Seventh Commandment," actually the Eighth); Rubens' portrayal of *Susanna and the Elders* ("Eighth Commandment," properly the Ninth); Rembrandt's *Bathsheba* ("Ninth Commandment," actually the Tenth); and James Smetham's contemporary painting of *Naboth's Vineyard* (another illustration to the Tenth Commandment). The order in which these reproductions are presented derives from the Catholic Bible, which holds sway in Latin America. A curious note is sounded by Domenico Morone's *St. Vincent Preaching in Verona,* a purely Christian motif, which is intended to portray the "Third" (i.e., Fourth) Commandment, "Remember the Sabbath day, to keep it holy . . . " (Ex. 20:8ff.)

A few other issues on Biblical subjects have been printed by African and Asian states. The ancient dynastic emblem of the Lion of the Tribe of Judah (the "Conquering Lion of Judah") has appeared on many Ethiopian postage stamps since 1894, and the "Throne of Solomon" on a stamp issued in 1909. An ancient "Portrait of King David" adorns a recent Ethiopian pictorial of 1971. Among the paintings reproduced on stamps which Togo produced in 1968 to honor the 20th anniversary of the World Health Organization was Michelangelo's fresco depicting Adam and Eve expelled from the Garden of Eden. A year later, in 1969, Liberia issued handsome, multicolored pictorials of Caravaggio's *David and Goliath* and Giorgione's *Judgment of Solomon.* Apart from the many "Biblical" stamps printed by the State of Israel (see below), Asia is represented by the Hashemite Kingdom of Jordan's "Dead Sea Scrolls" issue of 1965 and two large and impressive "State of Oman" pictorials depicting Rembrandt's *Jeremiah Lamenting the Destruction of Jerusalem* and Govert Flinck's *Isaac Giving his Blessing to Jacob*. Since these "State of Oman" issues were printed for rebels (c. 1971), and not for the legitimate government of Oman (and were in any case never used for internal postage purposes), they are properly classified as labels, rather than stamps.

A large number of commemoratives have been printed by many countries in honor of the Bible itself, generally on the occasion of some appropriate national anniversary. They include Brazil's "Bible Day" stamp of 1951, West Germany's issue to mark the 500th anniversary of the Gutenberg Bible (1954), a New Zealand stamp of 1968 commemorating the centenary of the Maori Bible, and Chile's issue of 1969 on the 400th anniversary of Cassiodoro de Reina's Spanish (Protestant) translation of the Scriptures. In 1967, the United Nations produced a Disarmament Campaign stamp inscribed with the Biblical quotation, "They Shall Beat Their Swords Into Ploughshares."

A wide selection of Biblical motifs have appeared on the postage stamps of the State of Israel. The national emblem of the Menorah figures on an early (1949) issue, together with the insignia of the Twelve Tribes, and on an Independence issue of 1955 (flanked by olive branches). Other Israeli stamps depict the dove and olive-branch (1950) and the arms of the Twelve Tribes (1955). On the tenth anniversary of the Universal Declaration of Human Rights (1958), a special stamp was printed bearing a plaque inscribed with the Hebrew legend, "*Ve-ahavta le-re'akha kamokha*" ("And thou shalt love thy neighbor as thyself," Lev. 19:18). A particularly colorful subject is Marc Chagall's painting of *David as King and Harpist*, which appears on a 1969 pictorial, together with a descriptive "tab" bearing the citation, "And David administered justice and equity to all his people" (2 Sam. 8:15). Postage stamps issued by the State of Israel on the occasion of the Jewish New Year have regularly featured Biblical motifs since the early years of independence. These include representations of the Four Species (palm-branch, myrtle, willow, and citron; cf. Lev. 23:40) in 1950; a Torah scroll (1951); two of Joshua's spies bearing an outsize bunch of grapes (1954); ancient Hebrew musicians (1955, 1956); Saul, David, and Solomon as multicolored "mosaics" (1960); Samson and Judah Maccabee as heroes of Israel (1961); the Six Days of Creation (1965); and scenes from the Flood (1969). The Six Days of Creation, designed in gold and a variety of delicate shades, illustrate "Light," "Heaven," "Earth," "Stars," "Birds and Beasts," and "Man." Biblical quotations accompany the designs on the New Year issues of 1962 (Isaiah), 1963 (Jonah), and 1971 (Exodus). Like the New Year pictorials, those issued for the *Shavu'ot* (Pentecost) festival of 1971 take the form of illuminated Scriptural verses. A set of 12 stamps reproducing Chagall's "Twelve Tribes of Israel" windows in the Hadassah Hospital Synagogue (Jerusalem) appeared in 1973, followed by a New Year issue portraying the three great Prophets—Isaiah, Jeremiah, and Ezekiel.

The U.S. art critic Bernard Berenson once wrote that "art is not based on actuality, but on the wishes, dreams, and aspirations of a people" (*Rumor and Reflections*, 1952). If the universal vision and yearning of any one nation have impressed themselves on almost every artistic genre known to humanity, that nation is Israel and the perennial motif is its matchless gift to the artist—the Hebrew Bible.

6

THE MUSICAL TRADITION

> Take up the melody, and sound
> the timbrel,
> The sweet harp with the psaltery
> (Ps. 81:3).

Among the ancient Hebrews, religious exultation often found expression in song and dance and these art forms assume great importance in the Bible. Long before the time of Abraham, Cain's descendant Jubal is described as "the father of all such as handle the harp and pipe" (Gen. 4:21), whence the tradition that music is the most ancient and honorable of all the arts known to man. When the Israelites were miraculously enabled to cross the Red ("Reed") Sea, leaving their Egyptian pursuers to be drowned when God caused the waters to flow back, Moses led the rescued host of Israel in a hymn of triumph and thanksgiving:

> I will sing unto the Lord, for He is highly exalted;
> The horse and his rider hath He thrown into the sea.
> The Lord is my strength and song,
> And He is become my salvation;
> This is my God, and I will glorify Him;
> My father's God, and I will exalt Him . . . .
> Who is like unto Thee, O Lord, among the mighty?
> Who is like unto Thee, glorious in holiness,
> Fearful in praises, doing wonders? . . . (Ex. 15:1–2, 11).

The Song of Moses was immediately echoed in song and dance by Miriam and the women of Israel(Ex. 15:20–21). This musical tradition was a powerful cultural influence in ancient Israel. After his momentous defeat of the Philistines, "David and all the house of Israel played before the Lord with all manner of instruments" (2 Sam. 6:5) and, when he later brought the Ark of the Lord up to Jerusalem, David performed an ecstatic dance "with shouting, and with the sound of the horn" (2 Sam. 6:14–15). This somewhat unregal behavior earned him a sarcastic rebuke attributed to his wife, Michal (2 Sam. 6:20), although the Biblical chronicler seems partly to sympathize with such criticism.

423

Jubal, the first musician mentioned in the Bible, portrayed in a stone relief by Giotto and Andrea Pisano (Florence Campanile, 14th century).

There are other notable examples of this musical current in the second Song of Moses (Deut. 32:1–43), Deborah's song of triumph (Judges 5), and in the Song of Songs ascribed to King Solomon. Further references to the dance include Judges 21:21 (as performed in the vineyards by the daughters of Shiloh); and there are also instances in the Apocrypha (Judith 15.12–13) and in the New Testament account of Salome's famous dance before Herod Antipas (Matthew 14:6; Mark 6:22).

THE RELIGIOUS DEVELOPMENT OF HEBREW MUSIC

Until the era of David and Solomon, music was more an expression of popular feeling on specific occasions than a formal part of religious ceremonial in Israel. During the wanderings of the Israelites in the wilderness, music played a very minor part in the cult of the Tabernacle, and it was only from the time when Solomon's Temple was first inaugurated that the religious function of music was fully appreciated. In view of Israel's obvious gift for singing and dancing this is a curious phenomenon; the cult of Orpheus was potent among the ancient Greeks and, in Babylon, Nebuchadnezzar ordered the three Hebrews to worship the image he had set up "at what time ye hear the sound of the horn, pipe, harp, trigon, psaltery, and bagpipe, and all kinds of music" (Dan. 3:15). The nations of antiquity were well aware of the almost magical effects which a melody can bring to bear on the listener, and these effects were readily exploited in the service of their various cults.

The religious foundations of Hebrew music were, however, laid in a genre which more fully revealed Israel's artistic genius—poetry. King David, the traditional author of the Book of Psalms, was an outstanding rhapsodist of the ancient world. David's significance in the history of music is demonstrated by a composition preserved in Ps. 18 and 2 Sam. 22. This is no primitive folk song, but an example of brilliant artistry, the work of a man who was at once king, warrior, prophet, poet, and musician. Renowned as a harpist (1 Sam. 16:18), David in his "last words" (2 Sam. 23:1) is described as "the sweet singer of Israel." One of the Bible's great poetic passages, in which Israel's future king bewails the tragic death of Saul and Jonathan, testifies to his mastery of the lament or dirge:

> Thy beauty, O Israel, upon thy high places is slain!
> How are the mighty fallen!
> Tell it not in Gath,
> Publish it not in the streets of Ashkelon;
> Lest the daughters of the Philistines rejoice . . .
> Saul and Jonathan, the lovely and the pleasant
> In their lives, even in their death they were not divided;
> They were swifter than eagles,
> They were stronger than lions . . .
> How are the mighty fallen,
> And the weapons of war perished! (2 Sam. 1:19–27)

It was thus in the Psalter that David, "a soul inspired by divine music and much other heroism, was wont to pour himself in song" (Carlyle). Almost half of the 150 Psalms bear the heading, *le-David* ("of David"), although it is now generally agreed that this may also mean "concerning David" or "dedicated to David," rather than simply "written by David." In a reference to the Psalms, Calvin asserted that "there is no movement of the spirit which is not reflected here, as in a mirror. All the sorrows,

David, inspired by the muse Melodia, playing the lyre. Full-page miniature from the 10th-century *Paris Psalter*.

troubles, fears, doubts, hopes, pains, perplexities, stormy outbursts, by which the hearts of men are tossed, have been depicted here to the very life."[1] Psalm 19 has been called the most magnificent of sacred songs and, alluding to Psalm 150, the English orientalist William Oesterley maintained that "the triumphant strains resounding in

---

[1] Quoted by Sir George Adam Smith in *The Legacy of Israel* (1927), pp. 21–22.

this Hallelujah finale make a noble and fitting conclusion to the Psalms, the grandest symphony of praise to God ever composed on earth" (*The Psalms in the Jewish Church*, 1910). The Psalter's unparalleled religious influence on men of different creeds was particularly stressed by Britain's late Chief Rabbi Joseph H. Hertz: "It translates into simple speech the spiritual passion of the profound scholar; and it also gives utterance, with the beauty born of truth, to the humble longing and petition of the unlettered peasant. It early found its way into the Temple as part of the daily service; and to-day, after thousands of years, it is still the inspiration of Jew and of Christian . . . the hymnbook of Humanity" (Introduction to *The Authorised Daily Prayer Book*, revised edition, London, 1959, p. xii). As we shall see, no other portion of the Hebrew Bible has inspired more settings by both Jewish and Christian composers.

Stylized representations of instruments played in the Second Temple, on coins of the Bar Kokhba Revolt, 132–35 C.E.: a pair of trumpets and the *nevel*.

From the Prophetical books it is clear that music was a feature of religious ceremonial outside Jerusalem in certain local sanctuaries: after anointing Saul, Samuel tells the young king that he will be met by "a band of prophets coming down from the high place with a psaltery, and a timbrel, and a pipe, and a harp, before them" (1 Sam. 10:5). Amos later condemns the pomp of another Israelite shrine with the noise of its songs and the melodies of its psalteries (5:23). David, the patron saint of Hebrew and Jewish music, may have planned the musical service of the Temple (1 Chron. 23:5, 25:1–7), but it was Solomon who appointed the Levites "who were the singers, all of them, even Asaph, Heman, Jeduthun, and their sons and their brethren" to join in praise with 120 trumpeters from among the priests at the dedication of the Sanctuary (2 Chron. 5:12ff.). Here the beginnings of Israel's liturgy may be traced, for the singers "lifted up their voice with the trumpets and cymbals and instruments of music, and praised the Lord: 'for He is good, for His mercy endureth for ever'...." This last phrase is an echo of Ps. 106:1 and foreshadows the *Hallel* ("Praise"; Ps. 113–118) which is still recited in the synagogue on festive occasions. Similarly, there are elements in Solomon's address and invocation which were to reappear in the penitential prayers of the Day of Atonement (2 Chron. 6:37) or in the regular liturgy when the Torah scrolls are returned to the Holy Ark (2 Chron. 6:41–42).

THE SERVICE OF THE TEMPLE

The singers and instrumentalists of ancient Israel may have borrowed some of their musical technique from the surrounding cultures. Psalm 150 mentions a number of instruments used in the Temple service which have equivalents elsewhere: the *nevel* (psaltery or lyre), a large harp; the *kinnor* (harp), a small lyrical harp or lyre; the *tof* (timbrel), a small drum; the *minnim* (stringed instruments), possibly a lute; the *ugav* (pipe), a small pipe or flute; the *zilzal* (cymbal), a loud-sounding copper instrument; and the *shofar* (ram's horn), which had no musical value, being used for signaling purposes and mainly in religious ceremonial. Because of its importance in the New Year ritual, the *shofar* was also employed in the synagogue and, as a result, it is the only instrument in current religious use that has survived since Temple times. Altogether, about 20 different musical instruments are referred to in the Bible, others including the *halil* (double-pipe), the *hazozerah* (trumpet), the *pa'amon* (a small bell attached to the tunic of the high priest), and other forms of the cymbal known as *meziltayim* and *mezillot*. In the musical service of the First Temple, the ten-stringed *kinnor* on which David was a virtuoso player found particular favor among the Levites; the twelve-stringed *nevel* ranked next in importance.[2]

It is therefore obvious that the Hebrews had evolved a considerable musical tradition during the era of the kings and the First Temple.

---

[2] For a detailed survey and description of the Temple instruments, see A. Z. Idelsohn, *Jewish Music in its Historical Development* (1929), pp. 7–17.

From an Assyrian document of the seventh century B.C.E. it is known that Sennacherib extorted a tribute of male and female musicians from Hezekiah. Moreover, when Nebuchadnezzar destroyed the first Jewish State and took the cream of its vanquished society into exile in Babylon, the foreign conquerors evidently displayed some interest in the musical talents of their slaves when they mocked these despondent Levites:

> By the rivers of Babylon,
> There we sat down, yea, we wept,
> When we remembered Zion.
> Upon the willows in the midst thereof
> We hanged up our harps.
> For there they that led us captive asked of us words of song,
> And our tormentors asked of us mirth:
> 'Sing us one of the songs of Zion.'
> How shall we sing the Lord's song
> In a foreign land?
> If I forget thee, O Jerusalem,
> Let my right hand forget her cunning.
> Let my tongue cleave to the roof of my mouth,
> If I remember thee not;
> If I set not Jerusalem
> Above my chiefest joy . . . (Ps. 137:1–6).

The words of this Psalm suggest that the Babylonians, hearing the Jews reciting their laments to the accompaniment of a favored instrument, maliciously ordered them to continue for the audience's amusement; but the captives refused and laid aside their harps, not wishing to have insult added to their sense of injury. The "songs of Zion" which the Babylonians requested were probably the sacred hymns of the Temple, and to have sung them in their present situation would have been a profanation of everything the Levites held dear.

Once the Temple was restored after the return under Ezra and Nehemiah, the musical service assumed its old importance and was arranged to cater for the demands of a more sophisticated era. The *kinnor* again figured as the leading instrument of the Temple orchestra, the components of which—*nevel* (2–6 in number), *kinnor* (no limit above a minimum of nine), cymbal (one), and *halil* (2–12) —are listed in the Mishnah (*Arakhin*, 2.3). In addition to these, the silver trumpet (*ḥaẓoẓerah*) and the ram's horn (*shofar*) were allotted specific non-orchestral functions in the Temple ceremonial. The *magrefah*, often referred to as an "org n," is more problematic. This term first occurs in the Mishnah (*Tamid*, 5.6) and there seems little doubt that it denoted a rake or similar implement used only as a signal for the Levite choristers. In the Talmud, however, *magrefah* was interpreted (in the light of the Rabbis' own musical knowledge) as denoting a pipe-organ of formidable capacity (*Arakhin*, 10b). According to the same Talmudic source, the Greek water organ (*hydraulis* or *organon hydraulium*) was banned from the Temple since its impressive tones might have diverted attention from the hallowed, if simpler, musical instruments. Moreover, the pipe-organ with which the Rabbis of the Talmud were familiar came into general use long after the Temple itself had been destroyed and its musical service reduced to a cherished memory. The earlier testimony of the Mishnah, on the other hand, seems based on eyewitness accounts of late Temple times.

Although there are only one or two allusions to religious dance in the Book of Psalms (149:3, 150:4), during the era of the Second Temple processions were made around the Sanctuary or altar on the Tabernacles festival (cf. Ps. 26:6), when the words "Save now, O Lord, we beseech Thee; make us now to prosper, O Lord, we beseech Thee!" (Ps. 118:25) were recited or sung.[3] The same festival was also marked by the Water Libation ceremony (*Simḥat Bet ha-Sho'evah*), a non-devotional entertainment latterly revived in Jerusalem, when men of prominence would add to the public rejoicing by the performance of skillful dances. The Temple choir was exclusively male and the minimum number of choristers was set at twelve adults aged between 30 and 50; boys of Levite descent were allowed to augment the chorus "in order to add sweetness to the song." Women were excluded from the vocal and instrumental ceremony of the Temple, but figured prominently as court singers and even as professional mourners. According to the Mishnah, "there were no happier days for Israel than the 15th of Av and the Day of Atonement, when the daughters of Jerusalem used to go out to dance in the vineyards, wearing borrowed white dresses (so as not to embarrass those who had none of their own) . . ." (*Ta'anit*, 4.8). This statement by Simeon ben Gamaliel subsequently makes it clear that this was a courtship dance: to the girls' warning not to consider

---

[3] There is authority for this in the Mishnah (*Sukkah*, 4.5).

beauty, but pedigree, the boys would reply by quoting Song of Songs 3:2.

More lasting importance must be attributed to the Levitical choir and its musical repertoire. Any talented Israelite might be admitted to the Temple orchestra, but only a Levite could sing in the choir and then only after a period of intensive training. The players enhanced the service, but the singers created it: indeed, according to the Talmud, the entire significance of the Temple music lay in the singing (*Sukkah*, 50b–51a; *Arakhin*, 11a). The high standard demanded of the choristers evidently led to professionalism and virtuosity in some instances, and the vocal effects cultivated by one singer, Agades or Hagros, roused the ire of the Rabbis (*Yoma*, 3.2). Some idea of the musical service of the Second Temple is conveyed in the Mishnaic tractate *Tamid*: after prescribed blessings and Scriptural passages (such as the Ten Commandments and the *Shema*) had been recited, the priests attended to the business of the sacrifices and one of their number then made a signal with the *magrefah*. At this, the main body of the priests entered the Temple, two trumpets were sounded and, after other preliminaries, the Levites began the musical service with the singing of the daily Psalm and of sections of the Pentateuch. How exactly the singing and instrumental music were coordinated is no longer clear, but the parallelism of the Psalter's literary structure was clearly reproduced in the renderings of the Temple chorale. Apart from obvious solo pieces (e.g., Ps. 3–5), there were Psalms of a responsive type in which the choir answered the soloist (e.g., Ps. 100, 118), antiphonal Psalms featuring two groups of singers (Ps. 136, 148), and other Psalms in which the soloist's rendering of the text was regularly punctuated by a choral refrain (Ps. 135:1–3). Standard acclamations such as *Amen, Hallelujah* ("Praise ye the Lord!"), and perhaps even the enigmatic *Selah* were an important part of the musical pattern, eventually gaining an honored place in the liturgy of the Church.

An "invitation to music" prefaces a number of the Psalms: "Sing aloud unto God our strength; shout unto the God of Jacob. Take up the melody, and sound the timbrel, the sweet harp with the psaltery . . ." (Ps. 81:2–3); "O come, let us sing unto the Lord, let us shout for joy to the Rock of our salvation . . ." (Ps. 95:1); "O sing unto the Lord a new song . . ." (Ps. 96:1, 98:1, 149:1); "O give thanks unto the Lord; for he is good; for His mercy endureth for ever" (Ps. 106:1, 107:1, 118:1, 136:1). Generally, too, the terms *mizmor* ("a Psalm") or *shir* ("a Song") introduce the text, either singly (as *mizmor le-David* or *le-David mizmor,* "a Psalm of David," etc.) or in combination (as *shir mizmor li-venei Korah,* "a Song; a Psalm of the sons of Korah;" *mizmor shir le-yom ha-Shabbat,* "a Psalm, a Song. For the Sabbath day"). Such formulas presumably once had some technical significance within the service of the Temple, but this has been lost. There are, however, many other phrases prefacing individual Psalms which clearly served as musical directions, beginning with *la-menazze'ah* ("for the Leader"), a word found in 2 Chron. 2:1 and used to describe the overseer in charge of the building of the Temple. Here, in the Psalter, *menazze'ah* evidently denotes the director of music (or choirmaster?) and a succeeding expression, such as *bi-neginot* or *al ha-sheminit* ("with string music"), indicates the kind of accompaniment which the actual text of the Psalm was to receive.

Although the Psalter—especially components such as the "Songs of Ascents" (Ps. 120–134) and the *Hallel* sequence (Ps. 113–118)—occupied a central position in the musical service of the Second Temple, other Biblical passages such as the two Songs of Moses (Ex. 15:1–18, Deut. 32:1–43) also assumed some importance. In addition, the Five Scrolls (Song of Songs, Ruth, Lamentations, Ecclesiastes, and Esther) were recited on specified festive or solemn occasions during the year, each to its own distinctive melody. Musical relics of these traditional tunes may survive in the service of the modern synagogue. Although the possibility of accident cannot be entirely ruled out, it is interesting to note that the plaintive Jewish melody for Lamentations has been traced in surviving liturgical elements of the early Church. Indeed, through Judeo-Christian tradition the ancient Temple song was a formative influence in primitive Christianity—and probably to a greater extent than it was in later Jewish worship.[4] Even when the Temple and its service still flourished (before 70 C.E.), a new and different musical structure was developing in the synagogues where Jews assembled for study and worship both in the Diaspora and the ancestral homeland. Instrumental performances were, of course, unknown outside the Temple and chanting replaced the Levites' elaborate chorale. In general, this was also true of Jewish sects—such as the Therapeutae of Egypt of whom Philo speaks—the adherents of which nevertheless maintained choirs and developed a musical theory and practice which modern scholars have linked with the hymnody of the Dead Sea Scrolls. With

---

[4] See below.

the destruction of the Temple, it was basically the chanting of the synagogue that survived and provided the source for all future musical development within the mainstream of Judaism.

JEWISH LITURGICAL MUSIC

Once the Temple had vanished into oblivion, Jewish religious music entirely abandoned the instrumental ensemble and the technical perfection of a professional choir. Biblical texts were chanted by the congregation in the synagogue, where a *sheli'ah zibbur* ("delegate of the community," i.e., prayer leader) recited certain passages and led the chanting. Except for a few isolated and shortlived instances in Renaissance Italy, instrumental music was totally banned until the innovations of religious Reform in the 19th century. Since the Rabbis maintained that prayer now replaced sacrifice in the dialogue between God and His people (*Rosh ha-Shanah*, 17b), the music of the synagogue became entirely vocal, prayer being a "service of the heart," and any layman possessed of a fine voice might act as precentor. In all Orthodox (and a few Conservative) synagogues, the ban on instrumental music remains in force to the present day. The spoken word—either a Scriptural text or a post-Biblical prayer—thus became the dominant factor in Jewish communal worship.

During the early centuries of the common era, Jewish congregational singing was rather simplified: complicated tunes and harmonies did not appear until recent times and the melodies favored were those easily grasped by the average male worshiper (women were not required to attend all statutory services and were, in any case, excluded from direct participation). As a result, the liturgy of the synagogue tended to comprise the chanting of the weekly Torah portion according to a system known as cantillation, the singing of Psalms, and the recitation of new prayers to simple melodic settings. This formed the basis of Judaism's sacred service throughout the lands of dispersion, although variations steadily developed from one far-flung community to the next. The oldest authentic form of synagogue chanting has survived in the Orient, especially in isolated regions such as the Yemen, and some scholars believe that there may be a direct connection between the lost melodies of the Temple and the musical traditions of Eastern Jewry. Much the same may be true of some musical elements preserved

Motifs from the masoretic cantillation of the German Jews in Italy, as notated by Athanasius Kircher in his *Musurgia Universalis* (Rome, 1650).

by the Sephardi Jews, whose ancestors were once established in Spain and Portugal; but the Ashkenazim (Jews of northern European descent) lost most, if not all, of their early musical tradition after the Middle Ages and had to reconstruct much of their distinctive melodic heritage within the past two centuries.

Jewish psalmody followed the textual pattern of the verses, a common melody being sung throughout each individual Psalm, although popular objection to such monotony led to the adoption of various enlivening techniques. Sometimes the precentor and the congregation recited alternate verses, or else the soloist sang the first hemistich and the congregation the second (or vice-versa). At other times, a verse served as an occasional refrain, a verse was repeated in some melodic variation, or a *Hallelujah!* was injected into the singing. These and other musical formulas contrast with the repetitive manner of the Gregorian chant or Christian Plain Song, which became standardized within Roman Catholicism, Church psalmody and the chanting of the synagogue both drawing from a common musical source. The Jews preferred to vary or escalate their Psalm-singing and the melodic patterns which they developed became rooted in tradition. The responsive method has retained general popularity down to the present day and in congregations affiliated with the United Synagogue in London, for example, *Ashrei* (Ps. 145) is sung in this manner, the acrostic verses (each begins with a consecutive letter of the Hebrew alphabet) being alternately intoned by the reader and choir or by two sections of the choir. On solemn occasions, as at the burial service, appropriate melodies are employed. The Book of Psalms has played a momentous part in Jewish worship throughout the ages and in every community and ritual: whether in public or private devotion, what the Yiddish-speaking Jewish masses of Eastern Europe called *Tehillim-zoggen* ("Psalm-saying") was a daily act of piety.

CANTILLATION AND "PRAYER MODES"

From earliest times, the "reading" of the Torah meant that it was chanted to a prescribed system based on the internal sense pattern of the Biblical verse. Those sections of the Pentateuch allocated to each Sabbath and festival (together with the associated portions from the Prophets) were recited according to this system of musical pitches and cadences (known as cantillation), and the Talmud provides evidence that such a method had become customary by the third century C.E. (*Megillah*, 3a; *Sanhedrin*, 99a). The Church Father Jerome, who was in regular contact with Jews in Palestine, also refers to the Jewish method of "chanting off the Divine injunctions." The cantillation of the Bible involves the use of entire musical phrases to which the individual words (or portions of words) are sung, and not our modern system of musical notation. During the Talmudic period (i.e., the first few centuries of the common era), these basic chants were passed down orally and, even after the masoretes devised a system of written "accents" at a later stage, the *te'amim* were ignored by certain Oriental communities, which continued to recite the Torah in a simpler manner. Among Ashkenazi Jews, on the other hand, cantillation became comparatively melodious, with musical flourishes often running to as many as 24 notes up and down the scale. The musical restriction of Biblical cantillation, even in its most elaborate form, nevertheless preserved and emphasized the meaning and clause structure of the Hebrew Bible, melodic considerations never interfering with the plain sense of the words. The masoretic *te'amim* were fixed by about the beginning of the tenth century C.E. and a similar form of notation is known to have developed in the Eastern Church. Sephardi and Oriental Jews still employ a relatively simple form of Biblical chant, while the Ashkenazim "read" the Torah in what strikes the average Western ear as a more musical and varied manner. Unlike their Orthodox and Conservative brethren, Reform Jews generally declaim Scriptural passages, radical congregations having tended to abandon the age-old system after the 19th century.

During the Middle Ages, the main Biblical influence in Jewish liturgical music centered in the work of anonymous "mode" adaptors, largely in the realm of the *piyyut* (religious hymn). These liturgical poets (*paytanim*) often composed the melodies for their own texts and a mystical note made its appearance as the Kabbalah began to penetrate Jewish thought and expression. According to the 13th-century *Tikkunei ha-Zohar* ("Emendations to the Zohar"), "there are palaces that open only to music." A curious, though neglected, *piyyut* in honor of Moses was composed by Obadiah the Proselyte, an early 12th-century Catholic priest who embraced Judaism (an extant manuscript contains the musical notation in his own handwriting). The Ḥanukkah hymn, *Ma'oz Ẓur* ("Rock of Ages"), which in acrostic fashion spells the name of Mordecai, an otherwise unknown liturgical poet, is of slightly later date and the tunes to which this poetic account of Israel's triumph over each fresh oppressor is sung are hallowed by tradition. Two other important developments throughout this period were the consolidation of regional "prayer modes" and the enhanced status of the precentor (*hazzan*). As Jewish art poetry became dominant in the synagogue, gifted soloists were increasingly sought after and professional cantors (*hazzanim*) replaced amateur prayer-leaders by about the tenth century; *hazzanut*, the cantorial art, soon became a hereditary vocation. Free harmonic evolution and improvisation now characterized the interpretation of the liturgy. After the decline of the great and influential Babylonian community, the musical traditions of the widely scattered Jewish dispersions went their separate ways. In Spain, and particularly in the Rhineland, non-Jewish elements infiltrated the music of the synagogue and the lovely melodies born of this union made such a powerful impression that later generations, unaware of their true origin, called them *"Mi-Sinai"* tunes (literally, "from Mount Sinai").

There were few notable developments apart from these before the dawn of the Renaissance. In Italy, where Sephardi refugees had begun to modify the native "modes" from the early 16th century onward, Salamone de' Rossi (c. 1565–c. 1630), court musician at Mantua and an important representative of the *stile nuovo* ("new style"), tried to revive the ancient choral tradition that had been abandoned since the Temple's destruction. With the backing of a prominent Venetian Rabbi, Leone (Judah) Modena, Rossi introduced contemporary techniques in the late Palestrina style and was induced to compose a series of liturgical works of a polyphonic nature for performance by a choir but without instrumental accompaniment. His collected *Shirim asher li-Shelomo* ("Solomon's Songs," 1622–23) were delightful examples of the a cappella style, but scarcely Jewish in their inspiration. By contrast, the 11 synagogal melodies which Benedetto Marcello, a non-Jewish composer, included in his *Estro armonico poetico* (1724–27) had a more authentic flavor and, as Marcello himself stated in his introduction, that was why he had seen fit to publish them in the collection.

While Eastern Jewry jealously preserved its ancient liturgical traditions, the Sephardim who quit Spain and Portugal from 1492 onward were open to other musical influences. Their Ladino "romances" on Biblical themes[5] remained authentically Iberian in language and melodic

---

[5] For further details of these "romances," see Chapter 4; their folk-music aspects are also discussed below.

technique, but Arab and Turkish elements soon entered synagogue song in the Sephardi diaspora. However, despite such "Orientalization," the fact that highly cultured Marranos continued to reinforce the aristocratic Sephardi communities of Western Europe (Amsterdam, London, Hamburg, etc.) was of some importance, since these newcomers tended to cultivate a taste for contemporary musical style. The Eastern "modes" imported by the foreign *hazzanim* whom they recruited slowly degenerated, although Oriental music continued to predominate in Italy and Provence. The English and Dutch Sephardim, on the other hand, promoted a more intensive study and development of sources and techniques: this activity reached its zenith in the compositions of David Aaron De Sola (1796–1860), *hazzan* of the London Sephardi community, whose many learned works included festival prayer books according to both the Spanish and Portuguese and the Ashkenazi rituals. Together with another composer, Emanuel Aguilar (whose sister was the Anglo–Jewish novelist Grace Aguilar), De Sola published *The Ancient Melodies of the Liturgy of the Spanish and Portuguese Jews* (1857), which contains his famous setting of the *Adon Olam* ("Lord of the Universe") hymn. The cultural impact of Western Sephardi music may be gauged from the fact that De Sola's *Adon Olam* soon entered the Ashkenazi repertoire, while London's United Synagogue congregations have also adopted a Sephardi "mode" for the cantillation of the first Song of Moses (Ex. 15:1–18).

THE REVIVAL OF *HAZZANUT*

The Ashkenazi Jews had meanwhile developed separate German and Russo-Polish variations of their traditional "prayer mode" (*nusah*). Throughout the 17th and 18th centuries, talented *hazzanim* popularized the beautiful compositions which they had written and which they regularly sang to appreciative worshipers as they traveled from one town or village to the next. During the penitential season between the New Year and the Day of Atonement, congregations were moved to tears by the characteristically emotional effect of this *hazzanut* which, from the late 18th century onward, became known as the "Polish style." With the rise of the Hasidic movement founded by Israel Ba'al Shem Tov (c. 1700–1760) a fresh mystical note entered Jewish religious song: the Biblical or liturgical text was only of secondary importance, the main emphasis being on a particular mood. The Hasidic *niggun* ("air" or "melody") ranges from profound grief to joy and ecstasy; verbal expression being unimportant, an extended tune may develop from a phrase or word or even from a meaningless syllable or syllabic sequence. The more gifted and successful composers of such *niggunim* often held official posts as "court musicians" to Ḥasidic Rabbis (*Admorim*). Their immensely popular settings of Scriptural phrases and passages entered Jewish musical folklore and, during the 19th and 20th centuries, Ḥasidic song powerfully stimulated melodic expression even in circles hostile to the movement itself.

From the late 17th century onward, the Jews of Western Europe became culturally integrated into their milieu and their taste for contemporary musical styles led to a rapid disintegration of the old "prayer modes." Lacking both formal training in music and any depth of Jewish knowledge, the Western Ashkenazi *hazzan* often sought to ingratiate himself with sophisticated congregants by borrowing popular melodies from the opera house or even from the Gentile ballad singer. A few of the more talented cantors produced original compositions, but even these marked a departure from the old norms, traditional improvisation serving as a vehicle for the *hazzan's* virtuoso performances. After the French Revolution (1789), many talented musicians preferred secular employment to a synagogue post and some even abandoned Judaism altogether in the quest for personal advancement. The religious Reform movement that gathered strength in Germany during the early 19th century tried to combat this drift by instituting prayers in the vernacular, introducing the organ and female choristers (a source of lasting contention with the Orthodox), and adopting "civilized" Sephardi melodies or even Lutheran chorales. Some Reform congregations actually did away with the *hazzan*, the traditional chanting of the liturgy, and the cantillation of the Torah, believing non-melodic declamation to be more in keeping with the "spirit of the age." These innovations finally proved unrewarding, even within the Reform community, but the controversy which they aroused at least stimulated more thoughtful traditionalists to effect some improvements in the synagogue service. Genuine ability and a thorough musical training were henceforth indispensable requirements for the appointment of a *hazzan*, and professional choirs were established in some of the larger synagogues of the West. In time, the whole of Jewish liturgical music was subjected to expert scrutiny in order to weed out extraneous matter and cultivate the best of the old and the new. A pioneer of the modern approach was

Salomon Sulzer (1804–1890), the cantor-composer of the Vienna Temple, whose musical achievements were praised by Franz Liszt. Sulzer was followed by men like Louis Lewandowski in Berlin and Samuel Naumbourg in Paris. Some of the outstanding compositions of these renovators—Sulzer's *Ein Kamokha* at the opening of the Holy Ark (Ps. 86:8, 145:13, 29:11; Num. 10:35–36) and Lewandowski's *Mah Tovu* (Num. 24:5; Ps. 5:8, 26:8, 69:14), *Shuvah Adonai* on the return of the Torah scrolls to the Ark (Num. 10:36; Ps. 132:8–10; Prov. 4:2, 3:18, 17; Lam. 5:21), and exultant *Hallelujah!* (Ps. 150)—are masterpieces of choral and cantorial music. In much the same tradition are the many popular settings of I. L. Mombach (1813–1880), such as *L'Adonai Ha-Arez* (Ps. 24) and *Havu l'Adonai* (Ps. 29), which virtually created the fine choral tradition of modern English synagogue music.

From the last quarter of the 19th century, Eastern Europe provided Ashkenazi Jewry with its great reservoir of artistry and inspiration in the liturgical sphere. *Ḥazzanim* of the "classical" type were succeeded by "Westernizing" cantors who acquired an extensive musical training (e.g., Jacob Bachmann, a pupil of Anton Rubinstein) and often developed an operatic manner, the better to display their phenomenal range and individual technique. A number of these *ḥazzanim* gradually came to rely on the liturgical compositions of other musicians, but there were some cantor-composers of eminence, such as A. M. Bernstein of Vilna, whose *Adonai Adonai* (Ex. 34:6–7)—one of the showpieces of the cantorial art—was eulogized by Rimsky-Korsakov as "among the elect of synagogal compositions." During this "Golden Age of *ḥazzanut*" many of the outstanding Russian cantors established worldwide reputations, touring Europe and the United States and winning the applause of Jew and Gentile alike. Concert performances and phonograph records enhanced the cantor's fame and stimulated a general revival of interest in the music of the synagogue. Prominent among these "Golden Age" cantors were Josef (Yossele) Rosenblatt (1880–1933), Mordechai Herschman (1888–1940), Moshe Koussevitzky (1899–1966), Zevulun (Zavel) Kwartin (1874–1953), and Gershon Sirota (1874–1943), all but the last of whom settled in the U.S.A. Great singers of this type movingly interpreted (and sometimes composed) settings to favorite Biblical passages such as Jer. 31:15–17 (*Raḥel Mevakkah al Baneha*) and Jer. 31:20 (*Ha-Ven Yakir Li Efrayim*), as well as a multitude of passages from the traditional liturgy. Rosenblatt, a tenor virtuoso who had an unusually eventful career, mostly sang his own compositions with choral accompaniment; his *Shir Ha-Ma'alot* (Ps. 126), over which the Hebrew poet Bialik enthused, has become the best-known setting for this Psalm. As a vocalist and composer, Rosenblatt had a close rival in Kwartin, whose interpretation of the High Holiday prayers was universally acclaimed. Sirota, who perished in the Warsaw Ghetto, was a tenor of world rank and one of the greatest cantors of all time. While in Vilna, he was engaged to sing annually for Czar Nicholas II of Russia. *Ha'azinah Elohim*, Sirota's interpretation of the first four verses of Ps. 55, based on an Italian art song attributed to Alessandro Stradella (*Pietà, Signore*), is so skillful that one is tempted to believe that the composer actually set his music to the Hebrew text.

Although a number of accomplished *hazzanim* continue to make their mark in the contemporary synagogue, few can hope to recapture the glories of the past. Thus, Jan Peerce and Richard Tucker have become internationally celebrated operatic tenors, while maintaining their links with the synagogue service through concert performances, recordings, and High Holiday and Passover *Seder* engagements. New training schools for *hazzanim* in Israel, the U.S.A., and Britain nevertheless assure a productive future for the cantorial art. "Sacred Services" have been written by leading Jewish composers such as Ernest Bloch and Darius Milhaud and other Biblical and liturgical pieces have been arranged for instrumental performance by several other composers of world rank. A number of American synagogues regularly sponsor musical creativity of this type with the aim of enhancing their own services while promoting the development of Israel's sacred melodies. This modern interest in Biblical and Jewish song has not been confined to adherents of Judaism: Franz Schubert was attracted to the services arranged by Sulzer in Vienna and himself composed a work ("*Tov l'hodos*") for his cantor friend, using the Hebrew of Ps. 92 as his text. Another non-Jew, Max Bruch, wrote an arrangement of the Ashkenazi *Kol Nidrei*[6](1880) on a commission from the Liverpool Jewish community, while Maurice Ravel's compositions include *Deux Mélodies Hébraïques* (1914), the first being an interpretation of the ancient *Kaddish* memorial prayer. From Temple times to the present day, Jewish song has retained all of its appeal to man's spiritual and emotional nature. Its influence has spread far and wide, accompanying the Biblical word, for, as Heine once noted, "the essence of music is a revelation."

[6] See below.

BIBLICAL ELEMENTS IN THE MUSIC OF THE CHURCH

The founders of the Church were Judeo-Christians for whom the Temple service and the life and worship of the synagogue were everyday realities. Indeed, the prayers which these "Nazarenes" recited in their *kenesiyah* ("house of assembly") were substantially the same as those said by "Orthodox" Jews, allowing for some textual variations in respect of the messiahship of Jesus. From the first-century Pharisees Judeo-Christianity took over a distinct hostility toward the use of instrumental music in public worship, and this attitude prevailed for some time in the early Gentile Church; Calvinists and Puritans later regarded the organ as a pagan element in the house of prayer, while some Eastern churches still maintain the old ban on instrumental music. The Church Fathers also tried to prohibit dancing, presumably because of the same fear that Christians might be affected by the rites of certain mystery cults. A significant proportion of basic Church music can be traced to the Jewish traditions of Jesus' time or to synagogue song of the pre-medieval period.

For the early Christians, as for the Jews, a central feature of public worship was the singing of Psalms. The roots of the Eight-Mode (or Eight-Tone) system which the Church adopted are in the Near East —some scholars have tried to link the eight Oriental "modes" with the superscription of Ps. 6 ("with string music; on the Sheminith")— and the psalmodic patterns evolved were, like the written text, "canonized" at a very early date. These patterns remained the basis of the single-voiced Gregorian chant (a development of plainsong or plainchant) until the 17th century. Scriptural parallelism (the Bible's antithetical sentence structure) gave rise to responsorial psalmody in its various forms, from which the antiphonal (alternating) principle of early Christian and later Western secular music ultimately derives. As in Jewish tradition, various forms of singing (soloist-group, group-group, etc.) emerged from this responsorial and antiphonal chant and it was from the technique of the 16th-century Venetian school that the concertizing of the Baroque era developed; from there it was only a short step to the modern orchestra. Melismatic (expanded coloratura) singing became a standard technique among virtuoso *hazzanim* of the synagogue, whose early Christian equivalents were known as "cantors," "lectors," or *psalmistae*; church choirs only became common after the rise of the monastic system. The same melismatic style was also adopted by the Church for its famous *Jubilus*—a florid rendition of *Alleluia* (*Hallelujah!*) often spun out with a prolonged final *a*—which Augustine and other Church Fathers regarded as the supreme achievement of their sacred music. The *Jubilus* in its definitive form was shorn of *Hallelujah*'s consonants and the vowels A-E-U-I-A exchanged for those of "*seculorum amen*" (E-U-O-U-A-E). Such wordless song apparently has partly Jewish roots and, though condemned by the Rabbis as a mystical deviation, it reemerged among the Jews as the Ḥasidic *niggun*. In the *Psalmus alleluiatus* of Christian tradition, the *Alleluia* was used as a decorative refrain, a practice also found among the Jews.

Despite Jesus' strictures against the Temple (Matthew 24:1–2, John 2:13ff., etc.) and Judeo-Christian hostility, leaders of both the Eastern and the Western Churches held the musical service of the Sanctuary in Jerusalem to be the religious ideal. This view was a logical one, since the aim of the Temple singers and Church choristers was one and the same: the creation of musical beauty to steal men's hearts and rival angelic song. The synagogue, on the other hand, spurned beauty for beauty's sake and insisted that the religious function of music must be the expression of human feeling in prayer. Christian typology, which plays so prominent a part in European painting and sculpture of the Middle Ages, also left its impress on music: in the Byzantine world, David the Psalmist was elected to a cultural trinity with Jesus and the divine Greek singer Orpheus; in the medieval West, "Saint Job" figured among the patrons of music and professional musicians on the basis of Job 30:31.

Psalm-singing was a powerful factor in the development of Roman Catholic liturgy and the Gregorian chant was not restricted to use with the Psalter. The Prayer of Hezekiah (Isa. 38:9–20) was included among the *cantica* (chants or canticles) of the Church of Rome and, as *Canticum Ezechiae*, it figures in the Lauds (dawn service) of the Office for the Defunct and is sung to a simple psalmodic formula. The same kind of psalmodic melody is used for the Psalm-like third and final chapter of Habakkuk in the *cantica* of many denominations, while the Roman Catholic rite again prescribes it for *Magnus es Domine in aeternum*, the song of praise in the 13th chapter of Tobit, and for the "Canticle of Judith," *Hymnum cantemus Domino* (Judith 16.15–21), intoned during the Lauds on Wednesday. Since the Church claimed to be the legitimate heir of the synagogue, it is not surprising to find that a very high proportion of Catholic music is of ancient Hebrew origin. So are all but one of the Christian liturgy's central components—the Psalter, the Doxology, and the Triple Sanctus (or "Thrice Holy"). The Lord's Prayer (Matthew 6:9–13; Luke 11:2–4), though never in itself part of the synagogal liturgy, contains distinct echoes of the *Kaddish* ("sanctification"), a prayer composed in Aramaic (the vernacular of Jesus' time) which is recited or sung at regular intervals during services in the synagogue. Apart from simple and responsorial psalmody and antiphonal prayer, Christian liturgical tradition also includes an ancient Jewish element in the litany, where a short passage recited by the precentor is answered by the whole congregation with a verse refrain of the "Help us, O Lord" (Hebrew, *Ana YHVH Hoshi'a-na*) type. All of these structures easily lend themselves to musical arrangement, as the Church speedily realized.

Another Jewish practice which Christianity adopted was cantillation, the chanting of Biblical texts. Aware of the need for organic continuity with Near Eastern liturgical sources, the early Christians fostered such Biblical chanting: the lesson from the Scriptures is thus often cantillated in the Roman Catholic Church, though in a comparatively simple form, while it is invariably chanted (more elaborately, on the Jewish pattern) in the Greek Orthodox rite. Indeed, to a Jewish ear, there is a remarkable resemblance between Greek and Russian Orthodox "prayer modes" with their use of cantor and choir and those of the synagogue. Although only one kind of melodic pattern now characterizes the recitation of Lamentations in the Catholic ritual, this is believed to contain the oldest surviving musical element of Jewish origin. In the Lamentations chanted during Holy Week, the melodic recitation includes not only the text itself but also the introductory phrase: *Incipit Lamentatio Jeremiae prophetae* ("So begins the lamentation of the prophet Jeremiah"), a common technique in Roman Catholic liturgical practice. Mingling cantillation and psalmody, this recitation includes the singing of the Hebrew letters *aleph, beth*, etc. which prefix each verse or group of verses in the acrostically composed first four chapters of the Book of Lamentations. Each section also concludes with the sentence: *Jerusalem, Jerusalem, convertere ad Dominum Deum tuum* ("O Jerusalem, Jerusalem, return to the Lord your God"). Closely associated with this solemn chant is the lament, *Quis dabit oculis meis* . . . ? ("Oh that mine eyes . . . ," Jer. 8:23), which occurs in the Catholic liturgy for Good Friday. Nor does the list of Christian borrowings from Jewish sacred music end here.

The third "mode" of Gregorian chant closely resembles Oriental Jewry's traditional manner of reciting the Pentateuch, as experts who have investigated the *Kyrie eleison—Domine miserere* ("Lord have mercy") prayer almost unanimously affirm. Moreover, as Greek notation symbols of the eighth–ninth centuries clearly prove, the Eastern Church and the Jewish masoretes employed closely related systems of accent-marking for Biblical cantillation. It is interesting to note that the Church Father Clement of Alexandria urged devout Christians not to imitate the melodies of Greece in its voluptuous decadence, but to praise God with the "modes" of ancient Greece—the *Tropos Spondeiakos* (spondaic trope)—which he identified with those of the Hebrew Psalms. Perhaps there is some distant reflection of this old musical dialogue in the word "*trop*" which Ashkenazi Jews still sometimes use to describe their method of cantillation.

A final instance of Christian indebtedness to the old Jewish liturgy is the Triple Sanctus of Isa. 6:3 ("Holy, holy, holy, is the Lord of hosts; the whole earth is full of His glory"). This constitutes the main text of the *Sanctus* portion of the Roman Catholic mass, where it is followed by the jubilant singing of *Hosanna in excelsis, Benedictus,* and of *Hosanna* once again (see Matthew 21:9, Mark 11:9–10, John 12:13). For this "Thrice Holy" text, Gregorian chant provides no less than 21 melodies dating from the tenth to the 13th century. The medieval Church undoubtedly borrowed the musical leitmotif from synagogue themes of the *Kol Nidrei*[7] type, and the *Sanctus* (which took its basic melody from Jewish "prayer modes" for the High Holidays) is a notable instance of this development. Immanuel of Rome, an eminent Hebrew poet of medieval Italy, thus made ironical use of a Biblical citation (Gen. 40:15) when he wrote: "What does the art of music say to the Christians? —'Indeed I was stolen away out of the land of the Hebrews' . . . "

RENAISSANCE, REFORMATION, AND BAROQUE TRENDS

Toward the end of the Middle Ages, when plainsong gave birth to polyphony, a new era of art music came into being and composers ceased

---

[7] *Kol Nidrei* (Aramaic for "All vows") is a formula used on the eve of *Yom Kippur* (the Day of Atonement) to nullify unfulfilled voluntary commitments between the individual and his Maker. The (Ashkenazi) *Kol Nidrei* melody has been remarkably influential in music.

to be anonymous. The first polyphonic settings of Biblical texts were written by musicians of the Franco-Flemish (or "Netherlands") school, notably Guillaume Dufay (c. 1400–1474), who was perhaps the outstanding composer of the 15th century. Textually related to the Book of Lamentations, Dufay's four-voice motet, *O très piteux* (1454), bewailed the Turkish seizure of Constantinople and was intended to launch a new Crusade against the infidels. From this time onward, musicians found new inspiration in the Psalms, seeing in them not only the "essence of sacred melody," but also an expression of individual and collective joy and sorrow which challenged the composer. Josquin Des Prés (c. 1450–1521), a successor of Dufay, composed religious works (motets, masses, etc.) that combined technical excellence with a transcendental spirituality. Des Prés, who served as court musician to Louis XII of France, wrote motets on the Biblical themes of David's lament on the death of Saul, David's elegy for Absalom (*Lugebat David Absalom: Absalom fili mi*), and the reign of King Solomon (*Stetit autem Salomon*). This "prince of musicians" also composed a setting of the Apocryphal Song of the Three Holy Children (*Canticum trium Puerorum*), which forms part of the Catholic liturgy.

Certain passages from the Bible and the Apocrypha assumed musical importance because of their close association with the ritual of the Church. Chapters 44–45 of the Wisdom of Ben Sira (Ecclesiasticus) thus provide one of the textual sources for Papal coronations, while the Vulgate text of the Song of Songs figured prominently in the liturgical music of the 15th–16th centuries, some verses and sections forming part of Marian celebrations. Among English settings of the Song of Songs at this period were those of John Constable (*Quam pulchra es*) and King Henry VIII.

The Reformation introduced new secular or revised "Gregorian" melodies into Psalm-singing in the vernacular, Luther sanctioning the use of old and familiar music in a famous quip: "Why should the Devil have all the good tunes?" Claude Le Jeune (c. 1528–1600), one of the great musicians of the age, headed the French and Swiss composers who wrote settings for the Reformed Church paraphrases of the Psalter by Marot and Calvin; Luther's German followers did the same in their Protestant chorales; while Jacobus Clemens non Papa (c. 1510–c. 1556) used popular folk tunes for his setting of the Dutch rhymed Psalter. Reformation composers arranged the Psalms for three or four voices, linking their tradition with that of the new art music. Continental melodies of Protestant origin were largely adopted by the English Reformers and eventually found their way into the Anglo-Scottish repertoire (Thomas Sternhold's *Whole Booke of Psalmes*, 1562; the Church of Scotland's *Psalms of David*, 1650); with local additions, these tunes were to accompany the Puritans and take root in North America. The stricter Protestants shared the old Jewish dislike for instrumental accompaniment: to quote Ben Jonson out of context, they maintained that "bells are profane, a tune may be religious" (*The Alchemist*, 1610). From the Psalter, this Protestant interest in the musical setting of Scripture broadened to encompass the whole range of Biblical and Apocryphal literature. Clemens non Papa wrote music for the laments of Jacob over Joseph and of David over Saul; Joachim à Burck composed the motet, *Da Jakob Labans Tochter nahm* (1599) on the romance of Jacob and Rachel; and many Bible songs were written by members of the Reformed churches as far afield as Hungary. From about 1600, Protestant composers were attracted by the half-verse, "I know that my Redeemer liveth" (Job 19:25), for which two settings were written by Heinrich Schütz (1585–1672), while German Lutheran arrangements of lines from the Song of Songs—at first used for wedding celebrations— became increasingly allegorical in tone. "Now Praise the Lord" (Ben Sira 50.22–24) was extensively used by Protestants: the English Catholic organist and composer William Byrd (1545–1623) arranged this passage as an impressive six-voiced anthem for the Anglican Church and Martin Rinkart's *Nun danket alle Gott* (1636) became famous when it was sung as the "German *Te Deum*" (to a chorale-melody by Johann Crüger) on the occasion of the peace treaty ending the Thirty Years' War (1648). As *Now thank we all our God*, the latter setting has enjoyed wide popularity among Anglicans; the German version was later reworked by both Bach and Mendelssohn. Byrd's *Behold now praise the Lord* entered the Anglican communion's *Book of Common Prayer* (1662), as did the opening of Ben Sira 44 ("Let us now praise famous men, and our fathers that begat us"), which the modern English composer Ralph Vaughan Williams has set for choir (1923). Though not strictly related to a Scriptural text, Melchior Franck's chorale, *Jerusalem, du hochgebaute Stadt* (1663), has a Biblical ring and an English version appeared as *Jerusalem, thou city built on high*. Most musical works on this theme were, however, inspired by the New Testament or Christian hymnology, one notable example being *Jerusalem the Golden* by John

Mason Neale, Alexander Ewing's setting of which appears in *Hymns Ancient and Modern* (1861).[8]

Side by side with this upsurge of Protestant music went the development of the Catholic Baroque. Palestrina (Giovanni Pierluigi, c. 1526–1594), one of the great masters of polyphony, was a prolific composer and a dominant influence even after his own lifetime. Palestrina's five-voice motet, *Quid habes Hester?* (1575), is based on the dialogue between Ahasuerus and his Jewish queen in the Apocryphal additions to the Book of Esther (15:9–14), while his setting of *Canite tuba in Syon* ("Blow ye the horn in Zion," Joel 2:1), written in 1590, met the demand for festive compositions providing "trumpet fanfare" imitations by the choir. Another typical Baroque practice was the arrangement of *Jerusalem, Jerusalem* . . . in the Book of Lamentations as a series of calls, preferably with echo effects. In the Papal Chancel, Palestrina's setting of Lamentations held sway between 1587 and 1641. The Baroque emphasis on notable scenes of repentance directed Catholic attention to some of the sadder passages in the Book of Job. Orlando di Lasso (Roland de Lassus, c. 1530–1594), a leading representative of the Franco-Belgian school, wrote two extended settings of passages from Job (1565; 1582), the first of which was an early musical best seller (a tenth edition appeared in 1587). A more joyful note appears in *Nigra sum* ("I am black") and *Pulchra es* ("Behold, thou art fair"), two chorales from the Song of Songs composed by Claudio Monteverdi (1567–1643), who revolutionized the musical idiom of his day and created Italian opera. Pietro Valentini's *Nodus Salomonis* ("Solomon's Knot," 1631) was a curiosity of musical technique: this canon for no less than 96 voices amounts to a kind of change-ringing on the G major chord.

After the 17th century, religious music lost its monopoly of Biblical themes, which gained new vitality in the sphere of secular composition. Bach, Handel, Verdi, Stravinsky, and other musical giants found contemporary or universal messages in those subjects which they drew from the Hebrew Bible and, from the motet and chorale, the scene shifted to the oratorio, cantata, opera, symphony, and even ballet. However, works on Biblical subjects are regularly commissioned from prominent composers by various Church bodies and organ and choral

---

[8] The status of much Biblical art music is complicated by the use of mixed texts (especially in the cantata), intermingling passages from the Hebrew Bible, the New Testament, and Church literature.

works are frequently written and performed. Coronations, state funerals, and other public events still call for a musical response, particularly in the English-speaking world, and this response often has a Scriptural inspiration. "O Music! miraculous art! . . . ," wrote Disraeli (in *Contarini Fleming*, 1832). "A blast of thy trumpet, and millions rush forward to die; a peal of thy organ, and uncounted nations sink down to pray." Despite the novelist's touch of irony, it remains true that many of the notes which the early Church borrowed from the Temple and the synagogue still echo in the chapel and concert hall of today.

BIBLICAL MOTIFS IN WESTERN SECULAR MUSIC

Although the main impact of Biblical song was felt in the sphere of liturgical music, countless works of a non-sacred character have also reflected this influence. Probably the oldest example in the West is *Daz Gedeones wollenvlius* ("Gideon's Woollen Fleece"), an allegorical song in Middle High German by the *Minnesänger* Rumelant (c. 1270), which combines a search for the Biblical prototypes of medieval chivalry with the mystical concept of Divine love. However, evidence of this musical current is far more abundant in 16th–19th-century compositions. The text of an anonymous French *chanson* entitled *Susanne un jour* ("One day Susanna," 1548) was reset by Orlando di Lasso, later used by Claude Le Jeune and others, and the melodic material eventually reworked by various composers as a piece for lute or keyboard instrument. The popularity which this *chanson* enjoyed is clear from William Byrd's English setting, *Susanna fayre sometime assaulted was*. Another English ballad on the same Apocryphal theme (for which Lasso may have provided the tune) began with the phrase: "There dwelt a man in Babylon"; Sir Toby Belch warbles the line in the "song scene" of Shakespeare's *Twelfth Night* (1600). Two Spanish polyphonic songs of the 17th century, *Siete años de pastor* ("Seven Years a Shepherd") and *Si por Rachel*, deal with the love of Jacob for Rachel. In France, Jean-Jacques Rousseau found time amid his philosophical writing to compose music, including a motet for solo voice and basso continuo on the Latin text of Lamentations (1772), while the first song which Schubert wrote was *Hagars Klage* ("Hagar's Lament," 1811). Lord Byron's *Hebrew Melodies* (1815) were originally requested by the Anglo-Jewish singer and composer Isaac Nathan (c. 1790–1864), who set them to a variety of airs (including a few traditional Jewish tunes). "On Jordan's Banks," one of the *Hebrew Melodies*, is the only authentic musical composition, being an arrangement of the Ḥanukkah hymn, *Ma'oz Ẓur*. "Jeph hah's Daughter," another of these poems by Byron, was set to music by Carl Loewe (1826) and Robert Schumann (in *Drei Gesänge*, Opus 95, 1849). Several "sacred ballads" and songs have been written by more recent composers such as Brahms, Mussorgsky, and Stravinsky. In terms of output and originality, however, the main importance of this genre lies in Jewish folk-song and the Negro spiritual.[9]

ORATORIO AND OPERA

Although they constitute two distinct musical genres, the oratorio and the opera possess certain common features, not least among which is the prominence of Biblical subjects in works of this type. The oratorio, which takes its name from the Oratory of S. Filippo Neri in Rome where musical performances of the type first took place (c. 1600), is a choral work (generally on a Scriptural theme) consisting in the main of arias, choruses, and recitatives with orchestral backing; while drama may be implicit in the text, there is neither action, costume, nor scenery throughout the performance. An opera, on the other hand, is a drama set to music and comprising vocal pieces (songs and recitatives) with costumes, scenery, and orchestral accompaniment; the orchestra usually plays an overture and interlude music between the acts, but (except in comic and light opera) there is no spoken dialogue. The first operas were also produced in early 17th-century Italy. A major precursor of the oratorio was *Ein Geystlich spiel von der Gottfürchtigen und keuschen Frawen Susannen* ("The Godly and Chaste Susanna," 1536), a musical school-play of the German Reformation by Paul Rebhun (c. 1505–1546), who was a close friend of Luther and Melanchthon. Luther encouraged the writing of Biblical drama and with Rebhun's *Susanna* music, too, was pressed into the service of Protestant ideology. During the next 200 years, however, oratorio composers largely hailed from Catholic Italy.[10]

---

[9] See the conclusion of this chapter.
[10] Censorship significantly delayed the production of Biblical oratorio in France (until the 18th century) and Russia (until 1917).

The pioneer of the oratorio seems to have been Giacomo Carissimi (1605–1674), whose *Jephte* (for six voices and organ) appeared in about 1648. He also wrote other oratorios about Hezekiah, Job, and Jonah and one with the Latin title *Judicium Salomonis* ("The Judgment of Solomon," 1669). Among Carissimi's successors were G. P. Colonna (*Mosè legato di Dio e liberatore del popolo ebreo*, 1686), Giovanni Battista Bononcini (*Il Giosuè*, 1688), and G. B. Bassani (*Giona*, 1689; *Ezechia*, 1737). Bassani's "Jonah" opens with an instrumental "Sea Symphony" and Bononcini's "Joshua" was the first of a series of oratorios (mostly about the fall of Jericho) which were evidently linked with contemporary political events, such as the victories of Prince Eugene of Savoy and the Duke of Marlborough over the French and of Charles of Lorraine over the Turks at Mohács (1687). Outweighing these were the compositions of Alessandro Scarlatti (1659–1725), who was one of the most talented and versatile musicians of the age. Scarlatti's Biblical oratorios include *Agar et Ismaele esiliati* ("Hagar and Ishmael in Exile," 1683), *La Giuditta vittoriosa* ("The Triumph of Judith," 1695), and *Il martirio di Santa Susanna* ("The Martyrdom of Susanna," 1706). The music which he wrote for *Samson vindicatus* ("The Vengeance of Samson," 1696) has been lost, but the score of *Cain, ovvero il primo omicidio* ("Cain, or the First Homicide," 1706), written in Scarlatti's own hand, was rediscovered in 1966. Alessandro Stradella's best-known oratorio, *Susanna* (1681), marks a significant departure from the pious, moralistic tradition that governed the treatment of this Apocryphal story, being noteworthy for its frivolity and eroticism. During the latter half of the 17th century, Italian composers became rather less predominant in the field of oratorio, although F. T. Richter's *L'incoronazione di Salomone* ("The Coronation of Solomon," 1696), which was premiered in Vienna, had an Italian and not a German text. Two early Biblical operas also came from the German-speaking milieu: J. A. Theile's *Der erschaffene, gefallene und wieder aufgerichtete Mensch* ("The Creation, Fall, and Restoration of Man," 1678) and *Von Jacobs doppelter Heyrath* ("Jacob's Double Marriage," 1700), a *Singspiel* (comic opera) by Johann Philipp Krieger.

The classic age of the oratorio dawned with the 18th century, when outstanding librettos by Apostolo Zeno and by the great poet and tragedian Pietro Metastasio (1698–1782) were set to music by leading composers. Marc-Antoine Charpentier (1634–1704), a pupil of Carissimi who became musical director at La Sainte-Chapelle in Paris, wrote a number of *histoires sacrées* (oratorios) including *Josué* (1700), *Judicium Salomonis* ("The Judgment of Solomon," 1702), and *Judith sive Bethulia liberata* ("Judith, or Bethulia Redeemed," c. 1702). The same theme inspired *Judith triumphans* (1716) by the celebrated Italian violinist and composer Antonio Vivaldi (c. 1680–1741), who also wrote an oratorio about Moses (1714), the music of which has been lost. The story of Judith had a great attraction for 18th-century musicians, particularly after the appearance of Metastasio's *Betulia liberata*, which was specially commissioned by the Emperor Charles VI of Austria. Apart from its intrinsic dramatic interest, the theme had obvious political overtones, since Austrians were inclined to regard the Empress Maria Theresa as a latter-day Judith defying the new Holofernes, Frederick the Great of Prussia! Georg Reutter's *Betulia liberata*, which had its premiere in Vienna in 1734, was the first of many musical settings for Metastasio's text. A year earlier, Reutter's *Il ritorno di Tobia* ("The Return of Tobias") had also been performed in the Austrian capital. Prominent among oratorio composers of the era was Antonio Caldara (1670–1736), who used librettos by Zeno for his works about Esther (1723), Tobias (1720), Jonathan (1728), Elijah (1729), and Isaiah (1729). His *Gioas, Re di Giuda* ("Joash, King of Judah," 1726), another setting of one of Zeno's texts, is an imitative sequel to Racine's classic French drama, *Athalie*. Apart from these oratorios, Caldara also wrote several operas on Biblical motifs.

Some of the minor 18th-century works in this genre have musical interest or are simply curiosities. Baldassare Galuppi's oratorio about Jael and Deborah, *Jahel* (first performed in Venice, 1747), featured an aria with mandolin accompaniment. Others of the same period treating the Jael theme were written in honor of Maria Theresa or women rulers of a like stamp. A few compositions are remembered not for their musical distinction, but because of their imitative or hybrid nature. Thus, *I trionfi di Giosuè* ("The Triumphs of Joshua," 1703), an "oratorio-pasticcio," was produced in Florence by more than ten separate composers, including Bononcini. Five years later, this record was beaten by *Sara in Egitto* ("Sarah in Egypt," 1708), a pastiche in which no less than 24 different hands have been detected. An achievement of another type was Johann Mattheson's *Der siegende Gideon* ("The Conquering Gideon," 1717), written for the celebration in Hamburg of Prince Eugene's great victory over the Turks at Belgrade. Mattheson's oratorio was begun, completed, and performed in the record time of 11 days.

HANDEL AND HIS SUCCESSORS

The composer who dominated the 18th-century scene was George Frederick Handel (1685–1759) who, though born in Germany, spent much of his life in England, where he established his international reputation from 1712 onward. Abandoning the Italianate operas of his early musical career, Handel turned to the oratorio and produced a series of choral works (mainly on Biblical subjects) that for sheer grandeur and melodic genius have never been rivaled. Early evidence of this musical creativity may be found in two compositions based on Racine's Biblical dramas (*Esther* and *Athalie*): *Haman and Mordecai* (1720) and *Athalia* (1733). The first of these, a masque staged at the Duke of Chandos' palace near Edgware, used a text written by John Arbuthnot and (probably also) by Alexander Pope. Reworked as a full oratorio entitled *Esther*, with additional text supplied by Samuel Humphreys, it had a triumphant reception at the King's Theatre in London twelve years later, in 1732. Humphreys also wrote the libretto for *Deborah* (1739), which with *Israel in Egypt* and *Saul* (also premiered in 1739) marks the beginning of Handel's "oratorio period." Both of the last two works used texts by Charles Jennens and were first performed at the King's Theatre. *Israel in Egypt*, one of Handel's major compositions and a masterpiece of its type, reaches a climax in its presentation of the Red Sea crossing and the "Song of Triumph," the chorus here symbolizing the Children of Israel. A different mood prevails in *Saul*, which is staged less frequently; since Handel's time, however, this oratorio has provided a standard musical accompaniment (the famous "Dead March in *Saul*") for the funerals of monarchs and other heads of state.

Although Christian elements are prominent in Handel's *Messiah* (premiered in Dublin, 1742; text by Jennens), this work contains many "Old Testament" passages. Here there are many textual links with the Book of Isaiah (beginning with "Comfort ye, comfort ye my people . . . ") in the first section and the contralto aria, "I know that my Redeemer liveth," is the most famous musical setting of Job 19:25, the opening words being engraved on a scroll held by the statue on Handel's grave in Westminster Abbey. The "Hallelujah Chorus" at the end of *Messiah*'s second part is renowned and it is often performed as a separate concert piece. Among the oratorios that followed were *Joseph and His Brethren* (text by James Miller) and *Samson* (text by

Newburgh Hamilton), both of which were first staged at Covent Garden in 1744, and the powerful *Belshazzar* (1745; libretto by Charles Jennens). Hamilton's text was based on the classic drama, *Samson Agonistes*, by John Milton. The genius of Handel was again displayed in *Judas Maccabaeus* (1747), which was written and performed to celebrate the Duke of Cumberland's historic victory over Charles Edward Stuart, the "Young Pretender," and his Scottish Jacobites at the battle of Culloden Moor (1746). For this work, the outstanding musical treatment of the Hasmonean saga, Thomas Morell wrote the libretto. Like *Israel in Egypt* and *Messiah*, *Judas Maccabaeus* is frequently performed; its most famous chorus, "*See, the conqu'ring hero comes*," has become an international favorite and, by an interesting process of inversion, it has entered the Israeli repertoire (with a Hebrew text) as a popular melody for the Ḥanukkah festival. Both *Joshua* (?1748) and *Alexander Balus* (1748), for which Morell also provided the librettos, similarly appealed to English patriotic sentiment, the second of these oratorios again touching on the Maccabean theme. *Solomon* and *Susanna* were premiered at Covent Garden in the following year (1749). Mendelssohn reworked *Solomon* in the 19th century, eliminating certain passages and adding a part for organ; the "Entry of the Queen of Sheba" which figures in this oratorio has become a standard concert piece. Handel's last work in the genre was *Jephtha*, performed at Covent Garden in 1752. Morell based his text on an Italian prototype, while the faltering notation in the musical score testifies to the composer's blindness during the last years of his life. *Nabal*, a work about King David for which Morell again wrote the libretto, appeared five years after Handel's death, in 1764; this was, however, no original composition, the music having been pilfered from various Handel oratorios.

With one exception, none of Handel's 18th-century successors wrote anything of lasting importance in the field. In England, Thomas Arne's *Judith* (1761) was notable only for the fact that it first brought female choristers onto the London stage, another oratorio of the period being Samuel Arnold's *The Cure of Saul* (1767). Scarcely more significent was *Betulia liberata* (1771; text by Metastasio), a work by Wolfgang Amadeus Mozart (1756–1791) which in no way compares with the operas of that great Austrian composer. The one exception was Joseph Haydn (1732–1809) who, though best known as the architect of the classical symphony, wrote two oratorios on Biblical themes. Haydn's *Il ritorno di Tobia* ("The Return of Tobias"), written in 1774–75 and revised and augmented in 1784, used a libretto by Giovanni Boccherini; both the overture and the entire work are still occasionally performed. But the composer's real claim to fame in this genre was his *Creation*, an undisputed masterpiece. The text, written by an obscure English librettist named Lidley, was originally intended for Handel, who died before the author could arrange for a musical setting. While on a visit to England in 1797, Haydn accepted this libretto and had it translated into German as *Die Schöpfung*; set to his music, it was privately performed in Vienna a year later and, after the public premiere there in 1799, *The Creation* became a worldwide success. This oratorio is also the outstanding musical work on the Genesis theme. It is interesting to recall that Haydn's Austrian national anthem, *Gott erhalte Franz den Kaiser* ("God Save our Emperor Francis," 1781)—the tune of which was later borrowed for Hoffmann von Fallersleben's *Deutschlandlied* ("Deutschland, Deutschland über alles")—was reworked in Hebrew and included by the Viennese cantor-composer Salomon Sulzer in his miscellany of airs for synagogal use (*Shir Ẓiyyon*, vol. 2, 1866)! With works by Purcell, Handel, Gluck, and Mozart, the opera had established itself in the musical field by the late 18th century, but as yet there were no major compositions of Biblical inspiration. Michel de Montéclair's *Jephté* (Paris, 1732) was the first opera on a subject drawn from the Bible that was licensed for performance on the French stage; two years later it was banned by Cardinal de Noailles. During the same period, Antonio Caldara wrote *Giuseppe* ("Joseph," 1722; text by A. Zeno) and a few other operas on Biblical themes (Daniel, Nebuchadnezzar) to match his oratorios.

Many leading composers of the 19th century devoted oratorio works to subjects from the Hebrew Bible, Moses and Saul being the most favored subjects. *La Mort d'Adam* ("The Death of Adam," 1809), based on Klopstock's German tragedy (*Der Tod Adams*), was written by Jean François Lesueur (1760–1837), who abandoned church music for French Revolutionary themes and spectacular operatic and choral works, later serving as court musician to Napoleon and Louis XVIII. Konradin Kreutzer's *Die Sendung Mosis* ("The Mission of Moses") followed in 1814.[11] Though better known for their operas, Gioacchino

---

[11] Kreutzer is perhaps best remembered for his comic opera, *Die Schlafmütze des Propheten Elias* (1814), which a meddlesome censor insisted on having retitled *Die Nachtmutze des Propheten Elias,* so "ennobling" the term used for Elijah's nightcap.

Antonio Rossini (1792–1868), Charles Gounod (1818–1893), and Camille Saint-Saëns (1835–1921) all wrote one Biblical oratorio apiece. Rossini composed *Saul* (1834), Gounod (a pupil of Lesueur) produced *Tobie* (c. 1866), while Saint-Saëns completed his musical version of the Noah story, *Le Déluge*, in 1876, premiering it at Boston, Mass., in 1880. Belgian by birth and French by adoption, César Franck (1822–1890) wrote *La Tour de Babel* (1865) and *Rebecca* (1881), the latter of which was reworked as a one-act "sacred opera" in 1918. Three Biblical oratorios were also written by the eminent English composer Sir Hubert (C.H.H.) Parry (1848–1918)—*Judith* (1888), *Job* (1892), and *Saul* (1894).

This "Age of Emancipation" was notable for the sudden appearan·e of many talented musicians who were Jews or of immediate Jewish origin. The Hebrew Bible naturally played an important seminal role in their choice of theme or melodic inspiration. Giacomo Meyerbeer (born Jakob Liebmann Beer, 1791–1864) made the earliest Jewish contribution to the oratorio genre with his *Jephtas Gelübde* ("Jephthah's Vow," 1813). The son of a Berlin pioneer of Reform Judaism, Meyerbeer enjoyed a great reputation as a composer in the 19th century, although he fell victim to the anti-Semitic attacks of Richard Wagner, whom he had once befriended. By 1840, the outstanding composer in Central Europe was Felix (Jakob Ludwig) Mendelssohn (1809–1847), a grandson of the eminent Jewish philosopher Moses Mendelssohn, but himself raised as a Lutheran. It is tempting to see in Mendelssohn's two great oratorios—*St. Paul (Paulus,* 1836) and *Elijah (Elias,* 1846)—a reflection of the two different religious traditions which the composer's birth and baptism represent. *Elijah*'s first performance at the Birmingham Festival in England was a triumph and this oratorio remains the one outstanding musical interpretation of the Hebrew prophet's character and career. It is also practically the only 19th-century work of the genre that is still regularly performed, especially in England, Germany (except during the Nazi period), and Israel.

Another converted Jew, the composer-conductor Ferdinand Hiller (1801–1885), wrote *Saul* (1853) and *Die Zerstörung Jerusalems* ("The Destruction of Jerusalem," 1840), the second of which is generally considered his best work. Hiller's Biblical interests also found expression in various settings of the Psalms.

Though baptized in his infancy, the Russian composer and pianist Anton Grigorevich Rubinstein (1829–1894) gave evidence of his Jewish background in several Biblical oratorios and operas, where the line dividing these two genres is not always clear. Rubinstein's compositions include *Das verlorene Paradies* ("Paradise Lost," 1855), the "scenic oratorios" *Der Turmbau zu Babel* ("The Tower of Babel," 1858) and *Sulamith* (1883), and *Moses* (1887). The first of these was based on Milton's *Paradise Lost*, while the other three display Jewish and Oriental elements in their melody and instrumental color. *Moses*, which was inspired by a German poem, reaches a dramatic climax with the giving of the Ten Commandments. Unsuccessful as an oratorio, Rubinstein's "Babel" was revised as an opera in 1872. Leopold Damrosch (1832–1885) and Marcus Hast (1840–1911) were more firmly rooted in Judaism. Damrosch, the head of an eminent musical family, established the Oratorio Society in New York (1873), where he composed *Ruth and Naomi* (1875) and *Sulamith* (1882). Hast was possibly the only Orthodox cantor-composer of the 19th century whose musical creativity ranged beyond the liturgical sphere. After leaving his native Poland, he served as ḥazzan at the Great Synagogue in Duke's Place (London) from 1871 and, apart from many works for the synagogue service, wrote *The Death of Moses* (1897) and other oratorios (*Bostanai, Azariah, The Destruction of Jerusalem*) in a skillful imitation of Handel.

VERDI AND THE GOLDEN AGE OF OPERA

The great age of the opera began in the early 19th century with the works of Beethoven and Rossini. However, the first composer of any distinction to deal with a Biblical theme was a Frenchman, Etienne Méhul (1763–1817), who is otherwise mainly remembered for his revolutionary *Chant du départ*. Méhul's best-known opera, *Joseph* (premiered in Paris, 1807), was set to a text by Alexandre Duval based largely on the Bible. The work, which employs only male vocalists, is still considered a classic. Rossini's *Mosè in Egitto* ("Moses in Egypt," 1818) was first produced in Naples with an Italian libretto by A. N. Tottola, but was later revised and enlarged in French as *Moïse* (Paris, 1827). This work has a "grand opera" plot and a most un-Biblical love story; it includes the famous "Prayer of Moses," a favorite subject for fantasias, variations, and arrangements throughout the later decades of the century. Among the operas that followed soon after were Samuele Levi's *Giuditta* (1844) and Luis Cepeda's Spanish *Jephté* (1845). Although the Apocryphal tale of Judith had long figured in oratorios, the censor obstinately banned its dramatic interpretation, and it was only toward the middle of the 19th century—by which time Biblical subjects were allowed on the stage and early Romantic "horror opera" had prepared audiences for the grisly sight of Holofernes' severed head—that Levi's *Giuditta* and its successors could begin regular production. Two later versions of the story, both entitled *Judith*, were Aleksandr Serov's highly successful presentation at St. Petersburg (1863) and an operatic fragment by Meyerbeer (1864).

Because of his choice of one particular subject from the Bible, Giuseppe Verdi (1813–1901) provides unusual interest and importance in the domain of opera. Closely identified with liberal, anti-clerical, and revolutionary ideals, he was frequently at odds with the censor before most of Italy was united under King Victor Emanuel of Piedmont in 1861. Political undercurrents run through several of Verdi's operas and, when the composer went to Naples in 1858, the slogan "*Viva Verdi!*" became a popular cheer with the hidden acrostic meaning, "*Viva Vittorio Emanuele Rè D'Italia!*" ("Long live Victor Emanuel King of Italy!"). Masked social and political comment has been widely detected in many of Verdi's works, notably *Rigoletto* (1851), *A Masked Ball* (1859), *Don Carlos* (1867), and even *Aida* (1871). In 1838, Verdi evidently saw the first performance of *Nabucodonosor* at La Scala, Milan, an opera marking the Emperor Ferdinand I's coronation as king of Lombardy and Venice. Inspired by the Biblical theme, Verdi subsequently acquired T. Solera's libretto of a similar title describing the enslavement of the Jews and their miseries in Babylonian exile. The chorus of the Hebrew captives, "*Va, pensiero, sull'ali dorate*" ("Fly, thought, on golden wings"), fired the composer's still dormant patriotism and the opera which he wrote under the shortened title, *Nabucco* (premiered at La Scala in 1842), created enormous enthusiasm throughout Italy. "With this opera my career as a composer may rightly be said to have begun," Verdi later wrote. In Act 3, Scene 2, Nebuchadnezzar has gone mad after having been struck by lightning for daring to proclaim himself a god and ordering the Jews to worship him. The king's daughter compels him to sign an edict for the massacre of the Jews and then has her father thrown into prison. On the banks of the Euphrates, the captives lament the destruction of the Temple and their exile, yearning for their lost homeland: "Oh inspire us with courage, Almighty God, that we may endure to the very last!" The Jews' prayer for deliverance ("*Va, pensiero . . .*") was seen as a barely concealed reference to Italy's state of subjugation to Austria or as the lament of Italian political exiles. The same interpretation, incidentally, was placed on the chorus of Scottish exiles in Verdi's opera, *Macbeth* (1847). *Nabucco* was principally meant for the Italy of Cavour and Garibaldi, but the composer's genius endowed it with a message and appeal far beyond the scope of its initial conception.[12]

Two other Biblical operas of some importance, both dealing with King Solomon and the Queen of Sheba, were written by Gounod and Karl Goldmark (1830–1915). *La Reine de Saba*, Gounod's four-act setting of a libretto after Gérard de Nerval, was first performed at the Paris Opera in 1862. Goldmark, the son of a Hungarian cantor, created an Oriental atmosphere in *Die Königin von Saba* (Vienna, 1875), which took him ten years to complete. In some of the motifs in this opera Jewish liturgical melodies have been traced. Goldmark's fine music and a first-rate libretto by S. H. Mosenthal ensured that the work ran successfully for many years. It was on a poem by Mosenthal that Anton Rubinstein fashioned his oratorio, *Moses*, and this Russian composer's earlier opera, *Die Makkabäer* ("The Maccabees," Berlin, 1875), used a text by the same writer for which Otto Ludwig's famous drama of the same title was the basic inspiration. Old Jewish melodies pervade Rubinstein's "Hasmonean" opera with its mingling of heroism and tragedy, and through later versions in Hebrew and Yiddish the work had profound repercussions among the Jews of Eastern Europe who were then subject to religious and political oppression. A pupil of Gounod and of the Jewish composer Jacques (François) Fromental Halévy,[13] Camille Saint-Saëns used a text by Fernand Lemaire for his most celebrated opera, *Samson et Dalila* (1877), which had its premiere in a German translation at Weimar. The "Bacchanale" section of this work is famous and Delilah's aria, "*Softly awakes my heart . . .*," has become a standby for every mezzo-soprano. With its spectacular and melodic qualities, *Samson and Delilah* has retained

---

[12] Biblical drama still being outlawed in Britain, *Nabucco* had to be restyled "*Nino*" and its characters disguised under other names for the opera's English premiere at Her Majesty's Theatre, London, in 1846.

[13] Because of their associations with Halévy, Saint-Saëns and Georges Bizet (Halévy's son-in-law) have been wrongly described as Jews; the same fallacy is current about Ravel.

its place in the operatic repertoire. By a strange chance, two separate productions were staged simultaneously for an Israel music festival in 1972.

The tremendous success which many of these operas enjoyed in the 19th century had some novel consequences. According to a contemporary report, a work entitled *Judith and Holofernes* was performed in 1861 by the imposingly named United Hebrew Opera Company, which was on tour in Boston, Mass. From the statement that this opera was "sung in German, with the program printed in Hebrew," it seems clear that Bostonians were treated neither to a German nor to a Hebrew production, but to one in Yiddish. On the other hand, parody was quite clearly the aim of two French works staged in Paris: Victor Roger's *Joséphine vendue par ses soeurs* ("Josephine sold by her Sisters," 1886) and Edmond Diel's operetta, *Madame Putiphar* (1897).

LATER WORKS

A very large number of oratorios and operas have been written by 20th-century composers, some of whom have distinguished themselves in both genres. Two oratorios produced in 1900 were by Frenchmen— Massenet's *La terre promise* ("The Promised Land"), about Moses and the Exodus, and Marcel Dupré's *La Vision de Jacob* (written at the age of 14). Enrico Bossi's *Il Paradiso perduto*, which was inspired by Milton's epic (*Paradise Lost*), appeared three years later in 1903. *Job*, an oratorio by Frederick Shepherd Converse, was one of the first American musical works presented in Europe, its premiere taking place in Hamburg (1908). Another *Job* (1932) was written by the Russian-born composer Nicolas (Nikolai) Nabokov, who used a text by Jacques Maritain based mainly on the Bible. More important than any of these were two works by Arthur Honegger (1892–1955) and Sir William Walton (1902–   ). Honegger's *King David* (*Le Roi David,* 1921), an anti-Romantic "dramatic psalm," is essentially an oratorio with spoken narration (text by R. Morax based on the Bible). Osbert Sitwell also used the Biblical source in his libretto for Walton's composition, *Belshazzar's Feast*, which was first performed at a music festival in Leeds (1931). Sometimes described as a cantata, this work for solo baritone, chorus, and orchestra is likewise best classified as an oratorio. Both *King David* and *Belshazzar's Feast* have entered the modern choral repertoire. The story of Jonah has particularly attracted musicians of the 20th century, inspiring oratorios by Lennox Berkeley (*Jonah*, 1935), the Russo-German composer Vladimir Vogel (*Jonah ging doch nach Ninive*, 1958), and others.

Some of the most interesting modern compositions in this genre are the work of Jews, notably Schoenberg, Milhaud, and Castelnuovo-Tedesco. Born in Austria, Arnold Schoenberg (1874–1951) made his name in Germany where, by 1923, he developed a revolutionary atonal (keyless) technique—the "twelve-tone" (or "twelve-note") system—which soon had worldwide influence. Ten years later, Schoenberg (or Schönberg, as he had hitherto spelled his name) was forced to leave Nazi Germany despite his early conversion to Roman Catholicism, and the effect of this was to revive his Jewish feeling and bring about his formal return to Judaism. *Die Jakobsleiter* ("Jacob's Ladder"), begun in 1913 but never completed, was the first work in which Schoenberg's original system of melodic manipulation clearly emerged, and it was typical of the composer that he wrote his own highly expressionistic text; variously described as an oratorio or a cantata, *Jacob's Ladder* was first performed in Vienna in 1961. Schoenberg's later works include an opera about Moses and a cycle of *Modern Psalms*, both of which were left unfinished at his death.

A native of Provence, Darius Milhaud (1892–   ) joined Honegger in the avant-garde "Group of Six" (*Les Six*), but later moved into more fruitful paths, exploring both Provençal folklore and traditional Jewish themes in his music. Milhaud's output includes a semi-Biblical opera, Psalms arranged for solo voices and orchestra, an elaborate *Service Sacré* for the Jewish Sabbath (1947), and various orchestral and vocal compositions on Jewish and Biblical motifs. Armand Lunel, a fellow Provençal, wrote the text for *David*, an oratorio in praise of the Hebrew king and musician, which the Israel authorities commissioned Milhaud to produce for the 3,000th anniversary of Jerusalem's establishment as the Davidic capital (1954). Biblical Israelites and modern Israelis figure in this colorful oratorio, which requires an unusually large vocal ensemble. Mario Castelnuovo-Tedesco (1895–1968) came of a traditional Italian-Jewish family and, after discovering some liturgical melodies written by his grandfather, began paying great attention to Biblical subjects from 1925. When Mussolini enforced the Nazi race laws against Italian Jewry, Castelnuovo-Tedesco moved to the U.S.A., where some of his best work was written. Apart from a Biblical opera, he composed the oratorios *Ruth* (1949), *Jonah* (1951), and *Naomi and Ruth* (1959), and a "scenic oratorio," *The Song of Songs*. This last theme also inspired a work by the modern Israeli composer Marc Lavry (*Shir ha-Shirim*), who also wrote a Biblical opera about Tamar. Other Jewish exponents of the Biblical oratorio include Hugo Chaim Adler (*Hiob*, 1933), Jacob Weinberg (*Isaiah,* 1947; *The Life of Moses*, 1955), Alexandre Tansman (*Isaïe le prophète*, 1951), and Franz Reizenstein (*Genesis,* 1958).

The output of operatic works on Biblical themes has also been considerable since the beginning of the 20th century. Eugène d'Albert's *Kain* (1900) and Felix Weingartner's *Kain und Abel* (1914) revived musical interest in a subject long ignored, as did the Egyptian-born Italian composer Vittorio Rieti with his *L'Arca di Noè* ("Noah's Ark," 1922). Carl Nielsen (1865–1931), generally reckoned Denmark's outstanding composer, wrote an oratorio-like opera, *Saul og David* (1902), the heroic theme of which also inspired Hermann Reutter's *Saul* (1928) and some more recent works. The Apocryphal story of Susanna has—in music as well as literature—come in for a good deal of irreverent treatment: liberties have often been taken with the details of this tale, which some composers have frankly parodied. Among modern operatic versions are Jean Gilbert's *Die keusche Susanne* ("The Modest Susanna," 1910), which was later made into an Argentine movie; Paul Hindemith's *Sancta Susanna* (1922); and Carlisle Floyd's *Susannah*, which had its premiere in New York in 1956. Some reflection of this theme's satirical interpretation may be seen in *Susanna's Secret* (*Il Segreto di Susanna*, 1909), a one-act comic opera by Ermanno Wolf-Ferrari, which makes its modern heroine a secret smoker!

A number of other 20th-century operas have also dealt with Biblical women. One rarity was Ildebrando Pizetti's *Dèbora e Jaele* (1922), for which the composer supplied his own text. The closest attention has, however, been paid to Judith, a perennial favorite, particularly between the two world wars. Leading the field was Emil von Resniček's *Holofernes* (1923), for which the composer again wrote his own libretto (based on Hebbel's drama, *Judith*); Resniček's overture, another arrangement of the *Kol Nidrei* melody, has also been performed as a separate concert piece. Operas entitled *Judith* were later written by Honegger (Monte Carlo, 1926), Eugene Goossens (London, 1929), and the Swedish composer Carl Natanael Berg (1935). Honegger's work developed from the music he originally wrote for a play by René Morax in 1925, while the libretto for Goossens' *Judith* was the work of Arnold Bennett.[14] In some of the more recent operas of this type the central figures are Biblical, rather than Apocryphal. Thus, the U.S. composer Randall Thompson used a story by Rudyard Kipling (*The Butterfly that Stamped*) for his *Solomon and Balkis* (1942), while Luigi Dallapiccola (an Italian practitioner of Schoenberg's "twelve-tone" system) wrote a "mystery play" entitled *Giobbe* ("Job") first performed in Rome in 1950. One of the later works of Sir Arthur Bliss (1891–   ), Master of the Queen's Music from 1953, was the opera *Tobias and the Angel* (1960), for which the text was supplied by Christopher Hassall.

Jewish composers have figured prominently among 20th-century exponents of the Biblical opera. Ernest Bloch's *Jézabel* (c. 1918) was never completed, but A. Z. Idelsohn, a leading musicologist, wrote the first Palestinian work in the genre, *Yiftaḥ* ("Jephthah," 1922), which was premiered in Jerusalem, and an unfinished opera about Elijah. The music in the first of these is an intriguing mixture of Jewish melodic traditions from both East and West, the product of Idelsohn's intensive ethno-musicological research. Darius Milhaud's *Esther de Carpentras* (1925; text by Armand Lunel) combines the composer's two favorite background elements (Provençal and Jewish folklore): here, the staging of an old Provençal Purim play is suddenly dramatized by a new and unforeseen development when a local bishop, intent on converting the Jews, unwittingly lends a menacing irony to their presentation of the Esther story. The son of a Rabbi, Mikhail Fabianovich Gnesin (1883–1957) studied under Rimsky-Korsakov and had a distinguished musical career in the U.S.S.R., where he taught at the Moscow and Leningrad conservatories. During his early "Jewish" period (ending in 1929), Gnesin visited Palestine (1921) and his impressions of the revived national life there inspired two opera-like compositions, one of which—*Makkavei* ("The Maccabeans," 1925)—is described as a "symphonic movement" for soloists, choir, and orchestra. Arnold Schoenberg's *Moses und Aron* ("Moses and Aaron") has a full libretto written by the composer, but the music (two acts completed in 1932; third act begun in 1951) was left unfinished at Schoenberg's death. A highly philosophical work, this musical drama expresses the triple conflict between the lawgiver, the wavering people, and the lawgiver's

---

[14] On the tendency of Bennett and several other modern writers to "debunk the Bible," see Chapter 4.

priestly brother (who acts as a glib mediator). Aaron fashions the golden
calf not merely in response to popular clamor, but also because he sees
in it a tangible symbol for worship, whence the clash with the invisible
God concept proclaimed by Moses. The first two acts, bereft of the
textual climax, were broadcast in concert form over Hamburg radio
in 1954 and the first stage production took place in Zurich three years
later. In the character of Aaron some have seen Schoenberg's view
of his critics, while others have made the figure a type of the conventional
modern composer.

Other recent works include Bernard Rogers' one-act opera, *The
Warrior* (1947; text by Norman Corwin), a treatment of the Samson
and Delilah romance premiered in New York; Castelnuovo-Tedesco's
Saul (1960); and Hugo Weisgall's *Athaliah* (1964), which used Jewish
liturgical motifs to enhance the "Biblical" atmosphere. In Israel,
Josef Tal (1910–   ) has achieved some distinction in the operatic field
with his concert opera, *Saul at Endor* (Ramat Gan, 1955), a "dramatic
cantata" for which the Biblical text served as libretto, and *Amnon
and Tamar* (1960; text by Recha Freier), which was first performed
as a concert piece in Jerusalem (1960). Tal has more recently achieved
international prominence with his opera, *Ashmedai*, which elaborates
the Talmudic legend according to which Satan (Asmodeus) once
temporarily assumed the identity of King Solomon—with dire consequences for the realm. This work, using a libretto by Israel Eliraz
and a score that includes electronic effects, had its premiere at the
Hamburg State Opera in 1971. Tal has developed an individual style
with a vocal emphasis deriving mainly from the Bible and from traditional
Jewish liturgy.

THE CANTATA AND OTHER CHORAL MUSIC

In modern terminology, a cantata is an extended choral work with or
without solo voices, and usually with orchestral accompaniment.
As we have seen, one and the same work is often described as a cantata,
an oratorio, or even a concert-opera, according to its presentation or
the whim of the music critic. Allied to these is the motet, originally
a type of choral work fostered by the Roman Catholic Church, which
developed into the anthem of the Anglican communion and even into
a "serious," but non-ecclesiastical form. However, all types of choral
music outside the scope of the oratorio will be considered under the

one heading. Among the earliest examples are Monteverdi's *Audi coelum* ("Give ear, ye heavens," 1610), based on the Second Song of Moses (Deut. 32), and *Fili mi Absalom* (David's lament for Absalom, 2 Sam. 19:1), a motet for bass solo and trombone quartet by Heinrich Schütz (in *Symphoniae Sacrae*, 1629). The Biblical motif became especially prominent in the 18th century, beginning with Bononcini's anthem for the funeral of the Duke of Marlborough, *When Saul was King over Israel* (1722). Johann Sebastian Bach (1685–1750) wrote almost 300 cantatas for solo voice(s) and orchestral accompaniment, but without choir: among these are his Cantata No. 46, *Schauet doch und sehet* ("Behold, and see . . . ," 1723–27), based on Lam. 1:12–13, and Cantata No. 160, *Ich weiss, dass mein Erlöser lebet* ("I know that my Redeemer liveth," Job 19:25), the authenticity of which is sometimes doubted. Handel's famous musical description of Solomon's enthronement, *Zadok the Priest*, was the first of a set of anthems especially composed for King George III in 1727, and it is still sung by a choir at the coronation of British monarchs in Westminster Abbey. Two later choral works of the 18th century were William Boyce's *Solomon, a Serenata . . . taken from the Canticles* (1743), with dialogues between King Solomon ("He"), the Shulammite ("She"), and the choirs, and Mozart's cantata, *Davidde penitente* ("The Penitent David," 1785), the music for which was mainly drawn from Mozart's own *Mass in C Minor*. The text which the composer set was probably written by Lorenzo da Ponte (1749–1838), a converted Italian Jew whose Casanova-like adventures tend to obscure a genuine talent in the libretto sphere (*Le nozze di Figaro*, 1786; *Don Giovanni*, 1787; *Cosi fan tutte*, 1790).

The art of the Jewish cantor made a deep impression on Franz Schubert (1797–1828), who was moved by Salomon Sulzer's rendering of the former's song, *The Wanderer* (1816), and composed a setting of one of the Psalms as a token of his gratitude to the Viennese cantor.[15] *Miriams Siegesgesang* ("Miriam's Song of Triumph"), which appeared in the year of Schubert's death (Opus 136, 1828; text by Franz Grillparzer), was written for soprano solo, mixed choir, and piano. The Book of Exodus also inspired Carl Gottfried Loewe's *Die eherne Schlange* ("The Brazen Serpent," 1834), a cantata for male choir, and Saint-Saëns' *Moïse sauvé des eaux* ("Moses Rescued from the Waters," 1851), the text of which was written by Victor Hugo. A later choral

[15] See above.

work by Saint-Saëns, arranged for eight male voices, is *Les soldats de Gédéon* ("The soldiers of Gideon," 1868). Samuel David (1836–1895), who served as musical director of the Paris synagogues, wrote two Biblical operas (*Absalon* and *I Macabei*), liturgical works, and a number of cantatas, foremost among which was his *Jephté* (1858), which gained the Prix de Rome of the Paris Conservatoire. Two much more famous French composers who also wrote Biblical cantatas were Emmanuel Chabrier (*La Sulamite*) and Georges Bizet (1838–1875), whose *L'Ange et Tobie* ("The Angel and Tobias," 1887; text by Léon Halévy) was never completed. *La Vision de Saül* (1896), a cantata, was the youthful work of the eminent Rumanian-born violinist and composer Georges Enesco (originally George Enescu, 1881–1955), whose pupils included Yehudi Menuhin. By contrast, Franz (Ferencz) Liszt (1811–1886) wrote his *Ossa arida* ("The Valley of Dry Bones") for choir and organ rather late in life (1879).

One of the most interesting of these 19th-century figures was the Russian composer Modest Petrovich Mussorgsky (or Moussorgsky; 1839–1881), a number of whose works were misleadingly "corrected" by Rimsky-Korsakov shortly after his death. Scarcely any other Russian musician who was not of Jewish origin showed as much regard for the Bible and it is perhaps significant that Mussorgsky, who expressed unusual sympathy for "the people," included a Jewish musical canvas among the ten described in his piano work, *Pictures at an Exhibition* (*Kartinki s vystavki*, 1874). One of his songs with piano, *King Saul*, was arranged for orchestral accompaniment by Glazunov and later, and more elaborately (for tenor or alto, mixed choir, piano or orchestra, trumpet, and side drum), by Lazare Saminsky (1929). The history of Mussorgsky's *Iysus Navin* ("Joshua, Son of Nun," c. 1864), practically the sole work of importance about Joshua in 19th-century music, is even more intriguing. This composition for baritone, alto, mixed choir, and piano was apparently based on melodies which Mussorgsky heard sung by Jewish neighbors in St. Petersburg. Some of the material was first used by the composer for the "Chorus of the Libyan Warriors" in *Salammbô*, an opera based on Flaubert's French novel which Mussorgsky never found time to complete. The music was eventually reworked as a choral scene on the battle of Gibeon (Josh. 10), the composer writing his own text after the Biblical source material. Two years after Mussorgsky's death, *Iysus Navin* was issued and performed by Rimsky-Korsakov, who rearranged the piano accompaniment for orchestra.

The opening choral theme, *"Thus saith the Lord of Hosts,"* is engraved on Mussorgsky's tombstone.

Choral works of the 20th century on Biblical themes present an even richer and more variegated panorama. The Hungarian composer Zoltán Kodály (1882–1967) produced a work of vast national significance (and greatly enhanced his own reputation) with *Psalmus Hungaricus* ("Hungarian Psalm," 1923), an opus for tenor, chorus, and orchestra based on a 16th-century Calvinist translation of Ps. 55 that has poignant associations for the Magyars. Farther West, a common subject inspired the English composer Granville Bantock's *Seven Burdens of Isaiah* for men's choir (1927) and *The Prophecy of Isaiah*, a cantata by Bohuslav Martinů (1890–1959), which was first performed in Jerusalem in 1963. The same was true of Natanael Berg with his chorale, *Das Hohelied* ("The Song of Songs"), and the U.S. composer Virgil Thomson (1896–   ) with his *Five Phrases from the Song of Solomon* for soprano and percussion.

The Hebrew Bible clearly fascinated Igor Stravinsky (1882–1971), a pupil of Rimsky-Korsakov, who left Russia in 1914 to settle first in Paris and later (from 1939) in the U.S.A. Several of this composer's major works are choral arrangements of Biblical texts. Stravinsky's *Symphony of Psalms* for chorus and orchestra (1930) is divided into three movements and uses the Latin wording of the Psalter; it was "composed to the glory of God, and dedicated to the Boston Symphony Orchestra." *Babel*, a cantata for narrator, male chorus, and orchestra, was written in 1944 and first published in 1952. In Hebrew, the Book of Lamentations is known as *Eikhah* ("How"), after the word that prefaces three of its four acrostic chapters; it is, however, popularly called *Sefer ha-Kinot* ("The Book of Lamentations," from the word *kinah* meaning "lament, dirge, elegy"). Since *Eikhah* was obviously meaningless in translation, equivalents for the alternative Hebrew title were found in Greek (*thrēni*) and Latin (*lamentationes*). Stravinsky thus called his (Latin) setting of part of the Biblical book *Threni, id est Lamentationes Jeremiae Prophetae*, and this work for soloists, choir, and orchestra had its premiere in 1958. Two old English Miracle Plays provided Stravinsky with the text on which he based another composition, *The Flood*, a "musical play" for singers, speakers, and orchestra which was first produced on American television in 1962. Stravinsky's most adventurous Biblical experiment was a "sacred ballad" about Abraham and his son written for baritone and chamber orchestra; his *Akedat Yizhak* ("The Binding of Isaac") has a text in Hebrew and was premiered in Jerusalem in 1964.

Technical experimentation characterizes the works of Karlheinz Stockhausen (1928–   ) who, using the "twelve-note" system as his point of departure, has widely exploited the "advanced" music produced electronically under laboratory conditions—a technique mainly pioneered in Germany during the 1950s. Thus Stockhausen's *Gesang der Drei Jünglinge* (the Apocryphal "Song of the Three Holy Children," 1956) dissolves and reconstitutes human speech by means of such electronic effects. More conventional works have been written by the English composers Ralph Vaughan Williams (1872–1958) and Benjamin Britten (1913–   ). One of two byproducts of Vaughan Williams' "Job" ballet (1931) was *The Voice out of the Whirlwind* for choir and organ, while Britten wrote *Noye's Fludde* (i.e., "Noah's Flood," 1958), a kind of operatic cantata for church performance based on the Chester Miracle Play, and *The Burning Fiery Furnace* (1966), a "parable" also intended for presentation in churches.

Once again, a significantly high proportion of 20th-century music in this genre has been produced by Jewish composers, some of world rank. In the U.S.A., Louis Gruenberg (1884–1964) pioneered the use of Negro elements (jazz and the spiritual) in serious music, notably in his setting of Vachel Lindsay's *The Daniel Jazz* for tenor and eight instruments (1923). Melodic elements from the Negro spiritual were also introduced in *The Creation* (1924). Another American musician, the cantor-composer Hugo Chaim Adler (1894–1955), began his career as a boy chorister in Hamburg under the celebrated *hazzan* Josef Rosenblatt. Adler wrote several Biblical cantatas in Germany —*Licht und Volk* ("Bearers of Light," 1931) about the Maccabean heroes, *Balak und Bileam* (1934), and *Akedah* ("The Binding of Isaac"), the last of which was denied performance following the notorious anti-Jewish *Kristallnacht* action by the Nazis (1938). Resuming his musical career in the U.S.A., Adler wrote *Jonah* (1943) and other cantatas on allied themes. Lazare Saminsky (1882–1959) became choirmaster at Temple Emanu-El in New York and composed fine settings of Psalms 102 and 137. He also wrote two choral works, *By the Rivers of Babylon* and *The Lament of Rachel*, and *The Daughter of Jephtha* (1937), a "cantata pantomime" for solo, choir, orchestra, and dancers. Apart from his Biblical opera, *The Warrior*, Bernard Rogers (1893–   ) composed two cantatas, *The Exodus* (1932) and *The Prophet Isaiah*

(1954), the latter theme also inspiring Robert Starer's *Ariel, Visions of Isaiah* (1959). David Diamond's *Young Joseph* (1947), for three-part women's chorus and string orchestra, was based on the novel by Thomas Mann. The works of another liturgical musician, Herbert Fromm (1905–), include *Song of Miriam* (1945), for women's choir and organ or piano, *Psalm Cantata* (1963), for mixed voices, organ, trumpet, viola, flute, and timpani, and various choral works for American Reform temples. A cantor-composer by the age of 18, Zavel Zilberts (1881–1949) worked in a more traditional milieu, composing liturgical music (notably his famous *Havdalah* setting) for Orthodox and Conservative synagogues. Zilberts wrote two Biblical cantatas, *Jacob's Dream* and *Am Yisra'el Hai!* ("Israel Lives!"). Preeminent among these American composers is Leonard Bernstein (1918–), best known for his successful Broadway and Hollywood musicals (e.g., *West Side Story*, 1957). Bernstein's first symphony, premiered in 1944, is the *"Jeremiah" Symphony*, which has an arrangement for mezzo-soprano solo in the last movement ("Lamentation") using a Hebrew text from the Book of Jeremiah. The use of a woman's voice in this elegy for Jerusalem is highly unconventional. Bernstein's *Symphony No. 3* is an interpretation of the *Kaddish* prayer. His *Chichester Psalms* for choir and orchestra (1965), written for Chichester Cathedral in England, created musical history because of the composer's stipulation that the text (based on Ps. 108, 100, 23, 131, 2, and 133) be sung only in Hebrew.

Outside the United States, modern Jewish choral music has also recorded some important achievements—in Europe and, especially, in Israel. Samuel Alman (1877–1947) studied at the Royal College of Music and later wrote works for Orthodox congregations in the East European style. However, Alman also made his name in the secular sphere with a Biblical opera, *Melekh Ahaz* ("King Ahaz," 1912), Psalm 15 for chorus and organ (1915), Psalm 133 for chorus and piano (1934), and various compositions for string instrument, notably *Ebraica* (1932). More recent contributions have been made by the pianist and composer Shula Doniach (1905–) with her settings of Hebrew texts, including *Voices of Jerusalem* for two soloists and chamber ensemble; and by Dudley Cohen (1932–), a former Royal Air Force bandmaster, who established the Zemel Choir (one of the leading mixed-voice chorales in Britain) and set various Biblical texts, notably *Ashrei* ("Happy are They," from Ps. 84, 144, 145) for men's voices in plainsong and women's in harmony. Under Cohen's direction, the Zemel Choir provided the choral background to *The Living Bible*, a series of LP records with readings by Sir Laurence (now Lord) Olivier. In France, the outstanding composer in this genre was Darius Milhaud, whose *Les deux Cités* ("The Two Cities," 1937), a cantata about Babylon and Jerusalem for augmented children's chorus and orchestra, used a text by Paul Claudel. Two later works by this composer were *Les Miracles de la foi* ("Miracles of the Faith," 1951), a cantata for tenor, chorus, and orchestra based on passages from the Book of Daniel, and *Invocation à l'ange Raphaël* (1965; text by Claudel), a choral piece for women's voices and orchestra, the theme of which was drawn from the Apocryphal Book of Tobit.

The immigrant musicians who arrived in Palestine before World War II inevitably imported the traditions of Europe in which they had been educated. Their sudden encounter with new cultures and conditions led, among other things, to experimentation with local folk material and to the emergence (before the State of Israel came into existence in 1948) of a nationalist sentiment which found expression in Biblical and Jewish historical motifs. This often naïve, "Mediterranean" style changed during the 1950s, when a freer cultural atmosphere began to prevail, but subjects drawn from the Hebrew Bible naturally continue to attract Israeli composers. One of the first to establish himself in Palestine was Erich-Walter Sternberg (1898–), who immigrated from Berlin in 1932. Most of Sternberg's compositions are of Biblical inspiration, including *David and Goliath*, a cantata for bass-baritone and chamber orchestra set to the Hebrew version of an 18th-century German text by Matthias Claudius. Another pioneer, Paul Ben-Haim (1897–), wrote several choral works, notably *Liturgical Cantata* (1950), *Three Psalms* (1952), and *Vision of a Prophet* (1959). Ben-Haim's characteristic lyricism gives way to drama in *Hymn from the Desert* (1962), a cantata based on a text in one of the Dead Sea Scrolls. Josef Tal who, like Paul Ben-Haim, is well-known outside Israel, has written a *Succoth Cantata* for the festival of Tabernacles (*Sukkot*); new techniques preoccupied him during and after the 1950s, as may be gauged from his *Exodus* chorale which exists in two versions, one instrumental and the other electronic.

Some Biblical works by the younger generation of Israeli composers are the cantata, *Jerusalem Eternal* (1967–68), of Haim Alexander (1915–) and *The Story of the Spies* (1953), a treatment of the Joshua theme by Ben-Zion Orgad (1926–), who used Biblical cantillation as a basis for his composition, a cantata for chorus and orchestra. Several choral settings of the Song of Songs have been written for the introductory portions of the Passover *Seder* recited in Israeli kibbutzim. The Song of Songs is chanted in the synagogue on Passover and secular "kibbutzniks" link the reading of this Biblical book with the celebration of Spring. While still a member of Kibbutz Yagur, Yehudah Sharett (1901–), a brother of the late prime minister of Israel (Moshe Sharett), composed a special "modernized" ritual (*Seder Pesaḥ Nusaḥ Yagur*, 1951) blending traditional text and melody with original elements; this has since become the Passover *Haggadah* most used in Israel's non-religious kibbutzim.

ORCHESTRAL WORKS

Since the year 70 C.E., the Hebrew genius for music has almost invariably found expression in the human voice rather than through instrumental media. Renaissance innovators, modern Jewish Reformers, and secular composers have all to varying degrees made use of instrumental accompaniment, but Israel's musical tradition remains essentially vocal and the accents of the Bible are more faithfully conveyed by the soloist or choir than by any orchestra. Nor, in this context, can the organ or violin replace man's own unaided singing. For 1,900 years, Jews have chanted the Pentateuch and Prophets and sung their liturgy with or without a cantor and choir, while Christians have used plainchant for their Mass and sung their hymns, with or without a choir and organ. In the realm of secular music, Biblical themes have again found more response in the spheres of oratorio, opera, and cantata than in instrumental and orchestral works. The few obvious exceptions only prove the rule. The *Miserere*, a setting of Psalm 50 in the Vulgate (Ps. 51 among Jews and Protestants), often occurs in Roman Catholic music. The version by Gregorio Allegri (1582–1652) was written down by Mozart and its best-known appearance in a secular work is the incorporation of a setting into the fourth act of Verdi's opera, *Il Trovatore* (1853). The only surviving relic of instrumental music in the Temple is the ram's horn or *shofar*, which is still blown ceremonially on the Jewish New Year festival. The sound of the *shofar* once heralded the advent of the Jubilee year and the blast of the ram's horn occasionally dramatizes events of historic importance in the Jewish world even today. Here, once again, an echo may be heard in a Christian milieu: the *shofar*'s peculiar associations inspired an instrumental simulation in Edward Elgar's oratorio, *The Apostles* (1903).

It is not surprising, therefore, that few composers devoted non-vocal works to Biblical motifs before the 20th century, while even the more recent instrumental or orchestral compositions mainly derive from liturgical sources. Perhaps the earliest interpreter of the Bible in this genre was the German composer and organist Johann Kuhnau (1660–1722), Bach's immediate predecessor as Cantor (director of music) at St. Thomas' Church in Leipzig. A Hebraist and scholar as well as a musician, Kuhnau wrote a series of Biblical sonatas (*Biblische Sonaten*, 1700), descriptive pieces for harpsichord which include *Der von David mittelst der Musik curierte Saul* ("Saul cured by David's Music," No. 2), *Jacobs Heyrath* ("The Marriage of Jacob," No. 3), *Der todtkranke und wieder gesunde Hiskias* ("Hezekiah Sick unto Death, then Made Whole," No. 4), and *Gideon—Der Heyland Israels* ("Gideon—Israel's Savior," No. 5). Later in the century, Haydn composed his *Symphony No. 26 in D Minor* (c. 1765), popularly known as the *"Lamentation" Symphony*: this nickname originates in the fact that Haydn's work contains certain themes that resemble plainchant settings of the Book of Lamentations which are sung in Roman Catholic churches during the week before Easter. A few more examples of this kind of melodic influence can be cited from music of the 19th century. In the third (and last) movement of his *"Reformation" Symphony* (Opus 5; written 1830, but published only in 1868), Mendelssohn included a powerful development of Luther's famous hymn, *Ein' feste Burg ist unser Gott* ("A safe stronghold our God is still . . . ;" cf. Ps. 46:2), also quoting the *"Dresden Amen"* of the Catholic Church in the first movement. Johannes Brahms (1833–1897) composed *Ein deutsches Requiem* ("A German Requiem," 1869) which, though written for soloists and chorus as well as for orchestra, may be mentioned here. The Requiem is, of course, the Roman Catholic Mass for the dead and takes its name from the initial Latin word meaning "repose." In the Catholic Church Requiem Mass is sung in plainchant, but various composers have written settings that are more appropriate for the concert hall than for the chapel (e.g., those of Berlioz, 1836–37; Verdi, 1873). Brahms, a Protestant, called his work a "German" Requiem because it was Lutheran and not Catholic, textually German and not Latin, and based on Biblical passages translated by the great Reformer. Instrumental adaptation of motifs from the Hebrew Bible were largely confined to the German-speaking milieu during the 19th century. Another composer who worked in this genre, Robert Schumann (1810–1856), expressed his dislike for the musical philistinism that surrounded him in the *Davidsbündler-Tänze* ("League of David Dances," 1834–37; revised 1850), piano works inspired by the composer's invention of a league founded by King David in opposition to the Philistine conception of art.

The introduction of choral sections into works of an orchestral nature has sometimes recurred in 20th-century compositions. Apart from Stravinsky (*Symphony of Psalms*) and Leonard Bernstein (*"Jeremiah" Symphony*), Vaughan Williams also provides an instance of this technique in his *Flos Campi* ("Rose of Sharon," literally "Flower of the Field," 1925), a suite for viola, small orchestra, and wordless chorus based on the Song of Songs. On the other hand, vocal elements are absent from *Belshazzar's Feast* (1906), a suite which the Finnish composer Jean Sibelius (1865–1957) drew from his incidental music to Hjalmar Procopé's drama, *Belsazars gästabud* (1905).

The vast majority of these modern interpretations of Biblical-Hebraic themes for instrument or orchestra have been written by Jewish composers. Foremost among them is Ernest Bloch (1880–1959) who, though born in Switzerland, spent much of his life in the United States. Generally regarded as the first important musician of the modern age who proclaimed his deep attachment to Judaism, Bloch is known to have composed the outline of an "Oriental Symphony" while still a boy and into this he wove Jewish liturgical melodies with which he was already familiar. Among his earliest published works are the *"Israel" Symphony* for five soloists and orchestra (1912–16) and *Trois Poèmes Juifs* (1913), both of which were immediate successes in New York. The *"Israel" Symphony*, originally conceived under the title, *"Fêtes juives,"* has musical associations with the major festivals of the Jewish calendar. In later years, Bloch declared that in his "Jewish" compositions he had "but listened to an inner voice, deep, secret, insistent, ardent . . . a voice which surged up within me on reading certain passages in the Bible." *Shelomo* ("Solomon," often spelled *"Schelomo"* in the German fashion), a "Hebrew rhapsody" for cello and orchestra written in 1916 and first performed a year later, has become a popular piece among soloists. The work was inspired by a figurine of King Solomon sculpted by the wife of a cellist, Alexander Barjanski. At the premiere of *Shelomo*, Barjanski played the solo instrumental part and Bloch himself was the conductor. Bloch was generally less indebted to Jewish liturgical "modes" than to his own musical intuition. He once wrote that it was "the Hebrew spirit that interests me—the complex, ardent, agitated soul that vibrates for me in the Bible; the vigor and ingenuousness of the Patriarchs, the violence that finds expression in the books of the Prophets, the burning love of justice, the desperation of the preachers of Jerusalem, the sorrow and grandeur of the Book of Job, the sensuality of the Song of Songs . . . This it is which I seek to feel within me and to translate in my music."

A similar development may be seen in Darius Milhaud. His *Opus Americanum 2* was originally composed as a ballet, *The Man of Midian*, but not produced; subsequently it reappeared as an orchestral suite and was performed in 1940. A parallel to the story of Bloch's *Shelomo* may be found in Milhaud's *Les Rêves de Jacob* ("Jacob's Dreams," Opus 294), a suite for five instruments composed in 1949 for a dance festival held in the Massachusetts village of Jacob's Pillow. On the occasion of Milhaud's first visit to Israel in April 1952, his descriptive piece for solo piano entitled *The Seven-Branched Candelabrum* was first performed by Frank Pelleg at the Ein Gev Festival held at a kibbutz by the shores of Lake Kinneret (or Tiberias). This work, composed in Paris in 1951, is a cyclic interpretation of the seven festivals of the Jewish year, beginning solemnly with "The New Year" (*Rosh ha-Shanah*) and "The Day of Atonement" (*Yom Kippur*) and then assuming a more joyful note with "Tabernacles" (*Sukkot*), "The Maccabeans" (*Ḥanukkah*), "The Feast of Queen Esther" (*Purim*), "Passover" (*Pesaḥ*), and "The Feast of Weeks" (*Shavu'ot*). *Le Candelabre a sept branches*, as this piano suite is generally known, has no significant counterpart in the musical sphere. Mario Castelnuovo-Tedesco is just as firmly rooted in the Jewish tradition and, like Ernest Bloch, he deliberately set out to create music of a Hebraic type. *La Danza del Rè David* ("King David's Dance," 1925), his rhapsody for piano, was followed by liturgical compositions and *The Prophets* (1931), a violin concerto written specially for Jascha Heifetz, which uses traditional Jewish melodies in its portrayal of Elijah, Isaiah, and Jeremiah.

Lazare Saminsky's symphony, *Jerusalem, City of Solomon and Christ* (1930), heralded several modern American works on Biblical motifs. Abraham Wolf Binder (1895–1960) helped to turn the musical tide in Reform temples when he reintroduced the traditional Torah chanting into the services at the Stephen Wise Free Synagogue in New York, where he was musical director from 1922. Binder, who subsequently founded the School of Sacred Music at Hebrew Union College, wrote nine cantatas and oratorios (including *Amos on Times Square*) and a symphonic work, *The Valley of Dry Bones* (1935). A self-taught musician, Ernst Toch (1887–1967) composed operas, a Passover oratorio entitled *Cantata of the Bitter Herbs* (1926), and *Jephta* (1963), a "rhapsodic poem" for orchestra, as well as many scores for Hollywood movies. Like Toch, Karol Rathaus (1895–1954) trained in Vienna, but made his reputation in the U.S.A., where he wrote music for the stage and screen. His compositions include a setting of the 23rd Psalm and orchestral music for the Habimah Theater production of *Jacob's Dream* (1941) by Richard Beer-Hofmann. Aaron Copland (1900–), a strong individualist, shocked staid Boston concertgoers with the aggressive jazz idiom of his early works. His compositions include *In the Beginning—the Seven Days of Creation* (1947). The impact of the Bible is particularly noticeable in the compositions of Moses Pergament (1893–) and Jan Meyerowitz (1913–). A leading Swedish music critic, Pergament has consistently employed motifs stemming from Biblical cantillation and Jewish folklore. His *Rapsodia ebraica* for orchestra (1935) and radio opera, *Eli* (1959), are representative of these preoccupations. Meyerowitz, a German-born U.S. composer who studied under Respighi, has written an oratorio-like opera about Esther (1957), a cantata entitled *Missa Rachel Plorans* ("Rachel Weeps"), and a symphony subtitled *Midrash Esther* (alluding to Jewish homiletical interpretation of Scripture).

Biblical and liturgical subjects have also played some part in the instrumental and orchestral composition of modern Israel. Erich-Walter Sternberg wrote *Joseph and His Brethren* (1938), a suite for string orchestra, *The Twelve Tribes of Israel* (1942), orchestral variations, and a symphony entitled *Noah's Ark*. Oriental melodic elements are interwoven with modern national rhythms in the music of Menahem Avidom (1908–), whose *"David" Symphony* (1947–48) is one of nine works he has written in this genre. Paul Ben-Haim's symphonic movement, *Sweet Psalmist of Israel*, won the Israel Prize in 1957. Of the younger generation of composers, Yeheskiel Braun (1922–) has written *Psalm for Strings* (1960) and *Illuminations to the Book of Ruth* (1966), another orchestral composition. No'am Sheriff (1935–), a native of Tel Aviv, is one of the most talented young Israeli musicians, his versatility extending to composition, orchestration, and conducting. His works include *Song of Degrees* (1959) and *Ashrei* ("Happy are they . . . ," 1961; cf. Ps. 84:5, 144:15) for alto, flute, two harps, and—two tom-toms.

BALLET

Biblical subjects are a 20th-century development in ballet. One pioneer was the German composer Richard Strauss (1864–1949), who used a libretto by Hugo von Hofmannsthal as the basis for *Die Josephslegende* ("The Legend of Joseph," 1914). After World War I, Ottorino Respighi (*Belkis, Regina di Saba*, 1923), Vittorio Rieti (*David Triomphant*, 1926), and Werner Josten (*Joseph and His Brethren*, 1936) all wrote music for ballet productions on Scriptural themes. Josten's "Joseph" was premiered in New York and later transformed into a symphonic suite (1939). More interesting than any of these is Ralph Vaughan Williams' *Job*, "a masque for dancing" composed for the Ballet Rambert, which was produced in London in 1931. The décor and the movements of the dancers follow Blake's original *Inventions to the Book of Job* (1826). The Swiss composer Arthur Honegger wrote the music for a ballet inspired by the Song of Songs (*Le Cantique des Cantiques*), while Marc Blitzstein (1905–1964), a pupil of Schoenberg noted for his works on radical themes, composed the music for *Cain* (1930). Despite its title, Darius Milhaud's *La Création du Monde* ("The Creation of the World," 1923) owes more to African mythology than it does to the Bible. The music for this ballet, first produced in Paris, is scored for 17 solo instruments in a jazz idiom.

Both from the musical and the choreographic viewpoint, ballet devoted to subjects drawn from the Bible owes its resuscitation in Israel to the efforts of three women and the interest of one leading composer. Rina Nikova (1898–1972), who was born and trained in Russia, made a vital contribution to Israeli ballet through her work as a dancer and choreographer. Bible themes were her speciality and she established a group known as the Jerusalem Biblical Ballet in 1949. In the same year, Sarah Levi-Tannai (1911–) founded the Inbal Dance Theater in Tel Aviv, she herself becoming the artistic director. The Inbal troupe has synthesized its basic Yemenite tradition with Ḥasidic folklore and Israeli shepherd dances, gaining an international reputation through its performances. Inbal's repertoire includes *The Boy Samuel*, *Deborah*, *Ruth*, and *The Queen of Sheba*. A third group, the Batsheva Dance Company, was founded by Baroness Bethsabée (Batsheva) de Rothschild in 1964

"A Psalm of David" performed by the Inbal Dance Theater, Israel.

and named in her honor. Biblical subjects figure prominently in the productions of this company. An important musical contribution has been made by the composer Mordechai Seter with works such as *Yehudit* ("Judith," 1963), a ballet written for the American dancer Martha Graham, who became Batsheva's first professional adviser, and *Bat Yiftaḥ* ("Jephthah's Daughter," 1965). Seter's "Judith" was rearranged in 1967 as a "symphonic chaconne" for orchestra.

STAGE MUSIC

Incidental music composed for plays and scores written for operetta, musical comedy, and the modern Broadway-style "musical" can be grouped conveniently under one heading. It was not until the 19th century that anything of importance emerged in the Biblical field. By that time, a new genre had come into being in the shape of the melodrama —not a sensational or sentimental play (as the term suggests today), but the dramatic use of spoken words against a musical background. An early example is *Die Makkabäer* ("The Maccabees," c. 1835), a melodrama written by Ignaz Seyfried. In a degenerate form, this later produced Hermann Cohn's five-act German parody, *Der Barbier von Schuschan* (1894), a pastiche of an earlier melodrama entitled *Der Barbier von Bagdad*. The satirical allusion to Rossini's opera, *The Barber of Seville* (1816), is also rather obvious. Meanwhile, instrumental (rather than vocal) accompaniment to plays had also developed, as in Eugène d'Albert's overture to Franz Grillparzer's unfinished *Esther* (music first performed in 1888).

In the Jewish sphere, stage music on Biblical motifs owes much to the Yiddish *Purim-Shpil* ("Purim Play"), traditionally performed in honor of Queen Esther on the festival of Purim.[16] Wandering theatrical troupes performed plays on this theme, generally accompanied by song and dance, before appreciative audiences in the Jewish communities of Central and Eastern Europe and it was from productions of this type that Abraham Goldfaden (1840–1908), the "father of the Yiddish theater," derived his own Yiddish operetta. A self-taught composer as well as a poet and dramatist, Goldfaden wrote songs in Hebrew and Yiddish and a number of important stage works on Biblical and historical themes in which Jewish folklore is a prime element. His *Shulamis* ("The Shulammite," 1880), a romantic operetta based on the Song of Songs, alternates between merriment and tragedy. It drew vast audiences and a performance by a visiting company in Prague fascinated the novelist Franz Kafka. Many of the songs that Goldfaden wrote for his plays have become hits, including *Rozhinkes mit Mandlen* ("Raisins and Almonds"), a Yiddish cradle song which the writer adapted and made famous in *Shulamis*. A work of the same type was Goldfaden's *Kenig Akhashverosh* ("King Ahasuerus," c. 1885).

Almost the only non-Jewish composer of eminence in the 20th century to become active in this genre was Arthur Honegger, who wrote the incidental music for *Saül* (1922), a drama by André Gide, and for *Sodome et Gomorrhe* (1943), a play by Jean Giraudoux. Most other composers have been of Jewish birth. For the premiere of Stefan Zweig's pacifist drama, *Jeremias* (1917), the stage music was composed by Arno Nadel (1878–1943), equally eminent as poet, playwright, and collector and composer of musical works. The Ohel Theater's production of *Jeremias*

---

[16] For fuller details, see Chapter 4 (The Yiddish-Speaking World).

during Palestine's Mandatory period had a separate musical score by Yedidyah Admon (1897–), who used a unified style blending Jewish Oriental (Yemenite and Persian), Arab, Ḥasidic, and prayer-chant melodies. Admon also wrote the music for other stage works on Biblical themes, such as Kadish Silman's *Megillat Ester* ("The Esther Scroll," c. 1934). Another Biblical production of the 1930s was by Kurt Weill (1900–1950), the son of a German cantor, who came to New York in 1935 in order to write the incidental music for a new version of Franz Werfel's drama, *Der Weg der Verheissung*. Under the direction of Max Reinhardt, this dramatic Jewish pageant had a long run in 1936 as *The Eternal Road*.

Since 1948, a good deal of music for Biblical drama has been composed in Israel. Emanuel Amiran (1909–), a noted writer of songs in the popular folk-style, provided the incidental music for Max Zweig's German-language play, *Saul*, staged in a Hebrew translation by the Habimah company in 1949. A far more important production was Sammy Gronemann's *"King Solomon and the Cobbler"* (*Der Weise und der Narr: König Salomo und der Schuster*, 1942), a comedy in a legendary Biblical setting which Nathan Alterman translated into Hebrew. As staged by the Cameri Theater, with music specially written by Alexander Argov, *Shelomo Ha-Melekh ve-Shalmai Ha-Sandelar* became the first successful Hebrew musical (1965). Another stage success of 1965 was an adaptation of Itzik Manger's *Megile-Lider* ("Scroll Songs," 1936) by the Burstein family. Eleven years previously, Pesach Burstein (1900–), a leading Yiddish actor, had emigrated to Israel from the United States together with his wife, the actress Lilian Lux, and son Michael. Their Yiddish version of *The Megillah*, a comedy about Queen Esther, King Ahasuerus, and Haman and Mordecai, was essentially a modern *Purim-Shpil*, but the acting was superb and the music, by Dov Seltzer, combined modern technique with a "revival style" reminiscent of traditional Jewish song and Yiddish theater. While Israel has become the focal point of musical comedy with a Biblical motif, there have been a few recent attempts in the United States. Among the latest productions have been *Two by Two* (1970), a musical about Noah and the Flood based on a play by Clifford Odets (*The Flowering Peach*, 1954), which was staged on Broadway with Danny Kaye in the star role and the attractive *Joseph and the Amazing Technicolor Dreamcoat* by Andrew Lloyd Webber and Tim Rice (who previously wrote the popular *Jesus Christ Superstar*).

THE BIBLE IN FOLK-SONG

Although a few isolated echoes of the Hebrew Bible can be detected in the musical folklore of the West, Biblical themes only achieve real significance in the Afro-American spiritual and in the folk song of the Jews. Wrenched from his ancestral culture and environment by Arab and European slavers, transported to North America and sold into perpetual servitude, the Negro found solace in the Book which his white masters taught him. It was only natural that he should identify with the people whose inspiring history, recurrent exile, and religious yearning were set forth in the Bible, and out of it he created a distinctive musical genre which expressed his inmost hopes and feelings. For the Jew, long separated from his homeland and scattered over a thousand dispersions, the Bible alone gave meaning to the life of indignity which he was often forced to lead. His daily prayers, Torah study, festivities, sorrow, and folklore were intimately bound up with the Book. In every age—as a Spanish exile, Kurdish villager, or Polish Hasid—the Jew also created a store of folk melodies which used familiar Biblical elements to give voice to his own Messianic vision. A sense of fulfillment and joy now pervades the folk song of modern Israel.

NEGRO SPIRITUALS

From the hymns and readings which he heard in Protestant (mainly Baptist and Methodist) churches of the American South a new type of religious song was evolved by the Negro. This "spiritual" often has a deeply emotional character and it usually consists of certain lines by a soloist to which a chorus responds with an appropriate refrain. Thus, in *Li'l David, Play on Your Harp*, the response is "Hallelu, Hallelu!," while in *Joshua Fit de Battle of Jericho*, the last word is twice repeated before the soloist resumes with "and the walls came a-tumblin' down," and so on throughout the song. A very high proportion of these Negro spirituals deal with subjects taken from the Hebrew Bible—(*Dese Bones Gwine Rise Again*), Noah and the Flood (*Didn't It Rain!, The Old Ark's A-Mov(er)in'*), the Exodus (*Go Down, Moses, March On*), and stories from the Prophets (*Samson, Ezek'el Saw the Wheel, Dry Bones*). In some instances, more than one theme is developed, as in *He Is Just the Same Today*, which refers to the crossing of the Red Sea, David's fight with Goliath, and Daniel's imprisonment in the lions' den, *Witness*, where Methuselah, Samson, and Daniel all appear, or *Wasn't That a Mornin'?*, which recalls Adam and Eve in the Garden of Eden and Samson's slaughter of the Philistines. Imaginative power and a keen poetic sense characterize most of these songs, a number of which have entered the international repertoire.

In their structure and narrative technique, many spirituals show points of originality. *Ezek'el Saw the Wheel* (based on Ezek. 1) is a simple, rhythmic tune in which the soloist's opening phrase is greeted by the chorus' response, but this song quickly turns from a description of "a wheel in a wheel—'way up in the middle o' the air" to criticism of the congregation's behavior. *Dry Bones*, often effectively arranged for vocal or instrumental ensembles, transforms the terrifying scene described in Ezek. 37 into a syncopated, jocular portrayal of the bones joining together one by one and then separating in reverse order. At the end of each section, the chorus joins in with the refrain, "Disconnect dem bones, dem dry bones" (or "Dem bones, dem bones gonna walk around"), and triumphantly proclaims: "Now hear the word of the Lord!" *Go Down, Moses*, a Negro slave's interpretation of Ex. 1–14, has become the world's best-known folk-interpretation of the Moses story. This powerful spiritual begins "When Israel was in Egypt's land" and retells the events leading up to the Exodus with the refrain, "Let My People Go!" More than any other song of its type, *Go Down, Moses* reflects the Negro slave's yearning for a liberator who would lead him out of his bondage in the plantations of the American South, a yearning which finds wistful expression in "Tell ol' Pharaoh—Let My People Go!"

Perhaps the best-loved and most beautiful of all the Negro spirituals is *Swing Low, Sweet Chariot*, in which "chariot" is pronounced "*shari-o*" in the French manner. This song has become immensely popular far beyond its original Negro milieu. The opening lines movingly relate the singer's vision of a blissful future: "I looked over Jordan, an' what did I see?/—Comin' for to carry me home—/A band of Angels coming after me,/Comin' for to carry me home." The vogue enjoyed by this musical genre has inspired many imitations. Among the most famous of these are the "plantation songs" written by the U.S. composer Stephen Foster (1826–1864) and Robert MacGinney's *Shadrack, Meshack, Abednego*, a description of the Three Hebrews and their ordeal in Nebuchadnezzar's fiery furnace which is often mistakenly regarded as an authentic Negro spiritual. *Darkies' Sunday School*, a well-known street corner song, is a good-humored parody of the spiritual. Here there are anachronistic accounts of Noah (who "sailed around the sea,/with half a dozen wives and a big menagerie"), Samson (whose "strong-man act just brought down the house"), Jezebel (who has "gone to the dogs"), Jonah (who "took a steerage passage in a transatlantic whale"), and other figures in "such Bible stories as you never heard before."[17] The source of these hilarious tales lies in the Negro's facility for relating Scriptural themes to the contemporary situation. The Afro-American spiritual, with its intense religious and emotional appeal, is one of the most important contributions to musical interpretation of the Bible.

THE PAGEANT OF JEWISH FOLK SONG

Jewish folk-music of the pre-modern period can be subdivided into Ashkenazi (Central and East European), Sephardi (Spanish-Portuguese), Oriental (Levantine and Persian), and Yemenite song. Among the Ashkenazim, Yiddish was the distinguishing factor, among the Sephardim it was Ladino (Judeo-Spanish). It is tempting to believe that the traditions of remote Yemen may have preserved an ancient substratum that was elsewhere obliterated by Islam's triumph in the Near East and North Africa. In any case, it is worth noting that the Yemenite interpretation of *Ozzi ve-zimrat Yah* ("The Lord is my strength and song," Ex. 15:2), *Mah Dodekh mi-Dod* ("What is thy beloved . . . ?," Song of Songs 5:9), *Be-ẓet Yisra'el mi-Miẓrayim* ("When Israel went forth out of Egypt," Ps. 114), and other kindred Biblical texts has readily been absorbed by the Israel folk-song and has also left its distinctive imprint upon it. The musical style evolved by the Jews of Kurdistan (a borderland region overlapping modern Iraq, Iran, and Turkey) may be taken as an example of the Oriental Jewish tradition. Contact with Arab music, Biblical cantillation, and *ḥazzanut* has also played an important part in the development of both sacred and secular song among the Jews of Kurdistan. One significant factor arising from the comparative freedom which the Jewish peasants of this region enjoyed side by side with their Muslim neighbors was the absorption of folkloristic elements in the Kurmanji language from the literature and song of the non-Jewish environment. In general, it is fair to say that the four basic

[17] See also Chapter 4 (The United States and Canada).

musical styles follow a linguistic divisional pattern: synagogal music (Hebrew); Biblical paraphrase and semireligious song (in *Targum*, i.e., Aramaic); secular artistic and social music (Arabic); and the folk-music of epic, ballad, and rural dance (in Kurmanji, or Kurdish). Biblical cantillation has evidently had some effect on the Kurdish Jews' melodic paraphrasing of stories and episodes from the Bible written as epic compositions in the Aramaic vernacular. As with the Yemenite Jews, songs of this type have only been properly analyzed in the land of Israel and not in their native milieu. These Aramaic epics from Kurdistan deal with certain characteristic themes: the story of Joseph, Moses and the daughter of Pharaoh, Israel's battle with the Amalekites, Jael and Sisera, King David. The opening stanza is often a quotation, or part-quotation of the original Hebrew text, which is then followed by a dramatic extension in Aramaic. Apocryphal material is rare in Ashkenazi folk-song, but not infrequent among Sephardim and Near Eastern Jewry. The story of Hannah and her Seven Sons thus figures prominently in the musical folklore of the Orient (generally sung as a vernacular ballad by the womenfolk on the Fast of Av).

The folk-music of Sephardi Jewry is peculiarly rich in Biblical subject matter and, because of its close association with medieval Spanish song and ballad, it has for some time past attracted the attention of musicologists and Hispanicists. With the disintegration of the once-flourishing Jewish communities of Spain after 1492, successive streams of exiles took many popular "romances" with them into the "Marrano diaspora."[18] The melodies that accompanied these poems made them easier to remember and to transmit, and the Ladino (Judeo-Spanish) *romancero* is therefore essentially an extension and adaptation of the Spanish *romancero* of the Middle Ages and the Renaissance. The various Biblical themes that occur in the Sephardi *romancero* deserve some mention. The story of Abraham figures in "romances" such as *Cuando el Rey Nimrod* ("King Nimrod") and *Abram Abinu* ("Father Abraham"), where the use of old Jewish legendary material is evident. Another ballad, *El Dios de ciel de Abraham* ("Abraham's God"), was formerly current in the Moroccan city of Tetuan. The life of David inspired many "romances" (e.g., *Un pregón pregono el Rey*), as did Amnon's rape of Tamar (*Un hijo tiene el Rey David*) and the tragedy

---

[18] For the literary background, see Chapter 4 (Spain, Portugal, and Latin America).

of Absalom's rebellion; *Triste está el Rey David* ("Sad is King David"), a song on this last theme, has recently been rearranged.[19] Other Ladino ballads about Hannah and her martyr sons ("The Song of Death"), Jerusalem, and the birth of Moses (*Cantar vos quiero un Mahase*) are also in the Sephardi repertoire. Biblical-liturgical pieces, such as *Yismah Moshe* ("Moses rejoiced"), are sung to a Hebrew text and several of these have been popularized in the Moroccan idiom by Jo Amar.

The folk-song of Ashkenazi Jewry has been subject to more external influence than any of the foregoing. Songs of liturgical, religious, or historical significance were occasionally sung to a "mode" associated with the Binding of Isaac (*Akedah*), and their later notation included the instruction that they be interpreted *be-niggun "Akedah"* ("to the *Akedah* tune").[20] Throughout the Jewish world, a rich and varied repertory of songs about the prophet Elijah came into existence and, in the Ashkenazi tradition, *Eliyahu ha-Navi* concludes the ceremonial rekindling of lights at the end of the Sabbath. Elijah is linked with Israel's Messianic hope, whence this song's explicit confidence that "Elijah the Prophet ... will soon come with Messiah son of David." Together with *Eliyahu ha-Navi*, Ashkenazi Jews also often sing *Al Tira Avdi Ya'akov* ("Fear not, My servant Jacob"), a melody for the Sabbath's departure based on an acrostic poem that echoes Biblical passages about the Hebrew patriarch. Other folk-songs in Hebrew and Yiddish are associated with the Jewish festivals. *Zingt-zhe alle Yidelakh* ("Let's all sing"), a typical example, is a lively tune referring in Yiddish to the three Pilgrim Festivals (Passover, Pentecost, and Tabernacles) and concluding with the greeting, "Next year in Jerusalem!" (*le-shanah ha-ba'ah bi-Yrushalayim!*). Here again, the Messianic hope is an essential ingredient, together with the hope for national restoration in the land of Israel. The theme recurs in *Az Moshiakh vet kummen* ("When Messiah comes"), a Yiddish folk-song

---

[19] Contemporary musicologists have made strenuous efforts to record and set down the finest elements of the *romancero* for fear that they may otherwise disappear.

[20] Some Yiddish and Hebrew poems of the early 18th century were similarly published with the direction: "to be sung to the tune of Haman in the Ahashverosh play" (i.e., the *Purim-Shpil*, in which Ahasuerus (Ahashverosh) is a leading figure).

for the Rejoicing of the Law festival (*Simḥat Torah*). In response to the question, "What will happen when Messiah comes?," the singer enumerates a series of wonderful events: the feast of the righteous (who eat Leviathan in Paradise), the Torah expounded by Moses himself, the wise remarks of Solomon, the playing of David, the dancing of Miriam, and so forth. Countless other examples of such Biblically inspired Ashkenazi folk-song might also be cited.

Vocal interpretation of phrases or verses from the Bible, no less popular among the Ashkenazim than elsewhere in the Jewish world, received its most powerful stimulus from the Ḥasidic movement, which made singing the focal point of religious expression. About half the Ḥasidic dance melodies (*niggunim*) are inspired by Biblical (or liturgical) texts, usually brief and repeated to fill out the tune. Other *niggunim* of the same type, not meant for dancing, are sung more slowly as informal "choir" pieces. In some Ḥasidic milieux, the actual text was reduced to a few words or even dissolved into a wordless harmonic chant. The Book of Psalms became a great reservoir of Ḥasidic song, inspiring melodies for *Or Zaru'a la-Ẓaddik* ("Light is sown for the righteous," Ps. 97:11), *Yevarekh et-Beit Yisra'el* ("He will bless the house of Israel," Ps. 115:12–18), *Kol Rinnah vi-Yshu'ah* ("The voice of rejoicing and salvation," Ps. 118:15–16), and numerous other passages. Other Ḥasidic favorites include *Ko Amar Ha-Shem* ("Thus saith the Lord," Jer. 2:2),[21] *Ha-Ven Yakkir Li Efrayim* ("Is Ephraim a darling son unto Me?," Jer. 31:20), the haunting *Zekhor Davar le-Avdekha* ("Remember the word unto Thy servant," Ps. 119:49–51), and *Tov Li Torat Pikha* ("The law of Thy mouth . . . ," Ps. 119:72). The constant repetition of individual words or word-groups is common in Ḥasidic song and has since become popular in cantorial music, where this practice often rouses the ire of purists and opponents of Ḥasidism. In some instances, Biblical sources are joined together, as in *Va-yehi vi-Yshurun Melekh* ("And there was a king in Jeshurun"), where the text is a mixture of Deut. 33:5 and Jer. 33:10–11. Because of this second text's reference to "the voice of mirth and the voice of gladness, the voice of the bride-

---

[21] On the substitution of "*Ha-Shem*" ("the Name") for *Adonai* (originally the Tetragrammaton, *YHVH*, meaning "the Lord") in pious Jewish usage, see Chapter 3. Outside the synagogue and religious ceremonial, "*Ha-Shem*" is customary among Orthodox Jews. The hybrid form, "*Adoshem*," is common in Jewish folk-song wherever the melody requires an extra syllable.

groom and the voice of the bride," the associated tune has become popular at the celebration of weddings. The Biblical songs of the Ḥasidim have in recent times been absorbed by Ashkenazi Jewry as a whole and their influence has spread even further, extending at the present day to the folk-music and pop of modern Israel.

MODERN HEBREW FOLK-SONG

Until the period of the British Mandate, Jewish folk-song in Palestine fell into two basic categories: that of the indigenous Ashkenazi-Ḥasidic or Sephardi and Oriental communities, and that brought over by the first generations of Zionist pioneers (the *haluẓim*); the latter was of a generally secular type, usually connected with the labor movement. In time, something approaching a new Hebrew folk-song tradition began to emerge, stimulated by the experimental compositions of European immigrants whose works were performed during the 1930s. In the evolving Palestinian song, East European and cantorial elements intermingled with Yemenite and Arab melodic patterns. The growth of the kibbutz movement, with its stress on agricultural themes, and the consolidation of Hebrew as an everyday language hastened the development of this new folk-song, which found powerful exponents in a number of leading composers. Biblical phrases and passages naturally inspired a significant proportion of these Hebrew folk-songs and also appealed to the widest section of Palestine's Jewish population. The Bible also retained its privileged position as a source for the many songs written after the declaration of the State of Israel in 1948. During the formative years of the Israel folk-dance movement (the late 1940s), settings of individual verses or combinations of verses from the Song of Songs assumed special importance, not least because the "historical" precedent of the Song of Songs helped to resolve the conflict that had arisen between the (Rumanian) *Hora*, a communal circle-dance, and the (Polish) *Krakowiak*, a couple-dance, both of which had been imported from Eastern Europe.

One of the pioneers of the Israel folk-song style was Emanuel Amiran, whose compositions include several based on the Song of Songs—*Al Tir'uni* ("Look not upon me," 1:6), *Dodi Ẓakh ve-Adom* ("My beloved is white and ruddy," 5:10–11), and *Anah Halakh Dodekh* ("Whither is thy beloved gone . . . ?," 6:1–2). Amiran has also set other Biblical texts, such as *Ha-Zore'im be-Dim'ah* ("They that sow in tears," Ps.

126:5), *Mayim, Mayim* ("With joy shall ye draw water," Isa. 12:3), and *Ki mi-Ziyyon teze Torah* ("For out of Zion shall go forth the Law," Isa. 2:3). Of these, *Mayim, Mayim* was particularly successful and became a popular dance in youth circles. A few of these first-generation composers were rooted in the kibbutz, notably David Zahavi of Na'an and Uri Giv'on (Ben-Ya'akov) of Sha'ar ha-Amakim. Zahavi's best-known song of this type is *Yesusum Midbar ve-Ziyyah* ("The wilderness and the parched land shall be glad," Isa. 35:1, 7); Uri Giv'on's *Ken Yovdu* ("So perish all Thine enemies," Judges 5:31) typically substituted "O Israel" for "O Lord" in this interpretation of a Biblical song of triumph, reflecting the secular spirit of the composer's environment. Another setting of *Ken Yovdu* was written by Sarah Levi-Tannai, founder of the Inbal Dance Theater, who also composed *El Ginnat Eggoz* ("I went down into the garden of nuts," Song of Songs 6:11). *Hafle va-Fele* ("Miracle of miracles"), a song by Yedidyah Admon known also by the alternative title, *U-Moshe Hikkah al Zur* ("And Moses struck the rock"), uses Biblical allusions (Num. 20:11, Deut. 32:13) to create a Jewish historical atmosphere. The "honey from the rock" theme similarly inspired Gil Aldema's *Va-Yenikehu* ("And He made him to suck," Deut. 32:13). Marc Lavry, represented here by *Mah Dodekh mi-Dod* ("What is thy beloved more than another . . . ?," Song of Songs 5:9–11), is best known for his art music. Mordechai Ze'ira (1905–1968). perhaps the outstanding creator of modern Israel song, mingled cantorial, Hasidic, Oriental, and even Russian revolutionary elements in his vast number of compositions, some 50 of which have proved enduring favorites. Ze'ira set *Al Tira Avdi Ya'akov* ("Fear not, My servant Jacob"), a poem by Emanuel Harussi about the patriarch's dream of the ladder, to a well-known *Hora* tune. He also composed a delightful melody for the liturgical piece, *David Melekh Yisra'el* ("David King of Israel"), and the vigorous music for Uri Avneri's *Shu'alei Shimshon* ("The Foxes of Samson," cf. Judges 15:4–5), a song about the Israeli "desert foxes" operating on the Egyptian front during the 1948 war.

The more recent generation of composers is represented by Nira Hen, who returned to the Song of Songs with *Dodi Li* ("My beloved is mine," 2:16, 4:9, 3:6, 4:16) and *Itti mi-Levanon* ("Come with me from Lebanon," 4:8), and Amittai Ne'eman, whose *Ha-Navah ba-Banot* ("Fairest of Maidens"), though not directly related to any one text, echoes the language of the same Biblical romance. Pageants based on the story of Jephthah were written for kibbutzim of the Gilboa region and Ne'eman composed two dances, both entitled *Bat Yiftah* ("Jephthah's Daughter"), which entered the Israel repertory. Some additional folk-style compositions are E. Gamliel's *Erez Zavat Ḥalav u-Devash* ("A land flowing with milk and honey," Ex. 3:8, etc.), one of Israel's favorite round-songs, and others by various writers, such as *Mezare Yisra'el* ("He that scattered Israel," Jer. 31:10), *Hineh Mah Tov* ("Behold, how good and how pleasant it is," Ps. 133:1), *Kol Dodi* ("Hark! my beloved!," Song of Songs 2:8), and *Ha-Yoshevet ba-Gannim* ("Thou that dwellest in the gardens," Song of Songs 8:13). Two curious instances of melodic borrowing deserve some mention. The Palestinian Arabs until recently organized mass pilgrimages to the legendary tomb of Moses on the festival of Nebi Musa, and this annual event gave rise to a Muslim repertory of mass chants. One of these, *Ya halila ya habibi, ya hawaja Musa*, became familiar to Jews as well and reappeared in a new setting as an Israel *Hora* song. Vastly more famous is the "conqu'ring hero" theme of Handel's oratorio, *Judas Maccabaeus*, which has taken firm root in Israel as a popular melody for the Hanukkah festival, on which occasion it is sometimes used in the synagogue as a setting for Ps. 118:21–24. [22]

Allied to these Biblical songs are others dealing with the Jerusalem theme, a number of which are textually related to the Bible. Emanuel Amiran's *Ki mi-Ziyyon* (Isa. 2:3) was composed during World War II and his *Al Homotayikh Yerushalayim* ("Upon thy walls, O Jerusalem," Isa. 62:6) was written during the Jordanian siege of 1948. Y. Zarai's *Va-Yiven Uzziyahu* ("Uzziah built towers," 2 Chron. 26:9) dates from 1956. Other songs of this type include Mordechai Ze'ira's *Lekhu ve-Nivneh et-Homat Yerushalayim* ("Come and let us build up the wall of Jerusalem," Neh. 2:17, 4:15), Moshe Wilensky's *Ziyyon, hoy Uri Livshi Uzzekh* ("Awake, awake, put on thy strength, O Zion," Isa. 52:1–2), and two traditional favorites, *Samakhti be-Omerim Li Beit Ha-Shem Nelekh* ("I rejoiced when they said unto me: 'Let us go unto the house of the Lord' . . . ," Ps. 122:1–3) and *Simhu et-Yerushalayim Gilu Vah* ("Rejoice ye with Jerusalem, and be glad with her," Isa. 66:10).

---

[22] In 1969, there was a curious intrusion of politics into music when a performance of Handel's *Israel in Egypt* at Strasbourg (France) was billed as *"Cantique de Moise,"* for fear that the composer's own title might offend Arab susceptibilities.

The most recent "Jerusalem" composition, which quotes Ps. 137:5, won first prize in the Israel Broadcasting Authority's Oriental Song Festival (1972).

During the 1960s, "Ḥasidic pop" made a sudden, unexpected appearance, this trend being inaugurated by Shlomo Carlebach (1926–), the famous "singing Rabbi." Carlebach actually created a neo-Ḥasidic style based on the familiar *niggun*, Israel folk-song, and the contemporary American folk-ballad; he himself provided the guitar accompaniment to his own compositions. Many of these are notable melodic interpretations of Biblical texts—"*Od Yeshoma*" ("Soon May There Be Heard," Jer. 7:34), "*Yismechu Hashomayim*" ("Let The Heavens Rejoice," Ps. 96:11), "*Esso Einai*" (I Lift Up My Eyes," Ps. 121:1–2), and "*Hashmi'ini*" ("Let Me Hear Thy Voice," Song of Songs 2:14). Through Shlomo Carlebach's radio, television, and personal appearances in the U.S.A., Israel, and other countries and through the sale of his LPs, these songs became international successes in the Jewish musical sphere and even gave rise to a pseudo-religious cult. "Ḥasidic pop" later found new exponents in *Avnei Ha-Kotel*, or "The Stones of the Wall," an English immigrant group led by Martin Davidson which enjoyed considerable success in Israel. *Oseh Shalom—Ya'aseh Shalom* ("He who maketh peace . . . may He make peace"), a lively Biblical-liturgical piece set to music by Nurit Hirsch, became a nationwide hit after gaining popularity with troops on the Suez Canal front after Israel's Six-Day War (1967). Individual singers and the Military Rabbinate Choir developed the vogue for such compositions. In this way, Biblical song made a startling and trend-setting entry into the pop idiom of the early 1970s.

EPILOGUE

My object in this book has been to provide the reader with a comprehensive survey of the Hebrew Bible's impact on world culture. Apart from the Scriptural texts themselves, many other sources have been adduced in the foregoing chapters to reveal the full extent of the Bible's influence from earliest times up to the present day. In selecting my material, I have had in mind the Biblical saying that "a word in season" or "fitly spoken" can add beauty and value to one's labors (Prov. 15:23, 25:11). The Rabbis of Mishnaic times commended those who identify their source material, believing that "whoever quotes something in the name of the one who said it brings redemption to the world" (*Avot,* 6.6). As far as possible, I have respected this teaching.

The Bible has given strength to the freedom fighter and new heart to the persecuted, a blueprint to the social reformer and inspiration to the writer and artist. Those sections of humanity nurtured by Judaism and Christianity clearly draw most from the Scriptures. Sometimes, however, tribute may come from an unexpected quarter. Not long ago, Zenon Kosidowski, a Polish Communist writer, published an anthology of Bible stories, the aim of which was to show how archaeological and historical data and literary analysis can be used to "demythologize" Israel's sacred Book and proclaim its "real" importance as a monument of world literature. In his postscript to the Russian edition of this work (*Bibleyskiye skazaniya,* Moscow, 1968, pp. 437–39), A. Osipov maintains that Kosidowski's "historical" approach has stripped the Bible of its Divine aura, proving it to be "nothing more nor less than a conglomeration of ancient folk tales and legends collected and reworked by the Jewish theologians of antiquity."[1] Nevertheless, while expressing reservations about Kosidowski's reliance on the Catholic text of the

---

[1]Basing themselves on the more sensational "findings" of outmoded Biblical criticism, militant atheists in various countries have written in similar terms.

Bible and his undisguised sympathy for certain Biblical figures, the Soviet critic parts company with upholders of the old Party line who dismissed the stories and personalities of Scripture as "utterly fictitious" and "bereft of historicity" (he notes that, "if we open a volume of the *Great Soviet Encyclopedia*'s second edition, we will find 'legendary figure,' 'myth,' or some such definition next to any Biblical name"). Osipov is thus caught on the horns of a dilemma: while averse to the idea of giving comfort to the religious believer, he cannot entirely disregard the general trend of modern scholarship. Hence this remarkable admission: "Some propagandists working for the cause of atheism have presented an oversimplified picture of the Bible as a collection of ancient legends remote from the facts of history. But present-day historical research indicates that the matter is by no means such a simple one." Osipov's own propagandist conclusion fails to obscure this significant confession.

Rousseau, who also lived in an iconoclastic age, is revered by politicians of the extreme left, yet his view of Scripture was very different from theirs. The Marxist critic of today prefers to ignore what the Frenchman wrote about denigrators of the Bible: "Behold the works of our philosophers; with all their pompous diction, how mean and contemptible they are by comparison with the Scriptures! Is it possible that a book at once so simple and sublime should be merely the work of man?"

In 1948, London played host to an exhibition on the theme of "The Bible in English Life." The objects on display included copies of the Bible that once belonged to men and women of prominence. Visitors were treated to a view of the Bible once used by the Quaker leader George Fox (1624–1691), the copy from which Elizabeth Fry (1780–1845) read while comforting those in prison, the Bible of another social reformer, Lord Shaftesbury (1801–1885), and the one which Florence Nightingale (1820–1910) took with her to the hospitals in which she pursued her errands of mercy. Among these exhibits were other Bibles, such as the copy cherished by General Gordon (1833–1885), a hero of the Victorian era, and the one which accompanied Viscount Montgomery (1887–) on his World War II campaigns from El Alamein to Berlin. Exhibitions of this type demonstrate the undiminished relevance and inspiration of God's word in the world of today.

One Bible that did not form part of this London display was the well-worn copy of another British soldier, Orde Charles Wingate (1903–1944). The savior of Italian-occupied Ethiopia and the leader of Britain's

Chindits in the Burma campaign against Japan, Wingate was described by Winston Churchill as "a man of genius who might well have become also a man of destiny," had he not died tragically in an air crash. Orde Wingate made the Bible his staple reading and, while serving in Palestine during the late 1930s, trained some of Israel's future army chiefs in his unorthodox methods of warfare; much of what he taught was suggested by the tactics of Joshua, Gideon, and David. "To stand on the places where the Old Testament prophets had lived, taught, fought and died was as sweet-smelling to him as the anointment oils of a newly proclaimed king. He tramped across the hills. He sang aloud . . . in a Hebrew which was daily growing more fluent the words of the 126th Psalm ('When the Lord turned again the captivity of Zion, we were like them that dream') . . ."[2] During Israel's War of Independence, the widow of this Christian Zionist arranged for his copy of the Bible to be dropped with a consignment of essential supplies into a children's village then under siege by Syrian troops. The dedication which she wrote on the flyleaf read:

7.5.48. To the Defenders of Yemin Orde. Since Orde Wingate is with you in spirit, though he cannot lead you in the flesh, I send you the Bible he carried in all his campaigns and from which he drew the inspiration of his victories. May it be a covenant between you and him, in triumph or defeat, now and always.

[2] Leonard Mosley, *Gideon Goes to War* (London, 1957 edn.), p. 29; the inscription cited below appears on p. 192. See also the standard biography by Christopher Sykes, *Orde Wingate* (London, 1959), p. 545.

BIBLIOGRAPHY

In a work of this scope, any bibliography must of necessity be selective. Jewish religious classics, such as the Soncino Press Bible (13 vols., Hebrew and English texts with commentary), Talmud (35 vols., English text), Midrash Rabbah (ten vols., English text), and Zohar (five vols., English text), have therefore not been included. Nor have many general works of reference been listed here. The reader will find more useful information in the following bibliographical guide.

GENERAL

The Legacy of Israel, planned by the late Israel Abrahams and edited by Edwyn R. Bevan and Charles Singer (Oxford, 1927).

The Hebrew Impact on Western Civilization, edited by Dagobert D. Runes (New York, 1951).

The Jews: Their History, Culture, and Religion, edited by Louis Finkelstein (two vols., New York, third edition, 1960).

Joseph H. Hertz, *A Book of Jewish Thoughts* (London, 1944 edn.).

Idem, The Pentateuch and Haftorahs (London, second edition, 1963).

Cecil Roth, *The Jewish Contribution to Civilisation* (London, 1956 edn.).

Encyclopaedia Judaica, edited by Cecil Roth and Geoffrey Wigoder (16 vols., Jerusalem, 1972).

CHAPTER 1: FROM RELIGION TO RACE RELATIONS

Legacy of Israel, pp. 1–96, 129–171, 283–375, 407–431.

Hebrew Impact, pp. 139–185.

The Jews, vol. II, pp. 1010–1075, 1234–1287.

F. W. Binder, *Education in the History of Western Civilization* (Toronto, 1970).

A. Cohen, *The Parting of the Ways. Judaism and the Rise of Christianity* (London, 1954).

Isidore Epstein, *The Faith of Judaism* (London, 1954).

Idem, Judaism. A Historical Presentation (London, 1959).

Maurice Fluegel, *The Humanity, Benevolence and Charity Legislation of the Pentateuch and Talmud* (Baltimore, 1908).

C. G. Montefiore and H. Loewe, *A Rabbinic Anthology* (London, 1938; reprinted 1963).

James Parkes, *Judaism and Christianity* (London, 1948).

Idem, The Conflict of the Church and the Synagogue (London, 1934; reprinted 1961).

François Secret, *Les Kabbalistes Chrétiens de la Renaissance* (Paris, 1964).

CHAPTER 2: THE LEGAL AND POLITICAL SPHERES

a. LAW

Legacy of Israel, pp. 377–406.

Hebrew Impact, pp. 1–61, 793–818.

An Introduction to Jewish Law, edited by Peter Elman (London, 1958).

Henry E. Baker, *The Legal System of Israel* (1961; revised edition, Jerusalem, 1968).

P. Biberfeld, "Judaism and International Law," in *Israel of Tomorrow*, edited by Leo Jung (New York, 1946), pp. 187–211.

Boaz Cohen, *Jewish and Roman Law. A Comparative Study* (two vols., New York, 1966).

R. W. M. Dias, *Jurisprudence* (London, 1964), pp. 502–505.

Menachem Elon, *Jewish Law in the State of Israel* (Jerusalem, 1970).

K. Kahana Kagan, *Three Great Systems of Jurisprudence* (London, 1955).

b. POLITICS

Legacy of Israel, pp. 407–431.

Hebrew Impact, pp. 1–61.

The Jews, vol. II, pp. 1430–1451.

The Ethic of Power: The Interplay of Religion, Philosophy, and Politics, edited by Harold D. Lasswell and Harlan Cleveland (New York, 1962).

J. W. Allen, *A History of Political Thought in the Sixteenth Century* (London, 1928; revised edition, 1960).

Sidney Dark, *The Red Bible. An Anthology* (London, 1942).

A. G. Dickens, *Reformation and Society in Sixteenth-Century Europe* (London, 1966).

William Irwin, *The Old Testament: Keystone of Human Culture* (New York, 1952).

Trygve Lie *et al., Peace on Earth* (New York, 1949).

D. D. Runes, *Despotism. A Pictorial History of Tyranny* (New York, 1963).
Steven S. Schwarzschild, "The Religious Demand for Peace," in *Judaism*, Vol. 15, No. 4, Fall 1966, pp. 412–418.
J. J. Stamm and H. Bietenhard, *Der Weltfriede im Alten und Neuen Testament* (Zurich, 1959).
Hayim Tadmor, " 'The People' and the Kingship in Ancient Israel: The Role of Political Institutions in the Biblical Period," in *Jewish Society through the Ages*, edited by H. H. Ben-Sasson and S. Ettinger (London, 1971), pp. 46–68.

CHAPTER 3: THE TESTIMONY OF EVERYDAY SPEECH

Legacy of Israel, pp. 473–481.
A New English Dictionary, edited by Sir James Murray *et al.* (ten vols., Oxford, 1888–).
The Interpreter's Dictionary of the Bible (four vols., New York, 1962).
Webster's Third New International Dictionary (Chicago, 1966 edition).
William Chomsky, *Hebrew: The Eternal Language* (Philadelphia, 1957).
Edward Horowitz, *How the Hebrew Language Grew* (New York, 1960).
J. Courtenay James, *Hebrew and English. Some Likenesses Psychic and Linguistic* (London, 1957).
F. A. Stoett, *Nederlandse Spreekwoorden en Gezegden* (1902; revised eighth edition, Zutphen, 1953).
E. Tannenbaum, *Philo Zitaten-Lexikon: Worte von Juden; Worte für Juden* (Berlin, 1936), pp. 17–61.
J. Trénel, *L'Ancien Testament et la Langue Française du Moyen-Age* (Paris, 1904).

CHAPTER 4. BIBLICAL THEMES AND ECHOES
IN WORLD LITERATURE

Legacy of Israel, pp. 483–505.
The Jews, vol. II, pp. 1452–1486.
The Penguin Books of French, German, Italian, Russian, and Spanish Verse.
Harold Fisch, *Jerusalem and Albion. The Hebraic Factor in Seventeenth-Century Literature* (London, 1964).
Solomon Goldman, *The Book of Human Destiny* (vols. 1–3, New York, 1948–58).
James D. Hart, *The Oxford Companion to American Literature* (fourth edn., New York, 1965).
Sir Paul Harvey, *The Oxford Companion to English Literature* (fourth edn., Oxford, 1967).

Sir Paul Harvey and Janet E. Heseltine, *The Oxford Companion to French Literature* (Oxford, 1959).

C. Lehrmann, *L'Elément Juif dans la Littérature Française* (two vols., Paris, 1960–61).

Sol Liptzin, *The Jew in American Literature* (New York, 1966).

Murray Roston, *Biblical Drama in England* (London, 1968).

CHAPTER 5: PAINTING AND SCULPTURE

Hebrew Impact, pp. 405–504.

The Jews, vol. II, pp. 1322–1348.

The Bible in Art (London, 1956).

The Larousse Encyclopedia of Renaissance and Baroque Art, edited by René Huyghe (English edition: London, 1964).

Peter Bloch, *Nachwirkungen des Alten Bundes in der christlichen Kunst* (Cologne, 1963).

Theodor Ehrenstein, *Das Alte Testament im Bilde* (Vienna, 1923).

Jacob Leveen, *The Hebrew Bible in Art* (London, 1944).

C. R. Morey, *Christian Art* (New York, 1958).

Bezalel Narkiss, *Hebrew Illustrated Manuscripts* (Jerusalem, 1969).

Louis Réau, *Iconographie de l'Art Chrétien* (Paris, 1956), vol. 2.

CHAPTER 6: THE MUSICAL TRADITION

Hebrew Impact, pp. 363–404, 505–526.

The Jews, vol. II, pp. 1288–1321.

James Daniel, "The Psalms: Hymnbook of Humanity," in *Christianity Today*, April 15, 1966.

Edith Gerson-Kiwi, *Musique dans la Bible* (Paris, 1956).

Artur Holde, *Jews in Music* (New York, 1959).

Abraham Z. Idelsohn, *Jewish Music in its Historical Development* (New York, 1929; reprinted 1967).

Arthur Jacobs, *A New Dictionary of Music* (1958; revised second edition, London, 1972).

Alan Lomax, *The Folk Songs of North America* (New York, 1960), pp. 447–479.

A. M. Rothmueller, *The Music of the Jews* (New York, 1954).

Lazare Saminsky, *Music of the Ghetto and the Bible* (New York, 1934).

ACKNOWLEDGMENTS

Penguin Books Ltd., U.K.: *Judaism. A Historical Representation* (1959), by Isidore Epstein, copyright © Isidore Epstein, 1959, p. 132; *The Penguin Book of French Verse,* vol. 4 (1959), *"Vantardises d'un marin breton ivre,"* by Max Jacob, edited and translated by Anthony Hartley, translation copyright © Anthony Hartley, 1959; *The Penguin Book of Italian Verse* (1958), *"Cantico delle creature,"* by San Francesco d'Assisi, edited and translated by George Kay, translation copyright © George Kay, 1958, 1965; *The Penguin Book of German Verse* (1957), *"Gebetslied in der Pest 1: Im anfang der Krankeit,"* by Huldrych Zwingli, and *"Morgenandacht,"* by Christian Knorr von Rosenroth, edited and translated by Leonard Forster, copyright © Leonard Forster, 1957, 1959; *The Penguin Book of Russian Verse* (1962), *"Prorok,"* by Aleksandr Pushkin, and *Plach Iosifa,* edited and translated by Dimitri Obolenski, translation copyright © Dimitri Obolenski, 1962, 1965.

The Clarendon Press, Oxford: *The Legacy of Israel* (1927), "The Hebrew Genius as exhibited in the Old Testament," by G. A. Smith, and "The Influence of the Old Testament on Puritanism," by W. B. Selbie, edited by E. R. Evans and C. Singer, pp. 12, 423.

Phaidon Press Ltd, London: Marcel Brion, Introd. to *The Bible in Art* (1956), pp. 7–8.

Alfred A. Knopf, Inc., New York: "These are the Chosen People," by Robert Nathan, in: *The Green Leaf* (1950).

Thames and Hudson Ltd., A. G. Dickens, *Reformation and Society in Sixteenth Century Europe* (1966).

Curtis Brown Ltd.: L. Mosley, *Gideon Goes to War* (1957).

N. V. Boekhandel en Drukkerij V/H E. J. Brill, Leiden: S. M. Paul, *Studies in the Book of the Covenant in the Light of Cuneiform and Biblical Law* (1970).

ILLUSTRATIONS

Photo David Harris, Jerusalem p.7, 14, 24, 234, 361.
Jerusalem, J. N. U. L. p.14.
Jerusalem, Israel Museum p.24, 361, 428.
Tel Aviv; Israel Gov't Press Office p. 27, 28, 65.

Courtesy Herbert Swartz, New York, p.29.

Photo K. Weiss, Jerusalem; p.31.

Liverpool, Walker Art Gallery p.40, 391.

New York, Jewish Theological Seminary p.50.

London, British Museum p.53, 205, 206, 300, 350.

Photo Alinari, Florence p.87, 365, 371, 424.

Copenhagen, Royal Museum of Fine Arts p.111.

Rome, Vatican Library p.122, 337.

Jerusalem, Armenian Patriarchate p.159.

London, *The Evening Standard,* May 26, 1960 p.173.

Winegerode, The Princely Library p. 209.

Photo Emka, Jerusalem p.222.

London, Tate Gallery p.230.

Cecil Roth Collection p.234.

Paramount Pictures Corporation p.244.

Photo Friedman-Abeles, New York p.245.

Photo Agence Presse Bernand, Paris p.252.

Photo Nahum Guttman, Tel Aviv p.304.

Jerusalem, Holyland Hotel p.325.

New Haven, Conn., Yale University p.330.

Vienna, Austrian National Library p.344.

Stuttgart, Württembergische Landesbibliothek. p.346.

New York, Pierpont-Morgan Library p.348.

Boston, Mass., Museum of Fine Art. p.355.

Frankfurt, Städelsche Kunstinstitut. p.374.

Vienna, Kunsthistorisches Museum p.376.

London, National Gallery p.386.

Ardmore, Pa., Sigmund Harrison Collection p.397.

Courtesy Bezalel Schatz, Jerusalem p.402.

Milan, Biblioteca Ambrosiana p.409.

Paris, Bibliothèque Nationale, p.426.

Jerusalem, Israel Department of Antiquities and Museum p.329, 428.

Photo Keren-Kidron, Tel Aviv p.477.